Cooking
for one

90 inspiring ways to cook for the *ProPoints*® plan

SIMON &
SCHUSTER
ILLUSTRATED

London · New York · Sydney · Toronto · New Delhi

A CBS COMPANY

D0274941

First published in Great Britain by Simon & Schuster UK Ltd, 2012
A CBS COMPANY

13579108642

Simon & Schuster UK Ltd, 1st Floor, 222 Gray's Inn Road, London WC1X 8HB
www.simonandschuster.co.uk
Simon & Schuster Australia, Sydney
Simon & Schuster India, New Delhi

A CIP catalogue copy for this book is available from the British Library.

Weight Watchers Publications Team: Jane Griffiths, Cheryl Jackson, Selena Makepeace,
Nina McKerlie and Imogen Prescott
Simon & Schuster Project Management: WordWorks *Photography*: Will Heap *Prop styling*: Polly Webb Wilson
Food styling: Emma Marsden *Design and typesetting*: Isobel Gillan
Cover photography: Dan Jones *Cover food styling*: Kim Morphew *Cover design*: Smith & Gilmour

Printed and bound in Singapore
Colour reproduction by Dot Gradations Ltd, UK

Pictured on the front cover: Steak 'Bearnaise', page 8

Pictured on the back cover, from top to bottom: Beef and Vegetable Noodles, page 10; Parma Wrapped Figs, page 32;
Lamb and Feta Burger, page 24; Butternut Squash and Tomato Penne, page 62

Cooking
for one

90 inspiring ways to cook for the *ProPoints*® plan

Sue Ashworth & Carol Tennant

ProPoints® value logo: You'll find this easy to read **ProPoints** value logo on every recipe throughout this book. The logo represents the number of **ProPoints** values per serving each recipe contains. It is not an indication of the fillingness of a recipe.

Weight Watchers **ProPoints** Weight Loss System is a simple way to lose weight. As part of the Weight Watchers **ProPoints** plan, you'll enjoy eating delicious, healthy, filling foods that help to keep you feeling satisfied for longer and in control of your portions.

Filling & Healthy foods are highlighted in green. Focus on these foods where you can – they are healthy choices that will help you to feel satisfied for longer.

V This symbol denotes a vegetarian recipe and assumes that, where relevant, free range eggs, vegetarian cheese, vegetarian virtually fat free fromage frais, vegetarian low fat crème fraîche and vegetarian low fat yogurts are used. Virtually fat free fromage frais, low fat crème fraîche and low fat yogurts may contain traces of gelatine so they are not always vegetarian. Please check the labels.

❄ This symbol denotes a dish that can be frozen. Unless otherwise stated, you can freeze the finished dish for up to 3 months. Defrost thoroughly and reheat until the dish is piping hot throughout.

Recipe notes

Egg size: Medium unless otherwise stated.

Raw eggs: Only the freshest eggs should be used. Pregnant women, the elderly and children should avoid recipes with eggs which are not fully cooked or raw.

All fruits and vegetables: Medium unless otherwise stated.

Low fat spread: Where a recipe states to use a low fat spread, a light spread with a fat content of no less than 38% should be used.

Stock: Stock cubes should be used in the recipes, unless otherwise stated. Prepare them according to the packet instructions, unless directed otherwise.

Low fat soft cheese: Where a recipe states to use low fat soft cheese, a soft cheese with a fat content of less than 5% should be used.

Recipe timings: These are approximate and meant to be guidelines. The preparation time includes all the steps up to and following the main cooking time(s), including making any other recipes.

Contents

 *Cooking for One* is the newest cookbook in the Weight Watchers 2012 range and is packed with 90 brand new recipes, all serving one. This fantastic new cookbook will inspire you to create fantastic meals just for you and will help to keep you on track with your weight loss. The recipes are easy to follow and have all been developed to work alongside the **ProPoints**® plan and many recipes include Filling & Healthy foods.

What are Filling & Healthy foods?

At the heart of the **ProPoints** plan are Filling & Healthy foods. These have been selected from each of the food groups and are the very best choices for satisfaction and health.

- *Filling & Healthy foods are filling* – they are low in energy density (in other words, they are bulky foods that are low in **ProPoints** values) and will help to keep you satisfied as you lose weight.
- *Filling & Healthy foods are healthier* – they are foods that have been carefully selected for their higher fibre content and/or lower salt, sugar and saturated fat content.
- *Filling & Healthy foods are great value* – whether they're zero **ProPoints** value fruit and veg, a medium salmon fillet for 6 **ProPoints** values or a 5 **ProPoints** value (150 g/5½ oz, cooked) portion of wholemeal pasta, you can be sure you're getting the best deal out of every **ProPoints** value that you spend.

You can find Filling & Healthy foods at a glance since they are shown throughout this cookbook highlighted in green, like this.

About the **ProPoints** *plan*

The **ProPoints** plan is based on the latest nutritional science and is Weight Watchers most flexible and liveable plan ever. Completely unique to Weight Watchers, it has been designed to work around your real life so you can control your weight whatever situation you find yourself in each day. The recipes in *Cooking for One* will help you stay on track by providing the **ProPoints** values per recipe, and highlighting foods that are Filling & Healthy. With *Cooking for One*, following the **ProPoints** plan couldn't be easier.

How do we develop the recipes?

The cookbook team at Weight Watchers works with some very talented cookery authors and home economists to develop the recipes, with the main focus being on taste and satisfaction. We ensure that everyone we work with has all the up-to-date information on the **ProPoints** plan so our Members can make the most of their **ProPoints** budget when deciding what to cook. Once the recipes are developed, we go along to watch them being photographed to make sure that what you see in this book is what you get at home, and we get to taste the recipes too.

In *Cooking for One*, each recipe has been created especially for one person and they are not simply reduced versions of larger recipes.

Steak 'Bearnaise' 10 ProPoints value

This lighter version of the famous sauce packs the same punch as the original, and goes so well with steak.

10 **ProPoints** values per recipe
30 minutes in total

100 g (3½ oz) **potato**, *peeled and cut into skinny fries*
calorie controlled cooking spray
150 g (5½ oz) **lean fillet steak**

For the 'Bearnaise' sauce
1 egg yolk
1 teaspoon Dijon mustard
1 teaspoon chopped **fresh tarragon**
2 teaspoons white wine vinegar or lemon juice
½ **shallot**, *chopped finely*
a handful of **watercress** *leaves, to serve*

1 Preheat the oven to Gas Mark 6/200°C/fan oven 180°C. Arrange the skinny fries in a single layer on a non stick baking tray. Spray with the cooking spray, toss and cook for 20–30 minutes, turning once, until golden and crisp.

2 Meanwhile, heat a non stick frying pan and spray with the cooking spray. Add the steak and cook over a high heat for 2 minutes on each side. Transfer to a roasting tray and place above the fries for 5 minutes for medium rare, 7 minutes for medium and 9 minutes for well done. Set aside to rest as you make the sauce.

3 Put all the 'Bearnaise' ingredients into a heatproof bowl along with 2 tablespoons of water. Set the bowl over a small pan of boiling water but don't allow the bowl to touch the water. Whisk constantly until the sauce thickens and becomes light and foamy, about 4–5 minutes.

4 Put the steak and skinny fries on a serving plate and pour over the sauce. Serve immediately, garnished with watercress.

beef, lamb and pork

Beef and bean hotpot

A simple, hearty and warming winter dish which needs no accompaniment.

10 *ProPoints* values per recipe

❄ • 15 minutes preparation, 35 minutes cooking

calorie controlled cooking spray
150 g (5½ oz) **lean sirloin steak**, visible fat removed, cut into small pieces
1 **onion**, chopped roughly
2 **carrots**, peeled and sliced thickly
75 g (2¾ oz) waxy **potatoes**, peeled and cut into large chunks
150 g can **baked beans**
1 teaspoon Worcestershire sauce
a handful of chopped **fresh parsley**, to garnish

1 Spray a lidded saucepan with the cooking spray and add the beef. Cook over a high heat, stirring often, until browned.

2 Add the onion, carrots and potatoes and 250 ml (9 fl oz) water. Bring to the boil then lower the heat. Cover and simmer for about 30 minutes, or until all the vegetables are tender.

3 Stir in the baked beans and Worcestershire sauce. Heat through for 5 minutes then serve, garnished with the parsley.

Beef and vegetable noodles

Instead of miso paste, you could use a 15 g sachet of dried instant miso soup.

8 *ProPoints* values per recipe
20 minutes in total

1 **carrot**, peeled and cut into matchsticks
1 small **leek**, sliced thinly
1 **celery** stick, sliced thinly
2–3 thin slices red **chilli** (optional)
2 teaspoons miso paste, dissolved in 450 ml (16 fl oz) boiling water
25 g (1 oz) dried fine egg noodles
calorie controlled cooking spray
100 g (3½ oz) rump steak, sliced into thin strips
1 teaspoon sesame seeds
1 tablespoon chopped **fresh coriander**
salt and freshly ground black pepper

1 Put the carrot, leek, celery, chilli (if using) and miso stock into a saucepan and bring to the boil. Reduce the heat and simmer for 2 minutes.

2 Add the noodles to the saucepan and cook over a low heat for a further 6 minutes, stirring occasionally.

3 Just before the noodles are ready, spray a non stick frying pan with cooking spray. Add the beef strips and stir-fry over a high heat for 2 minutes. Season, then stir in the sesame seeds and cook for a few seconds more, taking care that they don't burn.

4 Spoon the noodle and vegetable broth into a warmed bowl and top with the beef and sesame seeds. Serve sprinkled with the coriander.

TRY THIS
Use 100 g (3½ oz) **chicken** or **turkey** stir-fry strips instead of beef, for 6 *ProPoints* values per portion.

Steak burger with chilli salsa

Chilli salsa makes this filling burger intensely flavourful and satisfying.

7 *ProPoints* values per recipe
❄ (uncooked, without bread and salsa)
25 minutes in total

100 g (3½ oz) extra lean steak mince
½ small red onion or 1 shallot, chopped finely
1 small carrot, peeled and grated
½ teaspoon dried mixed herbs
a few drops of Worcestershire sauce
calorie controlled cooking spray
50 g (1¾ oz) slice rustic style bread,
   such as baguette
salt and freshly ground black pepper

For the salsa
1 large tomato, chopped finely
1 teaspoon finely chopped red or green chilli
5 cm (2 inch) cucumber, chopped finely
a few drops of balsamic, cider or white wine vinegar

1 In a bowl, combine the steak mince, onion or shallot, carrot, mixed herbs and Worcestershire sauce. Season and then, using wet hands, form into a burger.

2 Preheat a griddle pan or the grill. Spray the burger with cooking spray, then cook for 5–6 minutes on each side on a medium-high heat, until cooked to your liking.

3 Meanwhile, make the salsa by mixing together the tomato, chilli and cucumber. Season and add the vinegar.

4 When the burger is done, set it to one side to rest for a few moments. Meanwhile, spray one side of the bread with the cooking spray and grill until browned.

5 Place the bread on a warmed plate, sit the burger on top of the grilled side, and serve with the salsa.

Beef barley broth

Enjoy tender steak in a flavourful stock. If you prefer your beef less rare, you can cook it for longer in step 3.

7 *ProPoints* values per recipe
5 minutes preparation, 40 minutes cooking

75 g (2¾ oz) lean sirloin steak, visible fat removed
400 ml (14 fl oz) beef stock
1 bouquet garni
1 teaspoon Worcestershire sauce
25 g (1 oz) dried pearl barley
1 small carrot, peeled and diced
½ red pepper, de-seeded and diced
a handful of chopped fresh parsley

1 Put the steak in the freezer for 20 minutes to firm up for slicing.

2 Put the stock, bouquet garni, Worcestershire sauce and 250 ml (9 fl oz) water in a medium size lidded saucepan. Bring to the boil and add the pearl barley. Cover and simmer for 30 minutes then add the carrot and pepper. Return to the boil and simmer for a further 10 minutes until the barley is tender and puffed up and the vegetables are tender. Meanwhile, remove the steak from the freezer and slice it thinly. If you prefer your beef well done, add it for the final 3–5 minutes of cooking time until done to your liking, otherwise follow the next step.

3 If you prefer rare steak, put the steak slices in the bottom of a serving bowl and pour the hot soup over. The beef will cook on impact.

4 To serve, remove the bouquet garni and garnish with plenty of parsley.

SERVING SUGGESTION
Serve with 50 g (1¾ oz) French bread or a roll for 4 *ProPoints* values per portion.

Fillet steak on Mediterranean veg

5 ProPoints value

For a special dinner, try this succulent fillet steak, served on a pile of chargrilled vegetables.

5 *ProPoints* values per recipe
20 minutes in total

calorie controlled cooking spray
1 courgette, sliced diagonally into strips
1 red pepper, de-seeded and cut into large chunks
5 asparagus spears
125 g (4½ oz) lean fillet steak, visible fat removed
2 teaspoons chopped fresh rosemary
1 teaspoon balsamic vinegar
salt and freshly ground black pepper

To serve
3 cherry tomatoes, halved
4–5 fresh basil leaves

1 Preheat a griddle pan or the grill. Spray the vegetables with the cooking spray and then cook them in batches until tender. Remove and keep warm.
2 Spray the fillet steak with the cooking spray and rub the rosemary over both sides. Add the steak to the griddle pan, or a non stick frying pan. Cook for 2–3 minutes per side, depending on its thickness and how well done you like it. Add the vinegar and 1 tablespoon of water to the pan and heat for 1 minute to make a sauce.
3 Pile the vegetables on to a warm plate and arrange the steak on top. Sprinkle with the sauce, season, and serve with the cherry tomatoes and basil.

COOK'S TIP

When using a griddle pan, always lightly spray the food, not the pan, with cooking spray.

Beef and bean quesadillas

Quesadillas are deliciously crisp on the outside and melting on the inside.

9 *ProPoints* values per recipe
25 minutes in total

calorie controlled cooking spray
75 g (2¾ oz) **lean fillet steak**, trimmed of visible fat
1 Weight Watchers tortilla
2 tablespoons frozen **broad beans**, thawed
½ green **chilli**, de-seeded and chopped finely
1 **tomato**, de-seeded and chopped finely
2 tablespoons chopped **fresh coriander**
2 tablespoons hot salsa dip
25 g (1 oz) reduced fat Cheddar cheese, grated
salt and freshly ground black pepper

1 Heat a non stick frying pan and spray with the cooking spray. Season the steak and add to the pan. Cook for 2–3 minutes on each side for medium rare. For well done beef, cook for 4–5 minutes on each side. Remove from the pan and set aside to rest. Wipe out the pan.

2 Slice the steak thinly. Lay the tortilla on a chopping board and then arrange the steak over half of the tortilla. Sprinkle over the broad beans, chilli, tomato, coriander, salsa dip and cheese. Season then fold the tortilla over to enclose the filling.

3 Return the frying pan to the heat. When hot, put the tortilla in the pan and cook for 3–4 minutes on each side, turning with a fish slice, until the cheese is melted and the tortilla is golden and crisp. Serve immediately.

Lamb steaks with minty yogurt

Serve with 30 g (1¼ oz) dried couscous, cooked, for an extra 3 **ProPoints** values.

7 *ProPoints* values per recipe
20 minutes in total

125 g (4½ oz) lamb leg steak, trimmed of visible fat
2 teaspoons ras el hanout
calorie controlled cooking spray
salt and freshly ground black pepper
a lemon wedge, to garnish

For the yogurt sauce
50 g (1¾ oz) **0% fat Greek yogurt**
1 tablespoon chopped **fresh mint** leaves
1 **garlic clove**, crushed

For the griddled tomato salad
2 plum **tomatoes**, halved
1 teaspoon balsamic vinegar
1 tablespoon chopped **fresh coriander**

1 Put the lamb on a chopping board and sprinkle over about 1½ teaspoons of the ras el hanout. Season and rub the spices into the meat well.

2 For the yogurt sauce, mix together the yogurt, mint and garlic. Cover and refrigerate until needed. Toss the tomato halves with the remaining ras el hanout. Spray with the cooking spray and set aside.

3 Heat a griddle pan or non stick frying pan over a high heat until smoking hot. Spray the lamb steak with the cooking spray and add to the pan. Cook for 3–4 minutes on each side for medium, and 4–6 minutes on each side for well done, turning once. Remove and let rest for 5 minutes.

4 Add the tomatoes to the pan, cut side down, and cook for 2–3 minutes on each side, then transfer to a serving dish. Sprinkle with vinegar and coriander. Slice the lamb and serve with the tomato salad and the minty yogurt sauce.

Easy keema curry

If you're tempted by take away curries, try this one instead. It's delicious with a warm 44 g (1½ oz) Weight Watchers Mini Naan Bread, warmed in the toaster, for an extra 3 *ProPoints* values.

10 *ProPoints* values per recipe
❄ • 15 minutes preparation, 30 minutes cooking

80 g (3 oz) extra lean steak mince
1 small onion or 2 shallots, chopped finely
2 teaspoons medium curry paste
150 ml (5 fl oz) beef stock
1 tablespoon tomato purée
65 g (2¼ oz) canned chick peas in water, drained and rinsed
50 g (1¾ oz) mushrooms, sliced
50 g (1¾ oz) frozen peas
a handful of baby leaf spinach
a pinch of chilli powder (optional)
salt and freshly ground black pepper

For the raita
25 g (1 oz) low fat plain natural yogurt
1 tablespoon finely chopped cucumber

1 Heat a lidded non stick frying pan or saucepan, add the mince and cook over a high heat until sealed and browned. Add the onion or shallots and cook, stirring, for 2–3 minutes.

2 Add the curry paste, stock, tomato purée, chick peas and mushrooms, stirring to mix. Bring to the boil, reduce the heat then cover and simmer for 20–25 minutes.

3 Add the frozen peas and spinach. Cover and cook for a further 3–4 minutes until the spinach leaves have wilted. Check the seasoning and add the chilli powder, if using.

4 To make the raita, mix together the yogurt and cucumber in a bowl then serve with the curry.

Lime and cumin lamb cutlets

Here's an easy way to add a punch of flavour to a simple lamb chop.

12 *ProPoints* values per recipe
25 minutes in total

For the bulgur wheat salad
40 g (1½ oz) dried bulgur wheat
juice of a lime
5 cm (2 inch) cucumber, diced finely
½ yellow pepper, de-seeded and diced finely
6 cherry tomatoes, quartered
1 tablespoon chopped fresh coriander

For the lamb cutlets
2 x 100 g (3½ oz) lamb cutlets, trimmed of visible fat
1 teaspoon cumin seeds
calorie controlled cooking spray
salt and freshly ground pepper

1 Put the bulgur wheat in a saucepan and cook according to packet instructions until the liquid has been absorbed. Leave to stand for 5 minutes, then drain and refresh under cold running water. Drain well and transfer to a serving bowl. Stir in the juice of ½ the lime, the cucumber, pepper, tomatoes and coriander. Set aside.

2 Squeeze the remaining lime juice over the lamb cutlets then sprinkle with cumin seeds and season. Spray with the cooking spray. Heat a griddle pan until smoking, then cook the cutlets for 3–5 minutes on each side, according to taste, turning once. Set aside for 5 minutes.

3 Serve the lamb with the bulgur wheat salad.

Lamb steak with flageolet beans and bacon

9 ProPoints value

9 *ProPoints* values per recipe
40 minutes in total

100 g (3½ oz) lamb leg steak, trimmed of visible fat
zest and juice of ½ a lemon
2 fresh thyme sprigs, leaves only
calorie controlled cooking spray
1 shallot, chopped finely
1 small carrot, peeled and chopped finely
1 small celery stick, chopped finely
1 garlic clove, chopped finely
1 rasher (7 g) pancetta, chopped finely
4 tablespoons canned flageolet beans in water,
 drained and rinsed
100 ml (3½ fl oz) vegetable stock
salt and freshly ground black pepper

1 Put the lamb steak in a small, non metallic
 dish. Spoon over the lemon juice and zest
 and the leaves from the thyme sprig. Season
 and set aside.

2 Heat a small saucepan and spray with the
 cooking spray. Add the shallot, carrot and
 celery. Cook for 5–7 minutes until softened.
 Add the garlic and pancetta and cook for a
 further 5 minutes. Stir in the flageolet beans and
 the stock. Bring to the boil and simmer for
 15 minutes until the vegetables are tender and
 the sauce has thickened. Season and keep
 warm. If desired, remove from the heat and,
 using a food processor or hand-held blender,
 whizz until a rough purée; otherwise, serve the
 beans as they are.

3 Meanwhile, preheat the grill to high and
 cook the lamb leg steak under the grill for
 4–6 minutes in total, or until done to taste,
 turning once. Leave to rest for 5 minutes
 before serving with the flageolet bean purée.

Spiced lamb with aubergine braise

10 ProPoints value

10 **ProPoints** values per recipe
15 minutes preparation, 45 minutes cooking

½ teaspoon cumin seeds
½ teaspoon coriander seeds
75 g (2¾ oz) lamb neck fillet, trimmed of visible fat,
    and cut into chunks
calorie controlled cooking spray
1 small aubergine, cut into chunks
2 cm (¾ inch) fresh root ginger, peeled and
    chopped finely
1 garlic clove, chopped finely
1 small red chilli, de-seeded and chopped finely
2 plum tomatoes, skinned and chopped
1 heaped tablespoon canned chick peas in water,
    drained and rinsed
1 tablespoon chopped fresh parsley
1 tablespoon chopped fresh coriander
30 g (1¼ oz) dried couscous
¼ kettleful of boiling water

1 Put the cumin and coriander seeds in a dry, non
   stick frying pan and cook over a high heat for
   1–2 minutes until fragrant and starting to pop.
   Remove from the heat and grind roughly in a
   pestle and mortar. Add to the lamb. Mix well.

2 Heat a lidded medium saucepan and spray with
   the cooking spray. Add the lamb and cook for
   4–5 minutes until brown. Add the aubergine,
   ginger, garlic and chilli and cook for a further
   1–2 minutes. Add the tomatoes and
   3 tablespoons of water. Bring to the boil, cover
   and simmer for about 40 minutes until the lamb
   is tender and the sauce has thickened. Stir in the
   chick peas and cook, uncovered, for a further
   5 minutes. Stir in the parsley and coriander and
   season to taste.

3 Meanwhile, put the couscous in a bowl and add
   3 tablespoons of boiling water. Cover with a tea
   towel or plate. Leave to stand for 5 minutes until
   all the water is absorbed. Serve with the lamb.

Lamb masala kebabs

8 ProPoints value

8 **ProPoints** values per recipe
20 minutes in total + marinating

½ teaspoon ground coriander
a pinch of ground ginger
a pinch of ground cinnamon
½ teaspoon ground cumin
a pinch of chilli flakes
½ teaspoon turmeric
½ teaspoon garam masala
1 garlic clove, sliced finely
2 teaspoons lemon juice
100 g (3½ oz) boneless lamb leg steak,
    trimmed of visible fat, and cut into cubes
calorie controlled cooking spray
1 x 27 g wholemeal mini pitta
3 or 4 cherry tomatoes, halved
2 Little Gem lettuce leaves, shredded
15 g (½ oz) 0% fat Greek yogurt
5 or 6 fresh mint leaves

1 Mix all the spices, garlic and lemon juice
   together in a small bowl to make a paste. Add
   the lamb and mix well until all the meat is well
   coated. Cover and set aside to marinate at room
   temperature for 1 hour.

2 Preheat the grill to high and line the grill pan
   with foil. Thread the meat on to a metal skewer
   and put on the grill pan. Spray with the cooking
   spray and place under the grill for 4–6 minutes,
   turning once or twice until golden and tender.

3 Meanwhile, toast the pitta bread. Take the lamb
   from the skewer and serve on the pitta, along
   with the tomatoes, lettuce, Greek yogurt and
   mint leaves. Serve immediately.

TRY THIS

Cook with some grilled courgettes, peppers and
red onion for no additional **ProPoints** values.

Lamb mulligatawny

10 **ProPoints** values per recipe

❄ (after step 3) • 10 minutes preparation,
  40 minutes cooking

25 g (1 oz) dried red split lentils
calorie controlled cooking spray
50 g (1¾ oz) lean lamb leg, trimmed of visible fat,
  and diced
2 small shallots or onions, 1 chopped finely,
  1 sliced finely into rings
½ Granny Smith apple, peeled and grated
2 teaspoons medium curry powder
200 ml (7 fl oz) chicken stock
3 tablespoons reduced fat coconut milk
100 g (3½ oz) sweet potato, peeled and diced

1 Put the lentils in a saucepan and cover with
  100 ml (3½ fl oz) cold water. Bring to the boil
  and simmer until most of the water is absorbed
  and the lentils are soft. Drain and set aside.
2 Heat another saucepan and spray with the
  cooking spray. Add the lamb pieces and cook
  until browned. Remove from the pan. Set aside.
3 Spray the pan again and add the chopped
  shallot or onion, and grated apple. Cook,
  stirring, for 5–7 minutes until softened. Add the
  curry powder and cook for a further minute.
  Return the lamb to the pan, along with the
  stock, coconut milk and sweet potato. Bring to
  the boil and simmer for about 10–15 minutes
  until cooked through. Add the lentils to the pan.
4 Meanwhile, preheat the grill to high. Divide the
  sliced shallot or onion into rings and spread in a
  single layer on a non stick baking sheet. Spray
  with the cooking spray. Grill until golden. Top
  the soup with the onions or shallots to serve.

COOK'S TIP

Freeze any leftover coconut milk in an ice cube
tray, then keep in a freezer bag for up to 1 month.

Lamb and feta burger

Enjoy this burger with a 50 g (1¾ oz)
bread roll for an extra 4 **ProPoints** values.

7 **ProPoints** values per recipe
20 minutes in total

100 g (3½ oz) lean minced lamb
1 garlic clove, crushed
1 fresh rosemary sprig, leaves only,
  chopped finely
½ teaspoon dried oregano
25 g (1 oz) light feta cheese, crumbled
calorie controlled cooking spray
1 Little Gem lettuce leaf

For the tomato salsa
100 g (3½ oz) cherry tomatoes, quartered
1 spring onion, chopped finely
2 stoned black olives, chopped finely
1 tablespoon red wine vinegar
2 tablespoons chopped fresh parsley

1 Mix together the lamb, garlic, rosemary,
  oregano and feta. Using wet hands, shape into
  a patty and flatten.
2 Heat a non stick frying pan and spray with
  cooking spray. Add the lamb patty and cook for
  5–7 minutes on each side, until cooked through.
  Leave to rest for 5 minutes.
3 Meanwhile, make the salsa. Mix together the
  tomatoes, spring onion, olives, vinegar and
  parsley and then season.
4 Serve the burger in the lettuce leaf, topped with
  the tomato salsa.

Orange pork with Chinese greens

7 ProPoints value

Enjoy with 40 g (1½ oz) dried noodles, cooked, for an extra 4 *ProPoints* values.

7 *ProPoints* values per recipe
30 minutes in total + marinating

150 g (5½ oz) **lean pork fillet**, *trimmed of visible fat, and sliced*
1 tablespoon soy sauce
2 teaspoons sweet chilli sauce
1 teaspoon finely grated orange zest
3 tablespoons orange juice
1 teaspoon finely grated **fresh root ginger**
2 **spring onions**, *sliced thinly*
calorie controlled cooking spray
125 g (4½ oz) fine **green beans**, *trimmed*
1 head **pak choi**, *broken into separate leaves*
1 tablespoon chopped **fresh coriander**

1 Put the pork in a non metallic bowl. Add the soy sauce, sweet chilli sauce, orange zest, orange juice, ginger and spring onions. Cover and leave to marinate for at least 2–3 hours or overnight.

2 When ready to cook, spray a non stick frying pan with the cooking spray. Add the pork to the pan, reserving the marinade, and cook for 5–6 minutes on both sides. Add the marinade and simmer gently for 2–3 minutes until slightly reduced.

3 Meanwhile, bring a pan of water to the boil. Add the green beans and simmer for 4–5 minutes, adding the pak choi for the final 2 minutes. Drain well.

4 Serve the pork and vegetables, with the reduced marinade spooned over, sprinkled with the coriander.

TRY THIS

This recipe is also delicious with 165 g (5¾ oz) **skinless boneless chicken breast** instead of pork for 5 *ProPoints* values per serving.

Gammon and bean pepper pot

This speedy recipe ticks all the boxes and is ideal on a cold night when you want a cosy winter meal.

10 **ProPoints** values per recipe

❄ • 15 minutes preparation, 15 minutes cooking

calorie controlled cooking spray
125 g (4½ oz) gammon steak *(smoked or unsmoked)*,
  cut into chunks
1 small onion, *chopped*
½ red pepper, *de-seeded and chopped*
230 g can chopped tomatoes
300 g can mixed beans in water, *drained and rinsed*
1 tablespoon tomato purée
½ teaspoon chilli powder
25 g (1 oz) frozen sweetcorn
2 teaspoons chopped fresh parsley
freshly ground black pepper

1 Spray a saucepan with the cooking spray, then add the gammon chunks and onion. Cook, stirring, for 2–3 minutes until lightly browned. Add the pepper and cook for another minute.

2 Tip the tomatoes and beans into the saucepan then add the tomato purée and chilli powder. Bring to the boil, reduce the heat and simmer for 15 minutes, stirring occasionally. Add the sweetcorn and cook for a further 2 minutes.

3 Add the parsley then season and serve.

COOK'S TIP

If you're cutting the gammon from a larger piece, wrap and freeze the remainder, or keep it refrigerated. Use within 3 days.

Sausages with mash and red onion gravy

Enjoy this gastro-pub meal in your own home. It's comfort food at its best.

12 **ProPoints** values per recipe
20 minutes in total

300 g (10½ oz) sweet potato, *peeled and*
  cut into chunks
2 Weight Watchers Premium Pork Sausages
calorie controlled cooking spray
1 small red onion, *sliced thinly*
2 teaspoons instant gravy granules
2 teaspoons chopped fresh sage
salt and freshly ground black pepper

1 Bring a saucepan of water to the boil, add the sweet potato and cook until tender. Preheat the grill to medium.

2 Put the sausages on the grill pan and grill until thoroughly cooked.

3 Meanwhile, heat a small saucepan and spray with the cooking spray. Stir-fry the onion for 3–4 minutes, until softened, then add 200 ml (7 fl oz) water and bring up to the boil. Stir in the gravy granules and heat until thickened. Simmer over a very low heat until everything else is ready.

4 Drain the sweet potato and mash well, then stir in the sage and season.

5 Pile the mash on to a warmed plate and serve with the sausages and the red onion gravy.

TRY THIS

Make this recipe with 300 g (10½ oz) butternut squash instead of sweet potato if you prefer, for 4 **ProPoints** values.

Pork with garlic, lemon and thyme

6 ProPoints value

This quick and aromatic recipe is packed with flavour.

6 *ProPoints* values per recipe

❄ • 20 minutes in total

calorie controlled cooking spray
150 g (5½ oz) **pork tenderloin**, trimmed of visible fat,
   and cut into 1 cm (½ inch) slices
4 **spring onions**, sliced finely
1 small **garlic clove**, crushed
finely grated zest and juice of a small lemon
   (or ½ a large lemon)
1 teaspoon finely chopped **fresh thyme**
salt and freshly ground black pepper

1 Heat a non stick frying pan and spray with the cooking spray. Add the pork slices and cook over a high heat for 2 minutes on each side, until sealed and browned.
2 Add the spring onions and garlic to the pork, lower the heat and continue to cook for another 3–4 minutes. Add the lemon zest, lemon juice and thyme with 1 tablespoon of water.
3 Cook, stirring occasionally, for another 4–5 minutes, adding a splash of water if the ingredients start to stick. Season to taste, then serve.

TRY THIS

Why not use **fresh rosemary** instead of thyme for a change?

If you like, add half an eating **apple**, sliced thinly, to the pork when the spring onions are added, for no extra *ProPoints* values.

Pork and cashew nut stir-fry

11 ProPoints value

If you buy the pork tenderloin from a butcher or the supermarket's fresh meat counter, you can ask for the exact weight.

11 *ProPoints* values per recipe

20 minutes in total

40 g (1½ oz) dried fine egg noodles
¼ kettleful of boiling water
calorie controlled cooking spray
15 g (½ oz) unsalted cashew nuts
125 g (4½ oz) **pork tenderloin**, trimmed of visible fat,
   and cut into thin strips
3 **spring onions**, sliced finely
½ yellow or red **pepper**, de-seeded and sliced thinly
1 small **courgette**, sliced into strips
2 teaspoons soy sauce
2 teaspoons sweet chilli sauce

1 Put the noodles into a heatproof bowl and cover with boiling water. Soak for 5–6 minutes.
2 Meanwhile, heat a wok or non stick frying pan and spray with the cooking spray. Add the cashew nuts and stir-fry for about 1 minute until lightly browned. Remove and set aside.
3 Add the pork to the wok or frying pan and stir-fry briskly for 3–4 minutes, then add the spring onions, pepper and courgette. Continue stir-frying for a further 3–4 minutes.
4 Drain the noodles thoroughly, and add to the wok with the soy sauce and the sweet chilli sauce. Toss together. Serve, sprinkled with the cashew nuts.

COOK'S TIP

If you have a larger quantity of pork than needed, freeze the rest in 125 g (4½ oz) portions so it's ready when you make this dish again.

Chorizo and red pepper fusilli

A little chorizo adds a tasty kick to this simple pasta recipe.

9 *ProPoints* values per recipe
20 minutes in total

75 g (2¾ oz) dried **wholewheat fusilli pasta** *(or other pasta shapes)*

50 g (1¾ oz) fine **green beans**, *trimmed and sliced*

calorie controlled cooking spray

15 g (½ oz) chorizo, sliced thinly and cut into cubes

75 g (2¾ oz) roasted red peppers in a jar, drained and chopped roughly

25 g (1 oz) stoned olives, chopped

1 tablespoon chopped **fresh parsley** *(optional)*

salt and freshly ground black pepper

1 Bring a saucepan of water to the boil. Add the pasta and cook according to packet instructions, adding the green beans for the final 3–4 minutes.

2 Meanwhile, spray a non stick frying pan with the cooking spray and add the chorizo, cooking it for 1–2 minutes until sizzling.

3 Drain the pasta and beans, reserving 1–2 tablespoons of the cooking water in the saucepan. Return the pasta to the pan and add the chorizo, red peppers, olives and parsley, if using. Heat for a few moments, season and serve.

TRY THIS

This recipe is excellent served cold as a packed lunch.

Try substituting sliced **courgette** for the green beans, if you prefer. The *ProPoints* values remain the same.

You can use some of the remaining peppers in the recipe for Aubergine, Red Pepper and Lentil Curry on page 78.

Parma wrapped figs

5 ProPoints value

This starter is a knockout.

5 *ProPoints* values per recipe
10 minutes preparation, 20 minutes cooking

2 large ripe figs
40 g (1½ oz) low fat soft cheese
15 g (½ oz) Parmesan cheese, grated finely
2 x 15 g (½ oz) slices Parma ham
1 tablespoon balsamic vinegar
1 teaspoon clear honey
¼ teaspoon Dijon mustard
salt and freshly ground black pepper
mixed salad leaves, to serve

1 Preheat the oven to Gas Mark 5/190°C/fan oven 170°C.
2 Make deep cuts crossways in the tops of the figs, then open them out slightly. Mix together the soft cheese and Parmesan cheese and stuff this mixture into the figs. Wrap a slice of Parma ham around each fig, then put on a non stick baking tray.
3 Bake the figs for 18–20 minutes. Meanwhile, mix together the balsamic vinegar, honey and mustard. Season to taste.
4 Serve the figs with mixed salad leaves, with the dressing drizzled over.

COOK'S TIP

To prepare ahead, make the figs up to the point where they are baked, keeping them covered and chilled until ready to cook.

v TRY THIS

Make a vegetarian version by leaving out the Parma ham for 4 *ProPoints* values per recipe.

Pasta with Parmesan, bacon and mange tout

12 ProPoints value

A little sizzled bacon turns this simple pasta recipe into a great supper.

12 *ProPoints* values per recipe
25 minutes in total

calorie controlled cooking spray
1 smoked lean back bacon rasher, sliced into strips
75 g (2¾ oz) dried wholewheat pasta, *such as penne or farfalle*
50 g (1¾ oz) mange tout, *cut in half diagonally*
25 g (1 oz) frozen sweetcorn
50 g (1¾ oz) low fat soft cheese
2 tablespoons skimmed milk
1 teaspoon chopped fresh parsley
10 g (¼ oz) Parmesan cheese, grated
salt and freshly ground black pepper

1 Spray a non stick frying pan with the cooking spray and add the bacon. Cook for 3–4 minutes, stirring often, until crispy.

2 At the same time, bring a saucepan of water to the boil, add the pasta and cook according to packet instructions, adding the mange tout and sweetcorn for the final 2–3 minutes.

3 Drain the pasta and vegetables and set aside. Put the soft cheese and milk into the saucepan and stir over a low heat until smooth – about 1 minute. Tip in the pasta, vegetables and bacon and cook gently for about 30–40 seconds.

4 Transfer to a warm serving bowl or plate and sprinkle with the parsley and Parmesan cheese. Season to taste and serve.

TRY THIS
Use green beans or courgette instead of mange tout. The *ProPoints* values remain the same.

Peachy Parma sandwich

8 ProPoints value

Choose a ripe peach to bring out the best in this sensational sandwich.

8 *ProPoints* values per recipe
5 minutes in total

2 medium slices wholemeal bread
50 g (1¾ oz) low fat soft cheese
½ peach, *stoned and sliced*
2 thin slices Parma ham
15 g (½ oz) wild rocket
freshly ground black pepper

1 Spread both slices of bread with soft cheese and season with black pepper.

2 Arrange the peach slices on one slice of bread and add the Parma ham and the rocket leaves. Top with the second slice of bread and cut in half to serve.

Ham, mushroom and cheese bake

This clever little recipe only takes a few minutes to put together, and it bakes very quickly.

6 *ProPoints* values per recipe
10 minutes preparation, 15 minutes cooking

calorie controlled cooking spray
1 teaspoon wholegrain mustard
3 x 30 g (1¼ oz) slices wafer thin ham
100 g (3½ oz) closed cup mushrooms, sliced
3 spring onions, sliced thinly
½ red or yellow pepper, de-seeded and chopped
75 g (2¾ oz) reduced fat cottage cheese with chives
1 egg
1 tablespoon skimmed milk
½ teaspoon dried mixed herbs
salt and freshly ground black pepper

1 Preheat the oven to Gas Mark 5/190°C/fan oven 170°C.

2 Spray a shallow ovenproof serving dish, measuring about 20 x 12 cm (8 x 4½ inches), with the cooking spray and spread the mustard over the base. Arrange the slices of ham in the dish.

3 Spray a non stick frying pan with cooking spray and add the mushrooms, spring onions and pepper, cooking them for 3–4 minutes until lightly browned. Spoon them into the dish.

4 Beat the cottage cheese, egg, milk and dried herbs together. Season and pour over the mushroom mixture. Transfer to the oven and bake for 15 minutes then serve.

COOK'S TIP

You could use 75 g (2¾ oz) low fat soft cheese instead of cottage cheese if you prefer for 7 *ProPoints* values.

Summery chicken

5 ProPoints value

Creamy and bursting with flavour, this chicken dish is quick and tasty. It's sure to become a weeknight favourite. Serve with **broccoli** and **green beans** for no extra *ProPoints* values.

5 *ProPoints* values per recipe
10 minutes preparation, 25 minutes cooking

calorie controlled cooking spray
150 g (5½ oz) **skinless boneless chicken breast**
100 g (3½ oz) cherry **tomatoes***, halved*
25 g (1 oz) half fat crème fraîche
10 g (¼ oz) low fat pesto
a lemon wedge
salt and freshly ground black pepper
a few **fresh basil** *leaves, to serve*

1 Spray a non stick frying pan with the cooking spray. Season the chicken breast and add to the pan. Cook over a medium heat for about 20–25 minutes, turning often, until the chicken is cooked through and golden.

2 Add the cherry tomatoes to the pan and cook for a further 2–3 minutes. Add the crème fraîche and pesto, season, stir to combine, and squeeze over the lemon. Serve immediately, garnished with the fresh basil leaves.

COOK'S TIP

If you can't find low fat pesto use a standard variety and the *ProPoints* value will be 6.

chicken, duck and turkey

Poulet au vinaigre

Cooking the chicken in vinegar is a little unusual but it gives the sauce a delicious, rich piquancy.

8 *ProPoints* values per recipe

✳ • 20 minutes preparation, 20 minutes cooking

calorie controlled cooking spray
150 g (5½ oz) **skinless chicken leg**
2 **tomatoes**, skinned, de-seeded and chopped
   roughly (see Cook's tip)
150 ml (5 fl oz) good quality red wine vinegar
150 ml (5 fl oz) chicken stock
1 tablespoon chopped **fresh parsley**
salt and freshly ground black pepper

1 Spray a lidded medium saucepan with the cooking spray and place over a medium heat. Season the chicken leg and add to the pan. Cook for about 10 minutes, turning, until golden all over.

2 Add the tomatoes to the pan and cook until pulpy and reduced – about 5 minutes.

3 Pour in the red wine vinegar, increase the heat and simmer until nearly bubbled away.

4 Add the chicken stock, bring to the boil, cover and simmer for about 20 minutes until the chicken is tender. Increase the heat and boil to reduce the sauce until thickened. Stir in the parsley and serve.

COOK'S TIP

To skin a tomato, make a small cross at the base of the tomato with a sharp knife. Pour boiling water over just to cover and leave for 1 minute or a little longer if the tomato is less ripe. Drain and refresh under cold water until cool enough to handle. The skin should then peel away easily.

One pot spring chicken

This one-pot chicken is a great way to make a fuss-free meal.

9 *ProPoints* values per recipe

✳ • 20 minutes preparation, 45 minutes cooking

calorie controlled cooking spray
200 g (7 oz) **skinless boneless chicken breast**
1 **carrot**, peeled and sliced
3 baby **leeks**, or 1 large **leek**, sliced
2 **spring onions**, sliced
125 g (4½ oz) new **potatoes**, halved
450 ml (16 fl oz) chicken or vegetable stock
a few sprigs of **mint**, **sage** and **rosemary**
   (or 1 teaspoon dried mixed herbs)
25 g (1 oz) frozen **peas**
salt and freshly ground black pepper

1 Heat a lidded flameproof casserole dish and spray with the cooking spray. Add the chicken breast and cook for 1–2 minutes on each side until seared and browned.

2 Add the carrot, leeks, spring onions and potatoes. Pour in the stock, then add the herbs. Bring up to the boil, then reduce the heat to low. Cover and cook for 45 minutes, until the potatoes are tender.

3 Remove the lid and add the frozen peas. Simmer for 2–3 more minutes. Season to taste, remove the herb sprigs, if using fresh herbs, and then serve in a large bowl, seasoned with a little extra black pepper.

Roast chicken breast crown

This recipe uses a chicken breast crown – which is simply a chicken with the legs removed and the breasts left on the bone.

14 *ProPoints* values per recipe
30 minutes preparation, 1 hour cooking

1 chicken breast crown (from a 1.2 kg/2 lb 11 oz
   chicken), skin removed (see Cook's tip)
100 g (3½ oz) new **potatoes**
1 **carrot**, peeled and cut into chunks
1 **parsnip**, peeled and cut into chunks
1 **leek**, cut into chunks
calorie controlled cooking spray
¼ kettleful of boiling water
50 g (1¾ oz) stuffing mix (sage and onion)
100 ml (3½ fl oz) fresh chicken stock
1 teaspoon plain flour

For the marinade
1 **garlic clove**, chopped finely
2 **fresh thyme** sprigs, leaves only
2 finely chopped **fresh sage** leaves
a few finely chopped **fresh rosemary** leaves
zest and juice of ½ a lemon

1 Preheat the oven to Gas Mark 5/190°C/fan oven 170°C.
2 For the marinade, mix together the garlic, thyme, sage, rosemary, lemon juice and zest, then spread over the chicken. Place the squeezed out lemon half in a roasting tray and place the chicken on top.
3 Meanwhile, put the potatoes in a saucepan and cover with cold water. Bring to the boil and cook for 8–10 minutes until tender to the point of a knife, but not cooked through. Drain thoroughly. Put the potatoes and vegetable chunks around the chicken in the roasting tray and spray with the cooking spray.

4 Make up the stuffing balls by adding 5 tablespoons of boiling water to the mix, following the packet instructions. Shape into four balls and add these to the roasting tin.
5 Cover the chicken loosely with foil, leaving the vegetables uncovered, and put into the oven. Cook for 1 hour. Remove from the oven and transfer the chicken, vegetables and stuffing balls to a carving board. Cover loosely with foil, while you make the gravy.
6 Put the roasting tray on the hob over a medium heat. When hot, add the chicken stock and stir well to pick up any sticky bits from the bottom of the pan. Bring to the boil and simmer for 2–3 minutes until slightly reduced.
7 Mix the flour with 1 tablespoon of cold water to make a smooth paste. Reduce the heat under the gravy and gradually whisk in the paste. Continue to simmer for a further 2 minutes until the gravy has thickened. Season to taste.
8 Remove one breast from the chicken breast crown and reserve the other (see Cook's tip). Serve with the vegetables, stuffing balls and gravy.

COOK'S TIPS

A butcher can prepare the chicken breast crown, or you could make one yourself by removing both legs of a whole chicken and freezing the legs for later.

You can use the reserved chicken breast in another recipe, such as Lunchbox Caesar on page 42 or Lunchbox Slaw on page 42. Alternatively, use it to replace the lamb in the Lamb Mulligatawny on page 24.

Chicken lunchbox slaw

Since it's tricky to make small quantities of coleslaw, this recipe makes a larger amount than needed. The leftover half can be used in the Turkey Melt Open Sandwich on page 52 or simply kept in the fridge, undressed, for up to 1 week, to use another time.

9 *ProPoints* values per recipe
15 minutes in total

25 g (1 oz) walnuts
½ small green cabbage (such as pointed cabbage), shredded
1 small Granny Smith apple, cut into matchsticks
1 celery stick, sliced finely
1 small carrot, peeled and grated
1 spring onion, sliced finely
100 g (3½ oz) cooked skinless boneless chicken breast, torn into strips or chunks

For the low fat creamy dressing
25 g (1 oz) extra light mayonnaise
25 g (1 oz) low fat natural yogurt
2 tablespoons roughly chopped fresh coriander

1 Preheat the oven to Gas Mark 5/190°C/fan oven 170°C.
2 For the dressing, using a food processor or hand-held blender, mix all the ingredients together and whizz until smooth.
3 To toast the walnuts, spread them out on a baking sheet. Bake for 5–7 minutes until fragrant then leave to cool.
4 To make the coleslaw, mix together the cabbage, apple, celery, carrot, onions and walnuts. Divide the salad mixture in half and stir the dressing into one half, then add the chicken and serve.

Lunchbox Caesar salad

A truly scrummy salad to enjoy at the office or on a picnic.

9 *ProPoints* values per recipe
15 minutes in total

25 g (1 oz) extra light mayonnaise
1–2 tablespoons lemon juice, to taste
1 anchovy, drained and chopped finely or mashed
1 small garlic clove
½ teaspoon Worcestershire sauce
1 heart of Romaine lettuce, torn into bite size pieces
25 g (1 oz) read-made croutons
125 g (4½ oz) cooked skinless boneless chicken breast
10 g (¼ oz) Parmesan cheese, grated

1 To make the dressing, whisk together the mayonnaise, lemon juice, anchovy, garlic and Worcestershire sauce. If making for a lunchbox, pack this into a watertight container.
2 For a lunchbox, wrap the lettuce and the croutons separately in cling film and pack into a container.
3 Slice the chicken breast thickly. For a lunchbox, wrap it in clingfilm and pack next to the salad in the container.
4 Assemble the salad, pouring the dressing over the leaves and croutons. Place the chicken breast on top and sprinkle over the cheese. Serve immediately.

COOK'S TIP

Buy anchovies in a re-sealable jar and keep the unused ones in the fridge for up to 1 month.

Apricot glazed chicken

7 ProPoints value

Serve with 40 g (1½ oz) dried mixed wild and brown rice, cooked according to packet instructions, and finely sliced **mange tout** and **spring onions** for an extra 4 *ProPoints* values.

7 *ProPoints* values per recipe
5 minutes preparation, 35 minutes cooking

2 finely chopped **fresh sage** *leaves*
2 tablespoons apricot jam
1 small **garlic clove**, *crushed*
2 teaspoons cider vinegar
150 g (5½ oz) **skinless boneless chicken breast**
calorie controlled cooking spray

1 Preheat the oven to Gas Mark 4/180°C/fan oven 160°C.
2 In a small bowl, mix together the sage, jam, garlic and vinegar. Add the chicken breast and turn to coat evenly.
3 Spray the roasting tin with the cooking spray and transfer the chicken breast to the tin. Cover with foil, and cook for 25 minutes. Remove the foil and cook for a further 10 minutes until the chicken is golden and cooked through.

Chicken with capers and lemon

5 ProPoints value

Serve with a **green vegetable** and 100 g (3½ oz) new **potatoes** for an extra 2 *ProPoints* values.

5 *ProPoints* values per recipe
10 minutes preparation, 15 minutes cooking

calorie controlled cooking spray
165 g (5¾ oz) **skinless boneless chicken breast**, *sliced thickly*
zest and juice of ½ a lemon
1 teaspoon small capers in water, drained
1 teaspoon low fat spread
¼ kettleful of boiling water
salt and freshly ground black pepper

1 Spray a small non stick frying pan with the cooking spray. Season the chicken breast and add to the pan over a medium-low heat. Cook for 10–15 minutes, turning regularly, until golden and cooked through.
2 Remove the chicken to a serving plate and keep warm. Return the frying pan to a low heat and add the lemon juice, zest and capers. Stir to deglaze the pan, then swirl in the low fat spread and 1 tablespoon of boiling water.
3 To serve, pour the lemon and caper sauce over the chicken.

Chicken and black bean stew

8 ProPoints values per recipe

❄ • 30 minutes preparation, 40 minutes cooking

calorie controlled cooking spray
150 g (5½ oz) **skinless boneless chicken breast**,
    cut into chunks
1 small **onion** or **shallot**, chopped finely
1 small **garlic clove**, crushed
1 small **carrot**, peeled and chopped finely
1 small **celery** stick, chopped finely
½ red **pepper**, de-seeded and chopped finely
½ teaspoon ground cumin
½ teaspoon ground coriander
a pinch of cayenne pepper
100 g (3½ oz) canned **black beans in water**,
    drained and rinsed
3 tablespoons tomato salsa
125 ml (4 fl oz) chicken stock

1 Heat a lidded medium saucepan and spray with the cooking spray. Add the chicken pieces and brown on all sides. Remove from the pan and set aside.
2 Add the onion or shallot, garlic, carrot, celery and pepper to the pan. Cook for about 10–12 minutes until softened. Add the spices and stir well. Return the chicken to the pan along with the beans, salsa and stock. Bring to the boil, cover and simmer for about 40 minutes until the chicken is tender, then serve immediately.

TRY THIS

Serve with homemade tortilla chips for an additional 3 **ProPoints** values per serving. Preheat the grill to medium. Cut 1 reduced fat tortilla wrap into 6–8 triangles. Spray with the cooking spray and toast under the grill, turning once, until crisp and golden.

Chicken and sweet potato supper

14 ProPoints values per recipe

❄ • 30 minutes preparation, 35 minutes cooking

calorie controlled cooking spray
150 g (5½ oz) **skinless boneless chicken breast**,
    cut into 2½ cm (1 inch) chunks
1 small **onion** or **shallot**, chopped finely
1 **garlic clove**, chopped finely
1 **celery** stalk, chopped finely
1 **carrot**, peeled and chopped finely
2 teaspoons curry powder (mild or medium, to taste)
75 g (2¾ oz) dried **Puy lentils**
200 g can chopped **tomatoes**
200 ml (7 fl oz) chicken stock
100 g (3½ oz) **sweet potato**, peeled and cut
    into 2½ cm (1 inch) chunks
a large handful of baby leaf **spinach**
juice of ½ a lemon
salt and freshly ground black pepper

1 Spray a lidded, medium size, non stick saucepan with the cooking spray. Add the chicken breast pieces and cook over a high heat for about 5 minutes until lightly brown. Remove from the pan. Spray the pan again with cooking spray and add the onion, garlic, celery and carrot. Cover and cook gently for 7–10 minutes until softened. Return the chicken to the pan along with the curry powder and lentils. Stir well.
2 Add the chopped tomatoes and chicken stock and bring to the boil. Simmer for 10 minutes then add the sweet potato. Return to the boil and cook for a further 20–30 minutes, until the lentils and sweet potato are tender.
3 Add the spinach and stir well. Cook for a further 5 minutes until the spinach is just wilted. Add the lemon juice, season to taste and serve immediately.

Risotto solo

Someone, somewhere, has created the myth that risotto is tricky to cook. It really isn't – but don't be tempted to leave the kitchen.

11 *ProPoints* values per recipe
35 minutes in total

calorie controlled cooking spray
100 g (3½ oz) **skinless turkey breast steak**, cut into small chunks
75 g (2¾ oz) dried risotto rice
1 **leek**, sliced thinly
2 tablespoons dry white wine
350 ml (12 fl oz) chicken or vegetable stock
2 teaspoons chopped **fresh thyme**
1 teaspoon finely grated lemon zest
25 g (1 oz) frozen **peas**

1 Heat a medium size non stick frying pan and spray with the cooking spray. Add the turkey and cook for 3–4 minutes, until lightly browned.

2 Stir in the rice and leek. Cook, stirring, for another 1–2 minutes, then pour in the wine and allow it to bubble up.

3 Pour about one third of the stock into the pan and cook the risotto over a low heat, stirring often, until the liquid has almost been absorbed. Gradually add the remaining stock and continue to cook gently, stirring occasionally, until it has all been absorbed, and the rice is swollen and tender.

4 Add the thyme leaves, lemon zest and peas. Cook, stirring, for another 2–3 minutes, then serve.

Crispy oven-fried chicken

For a complete meal, serve with 150 g (5½ oz) new **potatoes**, **broccoli** and 2 tablespoons of ketchup for an extra 4 *ProPoints* values.

7 *ProPoints* values per recipe
5 minutes preparation + chilling, 40 minutes cooking

2 tablespoons **skimmed milk**
1 teaspoon finely chopped **fresh sage**
1 **garlic clove**, crushed
25 g (1 oz) cornflake cereal, crushed
a pinch of chilli flakes
1 teaspoon ground ginger
a large pinch of paprika
150 g (5½ oz) **skinless boneless chicken breast**
calorie controlled cooking spray
salt and freshly ground black pepper

1 Preheat the oven to Gas Mark 4/180°C/fan oven 160°C. Put the milk in a shallow dish, add the sage and garlic and mix well. In another shallow dish, mix together the crushed cornflakes, chilli flakes, ginger, paprika and seasoning.

2 Dip the chicken first in the milk mixture, then into the cornflake mixture, pressing well to coat. Put on a small plate and refrigerate for 1 hour.

3 Remove the chicken from the fridge and put on to a non stick baking tray. Spray with the cooking spray, cover with foil and bake for 25 minutes. Remove the foil, turn the breast over, and continue to cook for a further 10–15 minutes until golden and cooked through.

Honey-glazed chicken leg

5 ProPoints value

It's important to use reduced sodium soy sauce in this recipe, otherwise you may find the resulting sauce is too salty.

5 *ProPoints* values per recipe
5 minutes preparation + 1 hour marinating + standing, 40 minutes cooking

2 teaspoons clear honey
1 tablespoon reduced sodium soy sauce
1 garlic clove, crushed
1 cm (½ inch) fresh root ginger, peeled and sliced finely
125 g (4½ oz) skinless chicken leg
½ teaspoon sesame seeds, toasted (see Cook's tip)
1 spring onion, chopped finely

1 In a small non metallic dish, mix together the honey, soy sauce, garlic and ginger. Add the chicken leg and turn to coat. Cover and leave to marinate in the refrigerator for at least 1 hour, or overnight.

2 Preheat the oven to Gas Mark 6/200°C/fan oven 180°C. Transfer the chicken leg and marinade to an ovenproof dish. Cover with foil and bake for 30 minutes. Remove the foil, baste the chicken leg and return to the oven for a further 5–10 minutes until the meat is golden and the marinade has thickened to a glaze.

3 Remove from the oven and leave to stand for 10 minutes. Serve garnished with the sesame seeds and spring onion.

COOK'S TIP

To toast sesame seeds, put them in a large frying pan and cook on a medium heat for about 3–5 minutes. Watch them carefully and shake occasionally, until they are golden and release a fragrant aroma.

Barbecued chicken burger

9 ProPoints value

This burger lets you enjoy a barbecue flavour all year round.

9 *ProPoints* values per recipe
10 minutes preparation, 35 minutes cooking

calorie controlled cooking spray
1 small shallot, chopped finely
1 small garlic clove, crushed
1 tablespoon ketchup
1 tablespoon Worcestershire sauce
2 teaspoons American style mustard
1 teaspoon clear honey
125 g (4½ oz) skinless boneless chicken breast
50 g (1¾ oz) brown roll

To serve
lettuce leaves
sliced tomato

1 To make the sauce, heat a small saucepan and spray with the cooking spray. Add the shallot and garlic and cook for 3–4 minutes until softened, then add the ketchup, Worcestershire sauce, mustard and honey. Bring to the boil and simmer for 1–2 minutes. Remove from the heat and reserve 1 teaspoon of sauce for the roll.

2 Preheat the oven to Gas Mark 5/190°C/fan oven 170°C. Put the chicken in a small roasting tray and cover liberally with the sauce mixture. Cover with foil and bake for 20 minutes. Remove from the oven and then turn. Cover the chicken with any remaining sauce. Return to the oven and cook for a further 10 minutes, then remove the foil for a final 5 minutes until the chicken is golden and cooked through.

3 Cut the roll in half, toasting it if you wish. Spread the roll with the reserved sauce and then serve the chicken on the roll with lettuce and sliced tomato.

Turkey melt open sandwich

8 ProPoints value

If you're pressed for time, this quick and tasty hot sandwich is substantial enough for an evening meal.

8 *ProPoints* values per recipe
10 minutes in total

50 g (1¾ oz) cooked **skinless turkey breast**, chopped
    or shredded
15 g (½ oz) slice **reduced fat smoked ham**, chopped
    or torn into pieces
2 tablespoons low fat coleslaw
50 g (3¾ oz) crusty bread roll, cut in half lengthways
15 g (½ oz) Parmesan cheese, grated

1 Preheat the grill to high. Mix together the turkey breast, ham and coleslaw.

2 Lightly toast the halved roll on both sides. Divide the coleslaw mixture between the two halves of the roll and sprinkle each with the Parmesan. Return to the grill for 2–3 minutes until the cheese is melted and golden. Serve immediately.

COOK'S TIP

You could also use some of the leftover low fat coleslaw from the Chicken Lunchbox Slaw on page 42.

Chicken saltimbocca

4 ProPoints value

4 *ProPoints* values per recipe
25 minutes preparation + resting, 30 minutes cooking

125 g (4½ oz) **skinless boneless chicken breast**
1 **fresh sage** leaf
30 g (1¼ oz) **wafer thin ham**

For the tomato sauce
calorie controlled cooking spray
1 small **onion** or **shallot**, chopped finely
1 small **garlic clove**, crushed
200 g (7 oz) cherry **tomatoes**, halved
1 tablespoon chopped **fresh basil**
salt and freshly ground black pepper

1 Preheat the oven to Gas Mark 5/190°C/fan oven 170°C. Lay the chicken breast on a chopping board. Top with the sage leaf, then wrap the ham round to enclose the sage. If necessary, use a cocktail stick to keep everything together.

2 Transfer to a small roasting tin and cook for 20–30 minutes until the chicken is cooked through and the ham is golden. Set aside to rest for 10 minutes.

3 Meanwhile, heat a small saucepan and spray with the cooking spray. Add the onion or shallot and cook for 5–7 minutes until softened. Add the garlic and cook briefly before adding the tomatoes and 1–2 tablespoons water. Bring to the boil then simmer for 8–10 minutes until the tomatoes have softened and the sauce has thickened. Season to taste.

4 Slice the chicken breast in half at an angle and serve on top of the sauce, sprinkled with basil.

TRY THIS

Use the same amount of Parma ham in place of the wafer thin ham for 5 *ProPoints* values.

Use 125 g (4½ oz) **skinless turkey breast** instead of chicken for the same *ProPoints* values.

Italian stuffed cabbage

U8J®
ProPoints value

This lovely, warming recipe makes ideal comfort food for a cold night.

8 *ProPoints* values per recipe

❄ (parcels only) • 25 minutes preparation,
50 minutes cooking

15 g (½ oz) dried **brown basmati rice**
1 small **onion** or **shallot**, chopped
150 g (5½ oz) **chicken mince**
a large pinch of dried oregano
1 tablespoon chopped **fresh parsley**
10 g (¼ oz) Parmesan cheese, grated
2 large **Savoy cabbage** leaves
salt and freshly ground black pepper

For the tomato sauce

calorie controlled cooking spray
3 plum **tomatoes**, skinned and chopped
3 tablespoons red wine
a pinch of dried oregano
a pinch of chilli flakes
a pinch of cinnamon
1 bay leaf
125 ml (4 fl oz) chicken stock
1 tablespoon tomato purée

1 Bring a medium saucepan of water to the boil, add the rice and cook for 20 minutes until the rice is part-cooked. It is important that the rice is not fully cooked at this stage since it will continue to cook later. Drain well, and set aside.

2 In a medium bowl, mix together the onion or shallot, chicken mince, rice, oregano, chopped parsley and grated Parmesan cheese. Season well.

3 Cut the stalks from the cabbage leaves and lay them on a chopping board. Put half the chicken mixture on to one leaf and fold the leaf round to enclose it. Secure with a cocktail stick. Repeat with the second leaf and remaining chicken mixture. Refrigerate until needed.

4 Meanwhile, make the tomato sauce. Place a lidded medium saucepan over a high heat and spray with the cooking spray. Add the tomatoes. Immediately reduce the heat, cover, and cook for a couple of minutes until the tomatoes have started to soften. Add the red wine, oregano, chilli flakes, cinnamon, bay leaf and chicken stock and stir well. Cover and cook for a further 5 minutes.

5 Add the chicken parcels to the saucepan. The tomato sauce should cover the parcels by about two-thirds – if not, add a little more chicken stock or water. Bring to the boil, cover and simmer for 30 minutes, turning the parcels once and uncovering the pan for the final 15 minutes.

6 Remove the parcels to a serving plate and keep warm. Add the tomato purée to the pan, stir well and increase the heat. Simmer the sauce for 5–10 minutes until reduced and thickened.

7 Serve immediately with the parcels.

COOK'S TIP

If you can't find chicken mince, use 150 g (5½ oz) **skinless chicken fillet** and whizz in a food processor until fine.

Duck with cherries

Duck really suits sweet flavours and cherries make it taste fabulous.

9 *ProPoints* values per recipe
15 minutes in total

calorie controlled cooking spray
125 g (4½ oz) skinless duck breast or duck breast mini-fillets, cut into small pieces
15 g (½ oz) dried cherries
100 g (3½ oz) fresh cherries, stoned
1 small rosemary sprig, leaves removed and chopped finely
50 g (1¾ oz) frozen soya beans
50 ml (2 fl oz) dry white wine
75 ml (3 fl oz) chicken stock

1 Heat a non stick frying pan, spray with the cooking spray and add the duck pieces. Cook over a high heat for 2–3 minutes until browned. Add the dried cherries, fresh cherries, rosemary and soya beans to the pan and cook briefly. Remove from the pan and set aside.
2 Add the wine and swirl around to deglaze. Add the chicken stock, bring to the boil and simmer until reduced to 2 tablespoons. Return the duck and cherry mixture to the pan and warm through, then serve.

Chinese five spice braised duck

Most large supermarkets sell duck breast mini fillets, but if you can't find them, use a skinless duck breast of the same weight, sliced thinly. Serve with 40 g (1½ oz) dried rice, cooked according to packet instructions, for an extra 4 *ProPoints* values.

6 *ProPoints* values per recipe
15 minutes in total

1 teaspoon Chinese five spice powder
150 g (5½ oz) skinless duck breast mini-fillets
calorie controlled cooking spray
1 star anise
1 pak choi, halved
1 spring onion
1 tablespoon soy sauce
3 tablespoons chicken stock
1 teaspoon clear honey

1 Put the Chinese five spice powder on a small plate and dust the duck fillets in it. Heat a medium non stick frying pan and spray with the cooking spray. Add the duck fillets and cook for about 5 minutes, turning often, until nearly cooked through and browned. Add the star anise to the pan and cook for a further 1–2 minutes until the duck is firm to the touch. Remove the duck to a plate to rest.
2 Add the pak choi and spring onion to the pan and cook briefly before adding the remaining ingredients. Bring to the boil and bubble together until the pak choi has wilted.
3 Serve the pak choi with the duck and spoon over the sauce.

Duck with quinoa and pomegranate salad

11 *ProPoints* value

Quinoa (pronounced 'keen-wah') is a useful storecupboard staple and similar to couscous. Try it in this colourful salad, topped with delicious stir-fried duck.

11 *ProPoints* values per recipe
30 minutes in total + cooling

For the salad

75 g (2¾ oz) dried quinoa
225 ml (8 fl oz) vegetable stock
40 g (1½ oz) fine green beans, chopped finely
40 g (1½ oz) pomegranate seeds
    (from ½ a pomegranate)
1 very small red onion, chopped finely
1 small carrot, peeled and grated
2 teaspoons red or white wine vinegar
5–6 fresh mint leaves plus a few mint sprigs,
    to garnish
salt and freshly ground black pepper

For the duck

calorie controlled cooking spray
100 g (3½ oz) skinless duck breast
2 teaspoons sweet chilli sauce

1 Preheat the oven to Gas Mark 6/200°C/180°C fan oven. Rinse the quinoa in a sieve, then put it in a saucepan with the vegetable stock. Heat and simmer gently for 12–15 minutes, adding the green beans for the final 2–3 minutes of cooking time. The quinoa should be tender and have absorbed all the stock. Set aside to cool for 10 minutes.

2 Meanwhile, put the pomegranate seeds in a bowl with the red onion, carrot and vinegar. Snip in the mint leaves. Season and stir well.

3 Heat a non stick frying pan and spray with the cooking spray. Add the duck breast and cook for 2–3 minutes on each side. Transfer to a baking sheet and cook in the oven for 10 minutes. Return the duck to the pan and stir in the chilli sauce, then remove from the heat.

4 Mix the quinoa with the pomegranate mixture and pile on to a serving plate. Arrange the duck on top, then serve, with the warm chilli sauce. Garnish with mint sprigs.

TRY THIS

This dish is also delicious served cold, tossed with a generous handful of mixed salad leaves.

Butternut borlotti stew

8 ProPoints value

8 *ProPoints* values per recipe

V • ❄ (without topping) • 10 minutes preparation,
30 minutes cooking

100 g (3½ oz) canned **borlotti beans in water**,
   drained and rinsed
150 g (5½ oz) **butternut squash**, *peeled, de-seeded*
   and cut into 2 cm (¾ inch) cubes
4 **spring onions**, *chopped*
230 g can chopped **tomatoes**
200 ml (7 fl oz) vegetable stock
½ teaspoon dried mixed herbs
½ teaspoon paprika

For the topping
40 g (1½ oz) reduced fat halloumi cheese, cubed
15 g (½ oz) pine nut kernels
1 tablespoon chopped **fresh coriander** (optional)

1 Put the beans, butternut squash, spring onions,
tomatoes, stock, dried herbs and paprika in
a medium saucepan. Bring up to the boil, then
reduce the heat and simmer over a low heat,
for 20–25 minutes until the squash is tender
and the liquid has reduced.

2 A few minutes before the stew is ready, heat
a non stick frying pan and add the halloumi
cheese. Dry-fry until it turns light golden brown,
then add the pine nut kernels and cook for a
few more moments.

3 Spoon the stew into a warm serving bowl and
scatter the cheese and pine nut kernels on top.
Serve, sprinkled with the coriander, if using.

COOK'S TIP

Any leftover halloumi cheese can either be
refrigerated for a few days or frozen in 40 g
(1½ oz) portions, so you can make this recipe
again.

vegetarian
meals

Chinese spiced vegetable broth

This Chinese-style broth is full of flavour and it's ready in 15 minutes.

2 *ProPoints* values per recipe

V • 15 minutes in total

425 ml (15 fl oz) vegetable stock
½ teaspoon Chinese five spice powder
150 g (5½ oz) fresh stir-fry vegetables
225 g can bamboo shoots, drained
1 teaspoon finely chopped and de-seeded
    red or green chilli (optional)
100 g (3½ oz) silken tofu, cubed
a handful of chopped fresh chives or
    coriander, to garnish (optional)

1 Put the stock in a saucepan and bring to a boil. Stir in the Chinese five spice powder.
2 Add the stir-fry vegetables and bamboo shoots. If you like a spicy heat, add the chilli. Heat and simmer gently for 5–6 minutes, then add the tofu and cook for 2 more minutes.
3 Serve, topped with chopped fresh chives or coriander, if using.

COOK'S TIP

Wrap any remaining tofu from the packet in cling film and refrigerate, ready to use in a vegetable stir-fry within 2–3 days.

Midsummer minestrone

Make yourself feel good with a hearty portion of this summer vegetable soup. Serve with a 50 g (1¾ oz) wholemeal bread roll for an extra 3 *ProPoints* values.

7 *ProPoints* values per recipe

V • 20 minutes in total

calorie controlled cooking spray
3 spring onions, chopped finely
1 small courgette, chopped
50 g (1¾ oz) fine green beans, chopped
425 ml (15 fl oz) vegetable stock
1 teaspoon dried mixed Italian herbs
40 g (1½ oz) small dried pasta shapes
50 g (1¾ oz) frozen peas
10 g (¼ oz) green pesto sauce
salt and freshly ground black pepper
a handful of chopped fresh basil, to serve

1 Heat a saucepan and spray with the cooking spray. Add the spring onions, courgette and green beans and stir-fry over a medium-high heat for 1–2 minutes, until softened.
2 Add the vegetable stock and herbs. Bring up to the boil, then reduce the heat and simmer for 2 minutes.
3 Add the pasta to the saucepan and cook according to packet instructions or until tender. Stir in the peas and cook for 2 more minutes. Season to taste.
4 Ladle the soup into a warmed bowl and serve, topped with the pesto sauce and basil leaves.

COOK'S TIP

Keep any unused pesto sauce in the fridge, or freeze in 2 teaspoon portions in an ice cube tray.

Tagliatelle with chargrilled veg and goat's cheese

11 *ProPoints* value

Very easy and incredibly yummy.

11 *ProPoints* values per recipe

V • 25 minutes in total

1 small **courgette**, sliced diagonally into strips
calorie controlled cooking spray
60 g (2 oz) dried tagliatelle
15 g (½ oz) green or red pesto sauce
50 g (1¾ oz) roasted red pepper in a jar,
   cut into strips
25 g (1 oz) frozen **peas**, defrosted
25 g (1 oz) soft goat's cheese
5–6 **fresh basil** leaves
salt and freshly ground black pepper

1 Heat a griddle pan or preheat the grill. Spray the courgette strips with the cooking spray and griddle or grill until tender. You may have to do this in batches.
2 At the same time, bring a pan of water to the boil and cook the pasta according to packet instructions.
3 Drain the pasta, but not too thoroughly, so that you can return it to the saucepan with about 1 tablespoon of the cooking water. Add the pesto sauce, courgette strips, peppers and peas. Cook gently over a low heat for 1 minute.
4 Transfer to a warm serving bowl or plate and top with the goat's cheese and basil leaves. Season with black pepper, then serve.

COOK'S TIP

Instead of the courgette, you might like to try 75 g (2¾ oz) **asparagus** when it's in season. The *ProPoints* values remain the same.

Butternut squash and tomato penne

9 *ProPoints* value

If you love butternut squash, you'll adore this comforting pasta recipe.

9 *ProPoints* values per recipe

V • 25 minutes in total

250 g (9 oz) **butternut squash**, peeled, de-seeded
   and cut into 1 cm (½ inch) chunks
calorie controlled cooking spray
60 g (2 oz) dried **wholewheat penne**
   (or other pasta shapes)
75 g (2¾ oz) low fat soft cheese
2 tablespoons **skimmed milk**
25 g (1 oz) sun-blushed tomatoes, sliced
75 g (2¾ oz) cherry **tomatoes**, halved
freshly ground black pepper
a handful of **fresh basil** leaves, to garnish (optional)

1 Preheat the oven to Gas Mark 6/200°C/fan oven 180°C.
2 Spread out the butternut squash on a non stick baking tray and spray with the cooking spray. Roast for 20 minutes, turning after 10 minutes.
3 Meanwhile, bring a large saucepan of water to the boil and cook the pasta for 10–12 minutes, or according to packet instructions, until tender. Drain, reserving 1 tablespoon of cooking water in the saucepan.
4 Add the soft cheese and milk to the saucepan, mixing them with the reserved cooking water, stirring until smooth. Return the pasta to the pan and add the roasted squash, sun-blushed tomatoes and cherry tomatoes. Heat through for a few moments, then serve, sprinkled with black pepper and basil leaves, if using.

COOK'S TIP

Use pre-prepared butternut squash to save time.

Spaghetti frittata

11 ProPoints value

Discover another way to enjoy
spaghetti. This recipe works a treat.

11 **ProPoints** values per recipe

V • 25 minutes in total

50 g (1¾ oz) dried spaghetti
2 eggs
2 tablespoons skimmed milk
calorie controlled cooking spray
1 tomato, sliced thinly
40 g (1½ oz) reduced fat mozzarella cheese
½ teaspoon dried mixed Italian herbs
salt and freshly ground black pepper
a handful of fresh basil leaves, torn, to garnish

1 Bring a medium saucepan of water to the boil,
  add the pasta and cook according to packet
  instructions until tender. Drain well.

2 Preheat the grill to high. Heat a non stick frying
  pan and spray with the cooking spray. Beat the
  eggs and milk together then add the egg
  mixture to the pan. Arrange the pasta over the
  base of the pan and cook over a low heat for
  2–3 minutes to set.

3 Arrange the tomato and mozzarella over
  the surface of the frittata. Sprinkle the herbs
  on top and season. Place under the grill for
  2–3 minutes until the cheese has melted and
  started to bubble and brown.

4 Slide the frittata on to a warm plate and serve
  at once, garnished with the torn basil leaves.

COOK'S TIPS

Try 50 g (1¾ oz) small pasta shapes instead
of spaghetti for the same **ProPoints** values
per serving.

Be sure to use up the remaining mozzarella
cheese within 3 days.

Pepper and sweet potato stew

7 ProPoints value

Here's a tasty low *ProPoints* value vegetable stew that is simplicity itself.

7 *ProPoints* values per recipe

V • ❄ • 10 minutes preparation, 25 minutes cooking

1 small onion, sliced
1 carrot, peeled and sliced
1 celery stick, sliced
225 g (8 oz) sweet potato, peeled and cut into
    2 cm (¾ inch) cubes
½ red pepper, de-seeded and
    cut into chunks
230 g can chopped tomatoes
1 tablespoon tomato purée
¼ teaspoon chilli powder
150 ml (5 fl oz) vegetable stock
salt and freshly ground black pepper

To serve
15 g (½ oz) low fat plain yogurt
a handful of chopped fresh parsley

1 Put all the stew ingredients, except the seasoning, into a lidded medium saucepan and bring up to the boil. Reduce the heat, cover and simmer for 20–25 minutes, until the sweet potato is tender.
2 Season to taste. Serve topped with a spoonful of yogurt and sprinkled with parsley.

TRY THIS

If you really enjoy spicy food, go ahead and add some extra chilli.

Moroccan orange, feta and mint tabbouleh

6 ProPoints value

If you haven't tried bulgur wheat before, this delicious salad is a good way to start.

6 *ProPoints* values per recipe

V • 25 minutes in total

50 g (1¾ oz) dried bulgur wheat
250 ml (9 fl oz) vegetable stock
1 small orange
5 cm (2 inch) cucumber, chopped finely
3 spring onions, sliced finely
1 tablespoon chopped fresh parsley
1 tablespoon chopped fresh mint
45 g (1½ oz) light feta cheese

1 Put the bulgur wheat in a saucepan and add the stock. Cook over a medium heat according to packet instructions until the liquid has been absorbed. Set aside to cool for a few minutes.
2 Meanwhile, finely grate the zest from the orange and put it into a mixing bowl. Next, use a sharp, serrated knife to peel the orange, removing all the pith. Cut the orange into segments, removing all the membrane. Add to the bowl.
3 Stir in the cucumber, spring onions, parsley and mint, then crumble in the feta cheese. Tip in the cooled bulgur wheat, stir everything together, then serve.

Chilli non carne

This vegetarian chilli is incredibly low in **ProPoints** values so it's sure to become a favourite. Serve with 60 g (2 oz) dried **brown rice**, cooked according to packet instructions, for an extra 6 **ProPoints** values.

1 **ProPoints** value per recipe

V • ❄ • 10 minutes preparation, 25 minutes cooking

calorie controlled cooking spray
1 small red onion, chopped finely
1 small garlic clove, crushed
100 g (3½ oz) aubergine, chopped finely
75 g (2¾ oz) closed cup mushrooms, chopped finely
½ red chilli, de-seeded and chopped finely
230 g can chopped tomatoes
1 tablespoon tomato purée
1 tablespoon soy sauce
½ a vegetable stock cube
¼ kettleful of boiling water
salt and freshly ground black pepper
freshly chopped parsley, to garnish (optional)

1 Heat a medium saucepan and spray with the cooking spray. Add the onion, garlic, aubergine and mushrooms and cook for a few minutes, until softened.

2 Add the chilli, tomatoes, tomato purée and soy sauce.

3 Dissolve the vegetable stock cube in 3 tablespoons boiling water and add to the saucepan. Bring up to the boil, then reduce the heat and simmer gently for 20–25 minutes, until thick and pulpy, stirring occasionally.

4 Season to taste, then serve, garnished with parsley, if using.

TRY THIS

You can use chilli powder instead of fresh chilli if you prefer – ½ teaspoon should be enough, but add according to your taste. Try the Aubergine, Red Pepper and Lentil Curry on page 78 as it's a great way to use up the remaining aubergine.

Red rice salad

So many lovely textures and colours.

9 *ProPoints* values per recipe

V • 25 minutes in total

60 g (2 oz) dried Camargue red rice or brown rice
75 g (2¾ oz) cooked beetroot (not in vinegar),
    chopped
25 g (1 oz) baby leaf spinach
calorie controlled cooking spray
4 spring onions, sliced finely
10 g (¼ oz) pine nut kernels

For the dressing
finely grated zest and juice of ½ an orange
1 teaspoon clear honey
1 teaspoon wholegrain mustard
salt and freshly ground black pepper

1 Bring a saucepan of water to the boil, add the
rice and cook according to packet instructions
until tender.

2 Meanwhile, put the beetroot in a mixing bowl
and add the spinach.

3 Spray a non stick frying pan with the cooking
spray and gently fry the spring onions until soft.
Tip them into the bowl with the beetroot and
spinach. Brown the pine nut kernels in the frying
pan for 1–2 minutes, turning often. Cool slightly,
then stir them into the beetroot mixture.

4 Mix together all the dressing ingredients
and season.

5 Drain the rice, rinse with cold water and then
drain again thoroughly. Tip on to a serving plate
and top with the beetroot mixture. Drizzle with
the dressing, then serve.

COOK'S TIP

This salad is perfect for a packed lunch. Simply
keep it refrigerated and use within 3–4 days.

Caramelised apple and hazelnut salad

This salad is sensational. You could
enjoy it with a 50 g (1¾ oz) wholemeal
roll for an extra 3 *ProPoints* values.

8 *ProPoints* values per recipe

V • 10 minutes in total

calorie controlled cooking spray
1 apple, cored and sliced into thin wedges
a pinch of ground cinnamon (optional)
15 g (½ oz) whole blanched hazelnuts or almonds,
    chopped roughly
50 g (1¾ oz) mixed leaf salad
40 g (1½ oz) Cheshire cheese

For the dressing
1 tablespoon red or white wine vinegar
1 teaspoon olive oil
salt and freshly ground black pepper

1 Spray a non stick frying pan with the cooking
spray and add the apple slices, cooking them
over a medium-high heat until both sides are
lightly caramelised. Add the cinnamon (if using)
and hazelnuts or almonds. Stir well and cook
over a low heat for another few moments.

2 Put the salad leaves on a plate and pile the
warm apple slices and nuts on top. Crumble
the cheese over them.

3 For the dressing, mix together the vinegar and
olive oil. Season, then sprinkle the dressing over
the salad. Serve at once.

Halloumi with roast vegetable couscous

8 *ProPoints* values per recipe

V • 25 minutes in total + cooling

1 red onion, *cut into six wedges*
1 small courgette, *sliced at an angle*
calorie controlled cooking spray
¼ kettleful of boiling water
30 g (1¼ oz) dried couscous
½ roasted red pepper in a jar,
  chopped finely
1 tablespoon chopped fresh mint
1 tablespoon chopped fresh basil
5 cm (2 inch) cucumber, *chopped finely*
8 cherry tomatoes, *quartered*
zest and juice of ½ a lemon
2 x 40 g (1½ oz) slices reduced fat halloumi
salt and freshly ground black pepper

1 Preheat the grill to high. Lay the onion and courgette slices in a single layer on a baking tray or grill pan. Spray with the cooking spray and place under the grill for 5–7 minutes on each side, until golden and tender. Set aside until cool enough to handle.

2 Meanwhile, pour 3 tablespoons boiling water over the couscous and cover with a tea towel or plate. Leave to stand for 5 minutes until all the water is absorbed.

3 When the vegetables are cool enough to handle, chop everything finely. Stir into the couscous along with the pepper, mint, basil, cucumber, tomatoes and lemon zest and juice. Season and set aside.

4 Spray a non stick frying pan with the cooking spray and add the halloumi slices. Cook for 1–2 minutes on each side until golden. Serve immediately with the couscous.

Tomato crumpet with egg

5 *ProPoints* value

A few simple ingredients are put together in an ingenious way to make the perfect easy lunch.

5 *ProPoints* values per recipe

V • 20 minutes in total

1 egg
calorie controlled cooking spray
1 small onion, sliced thinly
2 tomatoes, skinned and sliced thickly
1 teaspoon paprika, plus a pinch to garnish
1 crumpet
salt and freshly ground black pepper

1 Bring a small pan of water to the boil, add the egg and cook for 12 minutes or less if you prefer.
2 Meanwhile, spray a non stick frying pan with the cooking spray, add the onion and cook for 3–4 minutes, until softened. Add the tomatoes and paprika and continue to cook for a further 4–5 minutes, until soft and pulpy. Season.
3 Shell the egg and slice it, or cut into quarters. Toast the crumpet.
4 Put the crumpet on a warm serving plate and spoon the tomato mixture over it. Arrange the egg on top, then serve, sprinkled with a little extra paprika and freshly ground black pepper.

TRY THIS

Use a toasted English muffin instead of the crumpet if you prefer, for 7 *ProPoints* values.

To find out how to skin a tomato, see the Cook's tip on page 38.

Spinach, tomato and ricotta torta

10 *ProPoints* value

A novel way to use fresh pasta.

10 *ProPoints* values per recipe

V • 10 minutes preparation, 30 minutes cooking

100 g (3½ oz) spinach
a kettleful of boiling water
100 g (3½ oz) ricotta cheese
calorie controlled cooking spray
1 x 45 g (1½ oz) fresh lasagne sheet
100 g (3½ oz) tomato and basil pasta sauce
½ teaspoon dried mixed Italian herbs
1 large tomato, sliced thinly
salt and freshly ground black pepper
5–6 fresh basil leaves, to serve

1 Preheat the oven to Gas Mark 5/190°C/fan oven 170°C.
2 Put the spinach into a colander and pour over the boiling water to wilt the leaves. Run cold water over the leaves and drain well. Squeeze out the excess moisture with your hands and place in a bowl. Add half of the ricotta and mix together.
3 Spray a shallow gratin or baking dish measuring about 15 x 23 cm (6 x 9 inches) with the cooking spray. Put the spinach mixture in the base of the dish. Lay the lasagne sheet on top.
4 Spoon the pasta sauce over the lasagne sheet and spread it over the base, then sprinkle with the herbs. Top with the sliced tomato and spoonfuls of the remaining ricotta cheese. Season and bake in the oven for 20–30 minutes, then serve, sprinkled with basil.

COOK'S TIP

If you freeze the remaining lasagne sheets, you can then defrost them one at a time when you need them.

Mushroom and aubergine parmigiana

Substantial and satisfying, you'll enjoy this generous portion.

8 *ProPoints* values per recipe

V • 20 minutes preparation, 30 minutes cooking

100 g (3½ oz) aubergine, sliced
calorie controlled cooking spray
100 g (3½ oz) mushrooms, sliced
250 g (9 oz) tomato and basil pasta sauce
75 g (2¾ oz) light mozzarella cheese, drained
   and sliced thinly
15 g (½ oz) fresh breadcrumbs
10 g (¼ oz) Parmesan cheese, grated finely
salt and freshly ground black pepper

1 Heat a griddle pan or non stick frying pan to a medium-high heat. Spray the aubergine slices with the cooking spray and chargrill or cook for a few minutes on each side, until lightly browned. Remove from the heat. Preheat the oven to Gas Mark 6/200°C/fan oven 180°C.

2 Place half of the aubergine slices in a shallow baking dish, measuring about 15 x 22 cm (6 x 8½ inches). Top with half of the mushrooms, then spoon half of the pasta sauce on top. Season lightly. Repeat these layers once more, then arrange the mozzarella evenly over the top.

3 Mix together the breadcrumbs and Parmesan, then scatter over the top. Bake for 25–30 minutes, until browned and bubbling.

COOK'S TIP

Why not use up the remaining aubergine from this recipe for Chilli Non Carne on page 67?

Caramelised onion and Stilton roll

This warm pastry tart is delicious served with **rocket** or mixed **salad** leaves.

7 *ProPoints* values per recipe

V • ❄ • 10 minutes preparation, 25 minutes cooking

calorie controlled cooking spray
1 red onion, sliced thinly
2 teaspoons balsamic vinegar
½ teaspoon sugar
½ teaspoon chopped fresh thyme
   or sage (or a pinch of dried herbs)
1 teaspoon pine nut kernels
1 x 45 g (1½ oz) sheet filo pastry, measuring
   50 x 24 cm (20 x 9½ inches), defrosted if frozen
25 g (1 oz) blue Stilton cheese, crumbled

1 Preheat the oven to Gas Mark 6/200°C/fan oven 180°C.

2 Spray a non stick frying pan with the cooking spray and add the onion, frying it over a medium-high heat for 4–5 minutes until softened and slightly caramelised. Add the vinegar, sugar, thyme or sage and pine nut kernels and cook for a few more moments.

3 Spray a baking sheet with cooking spray. Put the filo on top then fold the shortest edge over to make a square. Spoon the red onion mixture on to the square, leaving a border around the edge. Sprinkle the Stilton on top of the onion mix. Fold the filo around the filling to make a parcel, then bake in the oven for 20–25 minutes. Serve warm.

TRY THIS

Try crumbled Cheshire cheese instead of Stilton. The *ProPoints* values will be the same.

Leek and Cheddar bread pudding

9 ProPoints value

This is a great way to use up a few **vegetables** and any slightly stale bread.

9 *ProPoints* values per recipe

V • 15 minutes preparation, 20 minutes cooking

calorie controlled cooking spray
1 **leek**, sliced thinly
½ red **pepper**, de-seeded and chopped
100 g (3½ oz) **mushrooms**, sliced thinly
½ teaspoon dried mixed herbs
50 g (1¾ oz) fresh breadcrumbs
1 **egg**
150 ml (5 fl oz) **skimmed milk**
40 g (1½ oz) reduced fat Cheddar cheese, grated
salt and freshly ground black pepper

1 Preheat the oven to Gas Mark 5/190°C/fan oven 170°C.
2 Heat a non stick frying pan and spray with the cooking spray. Cook the leek, pepper and mushrooms for 4–5 minutes, stirring often, until softened. Add the herbs and season.
3 Spray a baking dish, measuring approximately 15 x 22 cm (6 x 8½ inches), with the cooking spray. Sprinkle half of the breadcrumbs over the base. Top with all the vegetables, then sprinkle the remaining breadcrumbs on top.
4 Beat the egg and milk together and pour evenly into the baking dish. Sprinkle the cheese over the top. Bake in the oven for 20 minutes until golden brown.

COOK'S TIPS

You might like to use up the other half of the pepper in the Ham, Mushroom and Cheese Bake on page 35.

Always keep some frozen breadcrumbs in your freezer, so they are handy for recipes like these.

Curry potato pie

7 ProPoints value

7 *ProPoints* values per recipe

V • 20 minutes preparation, 25 minutes cooking

100 g (3½ oz) **potato**, peeled and sliced medium thick
1 small **carrot**, peeled and sliced
calorie controlled cooking spray
1 **leek**, sliced finely
1 teaspoon chopped **fresh root ginger**
1 **garlic clove**, chopped finely
1 teaspoon mild or medium curry powder
100 ml (3½ fl oz) hot vegetable stock
1 x 45 g (1½ oz) sheet filo pastry, measuring
  50 x 24 cm (20 x 9½ inches), defrosted if frozen
salt and freshly ground black pepper

For the fresh coriander relish
a small bunch of finely chopped **fresh coriander**
¼ green **chilli**, de-seeded and chopped finely
juice of ½ a lime
1 tablespoon **0% fat Greek yogurt**
a pinch of sugar

1 Preheat the oven to Gas Mark 6/200°C/fan oven 180°C. To make the coriander relish, combine all the ingredients. Using a hand-held blender or food processor, whizz until well combined, adding a little water if it is too thick. Season, cover and refrigerate for up to 2 hours.
2 Bring a saucepan of water to the boil and cook the potato and carrot for about 4 minutes or until just tender. Drain well and set aside.
3 Spray a large non stick frying pan with the cooking spray. Add the leek, garlic and ginger. Cook for 5–7 minutes until softened but not brown, adding water if it starts to stick. Sprinkle over the curry powder and cook for 1 minute, stirring in the stock. Transfer to a bowl and add the potato and carrot. Mix well and season. Spoon into a 450 ml (16 fl oz) ovenproof dish.
4 Cut the pastry widthways into four thick strips. Scrunch it up over the top of the vegetable mix and spray with cooking spray. Bake for 20–25 minutes until golden then serve with the relish.

Aubergine, red pepper and lentil curry

9 ProPoints value

This delicious vegetarian curry is a doddle to make.

9 *ProPoints* values per recipe

V • ❄ • 15 minutes preparation, 30 minutes cooking

calorie controlled cooking spray
100 g (3½ oz) **aubergine**, cut into chunks
1 small **onion**, chopped finely
1 tablespoon medium curry paste
½ teaspoon cumin seeds
100 g (3½ oz) roasted red peppers in
  a jar, chopped
50 g (1¾ oz) dried red **lentils**
2 tablespoons tomato purée
400 ml (14 fl oz) vegetable stock
15 g (½ oz) **low fat natural yogurt**
a handful of chopped **fresh coriander**, to serve

1 Spray a large non stick frying pan with the cooking spray. Add the aubergine and onion and cook over a low heat for about 5–6 minutes, until softened.

2 Stir in the curry paste and cumin seeds, then add the red peppers, lentils, tomato purée and stock. Simmer over a low heat for 25–30 minutes, until the lentils are tender. Add a little extra water if the mixture begins to look dry.

3 Serve the curry, topped with the yogurt and sprinkled with chopped coriander.

COOK'S TIP

Some of the remaining peppers could be used in the recipe for Chorizo and Red Pepper Fusilli on page 31 or the Halloumi with Roasted Vegetable Couscous on page 70.

Paratha with spicy cauliflower

10 ProPoints value

You might like to enjoy this with 1 tablespoon of tomato chutney for an extra 1 *ProPoints* value.

10 *ProPoints* values per recipe

V • 25 minutes in total

½ small **cauliflower**, broken into florets
1 frozen paratha
calorie controlled cooking spray
2 **spring onions**, sliced finely
½ red **pepper**, de-seeded and chopped finely
6–8 thin slices red or green **chilli** (optional)
½ teaspoon black onion seeds
a pinch of cumin seeds (optional)
a pinch of turmeric
25 g (1 oz) paneer, cubed
a handful of chopped **fresh coriander**, to garnish
a lemon wedge, to serve (optional)

1 Bring a medium saucepan of water to the boil. Add the cauliflower and cook for about 5 minutes, until just tender. Be careful not to overcook it, as it will be stir-fried too, and needs to hold its shape. Drain well.

2 Heat a non stick frying pan and cook the paratha from frozen, according to packet instructions. Set aside on a warm plate.

3 Spray the frying pan with the cooking spray. Add the spring onions, pepper and chilli (if using) and stir-fry for 2–3 minutes, then add the cauliflower and spices. Cook for 2–3 minutes longer until the cauliflower is lightly browned.

4 Add the paneer, stir through, then pile the mixture on top of the paratha. Sprinkle fresh coriander over the top, then serve with the lemon wedge, if using.

Omelette burrito ⑥ ProPoints value

This quick dish is perfect as something different for breakfast, but also lovely for lunch or brunch.

6 **ProPoints** values per recipe
V • 10 minutes in total

calorie controlled cooking spray
2 spring onions, chopped finely
1 teaspoon chopped red or green fresh chilli
1 egg
2 tablespoons skimmed milk
1 tablespoon chopped fresh coriander
1 medium soft flour tortilla
salt and freshly ground black pepper

1 Heat a non stick frying pan and spray with the cooking spray. Add the spring onions and chilli and stir-fry for about 1 minute.
2 Beat the egg and milk together and pour into the frying pan. Cook for 1–2 minutes until the surface has set. Sprinkle with the coriander, then fold in half. Place the omelette on the centre of the tortilla. Season. Fold in the sides of the tortilla, then fold over the opposite edges to completely enclose the filling.
3 Cook the filled tortilla in the frying pan for about 30 seconds on each side, to warm it through. Remove from the pan, slice in half, then serve hot or cold.

TRY THIS

You could make the omelette with two eggs instead of one. This will increase the **ProPoints** values to 7.

Spinach and red onion pilaf ⑩ ProPoints value

Enjoy this pilaf hot as a main course, or cold for a packed lunch.

10 **ProPoints** values per recipe
V • 30 minutes in total

60 g (2 oz) dried brown basmati rice
½ vegetable stock cube
1 egg
calorie controlled cooking spray
1 small red onion, chopped
1 small garlic clove, crushed
½ teaspoon ground coriander
½ teaspoon cumin seeds
25 g (1 oz) raisins
100 g (3½ oz) spinach
a pinch of paprika
a handful of chopped fresh coriander,
    to garnish (optional)

1 Bring a saucepan of water to the boil and cook the rice with ½ a stock cube according to packet instructions, until tender. At the same time, bring another saucepan of water to the boil and hard-boil the egg in gently simmering water for 12 minutes.
2 Meanwhile, heat a non stick frying pan or wok and spray with the cooking spray. Add the onion and stir-fry for 2–3 minutes, until softened. Add the garlic, coriander and cumin seeds and stir-fry for a moment. Set aside until the rice is tender.
3 Drain the rice thoroughly and add to the wok or frying pan. Stir in the raisins and spinach and cook over a low heat for 3–4 more minutes, until the leaves have wilted.
4 Shell the egg and cut it into quarters. Spoon the pilaf on to a warm plate, top with the egg and sprinkle with the paprika. Sprinkle the fresh coriander over the top, if using, then serve.

Quorn korma

Create a tasty vegetarian curry with Quorn chicken-style pieces.

9 *ProPoints* values per recipe

V • ❄ • 15 minutes preparation, 20 minutes cooking

calorie controlled cooking spray
100 g (3½ oz) frozen Quorn chicken style pieces
4 spring onions or 2 shallots, chopped finely
75 g (2¾ oz) mushrooms, sliced
2 teaspoons Korma curry paste
230 g can chopped tomatoes
150 ml (5 fl oz) hot vegetable stock

To serve
40 g (1½ oz) dried long grain brown rice
15 g (½ oz) low fat plain yogurt
1 tablespoon chopped fresh coriander

1 Bring a saucepan of water to the boil and cook the rice according to packet instructions. Meanwhile, spray a saucepan with the cooking spray and add the frozen Quorn pieces and spring onions or shallots. Cook over a medium heat, stirring often, for 6–8 minutes.

2 Add the mushrooms, curry paste, tomatoes and stock. Bring up to the boil, then reduce the heat and simmer for 20 minutes, stirring occasionally. Add a little extra water if the mixture begins to look too dry.

3 Spoon the curry on to a warm serving plate and top with the yogurt and chopped coriander. Serve with the cooked rice.

COOK'S TIP

Frozen Quorn chicken-style pieces are available in 300 g packs. Keep the remainder of the packet in the freezer.

Peach, plum and Cheshire melt

With lightly caramelised peach and plum slices served on wholemeal toast, and topped with a melted Cheshire cheese, this is a real taste sensation.

7 *ProPoints* values per recipe

V • 15 minutes in total

calorie controlled cooking spray
1 peach, stoned and sliced into 8 wedges
1 plum, stoned and sliced thinly
a pinch of ground cinnamon or mixed spice
1 teaspoon light muscovado or caster sugar
2 x 20 g (¾ oz) slices calorie controlled wholemeal
    or granary bread
40 g (1½ oz) Cheshire cheese, sliced

1 Preheat the grill to medium-high.

2 Heat a non stick frying pan and spray with the cooking spray. Add the peach and plum slices and cook over a high heat for 3–4 minutes, turning occasionally, until lightly browned and beginning to soften. Add the cinnamon or mixed spice and sugar and cook over a low heat for another 1–2 minutes.

3 Meanwhile, toast the slices of bread. Place them on a heat-resistant plate or a baking sheet.

4 Pile the spiced fruits on to both slices of toast and arrange the sliced cheese on top. Grill for 1–2 minutes, to melt the cheese a little. Serve at once.

TRY THIS

This combination also works well with blue Stilton for an extra 1 ***ProPoints*** value. If you like, serve it with a mixed leaf salad or spinach sprinkled with a little balsamic vinegar or lemon juice.

Mezze platter

10 **ProPoints** values per recipe

V • 20 minutes in total

2 mini wholemeal pittas
calorie controlled cooking spray

For the houmous
100 g (3½ oz) canned chick peas in water,
    drained and rinsed
a pinch of ground cumin
juice of ½ a lemon
1 teaspoon sesame seeds
25 g (1 oz) 0% fat Greek yogurt
1 tablespoon chopped fresh coriander

For the tzatziki
2½ cm (1 inch) cucumber, grated
1 small garlic clove, grated
1 tablespoon chopped fresh mint

For the Greek salad
1 tomato, chopped
2½ cm (1 inch) cucumber, chopped
a pinch of dried oregano
3 stoned black olives, chopped
25 g (1 oz) light feta cheese
1 teaspoon red wine vinegar
salt and freshly ground black pepper

1 For the houmous, put the chick peas, cumin, lemon juice, sesame seeds and 1 tablespoon of the yogurt in a food processor or hand-held blender. Whizz until smooth, adding a little water if it seems too thick. Stir in the coriander.

2 For the tzatziki, mix the remaining yogurt with the cucumber, garlic and mint. For the Greek salad, mix together the tomato, cucumber, oregano, olives, cheese and vinegar. Season.

3 Preheat the grill to high. Cut the pittas in half horizontally, then cut each in half again. Lay in a single layer on a baking tray and spray with the cooking spray. Grill until golden then turn and grill again. Cool slightly and serve with the houmous, tzatziki and salad.

Chinese vegetable pancakes

These pancakes really are speedy and taste great with this Chinese-style filling.

9 **ProPoints** values per recipe

V • 25 minutes in total + resting

50 g (1¾ oz) plain flour
a pinch of salt
1 egg
125 ml (4 fl oz) skimmed milk
calorie controlled cooking spray
150 g (5½ oz) fresh or frozen stir-fry vegetables
a pinch of Chinese five spice powder
2 teaspoons sweet chilli sauce (optional)

1 Put the flour, salt, egg and milk in a large jug or mixing bowl. Beat the ingredients together, using a hand held whisk, to make a smooth batter. Set aside for 20 minutes to allow the flour to swell.

2 Heat a non stick frying pan and spray with the cooking spray. Pour in half the batter and swirl it over the base of the pan. Cook over a medium heat until the top has set, then flip over to cook the other side. Slide on to a warm plate and keep warm, covered with foil, whilst you make the second pancake. Slide this out of the pan and keep both pancakes warm whilst you make the filling.

3 Spray the frying pan once more with the cooking spray. Add the stir-fry vegetables and cook, stirring, for 3–4 minutes until done to your liking. Sprinkle with the Chinese five spice powder and add all of the sweet chilli sauce, if using, or reserve some for drizzling over at the end.

4 Share the stir-fried vegetables between the pancakes and fold them up into triangles. Serve at once, drizzling over any remaining chilli sauce.

Quick prawn and courgette curry

This seafood curry is great with 40 g (1½ oz) dried **brown basmati rice**, cooked according to packet instructions, for an extra 4 *ProPoints* values.

4 *ProPoints* values per recipe
20 minutes in total

calorie controlled cooking spray
1 large **garlic clove**, chopped finely
2½ cm (1 inch) **fresh root ginger**,
    peeled and grated
1 green **chilli** (or to taste), de-seeded and
    chopped finely
1 **courgette**, halved lengthwise
    then sliced across
a large pinch of turmeric
1 teaspoon ground cumin
200 g (7 oz) chopped **tomatoes**
200 g (7 oz) cooked peeled **prawns**,
    defrosted if frozen
3 tablespoons chopped **fresh coriander**
juice of ½ a lemon
salt and freshly ground black pepper

1 Heat a non stick frying pan or wok over a high heat and spray with the cooking spray. Add the garlic, ginger and chilli and cook briefly before adding the courgette. Stir-fry for 1 minute before adding the turmeric, cumin and tomatoes. Bring to the boil and simmer for 5 minutes until starting to thicken, then add the prawns.
2 Heat through for a further 1–2 minutes, then stir in the coriander and lemon juice. Season to taste and serve immediately.

fish and seafood

Couscous salad with prawns

7 ProPoints

It only takes 10 minutes to create this fabulous seafood salad. You can pack it for lunch if you wish.

7 **ProPoints** values per recipe
10 minutes in total

50 g (1¾ oz) dried couscous
5 tablespoons hot vegetable stock
a squeeze of lemon juice
2½ cm (1 inch) cucumber, diced
75 g (2¾ oz) cherry tomatoes, quartered
2 radishes, sliced into half moons
1 teaspoon chopped fresh dill
100 g (3½ oz) cooked peeled prawns
25 g (1 oz) baby leaf salad

1 Place the couscous in a bowl and pour in the hot stock. Stir briefly then cover the bowl with a tea towel or plate. Leave to absorb the stock for 5 minutes while you prepare the rest of the ingredients.
2 Fluff up the couscous with a fork, to break up the grains, then add a squeeze of lemon juice to taste. Stir in the cucumber, cherry tomatoes, radishes and dill, then top with the prawns.
3 If eating immediately, spoon the couscous salad on to the leaves to serve. If you are packing it in a lunchbox, place the salad leaves on top of the couscous salad, so that they don't wilt.

Prawns with shredded omelette

12 ProPoints

This easy dish is like a healthier version of egg fried rice. It's lovely served warm or cold.

12 **ProPoints** values per recipe
30 minutes in total

60 g (2 oz) dried long grain brown rice
calorie controlled cooking spray
1 egg
1 tablespoon skimmed milk
a pinch of chilli powder (optional)
4 spring onions, chopped finely
75 g (2¾ oz) raw peeled prawns
75 g (2¾ oz) frozen peas
1 tablespoon chopped fresh coriander
salt and freshly ground black pepper

1 Bring a saucepan of water to the boil, add the rice and cook according to packet instructions, until tender.
2 Meanwhile, spray a non stick frying pan with the cooking spray. Beat the egg and milk together, pour into the frying pan and let it flow over the surface. Cook over a medium heat until set. Sprinkle the surface with chilli powder, if using, then fold the omelette in half and slide it on to a plate. Set aside.
3 Wipe out the frying pan with a piece of kitchen paper, then spray once more with the cooking spray. Add the spring onions and gently fry for 3–4 minutes until softened, then add the prawns and peas. Cook over a low heat, stirring often, for about 5 minutes.
4 Drain the rice and add it to the frying pan, stirring it into the prawn mixture with the chopped coriander. Slice the omelette and add it to the pan, stirring it through gently. Season, then serve.

Chinese prawn and broccoli

8 ProPoints value

If you can't find tenderstem broccoli, ordinary broccoli works well too. Serve with 40 g (1½ oz) **dried brown rice**, cooked, for an extra 4 *ProPoints* values.

8 *ProPoints* values per recipe
15 minutes in total + chilling

1 teaspoon cornflour
a pinch of cayenne pepper
1 tablespoon soy sauce
100 g (3½ oz) raw peeled tiger **prawns**
calorie controlled cooking spray
25 g (1 oz) unsalted cashews
1 **garlic clove**, chopped
1 teaspoon grated **fresh root ginger**
100 g (3½ oz) tenderstem **broccoli**, trimmed
50 g (1¾ oz) shiitake **mushrooms**, sliced
2 tablespoons rice wine or dry sherry
1 **spring onion**, sliced finely at an angle

1 Mix together the cornflour and cayenne pepper. Add the soy sauce and mix well. Add the prawns and mix well with your hands. Set aside in the fridge to marinate for 30 minutes.

2 Heat a non stick frying pan or wok until hot then spray with the cooking spray. Add the cashews and stir-fry for 30 seconds or so, or until they start to colour. Remove and set aside.

3 Spray the pan again and add the garlic and ginger. Cook for a few seconds before adding the broccoli and mushrooms. Stir-fry over a high heat for about a minute. Add the rice wine, then the prawns and 5 tablespoons of water. Bring to the boil and simmer for 2–3 minutes until the prawns turn pink. Simmer for a further 1–2 minutes, then add the cashews and half of the spring onion. Cook for 1 minute.

4 Sprinkle over the remaining spring onion and serve immediately.

Crab Niçoise salad

6 ProPoints value

Traditionally, Niçoise salad uses tuna, but crab makes an excellent option in this hearty main course salad.

6 **ProPoints** values per recipe
25 minutes in total

75 g (2¾ oz) baby new potatoes, *halved if large*
75 g (2¾ oz) green beans, *trimmed*
1 egg
50 g (1¾ oz) baby leaf spinach
1 tomato, *cut into chunks*
2½ cm (1 inch) cucumber, *cubed*
1 spring onion, *chopped finely*
25 g (1 oz) stoned black olives
½ x 170 g can white crabmeat in brine, *drained*
    (or fresh crabmeat)
1 tablespoon finely chopped fresh basil
3 tablespoons low fat French dressing

1 Bring a saucepan of water to the boil and cook the potatoes for 8 minutes, before adding the beans. Return to the boil and cook for a further 4 minutes. Check that the potatoes are cooked, then drain and refresh the potatoes and beans under cold water. Leave to cool completely.

2 Meanwhile, bring a small pan of water to the boil and add the egg. Cook for 7–8 minutes then drain and refresh under cold running water. Leave to cool completely.

3 To assemble the salad, put a layer of spinach leaves on a serving plate. Top with the potatoes and beans, then add the tomatoes, cucumber, spring onions, olives and finally the crabmeat.

4 Peel and quarter the egg and add to the salad. Sprinkle the basil over, then drizzle with the French dressing. Serve immediately

Prawn and crab buns

11 ProPoints value

11 **ProPoints** values per recipe
15 minutes preparation + rising + standing,
    25 minutes cooking

75 g (2¾ oz) pizza base mix
calorie controlled cooking spray
1 small leek, *sliced finely*
50 g (1¾ oz) cooked, peeled prawns
½ x 170 g can white crabmeat in brine, *drained*
1 tablespoon chopped fresh dill
50 g (1¾ oz) low fat soft cheese
1 teaspoon plain flour
a large handful of cherry tomatoes, *halved if large*
a large handful of watercress leaves
a little balsamic vinegar

1 Make the pizza base by adding 3 tablespoons of warm water and mixing to make a dough. Set aside to rise until doubled in size, about 1 hour. Preheat the oven to Gas Mark 6/200°C/fan oven 180°C.

2 Heat a non stick frying pan and spray with the cooking spray. Add the leek and cook gently for about 5 minutes, until softened. Remove from the heat and set aside.

3 Put the prawns and crabmeat in a bowl. Add the leek, dill and soft cheese. Mix together well.

4 When the pizza dough is ready, sprinkle the work surface with flour, turn the dough out of the bowl and knead briefly. Divide the dough into two pieces, rolling each out to a 10 x 15 cm rectangle (4 x 6 inches). Spoon half of the filling on to each and fold the dough over to cover the filling.

5 Spray a baking sheet with cooking spray, place the buns on it and cook in the oven for 20–25 minutes until golden. Remove from the oven and allow to stand for 10 minutes before serving.

6 Put the tomatoes and watercress on a serving plate and drizzle with a little balsamic vinegar. Serve with the buns.

Thai tuna salad box

Red curry paste can be quite hot so be sure to adjust it to your taste.

7 **ProPoints** values per recipe
10 minutes in total

130 g tin **tuna in spring water**, *drained*
100 g (3½ oz) tinned **mixed beans in water**, *drained and rinsed*
1 teaspoon red curry paste
1 dried kaffir lime leaf, crumbled
juice and zest of a lime
2 **spring onions**, *chopped finely*
2 tablespoons chopped **fresh coriander**
25 g (1 oz) extra light mayonnaise
a few Little Gem **lettuce** *leaves*

1 Flake the tuna into a bowl and add the beans, red curry paste, lime leaf, lime juice and zest, spring onions, coriander and mayonnaise. Season and mix together thoroughly.
2 Serve the tuna mixture spooned into the lettuce leaves.

COOK'S TIP

This mixture will keep for up to 1 week in a sealed container in the fridge. Use as a sandwich filler, or pack the tuna mixture and lettuce leaves separately for your lunchbox.

Seared tuna on Savoy cabbage

Fresh tuna tastes sensational served on a bed of Savoy cabbage and sizzled pancetta.

9 **ProPoints** values per recipe
15 minutes in total

25 g (1 oz) pancetta rashers, cut into strips
150 g (5½ oz) **Savoy cabbage**, *shredded*
3–4 thin slices of red or green **chilli** (optional)
40 g (1½ oz) frozen **peas**
150 g (5½ oz) fresh **tuna** steak
calorie controlled cooking spray
salt and freshly ground black pepper
a lemon wedge, to serve

1 Heat a wok or non stick frying pan and add the pancetta cubes, stir-frying them over a high heat until lightly browned.
2 Add the Savoy cabbage and chilli (if using) and stir-fry for 2 minutes, then add the frozen peas and stir-fry for 2–3 more minutes. Season and tip on to a warm serving plate. Keep warm whilst you cook the tuna.
3 Spray both sides of the tuna steak with the cooking spray, then add to the frying pan and cook for about 2 minutes on each side, depending on the thickness of the tuna and how you like it cooked.
4 Place the tuna on top of the cooked cabbage, peas and pancetta and serve with the lemon wedge.

TRY THIS

You could use **curly kale** instead of Savoy cabbage, and a rasher of lean back bacon instead of the pancetta for 7 **ProPoints** values per serving.

Tuna fishcakes

7 **ProPoints** values per recipe

❄ (before cooking) • 30 minutes preparation
+ chilling, 14 minutes cooking

50 g (1¾ oz) small floury **potato** (such as King Edward
    or Maris Piper), peeled and cut into chunks
½ small **carrot**, peeled and cut into chunks
50 g (1¾ oz) **swede**, peeled and cut into chunks
calorie controlled cooking spray
½ small **onion** or **shallot**, chopped finely
80 g can **tuna in spring water**, drained
1 **thyme** sprig, leaves only
1 tablespoon chopped **fresh parsley**
zest of ½ a lemon
1 **egg**, beaten
2 tablespoons breadcrumbs
25 g (1 oz) low fat mayonnaise
15 g (½ oz) **0% fat Greek yogurt**
freshly ground black pepper

1 Bring a large saucepan of water to the boil and
  cook the potato, carrot and swede for 10–12
  minutes until tender. Drain well and then mash
  roughly (it's ok to leave a few chunky bits).

2 Meanwhile, heat a small non stick frying pan
  and spray with the cooking spray. Add the onion
  or shallot and cook gently until softened, about
  5–7 minutes. Add this to the mashed
  vegetables, along with the tuna, thyme leaves,
  parsley and half of the lemon zest. Season and
  mix together thoroughly. Shape into two patties.

3 Put the egg in a small bowl and the
  breadcrumbs on a small plate. Dip the patties
  first in the egg and then in the breadcrumbs,
  until coated. Refrigerate for 30 minutes.

4 Preheat the oven to Gas Mark 5/190°C/fan oven
  170°C. Transfer the patties to a baking sheet and
  spray with the cooking spray. Cook for 12–14
  minutes, turning once, until golden and crisp.

5 Meanwhile, mix together the mayonnaise, Greek
  yogurt and remaining lemon zest and plenty of
  black pepper. Serve with the hot tuna patties.

Miso roast salmon

Serve with 100 g (3½ oz) new **potatoes**
for an extra 2 **ProPoints** values.

8 **ProPoints** values per recipe
10 minutes preparation + marinating,
    15 minutes cooking

1 tablespoon miso paste
2 teaspoons mirin
a pinch of sugar
100 g (3½ oz) boneless **salmon** fillet
calorie controlled cooking spray
½ teaspoon sesame seeds
2 teaspoons soy sauce

For the cucumber and soya bean salad
½ **cucumber**
1 teaspoon rice vinegar or white wine vinegar
a pinch of sugar
1 tablespoon **soya beans**, defrosted if frozen

1 Mix together the miso paste, mirin and sugar.
  Put the salmon fillet on a plate and spread
  with the miso mixture. Refrigerate for at least
  30 minutes, or overnight if possible.

2 Preheat the oven to Gas Mark 6/200°C/fan oven
  180°C. Spray a non stick baking tray with the
  cooking spray. Using kitchen paper, wipe off the
  marinade (but do not wash the fish). Transfer
  the fish to the baking tray, skin-side down. Cook
  for 15 minutes, until the fish is golden, and
  flakes easily.

3 Meanwhile, toast the sesame seeds (see Cook's
  tip on page 50) and then make the cucumber
  and soya bean salad. Using a vegetable peeler,
  shave the cucumber into long, thin ribbons.
  Whisk together the vinegar and sugar. Toss with
  the cucumber ribbons and soya beans, then
  transfer to a plate. Serve with the salmon,
  sprinkled with the toasted sesame seeds and a
  drizzle of soy sauce.

Smoked salmon and asparagus pasta

7 ProPoints value

Pasta goes posh in this very tasty meal.

7 *ProPoints* values per recipe
20 minutes in total

75 g (2¾ oz) asparagus spears, *halved or left whole*
calorie controlled cooking spray
40 g (1½ oz) *dried* wholewheat pasta spirals
  (or other pasta shapes)
½ teaspoon finely grated lemon zest
25 g (1 oz) *frozen* peas, *defrosted*
2 tablespoons half fat crème fraîche
40 g (1½ oz) smoked salmon, sliced into strips
2 teaspoons chopped fresh dill *or* chives
freshly ground black pepper

1 Heat a griddle pan or preheat the grill to medium-high heat. Spray the asparagus with the cooking spray and chargrill or grill until tender, about 10 minutes, turning occasionally.

2 At the same time, bring a large saucepan of water to the boil and cook the pasta according to packet instructions.

3 Drain the pasta, but reserve some of the cooking water. Return the pasta to the saucepan with about 1 tablespoon of the cooking water. Add the lemon zest, peas, asparagus, crème fraîche and smoked salmon. Cook gently over a low heat for about 30–40 seconds.

4 Transfer to a warm serving bowl or plate and sprinkle with the dill or chives. Season with black pepper then serve.

TRY THIS

If asparagus is out of season, use fine green beans or mange tout instead. Boil them with the pasta for the final 5 minutes instead of chargrilling them. The *ProPoints* values remain the same.

Tuna, artichoke and caper linguine

9 ProPoints value

This sensational storecupboard lunch is ultra-quick.

9 **ProPoints** values per recipe
15 minutes in total

75 g (2¾ oz) dried linguine or spaghetti
80 g can tuna in brine, drained
1 tablespoon capers in brine, drained
25 g (1 oz) stoned black olives, chopped
50 g (1¾ oz) artichokes hearts in water, drained
    and chopped
1 teaspoon chopped red chilli (optional)
    or a pinch of dried chilli flakes
salt and freshly ground black pepper

1 Bring a large saucepan of water to the boil and cook the pasta according to packet instructions, until tender.
2 Drain the pasta and return to the saucepan. Gently stir in the tuna, capers, olives, artichokes and chilli (if using). Season and serve immediately.

Roasted Thai salmon

11 ProPoints value

11 **ProPoints** values per recipe
20 minutes in total + marinating

100 g (3½ oz) skinless salmon fillet
2 teaspoons fish sauce
juice of a lime
½ teaspoon brown sugar
1 garlic clove, crushed
1 small red chilli, de-seeded and chopped finely

For the noodles

40 g (1½ oz) dried rice noodles
10 g (¼ oz) roasted unsalted peanuts, chopped
1 spring onion, chopped finely
2 tablespoons chopped fresh coriander,
    plus a few leaves to garnish
1 tablespoon fish sauce
zest and juice of a lime
1 garlic clove, crushed
3 cherry tomatoes, chopped

1 Put the salmon steak in a shallow non metallic dish. Mix together the fish sauce, lime juice and sugar, stirring until the sugar has dissolved. Stir in the garlic and half of the chilli. Pour over the salmon. Set aside for 30 minutes to marinate.
2 Preheat the grill to high. Bring a medium saucepan of water to the boil. Add the noodles and cook according to packet instructions, then run under cold water. Drain well, then transfer to a serving bowl. Add the peanuts, spring onion, coriander and remaining chilli. Mix together the fish sauce, lime juice, lime zest and garlic and pour over the noodles. Add the chopped tomatoes and toss everything together well.
3 Put the salmon in an ovenproof tray or foil-lined grill pan. Discard the marinade and cook for 4–5 minutes on each side.
4 To serve, put the cooked salmon on top of the noodles. Garnish with a little more coriander and serve immediately.

Mackerel and ginger tartlet

Mackerel and ginger create a lovely flavour for this tartlet.

8 *ProPoints* values per recipe
25 minutes in total + cooling + chilling

15 g (½ oz) sheet filo pastry, measuring
   30 x 40 cm (12 x 16 inches), defrosted
   if frozen and cut into four
calorie controlled cooking spray
75 g (2¾ oz) mackerel fillet
15 g (½ oz) stem ginger in syrup, drained and
   chopped finely
15 g (½ oz) watercress, chopped finely
1 spring onion, chopped finely
1 tablespoon chopped fresh dill
50 g (1¾ oz) low fat soft cheese

1 Heat the oven to Gas Mark 6/200°C/fan oven 180°C. Take one piece of filo pastry and spray with the cooking spray. Use to line one hole of a muffin tray. Spray the next piece of filo and place it in the muffin tray, on top of the first, but at an angle. Repeat with the remaining filo. Bake for 5–7 minutes until golden and crisp. Leave to cool, then remove from the tin.

2 Meanwhile, heat a frying pan over a medium heat and spray with the cooking spray. Add the mackerel fillet, skin side down, and cook for 2 minutes. Turn and cook the second side for a further 2–3 minutes until the fish flakes easily. Remove from the heat. Set aside until cool.

3 Once cool, remove the skin from the fish and flake the flesh into a bowl. Add the ginger, watercress, spring onion, dill and low fat soft cheese. Mix everything together well and refrigerate for at least 2 hours or until needed.

4 When the filling is chilled, spoon into the filo pastry case and serve immediately.

Tomato, mackerel and basil salad

The dressing really lifts these ingredients to something special. Feel free to add any zero *ProPoints* value salad vegetables you have to hand.

9 *ProPoints* values per recipe
10 minutes in total

1 heart of Romaine lettuce, broken into leaves
   and torn into pieces
75 g (2¾ oz) cherry tomatoes, halved
5 cm (2 inch) cucumber, diced
1 small red onion or shallot, sliced finely into rounds
75 g (2¾ oz) smoked mackerel fillet, skinned and
   broken into large flakes

For the dressing
1 tablespoon balsamic vinegar
4 semi-dried tomatoes
1 small tomato, chopped coarsely
a large handful of fresh basil leaves
salt and freshly ground black pepper

1 To make the dressing, combine the vinegar, 3 tablespoons of water, the dried and fresh tomatoes and basil and, using a food processor or hand-held blender, whizz until smooth. Season and set aside.

2 To assemble the salad, put a layer of lettuce on a serving plate, top with tomatoes and cucumber then the onion and finally the mackerel. Drizzle over the dressing and serve immediately.

Smoked haddock pâté

There's a lot of flavour in this delicious fish pâté, so a little goes a long way. If you want to pack it for lunch, you could add 25 g (1 oz) crispbreads for 1 *ProPoints* value.

9 *ProPoints* values per recipe
20 minutes preparation + chilling

60 g (2 oz) skinless smoked haddock
1 egg
60 g (2 oz) low fat soft cheese
25 g (1 oz) low fat natural yogurt
2 tablespoons fresh wholemeal breadcrumbs
1 small shallot, chopped finely
zest of ½ a lemon
1 tablespoon chopped fresh parsley
1 tablespoon chopped fresh chives
a pinch of cayenne pepper
1 slice seeded wholegrain bread
salt and freshly ground black pepper
a handful of watercress, to serve

1 Put the fish in a small lidded saucepan and cover with cold water. Bring to the boil, then remove from the heat, cover and leave to stand for 5 minutes.

2 Meanwhile, put the egg into another saucepan and cover with cold water. Bring to the boil and simmer for 8 minutes, then drain and refresh under cold running water.

3 Put the cooked fish into a bowl and flake with a fork, checking carefully for bones as you do so. Peel the egg and chop, then add to the bowl along with the soft cheese, yogurt, breadcrumbs, shallot, lemon zest, parsley, chives and cayenne pepper. Beat together until smooth, and season to taste.

4 Transfer to a ramekin and refrigerate until needed, at least an hour. Preheat the grill to medium-high.

5 Put the bread under the grill and toast on one side. Cut into triangles and return the untoasted side to the grill until toasted. Watch carefully as it will brown very quickly.

6 Serve with the pâté and watercress.

Smoked haddock biryani

11 ProPoints value

Although this recipe requires a little effort, the result is really worth it.

11 **ProPoints** values per recipe
30 minutes in total

60 g (2 oz) dried long grain rice
125 g (4½ oz) **smoked haddock** fillet
calorie controlled cooking spray
1 small **onion** or 4 **spring onions**, chopped finely
1 teaspoon medium curry powder
½ teaspoon cumin seeds
75 g (2¾ oz) frozen **peas**
freshly ground black pepper
1 tablespoon chopped **fresh coriander**, to serve

1 Bring a saucepan of water to the boil and cook the rice according to packet instructions for 10–12 minutes, until tender. At the same time, put the haddock in a shallow pan and cover with water. Simmer gently for 6–7 minutes, until cooked and easy to flake.
2 Spray a large non stick frying pan with the cooking spray and gently fry the onion or spring onions for 3–4 minutes, until softened. Add the curry powder and cumin seeds and stir for another minute, then add the peas and cook for 2–3 minutes, stirring often.
3 Drain the rice thoroughly and add it to the frying pan. Season with pepper and stir together.
4 Pile the rice mixture on to a warm serving plate. Remove the skin from the haddock and flake the fish on top of the rice. Serve at once, sprinkled with the coriander.

TRY THIS

Frozen smoked haddock fillets are ideal for this recipe. Poach them as above, but add a few minutes to the cooking time.

Orange sole with summer veg

4 ProPoints value

This summery recipe really suits sole.

4 **ProPoints** values per recipe
15 minutes preparation, 30 minutes cooking

calorie controlled cooking spray
1 small **courgette**, sliced into matchsticks
6 cherry **tomatoes**, halved
50 g (1¾ oz) **sugar snap peas** or **mange tout**, sliced
1 small **orange**
2 **spring onions**, chopped finely
25 g (1 oz) fresh breadcrumbs
1 tablespoon chopped **fresh parsley**,
    plus extra, to garnish
150 g (5½ oz) **sole** fillet
salt and freshly ground black pepper

1 Preheat the oven to Gas Mark 5/190°C/fan oven 170°C.
2 Spray a shallow baking dish with the cooking spray and put the courgette, tomatoes and sugar snap peas or mange tout into it, spreading them over the base.
3 Finely grate the zest from half the orange and put it in a bowl. Squeeze the juice and add half to the bowl with the spring onions, breadcrumbs and the parsley. Season and mix together. Put the fish fillet on a work surface, skin side up, and spread the stuffing on top. Roll up and place on top of the vegetables. Sprinkle the remaining orange juice over the top.
4 Cover the dish with a lid or a piece of foil and bake for 25–30 minutes, or until the fish is done to your liking. It will be opaque and will flake easily. Serve, sprinkled with parsley.

TRY THIS

Enjoy this with some skinless boneless **cod** loin. Pile the stuffing mixture on top of the fish and bake as above for the same **ProPoints** values.

Baked Mediterranean cod

3 ProPoints value

This quick and flavourful fish dish makes an ideal midweek meal.

3 *ProPoints* values per recipe
15 minutes preparation, 15 minutes cooking

200 g can chopped tomatoes with herbs and garlic
2 teaspoons tomato purée
1 garlic clove, crushed
1 fresh thyme sprig, leaves only
1 tablespoon balsamic vinegar
1 teaspoon capers, drained and chopped if large
15 g (½ oz) stoned black olives
125 g (4½ oz) skinless cod fillet
salt and freshly ground black pepper
1 tablespoon chopped fresh basil, to garnish

1 Preheat the oven to Gas Mark 6/200°C/fan oven 180°C. Put the tomatoes, tomato purée, garlic and thyme leaves in a saucepan and bring to the boil. Simmer for about 10 minutes until slightly thickened.

2 Transfer the tomato sauce to an ovenproof gratin dish. Drizzle over the balsamic vinegar and sprinkle in the capers and olives. Lay the fish on top and season. Bake for 12–15 minutes until the fish is just cooked through.

3 Serve immediately, garnished with the basil.

SERVING SUGGESTIONS

Serve with 60 g (2 oz) dried tagliatelle, cooked according to packet instructions, for 6 *ProPoints* values per serving.

Try 60 g (2 oz) dried brown rice, cooked according to packet instructions, with a handful of spinach mixed in, for 6 *ProPoints* values per serving.

ProPoints value index

Beef, lamb and pork

5 *ProPoints* values

Fillet steak on Mediterranean veg 14

Parma wrapped figs 32

6 *ProPoints* values

Ham, mushroom and cheese bake 35

Pork with garlic, lemon and thyme 30

7 *ProPoints* values

Beef barley broth 12

Lamb and feta burger 24

Lamb steaks with minty yogurt 16

Orange pork with Chinese greens 26

Steak burger with chilli salsa 12

8 *ProPoints* values

Beef and vegetable noodles 10

Lamb masala kebabs 22

Peachy Parma sandwich 34

9 *ProPoints* values

Beef and bean quesadillas 16

Chorizo and red pepper fusilli 31

Lamb steak with flageolet beans and bacon 20

10 *ProPoints* values

Beef and bean hotpot 10

Easy keema curry 18

Gammon and bean pepper pot 28

Lamb mulligatawny 24

Spiced lamb with aubergine braise 22

Steak 'Bearnaise' 8

11 *ProPoints* values

Pork and cashew nut stir-fry 30

12 *ProPoints* values

Lime and cumin lamb cutlets 18

Pasta with Parmesan, bacon and
  mange tout 34

Sausages with mash and red onion gravy 28

Chicken, duck and turkey

4 *ProPoints* values

Chicken saltimbocca 52

5 *ProPoints* values

Chicken with capers and lemon 44

Honey-glazed chicken leg 50

Summery chicken 36

6 *ProPoints* values

Chinese five spice braised duck 54

7 *ProPoints* values

Apricot glazed chicken 44

Crispy oven-fried chicken 48

8 *ProPoints* values

Chicken and black bean stew 46

Italian stuffed cabbage 53

Poulet au vinaigre 38

Turkey melt open sandwich 52

9 *ProPoints* values

Barbecued chicken burger 50

Chicken lunchbox slaw 42

Duck with cherries 54

Lunchbox Caesar salad 42

One pot spring chicken 38

11 *ProPoints* values

Duck with quinoa and pomegranate
  salad 56

Risotto solo 48

14 *ProPoints* values

Chicken and sweet potato supper 46

Roast chicken breast crown 40

Vegetarian meals

1 *ProPoints* value

Chilli non carne 67

2 *ProPoints* values

Chinese spiced vegetable broth 60

5 *ProPoints* values

Tomato crumpet with egg 72

6 *ProPoints* values

Moroccan orange, feta and mint
  tabbouleh 66

Omelette burrito 80

7 *ProPoints* values

Caramelised onion and Stilton
  roll 74

Curry potato pie 76

Midsummer minestrone 60

Peach, plum and Cheshire melt 82

Pepper and sweet potato stew 66

8 *ProPoints* values

Butternut borlotti stew 58

Caramelised apple and hazelnut salad 68

Halloumi with roast vegetable couscous 70

Mushroom and aubergine parmigiana 74

9 *ProPoints* values

Aubergine, red pepper and lentil curry 78

Butternut squash and tomato penne 62

Chinese vegetable pancakes 84

Leek and Cheddar bread pudding 76

Quorn korma 82

Red rice salad 68

10 *ProPoints* values

Mezze platter 84

Paratha with spicy cauliflower 78

Spinach and red onion pilaf 80

Spinach, tomato and ricotta torta 72

11 *ProPoints* values

Spaghetti frittata 64

Tagliatelle with chargrilled veg and
  goat's cheese 62

Fish and seafood

3 *ProPoints* values

Baked Mediterranean cod 106

4 *ProPoints* values

Orange sole with summer veg 104

Quick prawn and courgette curry 86

6 *ProPoints* values

Crab Niçoise salad 92

7 *ProPoints* values

Couscous salad with prawns 88

Smoked salmon and asparagus pasta 98

Thai tuna salad box 94

Tuna fishcakes 96

8 *ProPoints* values

Chinese prawn and broccoli 90

Mackerel and ginger tartlet 102

Miso roast salmon 96

9 *ProPoints* values

Seared tuna on Savoy cabbage 94

Smoked haddock pâté 103

Tomato, mackerel and basil salad 102

Tuna, artichoke and caper linguine 100

11 *ProPoints* values

Prawn and crab buns 92

Roasted Thai salmon 100

Smoked haddock biryani 104

12 *ProPoints* values

Prawns with shredded omelette 88

soups

Fresh-tasting soups for all
seasons, from sustaining
winter potages to chilled
soups for hot summer days

baked red onion soup

This delicious variation of classic French onion soup is cooked entirely in the oven.

Serves 4-6
Preparation time: 20-25 minutes
Cooking time: 1¼-1½ hours
575-385 cals per serving

4 large red onions, each about 300g (10oz)
60ml (4 tbsp) olive oil
1 garlic clove, peeled and crushed
10ml (2 tsp) chopped fresh sage
salt and freshly ground black pepper
8 slices ciabatta, 1cm (½ inch) thick (cut on the diagonal)
900ml (1½ pints) hot vegetable stock
175g (6oz) gruyère or Cheddar cheese, grated
50g (2oz) Parmesan cheese, freshly grated

1 Peel the onions and cut each one into 8 wedges; place in a deep ovenproof dish. Combine the olive oil, garlic and sage, add to the onions and toss well. Roast in the oven at 200°C/fan oven 190°C (400°F) Mark 6 for 1 hour, stirring occasionally to ensure the onions brown evenly. Season generously with salt and pepper.
2 Divide about half of the roasted onions between 4-6 individual ovenproof soup bowls. Toast the ciabatta slices on both sides under the grill. Place one slice in each soup bowl. Add sufficient stock to cover, then scatter over half the gruyère or Cheddar and half the Parmesan.
3 Sprinkle with the remaining onions, then repeat the layers of toasted ciabatta, stock and grated cheese. Stand the bowls in a large shallow baking tin and bake in the oven for about 20 minutes until the cheese is melted and browned. Let stand for 5-10 minutes before serving.

stock

The secret of a successful soup is invariably a well-flavoured homemade stock, but if you are really short of time, use one of the 'fresh' stock products now available from the chilled delicatessen cabinets of larger supermarkets.

japanese noodle broth with pak choi and mooli

Mooli, the long white radish, is a popular Japanese ingredient and gives this dish a distinctive oriental flavour. If unavailable however, you use thinly sliced turnip instead. Similarly another variety of Chinese cabbage can be used in place of pak choi.

Serves 4
Preparation time: 15 minutes
Cooking time: 30 minutes
215 cals per serving

125g (4oz) flat rice or egg noodles
30ml (2 tbsp) sunflower oil
1 garlic clove, peeled and sliced
5ml (1 tsp) grated fresh root ginger
pinch of sugar
3 pak choi, about 350g (12oz) total weight, roughly chopped
1.1 litres (2 pints) vegetable stock
30ml (2 tbsp) miso (see note)
15ml (1 tbsp) lemon juice
15ml (1 tbsp) light soy sauce
125g (4oz) mooli, sliced
1 packet mustard and cress
15ml (1 tbsp) chopped fresh coriander

1 Cook the noodles according to the packet instructions. Drain, refresh under cold water, then drain thoroughly; set aside.
2 Heat the oil in a large, shallow pan and fry the garlic, ginger and sugar over a low heat for 2 minutes. Add the pak choi, in a single layer if possible, cover and cook over a low heat for 5 minutes. Add the stock, miso, lemon juice, soy sauce and mooli. Bring to the boil, cover and simmer for 15 minutes.
3 Stir in the noodles, mustard and cress, and coriander. Heat through for 1 minute and serve at once.

Note Miso is a thick paste made from fermented soya beans, used to flavour soups, sauces, stews etc. It is available from good health food stores and oriental food stores.

mushroom, garlic and thyme broth

A delicious, light mushroom soup, flavoured with wild mushrooms and scented with thyme oil.

Serves 4
Preparation time: 20 minutes, plus soaking
Cooking time: 25 minutes
195 cals per serving

15g (½oz) dried porcini mushrooms
900ml (1½ pints) water
1 head of garlic, peeled and lightly crushed
1 small onion, peeled and sliced
1 celery stick, peeled and chopped
salt and freshly ground black pepper
30ml (2 tbsp) extra-virgin olive oil
1 onion, peeled and sliced
15ml (1 tbsp) chopped fresh thyme
450g (1lb) mixed wild mushrooms, wiped
4 tomatoes, skinned, deseeded and diced
FOR THE THYME OIL:
60ml (2fl oz) extra-virgin olive oil
15ml (1 tbsp) chopped fresh thyme

1 To make the broth, place the dried porcini in a bowl, add 150ml (¼ pint) boiling water and leave to soak for 20 minutes. Strain the soaking liquid into a saucepan and add the garlic, onion, celery, 5ml (1 tsp) salt and a little pepper. Chop the soaked porcini and set aside.

2 Add the remaining 750ml (1¼ pints) water to the pan, bring to the boil, cover and simmer gently for 30 minutes. Strain the broth into a jug and set aside.

3 For the soup, heat the oil in a clean pan, add the onion and thyme and fry gently for 10 minutes until softened. Add the soaked porcini and fresh mushrooms and fry over a high heat for 5 minutes.

4 Pour in the mushroom broth and add the tomatoes. Bring to the boil, cover and simmer gently for 10 minutes. Season to taste.

5 Meanwhile, for the thyme oil, put the olive oil in a small pan, add the thyme leaves and heat gently for 2-3 minutes. Remove from the heat.

6 Spoon the soup into warmed bowls and drizzle with thyme oil. Serve with crusty French bread.

cream of jerusalem artichoke soup

An unusual combination of mild Jerusalem artichokes, the nutty taste of fresh Parmesan and a hint of spice.

Serves 6
Preparation time: 15 minutes
Cooking time: 30 minutes
Suitable for freezing (stage 3)
190 cals per serving

450g (1lb) Jerusalem artichokes
50g (2oz) butter
2 shallots, peeled and diced
5ml (1 tsp) mild curry paste
900ml (1½ pints) vegetable stock
150ml (¼ pint) single cream (or milk for a less rich soup)
freshly grated nutmeg, to taste
pinch of cayenne pepper
60ml (4 tbsp) freshly grated Parmesan cheese
salt and freshly ground black pepper
TO SERVE:
3-4 slices Melba toast (see page 22)

1 Scrub the Jerusalem artichokes thoroughly, pat dry, then slice thinly.
2 Melt the butter in a large saucepan, add the shallots and cook gently for 10 minutes until soft and golden. Stir in the curry paste and cook for 1 minute. Add the sliced artichokes and stock; stir well. Bring to the boil, cover and simmer for about 15 minutes until the artichokes are tender.
3 Add the cream, nutmeg and cayenne to the soup. Transfer to a blender or food processor and work until smooth, then pass through a sieve into a clean saucepan.
4 Reheat the soup and stir in the Parmesan cheese. Taste and adjust the seasoning. Serve at once, with the hot Melba toast.

Variation Replace the artichokes with 1 large cauliflower, divided into florets. Add to the shallots with the stock at stage 2 and bring to the boil. Simmer for about 10 minutes or until very soft, then continue as above.

tomato and harissa soup with coriander cream

Harissa, the North African spice paste, gives this soup a distinctive flavour. It is available in jars from larger supermarkets.

Serves 8
Preparation time: 20 minutes
Cooking time: 30 minutes
Suitable for freezing
215 cals per serving

90ml (6 tbsp) oil
450g (1lb) onions, peeled and finely chopped
4 garlic cloves, peeled and crushed
20ml (4 tsp) ground cumin
10ml (2 tsp) harissa
30ml (2 tbsp) tomato paste
two 400g (14oz) cans chopped plum tomatoes
10ml (2 tsp) sugar
2.5cm (1 inch) fresh root ginger, grated
2 litres (3½ pints) light vegetable stock
salt and freshly ground black pepper
FOR THE CORIANDER CREAM:
200ml (7fl oz) double cream
90ml (6 tbsp) roughly chopped fresh coriander leaves
TO GARNISH:
coriander sprigs

1 Heat the oil in a saucepan, add the onions and cook gently for 5 minutes or until soft but not coloured. Add the garlic and cumin; cook for 30 seconds. Add the harissa and tomato paste and fry, stirring, for 1 minute. Stir in the tomatoes, sugar, ginger and stock. Season and bring to the boil, then simmer gently for 20 minutes. Allow to cool slightly.
2 Purée the mixture in a blender until smooth. Pass through a sieve, then return the soup to the pan. Bring to the boil and check the seasoning.
3 For the coriander cream, lightly whip the cream in a bowl, season and fold in the chopped coriander.
4 To serve, spoon the soup into warmed soup bowls and top each portion with a spoonful of the coriander cream. Garnish with coriander and accompany with warm naan bread.

fresh tomato soup with basil

Serves 6
Preparation time: 20 minutes
Cooking time: 50 minutes
Suitable for freezing
90 cals per serving

30ml (2 tbsp) olive oil
1 onion, peeled and thinly sliced
2 garlic cloves, peeled and crushed
1 celery stick, thinly sliced
1 red pepper, quartered, cored and deseeded
900g (2lb) ripe plum tomatoes
900ml (1½ pints) chicken or vegetable stock
30ml (2 tbsp) sun-dried tomato paste
5ml (1 tsp) sugar
salt and freshly ground black pepper
TO SERVE:
basil leaves, shredded if preferred
freshly pared Parmesan cheese (optional)

1 Heat the oil in a saucepan, add the onion and garlic and fry gently for about 10 minutes until soft but not browned. Add the celery and fry for a further 5 minutes.
2 Meanwhile, place the pepper on the grill rack, skin-side up, and grill until charred. Cover with a damp cloth and leave until cool, then peel away the skin and slice finely.
3 Immerse the tomatoes in a bowl of boiling water for 10 seconds, then drain and refresh under cold running water. Peel the tomatoes and roughly chop the flesh.
4 Add the tomatoes and sliced pepper to the celery and onion with the stock, sun-dried tomato paste, sugar and seasoning. Bring to the boil, cover and simmer gently for about 30 minutes.
5 Ladle the soup into warmed bowls and scatter over some basil. Top with Parmesan shavings before serving if desired.

Note Make this delicious fresh-tasting soup during the summer months when tomatoes are inexpensive and full of flavour.

cream of mushroom soup with crème fraîche

Chestnut mushrooms and dried porcini give this creamy soup a superb depth of flavour.

Serves 4-6
Preparation time: 15 minutes, plus soaking
Cooking time: 35 minutes
Suitable for freezing
285-185 cals per serving

15g (½oz) dried porcini mushrooms
150ml (¼ pint) boiling water
50g (2oz) butter
1 large onion, peeled and chopped
1 garlic clove, peeled and crushed
15ml (1 tbsp) chopped fresh sage
700g (1½lb) chestnut mushrooms, or mixed chestnut
 and flat mushrooms, wiped and chopped
750ml (1¼ pints) vegetable stock
150ml (¼ pint) crème fraîche
salt and freshly ground black pepper
pinch of freshly grated nutmeg
TO GARNISH:
extra crème fraîche
snipped chives

1 Place the dried porcini in a bowl, pour on the boiling water and leave to soak for 20 minutes. Strain the liquid and reserve. Chop and reserve the porcini.
2 Melt half the butter in a saucepan, add the onion, porcini, garlic and sage and fry for 10 minutes until softened and lightly golden. Add the remaining butter, then add the mushrooms and increase the heat. Stir-fry for 5 minutes until the mushrooms are browned.
3 Stir in the reserved porcini liquid and stock. Bring to the boil, cover and simmer gently for 20 minutes. Transfer to a blender or food processor and purée until smooth. Return to the pan.
4 Stir in the crème fraîche and salt, pepper and nutmeg to taste; reheat gently. Spoon into warmed bowls and add a swirl of crème fraîche and a sprinkling of snipped chives to serve.

thai-style cauliflower and coconut soup

Serves 6
Preparation time: 25 minutes
Cooking time: 35-40 minutes
Suitable for freezing
540 cals per serving

two 400g (14oz) cans coconut milk
750ml (1¼ pints) vegetable stock
4 garlic cloves, peeled and finely chopped
5cm (2 inch) piece galangal or fresh root ginger, peeled and finely chopped
4 lemon grass stalks, roughly chopped
4 kaffir lime leaves, shredded (see note)
4 red chillies
30ml (2 tbsp) groundnut oil
10ml (2 tsp) sesame oil
1 large onion, peeled and thinly sliced
10ml (2 tsp) turmeric
10ml (2 tsp) sugar
900g (2lb) cauliflower florets
30ml (2 tbsp) lime juice
30ml (2 tbsp) light soy sauce
4 spring onions, shredded
60ml (4 tbsp) chopped fresh coriander
a little chilli or sesame oil, to serve

1 Put the coconut milk and vegetable stock into a saucepan. Add the garlic, galangal or ginger, lemon grass, lime leaves and whole chillies. Bring to the boil, cover and simmer for 15 minutes. Strain and reserve the liquid.
2 Heat the groundnut and sesame oils in a clean saucepan. Add the onion, turmeric and sugar and fry gently for 5 minutes. Cut the cauliflower into small pieces. Add to the pan and stir-fry for a further 5 minutes until lightly golden.
3 Add the reserved coconut stock, the lime juice and soy sauce. Bring to the boil, cover and simmer gently for 10-15 minutes until the cauliflower is tender. Check the seasoning. Stir in the shredded spring onion and chopped coriander.
4 Ladle into warmed soup bowls, drizzle over a little chilli or sesame oil and serve immediately.

Note If kaffir lime leaves are unobtainable, use the grated rind of 1 lime instead.

courgette, pea and pasta soup

A pretty green soup of grated courgettes, fresh or frozen peas, tiny soup pasta and stock, enriched with soured cream. Serve with crusty bread as a starter or light lunch.

Serves 4-6
Preparation time: 20 minutes
Cooking time: 30 minutes
215 cals per serving

60ml (4 tbsp) olive or sunflower oil
2 onions, peeled and finely chopped
1.4 litres (2½ pints) hot chicken or vegetable stock
450g (1lb) courgettes, trimmed and grated
450g (1lb) fresh peas, shelled, or 175g (6oz) frozen peas
125g (4oz) dried pastina (small soup pasta)
salt and freshly ground black pepper
squeeze of lemon or lime juice, to taste
30ml (2 tbsp) chopped fresh chervil
soured cream, to serve
chervil sprigs, to garnish

1 Heat the oil in a large saucepan. Add the onions, cover and cook gently for about 20 minutes until very soft but not coloured, stirring occasionally.
2 Pour in the stock and bring to the boil. Add the grated courgettes, fresh peas if using, and the pasta. Turn down the heat and simmer for 10-15 minutes or until the pasta is tender. Season with salt and pepper and add lemon or lime juice to taste. (If using frozen peas, add them 5 minutes before the end of cooking.)
3 Stir in the chopped chervil. Serve in warmed soup bowls, adding a swirl of soured cream to each portion. Garnish with sprigs of chervil.

miso soup with noodles

This healthy, Japanese clear soup contains fresh spinach, spring onions, carrot julienne and tofu.

Serves 4-6
Preparation time: 15 minutes
Cooking time: 25 minutes
335-225 cals per serving

125g (4oz) Japanese noodles (udon) or tagliatelle
10ml (2 tsp) oil
1.2 litres (2 pints) vegetable stock
60ml (2fl oz) sake or Japanese rice wine
5ml (1 tsp) sugar
5ml (1 tsp) dark soy sauce
2 carrots, peeled and cut into julienne strips
2 spring onions, trimmed and thinly sliced
30ml (2 tbsp) miso paste
125g (4oz) plain tofu, diced or cut into small batons
50g (2oz) spinach leaves, trimmed and finely shredded

1 Cook the noodles according to the packet instructions until just tender. Drain, refresh immediately under cold water and drain again. Toss with the oil to prevent sticking and set aside.
2 Meanwhile, pour the stock into a saucepan and add the sake or rice wine, sugar and soy sauce. Bring to the boil, cover and simmer for 10 minutes.
3 Add the carrots and spring onions to the broth and simmer for 10 minutes.
4 Blend the miso paste with a little of the hot stock, then stir into the soup. Add the tofu and spinach and heat gently, without boiling, for 5 minutes. Add the noodles to heat through. Serve immediately.

Note You can use any type of miso paste for this soup. Alternatively, stir in a sachet of instant miso soup, available from larger supermarkets.

to accompany soups

CROÛTONS are a classic accompaniment. Remove the crusts from 3-4 thick slices of day-old white bread, then cut into 2.5cm (1 inch) squares. Heat a 2.5cm (1 inch) depth of oil in a frying pan, then fry the bread cubes, turning constantly, until crisp and golden. Remove and drain on kitchen paper.
For a lower calorie alternative, simply toast the bread slices, then cut into cubes. Croûtons can be prepared ahead, allowed to cool, then stored in an airtight tin.

FLAVOURED CROÛTONS made with flavoured bread, such as walnut or sun-dried tomato bread, are delicious and easy to make. Toss cubes of the chosen bread in appropriate flavoured oil, such as walnut oil or sun-dried tomato oil (from a jar of sun-dried tomatoes). Place in a shallow roasting tin and bake in the oven at 200°C/fan oven 190°C (400°F) Mark 6 for about 15 minutes until golden; drain on kitchen paper.

MELBA TOAST is another classic complement. Toast 3-4 slices soft-grain bread lightly on both sides. Quickly cut off the crusts and split each slice in two. Scrape off any doughy bits. Sprinkle with Parmesan and paprika if desired. Place on a baking sheet and bake in the oven at 180°C/fan oven 170°C (350°F) Mark 4 for about 10 minutes until uniformly golden. If required Melba toast can be prepared ahead, allowed to cool, then stored in an airtight tin. Warm through in the oven before serving.

BRUSCHETTA is an Italian idea which goes well with most soups. Grill thick slices of day-old country-style bread lightly on both sides. Immediately rub all over with a whole peeled garlic clove. Drizzle with a little fruity extra-virgin olive oil and serve with the soup.

grilled pepper and aubergine soup

An intensely flavoured soup, served topped with a delicious saffron cream.

Serves 4-6
Preparation time: 25 minutes
Cooking time: 45 minutes
Suitable for freezing (without saffron cream)
390-300 cals per serving

2 large red peppers, quartered, cored and deseeded
90ml (3fl oz) olive oil
1 large aubergine, thinly sliced lengthways
1 large onion, peeled and chopped
2 garlic cloves, peeled and chopped
5ml (1 tsp) grated lemon rind
15ml (1 tbsp) chopped fresh thyme
5ml (1 tsp) dried oregano
400g (14oz) can chopped tomatoes
900ml (1½ pints) vegetable stock
1 bay leaf
30ml (2 tbsp) chopped fresh basil
salt and freshly ground black pepper
FOR THE SAFFRON CREAM:
small pinch of saffron strands
15ml (1 tbsp) boiling water
1 egg yolk
1 garlic clove, peeled and crushed
2.5ml (½ tsp) cayenne pepper
10ml (2 tsp) lemon juice
150-175ml (5-6fl oz) olive oil
TO GARNISH:
basil leaves

1 Brush the pepper quarters with a little olive oil and grill, skin-side up, for 3-4 minutes each side until charred and tender. Transfer to a plate, cover with a cloth and leave until cool enough to handle. Peel the peppers and roughly chop the flesh.

2 Brush the aubergine slices with olive oil and grill for 4-5 minutes each side until charred and tender. Leave until cool enough to handle, then chop roughly.

3 Heat the remaining oil in a large pan, add the onion, garlic, lemon rind, thyme and oregano and fry, stirring, for 10 minutes until browned. Add the peppers, aubergine, tomatoes, stock and bay leaf. Bring to the boil, cover and simmer for 20 minutes. Discard the bay leaf.

4 Meanwhile, make the saffron cream. Soak the saffron in the boiling water for 5 minutes. In a bowl, whisk the egg yolk with the garlic, cayenne, lemon juice and seasoning until pale and slightly thickened. Gradually whisk in the olive oil, until thick. Stir in the saffron liquid and check the seasoning.

5 Transfer the soup to a blender or food processor. Add the basil and work until smooth. Return the soup to the pan and heat through. Adjust the seasoning.

6 Pour into warmed soup bowls. Spoon a little saffron cream on top of each portion, garnish with basil leaves and serve at once.

finishing touches

CREAM OR CRÈME FRAÎCHE swirled onto each portion adds an attractive finish. If desired, feather the cream with a cocktail stick or sprinkle with a little contrasting pepper or paprika.

FRESH HERBS enhance most soups. Scatter snipped chives or freshly torn parsley, chervil, basil, coriander or mint over the surface, or garnish with herb sprigs.

PESTO is the ideal robust garnish for hearty vegetable potages, it also works well with fresh tomato soups.

FINELY PARED OR GRATED CHEESE such as gruyère, Parmesan, pecorino or Cheddar will melt deliciously into most soups.

CITRUS SLICES cut through the richness of creamy soups. Peel a small orange, lemon or lime, removing all pith, then cut into thin rounds. Finely pared strips of citrus zest also make a suitable garnish.

CITRUS BUTTERS make a tasty garnish. Simply blend a little finely grated orange, lemon or lime zest into some softened butter, form into a log, wrap and chill until firm. Thinly slice the butter and top each portion of soup with a few slices.

beetroot and orange soup

Serves 6
Preparation time: 15 minutes
Cooking time: 2½ hours
Suitable for freezing
230 cals per serving

700g (1½lb) raw beetroot, trimmed
50g (2oz) butter
225g (8oz) onions, peeled and roughly chopped
225g (8oz) potatoes, peeled and roughly chopped
1.3 litres (2¼ pints) vegetable stock
300ml (½ pint) sherry
300ml (½ pint) orange juice
salt and freshly ground black pepper
orange rind shreds, to garnish

1 Wrap the beetroot in foil and place in a large roasting tin. Bake in a preheated oven at 200°C/ fan oven 190°C (400°F) Mark 6 for 1½ hours. Allow to cool, then peel and roughly chop.
2 Heat the butter in a large heavy-based saucepan. Add the onions and fry gently for 10 minutes or until soft and golden. Add the beetroot and potatoes and stir to coat in the buttery juices.
3 Add the stock, sherry and orange juice, bring to the boil, then cover and simmer for 40 minutes or until the potatoes are tender. Let cool slightly.
4 Purée the soup in batches in a blender or food processor until smooth. Return to the pan and check the seasoning. Bring back to the boil.
5 Pour into individual soup bowls and serve garnished with orange rind shreds.

walnut soup with charmoula

Serves 4
Preparation time: 30 minutes
Cooking time: 30 minutes
Suitable for freezing
510 cals per serving

30ml (2 tbsp) walnut oil
1 onion, peeled and finely chopped
5ml (1 tsp) ground cinnamon
175g (6oz) walnuts, toasted and roughly chopped
50g (2oz) fresh breadcrumbs
15ml (1 tbsp) red wine vinegar
900ml (1½ pints) vegetable stock
salt and freshly ground black pepper
FOR THE CHARMOULA:
5ml (1 tsp) paprika
2.5ml (½ tsp) ground cumin
2.5ml (½ tsp) turmeric
1.25ml (¼ tsp) cayenne pepper
2 garlic cloves, peeled and chopped
30ml (2 tbsp) chopped fresh coriander
15ml (1 tbsp) lime juice
60ml (4 tbsp) olive oil
TO SERVE:
Greek-style yogurt (optional)
flat-leaf parsley

1 First make the charmoula. Place all the ingredients except the olive oil in a spice grinder or blender and work until smooth. Transfer to a bowl and stir in the oil. Season with salt and pepper to taste.
2 To make the soup, heat the walnut oil in a saucepan and add the onion, cinnamon and 30ml (2 tbsp) of the charmoula. Fry gently for 5 minutes until golden. Add the walnuts and breadcrumbs and fry for a further 5 minutes, stirring occasionally to prevent sticking.
3 Transfer the mixture to a blender or food processor, add the wine vinegar and 15-30ml (1-2 tbsp) of the stock, then work to a paste. Return to the pan, add the remaining stock and bring to the boil. Cover and simmer for 15 minutes. Adjust the seasoning.
4 Divide the soup between warmed bowls. Serve each portion topped with a spoonful of yogurt if desired, parsley and a little charmoula.

garlic soup with thyme croûtons

Although this soup uses a lot of garlic, it has a subtle, clean flavour. Thyme croûtons are the perfect complement.

Serves 6
Preparation time: 15 minutes
Cooking time: 1½ hours
Suitable for freezing (stage 3)
260 cals per serving

60ml (4 tbsp) olive oil
3 large onions, about 700g (1½lb)
16 garlic cloves, peeled and roughly chopped
150ml (¼ pint) white wine or cider
350g (12oz) potatoes, peeled and roughly chopped
1.6 litres (2¾ pints) vegetable stock
150ml (¼ pint) whipping cream
salt and freshly ground black pepper
TO SERVE:
thyme croûtons (see below)
thyme sprigs, to garnish

1 Heat the olive oil in a heavy-based pan and add the onions and garlic. Cover and cook over a very low heat, stirring occasionally, for 20-30 minutes until translucent and very soft; don't allow to colour.
2 Add the wine or cider and bring to the boil. Allow to bubble until the liquid is reduced by half. Add the potatoes and stock, bring to the boil and simmer, uncovered, for 45 minutes or until reduced slightly.
3 Allow to cool slightly, then transfer to a blender and process until smooth. Return the soup to the pan, add two thirds of the cream and season well.
4 Reheat the soup gently, stirring, then pour into warmed bowls. Drizzle with the remaining cream and serve topped with the croûtons and thyme.

thyme croûtons

Cut 3-4 slices of bread into cubes and toss in a bowl with 45-60ml (3-4 tbsp) olive oil and 5ml (1 tsp) dried thyme. Transfer to a shallow baking tin and bake at 200°C/fan oven 190°C (400°F) Mark 6 for about 10 minutes until golden; drain on kitchen paper. Sprinkle with salt and serve warm.

parsnip soup with parmesan crisps

A smooth, creamy soup enriched with spicy chorizo and served topped with deep-fried parsnip strips flavoured with Parmesan.

Serves 6
Preparation time: 30 minutes
Cooking time: 1 hour
Suitable for freezing (stage 3)
355 cals per serving

40g (1½oz) butter
150g (5oz) onion, peeled and roughly chopped
225g (8oz) floury potatoes, such as King Edward's, peeled and chopped
400g (14oz) parsnips, peeled and chopped
20ml (4 tsp) paprika, plus extra for dusting
1.1 litres (2 pints) fresh chicken or vegetable stock
450ml (¾ pint) milk
60ml (4 tbsp) double cream
salt and freshly ground black pepper
65g (2½oz) sliced chorizo sausage, cut into fine strips
FOR THE PARMESAN CRISPS:
1 large parsnip, weighing about 75g (3oz), peeled
vegetable oil, for frying
45ml (3 tbsp) freshly grated Parmesan cheese

1 Melt the butter in a large heavy-based pan. Add the onion and cook over a gentle heat for 5 minutes or until soft. Add the potatoes, parsnips and paprika; mix well. Cook gently, stirring occasionally, for about 15 minutes or until the vegetables are partially softened.

2 Add the stock, milk, cream and seasoning. Bring to the boil and simmer for 25 minutes or until the vegetables are very soft. Add 50g (2oz) of the chorizo.

3 Allow the soup to cool a little, then transfer to a blender or food processor and process until smooth. Return to the pan and thin with a little additional stock or milk, if wished. Check the seasoning.

4 To make the Parmesan crisps, using a wide swivel vegetable peeler, peel off as many long, wide strips from the parsnip as possible.

5 Heat a 2.5cm (1 inch) depth of oil in a large heavy-based saucepan or deep-sided frying pan.

6 Shallow-fry the parsnip strips in the hot oil in batches until golden and crisp. Drain on kitchen paper and sprinkle lightly with salt. Arrange the strips in 6 little mounds on a baking sheet, then sprinkle with half of the Parmesan cheese and the remaining chorizo. Bake at 200°C/fan oven 190°C (400°F) Mark 6 for 3-5 minutes or until the cheese begins to melt. Don't allow the crisps to brown or they'll taste bitter.

7 Meanwhile reheat the soup. Pour into warmed bowls and top with the Parmesan crisps. Sprinkle with the remaining Parmesan and dust with paprika to serve.

mexican bean soup with lime butter

A hearty bean soup, topped with crisp tortilla chips, diced avocado and a tangy lime butter.

Serves 6
Preparation time: 15 minutes
Cooking time: 25 minutes
Suitable for freezing (stage 4)
630 cals per serving

60ml (4 tbsp) extra-virgin olive oil
1 onion, peeled and chopped
2 garlic cloves, peeled and chopped
pinch of crushed red chillies
5ml (1 tsp) ground coriander
5ml (1 tsp) ground cumin
2.5ml (½ tsp) ground cinnamon
900ml (1½ pints) vegetable stock
300ml (½ pint) tomato juice
5-10ml (1-2 tsp) chilli sauce
two 400g (14oz) cans aduki or red kidney beans, drained
30ml (2 tbsp) chopped fresh coriander
salt and freshly ground black pepper
FOR THE LIME BUTTER:
50g (2oz) unsalted butter, softened
grated rind and juice of ½ lime
TO GARNISH:
1 small avocado
few tortilla chips

1. For the lime butter, beat the butter in a bowl with the lime rind and juice, salt and pepper. Shape into a log, wrap in cling film and refrigerate until required.
2. Heat the oil in a large saucepan, add the onion, garlic, chilli and spices and fry gently for 5 minutes until lightly golden.
3. Add the stock, tomato juice, chilli sauce and beans. Bring to the boil, cover and simmer gently for 20 minutes. Let cool slightly.
4. Purée in a blender until very smooth, then return the soup to the pan. Stir in the chopped coriander and heat through. Season with salt and pepper to taste.
5. Unwrap the lime butter and slice thinly. Peel, stone and thinly slice the avocado. Spoon the soup into warmed bowls and top each serving with a few slices of lime butter, some avocado and a few tortilla chips. Serve at once.

Variations

- Use aduki beans rather than red kidney beans.
- Flavour the butter with lemon or orange, instead of lime.

sweet potato and cumin soup

This soup is best made with the orange-fleshed variety of sweet potatoes which are available during the winter months.

Serves 6-8
Preparation time: 25 minutes
Cooking time: 50 minutes
Suitable for freezing
165-125 cals per serving

30ml (2 tbsp) olive oil
1 onion, peeled and chopped
2 garlic cloves, peeled and crushed
10ml (2 tsp) ground cumin
600g (1¼lb) peeled potatoes, diced
350g (12oz) peeled sweet potatoes, diced
1.2 litres (2 pints) hot vegetable stock
45-60ml (3-4 tbsp) chopped fresh coriander
15ml (1 tbsp) lemon juice
salt and freshly ground black pepper
a little extra-virgin olive oil, to serve

1 Heat the oil in a saucepan, add the onion, garlic and cumin and fry gently for 10 minutes.
2 Add all of the potatoes to the pan and fry for a further 5 minutes until they are lightly browned, stirring occasionally to prevent sticking.
3 Add the stock, bring to the boil, cover and simmer for 30 minutes. Transfer the soup to a blender or food processor and blend briefly until smooth.
4 Pour the soup into a clean pan and return to the boil. Stir in the coriander and simmer gently for 2-3 minutes.
5 Add the lemon juice and season with salt and pepper to taste. Serve the soup at once, drizzled with olive oil.

minestrone with pesto

This classic Italian soup is topped with pesto and freshly grated pecorino or Parmesan cheese. Serve it as a main course with plenty of good bread.

Serves 6-8
Preparation time: 20 minutes, plus overnight soaking
Cooking time: About 2-2½ hours
Suitable for freezing
540-400 cals per serving

175g (6oz) dried haricot, cannellini or flageolet beans, soaked overnight in cold water
salt and freshly ground black pepper
2.3 litres (4 pints) vegetable stock
1 dried red chilli
450g (1lb) potatoes, peeled and diced
450g (1lb) carrots, peeled and diced
2 large leeks, trimmed and thinly sliced
450g (1lb) courgettes, diced
225g (8oz) French beans, halved
425g (15oz) can chopped tomatoes
125g (4oz) dried pastina (tiny soup pasta)
TO SERVE:
classic basil pesto
50g (2oz) pecorino or Parmesan cheese, freshly grated

1 Drain the beans and put them in a large pan with enough fresh cold water to cover. Bring to the boil and boil steadily for 10 minutes, then lower the heat and simmer for 1-1½ hours or until the beans are tender, adding salt towards the end of the cooking time. Drain thoroughly.
2 Pour the stock into a large pan and add the chilli. Bring to the boil, then add the cooked beans, potatoes, carrots and leeks. Lower the heat, cover and simmer gently for 25 minutes or until the vegetables are very tender.
3 Add the courgettes, French beans, tomatoes and pasta to the soup and season generously. Re-cover and simmer for a further 10 minutes or until the pasta is just cooked.
4 Serve in warmed large soup plates, as a main course with plenty of good bread. Hand the pesto and grated cheese separately.

Variation Use two 425g (15oz) cans beans instead of dried ones. Drain and add to the soup towards the end of stage 3 to heat through.

tuscan bean soup

A substantial white bean soup with a fragrant, fried garlic and olive oil topping.

Serves 6
Preparation time: 20 minutes, plus soaking
Cooking time: 1¼ hours
Suitable for freezing (stage 3)
330 cals per serving

225g (8oz) dried haricot or cannellini beans, soaked
    overnight in cold water
4 garlic cloves, peeled
150ml (¼ pint) olive oil
salt and freshly ground black pepper
15-30ml (1-2 tbsp) chopped fresh parsley

1 Drain the beans, place in a flameproof casserole and add sufficient cold water to cover by 5cm (2 inches). Bring to the boil, cover tightly and bake in oven at 170°C/fan oven 160°C (325°F) Mark 3 for about 1 hour until tender (see note).
2 Meanwhile, finely chop half the garlic and thinly slice the remainder.
3 Transfer half of the beans and cooking liquid to a food processor or blender and process until smooth. Add this purée to the beans in the casserole and stir well.
4 Heat half the olive oil in a frying pan, add the chopped garlic and fry gently until soft and golden. Stir into the soup and reheat until boiling. Simmer gently for about 10 minutes, thinning the soup with a little water if it is too thick. Taste and season well with salt and pepper. Pour into a warmed tureen or individual soup bowls.
5 Heat remaining olive oil in the frying pan and fry the sliced garlic until golden. Spoon over the soup and serve at once, sprinkled with parsley.

Note The cooking time depends on the freshness of the beans. Older beans will take longer to cook. Begin testing them after 45 minutes.

Variations
• Stir 4 skinned, deseeded and chopped tomatoes into the soup as it is reheated.
• Stir 30ml (2 tbsp) chopped fresh sage or rosemary into the soup with the puréed beans.

butternut squash and haricot bean soup

This soup is equally good made with pumpkin. Olive pesto lends a superb flavour, though you could use classic basil pesto if preferred.

Serves 4-6
Preparation time: 20 minutes
Cooking time: 30 minutes
Suitable for freezing
350-235 cals per serving

900g (2lb) butternut squash
60ml (4 tbsp) olive oil
1 onion, peeled and chopped
2 garlic cloves, peeled and chopped
30ml (2 tbsp) chopped fresh sage
2.5ml (½ tsp) paprika
pinch of cayenne pepper
1.2 litres (2 pints) vegetable stock
400g (14oz) can haricot beans, drained
salt and freshly ground black pepper
TO SERVE:
60ml (4 tbsp) olive pesto (see note)

1 Peel and deseed the squash: you should have about 700g (1½lb) prepared weight. Cut the flesh into 1cm (½ inch) cubes.
2 Heat the oil in a large saucepan. Add the onion, garlic, squash, sage and spices, and fry gently for 10 minutes until lightly golden.
3 Add the stock and bring to the boil. Cover and simmer gently for 15 minutes. Transfer half of the soup to a blender or food processor and work until very smooth.
4 Return the puréed soup to the pan, stir in the haricot beans and return to a steady simmer. Cook gently for 5 minutes until the beans are heated through. Check the seasoning.
5 Serve the soup in warmed bowls topped with a spoonful of olive pesto.

Note Olive pesto is available from larger supermarkets and delicatessens.

bouillabaisse

Serves 4
Preparation time: 15 minutes
Cooking time: 45 minutes
285 cals per serving

1kg (2lb) mixed fish fillets and shellfish, such as red
    mullet, John Dory, monkfish, red snapper, whiting,
    mussels in shells, cooked large prawns and crab
    claws
large pinch of saffron strands
45ml (3 tbsp) olive oil
1 onion, peeled and sliced
1 leek, trimmed and sliced
2 celery sticks, sliced
2 garlic cloves, peeled and crushed
400g (14oz) can plum tomatoes, or skinned, deseeded
    flavourful fresh tomatoes, roughly chopped
1 bouquet garni
1 strip of pared orange zest
15ml (1 tbsp) sun-dried tomato paste
2.5ml (½ tsp) fennel seeds
1.2 litres (2 pints) fish stock
salt and freshly ground black pepper
30ml (2 tbsp) chopped fresh parsley
15ml (1 tbsp) chopped fresh thyme

1 Cut the fish fillets into bite-sized pieces.
2 Put the saffron strands in a bowl, pour over
   150ml (¼ pint) boiling water and leave to soak.
3 Heat the oil in a large pan, add the onion, leek,
   celery and garlic and cook until softened. Add
   the tomatoes, bouquet garni, orange zest, sun-
   dried tomato paste and fennel seeds; cook for
   1-2 minutes.
4 Add the fish stock with the saffron and its
   soaking liquid. Season with salt and pepper and
   bring to the boil. Lower the heat and simmer for
   about 30 minutes.
5 Add the fish pieces and mussels (not the prawns
   or crab claws) and cook for about 5-6 minutes,
   until the fish is just cooked and the mussels have
   opened; discard any unopened ones.
6 Stir in the prawns, crab claws and herbs. Heat
   through and serve with plenty of crusty bread.

Note This classic French fish soup originates from
Marseilles. If possible, buy whole fish and fillet
them yourself; use the bones and trimmings to
make the fish stock.

smoked fish chowder

Sliced smoked salmon and sweet potato add a
luxurious quality to this rich smoked haddock and
sweetcorn chowder. For a lighter soup, replace half
of the milk with water.

Serves 6
Preparation time: 20 minutes
Cooking time: 30 minutes
560-370 cals per serving

450g (1lb) skinless smoked haddock fillet
1.2 litres (2 pints) milk
2 celery sticks, sliced
2 onions, peeled and finely chopped
1 bay leaf
2 fresh parsley sprigs
6 white peppercorns
25g (1oz) unsalted butter
1 garlic clove, peeled and crushed
150ml (¼ pint) dry sherry
125g (4oz) piece smoked ham, chopped
225g (8oz) sweet potato, peeled and diced
125g (4oz) fresh or frozen sweetcorn kernels
125g (4oz) smoked salmon, sliced
TO SERVE:
croûtons (see page 22)
chopped parsley, to garnish

1 Lay the smoked haddock in a frying pan with the
   milk, celery, half of the onion, the herbs and
   peppercorns. Slowly bring to a simmer and poach
   for 1 minute, then turn off the heat and leave to
   cool.
2 Remove the fish from the pan and flake into
   pieces; set aside. Strain the milk and reserve. Melt
   the butter in a large saucepan, add the remaining
   onion and garlic and fry gently for 5 minutes
   until softened but not coloured. Add the sherry
   and boil rapidly for 4-5 minutes until almost
   totally reduced.
3 Add the chopped ham, sweet potato, fresh
   sweetcorn if using, and reserved poaching liquid.
   Bring to the boil, lower the heat, cover and
   simmer gently for 20 minutes. (If using frozen
   sweetcorn, add to the pan after 10 minutes.)
4 Stir in the flaked haddock and smoked salmon
   and heat through gently, without boiling, for
   3-4 minutes. Serve topped with croûtons and
   chopped parsley.

curried mussel soup

Serves 4
Preparation time: 15 minutes
Cooking time: 20 minutes
380 cals per serving

2kg (4½lb) mussels
small pinch of saffron strands
450ml (¾ pint) fish or vegetable stock
90ml (3fl oz) dry white wine
25g (1oz) butter
4 shallots, peeled and finely chopped
1 garlic clove, peeled and crushed
5ml (1 tsp) grated fresh root ginger
2.5ml (½ tsp) turmeric
2.5ml (½ tsp) garam masala
150ml (¼ pint) double cream
15ml (1 tbsp) chopped fresh dill
5ml (1 tsp) lemon juice, or to taste
freshly ground black pepper

1 Clean the mussels thoroughly under cold running water, removing their beards and discarding any with cracked or broken shells.

2 Put the saffron strands in a bowl, pour on the hot stock and leave to soak for 10 minutes.

3 Place the mussels in a large saucepan with the wine. Cover with a tight-fitting lid and steam for 4-5 minutes until the mussel shells have opened, shaking the pan frequently; discard any that remain closed.

4 Strain the mussel liquor through a muslin-lined sieve into a clean pan; set aside.

5 Remove the mussels from their shells, reserving 8 empty shells and 8 mussels for the garnish.

6 Melt the butter in a saucepan, add the shallots, garlic, ginger, turmeric and garam masala and fry gently for 5 minutes until soft. Add the saffron stock and mussel liquor and simmer gently, uncovered, for 10 minutes.

7 Stir in the cream, mussels and dill and heat through. Add the lemon juice and season with pepper to taste. Spoon the soup into warmed bowls. Pop a mussel into each of the reserved shells and float on top of the soup, as a garnish. Serve with warm crusty bread.

Note Garam masala and turmeric lend a subtle flavour to this soup; for a more pronounced curry flavour, use 5ml (1 tsp) curry powder instead.

pea and lettuce soup with lemon cream

You can serve this delicious spring soup either hot or chilled. If serving chilled, you might need to thin it down slightly with a little water or light vegetable stock.

Serves 6
Preparation time: 15 minutes
Cooking time: 30 minutes
Suitable for freezing (stage 2)
380 cals per serving

100g (3½oz) unsalted butter
pared rind of 1 lemon, plus 30 ml (2 tbsp) juice
1 bay leaf
75g (3oz) onion, finely chopped
800g (1lb 10oz) frozen peas or petit pois
150g (5oz) lettuce, finely shredded
2.5ml (½ tsp) caster sugar
salt and freshly ground black pepper
900ml (1½ pints) boiling water
FOR THE LEMON CREAM:
150ml (¼ pint) double cream
200g (7oz) frozen peas
finely grated rind of 1 lemon, plus 15ml (1 tbsp) juice
strips of lemon zest, to garnish

1 Melt the butter in a large pan. Tie the lemon rind and bay leaf together; add to the butter with the onion. Cook over a low heat for 10 minutes or until the onion is soft and golden. Add the frozen peas, lettuce, sugar, 5ml (1 tsp) salt, and pepper to taste; stir to coat with the butter.
2 Pour in the boiling water, return to the boil and simmer for 10 minutes or until the peas are very soft. Discard the lemon rind bundle. Allow the soup to cool a little, then pour into a blender and whizz until smooth. Add the lemon juice.
3 To make the lemon cream, heat the cream in a small pan and allow to bubble for 5 minutes. Meanwhile cook the frozen peas in boiling water for 1 minute; drain. Add the peas to the cream with the grated lemon rind. Season with salt and pepper to taste and cook for 2 minutes. Add the lemon juice and stir through.
4 Reheat the soup and check the seasoning. Ladle into warmed bowls and drizzle with the lemon cream. Garnish with the lemon zest to serve.

summer vegetable soup with herb pistou

The herb pistou adds flavour and fragrance, but you can serve the soup simply topped with grated Parmesan if preferred.

Serves 6
Preparation time: 45 minutes
Cooking time: 50 minutes
Suitable for freezing
290 cals per serving

45ml (3 tbsp) sunflower oil
1 medium onion, peeled and finely chopped
225g (8oz) waxy potatoes, peeled and finely diced
175g (6oz) carrots, peeled and finely diced
1 medium turnip, peeled and finely diced
1.7 litres (3 pints) vegetable stock or water
salt and freshly ground black pepper
4 bay leaves
6 large sage leaves
2 courgettes, about 375g (13oz), finely diced
175g (6oz) French beans, trimmed and halved
125g (4oz) shelled small fresh peas
225g (8oz) tomatoes, deseeded and finely diced
1 small head broccoli, divided into florets
FOR THE HERB PISTOU:
6 garlic cloves, peeled and chopped
1.75ml (¾ tsp) sea salt
15g (½oz) fresh basil leaves
175ml (6fl oz) olive oil

1 Heat the oil in a large pan, add the onion, potatoes, carrots and turnip and fry over a gentle heat for 10 minutes. Pour in the stock or water. Season well, bring to the boil and add the bay and sage leaves. Simmer for 25 minutes.
2 Add the courgettes, French beans, peas and tomatoes. Return to the boil and simmer for 10-15 minutes. Add the broccoli florets 5 minutes before the end of the cooking time.
3 In the meantime, make the herb pistou. Using a pestle and mortar, pound the garlic and sea salt together. Add the basil, pound to a paste, then gradually blend in the oil.
4 Remove the bay and sage leaves from the soup and adjust the seasoning. Pour the soup into warmed bowls, add a spoonful of herb pistou and serve with crusty bread.

vichyssoise with spinach cream

Serves 4-6
Preparation time: 20 minutes, plus chilling
Cooking time: 40 minutes
Suitable for freezing (stage 2)
575-385 cals per serving

50g (2oz) butter
350g (12oz) onions, peeled and roughly chopped
1kg (2¼lb) trimmed leeks, roughly chopped
1.1 litres (2 pints) vegetable or chicken stock
150ml (¼ pint) double cream
225g (8oz) potatoes, peeled and sliced
salt and freshly ground black pepper
FOR THE SPINACH CREAM:
15g (½oz) butter
125g (4oz) spinach leaves
grated rind of 1 lemon
150ml (¼ pint) double cream
TO GARNISH:
cooked peeled prawns (optional)
basil sprigs

1 Melt the butter in a large heavy-based pan. Add the onions and leeks and cook, stirring, for 10 minutes. Add the stock, cream and potatoes. Bring to the boil, cover and simmer for 30-40 minutes until the vegetables are tender.

2 Cool slightly, then process the soup in batches until smooth, using a blender or food processor. Pass through a fine sieve into a bowl if wished; season generously. Chill for at least 6 hours or overnight if serving cold.

3 Meanwhile, for the spinach cream, heat the butter in a pan. Add the spinach and lemon rind and cook, stirring, for 5 minutes. Add the cream and bubble for 1-2 minutes. Transfer to a blender or food processor and whizz until smooth. Season to taste; chill if serving the soup cold.

4 Ladle the soup into individual bowls and spoon in the spinach cream. Garnish with prawns if using, and basil to serve.

Note For puréed soup, a blender will give you a smoother result than a food processor.

gazpacho

This classic chilled tomato and pepper soup originates from Andalusia in Spain.

Serves 6-8
Preparation time: 25 minutes, plus chilling
Suitable for freezing (stage 4)
310-230 cals per serving

700g (1½lb) flavourful ripe tomatoes
1 cucumber, peeled and chopped
1 red pepper, halved, cored and deseeded
1 green pepper, halved, cored and deseeded
1 red chilli, halved and deseeded
3 garlic cloves, peeled and chopped
225g (8oz) fresh wholemeal breadcrumbs
15ml (1 tbsp) tomato paste
60ml (4 tbsp) wine vinegar
90ml (6 tbsp) olive oil
10ml (2 tsp) salt
freshly ground black pepper
600ml (1 pint) water
TO SERVE:
chopped cucumber
red and green pepper slices
chopped hard-boiled egg (optional)
chopped red or mild onion
ice cubes
croûtons (see page 22)

1 Immerse the tomatoes in a bowl of boiling water for 10 seconds, then drain and refresh under cold running water. Peel the tomatoes and roughly chop the flesh.
2 Put the tomatoes, cucumber, peppers, chilli and garlic into a large bowl. Add the breadcrumbs, tomato paste, wine vinegar, olive oil, salt and pepper to taste. Stir thoroughly.
3 Transfer half of the soup to a blender or food processor. Add about half of the water and process until fairly smooth. Transfer to a large serving bowl. Purée the remaining half of the soup mixture with the rest of the water. Add to the puréed soup and stir well.
4 Adjust the seasoning to taste. Cover and chill in the refrigerator for at least 2 hours.
5 To serve, put the garnishes in separate small bowls. Add a little ice to the gazpacho and serve accompanied by the garnishes.

cream of watercress soup

This soup is equally good served hot or cold. Use small, young watercress leaves for best results.

Serves 4
Preparation time: 15 minutes, plus optional chilling
Cooking time: 20 minutes
Suitable for freezing (stage 4)
300 cals per serving

2 bunches of watercress, about 175g (6oz) in total
50g (2oz) butter
1 onion, peeled and chopped
45ml (3 tbsp) plain flour
600ml (1 pint) milk
300ml (½ pint) chicken or vegetable stock
salt and freshly ground black pepper
90ml (6 tbsp) single cream or crème fraîche (optional)

1 Trim the watercress, discarding any coarse stalks and reserving a few sprigs for garnish. Roughly chop the watercress.
2 Melt the butter in a large saucepan, add the onion and cook gently for about 10 minutes, until soft but not browned.
3 Stir in the flour and cook gently for 1 minute, stirring. Remove from the heat and gradually stir in the milk, stock and seasoning. Bring to the boil slowly and continue to cook, stirring, until thickened.
4 Allow to cool very slightly, then purée with the watercress, in batches if necessary, using a blender or food processor.
5 To serve hot, return to the pan, reheat gently and adjust the seasoning. To serve the soup chilled, allow to cool, then place in the refrigerator for at least 4 hours or overnight.
6 Serve each portion topped with a swirl of cream if desired, and garnished with the reserved watercress sprigs.

iced asparagus and shallot soup

Serve this decadent soup ice-cool in chilled bowls to maximise its refreshing flavour.

Serves 6
Preparation time: 15 minutes, plus chilling
Cooking time: 35 minutes
95 cals per serving

1.1kg (2½lb) asparagus, trimmed
45ml (3 tbsp) oil
4 large shallots, peeled and finely chopped
200g (7oz) leeks, trimmed and finely chopped
1.3 litres (2¼ pints) water
salt and pepper
chervil sprigs, to garnish

1 Cut the tips off the asparagus and set aside. Thinly pare the lower part of the stalks, then cut into 2.5cm (1 inch) lengths.
2 Heat the oil in a large saucepan, add the shallots and cook gently for 2-3 minutes. Add the leeks and continue to cook for about 10 minutes until soft.
3 Add the asparagus, 900ml (1½ pints) water and seasoning. Bring to the boil, lower the heat and simmer very gently, uncovered, for 10-20 minutes or until the asparagus is very soft. Allow to cool slightly.
4 Transfer the soup to a blender or food processor and purée until smooth. Transfer to a bowl and allow to cool.
5 Cook the reserved asparagus tips in boiling salted water for 2-3 minutes until just tender, then drain and refresh under cold water.
6 Add the asparagus tips to the soup, cover and chill for several hours, or overnight.
7 To serve, stir approximately 450ml (¾ pint) iced water into the soup to obtain the required consistency. Season generously with salt and pepper. Serve in chilled soup bowls, garnished with chervil.

chilled tomato soup with avocado cream

Serves 6
Preparation time: 20 minutes, plus chilling
Suitable for freezing (stage 3)
145 cals per serving

1.4kg (3lb) ripe red tomatoes
750ml (1¼ pints) tomato juice
pinch of sugar
dash of Tabasco
15ml (1 tbsp) lemon juice
30ml (2 tbsp) chopped fresh mint
salt and freshly ground black pepper
FOR THE AVOCADO CREAM:
1 large ripe avocado
10-15ml (2-3 tsp) lemon juice
½ small onion
30ml (2 tbsp) chopped fresh mint
90ml (6 tbsp) soured cream
TO GARNISH:
mint sprigs

1 Halve the tomatoes, then squeeze out the seeds into a bowl. Reserve 4 tomato halves and cut into fine dice; cover and refrigerate. Strain the tomato seeds through a small sieve to extract any juices; discard the seeds.
2 Put the remaining tomatoes in a blender or food processor with the tomato juice, sugar, Tabasco, lemon juice, chopped mint and seasoning to taste. Process until smooth, then pass through a sieve into a clean bowl. Check the seasoning.
3 Cover and chill for at least 2 hours.
4 About 20 minutes before serving, halve the avocado, remove the stone, then peel. Mash the avocado flesh in a bowl, using a fork, adding lemon juice to taste. Peel and finely grate the onion and mix into the avocado with the chopped mint and soured cream.
5 Stir the reserved diced tomato into the chilled soup. Ladle the soup into serving bowls and add a dollop of the avocado cream to each one. Garnish with mint to serve.

Variation Substitute fresh basil for the mint. Dice the avocado and stir into the soup, leaving out the grated onion. Serve topped with soured cream.

chilled pea soup with mint salsa

Appreciate the superb flavour of fresh peas with this refreshing summer soup.

Serves 4
Preparation time: 20 minutes, plus chilling
Cooking time: 35-40 minutes
Suitable for freezing (without salsa)
350 cals per serving

450g (1lb) fresh peas in their pods
30ml (2 tbsp) extra-virgin olive oil
2 leeks, trimmed and sliced
1 garlic clove, peeled and crushed
1 potato, about 175g (6oz), peeled and cubed
1 litre (1¾ pints) vegetable stock
salt and freshly ground black pepper
150ml (¼ pint) double cream
FOR THE MINT SALSA:
juice of 1 lemon
25g (1oz) caster sugar
1 small onion, peeled and finely chopped
125g (4oz) cucumber, peeled, deseeded and diced
60ml (4 tbsp) chopped fresh mint
TO GARNISH:
mint sprigs
ice cubes (optional)

1 Pod the peas, reserving both the peas and the pods. String the pods and cut into small pieces.
2 Heat the oil in a saucepan, add the leeks, garlic and pea pods and fry gently for 5 minutes. Add the potato and stock, bring to the boil, cover and simmer gently for 20 minutes.
3 Transfer the soup to a blender or food processor and purée until smooth. Pass through a fine sieve into the cleaned pan and stir in the fresh peas. Cover and cook gently for a further 10 minutes until the peas are tender.

4 Meanwhile, make the salsa. Put the lemon juice and sugar into a small pan and heat gently to dissolve the sugar. Add the onion, cucumber and a pinch of salt. Remove from the heat, stir in the mint and set aside to cool.
5 Season the soup with salt and pepper, leave until cold, then chill for several hours.
6 To serve, stir in the cream and adjust the seasoning. Divide between individual bowls and serve garnished with the mint salsa, mint sprigs and some ice cubes, if wished.

Note The pea pods are included to add an extra depth of flavour to the soup.

starters & snacks

Sensational starters to stimulate the tastebuds and start off a special meal in style, plus a selection of original, tasty snacks

tomato bruschetta

For this Italian snack, generous slices of toast are rubbed with garlic and drizzled with extra-virgin olive oil, then topped with a fresh-tasting tomato and basil salsa.

Serves 4
Preparation time: 15 minutes, plus infusing
Cooking time: 1-2 minutes
180 cals per serving

6 ripe plum tomatoes, peeled and roughly diced
1.25ml (¼ tsp) caster sugar
15ml (1 tbsp) chopped fresh basil
60ml (2fl oz) extra-virgin olive oil
4 slices day-old country-style white bread
1 garlic clove, peeled and halved
salt and freshly ground black pepper
basil sprigs, to garnish

1 Put the tomatoes in a bowl with the sugar, chopped basil and half of the olive oil. Cover and set aside for 30 minutes to allow the flavours to mingle.
2 Toast the bread on both sides until crisp and golden, then rub all over with the cut garlic clove.
3 Spoon the tomato mixture on top of the toasted bread, pressing it firmly into the bread. Drizzle over the remaining olive oil and season generously with salt and pepper. Garnish with basil leaves to serve.

Variation

ASPARAGUS AND PARMA HAM BRUSCHETTA For the topping, use 225g (8oz) asparagus, trimmed; 50g (2oz) rocket leaves; 4 slices of Parma ham and some Parmesan cheese shavings. Toss the rocket in a light lemony vinaigrette. Brush the asparagus spears with olive oil and grill for 4-5 minutes until charred and tender. Arrange the rocket on the toasted bread, then top with the asparagus, Parma ham and Parmesan shavings. Drizzle with olive oil to serve.

deep-fried polenta sandwiches with fontina

Serves 4-6
Preparation time: 20 minutes, plus chilling
Cooking time: 10-15 minutes
535-355 cals per serving

900ml (1½ pints) water
15g (½oz) butter
2.5ml (½ tsp) salt
175g (6oz) quick-cook polenta
25g (1oz) Parmesan cheese, freshly grated
freshly ground black pepper
175g (6oz) fontina or mozzarella cheese
seasoned flour, for coating
2 eggs, beaten
75g (3oz) fresh white breadcrumbs
oil, for deep-frying

1 Bring the water to a rolling boil in a saucepan. Add the butter and salt. With the water at a steady simmer, gradually whisk in the polenta. Cook gently, stirring from time to time, for 6-8 minutes until the polenta is thickened and comes away from the sides of the pan.
2 Remove from the heat and beat in the Parmesan and plenty of black pepper. Pour the mixture into a greased 23x25cm (9x11 inch) shallow tin and level the surface with a palette knife. Leave until cold.
3 Turn the set polenta out on to a board. Using a plain 5cm (2 inch) cutter, stamp out 12 rounds, then halve each one horizontally to give 24 rounds. Cut the cheese into thin slices, then cut out 12 rounds, using the same cutter. Sandwich each disc of cheese between 2 polenta rounds.
4 Dip the sandwiches into the seasoned flour to coat on all sides, then carefully dip into the beaten egg and finally in the breadcrumbs to coat thoroughly. Chill for 30 minutes.
5 Heat a 10-12cm (4-5 inch) depth of vegetable oil in a deep heavy-based saucepan to 180°C (350°F), or until a cube of bread dropped into the oil crisps in 30 seconds.
6 Fry the polenta sandwiches in the hot oil, three at a time, for about 1-2 minutes until crisp and golden. Drain on kitchen paper and keep warm in a low oven whilst cooking the rest. Serve as soon as possible.

piadina with grilled pepper, mint and feta

Italian-style flat bread topped with grilled peppers, feta and chopped mint.

Serves 6
Preparation time: 20 minutes, plus resting
Cooking time: 20-25 minutes
305 cals per serving

FOR THE PIADINA:
225g (8oz) plain flour
2.5ml (½ tsp) salt
15g (½oz) butter, softened
150ml (¼ pint) tepid water
FOR THE TOPPING:
4 red peppers
60ml (4 tbsp) extra-virgin olive oil
15ml (1 tbsp) balsamic vinegar
1 small garlic clove, peeled and crushed
salt and freshly ground black pepper
150g (5oz) feta cheese
15ml (1 tbsp) chopped fresh mint
TO GARNISH:
mint sprigs

1 First grill the peppers, turning frequently, for 15-20 minutes, until evenly charred and softened. Transfer to a bowl, cover tightly and set aside until cool enough to handle.

2 To make the bread, sift the flour and salt into a bowl and make a well in the centre. Add the butter and water and work to a soft dough. Knead for 10 minutes until smooth, then wrap in cling film and leave to rest for 30 minutes.

3 Peel away the skin from the peppers, holding them over a bowl to catch the juices. Slice each pepper into strips, discarding the core and seeds. Place in the bowl and add the oil, vinegar, garlic and salt and pepper. Set aside until required.

4 Divide the dough into 6 equal pieces and roll each one out to an 18cm (7 inch) circle, about 3 mm (⅛ inch) thick. Preheat a griddle or heavy-based frying pan until really hot, add a dough round and cook for 1 minute until the base is cooked and flecked with brown. Flip over and cook the other side for 30 seconds. Remove and keep warm wrapped in a tea-towel while making five more piadina.

5 Lay the piadina on individual serving plates and top with the pepper mixture. Crumble over the feta and scatter with the chopped mint. Serve immediately, garnished with mint.

avocado and parma ham puffs

Puff pastry rounds topped with avocado slices, Parma ham slices and piquant gremolata.

Serves 6
Preparation time: 15 minutes, plus chilling
Cooking time: 12-15 minutes
320 cals per serving

350g (12oz) ready-made puff pastry
60ml (4 tbsp) sun-dried tomato paste
30ml (2 tbsp) mascarpone
1 small avocado
15ml (1 tbsp) lemon juice
6 slices prosciutto or Parma ham
FOR THE GREMOLATA:
2 garlic cloves, peeled and crushed
30ml (2 tbsp) chopped fresh basil
grated rind of 1 lemon
freshly ground black pepper

1 Roll out the pastry on a lightly floured surface and cut out six 12cm (5 inch) rounds, using an inverted fluted flan tin or saucer as a guide. Prick the bases and chill for 30 minutes.
2 Preheat a baking sheet on the middle shelf of the oven at 220°C/fan oven 210°C (425°F) Mark 7. Mix the tomato paste and mascarpone together and spread over the puff pastry bases.
3 Peel, halve and stone the avocado, then cut the flesh into wafer-thin slices and immediately brush with the lemon juice. Arrange on the pastry bases. Transfer to the preheated baking sheet and cook in the oven for 12-15 minutes until risen and golden.
4 Meanwhile, mix the gremolata ingredients together in a bowl. Arrange the Parma ham slices on the puffs; warm through in the oven for 1 minute if required. Scatter over the gremolata and serve immediately.

onion tartlets with tomato and caper salsa

Caramelised onions, shredded fresh basil and toasted pine nuts in puff pastry cases, complemented by a fresh-tasting salsa.

Serves 4
Preparation time: 25 minutes
Cooking time: 40 minutes
490 cals per serving

30ml (2 tbsp) olive or sunflower oil
450g (1lb) onions, peeled and sliced
300g (10oz) ready-made puff pastry
25g (1oz) pine nuts, toasted
12 basil leaves, shredded
salt and freshly ground black pepper
a little milk, to glaze
FOR THE SALSA:
1 tomato, halved, deseeded and finely chopped
1 red chilli, deseeded and finely chopped
25g (1oz) sun-dried tomatoes in oil, drained and chopped
25g (1oz) capers, chopped
15ml (1 tbsp) olive oil

1 Heat the oil in a large frying pan, add the onions and cook over a low heat, stirring occasionally, for about 20 minutes until golden brown and caramelised.
2 Meanwhile, roll out the puff pastry on a lightly floured surface to a 3-5 mm (⅛-¼ inch) thickness. Using a small plate as a guide, cut four 15cm (6 inch) circles. Knock up the edges using a round-bladed knife and flute them decoratively. Place the pastry discs on a greased baking sheet and prick with a fork.
3 Add the pine nuts and basil to the caramelised onions and season with salt and pepper to taste. Divide the mixture between the pastry discs, leaving a 2.5cm (½ inch) clear margin around the edges. Brush the edges with a little milk to glaze, then bake at 220°C/fan oven 210°C (425°F) Mark 7 for about 15 minutes until well risen, crisp and golden brown.
4 Meanwhile, combine all of the ingredients for the salsa in a bowl and mix well, seasoning with salt and pepper to taste.
5 Serve the tartlets hot or warm, with the salsa.

hummus with chilli oil and toasted pine nuts

This chick pea purée is quick to make and tastes far superior to ready-made hummus. Tahini paste is make from sesame seeds and is available from selected supermarkets.

Serves 6
Preparation time: 10 minutes
Cooking time: 2 minutes
285 cals per serving

150ml (¼ pint) olive oil
5ml (1 tsp) mild chilli powder
400g (14oz) can chick peas, drained and rinsed
15ml (1 tbsp) tahini paste
1 garlic clove, peeled and crushed
juice of 1 lemon
sea salt and freshly ground black pepper
25g (1oz) pine nuts, toasted
TO SERVE:
sesame seed sticks
pitta bread

1 Put 45ml (3 tbsp) olive oil into a pan and mix in the chilli powder. Warm over a gentle heat for 2 minutes; set aside.
2 Place the chick peas in a food processor with the tahini paste, garlic and lemon juice. With the motor running, add the remaining oil through the feeder tube and process to a rough paste. Season well.
3 Transfer the hummus to a serving bowl, drizzle the warm chilli oil over the surface and sprinkle with the toasted pine nuts. Serve with sesame seed sticks and warm pitta bread.

Note For convenience, the chilli oil and chick pea purée can be prepared a day in advance. To serve, warm the oil and finish as above.

pakoras

These tasty Indian fritters are best served with a cooling dish of yogurt or raita and a contrasting hot chutney.

Serves 4
Preparation time: 30 minutes
Cooking time: 12-15 minutes
Suitable for freezing
225 cals per serving

550g (1¼lb) mixed vegetables, such as courgettes, onion, potato, aubergine, red pepper, okra, spinach leaves, trimmed or peeled as necessary

FOR THE BATTER:
1 garlic clove, peeled and crushed
5ml (1 tsp) ground cumin
5ml (1 tsp) ground coriander
10ml (2 tsp) garam masala
5ml (1 tsp) chilli powder
5ml (1 tsp) turmeric
175g (6oz) gram flour or plain wholemeal flour
5ml (1 tsp) salt
30ml (2 tbsp) oil
200ml (7fl oz) water (approximately)
large handful of fresh mint leaves, shredded
large handful of fresh coriander leaves, shredded
15ml (1 tbsp) black poppy seeds

TO FINISH:
oil, for deep-frying
coriander sprigs, to garnish
raita (see right) and/or chutney, to serve

1 First make the batter. Mix the garlic, cumin, coriander, garam masala, chilli powder, turmeric, flour and salt together in a bowl. Add the oil, then gradually stir in about 200ml (7fl oz) cold water, to make a thick batter. Beat vigorously until smooth. Leave to stand for 30 minutes.

2 Cut the courgettes into thick slices. Thickly slice the onion. Peel the potato, cut into thick slices and blanch in boiling salted water for 2 minutes; drain and pat dry with kitchen paper. Cut the aubergine into thick slices, then cut each slice into 3 fingers. Halve, core and deseed the pepper, then cut into chunks. Wash and thoroughly dry the spinach leaves.

3 Add the shredded mint and coriander to the batter with the poppy seeds and beat well.

4 Heat the oil in a deep-fat fryer to 190°C (375°F), or until a teaspoonful of the batter dropped into the oil sizzles immediately on contact and rises to the surface.

5 When the oil is ready, cook the pakoras in batches. Dip a few vegetable pieces into the batter. Remove one piece at a time, carefully drop into the hot oil and cook for 4-5 minutes or until golden brown and crisp on all sides.

6 Drain the pakoras on crumpled kitchen paper and keep warm while cooking the remaining vegetables in batches. Don't try to cook too many pieces together or they will stick together. Serve warm, garnished with coriander and accompanied by raita, and/or chutney if desired.

vegetable samosas

Homemade samosas are much tastier than those you can buy and they are easy to make. Serve them with raita and a chutney.

Makes 24
Preparation time: 45 minutes
Cooking time: About 15 minutes
Suitable for freezing
150 cals per samosa

450g (1lb) potatoes
salt and freshly ground black pepper
15ml (1 tbsp) oil
1 onion, peeled and finely chopped
1 garlic clove, peeled and crushed
1-2 green chillies, deseeded and finely chopped
10ml (2 tsp) ground coriander
10ml (2 tsp) cumin seeds
5ml (1 tsp) ground fenugreek
1 large ripe tomato
50g (2oz) frozen peas
30ml (2 tbsp) chopped fresh coriander
15ml (1 tbsp) chopped fresh mint

FOR THE PASTRY:
450g (1lb) plain white flour
45ml (3 tbsp) chopped fresh coriander
60ml (4 tbsp) oil, melted ghee or butter
200ml (7fl oz) warm water (approximately)

TO FINISH:
oil, for deep-frying

1 Peel and halve the potatoes. Cook in salted water until just tender. Drain thoroughly and chop into fairly small pieces.

2 Heat the oil in a frying pan. Add the onion and garlic and cook until softened. Add the chilli and spices and cook, stirring for 2 minutes.

3 Chop the tomato, add to the pan and simmer until softened. Add the potatoes and stir to coat in the spice mixture. Add the peas and cook for 1-2 minutes until thawed. Add the herbs and plenty of seasoning. Take off the heat; let cool.

4 To make the pastry, mix the flour, 5ml (1 tsp) salt, and the coriander together in a bowl. Add the oil or melted fat and enough warm water to make a soft dough – about 200ml (7fl oz). Turn on to a lightly floured surface and knead for about 5 minutes.

5 Divide the dough into 12 pieces; keep covered with a damp cloth to prevent drying out. Roll one piece out to a 15cm (6 inch) round, using a plate as a guide to trim the edges. Cut in half to make 2 semi-circles.

6 Put a heaped teaspoon of filling on each semi-circle. Dampen the edges, fold over the filling and press together firmly to seal. Repeat with the remaining pastry and filling.

7 Heat the oil in a deep-fat fryer to 180°C (350°F) or until a small piece of pastry dropped into the oil sizzles on contact and rises to the surface.

8 Deep-fry the samosas, two or three at a time, for 3-5 minutes until golden. Drain on kitchen paper. Serve warm, with raita and a chutney.

Note For convenience, these samosas can be made in advance and reheated in the oven at 180°C/fan oven 170°C (350°F) Mark 4 for about 15 minutes.

coriander chutney

For a quick, fresh-tasting chutney to accompany these samosas, toss a few sliced spring onions with freshly torn mint and coriander leaves, crushed garlic, a splash of lemon juice, a dash of oil and plenty of seasoning.

raita

To make this cooling Indian side dish, flavour Greek-style yogurt with diced, deseeded cucumber, chopped fresh mint, a little crushed garlic and seasoning to taste.

falafel with minted yogurt dip

For falafel dried chick peas are soaked, but not pre-cooked. If possible, make the mixture well in advance – the flavour improves on standing.

Serves 4-6
Preparation time: 20-25 minutes, plus overnight soaking
Cooking time: 8-10 minutes
350-240 cals per serving

225g (8oz) dried chick peas, soaked overnight in cold water
15ml (1 tbsp) tahini paste
1 garlic clove, peeled and crushed
5ml (1 tsp) sea salt
5ml (1 tsp) turmeric
5ml (1 tsp) ground cumin
1.25ml (¼ tsp) cayenne pepper
30ml (2 tbsp) chopped fresh coriander
15ml (1 tbsp) chopped fresh mint
15ml (1 tbsp) lemon juice
a little seasoned flour
oil, for shallow-frying
FOR THE YOGURT DIP:
150ml (¼ pint) Greek yogurt
1-2 garlic cloves, peeled and crushed
15ml (1 tbsp) olive oil
30ml (2 tbsp) chopped fresh mint
salt and freshly ground black pepper

1 Drain the chick peas, place in a food processor and process to a fairly smooth paste.

2 Transfer to a bowl and add the tahini paste, garlic, salt, spices, herbs and lemon juice. Cover and leave to stand for at least 30 minutes.

3 Meanwhile, mix all the ingredients for the yogurt dip together in a bowl, seasoning to taste. Cover and set aside until required.

4 With floured hands, shape the chick pea mixture into 2.5cm (1 inch) balls. Flatten slightly and dust with the seasoned flour.

5 Heat a 1cm (½ inch) depth of oil in a frying pan. When hot, fry the patties in batches for 1-2 minutes on each side until evenly browned. Drain on kitchen paper; keep warm while cooking the rest.

6 Serve warm, with the yogurt dip and some warm pitta bread. Alternatively, serve cool.

wild mushroom and parmesan wafers

A medley of wild mushrooms in a delicious Champagne sauce are sandwiched between Parmesan puff pastry to make a decadent starter.

Serves 8
Preparation time: 35 minutes, plus chilling
Cooking time: 1 hour
480 cals per serving

75g (3oz) butter
350g (12oz) ready-made puff pastry
75g (3oz) Parmesan cheese, freshly grated
salt and freshly ground black pepper
225g (8oz) shallots, peeled and finely chopped
450g (1lb) mixed wild mushrooms, such as ceps morels, chanterelles, quartered
300ml (½ pint) Champagne or sparkling dry white wine
300ml (½ pint) vegetable stock
300ml (½ pint) double cream
thyme sprigs, to garnish

1 Melt 25g (1oz) of the butter. Roll out the pastry on a lightly floured surface to a 23x33cm (9x13 inch) rectangle and cut across into three even-sized pieces. Brush with the melted butter, sprinkle with half the grated Parmesan and season with pepper.
2 Stack the pieces of pastry on top of one another, then re-roll the pastry stack out to the same dimensions. Cover with cling film and chill in the refrigerator for 15 minutes.
3 Cut out eight 10cm (4 inch) rounds from the pastry and place on a greased baking sheet. Sprinkle with the remaining grated Parmesan, season with pepper and refrigerate for about 30 minutes.
4 Bake the pastry rounds at 200°C/fan oven 190°C (400°F) Mark 6 for 15 minutes. Set aside to cool, then carefully split each in two horizontally.
5 Heat the remaining butter in a large frying pan, add the shallots and cook, stirring, for 10 minutes or until soft. Add the mushrooms and cook for 5 minutes, stirring, then add the Champagne and stock. Bring to the boil and simmer for 5 minutes. Drain the mushrooms, reserving the liquor; set aside.
6 Return the liquor to the pan and stir in the cream. Bring to the boil and let bubble for 20 minutes or until syrupy. Season to taste and stir in the reserved mushrooms.
7 To serve, place a pastry base on each plate, then spoon the mushrooms and sauce on top. Position the pastry lids and garnish with thyme.

Note Most supermarkets now sell a selection of wild mushrooms. Make sure you rinse them thoroughly under cold running water; fine soil is often trapped in the gills.

grilled asparagus with bacon

Fresh plump asparagus spears are wrapped in bacon rashers and grilled until crisp. Serve with a herb-flavoured mayonnaise.

Serves 4-6
Preparation time: 15 minutes
Cooking time: 7 minutes
430-285 cals per serving

1.1kg (2½lb) plump asparagus, trimmed
salt and freshly ground black pepper
300g (10oz) thin rindless smoked streaky bacon rashers
30ml (2 tbsp) olive oil
snipped chives, to garnish
herb mayonnaise (see note), to serve

1 Blanch the asparagus in boiling salted water for 1 minute; drain and refresh in cold water.
2 Wrap a bacon rasher around the middle of each asparagus spear, starting about 2.5cm (1 inch) from the tip.
3 Place on a grill rack, brush with olive oil and season with pepper. Grill for about 6 minutes, turning frequently, until the bacon is crisp and the asparagus is tender.
4 Serve sprinkled with chives and accompanied by herb mayonnaise and crusty bread.

Note For the herb mayonnaise, flavour homemade or good quality bought mayonnaise with chopped fresh herbs, such as chervil, dill and parsley.

stuffed mushrooms with bacon and goat's cheese

Serves 4
Preparation time: 20 minutes
Cooking time: 20 minutes
270 cals per serving

4 large cup mushrooms
45ml (3 tbsp) extra-virgin olive oil
50g (2oz) rindless smoked bacon, finely diced
2 large garlic cloves, peeled and crushed
50g (2oz) fresh white breadcrumbs
50g (2oz) ground almonds
30ml (2 tbsp) chopped fresh basil
50g (2oz) goat's cheese, diced
30ml (2 tbsp) single cream
15ml (1 tbsp) lemon juice
salt and freshly ground black pepper
basil leaves, to garnish

1 Cut the stalks from the mushrooms and chop them finely, reserving the whole caps.
2 Heat 30ml (2 tbsp) of the oil in a frying pan, add the mushroom caps, rounded-side down, and fry quickly for about 1 minute to brown. Remove with a slotted spoon and arrange, cup-side up, in a baking dish.
3 Add the chopped mushroom stalks, bacon and garlic to the frying pan and fry for 5 minutes, then transfer to a bowl. Add the breadcrumbs, ground almonds, basil, goat's cheese, cream, lemon juice and seasoning; mix well. Divide the stuffing between the mushroom caps.
4 Drizzle the remaining oil over the top and bake at 200°C/fan oven 190°C (400°F) Mark 6 for 20 minutes until crisp and golden. Serve at once, garnished with basil.

fennel carpaccio

Wafer-thin slices of fennel are marinated in a piquant dressing, then topped with a handful of rocket leaves to make a stimulating, light starter.

Serves 4
Preparation time: 15-20 minutes, plus marinating
220 cals per serving

2 heads of fennel, about 700g (1½lb) total weight
120ml (4fl oz) extra-virgin olive oil
shredded zest and juice of ½ lemon
1 garlic clove, peeled and crushed
pinch of sugar
5ml (1 tsp) coriander seeds, crushed
2 fresh thyme sprigs, bruised
2 fresh rosemary sprigs, bruised
salt and freshly ground black pepper
15ml (1 tbsp) chopped fresh fennel fronds or dill
TO SERVE:
handful of rocket leaves
Parmesan cheese shavings (optional)
fennel flowers (optional)

1 Trim the fennel and slice the bulbs crosswise into wafer-thin slices, using a sharp knife. Place in a large shallow dish.
2 Combine the oil, lemon zest and juice, garlic, sugar, coriander seeds, thyme, rosemary and salt and pepper. Pour over the fennel and toss well until evenly coated. Cover and leave to marinate at room temperature for at least 1 hour.
3 Drain the fennel, reserving the juices. Divide between individual serving plates and top each serving with a few rocket leaves.
4 Taste the marinade and adjust the seasoning if necessary. Stir in the fennel fronds or dill and drizzle liberally over the fennel and rocket. Top with plenty of fresh Parmesan shavings and garnish with fennel flowers if available. Serve with walnut or olive bread.

Note The easiest way to shave wafer-thin slivers of Parmesan is to use a swivel potato peeler on a large wedge of cheese at room temperature (not hard from the refrigerator).

warm goat's cheese salad with rocket pesto

Serves 4
Preparation time: 20 minutes
Cooking time: 3-4 minutes
530 cals per serving

FOR THE ROCKET PESTO:
50g (2oz) rocket leaves
1 garlic clove, peeled
45ml (3 tbsp) freshly grated Parmesan cheese
25g (1oz) walnut halves, lightly toasted
90ml (6 tbsp) olive oil
freshly ground black pepper

FOR THE SALAD:
4 slices Bucheron chèvre (goat's cheese log with rind)
1 bunch of watercress, trimmed
50g (2oz) rocket leaves
40g (1½oz) walnut halves, toasted

FOR THE DRESSING:
15ml (1 tbsp) walnut oil
15ml (1 tbsp) sunflower oil
5ml (1 tsp) balsamic or sherry vinegar
salt and freshly ground black pepper

1 To make the rocket pesto, place all the ingredients in a blender or food processor and work until smooth. Alternatively pound the ingredients together using a pestle and mortar. Place in a jar, cover with a thin layer of oil and set aside.

2 Whisk the dressing ingredients together in a bowl, seasoning with salt and pepper to taste.

3 Place the goat's cheese slices on a foil-lined baking sheet and position as close to the grill as possible for 1-2 minutes, until browned.

4 Place a cheese slice on each serving plate and top with a spoonful of rocket pesto. Toss the salad leaves with the dressing and arrange around the goat's cheese. Scatter the toasted walnuts over the top and serve immediately.

Note Any leftover pesto can be stored in a screw-topped jar in the refrigerator for up to 3 days.

Variations Use halved *crottins de Chavignol* instead of Bucheron. Or simply serve a mound of soft fresh goat's cheese with the rocket pesto and salad.

chilled melon and ginger salad

Melon and ginger are a classic combination. The contrasting mellow tones of different melon varieties make this an attractive, light starter.

Serves 4-6
Preparation time: 15 minutes, plus chilling
Cooking time: 10 minutes
105-70 cals per serving

1 small charantais or cantaloupe melon
1 small ogen or galia melon
½ large honeydew melon
350g (12oz) watermelon

FOR THE DRESSING:
30ml (2 tbsp) caster sugar
15ml (1 tbsp) chopped preserved stem ginger in syrup, drained
120ml (4fl oz) water
30ml (2 tbsp) orange juice
10ml (2 tsp) lemon juice

1 First make the dressing. Put the sugar, ginger and water in a small saucepan and heat gently to dissolve the sugar, then bring to the boil and simmer for 10 minutes. Transfer to a bowl and stir in the orange and lemon juices. Set aside to cool.

2 Peel each melon and discard the seeds. Cut the flesh into thin wedges and mix together in a large bowl.

3 Pour the cooled dressing over the melon and toss gently to mix. Cover and chill in the refrigerator for 1 hour before serving.

Note Judging a melon's ripeness can be difficult. If the melon has a fruity aroma and feels slightly soft at the stalk end, it should be ready to eat.

summer melon salad with roquefort dressing

Make this refreshing starter during the summer months when charentais melons – with their scented orange flesh – are at their best.

Serves 4
Preparation time: 15 minutes
Cooking time: 2 minutes
435 cals per serving

225g (8oz) sugar snap peas
salt and freshly ground black pepper
½ charentais melon, about 700g (1½lb)
1 pear
juice of ½ lemon
125g (4oz) Roquefort cheese
FOR THE DRESSING:
30ml (2 tbsp) white wine vinegar
60ml (4 tbsp) walnut oil
60ml (4 tbsp) olive oil
TO GARNISH:
25g (1oz) walnuts, roughly chopped and toasted

1 Halve the sugar snap peas on the diagonal and cook in boiling salted water for 2 minutes. Drain, refresh in cold water and drain thoroughly.
2 Deseed, peel and slice the melon. Peel, quarter, core and slice the pear. Toss the pear and melon together with the lemon juice in a bowl. Crumble in the Roquefort cheese, then season with pepper and a little salt.
3 For the dressing, shake the vinegar, walnut oil, olive oil and seasoning together in a screw-top jar until amalgamated.
4 Arrange the pear, melon and Roquefort on a plate and top with the sugar snap peas. Drizzle the dressing over the salad and sprinkle with the toasted walnuts. Serve immediately.

grilled radicchio, chicory, stilton and caramelised walnut salad

Delicious grilled chicory, radicchio and sweet white onions tossed in a thyme and lemon dressing with spiced caramelised walnuts.

Serves 6
Preparation time: 25 minutes
Cooking time: 20 minutes, plus infusing
360 cals per serving

1 head of chicory
1 head of radicchio
2 white onions, peeled and quartered
2 red chillies, halved and deseeded
5ml (1 tsp) caster sugar
salt and freshly ground black pepper
125g (4oz) blue Stilton cheese, crumbled
FOR THE DRESSING:
100ml (3½fl oz) olive oil
2 fresh thyme sprigs
grated rind of 1 lemon
2 garlic cloves, peeled and bruised
30ml (2 tbsp) lemon juice
FOR THE CARAMELISED NUTS:
75g (3oz) walnuts
5ml (1 tsp) paprika
5ml (1 tsp) icing sugar
45ml (3 tbsp) oil
TO GARNISH:
flat-leafed parsley

1 First make the dressing. Put the olive oil in a small pan with the thyme sprigs, lemon rind and garlic cloves. Warm gently; do not boil. Set aside to infuse for 30 minutes.
2 For the caramelised nuts, cook the walnuts in boiling water for 5 minutes; drain and dry on kitchen paper. Mix together the paprika and icing sugar. Toss the walnuts in this mixture to coat. Heat the oil in a frying pan, add the walnuts and cook for 1-2 minutes until brown. Drain and let cool.
3 For the salad, quarter the chicory and radicchio lengthwise; separate the onions into 'petals'. Brush these vegetables and the chillies with half of the infused oil.

4 Place the onions in the grill pan, sprinkle with the sugar and cook under a hot grill for 5-10 minutes, turning once, until soft and slightly charred. Add the chicory and chillies and cook for 5 minutes, then add the radicchio and cook for a further 1 minute.

5 Allow the vegetables to cool slightly. Cut the chicory and radicchio into pieces if preferred; finely slice the chillies.

6 Whisk the lemon juice into the remaining infused oil and season with salt and pepper. Combine all of the vegetables and gently toss together with the dressing, cheese and caramelised walnuts. Arrange on individual plates and serve garnished with parsley.

salad with crisp-fried prosciutto and blueberries

This unusual warm salad is full of intriguing flavours. Serve it with warm foccacia.

Serves 4
Preparation time: 10 minutes
Cooking time: 3 minutes
340 cals per serving

30ml (2 tbsp) extra-virgin olive oil
6 slices prosciutto or Parma ham
125g (4oz) mixed salad leaves, such as rocket, lamb's lettuce, watercress, spinach
2 red or white chicory bulbs (or 1 of each), separated
60ml (4 tbsp) pine nuts, toasted
125g (4oz) blueberries
FOR THE DRESSING:
60ml (4 tbsp) extra-virgin olive oil
30ml (2 tbsp) balsamic vinegar
salt and freshly ground black pepper
TO SERVE:
Parmesan cheese shavings

1 Heat the oil in a frying pan. When hot, add the prosciutto and fry over a medium heat until crisp and golden. Drain on kitchen paper and, when cool, crumble into bite-sized pieces. Scrape the sediment and oil from the pan into a small saucepan and reserve.
2 Put the salad leaves into a large bowl. Add the chicory, prosciutto and toasted pine nuts; toss well.
3 To make the dressing, add the olive oil and vinegar to the pan. Season and add the blueberries. Heat gently until the liquid just reaches the boil.
4 Immediately pour the dressing over the salad, toss again and transfer to serving plates. Scatter over the Parmesan shavings to serve.

tomato, avocado and mozzarella salad

This simple salad makes a delicious summer starter. Make sure you use flavourful tomatoes – preferably homegrown or vine-ripened. If available, use a mixture of fresh plum tomatoes and small, sweet cherry tomatoes.

Serves 4
Preparation time: 15 minutes
510 cals per serving

2 small ripe avocados
175g (6oz) mozzarella cheese (preferably buffalo), thinly sliced
6 ripe tomatoes, thinly sliced
FOR THE DRESSING:
100ml (3½fl oz) olive oil
30ml (2 tbsp) white wine vinegar
pinch of sugar
salt and freshly ground black pepper
15g (½oz) fresh basil leaves
TO GARNISH:
basil sprigs

1 First make the dressing. Put all the ingredients into a food processor or blender and process for 1 minute until evenly blended.
2 Halve, stone and peel the avocados, then cut the flesh into slices.
3 Immediately arrange slices of mozzarella, tomato and avocado on a large serving platter or individual plates and spoon over the dressing. Garnish with basil sprigs and serve at once, with plenty of crusty bread.

Variation Omit the avocado. Scatter 30ml (2 tbsp) small French capers (rinsed and drained) and a handful of small black olives over the salad.

fast starters

- Serve thin slices of smoked salmon or ready-prepared gravadlax with thinly sliced brown bread and lime or lemon wedges.
- Drape thin slices of prosciutto over wedges of melon or fresh figs.
- Grill slices of courgette, peppers, aubergine, onion etc, drizzle with extra-virgin olive oil and serve with ready-made pesto.
- Halve and stone avocados and spoon a little herb or raspberry vinegar flavoured vinagrette into the cavities to serve.
- Arrange a selection of ready prepared meats, such as salami, prosciutto, cured pork, roast ham, smoked chicken and bresaola (cured beef) on a platter with a simple salad and black olive garnish.
- Serve freshly prepared seafood, such as cooked prawns in their shells or dressed crab with a good mayonnaise. Raw oysters on their half-shell are best served simply with brown bread and lemon wedges.
- Buy a selection of Italian antipasti from your local delicatessen, such as Parma ham, salami, black olives, marinated artichokes, anchovies and sliced tomatoes scattered with fresh basil. Arrange on a large platter and serve with warm foccacia or other Mediterranean-style bread.

butter bean, lemon and sage pâté

This easy vegetarian pâté is delicious spread on to toasted ciabatta or warm pitta bread.

Serves 6
Preparation time:10 minutes
Cooking time: 10 minutes
215 cals per serving

70ml (4½ tbsp) extra-virgin olive oil (approximately)
4 shallots, peeled and finely chopped
2 large garlic cloves, peeled and crushed
30ml (2 tbsp) chopped fresh sage
grated rind and juice of 1 small lemon
two 400g (14oz) cans butter beans or cannellini beans
salt and freshly ground black pepper
TO SERVE:
crudités
toasted ciabatta or pitta bread

1 Heat 60ml (4 tbsp) of the oil in a frying pan, add the shallots, garlic, sage and lemon rind and fry gently for 5 minutes until the shallots are softened.
2 Meanwhile, drain the beans, reserving 120ml (4fl oz) of the liquid. Add the beans and reserved liquid to the frying pan. Bring to the boil, cover and simmer gently for 5 minutes.
3 Transfer the mixture to a bowl and mash well, to a fairly smooth paste. Stir in the lemon juice and season with salt and pepper to taste. Gradually beat in a little extra olive oil until it is the required consistency.
4 Leave until cold. Serve with crudités and toasted ciabatta or pitta bread.

Note If preferred, serve this pâté straight from the pan whilst still warm. Alternatively it can be served chilled as a dip with a selection of crudités, such as baby carrots, cucumber sticks and cherry tomatoes.

aubergine, mushroom and coriander pâté

This luscious combination of smoky roasted aubergine, dark savoury mushrooms and fresh piquant coriander can be prepared as a chunky or smooth pâté as preferred. It is particularly good with toasted walnut bread.

Serves 4-6
Preparation time: 20 minutes
Cooking time: 1 hour
Suitable for freezing
140-95 cals per serving

2 medium aubergines
45ml (3 tbsp) olive oil
2 shallots, peeled and finely chopped
10-15ml (2-3 tsp) crushed coriander seeds
225g (8oz) large flat mushrooms, finely chopped
45ml (3 tbsp) dry white wine
60ml (4 tbsp) chopped fresh coriander
salt and freshly ground black pepper
coriander sprigs, to garnish

1 Place the aubergines on a baking sheet and bake in the oven at 200°C/fan oven 190°C (400°F) Mark 6 for about 45 minutes or until soft and the skins are beginning to char.
2 Meanwhile, heat the olive oil in a saucepan, add the shallots with the coriander seeds and cook gently for about 5 minutes until soft and golden. Stir in the chopped mushrooms and wine and cook over a high heat for 10 minutes or until all the liquid has evaporated, stirring occasionally.
3 Split the cooked aubergines, scoop out the flesh and chop roughly, then beat into the mushroom mixture. Stir in the chopped coriander and season well with salt and pepper.
4 Either serve warm or allow to cool, then chill. Serve garnished with coriander sprigs and accompanied by hot toast.

Variation For a milder flavour, stir 125g (4oz) fromage frais into the cold pâté.

grilled vegetable terrine

An elegant starter, vibrant with colourful roasted peppers, courgettes and aubergines.

Serves 6
Preparation time: 35 minutes, plus setting
Cooking time: About 15 minutes
250 cals per serving

3 large red peppers
2 large yellow peppers
2 large courgettes
1 long aubergine
75ml (5 tbsp) olive oil
450ml (¾ pint) tomato juice
15g (½oz) powdered gelatine or gelazone
60ml (4 tbsp) chopped mixed herbs, such as chervil, parsley and basil
FOR THE DRESSING:
90ml (3fl oz) virgin olive oil
30ml (2 tbsp) red wine vinegar
salt and freshly ground black pepper
TO GARNISH:
basil leaves

1 Quarter, core and deseed the peppers, then place skin-side up under a hot grill and cook until the skins are blackened. Transfer to a bowl, cover with a plate and leave to cool. When the peppers are cool enough to handle, remove the skins.

2 Slice the courgettes and aubergine lengthways, brush with oil and cook under the grill, turning occasionally, until tender and golden. (You may need to do this in two batches, depending on the size of your grill pan.)

3 Lightly oil a 1.5 litre (2½ pint) loaf tin or terrine and line with cling film, allowing it to overhang the sides.

4 Put 60ml (4 tbsp) of the tomato juice in a small bowl and sprinkle on the gelatine. Leave to soften for about 10 minutes, then place the bowl over a pan of simmering water until the gelatine is dissolved. Add to the remaining tomato juice, stirring well.

5 Place a layer of red peppers in the bottom of the terrine and pour in enough tomato juice to cover. Add a layer of aubergine slices, followed by courgette, yellow pepper and a sprinkling of herbs, pouring tomato juice onto each layer. Repeat the layers, finishing with red pepper.

6 Add the rest of the tomato juice to fill the loaf tin or terrine. Give the tin a sharp tap to disperse the juice through the vegetables. Cover and refrigerate for at least 3-4 hours until set.

7 To make the dressing, whisk together the oil, vinegar and seasoning.

8 To serve, cut the terrine into thick slices, using a serrated knife. Place on individual plates and drizzle with the dressing. Garnish with basil and serve with sun-dried tomato or olive bread.

aubergine timbales with roasted red pepper salsa

A stylish special occasion vegetarian starter, rich with the flavours of Mediterranean vegetables.

Serves 6
Preparation time: 40 minutes
Cooking time: 1½ hours, plus cooling
205 cals per serving

60ml (4 tbsp) olive oil, plus extra for brushing
4 garlic cloves, peeled and finely chopped
two 400g (14oz) cans chopped plum tomatoes
150ml (¼ pint) dry white wine
2 fresh thyme sprigs
15ml (1 tbsp) sun-dried tomato paste
5ml (1 tsp) caster sugar
salt and freshly ground black pepper
4 long, thin aubergines
90ml (6 tbsp) Greek yogurt
FOR THE RED PEPPER SALSA:
1 large red pepper
45ml (3 tbsp) olive oil
10ml (2 tsp) balsamic vinegar
TO SERVE:
thyme sprigs
rocket leaves

1 Heat the olive oil in a large saucepan, add the garlic and fry for 30 seconds. Add the chopped tomatoes, wine, thyme sprigs, sun-dried tomato paste, sugar, salt and pepper. Bring to the boil and simmer, uncovered, for about 45 minutes until thick, stirring occasionally. Discard the thyme sprigs and set aside to cool.

2 To make the salsa, roast the red pepper in the oven at 220°C/fan oven 210°C (425°F) Mark 7 for 30 minutes or until the skin is charred. Leave to cool, then remove the skin, core and seeds. Dice the pepper flesh and place in a bowl with the olive oil, balsamic vinegar and seasoning to taste. Mix well, then cover and refrigerate until needed.

3 Meanwhile, trim off the ends of the aubergines, then slice off 6 thin rounds. Cut the remaining aubergines lengthways into 5mm (¼ inch) thick slices. Brush both sides of the aubergine slices with olive oil and chargrill on a hot griddle or grill for 4-5 minutes, turning once, until brown.

4 Lightly oil six 175ml (6fl oz) timbales, large ramekins or other ovenproof moulds. Place an aubergine round in the bottom of each mould and use the long strips of aubergine to line the sides, making sure there are no gaps. Leave the excess aubergine overhanging the top edge.

5 Spoon 15ml (1 tbsp) yogurt into each mould, then add 45ml (3 tbsp) of the tomato mixture. Trim the excess aubergine and cover the tops with foil.

6 Place the moulds in a roasting tin half-filled with hot water. Cook at 180°C/fan oven 170°C (350°F) Mark 4 for 30-35 minutes. Allow to cool.

7 Turn the aubergine timbales out on to serving plates. Garnish with thyme sprigs and serve with the red pepper salsa and a rocket salad.

roquefort and walnut soufflés

Serves 6
Preparation time: 30 minutes, plus cooling
Cooking time: 20 minutes
175 cals per serving

15g (½oz) walnuts, toasted and finely chopped
15ml (1 tbsp) fresh white breadcrumbs
15ml (1 tbsp) freshly grated Parmesan cheese
25g (1oz) plain white flour
150ml (¼ pint) semi-skimmed milk
2 whole eggs, separated, plus 2 egg whites
125g (4oz) Roquefort cheese, crumbled
salt and freshly ground black pepper
TO SERVE:
salad leaves
olive oil, for drizzling
toasted walnuts, to garnish

1 Grease and base-line six 150ml (¼ pint) ramekin dishes. Mix the toasted walnuts with the breadcrumbs and Parmesan cheese. Coat the sides of the ramekins with about two thirds of this mixture; reserve the rest for the topping.
2 Put the flour into a saucepan, whisk in the milk to form a smooth paste and slowly bring to the boil, stirring continuously. Reduce the heat and cook gently for 1 minute until thick. Remove from the heat and allow to cool slightly.
3 Beat the egg yolks and Roquefort cheese into the sauce. Season generously with pepper and a little salt. In a separate bowl, whisk the 4 egg whites until they form soft peaks. Using a large metal spoon, carefully fold the egg whites into the cheese sauce.
4 Divide the mixture between the ramekins, then top with the reserved breadcrumbs. Stand the ramekins in a roasting tin and half-fill the tin with boiling water. Bake in the oven at 190°C/fan oven 180°C (375°F) Mark 5 for 15-20 minutes or until just firm to the touch.
5 Leave the soufflés in the ramekins for 10 minutes, then turn out, remove the paper and invert on to an oiled baking tray. Place under a hot grill for about 1 minute to brown the tops. Serve on individual plates, surrounded by salad leaves drizzled with a little olive oil. Garnish with toasted walnuts.

mussels with tomato and harissa

This recipe comes from south-west France. Serve with warm bread to mop up the delicious juices.

Serves 4
Preparation time: 30 minutes
Cooking time: 50 minutes
280 cals per serving

45ml (3 tbsp) olive oil
3 large shallots, peeled and finely chopped
4 garlic cloves, peeled and crushed
1.1kg (2½lb) ripe tomatoes (preferably plum), skinned, deseeded and roughly chopped
2 celery sticks, preferably with leaves, chopped
300ml (½ pint) white wine
20ml (4 tsp) balsamic vinegar
30ml (2 tbsp) harissa
2 bay leaves
2kg (4½lb) fresh mussels in shell
60ml (4 tbsp) chopped flat-leafed parsley

1 Heat the olive oil in a very large saucepan, add the chopped shallots and cook gently for 5-10 minutes or until soft and transparent. Add the garlic and cook for 2-3 minutes.
2 Add the chopped tomatoes, celery, white wine, balsamic vinegar, harissa and bay leaves. Bring to the boil and bubble gently for 20-30 minutes or until reduced by half.
3 Meanwhile, clean the mussels. Scrub the shells thoroughly under cold running water and pull any 'beards' from the shells. Discard any with damaged shells, and any which are open and do not close when sharply tapped.
4 Add the mussels to the saucepan, cover with a tight-fitting lid, bring to the boil and cook for about 5 minutes until the mussels have opened; discard any that do not open.
5 Spoon the mussels, along with some of the cooking liquid, into deep soup bowls for serving. Sprinkle generously with chopped parsley and serve with warm, crusty bread.

Note Harissa is a North African chilli paste available from larger supermarkets. If unobtainable, fry two large, finely chopped red chillies with the shallots at stage 1.

hot devilled crab

Fresh crabmeat spiked with mustard, horseradish and Worcestershire sauce, then warmed through in the oven. Don't overcook this dish or the texture of the crab will be spoilt.

Serves 4
Preparation time: 30 minutes
Cooking time: 15-20 minutes
420 cals per serving

6 spring onions, trimmed and finely chopped
20ml (4 tsp) Dijon mustard
10ml (2 tsp) horseradish sauce
10ml (2 tsp) Worcestershire sauce
60ml (4 tbsp) fromage frais
105ml (7 tbsp) fresh white breadcrumbs
2 medium cooked dressed crabs, each with about 225g (8oz) meat
2 eggs, separated
pinch of cayenne pepper
salt and freshly ground black pepper
30ml (2 tbsp) freshly grated Parmesan cheese
30ml (2 tbsp) ground almonds
25g (1oz) butter, melted
TO SERVE:
rocket leaves
lemon wedges

1 In a bowl, mix together the spring onions, mustard, horseradish, Worcestershire sauce and fromage frais. Add 60ml (4 tbsp) of the breadcrumbs, the crab meat and egg yolks; mix with a fork. Season with the cayenne, salt and pepper to taste.
2 Whisk the egg whites in a bowl until they form soft peaks; fold into the crab mixture. Transfer to a shallow ovenproof dish or individual ramekins.
3 Mix together the remaining breadcrumbs, Parmesan and ground almonds. Sprinkle over the crab, then drizzle over the melted butter. Bake at 220°C/fan oven 210°C (425°F) Mark 7 for 15-20 minutes or until hot through to the centre.
4 Serve each portion scooped on to a bed of rocket salad, garnished with lemon wedges.

smoked salmon and potato blinis

Serves 6
Preparation time: 30 minutes
Cooking time: 30 minutes
370 cals per serving

225g (8oz) floury potatoes, such as King Edward's, boiled and mashed with a little milk
45ml (3 tbsp) milk
75ml (5 tbsp) self-raising flour, sifted
4 large eggs, separated
45ml (3 tbsp) soured cream
salt and freshly ground black pepper
pinch of cayenne pepper
a little vegetable oil, for frying
300ml (½ pint) half-fat crème fraîche
275-350g (10-12oz) smoked salmon
fresh dill and lemon wedges, to garnish
FOR THE PICKLED VEGETABLES:
75ml (3fl oz) white wine vinegar
30ml (2 tbsp) caster sugar
225g (8oz) cucumber, deseeded and cut into strips
75g (3oz) radishes, cut into thin strips
1 spring onion, trimmed and cut into thin strips
5ml (1 tsp) mustard seeds
1 tbsp chopped fresh dill

1 For the pickled vegetables, put the vinegar and sugar in a saucepan and bring to the boil. Bubble for 2 minutes, then leave to cool. Stir in the vegetables, mustard seeds and dill. Set aside.
2 To make the blinis, place the mashed potato in a bowl, then beat in the milk with the flour, egg yolks, soured cream and seasoning. In a separate bowl, whisk the egg whites until they just hold their shape; fold into the potato mixture.
3 To cook the blinis, lightly oil a non-stick frying pan and place over a high heat. When hot, add 15-30ml (1–2 tbsp) batter and spread to a 9cm (3½ inch) round. Lower heat and cook for 1–2 minutes or until bubbles appear. Flip the blinis over and cook for about 1 minute. Remove from the pan and stack on a warmed plate, interleaved with greaseproof paper. Repeat to make 6 blinis.
4 To serve, place a blini on each plate and top with a dollop of crème fraîche, a generous tangle of smoked salmon and a scattering of pickled vegetables. Garnish with dill and lemon wedges.

warm mackerel and beetroot salad

Serves 4
Preparation time: 15 minutes
Cooking time: 1 ¼ hours
555 cals per serving

450g (1lb) baby beetroot, trimmed
12 garlic cloves, peeled
45ml (3 tbsp) olive oil
salt and freshly ground black pepper
2 large mackerel fillets
30ml (2 tbsp) plain flour
pinch of cayenne pepper
5ml (1 tsp) finely grated lemon rind
25g (1oz) butter
125g (4oz) mixed salad leaves, such as frisée,
    radicchio and watercress
few fresh herb sprigs, to include chives, parsley and
    tarragon
FOR THE DRESSING:
60ml (4 tbsp) extra-virgin olive oil
15ml (1 tbsp) lemon juice
10ml (2 tsp) creamed horseradish

1 Put the beetroot in a small roasting tin with the
garlic. Add the oil and season with salt and
pepper. Cover the tin with foil and bake in the
oven at 200°C/fan oven 190°C (400°F) Mark 6
for 45 minutes. Remove the foil and bake for a
further 30 minutes or until tender, depending on
size. Allow to cool slightly.
2 Remove any small bones from the mackerel
fillets, using a pair of tweezers, then flake the
flesh into bite-sized pieces. Season the flour with
salt, pepper and cayenne and mix with the
lemon rind. Toss the mackerel in the flour until
evenly coated.
3 Melt the butter in a frying pan and fry the
mackerel pieces for about 1 minute on each side
until golden and cooked through.
4 Place the salad leaves and herbs in a bowl.
Whisk the dressing ingredients together in a
small bowl to combine and season with salt and
pepper to taste. Toss the leaves with a little of
the dressing.
5 Arrange a pile of salad leaves in the centre of
each serving plate and top with the mackerel
pieces. Spoon the baby beets and garlic around
the leaves and drizzle over the remaining
dressing. Serve at once.

grilled king prawns with chilli soy sauce

Don't forget to provide finger bowls for this starter. If preferred the prawns can be threaded onto bamboo skewers and grilled or barbecued.

Serves 4
Preparation time: 25 minutes, plus marinating
Cooking time: 6-8 minutes
115 cals per serving

12 large raw tiger prawns
FOR THE MARINADE:
1 garlic clove, peeled and finely chopped
1 red chilli, deseeded and finely chopped
15ml (1 tbsp) sesame oil
30ml (2 tbsp) dark soy sauce
grated rind and juice of 2 limes
15-30ml (1-2 tbsp) soft brown sugar
FOR THE CHILLI SOY SAUCE:
5ml (1 tsp) crushed chilli flakes
15ml (1 tbsp) lime juice
30ml (2 tbsp) dark soy sauce
15ml (1 tbsp) Thai fish sauce
30ml (2 tbsp) soft brown sugar
TO SERVE:
chopped fresh coriander
lime wedges

1 Wash and dry the prawns and place in a shallow non-reactive dish. Mix the marinade ingredients together, pour over the prawns and stir well to coat. Cover the dish and leave to marinate in a cool place for at least 4 hours, preferably overnight.
2 For the chilli soy sauce, place all the ingredients in a small pan with 30ml (2 tbsp) cold water, heat gently until the sugar is dissolved, then bring to the boil, stirring. Remove from the heat and leave to cool.
3 When ready to eat, transfer the prawns to the grill rack. Grill under a high heat (as close to the heat source as possible) for 6-8 minutes, turning and basting frequently with the marinade juices until the prawns are pink and lightly charred.
4 Transfer the prawns to a warmed serving platter and scatter over some chopped fresh coriander. Serve with lime wedges and the chilli soy sauce for dipping.

crab, melon and cucumber salad

An imaginative combination of summer flavours to stimulate the tastebuds.

Serves 4
Preparation time: 20 minutes
340 cals per serving

225g (8oz) fresh white crab meat
½ cucumber, about 300g (10oz)
1 large chicory bulb, trimmed and separated into leaves
1 small Charentais melon, cut into quarters and deseeded
FOR THE DRESSING:
30ml (2 tbsp) white wine vinegar
150ml (¼ pint) olive oil
salt and freshly ground black pepper
30ml (2 tbsp) Japanese pickled ginger, chopped
2.5cm (1 inch) piece fresh root ginger, peeled and grated
TO GARNISH:
fresh crab claws (optional)
chives

1 First make the dressing. Whisk the wine vinegar, olive oil and seasoning together in a bowl. Add the pickled ginger and root ginger.
2 Flake the crab meat into a bowl, add half of the dressing and toss gently to mix.
3 Pare the cucumber into long thin ribbons, using a swivel vegetable peeler. Arrange a few chicory leaves, cucumber ribbons and a melon quarter on each serving plate. Pile the crab meat on top and drizzle with the remaining dressing. Garnish with crab claws if available and chives to serve.

Note Japanese pickled ginger is available in jars from oriental food stores and some supermarkets.

salmon and tarragon mousse

Serves 10
Preparation time: 1 hour, plus chilling
Cooking time: 20 minutes
340 cals per serving

finely grated rind and juice of 1 lemon
pinch of sugar
salt and freshly ground black pepper
90ml (6 tbsp) extra-virgin olive oil
300g (10oz) skinned fresh salmon fillet
450g (1lb) thinly sliced smoked salmon fillets
2 eggs
pinch of cayenne pepper
250ml (8fl oz) double cream
125g (4oz) full-fat soft cheese
30ml (2 tbsp) chopped fresh tarragon
FOR THE FENNEL AND TOMATO SALSA:
1 small fennel bulb, cut into fine strips
4 tomatoes, skinned, deseeded and cut into strips

1 Mix a little lemon rind with 20ml (4 tsp) lemon juice, the sugar, seasoning and oil; set aside.
2 Roughly chop the fresh salmon and 125g (4oz) of the smoked salmon. Process in a blender or food processor until smooth. With the motor running, add the eggs, one at a time, processing briefly. Turn into a bowl, beat in the remaining lemon rind and season with the cayenne, salt and pepper. Cover and refrigerate for at least 30 minutes.
3 Slowly beat 200ml (7fl oz) of the cream into the salmon mixture, a spoonful at a time. In another bowl, beat the cheese with the tarragon, remaining cream and seasoning until smooth. Cover and chill both mixtures for 30 minutes.
4 Line ten 120ml (4fl oz) ramekins with half of the remaining smoked salmon, cutting discs to fit the bases and strips to line sides; reserve trimmings.
5 Half-fill the ramekins with the salmon mousse. Put a teaspoonful of tarragon cheese in the centre, then top with the remaining mousse. Cover with the remaining smoked salmon. Chill for 30 minutes.
6 Stand the ramekins in a roasting tin and pour in enough boiling water to come halfway up their sides. Cover the tin with foil and bake at 170°C/fan oven 160°C (325°F) Mark 3 for 20 minutes, or until the mousses are just set and firm to the touch. Remove from the water and leave to cool.
7 Meanwhile, for the salsa, toss the fennel and tomato with the reserved lemon dressing.
8 Turn out the salmon mousses on to individual serving plates. Surround with the salsa and serve with wholemeal bread.

to open or 'shuck' oysters

Hold the oyster, wrapped in a cloth, on a surface with the flatter shell uppermost and the hinge pointing towards you. Grip the oyster knife firmly and insert into the small gap in the hinge. Twist to snap the shells apart. Slide the blade of the knife along the inside of the upper shell to sever the muscle that holds the shells together. Lift off the top shell, taking care to avoid spilling any of the juice. Clean away any pieces of broken shell from the lower shell. Run the blade of the knife under the oyster to loosen it from the shell.

creamy grilled oysters with sun-dried tomatoes

Serves 4
Preparation time: 10 minutes
Cooking time: 1 minute
280 cals per serving

12 oysters, shucked
2 shallots, peeled and finely chopped
300ml (½ pint) single cream
4 sun-dried tomatoes in oil, drained and chopped
15ml (1 tbsp) chopped fresh chervil
15g (½oz) dried breadcrumbs
15g (½oz) freshly grated Parmesan cheese
pinch of cayenne pepper
salt
chervil sprigs, to garnish

1 Discard the flatter half of each oyster shell and strain the juices into a small saucepan. Place the oysters in their cleaned half-shells in a large gratin dish.

2 Add the shallots and cream to the juices in the pan and bring to the boil, reduce by half and strain through a fine sieve into a bowl. Leave to cool.

3 Stir the sun-dried tomatoes and chervil into the cream and spoon a little over each oyster.

4 Mix the breadcrumbs with the Parmesan and cayenne and scatter over the top of the oysters. Place under a hot grill for 30 seconds to 1 minute until bubbling and golden. Serve at once, garnished with chervil.

grilled stuffed mussels

These appetising morsels are easy to eat and tend to disappear quickly served as they are here, hot from the grill. Accompany with warm bread.

Serves 4-6
Preparation time: 15 minutes
Cooking time: 5-6 minutes
325-215 cals per serving

1.4kg (3lb) large mussels in their shells
75ml (5 tbsp) dry white wine
2 slices prosciutto or Parma ham, finely chopped
25g (1oz) fresh white breadcrumbs
45ml (3 tbsp) chopped fresh parsley
15ml (1 tbsp) chopped fresh oregano
1-2 garlic cloves, peeled and crushed
salt and freshly ground black pepper
75ml (5 tbsp) olive oil
lemon wedges, to serve

1 Scrub the mussels thoroughly under cold water and remove their 'beards'. Throw away any with damaged shells. Rinse the mussels and discard any that do not close when tapped firmly.

2 Put the mussels in a large saucepan with the wine, cover with a tight-fitting lid and place over a high heat. Steam for 3-4 minutes or until the shells open. Strain, reserving the liquid. Discard any mussels that have not opened.

3 Remove and discard the empty half-shell from each mussel. Arrange the mussels in their half-shells on baking sheets.

4 Put the prosciutto, breadcrumbs, herbs and garlic in a bowl and season with salt and pepper. Add half of the olive oil and moisten with a little of the reserved mussel liquor, mixing with a fork.

5 Spoon the breadcrumb mixture on top of the mussels in their half-shells. Sprinkle with the remaining olive oil and place under the grill for 2 minutes or until the topping is crisp and golden. Serve hot, with lemon wedges.

Variation Replace the prosciutto with 2 rashers smoked bacon, finely diced. Dry-fry the bacon in its own fat until beginning to crisp, then mix with the other stuffing ingredients. Continue as above; sprinkle with grated Parmesan before grilling.

smoked salmon and scallop parcels

Serves 6
Preparation time: 40 minutes
Cooking time: 6 minutes
235 cals per serving

FOR THE SALMON PARCELS:
6 large scallops or 12 small queen scallops with corals attached, about 225g (8oz) total weight, cleaned
1 large ripe avocado, halved, peeled and stoned
1 garlic clove, peeled and crushed
4 small spring onions, finely chopped
1 green chilli, deseeded and finely chopped
15ml (1 tbsp) grapeseed oil
grated rind and juice of 1 lime
6 large slices of smoked salmon, about 300g (11oz) total weight and 23cm (9 inches) in length
FOR THE CORIANDER DRESSING:
25g (1oz) coriander sprigs
1 small garlic clove, peeled and crushed
50ml (2fl oz) grapeseed oil
15ml (1 tbsp) lime juice
salt and freshly ground black pepper
pinch of caster sugar
TO SERVE:
squeeze of lime, to taste
rocket or other salad leaves

1 Remove any tough outer membrane from the scallops, then season. Place in a steamer and cook for 3-5 minutes or until the flesh is just white. Drain on kitchen paper and allow to cool.

2 To make the coriander dressing, whizz all the ingredients in a blender until smooth; set aside.

3 Meanwhile, put the avocado, garlic, spring onions, chilli, grapeseed oil, lime rind and juice in a bowl. Crush the avocado flesh with a fork, then mix together with the other ingredients. Season well.

4 Lay the salmon slices on a clean surface. Place a large scallop or two small ones on each slice and spoon the avocado mixture on top. Roll the salmon around the filling.

5 To serve, place a salmon parcel on each serving plate and squeeze over a little lime juice. Drizzle with the coriander dressing and garnish with salad leaves and a sprinkling of pepper.

potted seafood

Asian flavourings and olive oil give this attractive classic starter a modern twist.

Serves 6
Preparation time: 30 minutes, plus chilling
210 cals per serving

700g (1½lb) mixed cooked seafood (see note)
FOR THE DRESSING:
1 lemon grass stalk (outside leaves discarded), finely
    chopped
5ml (1 tsp) finely chopped fresh root ginger
1 red chilli, deseeded and finely chopped
2 garlic cloves, peeled and crushed
10ml (2 tsp) caster sugar
freshly ground black pepper
juice of 1 lime
15ml (1 tbsp) Thai fish sauce
90ml (6 tbsp) olive oil
TO SERVE:
coriander and chervil sprigs
lime wedges

1 Lightly oil and base-line six 150ml (¼ pint) ramekins. For the dressing, combine the lemon grass, ginger, chilli, garlic, sugar, pepper, lime juice and fish sauce in a bowl, then whisk in the olive oil.
2 Toss the seafood with the dressing and check the seasoning. Spoon the seafood into the ramekins and press down. Drizzle with any remaining dressing, cover, lightly weight down and chill for at least 1 hour.
3 To serve, run a knife around each ramekin and turn out on to individual serving plates. Garnish with coriander and chervil and serve with lime wedges and grilled slices of focaccia.

Notes
• Packets of mixed seafood, or seafood cocktail are available from supermarkets. Or buy a selection of fresh seafood and prepare yourself.
• Thai fish sauce is available from most major supermarkets, though you can substitute light soy sauce if wished.
• To prepare ahead, complete the recipe to the end of step 2, then cover and chill overnight.

chicken liver pâté with pistachios

Serves 8-10
Preparation time: 20 minutes, plus chilling
Cooking time: 15 minutes
Suitable for freezing
435-350 cals per serving

2 rashers rindless streaky bacon, finely chopped
about 225g (8oz) butter
700g (1½lb) chicken livers, trimmed and roughly
   chopped
1-2 garlic cloves, peeled and chopped
large pinch of ground allspice
125g (4oz) flat mushrooms, finely chopped
1 onion, peeled and finely chopped
200g (7oz) low-fat soft cheese
30ml (2 tbsp) double cream
40g (1½oz) pistachio nuts, roughly chopped
45ml (3 tbsp) chopped mixed fresh parsley, chives and
   thyme
salt and freshly ground black pepper
few herb leaves and pistachio nuts, to garnish

1 Put the bacon in a heavy-based frying pan and
   heat gently until the fat starts to run, then
   increase heat and cook until lightly browned.
2 Add 50g (2oz) of the butter to the pan, heat
   until just melted, then add the chicken livers,
   garlic and allspice. Cook briskly over a high heat
   until the livers are sealed and browned, but still
   a little pink on the inside. Remove the bacon
   and livers with a slotted spoon; set aside.
3 Add the mushrooms and onion to the pan and
   cook gently until the onion is softened.
4 Transfer the livers and bacon to a blender or
   food processor. Add the onion and mushrooms,
   with the pan juices. Add the soft cheese and
   cream and work until smooth. Turn into a bowl.
5 Fold in the nuts and herbs, and season with salt
   and pepper to taste. Spoon the pâté into small
   individual dishes and level the surface.
6 Melt the remaining butter in a small pan over a
   very low heat. Slowly pour into a jug, leaving
   the milky sediment behind. Slowly pour the
   clarified butter onto the pâtés to cover them
   completely. Immerse a few herb and pistachios
   in the butter to garnish. Chill overnight to set.
7 Serve with plenty of good bread or toast.

parma ham with mint and mango relish

A tangy mint and mango relish enhances the
wonderfully light, refreshing combination of Parma
ham and mango.

Serves 6
Preparation time: 15 minutes
155 cals per serving

3 ripe mangoes
1 passion fruit
60ml (4 tbsp) grapeseed oil
45ml (3 tbsp) lemon juice
salt and freshly ground black pepper
25ml (5 tsp) chopped fresh mint
50-75g (2-3oz) prosciutto or Parma ham

1 Peel the mangoes, using a potato peeler, then cut
   down either side of the central stone; cut away
   as much of the remaining flesh as possible.
   Halve the passion fruit and scoop out the pulp.
2 In a blender or food processor, purée the flesh of
   one mango with the pulp of the passion fruit.
   With the motor running, slowly add the
   grapeseed oil and lemon juice. Season with salt
   and pepper to taste, then fold in the chopped
   mint. Divide between small individual serving
   dishes.
3 Thickly slice the remaining mangoes and arrange
   on serving plates with the Parma ham. Serve
   with the mint and mango relish.

glazed spare ribs

Serves 4
Preparation time: 15 minutes
Cooking time: 1½ hours
Suitable for freezing (see note)
280 cals per serving

900g (2lb) pork spare ribs
30ml (2 tbsp) malt vinegar
30ml (2 tbsp) sesame oil
90ml (3fl oz) rice or wine vinegar
60ml (2fl oz) dark soy sauce
10ml (2 tsp) grated fresh root ginger
1 garlic clove, peeled and crushed
grated rind of 1 lime
60ml (4 tbsp) soft brown sugar
2.5ml (½ tsp) Chinese five-spice powder
90ml (3fl oz) water
lime wedges, to garnish

1 Wash and dry the spare ribs and place in a saucepan. Cover with plenty of cold water and add the vinegar. Bring to the boil and simmer for 20 minutes, skimming from time to time.
2 Meanwhile, place all the remaining ingredients in a small pan, bring to the boil and simmer for 5 minutes until reduced and thickened slightly.
3 Drain the ribs and transfer to a roasting dish that will hold them in a single layer. Pour over the soy mixture and toss the ribs to coat evenly.
4 Cover the tin loosely with foil and roast at 220°C/fan oven 210°C (425°F) Mark 7 for 30 minutes. Remove the foil and cook for a further 30 minutes, turning and basting the ribs every 5 minutes. Leave to stand for 5 minutes before serving, with lime wedges. Provide finger bowls and napkins.

Note If frozen, allow to thaw at room temperature, then reheat in a covered dish in a moderate oven for 20 minutes.

Variation For barbecued chicken wings omit the par-boiling. Roast as above, coated with glaze, for 30-40 minutes in total or until glazed and tender.

chunky pâté with port and peppercorns

Serves 8
Preparation time: 25 minutes, plus setting
Cooking time: About 1½ hours
325 cals per serving

350g (12oz) boneless belly pork, derinded and roughly chopped
1 large skinless chicken breast fillet
225g (8oz) chicken livers, trimmed
1 large duck breast, skinned and chopped into small pieces
125g (4oz) streaky bacon, derinded and diced
45ml (3 tbsp) white or red port, or brandy
salt and freshly ground black pepper
15ml (1 tbsp) finely chopped fresh rosemary
30ml (2 tbsp) green or pink peppercorns
TO FINISH:
few bay leaves
10ml (2 tsp) powdered gelatine
150ml (¼ pint) white port or dry sherry

1 Coarsely mince the belly pork in a food processor, retaining some small chunks; take out and set aside. Mince the chicken breast in the processor; repeat with the chicken livers.
2 Combine all the meats in a large bowl. Add the port or brandy, 5ml (1 tsp) salt, pepper to taste, rosemary and peppercorns. Mix thoroughly.
3 Pack the mixture into a 1.1 litre (2 pint) terrine or ovenproof dish. Stand in a roasting tin and surround with a 2.5cm (1 inch) depth of boiling water. Cover the tin with foil and bake at 170°C/fan oven 160°C (325°F) Mark 3 for 1 hour.
4 Remove foil and arrange the bay leaves on top of the pâté. Cook for a further 30 minutes until the juices run clear when pierced with a skewer.
5 Drain the meat juices into a small heatproof bowl and leave to cool completely. Skim off any fat, then sprinkle over the gelatine and leave to soften for 5 minutes. Stand the bowl in a little simmering water until the gelatine is dissolved. Stir in the port or sherry, then make up to 450ml (¾ pint) with water, if necessary.
6 Pour the liquid over the pâté and chill until it has set. Store in the refrigerator for up to 2 days. Serve individual portions scooped onto a bed of salad leaves. Accompany with warm bread.

potato pancakes with mustard chicken livers

Serves 4
Preparation time: 20 minutes
Cooking time: 25-30 minutes
Suitable for freezing (pancakes only)
335 cals per serving

FOR THE PANCAKES:
225g (8oz) floury potatoes, peeled
1 small egg
30ml (2 tbsp) milk
20ml (4 tsp) self-raising flour
5ml (1 tsp) chopped fresh thyme
1.25ml (¼ tsp) salt
1 egg white
a little oil, for frying

FOR THE SAUCE:
50g (2oz) crème fraîche
15ml (1 tbsp) wholegrain mustard
7.5ml (1½ tsp) lemon juice
15ml (1 tbsp) chopped fresh chives

TO ASSEMBLE:
25g (1oz) butter
2 shallots, peeled and sliced
225g (8oz) chicken livers, trimmed
salt and freshly ground black pepper
50g (2oz) lamb's lettuce
extra virgin olive oil
lemon juice, to taste

1 Cut the potatoes into even chunks and boil until tender. Drain and mash smoothly. Cool slightly, then whisk in the egg, milk, flour, thyme and salt to form a thick smooth batter.
2 Meanwhile, make the sauce. In a bowl, mix together the crème fraîche, mustard, lemon juice and chives; set aside.
3 Whisk the egg white in a bowl until soft peaks form, then carefully fold into the pancake batter.
4 Heat a thin layer of oil in a heavy-based frying pan. Add 2-3 large spoonfuls of batter to form small pancakes and cook for 1-2 minutes until golden. Flip the pancakes over and cook the underside until golden. Drain on kitchen paper; keep warm. Repeat, to make 8 pancakes.
5 Melt the butter in a small frying pan and fry the shallots gently for 5 minutes until golden. Increase heat, add chicken livers and stir-fry for 3-4 minutes until well browned on the outside, but still a little pink in the centre. Season.
6 Toss the lamb's lettuce with a little olive oil and lemon juice. Arrange the pancakes on warmed plates. Spoon on the chicken livers, adding any pan juices. Top with a spoonful of the mustard sauce and garnish with the salad.

salads

Make the most of the
excellent variety of salad
ingredients now available
with these inspirational
flavour combinations

smoked mackerel salad with new potatoes and chives

This robust salad makes an excellent fast lunch or supper dish – served with plenty of crusty bread to mop up the delicious dressing. Make sure you buy hot-smoked mackerel, the most common type, which doesn't require further cooking.

Serves 4
Preparation time: 15 minutes, plus cooling
Cooking time: About 10 minutes
560 cals per serving

450g (1lb) small new potatoes, scrubbed
2 large smoked mackerel fillets, skinned
225g (8oz) cherry tomatoes, halved
4 spring onions, diagonally sliced
FOR THE DRESSING:
25g (1oz) fresh chives, roughly chopped
120ml (4fl oz) extra-virgin olive oil
15ml (1 tbsp) lemon juice
15ml (1 tbsp) wholegrain mustard
salt and freshly ground black pepper

1 Cook the new potatoes in a pan of lightly salted boiling water for 10-12 minutes until tender. Drain and place the potatoes in a large bowl.
2 For the dressing, blanch the chives in boiling water for 30 seconds, drain and immediately refresh under cold water; drain and pat dry. Place the chives in a blender or food processor with the oil and purée until smooth. Add the lemon juice, mustard and seasoning to taste; process briefly to mix.
3 Pour half of the dressing over the warm potatoes and toss until evenly coated. Set aside until the potatoes are cool.
4 Add the mackerel, tomatoes and spring onions to the cooled potatoes with the remaining dressing; toss lightly to mix. Serve at once, with crusty bread.

salade niçoise

There are many variations of this wonderful Provençal salad – this one uses fresh tuna. Serve with plenty of warm crusty bread as a lunch.

Serves 4
Preparation time: 20 minutes, plus cooling
Cooking time: 15 minutes
465 cals per serving

2 tuna steaks, each about 200g (7oz)
olive oil, for basting
4 eggs
175g (6oz) thin French beans, trimmed
1 lettuce heart, or a handful of salad leaves
1 red or mild onion, peeled and thinly sliced
½ cucumber, peeled and thinly sliced
225g (8oz) ripe tomatoes, quartered
50g (2oz) can anchovies, drained
handful of black olives (preferably Niçoise)
FOR THE DRESSING:
75ml (5 tbsp) olive oil
15ml (1 tbsp) white wine vinegar
1 garlic clove, peeled and crushed
salt and freshly ground black pepper
TO GARNISH:
30ml (2 tbsp) roughly torn flat-leaf parsley

1 Place the tuna steaks on the grill rack, brush with olive oil and grill under a medium heat for about 7 minutes each side, until firm and cooked through, basting frequently with the oil. Allow to cool, then cut into chunks.
2 Boil eggs for 6-8 minutes; cool under cold running water, shell and cut into quarters.
3 Cook the beans in boiling salted water for 2-3 minutes until barely tender. Drain and refresh under cold running water; dry on kitchen paper.
4 Tear the lettuce into bite-sized pieces and place in a large salad bowl with the beans, onion and cucumber; toss to mix. Add the eggs, tuna, tomatoes, anchovies and olives. Toss lightly.
5 For the dressing, whisk the ingredients together in a small bowl or shake together in a screw-topped jar. Pour over the salad and sprinkle with the parsley. Serve at once.

Variation   Instead of fresh tuna, use a 200g (7oz) can tuna in oil, drained and flaked.

chicory and crab salad with lime dressing

For optimum flavour, buy a freshly cooked crab for this salad and prepare it yourself. You will need one that weighs about 1.5kg (3lb). Alternatively, buy a fresh dressed crab from a good fishmonger or supermarket fresh fish counter.

Serves 4
Preparation time: 10 minutes
170 cals per serving

450g (1lb) fresh white crab meat
15ml (1 tbsp) groundnut oil
30ml (2 tbsp) chopped fresh coriander
1 red chilli, deseeded and finely chopped
5-10ml (1-2 tsp) chopped Japanese pickled ginger
45ml (3 tbsp) lime juice
2.5ml (½ tsp) sea salt
white pepper, to taste
2 chicory bulbs
coriander leaves, to garnish

1 Pick over the crab meat, discarding any small pieces of cartilage that may remain, then place in a large bowl. Add the oil, coriander, chilli, ginger, lime juice, salt, and pepper to taste. Toss gently to mix.
2 Separate out the chicory leaves and arrange on a large plate. Spoon the crab salad into the centre and serve immediately, garnished with coriander.

Note Japanese pickled ginger is available in jars from larger supermarkets and oriental food stores. Drain before using.

salad herbs

Fresh herbs will enhance most salads and it is well worth growing your own supply. The flowers from herbs such as borage, chives, fennel and thyme can also be added to salads. Not all herbs are good in raw salads, but most work well.

Basil is almost indispensable in tomato salads; it complements leaf salads too. Chervil, chives and flat-leaved parsley will flatter most salads. Coriander is excellent in robust green salads, bulghar salads and couscous dishes. Dill and fennel are particularly good in fish salads, while mint combines well with oranges and peas. Oregano is a classic ingredient in Greek salad; like marjoram and thyme, it works well in cooked salads, too. Strongly flavoured tarragon is great with chicken salads – it also enhances creamy salad dressings, particularly those containing mustard.

pasta salad with prawns, chillies and french beans

This colourful main-course pasta salad is both unusual and fresh-tasting.

Serves 4-6
Preparation time: 20 minutes, plus infusing
Cooking time: 10 minutes
670-450 cals per serving

150ml (¼ pint) extra-virgin olive oil
2 whole dried red chillies
2 garlic cloves, peeled and roughly chopped
grated rind and juice of 1 large lemon
350g (12oz) dried pasta twists
salt and freshly ground black pepper
175g (6oz) French beans, halved
450g (1lb) cooked Mediterranean prawns (shelled if preferred)
60ml (4 tbsp) chopped fresh herbs, such as basil, chervil, chives, mint and parsley
50g (2oz) pine nuts, toasted

1 Place the oil, chillies, garlic and lemon rind in a small pan and heat gently without boiling for 10 minutes. Remove from the heat and set aside to infuse and cool. Strain and reserve the flavoured oil.
2 Cook the pasta in a large pan of lightly salted boiling water for 8-10 minutes or until *al dente*. Drain well and immediately toss with the lemon juice and half of the flavoured oil. Leave to cool to room temperature.
3 Meanwhile, cook the beans in lightly salted boiling water for 3 minutes until just cooked; drain and immediately refresh under cold water. Pat dry.
4 Add the prawns, beans and herbs to the cooled pasta and stir well to combine. Add extra flavoured oil and seasoning to taste. Serve sprinkled with the pine nuts.

Variation Use fresh peas in place of French beans.

squid and roasted pepper salad

Serves 4
Preparation time: 20 minutes, plus cooling
Cooking time: 45 minutes
400 cals per serving

3 large red peppers, cored, deseeded and cut into
    broad strips
16 small shallots, peeled
4 fresh rosemary sprigs, bruised
4 fresh thyme sprigs, bruised
60ml (4 tbsp) olive oil
8 garlic cloves, peeled
600g (1¼lb) baby squid, cleaned
finely pared zest of 2 lemons, in strips
vegetable oil, for frying
sea salt
5ml (1 tsp) chopped fresh thyme
FOR THE DRESSING:
75ml (5 tbsp) extra-virgin olive oil
juice of ½ lemon
30ml (2 tbsp) chopped fresh parsley
pinch of sugar
salt and freshly ground black pepper

1 Place the peppers in a small roasting tin with the shallots and herb sprigs. Add 45ml (3 tbsp) of the olive oil and toss well. Roast at 220°C/fan oven 210°C (425°F) Mark 7 for 20 minutes.

2 Add the garlic cloves to the roasting tin, stir once and roast for a further 20 minutes or until all the vegetables are tender; let cool.

3 Meanwhile slice open the squid pouches and lay flat on a board, inside upwards; score a criss-cross pattern, using a sharp knife. Leave tentacles whole. Rinse and pat dry on kitchen paper.

4 Fry the lemon zest in a little hot oil for 30 seconds until crisp. Drain on kitchen paper and sprinkle with a little sea salt.

5 Shake all the dressing ingredients together in a screw topped jar until combined. Pour over the cooled vegetables and toss well.

6 Heat the remaining 15ml (1 tbsp) olive oil in a non-stick heavy-based frying pan until very hot. Add the squid and stir-fry for 1 minute. Stir in the thyme, then add to the vegetables. Leave to stand for 10 minutes before serving, topped with the lemon zest.

salad dressings

A salad is rarely complete without a dressing, whether it's a piquant vinaigrette, a creamy mayonnaise, or simply a squeeze of lemon or lime juice. Oils and vinegars form the basis of most salad dressings. For optimum results, make sure you use the correct oil, and/or vinegar, for the particular dressing. Olive oil is synonymous with good salad dressings. Extra-virgin olive oil, cold pressed and from a single estate, is the premium type. Although expensive, a good extra-virgin olive oil can be used with great effect in salads. It is particularly good drizzled liberally over raw vegetables, tomatoes or salad leaves with just a little lemon juice or balsamic vinegar. Light or pure olive oils are the best choice for making mayonnaise as extra-virgin oil is too overpowering.

caribbean chicken salad

Spicy and succulent, this substantial salad is great for a quick midweek supper.

Serves 4
Preparation time: 10 minutes
Cooking time: 25 minutes
600 cals per serving

4 chicken breast fillets (with skin)
salt and freshly ground black pepper
20ml (4 tsp) jerk seasoning (see note)
450g (1lb) Jersey royal potatoes
100ml (3½fl oz) mayonnaise
30ml (2 tbsp) wholegrain mustard
30ml (2 tbsp) vegetable oil
200g (7oz) onion, peeled and sliced
125g (4oz) brown cap mushrooms, sliced
225g (8oz) young spinach leaves
45ml (3 tbsp) chopped fresh chives
lemon juice, to taste

1 Season the chicken breasts with salt and pepper and rub with jerk seasoning. Place the chicken breasts on the grill rack and cook under a high grill for 5 minutes on each side or until cooked through to the centre. Set aside.
2 Meanwhile, cook the potatoes in boiling salted water for 10 minutes or until tender. Drain, cool slightly, then cut into chunks. Mix the mayonnaise and mustard together, then add to the potatoes, toss to mix and set aside.
3 Heat the oil in a large frying pan, add the onion and fry for 5 minutes. Add the mushrooms and cook for a further 2 minutes, then season.
4 Combine the potatoes and mushrooms in a bowl and add the spinach. Toss with the chives, add the lemon juice and check the seasoning. Cut the chicken into thick slices on the diagonal. Arrange the salad on individual plates and top with the chicken.

Note Jerk seasoning is a mix of Caribbean herbs and spices, available in jars from supermarkets.

duck and mango salad

Serves 4
Preparation time: 30 minutes
Cooking time: 15 minutes
560 cals per serving

2 small duck breasts, each about 125g (4oz)
30ml (2 tbsp) thin honey
5ml (1 tsp) Chinese five-spice powder
2.5ml (½ tsp) sea salt
30ml (2 tbsp) olive oil
1 onion, peeled and thinly sliced
125g (4oz) sugar snap peas, trimmed
175g (6oz) assorted salad leaves, such as frisée, watercress, chicory, baby spinach
1 mango, peeled, stoned and thinly sliced
FOR THE DRESSING:
60ml (4 tbsp) peanut oil
30ml (2 tbsp) sesame oil
15ml (1 tbsp) rice wine vinegar
15ml (1 tbsp) soy sauce
5ml (1 tsp) grated fresh root ginger
30ml (2 tbsp) chopped fresh coriander
freshly ground black pepper
TO GARNISH:
30ml (2 tbsp) sesame seeds, toasted

1 Rinse and dry the duck breasts. Blend the honey, five-spice powder and salt together and brush all over the duck.
2 Heat half of the oil in a heavy-based frying pan and fry the duck breasts for 1-2 minutes on each side until well browned. Transfer to a baking tray and roast at 200°C/fan oven 190°C (400°F) Mark 6 for 6-8 minutes. Leave to rest for 5 minutes.
3 Meanwhile, fry the onion in the remaining oil for 10 minutes until crisp and golden; set aside.
4 Blanch the sugar snap peas in lightly salted boiling water for 2 minutes. Drain, refresh under cold water and set aside.
5 Shake the dressing ingredients together in a screw-topped jar until evenly combined. Toss the salad leaves with a little of the dressing, then arrange on individual plates. Gently heat the remaining dressing.
6 Thinly slice the duck breasts and arrange on the salad leaves. Add the mango slices, sugar snaps and onions. Drizzle over the warm dressing and scatter on the sesame seeds. Serve immediately.

warm chorizo and chick pea salad

Serves 4
Preparation time: 20 minutes
Cooking time: 17 minutes
565 cals per serving

75ml (5 tbsp) olive oil
200g (7oz) chorizo sausage, thinly sliced
225g (8oz) red onion, peeled and chopped
1 large red pepper, cored, deseeded and sliced
3 garlic cloves, peeled and finely chopped
5ml (1 tsp) cumin seeds
two 440g (15½oz) cans chick peas, drained and rinsed
30ml (2 tbsp) chopped fresh coriander
juice of 1 lemon
salt and freshly ground black pepper
coriander sprigs, to garnish

1 Heat 15ml (1 tbsp) olive oil in a non-stick frying pan and cook the chorizo over a medium heat for 1-2 minutes or until lightly browned. Remove with a slotted spoon, transfer to a bowl and set aside.
2 Fry the onion in the oil remaining in the pan for 10 minutes or until browned. Add the red pepper, garlic, cumin and chick peas and cook for a further 5 minutes, stirring frequently to prevent sticking. Add to the chorizo.
3 Add the chopped coriander, lemon juice and remaining olive oil. Season well and serve immediately, garnished with coriander.

Note Chorizo is a cured, spicy Spanish sausage made from pork and paprika which is available from most supermarket delicatessen counters.

Variation For an extra kick, drizzle over a little chilli oil to serve. Flavoured oils are available from supermarkets, or you can make your own.

spring lamb and flageolet bean salad

Serves 4
Preparation time: 10 minutes
Cooking time: 12-20 minutes
725 cals per serving

2-3 lamb fillets, about 700g (1½lb) in total
15ml (1 tbsp) Dijon mustard
salt and freshly ground black pepper
75ml (5 tbsp) olive oil
5ml (1 tsp) chopped fresh parsley
2 garlic cloves, peeled
juice of 1 lemon
400g (14oz) can flageolet beans, drained and rinsed
125g (4oz) frisée or curly endive
250g (9oz) baby plum or cherry tomatoes, halved

1 Rub the lamb fillets with the mustard and season with pepper. Heat 15ml (1 tbsp) olive oil in a non-stick frying pan, add the lamb fillets and fry over a medium heat for 6-7 minutes on each side for medium rare, 8-10 minutes for well done. Lift the lamb on to a plate, cover and leave to rest for 5 minutes.
2 To make the dressing, put the parsley, garlic, lemon juice and remaining olive oil in a blender or food processor and process for 10 seconds.
3 Place the flageolet beans, frisée and tomatoes in a bowl, add the dressing and toss lightly to mix, seasoning to taste.
4 Divide the salad between individual plates. Cut the lamb into 1cm (½ inch) slices and place on top of the salad. Serve immediately.

Note If you can't find canned flageolet beans, use canned cannellini beans instead.

beef and roasted summer vegetable salad

Serves 6
Preparation time: 30 minutes, plus chilling
Cooking time: 45 minutes
350 cals per serving

600g (1¼lb) fillet of beef
dash of mushroom ketchup or Worcestershire sauce, to taste
salt and freshly ground black pepper
150ml (¼ pint) olive oil
2 purple or red onions
1 each red and yellow pepper, cored, deseeded and cut into chunks
3 small round squash or courgettes, about 450g (1lb) in total, halved or quartered
1 small aubergine, about 250g (9oz), cut into chunks
2 fresh thyme sprigs
30ml (2 tbsp) balsamic vinegar (approximately)
basil leaves, to garnish
Garlic and Basil Mayonnaise (see right), to serve

1 Trim the beef of any membrane or fat and sprinkle with mushroom ketchup or Worcestershire sauce, and pepper. Heat 30ml (2tbsp) of the oil in a heavy roasting tin and sear the meat on all sides over a high heat to seal in the juices and brown.

2 Roast the meat at 200°C/fan oven 190°C (400°F) Mark 6 for 15 minutes. Leave to cool, then cover and refrigerate until required.

3 Quarter the onions vertically, keeping the roots intact, then peel. Place the onion wedges in a large roasting tin with the peppers, squash and aubergine.

4 Pour the rest of the oil over the vegetables and toss well. Roast at 220°C/fan oven 210°C (425°F) Mark 7 for about 35 minutes, until lightly coloured and tender, but not disintegrating, turning twice, and adding the thyme 10 minutes before the end. Season generously, turn into a bowl and leave to cool completely.

5 Just before serving, cut the beef into strips. Drain the vegetables, reserving liquor. Flavour the liquor with balsamic vinegar to taste, to make a dressing. Carefully toss the beef and vegetables with the dressing. Serve garnished with basil and accompanied by the flavoured mayonnaise.

mayonnaise

Mayonnaise ingredients must be at room temperature. If eggs are used straight from the refrigerator the mayonnaise is liable to curdle. Light olive oil is the best choice for mayonnaise as extra-virgin oil is too overpowering.

Makes 300 ml (½ pint)
Preparation: 10 minutes
140 cals per 15 ml (1 tbsp)

2 egg yolks
10 ml (2 tsp) lemon juice or white wine vinegar
5 ml (1 tsp) Dijon mustard
salt and pepper
pinch of sugar
300 ml (½ pint) light olive oil

- Place all the ingredients except the oil in a blender or food processor and blend briefly until pale and creamy.
- With the blade motor running, pour in the oil through the feeder tube, in a steady stream, until the mayonnaise is thick. Thin to the required consistency, if necessary, with a little hot water.
- Store in a screw-topped jar in the refrigerator for up to 3 days.

Note If preferred, make the mayonnaise by hand. Mix the egg yolks, mustard and seasoning together in a bowl, then whisk in the oil, drop by drop to begin with, then in a slow, steady stream. Finally add the vinegar or lemon juice.

Variations

HERB MAYONNAISE Fold in 30 ml (2 tbsp) chopped fresh herbs, such as chives, chervil, basil, tarragon or coriander.

LEMON MAYONNAISE Use lemon juice. Add 5 ml (1 tsp) grated lemon zest and an extra 15 ml (1 tbsp) lemon juice at the end.

GARLIC AND BASIL MAYONNAISE Add 1 crushed garlic clove at stage 1. Fold 30 ml (2 tbsp) shredded fresh basil in at the end.

BLUE CHEESE DRESSING Blend 50 g (2 oz) diced Gorgonzola in a food processor with 30 ml (2 tbsp) milk, 15 ml (1 tbsp) white wine vinegar, pepper and 90 ml (6 tbsp) olive oil.

lentil and vegetable salad with goat's cheese

For this vegetarian salad Puy lentils, mangetout, asparagus tips and French beans are tossed in a lemony dressing with crumbled goat's cheese.

Serves 4-6
Preparation time: 25 minutes, plus standing
Cooking time: 35 minutes
370-250 cals per serving

1 small onion, peeled
1 small carrot, peeled
1 small leek, trimmed
1 small celery stick, trimmed
30ml (2 tbsp) olive oil
225g (8oz) Puy lentils
2 bay leaves
600ml (1 pint) vegetable stock
125g (4oz) mangetout
125g (4oz) French beans, trimmed
125g (4oz) asparagus tips
125g (4oz) goat's cheese, crumbled
FOR THE DRESSING:
90ml (6 tbsp) extra-virgin olive oil
30ml (2 tbsp) lemon juice
1 garlic clove, peeled and crushed
1.25ml (¼ tsp) paprika
pinch of cayenne pepper
salt and freshly ground black pepper

1 Finely chop the onion, carrot, leek and celery. Heat the oil in a large pan and sauté the chopped vegetables for 10 minutes. Stir in the lentils, bay leaves and stock. Bring to the boil, cover and simmer for 20-30 minutes until tender. Discard the bay leaves.
2 In the meantime, place the ingredients for the dressing in a small bowl and whisk to emulsify.
3 Drain the lentils and vegetables. Place in a large bowl, add the dressing, toss to mix and cool to room temperature.
4 Cook the mangetout, French beans and asparagus separately in boiling water for 2-3 minutes until just tender. Drain, refresh under cold water and pat dry.
5 When the lentils are cool, add the green vegetables and goat's cheese; toss well and check the seasoning before serving.

caesar salad

This classic salad is traditionally made with crunchy cos lettuce, but this version uses sweet tender, little gem lettuce instead.

Serves 4
Preparation time: 15 minutes
Cooking time: 12 minutes
510 cals per serving

75g (3oz) one day-old rustic white bread
30ml (2 tbsp) olive oil
5ml (1 tsp) paprika
pinch of cayenne pepper
4 little gem lettuce, separated into leaves
25g (1oz) Parmesan cheese, finely pared into
    shavings
FOR THE DRESSING:
75ml (5 tbsp) light olive oil
4 garlic cloves, peeled
2 anchovy fillets in oil, drained and chopped
15ml (1 tbsp) balsamic vinegar
22ml (1½ tbsp) Dijon mustard
salt and freshly ground black pepper
1 egg

1 Cut the bread into 2.5cm (1 inch) cubes. Combine the oil, paprika and cayenne in a bowl, add the bread cubes and toss until thoroughly coated. Spread the bread cubes out on a baking sheet and roast at 220°C/fan oven 210°C (425°F) Mark 7 for 6-8 minutes until crisp and golden. Set aside.
2 To prepare the dressing, put the oil in a small saucepan, add the garlic and anchovies and heat gently for 5-6 minutes until soft and golden. Set aside until cold, then drain the garlic and anchovies, reserving the oil.
3 Mash the garlic and anchovies to a paste in a bowl, then mix in the vinegar, mustard and seasoning. Gradually whisk in the strained oil in a steady stream until thickened.
4 Cook the egg in boiling water for 2 minutes only, cool under running water, then shell and whisk directly into the dressing until evenly combined.
5 Place the lettuce leaves in a large salad bowl, then scatter over the croûtons and Parmesan shavings. Pour on the dressing and toss well. Serve immediately.

warm salad with quorn and berries

Quorn is a high-protein, low-fat vegetarian alternative to meat. Look out for it in your supermarket chilled cabinet.

Serves 4
Preparation time: 5 minutes
Cooking time: 12 minutes
200 cals per serving

30ml (2 tbsp) olive oil
1 white onion, sliced
175g (6oz) packet Quorn pieces
salt and pepper
30ml (2 tbsp) raspberry vinegar
150g (5oz) punnet blueberries
225g (8oz) mixed salad leaves, such as baby spinach, rocket or batavia

1 Heat the olive oil in a frying pan, add the onion and cook for 5 minutes or until soft and golden. Increase the heat and add the Quorn pieces. Cook, stirring, for 5 minutes or until golden brown. Season with salt and pepper and place in a large bowl; set aside.
2 Add the raspberry vinegar, 90ml (3fl oz) water and the blueberries to the frying pan. Bring to the boil and let bubble to a syrupy consistency, about 1-2 minutes.
3 Toss the Quorn, blueberry mixture and salad leaves gently together. Serve immediately.

Note Flavoured vinegars and oils enhance salads and can transform a dish into something special. Buy them little and often, as the flavour diminishes over time.

potato, pea and walnut salad

Minted baby new potatoes, sugar snaps and freshly podded peas tossed in a walnut dressing to make a tempting vegetarian summer salad.

Serves 4
Preparation time: 10 minutes
Cooking time: 15 minutes
425 cals per serving

350g (12oz) baby new potatoes, scrubbed and halved
    if large
4 fresh mint sprigs, bruised
salt and freshly ground black pepper
225g (8oz) sugar snap peas, trimmed
225g (8oz) shelled fresh peas
50g (2oz) sprouted seeds
50g (2oz) walnuts, toasted and roughly chopped
FOR THE DRESSING:
90ml (3fl oz) walnut oil
60ml (2fl oz) light olive oil
15-30ml (1-2 tbsp) white wine vinegar
5ml (1 tsp) Dijon mustard

1 Put the potatoes in a saucepan, add cold water to cover, the mint and a little salt. Bring to the boil and cook for 8-10 minutes until tender. Drain off the water into a clean pan; put the potatoes into a bowl.
2 Meanwhile, whisk the dressing ingredients together in a small bowl; season with salt and pepper.
3 Pour half of the dressing over the hot potatoes, toss well and leave to cool.
4 Cook the sugar snaps and fresh peas in the reserved water for 3-4 minutes until tender. Drain, refresh under cold water and toss with the remaining dressing.
5 When the potatoes are cool, add the peas, sugar snaps and sprouts; toss to mix and check the seasoning. Scatter the chopped walnuts over the salad and serve at once.

roasted vegetable salad with fontina

Serves 8
Preparation time: 20 minutes, plus standing
Cooking time: 45-50 minutes
250 cals per serving

2 aubergines
2 courgettes
salt and freshly ground black pepper
2 red peppers, halved, cored and deseeded
2 small red onions, peeled and cut into wedges
1 fennel bulb, quartered, cored and diced
15ml (1 tbsp) chopped fresh thyme
15ml (1 tbsp) chopped fresh sage
60ml (4 tbsp) olive oil, plus extra for drizzling
1 small head of garlic
125g (4oz) fontina or mozzarella cheese, diced
30ml (2 tbsp) chopped fresh basil
25g (1oz) pitted black olives
25g (1oz) pine nuts, toasted
FOR THE DRESSING:
10ml (2 tsp) balsamic or sherry vinegar
60ml (4 tbsp) extra-virgin olive oil

1 Cut the aubergines and courgettes into 2.5cm (1 inch) cubes. Layer in a colander, sprinkling with 10ml (2 tsp) salt. Set aside for 30 minutes, then rinse well and dry on kitchen paper.
2 Cut the peppers into 2.5cm (1 inch) squares and place in a large bowl with the aubergines, courgettes, onions, fennel, thyme, sage and olive oil. Toss well, then place in a large roasting tin, in a single layer. (If necessary, use 2 roasting tins.)
3 Slice the top from the head of garlic and stand on a small sheet of foil. Drizzle over a little oil, season and seal the foil to form a parcel. Sit the parcel amongst the vegetables.
4 Roast at 230°C/fan oven 220°C (450°F) Mark 8 for 45-50 minutes, stirring from time to time to ensure even browning. Transfer the vegetables to a large bowl and stir in the cheese.
5 Unwrap the garlic and scoop the flesh into a bowl. Whisk in the dressing ingredients and season with salt and pepper.
6 Pour the dressing over the vegetables, add the basil, olives and pine nuts and toss lightly. Serve warm, with crusty bread.

greek salad

Serve this colourful, gutsy salad *al fresco* with a glass of chilled white wine and rustic bread.

Serves 4
Preparation time: 15 minutes
425 cals per serving

450g (1lb) ripe, flavourful tomatoes, cut into chunks
1 cucumber, halved, deseeded and cut into chunks
1 large onion, peeled and thinly sliced
75g (3oz) black olives
225g (8oz) feta cheese, cut into chunks
FOR THE DRESSING:
90ml (6 tbsp) extra-virgin olive oil
30ml (2 tbsp) lemon juice
1 garlic clove, peeled and crushed
30-45ml (2-3 tbsp) chopped fresh oregano
pinch of sugar
sea salt and freshly ground black pepper
TO GARNISH:
chopped herbs

1 To make the dressing, whisk the ingredients together in a bowl or shake in a screw-topped jar until combined.
2 Combine the tomatoes, cucumber and onion in a large bowl, then add the olives.
3 Pour on the dressing and toss gently to mix. Scatter the feta cheese on top and serve, garnished with chopped herbs and accompanied by plenty of crusty bread.

Variation Flavour the salad dressing with basil rather than oregano.

sprouting beans

Larger supermarkets sell bags of mixed bean sprouts, which are often termed salad sprouts. Alternatively, you can sprout your own seeds at home, though it is important to buy ones which are specifically produced for sprouting, from a healthfood shop or other reliable source.

sprouted bean salad with avocado and bacon

Sprouted beans are full of goodness and add a delicious bite to this attractive salad. Serve as a light lunch or side salad.

Serves 4-6
Preparation time:10 minutes
Cooking time: 5-6 minutes
470-315 cals per serving

175g (6oz) streaky bacon rashers, derinded
175g (6oz) assorted salad leaves, such as frisée, oak leaf, cos, batavia
50g (2oz) salad sprouts or sprouting beans (see below, left)
25g (1oz) alfalfa sprouts
25g (1oz) mustard and cress
1 ripe avocado
FOR THE DRESSING:
10ml (2 tsp) raspberry vinegar
5ml (1 tsp) wholegrain mustard
5ml (1 tsp) grated fresh root ginger
1.25ml (¼ tsp) thin honey
60ml (4 tbsp) walnut oil
30ml (2 tbsp) sunflower oil
salt and freshly ground black pepper

1 First make the dressing. In a small bowl, whisk together the vinegar, mustard, ginger and honey. Gradually whisk in the walnut and sunflower oils; season with salt and pepper to taste. Set aside.
2 Grill the bacon for 2-3 minutes on each side until crisp and golden. Let cool, then break into bite-sized pieces.
3 Place the salad leaves, bean sprouts and mustard and cress in a large bowl, add a little of the dressing and toss gently to coat the leaves.
4 Peel, halve and stone the avocado, then cut the flesh into thin slices. Arrange the salad on individual serving plates and top with the avocado slices and crispy bacon. Drizzle over a little more dressing and serve at once.

indonesian vegetable salad

Based on a traditional Indonesian salad of raw and cooked vegetables, this version is scattered with toasted peanuts rather than served with a peanut dipping sauce.

Serves 4-6
Preparation time: 30 minutes, plus marinating
Cooking time: 20 minutes
350-235 cals per serving

60ml (4 tbsp) vegetable oil
20ml (4 tsp) sesame oil
1 medium sweet potato, or small butternut squash, peeled and thinly sliced
2 large raw beetroot, peeled and thinly sliced
1 fennel bulb, trimmed and thinly sliced lengthways
2 large carrots peeled and thinly sliced lengthways
1 medium courgette, trimmed and finely sliced
125g (4oz) cucumber, finely sliced
125g (4oz) radishes, finely sliced
125g (4oz) bean sprouts
salt and freshly ground black pepper
FOR THE DRESSING:
2.5cm (1 inch) piece fresh root ginger, peeled and grated
1 red chilli, deseeded and finely chopped
1 garlic clove, peeled and crushed
5ml (1 tsp) thin honey
grated rind and juice of 1 lime
15ml (1 tbsp) chopped fresh coriander
TO SERVE:
50g (2oz) raw peanuts, toasted
coriander sprigs, to garnish

1 Mix the two oils together. Brush the sweet potato or squash slices with some of the oil and place on the grill rack. Grill as close to the heat as possible for 6-8 minutes on each side until charred and cooked through.
2 Repeat with the beetroot and fennel, grilling for 5-6 minutes on each side, then the carrot, grilling for 4-5 minutes each side. Transfer to a large bowl and set aside to cool.
3 Put the courgette, cucumber and radish slices in another bowl with the bean sprouts.

4 To make the dressing, put the ingredients in a screw-topped jar with the remaining oil and salt and pepper to taste. Shake until evenly blended.
5 Combine the raw vegetables with the cooked ones, pour over the dressing, toss well and leave to marinate for 1 hour. Check the seasoning.
6 Just before serving, scatter the peanuts over the salad and garnish with coriander sprigs.

tomato and mozzarella pasta salad

This simple salad is great served as a light supper with warm, crusty bread.

Serves 4
Preparation time: 20 minutes
Cooking time: 10-12 minutes
710 cals per serving

350g (12oz) penne or pasta shells
250g (9oz) mozzarella cheese, cut into chunks
700g (1½lb) vine-ripened tomatoes, skinned, deseeded and cut into chunks
½ large red chilli, deseeded and finely sliced
½ large green chilli, deseeded and finely sliced
FOR THE DRESSING:
10ml (2 tsp) lemon juice
105ml (7 tbsp) basil-flavoured olive oil
2 garlic cloves, peeled and crushed
salt and freshly ground black pepper
TO GARNISH:
basil leaves

1 For the dressing, whisk the ingredients together in a bowl to combine; set aside.
2 Add the pasta to a large pan of boiling salted water and cook until *al dente*; drain well and place in a bowl. Toss with 30ml (2 tbsp) of the dressing to prevent the pasta from sticking together; set aside to cool.
3 Put the mozzarella in a large bowl and toss with the remaining dressing; set aside.
4 When ready to serve, add the pasta to the mozzarella with the tomatoes and chillies. Toss together and season well. Garnish with basil leaves to serve.

grilled ciabatta and mozzarella salad

This scrumptious salad is full of Mediterranean flavours. Serve it as a sustaining supper.

Serves 4
Preparation time: 10 minutes
Cooking time: 5 minutes
610 cals per serving

8 thick slices ciabatta or other Italian bread
10ml (2 tsp) tapenade or sun-dried tomato paste
two 150g (5oz) packs buffalo mozzarella cheese, drained and sliced
60ml (4 tbsp) olive oil, plus extra for drizzling
30ml (2 tbsp) balsamic vinegar
salt and freshly ground black pepper
280g (10oz) jar artichoke hearts in oil, drained and sliced
100g (3½oz) salad leaves, such as rocket and batavia
50g (2oz) sun-dried tomato halves

1 Toast the bread slices on one side. Spread the untoasted side with tapenade or sun-dried tomato paste, then top with the mozzarella slices and drizzle lightly with olive oil.
2 Mix the balsamic vinegar with salt and pepper in a bowl and whisk in the olive oil. Add the artichoke hearts and toss to mix.
3 Place the bread slices on the grill rack and grill for 2-3 minutes or until the mozzarella is lightly browned.
4 Toss the salad leaves with the artichoke mixture and divide between individual plates. Top each serving with two slices of grilled bread and scatter over the sun-dried tomatoes.

Note Most supermarkets sell jars of marinated artichokes, though if unobtainable you can buy canned artichoke hearts instead. Simply drain, slice and cover in olive oil. They will keep in the fridge for up to 1 week.

Variation Replace the sun-dried tomatoes with prosciutto, cut into strips.

grilled stuffed pepper salad

A colourful salad of smoky grilled peppers, filled with grilled onions and capers, and drizzled with a sweet balsamic dressing. Serve as a starter, accompaniment, or light lunch with country-style bread to mop up the delicious juices.

Serves 6
Preparation time: 20 minutes
Cooking time: About 20 minutes
200 cals per serving

3 small onions
3 red peppers, halved, cored and deseeded
3 yellow peppers, halved, cored and deseeded
3 garlic cloves, peeled
45ml (3 tbsp) capers
25ml (1½ tbsp) fennel seeds
90ml (6 tbsp) olive oil
30ml (2 tbsp) balsamic vinegar
45ml (3 tbsp) roughly torn fresh flat-leaf parsley
coarse sea salt and freshly ground black pepper

1 Peel the onions, leaving the root ends intact, then cut into quarters. Add to a pan of boiling water and cook for 1 minute; drain well.
2 Place the pepper halves on a grill rack, skin-side up. Add the onion quarters and garlic cloves (see note). Grill until the pepper skins are blistered and well charred. Turn the onions and garlic as necessary, but let them char slightly too.
3 Cover the peppers with a damp cloth and allow to cool slightly, then peel away their skins. Arrange the peppers on a serving platter. Fill the cavities with the grilled onions and capers.
4 Toast the fennel seeds in a dry frying pan over a moderate heat for a few minutes until they begin to pop and release their aroma. Transfer to a mortar and grind coarsely, using a pestle. Add the grilled garlic and grind to a paste. Transfer the garlic paste to a small bowl and whisk in the oil and vinegar.
5 Sprinkle the parsley, sea salt and pepper over the salad and spoon on the dressing. Serve at room temperature.

Note If your grill is small, it may be necessary to grill the vegetables in two batches.

mixed bean salad

This mildly spiced mix of beans, fresh coriander and grilled peppers makes a delicious side salad.

Serves 6
Preparation time: 10 minutes, plus standing
Cooking time: 10-15 minutes
330 cals per serving

1 red pepper, halved, cored and deseeded
1 yellow pepper, halved, cored and deseeded
425g (15oz) can black-eye beans
215g (7oz) can red kidney or aduki beans
425g (15oz) can chick peas
60ml (4 tbsp) chopped fresh coriander
salt and freshly ground black pepper
FOR THE DRESSING:
5ml (1 tsp) curry paste
2.5ml (½ tsp) thin honey
1 garlic clove, peeled and crushed
25ml (1½ tbsp) white wine vinegar
90ml (6 tbsp) sunflower oil

1 Place the pepper halves, cut-side down, on the grill rack and grill under a high heat until the skins are black and blistered. Cover with a damp cloth and let cool slightly, then peel away the skins and cut the flesh into strips.
2 Drain the beans and chick peas, rinse under cold running water, drain well and place in a bowl.
3 To make the dressing, put the curry paste, honey and garlic in a small bowl and whisk together with a fork. Add the vinegar, then gradually whisk in the oil. Season with salt and pepper.
4 Add the peppers and coriander to the beans, then pour on the dressing. Toss well and leave at cool room temperature for 2-3 hours before serving, to allow the flavours to develop. Check the seasoning before serving.

salad leaves

There is now a wonderful array of lettuces and other salad leaves to choose from, ranging from the soft delicate, round lettuce, russet-coloured Oak leaf and frilly-leaved lollo rosso – to the crisp Cos, Iceberg and Little Gem. In addition, there are the deliciously bitter leaves such as dark red radicchio, peppery rocket, crisp chicory, watercress, frisée and curly endive. Other interesting salad leaves are tender baby spinach and delicate lamb's lettuce, also known as corn salad and mâche.

Ready-prepared bags of mixed salad leaves are widely available from supermarkets; these are a convenient way of buying salad leaves if you want a selection but only require a small quantity. Leaf salads are simple, refreshing and easily enhanced by the addition of fresh herbs or edible flowers.

When choosing salad plants, look for fresh, crisp leaves and a tightly packed head where appropriate. Avoid wilted or damaged ones. Store salad leaves loosely wrapped in the salad drawer of the refrigerator.

To prepare, pull off and discard any coarse or damaged outer leaves, then divide the salad plant if appropriate. Wash the leaves in cold water. Drain and dry well, using a clean tea-towel or a salad spinner.

mixed leaf salad with croûtons

A crisp, colourful leafy salad of peppery rocket, watercress, spinach and crunchy croûtons.

Serves 6-8
Preparation time: 10 minutes
140-105 cals per serving

1 head of radicchio
1 bunch of watercress, stalks removed
½ head of frisée, separated into leaves
50g (2oz) baby spinach leaves
50g (2oz) rocket leaves
handful of radishes (optional)
FOR THE DRESSING:
30ml (2 tbsp) olive oil
30ml (2 tbsp) sunflower oil
15ml (1 tbsp) white wine vinegar
pinch of sugar
1 small garlic clove, peeled and crushed
salt and freshly ground black pepper
FOR THE CROÛTONS:
5 thick slices of white bread
oil, for shallow frying

1 Tear the radicchio into bite-sized pieces. Combine the salad leaves, and radishes if using, in a large salad bowl.
2 For the dressing, put all the ingredients in a screw-topped jar and shake vigorously to combine.
3 To make the croûtons, cut the bread into cubes. Heat a layer of oil in a frying pan and fry the bread cubes, turning frequently, until crisp and golden.
4 To serve, transfer the salad leaves to a serving bowl. Pour on the dressing and toss lightly. Serve at once.

mesclun

The French term *mesclun* refers to an assortment of wild salad greens that once would have been picked fresh from the fields for this salad. This version is enhanced with toasted seeds.

Serves 4
Preparation time: 5 minutes
Cooking time: 2-3 minutes
215 cals per serving

175g (6oz) assorted salad leaves, such as rocket, lamb's lettuce, watercress, oak leaf, red chicory
25g (1oz) assorted fresh herb leaves, such as parsley, chives, basil, chervil and tarragon
25g (1oz) sunflower seeds
25g (1oz) pumpkin seeds
30ml (2 tbsp) poppy seeds
FOR THE DRESSING:
60ml (4 tbsp) extra-virgin olive oil
10ml (2 tsp) wine or sherry vinegar
pinch of sugar
salt and freshly ground black pepper
TO GARNISH:
edible flowers (optional)

1 Place the salad leaves and herbs in a large salad bowl.
2 Place a heavy-based frying pan over a medium heat. Add the sunflower, pumpkin and poppy seeds and stir-fry for 2-3 minutes until golden and beginning to release their aroma. Immediately transfer to a plate and allow to cool.
3 Shake all the dressing ingredients together in a screw-topped jar until evenly combined.
4 Pour the dressing over the salad leaves and herbs, and toss gently until coated. Scatter over the toasted seeds and edible flowers if using. Serve at once.

Note For convenience, use one of the ready-prepared packs of mixed salad leaves which are readily available from supermarkets.

fennel and orange salad

Serves 4
Preparation time: 15 minutes
280 cals per serving

2 large oranges
1 fennel bulb
1 small red onion, peeled and finely sliced
50g (2oz) rocket leaves
FOR THE DRESSING:
15g (½oz) pitted black olives, chopped
1 sun-dried tomato in oil, drained and roughly
  chopped
1 small garlic clove, peeled and crushed
7.5ml (½ tbsp) chopped fresh parsley
90ml (6 tbsp) extra-virgin olive oil
10ml (2 tsp) balsamic vinegar
salt and freshly ground black pepper

1 First make the dressing. Put the olives, sun-dried
  tomato, garlic and parsley in a blender or food
  processor with 15ml (1 tbsp) oil. Blend to a fairly
  smooth paste. Transfer to a bowl and whisk in
  the remaining oil, vinegar and seasoning to
  taste.
2 Peel the oranges, removing all the white pith,
  then cut into segments between the membranes
  (do this over a bowl to catch the juice and add it
  to the dressing); place the orange segments in a
  large bowl.
3 Discard the tough outer layer from the fennel,
  then slice very finely.
4 Add the fennel, onion and rocket leaves to the
  orange segments. Add the dressing and toss
  lightly to serve.

Note Sweet, ruby-fleshed blood oranges are the
ideal choice for this salad when in season.

tomato salad with basil

The individual flavours and textures of different tomatoes are combined here to delicious effect. It is essential to use full-flavoured tomatoes – preferably either homegrown or vine-ripened.

Serves 4-6
Preparation time: 10 minutes, plus standing
215-110 cals per serving

30ml (2 tbsp) capers, preferably small French ones
   (optional)
2 large ripe beef tomatoes
3 ripe plum tomatoes
125g (4oz) red or yellow cherry tomatoes
40g (1½oz) small Nicoise olives (optional)
FOR THE DRESSING:
60ml (4 tbsp) extra-virgin olive oil
30ml (2 tbsp) lemon juice
5ml (1 tsp) Dijon mustard
1.25ml (¼ tsp) thin honey
salt and freshly ground black pepper
TO FINISH:
15g (½oz) fresh basil leaves
40g (1½oz) pecorino or Parmesan cheese (optional)

1 1 If using capers, soak in cold water for 30 minutes, then drain and pat dry.
2 Thinly slice the beef tomatoes and arrange them in overlapping slices on a large plate. Slice the plum tomatoes lengthwise and arrange on top. Halve the cherry tomatoes and place in the centre of the plate. If using capers and olives, scatter them over the tomatoes.
3 Place all the ingredients for the dressing in a screw-topped jar and shake well.
4 Scatter the basil leaves over the salad, then top with wafer-thin slivers of pecorino or Parmesan cheese if desired. Serve immediately.

Note For a simplified version, use about 600g (1¼lb) of one variety of vine-ripened tomatoes instead of the three different ones.

red cabbage slaw

This coleslaw variation is particularly good. As the flavours develop on standing, it is best prepared an hour or so in advance.

Serves 4-6
Preparation time: 20 minutes, plus standing
495-335 cals per serving

225g (8oz) red cabbage, cored
2 medium carrots, peeled
50g (2oz) raw beetroot, peeled
2 green apples
1 red onion, peeled and finely sliced
1 garlic clove, peeled and crushed
50g (2oz) pecan nuts, toasted and roughly chopped
FOR THE DRESSING:
½ quantity Mayonnaise (see page 79, see note)
60ml (4 tbsp) Greek yogurt
15ml (1 tbsp) orange juice
15ml (1 tbsp) red wine vinegar
salt and freshly ground black pepper
30ml (2 tbsp) chopped fresh chives

1 Coarsely grate or shred the cabbage, carrots and beetroot, using a food processor fitted with a medium grating disc.
2 Quarter, core and grate the apples. Place in a large bowl with the grated vegetables, onion, garlic and pecan nuts.
3 To make the dressing, beat the mayonnaise, yogurt, orange juice, vinegar and seasoning together in a bowl. Stir in the chives.
4 Spoon the dressing over the vegetables and nuts and toss well until coated. Cover and set aside for at least 30 minutes to allow the flavours to develop. Toss the salad before serving.

Note Use a good ready-made mayonnaise if you haven't time to make your own or if you are unhappy about using raw egg yolks; you will need 150ml (¼ pint).

marinated mushroom and herb salad

Serves 4
Preparation time: 10 minutes, plus marinating
370 cals per serving

225g (8oz) very fresh chestnut mushrooms
1 small fennel bulb, trimmed
2 garlic cloves, peeled
150ml (¼ pint) extra-virgin olive oil, plus extra for
    drizzling
30ml (2 tbsp) lemon juice
salt and freshly ground black pepper
15ml (1 tbsp) chopped fresh dill
15ml (1 tbsp) chopped fresh chives
25g (1oz) pecorino or Parmesan cheese, finely pared
    into shavings
4 slices one day-old rustic white bread
chives, to garnish

1 Thinly slice the mushrooms and fennel,
  chopping any fennel fronds; place in a large
  shallow bowl.
2 Crush one of the garlic cloves and mix with the
  olive oil, lemon juice, salt and pepper in a bowl.
  Pour this dressing over the mushrooms and
  fennel and toss well. Cover and leave to
  marinate for 1½-2 hours until the mushrooms
  are softened, stirring from time to time.
3 Add the herbs and most of the cheese shavings;
  toss lightly to mix and season with salt and
  pepper to taste.
4 Grill the bread on both sides, then immediately
  rub all over with the remaining garlic clove and
  drizzle with olive oil.
5 Spoon the mushroom salad onto the bread.
  Serve at once, topped with the remaining cheese
  shavings and chives.

courgette and lemon salad

If available, use a mixture of yellow and green
courgettes for this zesty side salad.

Serves 6
Preparation time: 10 minutes, plus standing
115 cals per serving

900g (2lb) courgettes
grated rind and juice of 1 lemon
small handful of fresh oregano leaves
1 large garlic clove, peeled and crushed
60ml (4 tbsp) extra-virgin olive oil
salt and freshly ground black pepper

1 Trim and thinly slice the courgettes. Place in a
  large bowl.
2 Add the lemon rind and juice, oregano, garlic
  and olive oil. Season generously with salt and
  pepper. Cover and leave to marinate in the
  refrigerator for about 3 hours.
3 Toss lightly and check the seasoning to serve.

rocket and onion salad

Serves 8
Preparation time: 10 minutes
55 cals per serving

1 small white onion, peeled and finely sliced
225g (8oz) rocket leaves
FOR THE DRESSING:
30ml (2 tbsp) lemon juice
60ml (4 tbsp) olive oil
salt and freshly ground black pepper
TO GARNISH:
lemon zest

1 Toss the onion and rocket leaves together in a
  large bowl.
2 To make the dressing, whisk the ingredients
  together in a small bowl.
3 Drizzle the dressing over the salad and toss to
  mix. Serve garnished with lemon zest.

sweet and sour beetroot salad

Serves 4

Preparation time: 10 minutes, plus marinating

165 cals per serving

450g (1lb) raw beetroot
1 small red onion, peeled and sliced
1 garlic clove, peeled and crushed
30ml (2 tbsp) small French capers in brine, rinsed (see note)
30ml (2 tbsp) chopped fresh parsley
FOR THE DRESSING:
60ml (4 tbsp) extra-virgin olive oil
15ml (1 tbsp) red wine vinegar
15ml (1 tbsp) thin honey
salt and pepper

1 Peel the beetroot, then immediately grate finely, using the fine grater attachment on a food processor if possible, or the fine side of a box grater.

2 Turn the grated beetroot into a bowl and add the onion, garlic, capers and chopped parsley; toss well.

3 Whisk the dressing ingredients together in a bowl, seasoning with salt and pepper to taste. Pour the dressing over the salad and stir well. Leave to marinate for about 30 minutes before serving, garnished with extra parsley if wished.

Note If you are unable to obtain the superior small French capers, use ordinary larger ones, roughly chopping them.

tabbouleh

A simple version of the classic Middle eastern bulghar wheat side salad, fragrant with fresh mint and parsley.

Serves 4
Preparation time: 30 minutes, plus standing
270 cals per serving

125g (4oz) bulghar wheat
90ml (6 tbsp) extra-virgin olive oil
juice of 1 small lemon
1 garlic clove, peeled and crushed
½ cucumber
2 ripe tomatoes
6 spring onions, finely chopped
60ml (4 tbsp) chopped fresh parsley
30ml (2 tbsp) chopped fresh mint
salt and freshly ground black pepper
mint sprigs, to garnish

1 Put the bulghar wheat in a bowl, add plenty of cold water to cover and leave to soak for 30 minutes.
2 Meanwhile, put the olive oil, lemon juice and garlic in a small bowl; stir to mix and set aside until required.
3 Peel, halve, deseed and dice the cucumber. Skin the tomatoes if preferred, then dice.
4 Drain the bulghar wheat thoroughly, shaking off as much excess liquid as possible. Place in a bowl with the cucumber, tomatoes, spring onions and herbs.
5 Pour in the lemon oil and toss well. Season with salt and pepper to taste. Cover and leave to infuse for several hours or overnight until ready to serve. Garnish with mint to serve.

gingered rice salad

This, nutty brown rice salad is liberally flavoured with coriander and mint and tossed in a fresh ginger, soy and sesame dressing.

Serves 6
Preparation time: 15 minutes, plus cooling
Cooking time: 45 minutes
240 cals per serving

175g (6oz) brown rice
salt and freshly ground black pepper
30ml (2 tbsp) sesame oil
60ml (4 tbsp) sunflower oil
30ml (2 tbsp) dark soy sauce
juice of ½ orange
½ cucumber
2cm (¾ inch) piece fresh root ginger, peeled and finely chopped
2 spring onions, finely chopped
1 red pepper, halved, cored, deseeded and thinly sliced
3 ripe tomatoes, halved, deseeded and diced
15ml (1 tbsp) sesame seeds
45ml (3 tbsp) chopped fresh coriander
15ml (1 tbsp) chopped fresh mint

1 Cook the rice in twice its volume of boiling salted water for about 45 minutes until all the water is absorbed.
2 Turn the rice into a sieve and rinse under cold running water. Drain thoroughly and transfer to a large bowl. Add the sesame and sunflower oils, soy sauce and orange juice; toss well. Leave to cool.
3 Halve the cucumber lengthways, scoop out the seeds, then dice the flesh. Add to the rice, with the ginger, spring onions, red pepper and tomatoes; mix well.
4 Preheat a small frying pan and dry-fry the sesame seeds, stirring, until golden. Add to the salad with the coriander, mint and seasoning to taste. Toss before serving.

Note This salad is best made the day before you intend to serve it – to allow the flavours to mingle. Keep it covered in the refrigerator, but bring to room temperature before serving. Moisten with a little more sunflower oil, if necessary.

potato salad with basil

Serve this quick and easy potato salad warm or cold as you prefer.

Serves 4
Preparation time: 10 minutes, plus standing
Cooking time: 10-12 minutes
345 cals per serving

700g (1½lb) firm, waxy potatoes, such as Pink Fir
    Apple, scrubbed
salt and freshly ground black pepper
4 spring onions, finely chopped
25g (1oz) pine nuts, toasted
FOR THE DRESSING:
90ml (3fl oz) extra-virgin olive oil
1 garlic clove, peeled and crushed
grated rind of 1 lemon
15ml (1 tbsp) sherry vinegar
30-45ml (2-3 tbsp) chopped fresh basil

1 Place the potatoes in a saucepan, add cold salted water to cover, bring to the boil and cook for about 10 minutes until just tender.
2 Meanwhile, make the dressing. Heat 30ml (2 tbsp) of the oil in a large frying pan, add the garlic and lemon rind and fry gently for 5 minutes until soft but not golden.
3 In a bowl, blend the remaining oil with the sherry vinegar and seasoning. Stir in the basil.
4 Drain the potatoes and shake off excess water. Add to the frying pan and stir-fry for 1 minute. Stir in the basil mixture and remove from the heat. Set aside to cool to room temperature.
5 Just before serving, add the spring onions and toasted pine nuts to the salad and toss lightly; check the seasoning.

pizzas, pies & savoury tarts

Irresistible pizzas piled high
with lavish toppings,
comforting deep-filled pies
and tasty flans brimming
with delicious creamy fillings

pizza base dough

It is surprisingly quick and easy to make your own pizza dough, using fast-action dried yeast. If you are very short of time, use a pizza base mix instead: a 145g (5oz) packet is roughly equivalent to this basic recipe quantity.

Makes 1 large 30-35cm (12-14 inch) pizza base or two 20cm (8 inch) pizza bases
Preparation time: 15 minutes, plus rising

225g (8oz) strong plain white flour
2.5ml (½ tsp) salt
2.5ml (½ tsp) fast-action dried yeast
150ml (¼ pint) warm water
15ml (1 tbsp) extra-virgin olive oil

1 Sift the flour and salt into a bowl and stir in the yeast. Make a well in the centre and gradually work in the water and oil to form a soft dough.
2 Knead the dough on a lightly floured surface for 8-10 minutes (or using a large food mixer with a dough hook) until smooth and elastic.
3 Place in an oiled bowl, turn the dough once to coat the surface with oil and cover the bowl with cling film. Leave to rise in a warm place for approximately 1 hour until doubled in size.
4 Knock back the pizza dough and shape as required.

Note If preferred, use 15g (½oz) fresh yeast instead of fast-action dried yeast. Mix with 30ml (2 tbsp) of the flour, a pinch of sugar and the warm water. Leave in a warm place for 10 minutes until frothy, then add to the rest of the flour and salt. Mix to a dough and continue as above.

pizzette with pancetta, onion and taleggio

Serves 4
Preparation time: 30 minutes, plus rising
Cooking time: 30-35 minutes
630 cals per serving

two 145g (5oz) packets pizza-base mix
60ml (4 tbsp) Dijon mustard
50g (2oz) fresh basil leaves
1 red onion, peeled and cut into wedges
4 garlic cloves, peeled and finely sliced
200g (7oz) pancetta or streaky bacon rashers
300g (10oz) taleggio cheese (or brie), sliced
16 fresh thyme sprigs, or 15ml (1 tbsp) dried
freshly ground black pepper
extra-virgin olive oil, for drizzling

1 In a large mixing bowl, make up the pizza-base mix according to the packet instructions. Divide the dough into 4 equal portions. On a lightly floured board, roll each portion out thinly to a 22cm (8½ inch) round.
2 Preheat 2 baking sheets in the oven at 200°C/fan oven 190°C (400°F) Mark 6 for 5-10 minutes.
3 Meanwhile, spread each pizza base with 15ml (1 tbsp) mustard, then scatter over the basil leaves, red onion, garlic and pancetta. Place the taleggio cheese in the middle with the thyme sprigs or a pinch of dried thyme. Season with pepper. Transfer to 2 large greased baking sheets and drizzle lightly with oil.
4 Lift the pizzas on to the hot baking sheets and bake for 30-35 minutes or until golden.

baking pizzas

- For baking pizzas, you need good quality baking sheets, made of thick-gauge metal that won't buckle under high temperatures. Pizzas need maximum exposure to heat in order to crisp and brown properly.
- To ensure pizza bases cook through and crisp, preheat baking sheets in the oven for 5-10 minutes before adding the pizzas.

- If cooking two or more pizzas on different oven shelves, transpose them halfway through baking to ensure even cooking.
- If you enjoy making pizzas, you may want to invest in a special pizza stone – a clay slab which reproduces the intense dry heat of a professional pizza oven. Like a baking sheet, the stone should be preheated.

roquefort, prosciutto and spinach pizza

Serves 6
Preparation time: 25 minutes
Cooking time: 50 minutes
Suitable for freezing
340 cals per serving

1 quantity Pizza Base Dough (see page 98)
FOR THE TOMATO SAUCE:
225g (8oz) plum tomatoes, halved
1 shallot, peeled and chopped
1 large garlic clove, peeled and halved
15ml (1 tbsp) olive oil
150ml (¼ pint) dry white wine
30ml (2 tbsp) tomato paste
pinch of caster sugar
salt and freshly ground black pepper
FOR THE TOPPING:
100g (3½oz) Roquefort cheese, cut into 1cm (½ inch)
   pieces
15ml (1 tbsp) raisins
6 slices prosciutto or Parma ham
25g (1oz) trimmed spinach leaves, washed and dried
15ml (1 tbsp) pine nuts, toasted
15-30ml (1-2 tbsp) olive oil

1 Make up the pizza dough and leave to rise for 1 hour or until doubled in size.

2 Meanwhile make the tomato sauce. Put the tomatoes, shallot, garlic, olive oil and wine in a roasting tin and cook at 200°C/fan oven 190°C (400°F) Mark 6 for 30 minutes. Allow to cool slightly, then transfer the mixture to a food processor and whizz until smooth. Turn into a bowl and stir in the tomato paste. Add the sugar and season with salt and pepper to taste.

3 Increase the oven temperature to 220°C/fan oven 210°C (425°F) Mark 7 and preheat a baking sheet on the top shelf. Knock back the pizza dough and roll out thinly on a lightly floured surface to a 30-35cm (12-14 inch) round. Place on a lightly floured baking sheet and press up the edge to make a rim.

4 Spread the tomato sauce over the pizza base, slide on to the preheated baking sheet and bake for 8-10 minutes. Top with the Roquefort, raisins and prosciutto and bake for 5 minutes or until the prosciutto is crisp.

5 Scatter over the spinach leaves and pine nuts, drizzle with olive oil and return to the oven for 5 minutes. Serve at once.

Variation Use bresaola instead of prosciutto and rocket leaves instead of spinach.

four cheese pizza with sun-dried tomatoes

Thin, crisp pizzas with a deliciously rich topping of mozzarella, dolcelatte, ricotta and Parmesan. Serve with a mixed leafy salad and a glass of red wine.

Serves 4
Preparation time: 30 minutes, plus rising
Cooking time: 10-15 minutes
690 cals per serving

1 quantity Pizza Base Dough (see page 98)
50g (2oz) drained sun-dried tomatoes in oil, sliced
125g (4oz) mozzarella cheese, grated
125g (4oz) dolcelatte cheese, diced
125g (4oz) mascarpone
50g (2oz) Parmesan cheese, freshly grated
5ml (1 tsp) dried oregano
salt and freshly ground black pepper

1 Make the pizza dough and leave to rise for 1 hour or until doubled in size.
2 Preheat a baking sheet on the top shelf of the oven at 230°C/fan oven 220°C (450°F) Mark 8. Knock back the risen dough and divide into 4 equal pieces.
3 On a well floured board, roll out each piece of dough to a thin 18cm (7 inch) round. Top with the sun-dried tomatoes and cheeses, then sprinkle with the oregano and seasoning.
4 Carefully transfer the pizzas to the hot baking sheet and bake for 10-15 minutes until bubbling and golden. Serve at once.

Note You will need a large baking sheet to take all four pizzas; alternatively you may prefer to cook them in two batches.

roasted red onion and olive calzone

A calzone is simply a regular pizza folded in half before baking to form a double crust pizza.

Serves 4
Preparation time: 40 minutes, plus rising
Cooking time: 45 minutes
Suitable for freezing
475 cals per serving

1 quantity Pizza Base Dough (see page 98)
FOR THE FILLING:
4 red onions, peeled and cut into wedges
1 garlic clove, peeled and crushed
5ml (1 tsp) chopped fresh rosemary
5ml (1 tsp) grated lemon rind
60ml (4 tbsp) olive oil
125g (4oz) ricotta cheese
125g (4oz) fontina or mozzarella cheese, diced
30ml (2 tbsp) olive paste
salt and freshly ground black pepper

1 Make up the pizza base dough and leave to rise for 1 hour or until doubled in size.
2 Meanwhile, make the filling. Place the onions in a roasting tin with the garlic, rosemary and lemon rind, add the oil and toss well. Roast at 230°C/fan oven 220°C (450°F) Mark 8 for 30 minutes, stirring occasionally until the onions are softened and browned. Turn into a bowl; allow to cool.
3 Add the ricotta, fontina or mozzarella, and olive paste to the cooled onion mixture. Season with salt and pepper to taste. Preheat a baking sheet on the top shelf of the oven.
4 Knock back the risen dough and divide into 4 equal pieces. Keeping the other 3 pieces covered with cling film, roll out one piece thinly on a well floured board to a 20cm (8 inch) round.
5 Spoon a quarter of the onion mixture on to one half of the dough and dampen the edges with a little water. Fold over the other half of the dough and press the edges together well to seal. Repeat to make 4 calzone in total.
6 Transfer the calzone to the hot baking sheet and bake on the top shelf of the oven for 15 minutes until puffed slightly and golden. Leave to stand for 5 minutes, then serve with a tomato salad.

tomato pizza with prosciutto, rocket and parmesan

A stylish pizza topped with slices of prosciutto, a tangle of rocket leaves and Parmesan shavings.

Serves 2-4
Preparation time: 30 minutes, plus rising
Cooking time: 10-15 minutes
750-375 cals per serving

1 quantity Pizza Base Dough (see page 98)
400g (14oz) can chopped tomatoes
2 garlic cloves, peeled and crushed
grated rind of ½ lemon
45ml (3 tbsp) extra-virgin olive oil
30ml (2 tbsp) chopped fresh basil
pinch of caster sugar
salt and freshly ground black pepper
50g (2oz) rocket leaves
6 slices prosciutto or Parma ham
25g (1oz) Parmesan cheese shavings

1 Make the pizza dough and leave to rise for 1 hour or until doubled in size.
2 Meanwhile, place the tomatoes, garlic, lemon rind, 30ml (2 tbsp) oil, the basil, sugar, salt and pepper in a saucepan and bring to the boil. Cover and simmer gently for 15 minutes, then cook uncovered for a further 10 minutes until reduced and thickened. Leave to cool.
3 Preheat a baking sheet on the top shelf of the oven at 230°C/fan oven 220°C (450°F) Mark 8. Knock back the pizza dough and roll out thinly on a floured board to a 30-35cm (12-14 inch) round, according to preferred thickness of pizza. Transfer to a second baking sheet.
4 Spread the tomato sauce over the dough, almost to the edges. Transfer the pizza to the hot baking sheet and bake for 10-15 minutes until the dough is crisp and golden.
5 Meanwhile, toss the rocket in the remaining 15ml (1 tbsp) olive oil. On removing the pizza from the oven, immediately top with the slices of Parma ham, rocket, salt and pepper, and finally the Parmesan shavings. Serve at once.

pissaladière parcel

In this variation of the famous Provençal onion pizza, meltingly soft onions, goat's cheese and anchovies are baked in a crisp dough crust.

Serves 6-8
Preparation time: 1 hour, plus rising
Cooking time: 45 minutes-1 hour
470-355 cals per serving

FOR THE YEAST DOUGH:
375g (12oz) strong plain white flour
5ml (1 tsp) salt
2.5ml (½ tsp) fast-action dried yeast
30ml (2 tbsp) olive oil
FOR THE FILLING:
60ml (4 tbsp) olive oil
900g (2lb) onions, peeled and finely sliced
3 garlic cloves, peeled and finely sliced
10ml (2 tsp) finely chopped fresh rosemary
200g (7oz) goat's cheese, crumbled
8 anchovy fillets, chopped
TO FINISH:
beaten egg, for brushing
rosemary sprigs
sea salt, for sprinkling

1 For the filling, heat the oil in a pan, then add the onions, garlic and rosemary. Lay a disc of greaseproof paper on top and cover the pan with a tight-fitting lid. Simmer over a low heat for 45 minutes, stirring occasionally, and adding a little water if dry. Drain onions, reserving liquid.
2 Meanwhile make the dough. Sift the flour and salt into a bowl and stir in the yeast. Make a well in the centre. Make the reserved onion liquid up to 300ml (½ pint) with warm water, then add to the well with the oil and mix to a soft dough. Knead for 10 minutes until smooth. Shape into a ball and place in an oiled bowl. Cover the bowl with cling film and leave to rise for 45 minutes or until doubled in size.
3 Mix the goat's cheese and anchovies into the cooked onion mixture.
4 Roll the dough out to a 30cm (12 inch) round. Lift on to a lightly floured baking sheet. Spread with the onion mixture, leaving a 6cm (2½ inch) border. Lightly brush border with water. Bring up the edges of the dough over the filling to make a parcel and press together to seal well.

5 Place another non-stick baking sheet on top of the parcel, then invert both baking sheets to turn the parcel over, so the seal is underneath. Press down lightly, then remove the top baking sheet. Make deep, diagonal slashes across the top of the dough, 1cm (½ inch) apart. Leave to prove for 30 minutes or until spongy.
6 Brush the dough lightly with beaten egg, then sprinkle with rosemary and sea salt. Bake at 220°C/fan oven 210°C (425°F) Mark 7 for 45 minutes-1 hour until the pastry is crisp, covering with greaseproof paper if it appears to be overbrowning. Leave to stand for 5 minutes before serving.

artichoke and dolcelatte pizza

Serves 2-4
Preparation time: 25 minutes, plus rising
Cooking time: 15-20 minutes
995-495 cals per serving

1 quantity Pizza Base Dough (see page 98)
FOR THE TOPPING:
45ml (3 tbsp) sun-dried tomato paste
400g (14oz) can artichoke hearts, drained, rinsed and halved
175g (6oz) dolcelatte cheese, derinded and diced
25g (1oz) pitted black olives
10ml (2 tsp) dried oregano
25g (1oz) Parmesan cheese, freshly grated
freshly ground black pepper

1 Make the pizza dough and leave to rise for 1 hour or until doubled in size.
2 Preheat a baking sheet on the top shelf of the oven at 230°C/fan oven 220°C (450°F) Mark 8. Knock back the risen dough and roll out on a lightly floured board to a 30cm (12 inch) round. Using fingertips and thumbs, form a shallow rim around the edge of the dough. Prick with a fork.
3 Transfer the dough to a lightly greased baking sheet and spread with the tomato paste. Scatter over the artichokes, dolcelatte cheese, olives, oregano, Parmesan and pepper to taste.
4 Slide the pizza on to the hot baking sheet and bake for 15-20 minutes until the base is crisp and the topping is golden.

pizza with feta, spinach and pine nuts

Spinach and garlic pizzas dotted with feta cheese, creamy mascarpone, pine nuts and raisins.

Serves 2-4
Preparation time: 30 minutes, plus rising
Cooking time: About 15 minutes
1200-600 cals per serving

1 quantity Pizza Base Dough (see page 98)
45ml (3 tbsp) olive oil, plus extra for drizzling
1 large onion, peeled and thinly sliced
2 garlic cloves, peeled and crushed
450g (1lb) frozen leaf spinach, thawed and drained
salt and freshly ground black pepper
25g (1oz) raisins (optional)
30ml (2 tbsp) sun-dried tomato paste
125g (4oz) feta cheese
150g (5oz) mascarpone cheese
15g (½oz) pine nuts

1 Make the pizza dough and leave to rise for 1 hour or until doubled in size.
2 Preheat 2 baking sheets on the top shelf of the oven at 230°C/fan oven 220°C (450°F) Mark 8. Heat 30ml (2 tbsp) olive oil in a frying pan, add the onion and garlic and fry gently for 10 minutes until softened.
3 Squeeze out excess water from the spinach and chop finely, then mix with the onion, remaining olive oil, seasoning, and raisins if using.
4 Knock back the risen dough and divide in half. Roll out each piece on a lightly floured board to a 23cm (9 inch) round and place on cool baking sheets. Spread each one with tomato paste and top with the spinach mixture.
5 Cream the feta and mascarpone together in a bowl, then dot over the pizza. Sprinkle with the pine nuts.
6 Slide the pizzas on to the hot baking sheets and bake for 15 minutes or until melted and bubbling. Serve at once.

salmon in a brioche crust

This recipe is a light version of a traditional Russian fish dish. It's delicious hot, but also wonderful eaten cold as it slices beautifully. If you don't want to make your own brioche dough use 450g (1lb) ready-made puff pastry instead.

Serves 8
Preparation time: 45 minutes
Cooking time: 55 minutes
Suitable for freezing: (stage 5)
580 cals per serving

FOR THE BRIOCHE DOUGH:
375g (13oz) strong white bread flour
10ml (2 tsp) fast-action dried yeast
5ml (1 tsp) caster sugar
1.25ml (¼ tsp) salt
2 large eggs, beaten
100g (3½oz) unsalted butter, melted and cooled
100ml (3½fl oz) cold water (approximately)

FOR THE FILLING:
450g (1lb) sliced smoked salmon, chilled
1 large egg white
45ml (3 tbsp) double cream, chilled
finely grated rind of 1 lemon, plus 15ml (1 tbsp) juice
15ml (1 tbsp) finely chopped chives
salt and freshly ground black pepper
225g (8oz) spinach, stalks removed
800g (1¾lb) salmon fillet, cut from the middle, skinned

TO FINISH:
1 egg yolk, beaten with 15ml (1 tbsp) water
5ml (1 tsp) pink peppercorns
lemon wedges, chives and crushed pink peppercorns, to garnish

1 To make the brioche dough, sift the flour into a large bowl. Stir in the yeast, sugar and salt and make a well in the centre. Gradually mix in the beaten eggs, melted butter and enough cold water to make a soft, pliable dough.

2 Turn the dough out on to a lightly floured surface and knead for about 5 minutes until smooth and elastic (see note). Place the brioche dough in a large greased bowl and cover with greased cling film. Leave to rise at room temperature for approximately 1½ hours or until doubled in volume.

3 Meanwhile, make the filling. Put 125g (4oz) of the smoked salmon in a food processor and process for 10 seconds or until smooth. Using the pulse button, slowly mix in the egg white. Turn into a small bowl and gradually beat in the cream, then add the lemon rind and juice, and the chives. Season with pepper only. Cover and chill for 10 minutes.

4 Briefly blanch the spinach leaves in boiling water to soften slightly. Halve the salmon fillet horizontally. Spread the bottom half with the smoked salmon mixture and place the other piece on top. Place a sheet of cling film three times the width of the fillet on a clean surface. Cover two thirds of the cling film with the remaining smoked salmon, season with pepper, then cover with spinach leaves. Place the stuffed fillet at one end; season. Use the cling film to help wrap the fillet neatly in the spinach and smoked salmon. Chill for 5-10 minutes.

5 Preheat a large baking sheet in the oven at 200°C/fan oven 190°C (400°F) Mark 6. On a lightly floured surface, roll out the brioche dough to a rectangle measuring about 33x40cm (13x16 inches) or large enough to wrap around the salmon easily. Place the salmon in the centre and lightly brush the edges of the dough with beaten egg. Fold the brioche around, sealing the edges; trim off any excess. Place the salmon on a floured baking sheet, seam-side down.

6 Brush with egg and decorate with the brioche trimmings. Brush again with egg and score the surface lightly with the back of a knife. Dot with pink peppercorns and leave to prove in a warm place for 20 minutes or until the brioche feels spongy. Place the baking sheet directly on the hot baking sheet and bake for 50-55 minutes or until deep golden brown. Serve hot or cold, cut into slices and garnished with lemon wedges, chives and peppercorns.

Notes
- A soft dough will give a light texture; try not to add any extra flour when kneading.
- To prepare ahead, follow steps 1 and 2, but don't set the dough to rise. Instead, place in a greased bowl, cover with cling film and refrigerate overnight. Prepare the salmon as in steps 3 and 4, wrap and chill overnight. To use, allow the brioche to rise at room temperature for about 3 hours, then complete the recipe.

wild mushroom and potato pithiviers

This elegant dish makes an ideal vegetarian alternative to a traditional Christmas dinner.

Serves 6
Preparation time: 1 hour, plus chilling
Cooking time: 20-25 minutes
Suitable for freezing (stage 5)
1040 cals per serving

two 500g packets ready-made puff pastry
1 egg, beaten
FOR THE FILLING:
450g (1lb) assorted wild mushrooms
450g (1lb) floury potatoes
300ml (½ pint) milk
200ml (7fl oz) double cream
2 garlic cloves, peeled and crushed
salt and freshly ground black pepper
freshly grated nutmeg
50g (2oz) butter
10ml (2 tsp) chopped fresh thyme
FOR THE PORT SAUCE:
40g (1½oz) butter
4 shallots, peeled and finely chopped
150ml (¼ pint) port or Madeira
600ml (1 pint) vegetable stock
TO GARNISH:
thyme sprigs

1 To make the filling, rinse the wild mushrooms to remove any grit, then pat dry with kitchen paper and slice thickly.

2 Peel and thinly slice the potatoes. Pour the milk and cream into a large, heavy-based saucepan, add the garlic and bring to the boil. Add the potatoes, return to the boil and simmer gently, stirring occasionally, for 15-20 minutes or until tender. Season generously with salt, pepper and nutmeg. Cool.

3 Melt the butter in a large frying pan. As it starts sizzling, add the mushrooms and fry, stirring, over a high heat, for 5-7 minutes or until they are cooked and the juices have completely evaporated. Season with salt and pepper, stir in the chopped thyme, then set aside to cool.

4 Roll out the pastry thinly on a lightly floured surface. Cut out six 15cm (6 inches) rounds for the lids and six 14cm (5½ inches) rounds for the bases. Place the smaller pastry bases on a large baking sheet and brush the edges with beaten egg.

5 Spoon the cooled potato mixture on to the pastry bases, leaving a 1cm (½ inch) margin. Top with the mushroom mixture. Position the pastry lids and press the pastry edges together to seal. Chill for 30 minutes-1 hour.

6 Preheat another large baking sheet in the oven at 220°C/fan oven 210°C (425°F) Mark 7. Knock up and scallop the pastry edges, then brush the tops with beaten egg. If wished, use the back of a knife to lightly score the tops of the pithiviers in a decorative pattern. Slide the tray of pithiviers on to the hot baking sheet and bake for 20-25 minutes or until deep golden brown.

7 Meanwhile, make the port sauce. Melt the butter in a frying pan, add the shallots and cook for 2-3 minutes. Pour in the port and bubble to reduce by half. Add the stock, bring to the boil and bubble for 10-15 minutes or until syrupy; season.

8 Transfer the pithiviers to warmed plates, garnish with thyme and serve with the port sauce and steamed baby leeks.

Note The pithiviers can be baked from frozen; allow an extra 10-15 minutes.

lamb and chestnuts en croûte

Lamb fillets are wrapped in spinach leaves and ham to seal in the juices, keeping the meat deliciously moist and tender, and ensuring that the pastry crust stays crisp.

Serves 8
Preparation time: 40 minutes, plus chilling
Cooking time: 35-50 minutes
Suitable for freezing (stage 5)
645 cals per serving

2 racks of lamb, trimmed, each 350g (12oz)
100g (3½oz) trimmed spinach leaves
50g (2oz) butter
75g (3oz) shallots, peeled and chopped
225g (8oz) mixed mushrooms, chopped
3 garlic cloves, peeled and crushed
45ml (3 tbsp) balsamic vinegar
100g (3½oz) cooked, vacuum-packed chestnuts, chopped
5ml (1 tsp) chopped fresh thyme
150ml (¼ pint) double cream
salt and freshly ground black pepper
4 thin slices cooked ham
500g (1lb 2oz) packet ready-made puff pastry
1 egg, beaten
FOR THE PORT GRAVY:
750ml (1¼ pints) well flavoured lamb stock
150ml (¼ pint) port
5ml (1 tsp) redcurrant jelly

1 Bone the lamb racks, removing each fillet in one piece (use the bones to make stock). Immerse the spinach in boiling water for 1-2 seconds. Drain, refresh with cold water and pat dry.

2 Melt the butter in a pan, add the shallots and cook, stirring, for 2-3 minutes. Add the mushrooms and cook for 3-4 minutes. Stir in the garlic and vinegar; cook for 1 minute. Add the chestnuts, thyme and cream. Bring to the boil and let bubble for 10 minutes or until reduced to a sticky glaze. Season with salt and pepper to taste; set aside to cool slightly.

3 Lay 2 ham slices on a piece of cling film, overlapping them slightly to form a 20x15cm (8x6 inch) rectangle. Cover with half of the spinach. Season one lamb fillet; place in the middle. Spread with half of the mushroom mixture. Wrap the meat tightly in the spinach and ham, sealing with the cling film. Repeat with the other lamb fillet. Refrigerate.

4 Roll out 125g (4oz) of the pastry to a 30x20cm (12x8 inch) rectangle. Place on a baking sheet and prick well; chill for 30 minutes. Cook at 220°C/fan oven 210°C (425°F) Mark 7 for 15 minutes. Cool, then cut into two 20x15cm (8x6 inch) rectangles. Place one lamb fillet on each piece of baked pastry. Trim pastry to the same dimensions.

5 Thinly roll out the remaining pastry to an oblong, 56x23cm (22x9 inches). Cut into two 28x23cm (11x9 inch) pieces. Brush with beaten egg, then wrap around the lamb (glazed-side down). Trim, leaving 2.5cm (1 inch) to tuck under the cooked pastry base. Brush with egg; decorate with leaves cut from the pastry trimmings. Cover lightly with cling film; chill for 1 hour.

6 Brush the pastry again with egg. Bake at 230°C/fan oven 220°C (450°F) Mark 8 allowing 20-30 minutes for medium-rare lamb; 30-35 minutes for well done meat. Cover the pastry towards the end of the cooking time if it appears to be overbrowning.

7 Meanwhile make the gravy. Add the port and jelly to the stock and boil briskly for 20-30 minutes until syrupy and reduced to about 450ml (¾ pint). Check the seasoning.

8 Allow the meat to stand for 5 minutes before slicing. Serve with the port gravy.

1 To make the filling, put the halloumi in a bowl with the ricotta, pine nuts, olives, oil, chopped coriander and mustard seeds. Toss to mix and season with pepper to taste. (As halloumi is naturally salty, there is no need to add extra salt.)

2 Roll out half of the pastry on a lightly floured surface to a 25cm (10 inch) square, then cut into four 12cm (5 inch) squares. Repeat with the rest of the pastry to make 8 squares.

3 Brush the edges of the squares with beaten egg. Spoon the filling on to one side of the squares. Fold the pastry over the filling to enclose and press the edges together to seal; flute the edges. Transfer the pastries to a lightly greased large baking sheet.

4 Lightly brush the pastries with beaten egg, then score the top of each one with a sharp knife. Scatter with extra mustard seeds. Bake at 220°C/fan oven 210°C (425°F) Mark 7 for about 15 minutes until well risen and golden. Serve warm, with a selection of roasted vegetables, such as aubergine, peppers and tomato.

Variations Flavour the filling with basil, thyme or rosemary instead of coriander.

mediterranean cheese puffs

Puff pastry parcels filled with ricotta, halloumi cheese, pine nuts, olives and fresh coriander.

Makes 8
Preparation time: 25 minutes
Cooking time: 15 minutes
345 cals per puff

450g (1lb) ready-made puff pastry
FOR THE FILLING:
150g (5oz) halloumi cheese, diced
200g (7oz) ricotta cheese
25g (1oz) pine nuts, toasted
12 black olives, pitted
30ml (2 tbsp) extra-virgin olive oil
30ml (2 tbsp) chopped fresh coriander
2.5ml (½ tsp) black mustard seeds
freshly ground black pepper
TO FINISH:
beaten egg, to glaze
extra black mustard seeds, for sprinkling

pepper, parmesan and almond filos

A medley of sweet peppers, tomatoes, nuts and herbs, sandwiched between cheesy filo layers.

Serves 6
Preparation time: 30 minutes
Cooking time: 25 minutes
Suitable for freezing (stage 5)
400 cals per serving

270g (9½oz) packet filo pastry
FOR THE FILLING:
60ml (4 tbsp) extra-virgin olive oil
350g (12oz) onions, peeled and sliced
4 garlic cloves, peeled and crushed
50g (2oz) chopped mixed nuts
2 red peppers, halved, cored and deseeded
1 yellow pepper, halved, cored and deseeded

50g (2oz) sun-dried tomatoes in oil, drained and
    roughly chopped
400g (14oz) can chopped tomatoes
large handful of basil leaves
large pinch of sugar
salt and freshly ground black pepper
TO ASSEMBLE:
30ml (2 tbsp) olive oil
40g (1½oz) Parmesan cheese, grated
TO GARNISH:
basil leaves

1 To make the filling, heat the oil in a large
saucepan. Add the onions, garlic and nuts and
fry for 3 minutes. Add the peppers and fry for
2 minutes.

2 Stir in the sun-dried and canned tomatoes. Bring
to the boil and cook for 10 minutes until pulpy.
Stir in the basil, sugar and seasoning to taste;
leave to cool.

3 Lay one filo pastry sheet in a 23cm (9 inch)
square baking tin, about 3cm (1¼ inches) deep,
allowing the excess pastry to overhang the
edges. Brush with a little oil and sprinkle with a
little Parmesan.

4 Lay another sheet of pastry on top, crumpling it
up slightly over the base and letting the excess
fall over the sides. Brush with more oil and
sprinkle with Parmesan. Repeat the layers until
you have used half of the filo pastry sheets.

5 Spread the filling in the tin, then fold the
overhanging pastry over the top. Crumple the
remaining filo sheets and layer on top of the
filling, brushing with more oil and sprinkling
with Parmesan. Sprinkle the top sheets with the
remaining Parmesan.

6 Bake at 190°C/fan oven 180°C (375°F) Mark 5 for
25 minutes until the pastry is deep golden and
crisp. Cut into squares to serve. Garnish with
basil and serve with a crisp green salad.

filo pastry

Packets of ready-made filo sheets are widely available
and give excellent results. Note that the size of filo
sheets varies considerably between brands – check
whether the recipe states a specific size before buying.
It is essential to keep filo sheets covered as you work to
prevent them from drying out and becoming brittle.

moroccan filo pie

A delicious, mildly spiced spinach, lentil and feta
cheese filo pie – scented with garlic and herbs.

Serves 6-8
Preparation time: 20 minutes
Cooking time: 40-45 minutes
Suitable for freezing (stage 5)
540-410 cals per serving

12 sheets filo pastry (or 6 large ones, halved)
75g (3oz) unsalted butter, melted
FOR THE FILLING:
60ml (4 tbsp) olive oil
1 onion, peeled and finely chopped
2-3 garlic cloves, peeled and crushed
10ml (2 tsp) ground coriander
5ml (1 tsp) ground cumin
450g (1lb) spinach leaves, shredded
two 400g (14oz) cans green lentils, drained
2 eggs, beaten
175g (6oz) feta cheese, crumbled
25g (1oz) Parmesan cheese, freshly grated
60ml (4 tbsp) chopped fresh herbs, such as coriander,
    mint and parsley
salt and freshly ground black pepper

1 To prepare the filling, heat the oil in a saucepan,
add the onion, garlic and spices and fry gently
for 10 minutes.

2 Add the spinach and cook until wilted. Stir in
the lentils, cover and heat through for
5 minutes. Mash the lentils slightly with a fork,
then transfer to a bowl; let cool slightly.

3 Stir the eggs into the cooled filling, then add the
feta, Parmesan, herbs and seasoning. Toss to
mix, then set aside.

4 Lay one sheet of filo pastry in the base of a
lightly oiled 25x20cm (10x8 inch) baking tin,
trimming to fit as necessary, and brush with
butter. Layer five more filo sheets in the tin,
brushing each with butter.

5 Spoon in the filling and level the surface. Layer
the remaining filo sheets on top, again brushing
each with butter.

6 Score the top of the pie in a diamond pattern,
using a sharp knife. Bake at 180°C/fan oven
170°C (350°F) Mark 4 for 40-45 minutes until
golden brown. Leave to stand for 5 minutes,
then cut into squares and serve with a salad.

rolling out pastry

Dust the work surface and rolling pin – never the pastry – very lightly with flour. Roll the dough lightly and evenly in one direction only – until thin. Always roll away from you, using light, firm strokes and rotate the pastry frequently to keep an even shape and thickness. Avoid over-rolling, pulling or stretching the pastry as you roll or it will shrink badly during cooking. The usual thickness for rolling out pastries is 3mm (⅛ inch), though puff pastry is sometimes rolled out to a 5 mm (¼ inch) thickness, depending on use.

lining a flan case

Roll out the pastry on a lightly floured surface until it is 5-7.5cm (2-3 inches) larger all round than the flan tin, depending on depth of tin. Using the rolling pin, lift the pastry over the tin. Lift the edges of the pastry so that it falls down into the tin, then gently press the pastry against the side of the tin so there are no gaps between pastry and tin. Turn any surplus pastry outwards over the rim, then trim away using a sharp knife to leave a neat edge. Chill in the refrigerator for 20-30 minutes to rest the pastry; this helps to minimise shrinkage during baking.

baking blind

If a recipe tells you to 'bake blind' you need to bake, or part-bake the pastry case without its filling. It is either partially cooked before filling, or completely cooked if the filling doesn't need baking. Prick the base with a fork, then line with a large piece of greaseproof paper. Fill with ceramic baking beans or dried pulses. Bake at the suggested temperature for 10-15 minutes or until the case looks set, then remove paper and beans and bake for a further 5 minutes until the base is firm and lightly coloured; or a further 15 minutes until crisp and golden brown if the pastry requires complete baking.

to unmould a flan

Place the flan tin on a can of beans and gently pull down the ring, leaving the finished tart on the base suspended on the can.

creamy leek tart

Serves 6
Preparation time: 30 minutes, plus chilling
Cooking time: 35-40 minutes
640 cals per serving

FOR THE PÂTE BRISÉE:
250g (9oz) plain white flour
5ml (1 tsp) salt
125g (4½oz) butter, softened
1 large egg yolk
FOR THE FILLING:
50g (2oz) butter
1.4 kg (3lb) leeks, trimmed and sliced
30ml (2 tbsp) water
salt and freshly ground black pepper
3 egg yolks
300ml (½ pint) crème fraîche or double cream
freshly grated nutmeg

1 To make the pastry, sift the flour and salt onto a sheet of greaseproof paper. Put the butter and egg yolk in a food processor and blend until smooth. Shoot in the flour and work until just combined. Turn out onto a lightly floured work surface and knead gently until smooth. Form into a ball, flatten and wrap in cling film. Chill in the refrigerator for at least 30 minutes. Allow to come to room temperature before rolling out.

2 Meanwhile, prepare the filling. Melt the butter in a large saucepan, add the leeks and stir to coat in the butter. Add the water, cover and cook gently, stirring occasionally, for about 20 minutes until very soft, but not coloured. Season well. Set aside to cool.

3 Roll out the pastry thinly on a lightly floured surface and use to line a 25cm (10 inch) loose-bottomed flan tin. Chill for 20 minutes, then lightly prick the base with a fork.

4 Beat the egg yolks and cream together, adding a little freshly grated nutmeg. Spread the leeks in the pastry case and pour over the egg and cream mixture.

5 Bake in the oven at 200°C/fan oven 190°C (400°F) Mark 6 for 15 minutes, then lower the oven setting to 190°C/fan oven 180°C (375°F) Mark 5 and bake for a further 20-25 minutes until the filling is set and browned on top. Serve warm or cold.

mediterranean vegetable flan

A vibrant assortment of Mediterranean vegetables set in a creamy ricotta custard.

Serves 4-6
Preparation time: 25 minutes, plus chilling
Cooking time: 45 minutes
Suitable for freezing
845-565 cals per serving

FOR THE PASTRY:
225g (8oz) plain white flour
pinch of salt
125g (4oz) butter, diced
45-60ml (3-4 tbsp) cold water

FOR THE FILLING:
45ml (3 tbsp) extra-virgin olive oil
1 red onion, peeled and thinly sliced
1 small red pepper, cored, deseeded and thinly sliced
1 small yellow pepper, cored, deseeded and thinly sliced
1 small courgette, sliced
1 garlic clove, peeled and crushed
15ml (1 tbsp) chopped fresh thyme
10ml (2 tsp) dried oregano
225g (8oz) ricotta cheese
25g (1oz) Parmesan cheese, freshly grated
2 eggs
150ml (¼ pint) double cream
salt and freshly ground black pepper
25g (1oz) pitted black olives

1 To make the pastry, sift the flour and salt into a bowl, then rub in the butter until the mixture resembles fine breadcrumbs. Add sufficient water to mix to a firm dough. Knead lightly, then wrap in cling film and chill for 30 minutes.

2 Preheat a baking sheet in the oven. Roll out the pastry on a lightly floured surface and use to line a 25cm (10 inch) loose-bottomed flan tin. Chill in the refrigerator for 20 minutes.

3 Prick the base, then line with greaseproof paper and baking beans. Place on the preheated baking sheet and bake blind at 200°C/fan oven 190°C (400°F) Mark 6 for 10 minutes. Remove paper and beans and bake for a further 10 minutes until the pastry is golden. Lower the oven setting to 190°C/fan oven 180°C (375°F) Mark 5.

4 Meanwhile, heat the oil in a large frying pan, add the vegetables, garlic and herbs and stir-fry over a high heat for 5-6 minutes until lightly golden. Drain on kitchen paper.

5 In a bowl, beat the ricotta, Parmesan and eggs together until evenly blended, then stir in the cream; season generously.

6 Spoon the vegetables into the pastry case and scatter the olives on top. Pour on the ricotta mixture and bake for 25 minutes, or until risen and firm. Let cool slightly. Serve warm or cold, with a tomato and basil salad.

1. Put the saffron strands in a small bowl, pour on the boiling water and set aside to infuse until cool. Sift the flour with a pinch of salt into a bowl and add a little pepper. Rub in the butter until the mixture resembles fine breadcrumbs. Stir in the saffron-infused liquid and sufficient cold water to mix to a firm dough. Knead lightly, wrap in cling film and chill for 30 minutes.

2. Roll out the pastry on a lightly floured surface and use to line a 24cm (9½ inch) loose-based flan tin, about 2.5cm (1 inch) deep. Line with greaseproof paper and baking beans and bake blind in the oven at 200°C/fan oven 190°C (400°F) Mark 6 for 15 minutes until beginning to colour around the edges. Remove the beans and paper and bake for a further 5 minutes.

3. Meanwhile, prepare the filling. Melt the butter in a frying pan, add the onion and garlic and fry for 3 minutes. Add the mushrooms and fry for a further 2 minutes. Turn into the pastry case.

4. In a bowl, beat together the eggs, cream and seasoning, then pour over the mushrooms. Bake in the oven for about 25-30 minutes until the custard is just set in the centre. Serve topped with Parmesan shavings if desired.

saffron tart with wild mushrooms

A saffron flavoured pastry case with an exquisite garlicky wild mushroom filling. If wild mushrooms are unavailable, use a mixture of chestnut, button and oyster mushrooms.

Serves 6
Preparation time: 25 minutes, plus chilling
Cooking time: 45-50 minutes
Suitable for freezing
550 cals per serving

FOR THE SAFFRON PASTRY:
large pinch of saffron strands
10ml (2 tsp) boiling water
225g (8oz) plain white flour
salt and freshly ground black pepper
125g (4oz) lightly salted butter, diced
5-10ml (1-2 tsp) chilled water
FOR THE FILLING:
50g (2oz) lightly salted butter
1 large onion, peeled and finely chopped
2-3 garlic cloves, peeled and crushed
450g (1lb) mixed wild mushrooms, cleaned
2 eggs
200ml (7fl oz) double cream
TO GARNISH:
Parmesan cheese shavings (optional)

spinach and sweet onion tart

Caramelised whole baby onions, fresh spinach and crème fraîche in a melting crust.

Serves 6-8
Preparation time: 45 minutes, plus chilling
Cooking time: 40 minutes
480-360 cals per serving

FOR THE PASTRY:
200g (7oz) plain white flour
pinch of salt
75g (3oz) butter, diced
15g (½oz) walnuts, toasted and ground
1 egg yolk
30-45ml (2-3 tbsp) cold water
FOR THE FILLING:
225g (8oz) baby onions, peeled
50g (2oz) butter
6 garlic cloves, peeled
2 fresh thyme sprigs, bruised

2 fresh bay leaves, bruised
salt and freshly ground black pepper
30ml (2 tbsp) balsamic vinegar
450g (1lb) spinach leaves, stalks removed
pinch of freshly grated nutmeg
200ml (7fl oz) crème fraîche
25g (1oz) Parmesan cheese, freshly grated

1 To make the pastry, sift the flour and salt into a bowl and rub in the butter until the mixture resembles fine breadcrumbs. Stir in the walnuts, then gradually work in the egg yolk and water to form a soft dough. Wrap in cling film and chill for 30 minutes.

2 Preheat a baking sheet in the oven at 200°C/fan oven 190°C (400°F) Mark 6. Roll out the dough on a lightly floured surface and use to line a 3cm (1¼ inch) deep, 23cm (9 inch) loose-based flan tin. Prick the base and chill for 15 minutes.

3 Line the pastry case with greaseproof paper and baking beans and bake on the hot baking sheet for 10-12 minutes. Remove paper and beans and bake for a further 10 minutes; set aside to cool. Increase oven setting to 230°C/fan oven 220°C (450°F) Mark 8.

4 Meanwhile, for the filling, blanch the whole onions in boiling water for 2 minutes; drain and dry on kitchen paper. Melt half of the butter in a frying pan. Add the whole onions and garlic cloves with the thyme and bay leaves. Fry over a medium heat for 20 minutes until golden and caramelised. Stir in 2.5ml (½ tsp) salt and the balsamic vinegar; cook for a further 5 minutes. Discard the herbs; allow to cool.

5 Cook the spinach in a large saucepan over a low heat, with just the water clinging to the leaves after washing, for 3-4 minutes until wilted. Refresh under cold water and squeeze out excess liquid. Chop finely and return to the pan. Heat gently to dry thoroughly, stir in the remaining butter and season with the nutmeg, salt and pepper.

6 Arrange the onion mixture and spinach in the pastry case and spoon over the crème fraîche, spreading to the edges. Sprinkle with the grated Parmesan and bake for about 20 minutes until golden and bubbling. Leave to stand for approximately 10 minutes. Serve warm.

Note The creamy filling should still be soft when the tart is served.

courgette quiche

Serves 6
Preparation time: 25 minutes, plus chilling
Cooking time: About 1 hour
515 cals per serving

FOR THE OATMEAL PASTRY:
50g (2oz) plain white flour
50g (2oz) plain wholemeal flour
pinch of salt
50g (2oz) medium oatmeal
40g (1½oz) lightly salted butter, diced
40g (1½oz) white vegetable fat, diced
FOR THE FILLING:
450g (1lb) small courgettes
60ml (4 tbsp) olive oil
350g (12oz) onions, peeled and sliced
2 eggs, plus 1 egg yolk
200ml (7fl oz) crème fraîche
30ml (2 tbsp) grainy mustard (optional)
salt and freshly ground black pepper
30ml (2 tbsp) pine nuts
30ml (2 tbsp) Parmesan cheese, grated

1 To make the pastry, place the flours, salt and oatmeal in a bowl, then rub in the fats until the mixture resembles breadcrumbs. Add enough cold water to mix to a firm dough. Knead lightly, then wrap in cling film and chill in the refrigerator for 30 minutes.

2 Roll out the pastry on a lightly floured surface and use to line a 2.5cm (1 inch) deep, 28x20cm (11x8 inch) rectangular loose-based flan tin, or 24cm (9½ inch) round flan tin. Line with greaseproof paper and baking beans and bake blind in the oven at 200°C/fan oven 190°C (400°F) Mark 6 for 15 minutes until beginning to colour around the edges. Remove the beans and paper and bake for a further 5 minutes.

3 Meanwhile, prepare the filling. Halve the courgettes lengthwise, then cut across into small chunks. Heat the oil in a frying pan, add the onions and fry for 2 minutes. Add the courgettes and fry for a further 3-5 minutes until turning golden. Spread the mixture in the pastry case.

4 In a bowl, beat the eggs, egg yolk and crème fraîche with the mustard if using, and seasoning. Pour over the courgettes and onions. Sprinkle with the pine nuts and cheese and bake for 35-40 minutes until golden. Serve warm.

roquefort tart

This classic French flan is served drizzled with a delicious fried garlic and walnut topping.

Serves 6-8
Preparation time: 30 minutes, plus chilling
Cooking time: 45-50 minutes
905-680 cals per serving

FOR THE PÂTE BRISÉE:
250g (9oz) plain white flour
5ml (1 tsp) salt
125g (4½oz) butter, softened
1 egg yolk
FOR THE FILLING:
225g (8oz) cream cheese
150ml (¼ pint) crème fraîche or double cream
3 eggs, beaten
175g (6oz) Roquefort cheese, crumbled
freshly ground black pepper
freshly grated nutmeg
45ml (3 tbsp) chopped fresh chives
FOR THE TOPPING:
30ml (2 tbsp) olive oil
3 garlic cloves, peeled and sliced
125g (4oz) walnut halves
15ml (1 tbsp) walnut oil
45ml (3 tbsp) chopped fresh parsley

1 To make the pastry, sift the flour and salt on to a sheet of greaseproof paper. Put the butter and egg yolk in a food processor and process briefly until smooth. Shoot in the flour and work until just combined. Turn out on to a lightly floured surface and knead gently until smooth. Wrap in cling film and leave to rest in the refrigerator for at least 30 minutes. Bring to room temperature before rolling out.
2 For the filling, beat the cream cheese in a bowl until soft. Add the cream and eggs and beat until smooth. Mix in the Roquefort gently. Season liberally with pepper and a little nutmeg. Stir in the chives; set aside.
3 Roll out the pastry on a lightly floured surface and use to line a 25cm (10 inch) loose-based flan tin. Chill for 20 minutes.

4 Prick the pastry base. Line with greaseproof paper and baking beans and bake blind at 200°C/fan oven 190°C (400°F) Mark 6 for 10 minutes. Remove paper and beans; bake for a further 5 minutes. Let cool slightly. Lower oven setting to 190°C/fan oven 180°C (375°F) Mark 5.
5 Pour the filling into the pastry case. Bake for 30-35 minutes until puffed and lightly browned.
6 Meanwhile, prepare topping. Heat the olive oil in a frying pan and fry the garlic and walnuts, stirring, until the garlic is golden and the nuts are browned. Stir in the walnut oil and parsley.
7 Scatter the topping over the tart and serve warm or cold, with a salad.

sweet potato and smoked cheese flan

Wafer-thin sweet potato slices, spicy chorizo and smoked Cheddar cheese in a puff pastry case.

Serves 6-8
Preparation time: 15 minutes, plus chilling
Cooking time: 15-20 minutes
475-355 cals per serving

350g (12oz) packet ready-made puff pastry
350g (12oz) sweet potatoes, scrubbed
15ml (1 tbsp) olive oil
125g (4oz) smoked Cheddar cheese, grated
125g (4oz) spicy chorizo sausage, thinly sliced
salt and freshly ground black pepper

1 Roll out the pastry thinly on a lightly floured surface, trim to a 23x33cm (9x13 inch) rectangle and press into a Swiss roll tin (of the same dimensions). Prick the base with a fork and chill for 30 minutes.
2 Preheat a baking sheet on the middle shelf of the oven at 220°C/fan oven 210°C (425°F) Mark 7. Cut the sweet potatoes into thin slices, no more than 3mm (⅛ inch) thick. Brush with oil and place on the grill rack. Grill for 3-5 minutes each side until golden and just tender. Allow to cool.
3 Arrange the sweet potato slices and chorizo slices over the pastry base and scatter with the grated cheese. Bake on the preheated baking sheet for 15-20 minutes until risen and golden. Serve with a green salad.

onion and potato tart

A simple, tasty cheese-topped flan, enriched with capers, olive pesto and fresh herbs.

Serves 4
Preparation time: 30 minutes, plus chilling
Cooking time: 35-40 minutes
605 cals per serving

FOR THE SHORTCRUST PASTRY:
175g (6oz) plain white flour
pinch of salt
75g (3oz) butter, diced
30-45ml (2-3 tbsp) chilled water
FOR THE FILLING:
3 small potatoes, about 225g (8oz)
60ml (4 tbsp) olive oil
2 onions, peeled and sliced
2 garlic cloves, peeled and crushed
10ml (2 tsp) chopped fresh thyme
10ml (2 tsp) chopped fresh sage
30ml (2 tbsp) olive paste
30ml (2 tbsp) capers in brine, drained
125g (4oz) gruyère or Cheddar cheese, grated
salt and freshly ground black pepper

1 To make the pastry, sift the flour and salt into a bowl, then rub in the butter until the mixture resembles fine breadcrumbs. Add sufficient water to mix to a firm dough. Knead lightly, then wrap in cling film and chill for 30 minutes.

2 Preheat a baking sheet in the oven at 220°C/fan oven 210°C (425°F) Mark 7. Roll out the pastry on a lightly floured surface to a 30cm (12 inch) round, then lift on to a cold baking sheet. Using fingers and thumbs, form a slight rim around the edge. Prick the base and line with greaseproof paper and baking beans.

3 Slide the baking sheet on to the hot baking sheet and bake blind for 10 minutes. Remove the paper and beans and bake for a further 5-8 minutes or until the pastry is crisp.

4 Meanwhile, cook the potatoes in lightly salted boiling water for 10-15 minutes until just tender. Drain and immediately refresh under cold water. Pat dry and cut into thin slices.

5 Heat the oil in a frying pan, add the onions, garlic and herbs and fry gently for 10 minutes until softened and light golden.

6 Spread the olive paste over the pastry base, then top with the potatoes, onion mixture and capers. Scatter over the cheese and season well. Bake for 20-25 minutes until the filling is golden. Serve at once, with a tomato salad.

Note For convenience, you can buy a 225g (8oz) packet ready-made shortcrust pastry, rather than make your own.

fennel, onion and gruyère tartlets

Serves 4
Preparation time: 25 minutes, plus chilling
Cooking time: 35 minutes
Suitable for freezing
670 cals per serving

FOR THE CHEESE PASTRY:
175g (6oz) plain white flour
75g (3oz) lightly salted butter, in pieces
50g (2oz) gruyère cheese, grated
1 egg yolk
30ml (2 tbsp) cold water
FOR THE FILLING:
225g (8oz) onion, peeled
225g (8oz) fennel bulb
45ml (3 tbsp) olive oil
5ml (1 tsp) fennel seeds
1 egg
150ml (¼ pint) double cream
salt and freshly ground black pepper
25g (1oz) gruyère cheese, grated

1 To make the pastry, sift the flour into a bowl.
   Rub in the butter, using your fingertips, then stir
   in the cheese. Add the egg yolk and cold water
   and mix to a firm dough. Knead lightly until
   smooth, then wrap in cling film and chill in the
   refrigerator for 30 minutes.
2 Roll out the pastry thinly on a lightly floured
   surface and use to line four 2cm (¾ inch) deep,
   10cm (4 inch) individual flan tins.
3 Line with greaseproof paper and baking beans
   and bake blind at 200°C/fan oven 190°C (400°F)
   Mark 6 for 10 minutes until beginning to colour
   around the edges. Remove the paper and beans
   and bake for a further 5 minutes.
4 Meanwhile, prepare the filling. Slice the onion
   and fennel as thinly as possible. Heat the oil in a
   large frying pan and add the onion and fennel,
   with the fennel seeds. Fry very gently for 10
   minutes or until softened. Allow to cool slightly.
5 In a bowl, beat together the egg, cream and a
   little seasoning. Divide the fennel mixture
   between the pastry cases and pack down lightly.
   Pour on the egg mixture and sprinkle with the
   cheese. Bake for about 20 minutes until the
   custard is just set. Serve warm.

tomato and basil tarte tatin

Roasted plum tomatoes baked under a layer of pastry, then inverted to serve and scattered with garlic and basil flavoured ciabatta crumbs.

Serves 6
Preparation time: 50 minutes, plus chilling
Cooking time: 30-40 minutes
310 cals per serving

90ml (6 tbsp) olive oil
30ml (2 tbsp) tomato paste
400g (14oz) can chopped tomatoes
1 fresh thyme sprig
salt and freshly ground black pepper
20ml (4 tsp) caster sugar
1.1kg (2½lb) plum tomatoes
50g (2oz) ciabatta, roughly chopped
2 garlic cloves, crushed
45ml (3 tbsp) chopped fresh basil or thyme
FOR THE PASTRY:
75g (3oz) chilled butter, cut into cubes
125g (4oz) plain white flour
60-75ml (4-5 tbsp) soured cream
TO SERVE:
garlic-infused olive oil (see note)
chervil or parsley sprigs
crushed black peppercorns

mixing pastry in a food processor

Short pastries can be made very successfully and quickly in a food processor. To ensure that the dough is not over-worked, use the pulse button in short bursts, checking the consistency all the time. Blend the dry ingredients first for 5-10 seconds, then add the fat and blend for another 10-15 seconds. Add the water 15ml (1 tbsp) at a time and pulse until the dough starts to hold together. Avoid making too large a quantity at one time or the result will be disappointing.

1 Heat 30ml (2 tbsp) olive oil in a pan, add the tomato paste and cook, stirring, for 1 minute. Add the canned tomatoes, thyme, seasoning and 5ml (1 tsp) caster sugar. Bring to the boil, lower the heat and simmer gently, uncovered, for 45 minutes or until the sauce is reduced and very thick. Discard the thyme; allow to cool.

2 Meanwhile, halve the plum tomatoes lengthwise and place on a baking sheet, cut-side up. Season, sprinkle with remaining sugar and drizzle with 15ml (1 tbsp) olive oil. Cook under a preheated grill for about 15 minutes until charred. Cool.

3 To make the pastry, place the butter and flour in a food processor. Pulse until the resembles coarse crumbs, add the soured cream and pulse again until the dough just comes together. Wrap in cling film and chill for at least 30 minutes.

4 Process the ciabatta with the garlic and 45ml (3 tbsp) olive oil to rough crumbs; season well and place on a baking sheet. Bake at 200°C/fan oven 190°C (400°F) Mark 6 for 5-10 minutes or until golden. Mix with the chopped basil or thyme.

5 Arrange the tomatoes, cut-side down, over the base of a 25cm (10 inch) ovenproof frying pan or non-stick cake tin. Spoon over any juices and season. Spread the tomato sauce over the tomatoes.

6 Roll the pastry out on a lightly floured surface to a 25cm (10 inch) round, place on top of the tomatoes and trim the edges. Cut steam holes in the pastry and bake in the oven for 30-40 minutes or until golden.

7 Invert the tart on to a serving plate and scatter over the garlic and herb crumb mixture. Drizzle with garlic-infused oil, garnish with herbs and season with crushed peppercorns.

Note For garlic-infused oil, put 2 thinly sliced garlic cloves in a pan with 90ml (6 tbsp) olive oil and warm gently until the garlic is golden; remove from the heat.

crab filo tart with ginger and coriander

Serves 8
Preparation time: 20 minutes, plus cooling
Cooking time: 55 minutes
260 cals per serving

175g (6oz) filo pastry
30ml (2 tbsp) olive oil
FOR THE FILLING:
25g (1oz) butter
1 bunch spring onions, finely chopped
10-15ml (2-3 tsp) grated fresh root ginger
450g (1lb) fresh or frozen white crab meat (see note)
200ml (7fl oz) single cream
3 egg yolks
30ml (2 tbsp) chopped fresh coriander
salt and freshly ground black pepper
TO GARNISH:
coriander leaves

1 Preheat a baking sheet on the middle shelf of the oven at 200°C/fan oven 190°C (400°F) Mark 6. Keep the filo pastry covered with a damp tea-towel. Taking one sheet at a time, brush with oil and place in a deep 23cm (9 inch) flan tin, allowing the edges to overhang slightly. Continue to add oiled filo sheets to fill the tin and form a shell. Prick the base.

2 Bake on the preheated baking sheet for 10 minutes, then set aside to cool. Reduce oven setting to 190°C/fan oven 180°C (375°F) Mark 5.

3 To make the filling, melt the butter in a frying pan and gently fry the spring onions and ginger for 2-3 minutes until softened. Allow to cool.

4 Flake the crab meat into a bowl. Add the cooled onion mixture, with all of the remaining filling ingredients. Stir well, seasoning generously. Spoon into the filo case.

5 Carefully cover the overhanging filo edges with foil to prevent them overbrowning and bake for 45 minutes until golden and just set. Leave to stand for 10 minutes. Serve warm, garnished with coriander.

Note Vacuum packed fresh crab meat is available from fishmongers, but frozen or even canned crab meat can be used; make sure it is well drained.

filo mushroom tartlets

Attractive, individual filo cases filled with a tasty mixture of mushrooms, topped with a whole egg, then baked to perfection.

Serves 6
Preparation time: 30 minutes
Cooking time: 25-30 minutes
375 cals per serving

8-10 sheets filo pastry
sunflower oil, for brushing
FOR THE FILLING:
15ml (1 tbsp) sunflower oil
2 small red onions, peeled and finely chopped
2 garlic cloves, peeled and crushed
125g (4oz) chestnut mushrooms, finely chopped
125g (4oz) flat mushrooms, finely chopped
5 sun-dried tomatoes in oil, drained and finely chopped
10ml (2 tsp) lemon juice
15ml (1 tbsp) chopped fresh parsley
salt and freshly ground black pepper
6 medium eggs
15g (½oz) Parmesan cheese, freshly grated

1 Lightly oil six 2.5cm (1 inch) deep, 9cm (3½ inch) individual flan tins. Cut eighteen 11cm (4½ inch) squares from the filo pastry. Brush each square with a little sunflower oil. Layer 3 filo squares in each tin, arranging them at an angle to each other so the points form a star. Press the pastry into the edges of the tins. Bake at 190°C/fan oven 180°C (375°F) Mark 5 for 10-15 minutes until just golden.

2 Meanwhile, heat the oil in a pan, add the onions and fry until softened but not coloured. Add the garlic and mushrooms to the pan and cook until the juices start to run. Add the sun-dried tomatoes, lemon juice, parsley and seasoning.

3 Divide the filling between the filo pastry cases. Press a hollow in the centre of one with the back of a spoon. Break an egg into a small saucer or small cup, then slide into one of the hollows; repeat with the other eggs. Sprinkle with the Parmesan and bake for 14-16 minutes until the eggs are softly set and creamy. Serve with a mixed leaf salad drizzled with balsamic vinegar.

onion, feta and pine nut tarts

Sweet caramelised onions, olives, pine nuts, sun-dried tomatoes and feta in puff pastry cases.

Serves 4
Preparation time: 30 minutes, plus chilling
Cooking time: 15 minutes
Suitable for freezing (see note)
710 cals per serving

450g (1lb) ready-made puff pastry
60ml (4 tbsp) olive oil, plus extra for brushing
700g (1½lb) onions, peeled and sliced
25g (1oz) pine nuts
25g (1oz) raisins (optional)
50g (2oz) feta cheese, crumbled
25g (1oz) pitted black olives
25g (1oz) sun-dried tomatoes, roughly chopped
25g (1oz) capers
salt and freshly ground black pepper
oregano sprigs, to garnish

1 Roll out the pastry on a lightly floured surface and cut out four 15cm (6 inch) rounds, using an inverted saucer as a guide. Chill for 30 minutes.

2 Preheat two baking sheets in the oven at 220°C/fan oven 210°C (425°F) Mark 7. Meanwhile, heat the oil in a large heavy-based frying pan. Add the onions and cook over a low heat for 10-15 minutes, stirring occasionally, until golden and caramelised. Allow to cool, then stir in the pine nuts, raisins if using, feta cheese, olives, sun-dried tomatoes and capers.

3 Prick the pastry rounds with a fork and brush with a little oil. Divide the onion mixture between them, leaving a 1cm (½ inch) margin round the edges. Season with salt and pepper.

4 Place the tarts on the hot baking sheets and bake in the oven for 15 minutes or until the pastry is crisp, golden and risen around the edges. Garnish with oregano sprigs to serve.

Note These tarts can be reheated from frozen at the above temperature for 10 minutes.

Variation Flavour the filling with anchovies instead of raisins. Season with pepper only.

pasta & noodles

Versatile, colourful pasta
dishes for all kinds of meals
from quick after-work
suppers to elegant main
courses for special occasions

pasta shapes

The choice of pasta is largely a matter of personal taste, but you will find that some pasta shapes are more suited to particular recipes than others. Broad pappardelle noodles, for example, tend to work best in dishes where the other ingredients are chunky. Smoother-textured sauces are generally better served with finer pastas, such as spaghetti or linguine. Where a recipe includes a lot of sauce, shapes such as conchiglie (shells) and penne (tubes) are ideal because they hold the sauce well.

quantities

It is difficult to give specific quantity guidelines for pasta, because there are so many factors, including the nature of the sauce and whether you are serving the pasta as a starter, lunch or main meal. Individual appetites for pasta seem to vary enormously too. As a very approximate guide, allow about 75-125g (3-4oz) uncooked weight per person.

cooking pasta

All pasta, fresh and dried, should be cooked until *al dente* – firm to the bite, definitely not soft, and without a hard, uncooked centre. Always add pasta to a large pan containing plenty of fast-boiling water; insufficient water will result in stodgy unevenly cooked pasta. Fresh pasta needs only the briefest of cooking time, so watch it carefully. Most dried pasta takes around 8-12 minutes. Manufacturer's recommended cooking times provide a rough guide, but the only way to determine when pasta is cooked is by tasting. Avoid overcooking at all costs!

serving suggestions

Have warmed serving plates or bowls ready as pasta quickly loses its heat once it is drained. Toss the pasta with the chosen sauce, butter or olive oil as soon as it is cooked, or it may start to stick together. Parmesan cheese provides the finishing touch for many pasta dishes. Either grate the Parmesan over the finished dish or shave off thin flakes, using a swivel potato peeler.

spaghetti with courgettes, lemon and pistachio nuts

During the summer months, look out for vibrant yellow courgettes. They taste the same as green ones, but the colour combination makes this an attractive dish.

Serves 4
Preparation time: 10 minutes
Cooking time: 15 minutes
550 cals per serving

350g (12oz) dried spaghetti
salt and freshly ground black pepper
90ml (6 tbsp) extra-virgin olive oil
600g (1¼lb) courgettes (preferably mixed green and
    yellow ones), trimmed and thinly sliced
2 garlic cloves, peeled and thinly sliced
1 small red chilli, deseeded and finely chopped
grated rind and juice of 2 lemons
30ml (2 tbsp) chopped fresh chives
TO SERVE:
50g (2oz) toasted pistachio nuts, finely chopped
Parmesan cheese shavings (optional)
extra-virgin olive oil (optional)

1 Cook the spaghetti in a large saucepan of boiling salted water until *al dente*.
2 Meanwhile, heat the oil in a large frying pan. Add the courgettes, garlic, chilli and lemon rind and stir-fry over a high heat for 4-5 minutes until the courgettes are golden. Remove from the heat and stir in the lemon juice.
3 Drain the pasta and add to the courgettes with the chives. Season with salt and pepper and toss over a low heat for 30 seconds.
4 Divide the spaghetti between warmed serving plates and top with toasted pistachios. Scatter over some Parmesan shavings and drizzle with a little extra olive oil to serve if you like.

Variation Replace the pistachios with pine nuts.

sweet and sour red pepper pasta

Serves 4
Preparation time: 5 minutes
Cooking time: 22 minutes
455 cals per serving

2 large red peppers, halved, cored and deseeded
30ml (2 tbsp) olive oil
30ml (2 tbsp) white wine vinegar
5ml (1 tsp) brown sugar
350g (12oz) jar tomato and chilli sauce (see note)
350g (12oz) dried spaghetti
salt and freshly ground black pepper

1 Cut the peppers into large chunks. Heat the oil in a frying pan, add the peppers and cook over a high heat for 7-10 minutes or until tinged with brown. Add the vinegar and brown sugar and cook for a further 2 minutes. Add the tomato and chilli sauce, bring to the boil and simmer for 7-10 minutes. Season.
2 Meanwhile, cook the pasta in a large pan of boiling salted water until *al dente*. Drain, add to the sauce and toss to mix. Check the seasoning and serve.

Note Most supermarkets stock a good range of ready-made pasta sauces.

buckwheat pasta with grilled radicchio

Grilling mellows the bitter taste of radicchio and imparts a wonderful smoky flavour. Sweet sour caramelised onions provide the perfect balance in this main course pasta dish.

Serves 4
Preparation time: 20 minutes
Cooking time: 15 minutes
575 cals per serving

60ml (4 tbsp) extra-virgin olive oil, plus extra for brushing
2 small red onions, peeled and thinly sliced
1 garlic clove, peeled and crushed
15ml (1 tbsp) chopped fresh thyme
pinch of sugar
2 heads of radicchio, cut into thick wedges
450g (1lb) fresh or 400g (14oz) dried buckwheat tagliatelle (see note)
salt and freshly ground black pepper
30ml (2 tbsp) balsamic vinegar
25g (1oz) capers in wine vinegar, drained
50g (2oz) pine nuts, toasted
30ml (2 tbsp) chopped fresh basil
freshly grated Parmesan cheese, to taste (optional)

1 Heat the 60ml (4 tbsp) oil in a deep frying pan, add the onions, garlic, thyme and sugar and fry for 10-15 minutes until golden and tender.
2 Meanwhile, lay the radicchio wedges on the grill rack, brush with a little oil and grill under a high heat for 2-3 minutes. Turn the wedges over, brush with oil and grill for a further 2-3 minutes until charred and tender; keep warm.
3 Cook the buckwheat pasta in a large pan of boiling salted water until *al dente*; fresh pasta will only take 1-2 minutes.
4 Add the balsamic vinegar, capers, pine nuts and basil to the onions and stir well; keep warm.
5 Drain the pasta, reserving 60ml (4 tbsp) cooking water. Add both to the caramelised onions with the radicchio. Stir briefly over a medium heat, then season with salt and pepper and serve at once, with Parmesan, if wished.

Variation Use 4 heads of chicory, quartered, instead of radicchio.

tagliatelle with pumpkin and blue cheese sauce

This deliciously rich combination is best served with a simple salad and, perhaps, some good brown bread. Other firm squash, such as butternut or acorn squash, can be used with equal success when pumpkin is out of season.

Serves 4-6
Preparation time: 15 minutes
Cooking time: About 12 minutes
930-620 cals per serving

350g (12oz) wedge of pumpkin, peeled and deseeded
25g (1oz) butter
1 garlic clove, peeled and crushed
30ml (2 tbsp) chopped fresh parsley
300ml (½ pint) extra-thick double cream
1.25ml (¼ tsp) freshly grated nutmeg
400g (14oz) dried tagliatelle, pappardelle or fusilli
175g (6oz) dolcelatte cheese, cut into small pieces
salt and freshly ground black pepper
TO GARNISH:
30ml (2 tbsp) pine nuts, toasted
15ml (1 tbsp) chopped fresh parsley

1 Grate the pumpkin flesh, using a food processor fitted with a medium grating attachment, or a box grater.
2 Melt the butter in a large frying pan. Add the pumpkin and garlic and cook, stirring, over a medium heat for about 5 minutes, until softened. Stir in the parsley, cream and nutmeg and cook for a further 2 minutes.
3 Cook the pasta in a large pan of boiling salted water until *al dente*.
4 Add the dolcelatte to the sauce and heat gently, stirring, until melted. Season with salt and pepper to taste.
5 Drain the pasta thoroughly and return to the pan. Add the sauce and toss well to mix. Serve at once, sprinkled with toasted pine nuts and chopped parsley.

Variation Replace the dolcelatte with Boursin or other garlic and herb-flavoured cream cheese.

fettucine with gorgonzola and spinach

The rich, creamy flavour of this pasta sauce belies its few simple ingredients. Use small young, tender spinach leaves for best results. Serve with crusty bread and a mixed salad.

Serves 4-6
Preparation time: About 15 minutes
Cooking time: 2-10 minutes
630-420 cals per serving

350g (12oz) young leaf spinach, trimmed
400g (14oz) fresh or dried fettucine, tagliatelle or long fusilli
salt and freshly ground black pepper
225g (8oz) gorgonzola cheese, diced
90ml (3fl oz) milk
25g (1oz) butter
freshly grated nutmeg, to taste

1 Place the spinach in a saucepan with just the water clinging to the leaves after washing and cook, stirring, over a medium high heat for 2-3 minutes until wilted. Drain well in a colander or sieve, pressing out any excess liquid.
2 Cook the pasta in a large pan of boiling salted water until *al dente*
3 Meanwhile, place the gorgonzola in a clean pan with the milk and butter. Heat gently, stirring, until melted to a creamy sauce. Stir in the drained spinach. Season to taste with pepper; it shouldn't be necessary to add salt.
4 Drain the pasta and add to the sauce. Toss well to mix. Serve at once, sprinkled with a little freshly grated nutmeg.

Variations
- For a milder alternative, use dolcelatte rather than gorgonzola cheese.
- Add 125g (4oz) diced cooked smoked ham to the sauce with the wilted spinach.

tagliatelle with broad beans, chicory and cream

Tender, bright green broad beans and chicory are tossed in a creamy sauce, with herbs, and served with tagliatelle and Parmesan. Slipping the beans out of their waxy skins takes a little time, but it's worth the effort. If you think you'll find it tiresome, opt for the variation rather than use frozen broad beans in their skins.

Serves 4
Preparation time: 25 minutes
Cooking time: 10 minutes
880-590 cals per serving

350g (12oz) frozen broad beans, thawed
40g (1½oz) butter
1 onion, peeled and finely chopped
400g (14oz) dried paglia e fieno (egg and green tagliatelle)
2 heads chicory, about 200g (7oz) total weight, sliced
45ml (3 tbsp) chopped fresh parsley or chervil
300ml (½ pint) extra-thick double cream
60ml (4 tbsp) freshly grated Parmesan cheese
salt and freshly ground black pepper
Parmesan cheese shavings, to serve

1 Slip the broad beans out of their waxy outer skins and place in a bowl; set aside.
2 Melt the butter in a large frying pan. Add the onion and cook over a medium heat, stirring frequently, for 5-6 minutes until soft.
3 Cook the pasta in a large pan of boiling salted water until *al dente*.
4 Meanwhile, add the broad beans to the onion in the frying pan and continue cooking for 2 minutes, then stir in the chicory and parsley or chervil. Cook for a further 2 minutes, then stir in the cream. Bring to the boil and add the grated Parmesan. Season with salt and pepper to taste.
5 Drain the pasta and toss with the sauce. Serve at once, topped with Parmesan shavings.

Variation Replace the skinned broad beans with 300g (10oz) frozen peas. Add them to the onion with the chicory.

pasta with caper sauce and grilled halloumi

Halloumi is a firm-textured Cypriot cheese with a salty flavour. It is wonderful for grilling or frying as it softens, rather than melts, and develops a golden crust. Most supermarkets sell halloumi.

Serves 4-6
Preparation time: 30 minutes
Cooking time: 15 minutes
755-505 cals per serving

2 red peppers
90ml (6 tbsp) extra-virgin olive oil
2 onions, peeled and chopped
2 garlic cloves, peeled and chopped
45ml (3 tbsp) chopped fresh parsley
50g (2oz) capers in wine vinegar, rinsed and drained
salt and freshly ground black pepper
400g (14oz) dried penne, rigatoni or tagliatelle
225g (8oz) halloumi cheese, cut into 1cm (½ inch) cubes

1 Grill the whole peppers under a preheated high grill, turning occasionally until the skin is blistered and blackened all over; this will take about 20 minutes. Cool slightly then, over a bowl to catch the juices, peel away the charred skin and remove the seeds. Cut the flesh into strips and add to the bowl; set aside.
2 Meanwhile, heat 75ml (5 tbsp) olive oil in a large frying pan. Add the onions and cook over a medium heat, stirring frequently, for 7-8 minutes until soft. Stir in the garlic and continue cooking for 2-3 minutes. Stir in the parsley.
3 Transfer the mixture to a food processor and add the capers and seasoning. Process briefly to chop coarsely.
4 Cook the pasta in a large pan of boiling salted water until *al dente*.
5 Meanwhile, put the halloumi cubes on a baking tray in a single layer. Sprinkle with the remaining 15ml (1 tbsp) olive oil and plenty of pepper; toss to coat the cheese. Grill, turning occasionally, for about 8 minutes until evenly golden on all sides.
6 Drain the pasta and return to the pan. Add the caper sauce and pepper strips; toss to mix. Serve at once, topped with the grilled halloumi.

spaghetti with leek and mascarpone sauce

This fast, creamy pasta dish tastes delicious. For a special supper, prepare Parmesan wafers in advance to use as a garnish (see below).

Serves 4
Preparation time: 10 minutes
Cooking time: 25 minutes
930 cals per serving

75g (3oz) butter
450g (1lb) leeks, trimmed and finely diced
150ml (¼ pint) dry white wine
250g (9oz) mascarpone
75g (3oz) Parmesan cheese, freshly grated
freshly ground black pepper
450g (1lb) fresh or dried spaghetti
Parmesan wafers, to garnish (optional)

1 Melt the butter in a large deep frying pan. Add the leeks and cook gently for about 15 minutes or until very soft but not coloured. Pour in the wine and let bubble until reduced by half.
2 Meanwhile, cook the pasta in a large pan of boiling salted water until *al dente*.
3 To finish the sauce, lower the heat and add the mascarpone. Stir until it has melted through the leeks, then add two thirds of the Parmesan and season with pepper. Take off the heat.
4 Drain the pasta and toss with the sauce. Serve sprinkled with the remaining Parmesan and garnished with Parmesan wafers if you like.

Parmesan wafers Finely grate 40g (1½oz) Parmesan cheese and sprinkle in 4 thin piles on a baking tray. Place under a medium grill for about 30 seconds until melted and golden. Leave on the tray for 10 seconds, then carefully lift off using a palette knife and cool on a wire rack. Store the wafers in an airtight container for up to 24 hours.

linguine with mushrooms and truffle oil

Truffle oil has a distinctive aroma and transforms this quick dish into a special mid-week supper.

Serves 4
Preparation time: 10 minutes
Cooking time: 15 minutes
515 cals per serving

30ml (2 tbsp) olive oil
50g (2oz) butter
3 large garlic cloves, peeled and crushed
600g (1¼lb) large field mushrooms, chopped
350g (12oz) fresh linguine or pappardelle
salt and freshly ground black pepper
15-30ml (1-2 tbsp) truffle oil (optional)
15ml (1 tbsp) chopped fresh sage
fried sage leaves, to garnish (optional, see note)

1 Heat the oil and butter in a large frying pan, add the garlic and cook for 30 seconds. Add the mushrooms and cook over a moderate heat for 5-10 minutes or until cooked and all the liquid has evaporated.

2 Meanwhile, cook the pasta in a large saucepan of boiling salted water until *al dente*.

3 Drain the pasta and add to the mushroom mixture with the truffle oil if using, and chopped sage. Toss well and season with salt and pepper to taste. Serve garnished with fried sage leaves if wished.

Note For the fried sage leaf garnish, heat a 2.5cm (1 inch) depth of oil in a deep frying pan until a cube of bread dropped in browns in 30 seconds, then fry the sage leaves in batches for 30 seconds or until crisp. Drain on kitchen paper.

orecchiette with rocket and cherry tomatoes

This quick, fresh-tasting dish relies on the inclusion of peppery rocket leaves for its success. Serve this pasta dish as a light lunch, with a crisp leafy salad and warm crusty bread.

Serves 4
Preparation time: 10 minutes
Cooking time: About 10 minutes
580 cals per serving

400g (14oz) dried orecchiette, or other pasta shapes
salt and freshly ground black pepper
45ml (3 tbsp) olive oil
30ml (2 tbsp) pine nuts
450g (1lb) very ripe cherry tomatoes, halved
75g (3oz) rocket leaves
50g (2oz) Parmesan cheese shavings, to serve

1 Cook the pasta in a large pan of boiling salted water until *al dente*.

2 A few minutes before the pasta will be ready, heat 30ml (2 tbsp) of the oil in a large saucepan. Add the pine nuts and cook for 1-2 minutes until golden. Add the tomatoes and cook for barely 1 minute until only just heated through, not disintegrated.

3 Drain the pasta and toss with the remaining olive oil. Add the pasta to the tomatoes, then add the rocket. Carefully stir to mix and heat through. Season generously with salt and pepper. Serve immediately, topped with plenty of Parmesan shavings.

Note Orecchiette – literally 'tiny ears' in Italian – is available from Italian delicatessens.

Variations
• Use young spinach leaves in place of the rocket.
• For extra colour, use a mixture of red cherry and yellow pear tomatoes.

pasta primavera with herbs

In this colourful dish, ribbon pasta perfectly offsets spring vegetables – or primavera as they are known in Italy. Some of the vegetables are cooked slowly until meltingly soft, sweet and buttery, while in contrast young asparagus, whole tiny carrots and sugar snap peas are cooked briefly to retain their fresh crispness.

Serves 4-6
Preparation time: 25 minutes
Cooking time: About 25 minutes
950-635 cals per serving

175g (6oz) thin asparagus, halved
125g (4oz) sugar snap peas, topped and tailed
225g (8oz) carrots, preferably baby ones
50g (2oz) butter
1 small onion, peeled and chopped
1 red pepper, skinned, cored, deseeded and diced
2 celery stalks, diced
2 courgettes, diced
6-8 spring onions, white parts only, diced
400g (14oz) dried tagliatelle or pappardelle
300ml (½ pint) double cream
60ml (4 tbsp) freshly grated Parmesan cheese
salt and freshly ground black pepper
15ml (1 tbsp) oil
20ml (4 tsp) snipped chives
20ml (4 tsp) chopped fresh chervil
20ml (4 tsp) chopped fresh dill

1 Cook the asparagus in boiling salted water for 3-4 minutes, adding the sugar snaps after 2 minutes so that both are cooked until just tender. Drain, refresh with cold water and drain again; set aside.
2 If the carrots are tiny baby ones, leave whole; otherwise peel and cut into matchsticks.
3 Melt the butter in a large frying pan. Add the chopped onion and sauté over a medium heat for 7-8 minutes until softened and golden. Add the red pepper and celery and cook for 5 minutes. Stir in the courgettes, carrots and spring onions and cook for 12-15 minutes, stirring frequently, until the vegetables are tender and beginning to colour.

4 Cook the pasta in a large pan of boiling salted water until *al dente*.
5 Meanwhile, stir the cream into the vegetables and bring to the boil. Allow to bubble, stirring frequently, for a few minutes until it is reduced by about one third. Stir in the asparagus and sugar snaps. Add the Parmesan and heat gently. Season with salt and pepper to taste.
6 Drain the pasta thoroughly and toss with the oil to prevent sticking. Pour the sauce over the pasta and sprinkle with the herbs. Toss to mix and serve at once.

Variations
- Vary the vegetables according to availability. Fennel, broccoli florets, fresh peas and fine beans are suitable options.
- Replace some of the herbs with 40g (1½oz) chopped walnuts.

pasta with mediterranean vegetables and walnut paste

Pasta tossed in walnut paste is a wonderful combination and a delicious dish in its own right. Topped with grilled Mediterranean vegetables it makes a robust, colourful dish.

Serves 4-6
Preparation time: 25 minutes
Cooking time: 20 minutes
950-630 cals per serving

1 fennel bulb, cut into wedges
2 small red onions, peeled and cut into wedges
2 courgettes, halved and thinly sliced lengthwise
1 large red pepper, cored, deseeded and cut into broad strips
6 small tomatoes, halved
45ml (3 tbsp) extra-virgin olive oil
15ml (1 tbsp) chopped fresh thyme
5ml (1 tsp) finely grated lemon rind
coarse sea salt and freshly ground black pepper
400g (14oz) dried tagliatelle

FOR THE WALNUT PASTE:
150g (5oz) walnuts, roughly chopped
1 garlic clove, peeled and chopped
45ml (3 tbsp) chopped fresh parsley
75ml (5 tbsp) extra-virgin olive oil
50g (2oz) ricotta or other soft cheese
TO GARNISH:
thyme sprigs

1 Add the fennel and onions to a large pan of boiling water, bring back to the boil and cook for 2 minutes. Add the courgette strips and cook for a further 1 minute. Drain in a colander and refresh under cold running water. Drain and set aside.

2 Preheat the grill to high. Put the blanched vegetables in a bowl with the red pepper and tomatoes. Add the olive oil, thyme, lemon rind and seasoning; toss to coat.

3 Transfer the vegetables to the foil-lined grill pan and grill for 15-20 minutes, turning occasionally until they are tender and patched with brown.

4 Meanwhile, cook the pasta in a large pan of boiling salted water until *al dente*.

5 Meanwhile, prepare the walnut paste. Put the walnuts and garlic into a food processor and process briefly to chop finely. Add the parsley and process for 1 second. Add the oil and work to a coarse paste. Transfer to a bowl and stir in the ricotta and seasoning.

6 Drain the pasta thoroughly in a colander. Meanwhile, gently heat the walnut paste in the large pasta pan for a few seconds, then remove from the heat, add the pasta and toss to mix. Serve at once, topped with the grilled vegetables, drizzling over any oil and juices from the grill pan. Garnish with thyme sprigs.

Variation Use olive paste rather than walnut paste. Buy ready-made, or make your own – by processing stoned olives with a chopped garlic clove, olive oil and some chopped herbs.

calabrian pasta

The finest broccoli is grown in 'the toe' of Italy in the region of Calabria – and is called calabrese. Fried with pine nuts, sultanas, garlic and breadcrumbs, it makes a delicious sauce to serve with pasta.

Serves 4-6
Preparation time: 10 minutes
Cooking time: 12-15 minutes
695-465 cals per serving

50g (2oz) sultanas
150g (5oz) broccoli
300-350g (10-12oz) ziti, long fusilli or spaghetti
salt and freshly ground black pepper
125ml (4fl oz) olive oil
75g (3oz) white breadcrumbs
2 garlic cloves, peeled and finely chopped
25g (1oz) pine nuts
15ml (1 tbsp) sun-dried tomato paste
45ml (3 tbsp) chopped fresh parsley
cayenne pepper, to taste

1 Put the sultanas in a bowl, pour on a little boiling water and leave to soak. Break the broccoli into small florets, cutting the stems into similar sized pieces. Add the broccoli to a pan of boiling water, return to the boil and simmer for 30 seconds; drain.

2 Cook the pasta in a large pan of boiling salted water until *al dente*.

3 In the meantime, heat the oil in a frying pan, add the breadcrumbs and fry, stirring, until they begin to crisp. Add the garlic and pine nuts and continue to fry, stirring, until the pine nuts begin to colour. Add the broccoli and stir over the heat until it is thoroughly heated through.

4 Drain the pasta in a colander, setting it back on the pan to catch the last 15ml (1 tbsp) cooking water. Stir the tomato paste and drained sultanas into this liquid, then return the pasta to the pan. Toss with a generous grinding of pepper and half of the parsley. Transfer to a heated serving bowl.

5 Mix the remaining parsley with the broccoli and crumb mixture. Add to the pasta and toss to mix. Sprinkle with cayenne pepper to serve.

Variation Replace the sun-dried tomato paste with 10ml (2 tsp) anchovy essence.

vegetarian lasagne

This lasagne has a rich Mediterranean vegetable filling complemented by a creamy topping made from goat's cheese, eggs and cream. Use the mild soft young goat's cheese – chèvre frais – sold in tubs. Or use cream or curd cheese instead.

Serves 6
Preparation time: About 1 hour
Cooking time: 40 minutes
Suitable for freezing (stage 5)
685 cals per serving

4 red, orange or yellow peppers
2 medium aubergines, diced
salt and freshly ground black pepper
75ml (5 tbsp) extra-virgin olive oil
2 onions, peeled and chopped
4 garlic cloves, peeled and thinly sliced
75ml (5 tbsp) red wine or water
45ml (3 tbsp) chopped fresh oregano
90ml (6 tbsp) sun-dried tomato paste
12 sheets dried lasagne
FOR THE TOPPING:
350g (12oz) fresh soft goat's cheese
2 eggs
150ml (¼ pint) single cream
45ml (3 tbsp) day-old white breadcrumbs
30ml (2 tbsp) freshly grated Parmesan cheese

1 Grill the peppers under a high heat, turning from time to time, until the skins are charred and blistered all over; this will take about 20 minutes. Allow to cool slightly, then over a bowl to catch the juices, peel away the skins. Chop the flesh, discarding the seeds; set aside with the juices.

2 Put the diced aubergines in a colander, rinse, then sprinkle liberally with salt. Leave for 20 minutes, to extract the bitter juices. Rinse, then blanch in boiling water for 1 minute; drain well.

3 Heat the oil in a large saucepan. Add the onions and cook, stirring, for 8 minutes or until soft and golden. Add the garlic and cook for 2 minutes. Add the wine and let bubble for 1 minute, then stir in the aubergine, oregano and sun-dried tomato paste. Cover and cook over a medium heat for 15-20 minutes, stirring frequently. Take off the heat and stir in the grilled peppers; season.

4 Cook the lasagne in a large pan of boiling salted water until *al dente* or according to packet instructions. Drain, then drop into a bowl of cold water with 30ml (2 tbsp) oil added to prevent the sheets sticking. Drain and lay on a clean tea towel.

5 Oil a baking dish, measuring about 25x18x8cm (10x7x3½ inches). Spread one third of the filling in the base of the dish and then cover with a layer of pasta, trimming the sheets to fit the dish as necessary. Add another third of the filling and cover with pasta as before. Cover with the last of the filling and arrange the remaining pasta sheets on top.

6 To make the topping, place the goat's cheese in a bowl, add the eggs and beat well. Stir in the cream and season with salt and pepper. Pour over the lasagne and spread evenly. Sprinkle with the breadcrumbs and Parmesan, then bake at 190°C/fan oven 180°C (375°F) Mark 5 for about 35-40 minutes, until heated through and lightly browned on top.

Variation Replace the goat's cheese topping with 350g (12oz) mozzarella, cut into slices.

fresh tomato sauce

A simple fresh-tasting sauce to serve with pasta. Make it during the summer when tomatoes are at their best and freeze some for later use.

• Put 900g (2lb) roughly chopped vine-ripened tomatoes in a saucepan with 30ml (2tbsp) extra-virgin olive oil, 2 crushed garlic cloves, the grated rind of 1 lemon and 5ml (1 tsp) dried oregano. Bring to the boil, cover and simmer gently for 30 minutes.

• Add the basil, salt and freshly ground black pepper to taste, and a pinch of sugar if required. Simmer, uncovered, for a further 20-30 minutes until thickened. If a smooth sauce is preferred, pass through a sieve.

sicilian aubergine and ricotta pasta

Serve this delicious combination of hot pasta, creamy ricotta, tomato, aubergine and basil as a lunch or light supper dish.

Serves 4-6
Preparation time: 15 minutes, plus standing
Cooking time: 35 minutes
870-580 cals per serving

2 medium thin aubergines
salt and freshly ground black pepper
450g (1lb) penne or pasta shells
light olive oil, for shallow-frying
600ml (1 pint) Fresh Tomato Sauce (see left)
30-45ml (2-3 tbsp) shredded fresh basil leaves
225g (8oz) ricotta cheese, crumbled
basil leaves, to garnish

1 Slice the aubergines thinly. Sprinkle with salt, place in a colander and leave to drain for 1 hour. Rinse well, drain and pat dry.

2 Cook the pasta in a large pan of boiling salted water until *al dente*.

3 Meanwhile, heat the oil in a deep frying pan. When hot, shallow-fry the aubergines in batches until golden. Drain well on kitchen paper. Reheat the tomato sauce.

4 Drain the pasta thoroughly, then add the tomato sauce, shredded basil and half of the ricotta. Toss well and transfer to a warmed serving bowl. Arrange the aubergine slices on top. Sprinkle over the remaining ricotta and serve immediately, garnished with basil.

spaghetti with wild mushrooms and sage

Not everyone is able to buy – or pick – wild mushrooms, but cultivated large field mushrooms work well in this dish too. Whichever mushrooms you choose, the dried porcini will add a superb depth of flavour to the sauce.

Serves 4-6
Preparation time: 25 minutes, plus soaking
Cooking time: 20 minutes
660-440 cals per serving

15g (½oz) dried porcini mushrooms
600g (1¼lb) mixed fresh mushrooms, such as field, chestnut, oyster, plus chanterelles or other wild mushrooms as available, cleaned
75ml (5 tbsp) extra-virgin olive oil
3 shallots, peeled and chopped
2-3 garlic cloves, peeled and chopped
300ml (½ pint) dry white wine
30ml (2 tbsp) chopped fresh sage
30ml (2 tbsp) chopped fresh parsley
salt and freshly ground black pepper
400g (14oz) dried spaghettini
Parmesan cheese shavings, to serve (optional)

1 Put the dried porcini in a small bowl and pour on 120ml (4fl oz) boiling water. Leave to soak for 20 minutes, then drain, reserving the soaking liquor. Rinse and chop the mushrooms.
2 Slice large field mushrooms; quarter chestnut mushrooms; leave oyster mushrooms and any others whole (unless very large).
3 Heat the olive oil in a large frying pan. Add the shallots and sauté over a medium heat for 5 minutes until softened. Stir in the garlic and cook for a further 1-2 minutes.
4 Add the chopped dried mushrooms to the frying pan with the soaking liquor and wine. Bring to the boil, then lower the heat a little and allow to bubble for 8-10 minutes until the liquid has reduced by about half.
5 Add the fresh mushrooms, except oyster mushrooms, to the pan with the sage. Cook for about 6 minutes until they are tender. Stir in the oyster mushrooms, parsley and seasoning. Cook for a further 2 minutes.
6 Meanwhile, cook the spaghettini in a large pan of boiling salted water until *al dente*. Drain thoroughly and return to the pan.
7 Add the mushroom mixture to the pasta and toss lightly to mix. Check the seasoning and serve, topped with Parmesan shavings if wished.

artichoke and mushroom lasagne

Serves 4
Preparation time: 20 minutes
Cooking time: 1 hour 40 minutes
785 cals per serving

45ml (3 tbsp) olive oil
225g (8oz) onions, peeled and roughly chopped
3 garlic cloves, peeled and crushed
25g (1oz) walnuts
1.1kg (2½lb) mixed mushrooms, such as brown-cap and button, quartered
125g (4oz) cherry tomatoes
50g (2oz) butter
50g (2oz) plain flour
1.1 litres (2 pints) milk
2 bay leaves
30ml (2 tbsp) lemon juice
salt and pepper
200g (7oz) chilled fresh lasagne
400g (14oz) can artichoke hearts in water, drained and halved
75g (3oz) Parmesan cheese, freshly grated

1 Heat the oil in a large pan, add the onions and fry gently for 10 minutes until soft. Add the garlic and walnuts and fry for 3-4 minutes.

2 Stir in the mushrooms and cook for 10 minutes. Bubble briskly for a further 10 minutes or until the liquid is totally evaporated. Add the tomatoes and set aside.

3 Melt the butter in a saucepan, add the flour and stir over a low heat for 1 minute. Slowly whisk in the milk to make a smooth sauce. Bring to the boil, add the bay leaves and stir over a gentle heat for 10 minutes. Add the lemon juice and seasoning to taste. Discard the bay leaves.

4 Arrange a layer of lasagne over the base of a greased shallow ovenproof dish. Spoon on half of the mushroom mixture, then half the artichokes. Cover with another layer of lasagne, then half the sauce. Repeat the mushroom and artichoke layers, then top with the rest of the lasagne.

5 Stir the Parmesan into the remaining sauce and spoon over the top. Bake at 200°C/fan oven 190°C (400°F) Mark 6 for 40-50 minutes until golden and bubbling.

mushroom and pasta gratin

A quick and easy gratin of pasta shells and mushrooms under a rich creamy sauce.

Serves 4
Preparation time: 10 minutes
Cooking time: 40-45 minutes
700 cals per serving

225g (8oz) dried pasta shells
salt and freshly ground black pepper
10ml (2 tsp) olive oil
25g (1oz) butter
450g (1lb) button mushrooms, halved, or quartered if large
90ml (3fl oz) brandy (optional)
15ml (1 tbsp) chopped fresh tarragon
15ml (1 tbsp) chopped fresh chives
300ml (½ pint) double cream
50g (2oz) Parmesan cheese, freshly grated

1 Cook the pasta in a large pan of boiling salted water until *al dente*. Drain and immediately refresh under cold water, then drain well and toss with a little oil to prevent sticking.

2 Melt the butter in a large frying pan, add the mushrooms and stir-fry for 4-5 minutes until golden. Add the brandy if using and boil rapidly until only 30ml (2 tbsp) liquid remains. Stir in the chopped herbs and remove from the heat.

3 Toss the mushrooms with the pasta and transfer to a lightly oiled gratin dish. Mix the cream with half of the Parmesan and pour over the pasta. Sprinkle the remaining cheese on top and bake at 190°C/fan oven 180°C (375°F) Mark 5 for 20-25 minutes until bubbling and golden.

penne with broccoli pesto

This original pasta dish makes a sustaining vegetarian supper. It is also a good accompaniment to grilled chicken.

Serves 4
Preparation time: 10 minutes
Cooking time: 30 minutes
535 cals per serving

700g (1½lb) broccoli
salt and freshly ground black pepper
60ml (4 tbsp) olive oil
2 garlic cloves, peeled and chopped
350g (12oz) dried penne or other pasta shapes
45ml (3 tbsp) lemon juice
150ml (¼ pint) double cream
15g (½oz) Parmesan cheese, freshly grated
TO SERVE:
classic basil pesto (optional)
basil leaves, to garnish

1 Trim the thick stalks from the broccoli and divide the tops into small florets.
2 Cook the broccoli in a pan of boiling salted water for 5-6 minutes until tender. Drain, reserving 50ml (2fl oz) cooking liquor. Refresh the broccoli in cold water; drain well.
3 Heat the olive oil in a medium pan, add the chopped garlic and cook for 1-2 minutes. Stir in the broccoli and cook over a medium heat for about 15 minutes, stirring all the time, until the broccoli is reduced to a thick pulp.
4 Meanwhile, cook the pasta in a large pan of boiling salted water until *al dente*. Drain well.
5 Stir the lemon juice and cream into the broccoli mixture and simmer gently for a further 3-4 minutes. Thin the sauce to the consistency of single cream with some of the reserved cooking liquor. Stir in the grated Parmesan and season generously.
6 Toss the pasta with the broccoli pesto. Serve immediately, with a little classic pesto spooned over if desired. Garnish with basil leaves.

four fast pasta sauces

Toss each of these sauces with 350g (12oz) dried pasta, cooked and drained. Each recipe serves 4.

BROCCOLI AND CHILLI Fry 3 chopped garlic cloves in 60ml (4 tbsp) olive oil; add 2.5ml (½ tsp) dried chilli flakes and 450g (1lb) cooked broccoli florets. Add to the pasta, season, drizzle with olive oil and serve with grated Parmesan.

OLIVE AND AUBERGINE Fry 400g (14oz) cubed aubergine in 60ml (4 tbsp) olive oil until soft and brown. Add 3 crushed garlic cloves, 500g (1lb 2oz) passata and 120ml (4fl oz) water. Season, bring to the boil and simmer for 2-3 minutes. Add 25g (1oz) chopped black olives and 30ml (2 tbsp) chopped basil.

SEAFOOD AND PESTO Combine 60ml (4 tbsp) olive oil with 60ml (4 tbsp) ready-made pesto. Add 225g (8oz) cooked peeled prawns and 4 chopped fresh tomatoes. Season to taste.

ARTICHOKE AND MUSHROOM Drain a 250g (9oz) jar of artichoke antipasto, reserving 30ml (2 tbsp) of the oil. Heat this oil in a frying pan and cook 225g (8oz) chopped mushrooms with 2 crushed garlic cloves and 30ml (2 tbsp) chopped fresh rosemary until tender. Mix with the drained artichokes and 150g (5oz) diced mozzarella cheese.

cooking pasta to perfection

Cook pasta in your largest saucepan, using plenty of water. If the pan is too small or you don't use enough water, the pasta will become sticky and stodgy. When cooked, the strands (or shapes) should separate easily and be firm to the bite (*al dente*).

Italians rarely add any oil to the cooking water to prevent sticking – it's not necessary if you're going to mix the pasta and sauce together immediately after cooking. If the pasta is ready before you've finished making the sauce however, toss it with a tablespoon of olive oil after draining to prevent it from sticking together before you're ready to serve the meal.

clam spaghetti

Serves 6
Preparation time: 10 minutes
Cooking time: 12-15 minutes
520 cals per serving

150ml (¼ pint) olive oil
3 garlic cloves, peeled and crushed
150ml (¼ pint) dry white wine
two 400g (14oz) cans chopped tomatoes
salt and freshly ground black pepper
squeeze of lemon juice
450g (1lb) spaghetti or linguine
1.1kg (2½lb) fresh clams in shells, cleaned
chives and chopped parsley, to garnish
lemon wedges, to serve

1 Heat the oil in a large heavy-based pan. Add the garlic and cook for 30 seconds. Add the wine and allow to bubble for 1 minute, then add the tomatoes and bubble for a further 2 minutes. Add salt, pepper and the lemon juice.
2 Cook the pasta in a large pan of boiling salted water until *al dente*. Drain and return to the pan with a little of the cooking liquid.
3 Add the clams to the tomato sauce, cover and simmer for 1 minute or until the shells have opened up; discard any that remain closed.
4 Toss the cooked pasta with the sauce and divide between warmed serving bowls. Add a generous grinding of pepper and garnish with chives and parsley. Serve with lemon wedges.

Note If fresh clams are unavailable, replace with 2 jars of clams. Simply add at stage 3.

mussels with linguine and saffron

Saffron is often used in Mediterranean seafood dishes and, although expensive, only a small amount is needed to impart a great flavour.

Serves 4
Preparation time: 20 minutes
Cooking time: 10-12 minutes
590 cals per serving

350g (12oz) linguine
salt and freshly ground black pepper
25g (1oz) butter
15ml (1 tbsp) olive oil
2 onions, peeled and separated into petals
3 garlic cloves, peeled and chopped
pinch of saffron threads
900g (2lb) fresh mussels in shells, cleaned
100ml (3½fl oz) dry white wine
200ml (7fl oz) crème fraîche
saffron threads and chives, to garnish

1 Cook the linguine in a large pan of boiling salted water until *al dente*.
2 Meanwhile, heat the butter and olive oil in a heavy-based pan, add the onions and cook gently for 10 minutes or until softened. Add the garlic and saffron and cook for 1 minute.
3 Increase the heat, add the mussels and wine, cover with a tight-fitting lid and cook for 3-4 minutes or until the shells have opened. Discard any that remain closed. Add the crème fraîche and stir to heat through.
4 Drain the pasta and add to the mussel and cream mixture, toss together and season to taste. Serve garnished with saffron threads and chives.

Note To prepare mussels, rinse under cold, running water to remove grit and sand, then scrub the shells using a small, stiff brush to remove any barnacles. Pull off the hairy 'beards' and tap any open mussels with the back of a knife; discard any that remain open. Give the mussels a final rinse before cooking.

stir-fried orzo with prawns and thai flavourings

Orzo pasta – also known as puntalette – looks like grains of rice. In this recipe, it is cooked until almost *al dente*, then stir-fried with large prawns and vegetables, together with coconut, coriander and Thai red curry paste. It's an unusual combination, but one that works well.

Serves 4
Preparation time: 15 minutes
Cooking time: 15 minutes
550 cals per serving

225g (8oz) orzo pasta
350g (12oz) large raw or cooked prawns, shelled
15ml (1 tbsp) vegetable oil
5ml (1 tsp) sesame oil
4 shallots, peeled and chopped
1 red pepper, cored, deseeded and thinly sliced
6 spring onions, trimmed and sliced
125g (4oz) sugar snap peas
125g (4oz) creamed coconut, crumbled
20ml (4 tsp) Thai red curry paste
60ml (4 tbsp) chopped fresh coriander

1 Cook the pasta in a large pan of boiling salted water until almost *al dente* (about 1 minute less than the cooking time). Drain, refresh under cold water and set aside.
2 If using raw prawns, slit them down the back and remove the black intestinal vein. Rinse under cold water, drain and pat dry with kitchen paper.
3 Heat the vegetable and sesame oils in a wok or large sauté pan. Add the shallots, pepper and spring onions, and stir-fry for 2-3 minutes until softened.
4 Add the sugar snaps, with the raw prawns if using. Continue to cook for 2-3 minutes, until the prawns have turned pink.
5 Stir in the creamed coconut and curry paste. As soon as the coconut cream has melted, add 100ml (3½fl oz) water, the pasta and cooked prawns if using. Continue cooking and stirring for a further 1-2 minutes until the pasta is heated through. Stir in the coriander and serve.

pasta with fresh crab and ginger

For this recipe, you do not necessarily have to prepare a whole crab. Many fishmongers and supermarket fresh fish counters sell ready-dressed crab or vacuum-packed fresh crab meat. However, the quality of ready-prepared crabmeat can be variable – seek out a reliable source!

Serves 4-6
Preparation time: 10 minutes
Cooking time: 8-10 minutes
705-460 cals per serving

450g (1lb) mixed white and brown fresh crab meat, or a 1.5kg (3lb) crab, dressed
juice of 2 lemons
90ml (6 tbsp) extra-virgin olive oil
1 small red onion, peeled and thinly sliced
2 garlic cloves, peeled and crushed
5ml (1 tsp) grated fresh root ginger
grated rind of 1 lemon
pinch of crushed red chillies
450g (1lb) fresh, or 400g (14oz) dried linguine
salt and freshly ground black pepper
60ml (4 tbsp) chopped fresh parsley
TO SERVE:
lemon wedges
extra-virgin olive oil (optional)

1 Flake through the crab meat to ensure there are no pieces of shell remaining, then toss in the lemon juice.
2 Heat the oil in a large frying pan, add the onion, garlic, ginger, lemon rind and chillies and stir-fry for 5 minutes until golden.
3 Cook the pasta in a large pan of boiling salted water until *al dente*; fresh linguine will only take about 1 minute.
4 Meanwhile, add the crab to the frying pan, stir well and heat through for 1-2 minutes.
5 Drain the pasta, reserving 60ml (4 tbsp) of the cooking water. Add the reserved pasta and water to the crab mixture, together with the parsley. Toss over the heat for 30 seconds. Season with salt and pepper to taste. Serve at once, with lemon wedges, drizzling a little extra olive oil over each portion, if wished.

pasta with salmon and dill

This dish combines the distinctive flavours of fresh and smoked salmon to delicious effect. It is important to add the smoked salmon at the end of cooking in order to preserve its texture and flavour. If preferred, use tagliatelle, linguine, or paglia e fieno instead of pasta shells.

Serves 4-6
Preparation time: 15 minutes
Cooking time: 18-20 minutes
1000-670 cals per serving

300g (10oz) fresh salmon fillet, skinned
125g (4oz) sliced smoked salmon
40g (1½oz) butter
1 onion, peeled and chopped
250ml (8fl oz) dry white wine
30ml (2 tbsp) wholegrain mustard
400g (14oz) dried pasta shells
salt and freshly ground black pepper
300ml (½ pint) extra-thick double cream
30-45ml (2-3 tbsp) chopped fresh dill
TO GARNISH:
dill sprigs
toasted pine nuts, for sprinkling (optional)

1 Cut the fresh salmon fillet into 2.5cm (1 inch) cubes. Cut the smoked salmon into strips.
2 Melt the butter in a large frying pan. Add the onion and cook over a medium heat for about 7 minutes until soft and golden. Stir in the wine and mustard and bring to the boil. Cook for 5-7 minutes until reduced by about half.
3 Meanwhile, cook the pasta in a large pan of boiling salted water until *al dente*.
4 Add the cream to the sauce and simmer for 1 minute, then lower the heat. Add the fresh salmon and cook gently for 2-3 minutes until firm. Stir in the dill and season with pepper. Remove from the heat.
5 Drain the cooked pasta. Toss with the sauce and smoked salmon strips. Serve at once, garnished with tiny sprigs of dill and sprinkled with toasted pine nuts, if wished.

shellfish pasta with roasted cherry tomatoes

Roasting cherry tomatoes intensifies the flavour and accentuates their natural sweetness. The soft roasted tomatoes are tossed into pasta – together with roasted onions and a medley of seafood. The result tastes as good as it looks!

Serves 4-6
Preparation time: 30 minutes
Cooking time: 1-1¼ hours
760-505 cals per serving

4 medium-small onions, peeled
450g (1lb) cherry tomatoes
75ml (5 tbsp) extra-virgin olive oil
15ml (1 tbsp) chopped fresh thyme
salt and freshly ground black pepper
1 kg (2lb) mussels in shells
12 large raw prawns
450g (1lb) squid, cleaned
3-4 garlic cloves, peeled and sliced
175ml (6fl oz) dry white wine
few parsley stalks
400g (14oz) dried spaghetti
chopped fresh parsley, to garnish

1 Cut each onion into 6 wedges, leaving the root end intact. Arrange the onions in one layer in a roasting tin. Halve the cherry tomatoes and arrange cut-side up in the tin. Drizzle over 45ml (3 tbsp) of the olive oil and sprinkle with the thyme, and salt and pepper. Roast in the oven at 200°C/fan oven 190°C (400°F) Mark 6 for 1-1¼ hours until the onions are tender; the tomatoes will be soft.
2 Meanwhile, prepare the shellfish. Scrub the mussels thoroughly under cold running water and pull off the beards. Discard any mussels with cracked or broken shells and those which do not close when tapped firmly. Wash the prawns and remove the black intestinal vein, but leave them whole. Slice the squid.
3 About 20 minutes before serving, heat 30ml (2 tbsp) oil in a large saucepan, add the garlic and cook over a medium heat for 1 minute. Add the wine and parsley stalks, bring to the boil and cook for 2 minutes.

4 Add the prawns to the pan and cook gently, covered, for 2 minutes. Add the squid and cook for a further 1-2 minutes until both are cooked. Transfer with a slotted spoon to a plate; set aside.

5 Add the mussels to the pan, cover and cook for 3-4 minutes, shaking the pan frequently, until they open. Drain, reserving the liquid but discarding the garlic and parsley. Discard any mussels which have not opened. Strain the liquor through a muslin-lined sieve and return to the pan with the cooked shellfish.

6 Meanwhile, cook the pasta in a large pan of boiling salted water until almost *al dente*, about 1 minute less than the suggested cooking time. Drain thoroughly, then return to the pan. Add the cooked shellfish and cooking liquor, toss to mix and heat through gently for 1 minute.

7 Add the roasted onion and cherry tomato mixture to the pan and toss lightly. Adjust the seasoning and serve at once, sprinkled with chopped parsley.

spaghettini carbonara with salami crisps

Crisp fried salami strips give this ever-popular pasta dish with its rich smoky flavour and light, soft scrambled egg texture a delicious new twist.

Serves 4
Preparation time: 15 minutes
Cooking time: 15 minutes
825 cals per serving

2 large eggs, plus 2 large egg yolks
90ml (6 tbsp) single cream
2 garlic cloves, peeled and crushed
50g (2oz) Parmesan cheese, freshly grated
salt and freshly ground black pepper
30ml (2 tbsp) sunflower oil
125g (4oz) Italian salami, cut into thin strips
3 red onions, peeled and cut into wedges
350g (12oz) spaghettini, or other fine pasta
Parmesan cheese shavings, to serve

1 Place the eggs, egg yolks, cream, garlic and Parmesan cheese in a bowl and beat together until smooth. Season generously with salt and pepper and set aside.

2 Heat the oil in a large frying pan. Add the salami strips and cook, stirring, for 5 minutes until golden and crisp. Remove with a slotted spoon and drain on kitchen paper.

3 Add the onions to the pan and fry briskly for 5 minutes or until crisp: drain on kitchen paper.

4 Cook the spaghettini in a large pan of boiling salted water until *al dente*. Drain and return to the pan. Add the egg mixture and toss well. Stir over a low heat for about 2 minutes until the sauce thickens slightly. Season with plenty of pepper.

5 Divide the pasta between serving bowls and top with the salami strips and onion. Scatter with Parmesan shavings to serve.

Note This recipe isn't suitable for those who should avoid lightly cooked eggs, owing to the slight risk of salmonella.

pappardelle with frazzled prosciutto and asparagus

A delicious combination of flavours and textures. For a less substantial dish, omit the goat's cheese.

Serves 4-6
Preparation time: 30 minutes
Cooking time: About 12 minutes
850-565 cals per serving

350g (12oz) frozen young broad beans, thawed
350g (12oz) asparagus, trimmed
90ml (6 tbsp) extra-virgin olive oil
175g (6oz) prosciutto or Parma ham, in thin slices
3 shallots, peeled and finely chopped
2 garlic cloves, peeled and crushed
400g (14oz) dried pappardelle or tagliatelle
45ml (3 tbsp) chopped fresh parsley
salt and freshly ground black pepper
300g (10oz) goat's cheese log, with rind

1 Slip the broad beans out of their waxy outer skins into a bowl and set aside.
2 Cook the asparagus in a pan of boiling water for about 4 minutes until almost tender. Drain and refresh under cold running water; drain well. Cut into 5cm (2 inch) lengths; set aside.
3 Heat the oil in a large frying pan. Fry the prosciutto, in batches if necessary, over a high heat for a few seconds; remove and set aside.
4 Add the shallots and garlic to the frying pan and cook gently for 5 minutes to soften; do not allow to brown. Increase the heat to medium and add the broad beans. Cook, stirring, for 4 minutes.
5 Meanwhile, cook the pasta in a large pan of boiling salted water until *al dente*.
6 Add the asparagus to the frying pan with the parsley. Cook, stirring, for 2 minutes, then return the prosciutto to the pan. Season with salt and pepper. Remove from the heat.
7 Meanwhile, cut the goat's cheese into slices and place on a lightly greased baking sheet. Grill under a preheated hot grill for 3-4 minutes until lightly browned.
8 Drain the pasta thoroughly and toss with the prosciutto mixture. Arrange on warmed serving plates and top with the grilled goat's cheese. Serve at once.

pasta with chorizo

Chorizo, the spicy Spanish sausage liberally flavoured with paprika, is available both raw by the piece, and cured ready to slice and eat. If you are unable to buy it raw in one piece, use cured chorizo – sold pre-packed in supermarkets – and cook in the sauce for 5 minutes only.

Serves 4-6
Preparation time: 10 minutes
Cooking time: About 50 minutes
950-630 cals per serving

30ml (2 tbsp) olive oil
1 onion, peeled and finely chopped
2 garlic cloves, peeled and crushed
30ml (2 tbsp) tomato paste
30ml (2 tbsp) mild paprika
1 dried chilli
2 bay leaves
2 fresh thyme sprigs
2 fresh rosemary sprigs
150ml (¼ pint) dry red wine
425g (15oz) can chopped tomatoes
salt and freshly ground black pepper
450g (1lb) raw chorizo sausage, in one piece
400-450g (14 oz-1lb) fresh or dried pasta
chopped parsley, to garnish

1 Heat the oil in a heavy-based saucepan, add the onion and garlic and sauté for about 5 minutes or until softened. Add the tomato paste and paprika and cook for 2 minutes, stirring all the time.
2 Crumble in the chilli, then add the bay leaves, thyme and rosemary. Pour in the wine and bring to the boil. Cook for 2 minutes, stirring. Add the tomatoes with their juice and bring to the boil again. Lower the heat and simmer gently for 30 minutes. Season with salt and pepper to taste.
3 Cut the chorizo sausage into thick slices and add to the sauce. Cook for 15 minutes.
4 Meanwhile, cook the pasta in a large pan of boiling salted water until *al dente*. Drain thoroughly. Serve at once, topped with the sauce and sprinkled with plenty of chopped parsley.

Serves 4
Preparation time: 10 minutes
Cooking time: About 1 hour
Suitable for freezing (sauce only)
540 cals per serving

400g (14oz) dried spaghetti
FOR THE BOLOGNESE SAUCE:
15ml (1 tbsp) olive oil
1 large onion, peeled and finely chopped
1 carrot, peeled and finely chopped
1 celery stick, finely chopped
1 garlic clove, peeled and crushed
125g (4oz) button mushrooms, chopped
450g (1lb) minced beef
300ml (½ pint) dry red or white wine
300ml (½ pint) beef stock
400g (14oz) can chopped tomatoes
15ml (1 tbsp) tomato paste
10ml (2 tsp) dried oregano
salt and freshly ground black pepper
30ml (2 tbsp) chopped fresh parsley
TO SERVE:
25-50g (1-2oz) Parmesan cheese, freshly pared

1 To make the Bolognese sauce, heat the oil in a frying pan. Add the onion, carrot, celery and garlic, and fry gently for 5 minutes or until softened. Add the mushrooms and fry for 1 minute.
2 Stir in the beef and cook, stirring, over a high heat until browned. Stir in the wine, stock, tomatoes, tomato paste, oregano and seasoning. Bring to the boil, cover and simmer for 1 hour or until the meat is tender and the sauce is well reduced. Check the seasoning and stir in the parsley.
3 Cook the pasta in a large pan of boiling salted water until *al dente*. Drain thoroughly and divide between warmed serving plates. Serve immediately, topped with Parmesan shavings.

rich tomato sauce

Made with fresh tomato and enriched with sun-dried tomato paste, this sauce is substantial enough to serve on plain pasta as a meal, but it is also good served with ready-made filled pastas such as ravioli, tortelloni etc. Full-flavoured ripe, fresh tomatoes give the best result but canned plum tomatoes are a better choice than under-ripe or flavourless fresh ones. You will need 1 kg (2lb) ripe tomatoes, preferably plum, or two 400g (14oz) cans plum tomatoes with their juice.

• Melt 50g (2oz) butter in a saucepan, add 1 finely chopped onion and 2 finely chopped garlic cloves and cook over a medium-low heat for about 8 minutes while preparing the tomatoes.
• If using fresh tomatoes, first skin them. Immerse in a bowl of boiling water for 30 seconds, then drain and refresh under cold running water. Peel away the skins. Quarter the tomatoes, discard the seeds, then roughly chop the flesh. If using canned plum tomatoes, chop them roughly.
• Add the tomatoes to the onion and garlic mixture together with 45ml (3 tbsp) sun-dried tomato paste and 2 oregano sprigs. Cook, uncovered, over a low heat for 25-30 minutes, stirring occasionally, until the sauce is thick and pulpy. Discard the oregano and season with salt and freshly ground black pepper to taste.

spaghetti with spiced meatballs

Serves 4-6
Preparation time: 30 minutes
Cooking time: 20 minutes
Suitable for freezing (stage 4)
965-645 cals per serving

350g (12oz) shoulder of pork
175g (6oz) piece of gammon
175g (6oz) belly pork
2 garlic cloves, peeled
5ml (1 tsp) coarse sea salt
5ml (1 tsp) granulated sugar
15ml (1 tbsp) coarsely crushed black pepper
5ml (1 tsp) fennel seeds
1.25ml (¼ tsp) dried chilli flakes
30ml (2 tbsp) oil
1 quantity Rich Tomato Sauce (see left)
450g (1lb) dried spaghetti
oregano sprigs, to garnish
freshly grated Parmesan cheese, to serve

1 Trim the shoulder of pork, gammon and belly pork of any skin or connective tissue, then cut into rough chunks. Place the meat in a food processor, add all the remaining ingredients and process until smooth. The sausagemeat is ready to use at this stage, but it can be covered and left to mature in the fridge overnight if preferred.
2 With moist hands, roll the sausagemeat into small, even-sized balls.
3 Heat the oil in a heavy-based frying pan and fry the meatballs in batches if necessary until evenly browned.
4 Pour over the tomato sauce, bring to the boil, lower the heat and simmer for 10-15 minutes.
5 Meanwhile, cook the pasta in a large pan of boiling salted water until *al dente*. Drain well and toss with the spiced meatballs and tomato sauce. Serve garnished with oregano and topped with grated Parmesan.

Variation For a quicker version of the meatballs, replace the above meats with 450g (1lb) minced pork and 225g (8oz) unsmoked streaky bacon, derinded and finely chopped.

classic italian lasagne

Many regions of Italy have their own lasagne recipe and this one comes from the Marche region which borders Tuscany.

Serves 6
Preparation time: 20 minutes
Cooking time: About 2 hours
Suitable for freezing
745 cals per serving

350g (12oz) fresh egg lasagne or 225g (8oz) dried 'no need to pre-cook' lasagne (about 12 sheets)

FOR THE MEAT SAUCE:
10g (⅓oz) dried porcini mushrooms
15ml (1 tbsp) olive oil
275g (10oz) onion, peeled and finely chopped
75g (3oz) carrot, peeled and finely chopped
75g (3oz) celery, finely chopped
125g (4oz) brown-cap or large button mushrooms, chopped
2 garlic cloves, peeled and crushed
450g (1lb) minced beef
125g (4oz) rindless streaky bacon, chopped
300ml (½ pint) dry white wine
300ml (½ pint) beef or vegetable stock
15ml (1 tbsp) tomato paste
10ml (2 tsp) dried oregano
125g (4oz) chicken livers, trimmed and chopped
90ml (6 tbsp) double cream
30ml (2 tbsp) chopped fresh parsley
salt and freshly ground black pepper

FOR THE WHITE SAUCE:
50g (2oz) butter
40g (1½oz) flour
750ml (1¼ pints) milk
60ml (4 tbsp) double cream

TO FINISH:
50-75g (2-3oz) Parmesan cheese, freshly grated

1 To prepare the meat sauce, put the dried porcini in a bowl, pour on 100ml (3½fl oz) water and leave to soak for about 30 minutes.

2 Heat the oil in a frying pan. Add the onion, carrot and celery and fry gently for 5 minutes or until softened. Add the fresh mushrooms and garlic; fry for 1 minute.

3 Stir in the beef and bacon; cook, stirring, over a high heat until browned. Stir in the wine, stock, tomato paste and oregano. Bring to the boil, cover and simmer for 45 minutes.

4 Meanwhile make the white sauce. Melt the butter in a large saucepan, add the flour and cook, stirring, for 1 minute. Off the heat, gradually whisk in the milk. Return to the heat. Bring to the boil, stirring, and simmer for 3-4 minutes or until thickened. Season with salt and pepper to taste. Stir in the cream. Set aside.

5 Uncover the meat mixture, stir in the dried mushrooms with their liquor and the chicken livers. Simmer for 7-10 minutes, until the livers are cooked and the liquid is reduced by half. Add the cream and parsley and allow to bubble for 1 minute. Check the seasoning.

6 Grease a 2.3 litre (4 pint) rectangular or square ovenproof dish with butter. Spread a thin layer of white sauce over the base of the dish, then layer the pasta, meat, white sauce and Parmesan in the dish to make 3 layers of each. Ensure that the top is well covered with white sauce and a generous sprinkling of Parmesan. Cook in the oven at 190°C/fan oven 180°C (375°F) Mark 5 for 1 hour, covering the top loosely with foil after about 20 minutes when the top is browned and bubbling.

Notes
- If using 'no need to precook' lasagne, add a little extra stock to the meat sauce and a little extra milk to the white sauce.
- To prepare ahead, make both sauces the day before; cover and refrigerate separately. Warm the sauces through before layering up with the pasta as in stage 6.

pappardelle with chicken, parma ham and tarragon

Serves 4
Preparation time: 10 minutes
Cooking time: 25 minutes
690 cals per serving

25g (1oz) unsalted butter
4 skinless chicken breasts, about 450g (1lb) in total,
    cut into thin strips
5ml (1 tsp) olive oil
175g (6oz) prosciutto or Parma ham, torn into pieces
300ml (½ pint) chicken stock
150ml (¼ pint) double cream
salt and freshly ground black pepper
350g (12oz) pappardelle or other ribbon pasta
juice of ½ lemon
45ml (3 tbsp) chopped fresh tarragon
tarragon leaves and crushed black pepper, to garnish

1 Heat half of the butter in a non-stick frying pan
   until foaming and fry half of the chicken over a
   moderate heat for 5-6 minutes until golden. Lift
   the chicken from the pan with a slotted spoon
   and set aside. Repeat with the remaining butter
   and chicken, then remove and set aside.
2 Add the oil to the pan and heat gently. Fry the
   Parma ham in batches for about 5 minutes until
   brown. Remove and set aside.
3 Add the stock to the pan, bring to the boil and
   bubble for about 4 minutes or until reduced by
   half. Add the cream and cook for 3-4 minutes or
   until syrupy.
4 Meanwhile, cook the pasta in a large saucepan of
   boiling salted water until *al dente*; drain.
5 Return the chicken to the frying pan and add
   the lemon juice and tarragon. Stir to heat
   through and season with salt and pepper to
   taste. Add the pasta and Parma ham to the
   chicken and toss well. Serve garnished with
   tarragon and pepper.

Note Pappardelle are broad, flat noodles made
from egg pasta, sometimes with wavy edges.

Variation For a cheaper alternative to Parma ham,
use 225g (8oz) unsmoked bacon lardons.

linguine with chicken livers and vermouth

Serve this rich, sustaining dish accompanied by a
salad, or steamed French beans.

Serves 4
Preparation time: 10 minutes
Cooking time: 12 minutes
830 cals per serving

700g (1½lb) chicken livers
400g (14oz) dried linguine
salt and freshly ground black pepper
45ml (3 tbsp) vegetable oil
6 spring onions, trimmed and sliced
5ml (1 tsp) cornflour
150ml (¼ pint) dry vermouth
30ml (2 tbsp) chopped fresh sage
50g (2oz) butter, cubed

1 Trim any fat and white membrane from the
   chicken livers. Rinse the livers and pat dry with
   kitchen paper.
2 Cook the pasta in a large pan of boiling salted
   water until *al dente*.
3 Meanwhile, heat the oil in a frying pan until
   smoking. Add the spring onions, followed by the
   chicken livers. Fry, stirring, for about 2 minutes
   until the livers are evenly browned, then
   sprinkle over the cornflour and stir in. Pour on
   the vermouth, add the sage, cover and cook for
   2 minutes. Season with salt and pepper to taste.
4 Drain the pasta thoroughly, toss with the butter
   and pile into a warmed serving dish. Pour over
   the chicken liver sauce and serve at once.

beef with pak choi and noodles

Noodles are a great time-saving ingredient and quicker to cook than either pasta or rice.

Serves 4
Preparation time: 15 minutes
Cooking time: 6-10 minutes
305 cals per serving

60ml (4 tbsp) dark soy sauce
5ml (1 tsp) hot horseradish sauce
2.5cm (1 inch) piece fresh root ginger, chopped
juice of ½ lime
2 sirloin steaks, each about 175g (6oz)
200g (7oz) egg noodles
45ml (3 tbsp) oil
4 spring onions, trimmed and sliced
200g (7oz) pak choi or young spinach, thickly sliced
salt and freshly ground black pepper
15ml (1 tbsp) sesame seeds, toasted, to garnish

1 Combine the soy sauce, horseradish sauce, ginger and lime juice in a bowl. Spoon half of the mixture over the steaks; set aside the remainder.
2 Cook the noodles according to the packet instructions. Drain, rinse under cold water and set aside.
3 Heat 15ml (1 tbsp) oil in a non-stick frying pan. Fry the steaks for 2 minutes on each side for medium rare, or 3-4 minutes if you prefer them well done; remove and set aside.
4 Wipe out the pan, then add the remaining oil and heat. Add the spring onions and cook for 1 minute. Add the pak choi and noodles and cook for 1 minute or until the pak choi is just wilting and the noodles are warmed through. Season with salt and pepper to taste.
5 Slice the steak into 1cm (½ inch) strips, then add to the noodles and pak choi. Pour on the reserved dressing and serve, sprinkled with sesame seeds.

Note Available from major supermarkets, pak choi (or bok choi) has long green leaves and white stalks. If you can't find it, use fresh spinach.

oriental noodles

Serve this simple noodle dish as a fast snack, or with stir-fried or grilled vegetables as a light meal.

Serves 4
Preparation time: 10 minutes
Cooking time: 12-15 minutes
360 cals per serving

250g (9oz) packet medium egg noodles
60ml (4 tbsp) light olive oil
10ml (2 tsp) sesame oil
2 garlic cloves, peeled and sliced
2.5ml (½ tsp) grated fresh root ginger
2 small red chillies, deseeded and finely chopped
grated rind and juice of 1 lime
30-45ml (2-3 tbsp) chopped fresh coriander
15-30ml (1-2 tbsp) chopped fresh basil
salt and freshly ground black pepper
coriander sprigs, to garnish

pad thai

1 Bring a large saucepan of salted water to the boil, add the egg noodles and remove from the heat. Leave to stand for 4 minutes; the noodles will cook in the residual heat. Drain, reserving 90ml (6 tbsp) of the cooking water. Immediately refresh under cold water, then drain well and toss the noodles with a little oil to prevent sticking; set aside.

2 Heat the two oils together in a large wok. Add the garlic, ginger, chillies and lime rind and fry gently for about 30 seconds until the garlic starts to release its aroma. Whisk in the reserved 90ml (6 tbsp) water and bring to the boil.

3 Stir the egg noodles into the sauce with the chopped herbs and lime juice and toss over the heat for a few seconds until heated through. Season with salt and pepper to taste and serve immediately, garnished with coriander sprigs.

Serves 4
Preparation time: 20 minutes
Cooking time: 8-10 minutes
410 cals per serving

225g (8oz) plain tofu
vegetable oil, for deep-frying
125g (4oz) flat rice or egg noodles
30ml (2 tbsp) sunflower oil
2 eggs, lightly beaten
salt and freshly ground black pepper
1 garlic clove, peeled and crushed
2 red chillies, deseeded and chopped
6 spring onions, trimmed and sliced
50g (2oz) bean sprouts
30ml (2 tbsp) smooth peanut butter
30ml (2 tbsp) dark soy sauce
30ml (2 tbsp) lime juice
15ml (1 tbsp) sugar
60ml (4 tbsp) water
15ml (1 tbsp) chopped fresh coriander
15ml (1 tbsp) chopped fresh mint

1 Cut the tofu into 2.5cm (1 inch) cubes and drain well on kitchen paper. Heat the oil in a deep saucepan until it registers 180°C (350°F) on a sugar thermometer or until a cube of bread dropped in crisps in 30 seconds. Deep-fry the tofu in batches for 2-3 minutes until golden; drain on kitchen paper and set aside.

2 Cook the noodles according to the packet instructions; drain. Refresh under cold water, drain and dry well.

3 Heat half of the sunflower oil in a large frying pan. Season the eggs with a little salt and pepper and swirl into the pan. Cook over a gentle heat until the omelette is just set, then remove from the pan. Let cool slightly, then cut into thin strips; set aside.

4 Heat the remaining oil in a large wok, add the garlic, chillies, spring onions and bean sprouts and stir-fry for 1 minute.

5 Put the peanut butter, soy sauce, lime juice, sugar and water in another pan and heat gently until smooth.

6 Add the noodles to the wok with the tofu. Stir in the sauce and toss over the heat until the noodles are well coated with the sauce. Add the egg strips and herbs. Serve immediately.

rice & grains

Tempting creamy risottos,
saffron spiced paellas and
pilafs, plus a selection of
fragrant couscous dishes and
tasty ways to serve polenta

spinach risotto

A tasty, colourful risotto – ideal for a quick and effortless midweek supper.

Serves 4
Preparation time: 10 minutes
Cooking time: 30 minutes
345 cals per serving

25g (1oz) butter
1 onion, peeled and finely chopped
1 garlic clove, peeled and sliced
225g (8oz) arborio rice
salt and freshly ground black pepper
750ml (1¼ pints) vegetable stock
400g (14oz) fresh spinach leaves, trimmed and
    chopped, or 125g (4oz) frozen leaf spinach
60ml (4 tbsp) freshly grated Parmesan cheese
extra Parmesan cheese, to serve

1 Melt the butter in a heavy-based saucepan. Add the onion and garlic and cook for about 5 minutes or until the onion is beginning to soften.
2 Add the rice, salt and pepper and cook, stirring, for about 2 minutes. Add just enough stock to cover the rice and continue cooking, stirring all the time until most of the stock has been absorbed. Continue adding the stock in this way until it is completely absorbed and the rice is tender.
3 Squeeze the excess liquid from the frozen spinach, if using. Stir the fresh or frozen spinach into the rice. Heat through for 1-2 minutes or until the fresh spinach is just wilted.
4 Remove from the heat and stir in the Parmesan. Adjust the seasoning and serve immediately, with extra Parmesan.

risotto rice

Arborio rice is the classic Italian risotto variety with plump medium grains. It has the capacity to absorb plenty of liquid during cooking without turning mushy. Once cooked, arborio has a wonderfully creamy texture, whilst still retaining a slight bite. Carnaroli is another excellent Italian risotto rice.

baby onion and pea risotto

Serves 4
Preparation time: 30 minutes
Cooking time: 35 minutes
495 cals per serving

225g (8oz) baby onions
50g (2oz) butter
30ml (2 tbsp) olive oil
4 garlic cloves, peeled
30ml (2 tbsp) chopped fresh sage
10ml (2 tsp) soft brown sugar
5ml (1 tsp) sea salt
225g (8oz) arborio rice
150ml (¼ pint) red wine
60ml (2fl oz) port (optional)
900 ml-1.2 litres (1½-2 pints) vegetable stock
300g (10oz) fresh peas in the pod, shelled, or 125g
    (4oz) frozen peas, thawed
15-30ml (1-2 tbsp) olive paste
25g (1oz) Parmesan cheese, freshly grated

1 Put the onions in a pan, cover with cold water and bring to the boil. Simmer for 30 seconds, then drain, refresh under cold water and peel.
2 Melt half the butter with the oil in a frying pan. Add the onions and garlic cloves and fry over a medium heat for 15 minutes, stirring occasionally, until caramelised. Stir in the sage, sugar and salt and fry for a further 10 minutes.
3 Meanwhile, melt remaining butter in a heavy-based frying pan. Add the rice and stir-fry for 1-2 minutes until glossy. Add the wine, and port if using, and boil rapidly until well reduced.
4 Heat the stock in a small pan; keep at a gentle simmer. Gradually add to the rice, a ladleful at a time, stirring constantly and ensuring each addition is absorbed before adding the next. Continue for about 20 minutes, until most stock has been added and the rice is almost cooked.
5 Add the onion mixture to the rice with the remaining stock and fresh peas (if using) and continue to cook, stirring, until the liquid is absorbed and the rice is just tender. Stir in frozen peas (if using) towards the end.
6 Off the heat, stir in the olive paste and most of the Parmesan. Season, cover and let stand for 5 minutes. Serve topped with remaining cheese.

wild mushroom risotto

Serves 4
Preparation time: 25 minutes, plus soaking
Cooking time: 30 minutes
550 cals per serving

15g (½oz) dried porcini mushrooms
90ml (6 tbsp) extra-virgin olive oil
1 red onion, peeled and finely chopped
2 garlic cloves, peeled and finely chopped
10ml (2 tsp) chopped fresh thyme
5ml (1 tsp) grated lemon rind
350g (12oz) arborio rice
150ml (¼ pint) dry white wine
900ml (1½ pints) vegetable stock
450g (1lb) mixed fresh mushrooms, such as oyster,
    shiitake, ceps, halved or sliced if large
25g (1oz) Parmesan cheese, freshly grated
30ml (2 tbsp) chopped fresh parsley
salt and freshly ground black pepper
extra Parmesan cheese, to serve (optional)

1 Soak the porcini in 150ml (¼ pint) boiling water for 20 minutes, then drain and finely chop; strain and reserve the liquid.
2 Heat half the oil in a heavy-based pan. Add the porcini, onion, garlic, thyme and lemon rind and fry for 5 minutes to soften. Add the rice and stir-fry for 1 minute until the grains are glossy.
3 Add the wine and boil rapidly until almost totally evaporated. In the meantime, put the stock and mushroom liquid in a separate pan and bring to a steady, low simmer.
4 Gradually add the stock to the rice, a ladleful at a time, ensuring it is absorbed before adding more, stirring constantly. Continue until the rice is tender; this will take about 20 minutes; it may not be necessary to add all of the stock.
5 About 5 minutes before the rice will be ready, heat the remaining oil in a large frying pan and stir-fry the mushrooms over a high heat for 4-5 minutes.
6 Immediately stir the mushrooms into the rice with the Parmesan and parsley. Season with salt and pepper to taste and serve at once, with extra Parmesan if wished.

pumpkin and barley risotto

Serves 4
Preparation time: 20 minutes
Cooking time: 35 minutes, plus resting
560 cals per serving

60ml (4 tbsp) extra-virgin olive oil
2 leeks, trimmed and thinly sliced
2 garlic cloves, peeled and finely chopped
1 red chilli, deseed and finely diced
15ml (1 tbsp) finely chopped fresh rosemary
15ml (1 tbsp) chopped fresh sage
350g (12oz) pearl barley
1.2 litres (2 pints) vegetable stock
450g (1lb) peeled and deseeded pumpkin, diced
65g (2½oz) Parmesan cheese, freshly grated
60ml (4 tbsp) double cream
salt and freshly ground black pepper

1 Heat the oil in a large saucepan, add the leeks, garlic, chilli and herbs and fry for 5 minutes until softened.
2 Add the barley and stir-fry for 1 minute until all the grains are glossy.
3 Meanwhile bring the vegetable stock to a steady simmer in another saucepan.
4 Add the pumpkin to the barley and stir well. Pour in 150ml (¼ pint) of the hot stock and stir over a medium heat until absorbed.
5 Gradually add the remaining simmering stock a ladleful at a time, stirring occasionally, and making sure each addition is absorbed before adding the next. Continue until the barley is tender and all the stock absorbed; this will take about 30 minutes.
6 Remove from the heat and stir in most of the Parmesan with the cream. Cover and allow to stand for 5 minutes. Season with salt and pepper to taste and serve at once, with topped with the remaining Parmesan.

Variation

PUMPKIN AND BARLEY BAKE Follow the recipe to the end of step 2. Add the pumpkin and 900ml (1½ pints) stock, bring to the boil and transfer to a deep baking dish. Cover with foil and bake in the oven at 180°C/fan oven 170°C (350°F) Mark 4 for about 1 hour. Remove foil, scatter some grated Parmesan over the top and grill until golden.

pearl barley

Pearl barley – the polished barley grain – is typically added to soups and stews. However it works well in a vegetarian risotto, such as this one, as it has a creamy cooked texture similar to arborio rice.

risotto galette

Rich, soft Italian taleggio with its wonderful melting texture makes a delicious filling for this risotto 'cake'. Use either mozzarella or fontina as an alternative if you are unable to find taleggio.

Serves 6-8
Preparation time: 15 minutes, plus cooling
Cooking time: 1 hour
540-405 cals per serving

large pinch of saffron strands
900ml (2 pints) hot vegetable stock
50g (2oz) butter
1 onion, peeled and finely chopped
3 garlic cloves, peeled and crushed
350g (12oz) arborio rice
120ml (4fl oz) dry white wine
60ml (4 tbsp) chopped mixed fresh herbs, such as
    basil, chives, parsley and tarragon
25g (1oz) Parmesan or Cheddar cheese, freshly grated
2 large eggs, beaten
225g (8oz) derinded taleggio cheese, diced
salt and freshly ground black pepper
oil, for shallow-frying

1 Infuse the saffron strands in the hot stock for 10 minutes, then transfer to a saucepan.
2 Melt the butter in a large heavy-based frying pan, add the onion and garlic and fry gently for 10 minutes until soft and golden.
3 Add the rice and cook, stirring, for 1 minute until the grains are glossy. Add the wine and boil rapidly until almost totally evaporated. Heat the saffron infused stock and keep at a low simmer.
4 Add a ladleful of the saffron stock to the rice. Simmer gently, stirring constantly, until it is absorbed. Continue to add the stock and stir the rice for 20-25 minutes until all the liquid is used up and the rice is just cooked.
5 Remove from the heat; stir in the herbs and Parmesan or Cheddar. Cover the surface with a piece of greaseproof paper and leave to cool.
6 Stir the eggs into the risotto, then divide the mixture in half. Gently heat a little oil in a 23cm (9 inch) non-stick (grillproof) frying pan. Spoon half the risotto into the pan and spread evenly to the edges with a palette knife. Sprinkle over the taleggio.
7 Carefully spread the remaining risotto on top and cook over a low heat for 20 minutes until golden underneath.
8 Position the frying pan under the grill and cook for 10 minutes until the top is golden all over. Turn out onto a large plate and allow to cool slightly for 10-15 minutes. Serve warm, cut into wedges, accompanied by a green salad.

oven-baked thai chicken risotto

An easy 'cheat's' risotto which is left to cook in the oven rather than stirred on the hob.

Serves 4
Preparation time: 10 minutes
Cooking time: 35 minutes
950 cals per serving

8 skinless, boneless chicken thighs
30ml (2 tbsp) oil
2 onions, peeled and roughly chopped
225g (8oz) arborio or other risotto rice
330ml (11fl oz) jar Thai red or green curry sauce
600ml (1 pint) boiling water
salt and freshly ground black pepper
handful of fresh coriander leaves

1 Cut the chicken into large pieces, discarding the bones; set aside.
2 Heat the oil in a large, shallow flameproof dish. Add the onions and fry gently for about 5 minutes until light golden. Add the chicken pieces to the pan and cook for 2 minutes.
3 Add the risotto rice and stir to coat with the oil. Add the Thai curry sauce, then half of the water and bring to the boil.
4 Cook, uncovered, in the oven at 200°C/fan oven 190°C (400°F) Mark 6 for 10 minutes. Stir in the remaining 300ml (½ pint) boiling water and return to the oven for a further 20 minutes or until all the liquid has been absorbed and the rice is tender, stirring from time to time. Check the seasoning.
5 Add the coriander leaves and fork through just before serving. Serve with a green salad.

mozzarella rice balls

These are a good way to use up leftover risotto, but worth making from scratch too. Serve with a salad as a supper, or alone as a filling snack.

Serves 4
Preparation time: 45 minutes
Cooking time: 10-15 minutes
765 cals per serving

75g (3oz) butter
1 red onion, peeled and finely copped
150ml (¼ pint) dry white wine
275g (10oz) arborio rice
1 litre (1¾ pints) vegetable stock
salt and freshly ground black pepper
25g (1oz) freshly grated Parmesan cheese
2 eggs, beaten
about 16 small basil leaves
125g (4oz) mozzarella cheese, cut into small cubes
125g (4oz) dried white breadcrumbs
oil, for deep-frying

1 To make the risotto, melt the butter in a large pan, add the onion and fry gently for 5 minutes or until soft but not coloured. Pour in the wine and boil rapidly until almost totally reduced. Add the rice and stir to coat with the butter and wine.
2 Add a ladleful of stock and simmer, stirring, until absorbed. Continue adding stock a ladleful at a time until the rice is tender and creamy but retains some bite; this should take about 20 minutes. Make sure each addition of stock is absorbed before adding the next. Season well and stir in the Parmesan. Leave to cool.
3 Beat the eggs into the cold risotto.
4 With moistened hands, spread 15ml (1 tbsp) risotto in the palm of one hand. Lay a basil leaf and a cube of mozzarella in the middle. Take another 15ml (1 tbsp) of risotto and press over the mozzarella and basil to enclose. Shape into a smooth ball. Repeat to make about 16 in total.
5 Roll the rice balls in the breadcrumbs to coat.
6 Heat the oil in a deep-fryer to 180°C (350°F) or until a crumb dropped in sizzles immediately. Fry the rice balls, a few at a time, for 3-5 minutes until golden and crisp. Drain on kitchen paper; keep hot while cooking the rest. Serve at once.

spanish rice with aïoli

Spanish short-grain rice is sold in Spanish food stores and delicatessens. It is similar to arborio rice, which is therefore a suitable substitute. Refrigerate leftover aïoli and use within 1 week.

Serves 4-6
Preparation time: 20 minutes
Cooking time: 45 minutes
750-500 cals per serving

60ml (4 tbsp) olive oil
2 onions, peeled and chopped
4 garlic cloves, peeled and chopped
10ml (2 tsp) hot paprika
5ml (1 tsp) turmeric
pinch of cayenne pepper
350g (12oz) Spanish short-grain or arborio rice
900ml (1½ pints) hot vegetable stock
450g (1lb) ripe tomatoes, skinned and chopped
30ml (2 tbsp) sun-dried tomato paste
30ml (2 tbsp) chopped fresh parsley
FOR THE AÏOLI:
2-4 garlic cloves, peeled
2.5ml (½ tsp) coarse sea salt
2 egg yolks
15ml (1 tbsp) lemon juice
300ml (½ pint) light olive oil

1 Heat the oil in a large, deep frying pan or saucepan, add the onions, garlic and spices and fry gently for 10 minutes until golden.
2 Add the rice and stir-fry for 1 minute until the grains are glossy. Stir in the stock, bring to the boil and simmer for 10 minutes.
3 Add the tomatoes and tomato paste. Simmer over a low heat for a further 20 minutes or until the liquid is absorbed and the rice is tender. Add a little hot water during cooking if it appears dry.
4 Meanwhile, make the aïoli. Put the garlic, salt, egg yolks and lemon juice in a food processor and blend for 30 seconds until pale and frothy. Then with the motor running, pour in the oil in a steady stream through the feeder tube, until the aïoli is thickened and glossy. Season with salt and pepper to taste.
5 Add the chopped parsley to the rice and fork through. Season with salt and pepper to taste. Serve hot, with the aïoli handed separately.

crisp chicken liver risotto

Serves 4
Preparation time: 15 minutes
Cooking time: 40 minutes
885 cals per serving

50g (2oz) Italian salami, sliced
225g (8oz) rindless streaky bacon rashers, thinly sliced
100g (3½oz) butter
225g (8oz) chicken livers, halved if very large
225g (8oz) onions, peeled and roughly chopped
350g (12oz) arborio rice
30ml (2 tbsp) tomato paste
1.4-1.7 litres (2½-3 pints) chicken or vegetable stock
200ml (7fl oz) white wine
30ml (2 tbsp) finely chopped fresh rosemary
freshly grated Parmesan cheese, to serve
salt and freshly ground black pepper
rosemary sprigs, to garnish

1 Scatter the salami and bacon in an even layer in a large roasting tin. Cook at 200°C/fan oven 190°C (400°F) Mark 6 for 15-20 minutes or until crisp and brown, then drain on kitchen paper.

2 Meanwhile, melt 25g (1oz) butter in a large pan, add the chicken livers and fry briskly for 2-3 minutes. Drain and set aside; wipe out the pan.

3 Melt the remaining butter in the pan, add the onions and cook over a medium heat for 10 minutes until soft. Stir in the rice and tomato paste and cook for 1 minute. Meanwhile, pour the stock and wine into another pan and bring to the boil. Keep at a low simmer.

4 Add a ladleful of the hot liquid to the rice. Cook gently, stirring, until absorbed. Keep adding stock in ladlefuls as each one is absorbed and stirring, until the rice is tender and the risotto is thick and creamy; this should take about 20 minutes.

5 To serve, drain the chicken livers, then add them to the risotto with the chopped rosemary, Parmesan, crisp salami and bacon. Check the seasoning. Stir for 1 minute over the heat then serve, garnished with rosemary.

vegetable and rice tian

A tasty vegetarian bake, with a crunchy breadcrumb, almond and Parmesan topping.

Serves 4
Preparation time: 20 minutes
Cooking time: 1½ hours
310 cals per serving

125g (4oz) long-grain white rice
30ml (2 tbsp) olive oil
1 onion, peeled and chopped
2 garlic cloves, peeled and crushed
5ml (1 tsp) ground cumin
5ml (1 tsp) ground cinnamon
5ml (1 tsp) ground coriander
10ml (2 tsp) chopped fresh thyme
1 each red and yellow pepper, halved, cored,
    deseeded and chopped
1 red chilli, deseeded and finely chopped
2 courgettes, diced
30ml (2 tbsp) sun-dried tomato paste
two 400g (14oz) cans chopped tomatoes
200ml (7fl oz) vegetable stock
5ml (1 tsp) sugar
1 bay leaf
salt and freshly ground black pepper
FOR THE TOPPING:
15g (½oz) ground almonds
15g (½oz) fresh breadcrumbs
15g (½oz) Parmesan cheese, freshly grated (optional)
30ml (2 tbsp) chopped fresh parsley
TO FINISH:
olive oil, for drizzling

1 Put the rice in a bowl, add plenty of cold water to cover and leave to soak for 30 minutes. Drain thoroughly in a sieve and shake dry.
2 Heat the olive oil in a saucepan, add the onion, garlic, spices and thyme and fry gently for 10 minutes, stirring frequently. Add the chopped peppers, chilli and courgettes with a little more oil if necessary. Stir-fry for 5 minutes until lightly golden.
3 Stir in the tomato paste, tomatoes, stock, sugar and bay leaf. Bring to the boil, cover and simmer gently for 30 minutes. Remove the bay leaf. Season with salt and pepper to taste.
4 Spoon half of the vegetables into a lightly oiled baking dish. Sprinkle the rice evenly over the surface, then top with the rest of the vegetables.
5 Cover the dish with foil and bake at 190°C/fan oven 180°C (375°F) Mark 5 for 40 minutes. Meanwhile, mix the topping ingredients together. Remove the foil from the baking dish, sprinkle the topping over the vegetables and drizzle liberally with oil. Bake for a further 15-20 minutes until the topping is golden.
6 Allow to stand for a few minutes before serving.

Variation Omit Parmesan and scatter some grated Cheddar or gruyère over the crumb topping.

fried rice cakes with sage butter

These saffron risotto cakes are enriched with ricotta and served with a fragrant sage butter. Serve them with a salad as a lunch or supper dish, or on their own as a starter or snack.

Serves 6-8
Preparation time: 30 minutes, plus cooling
Cooking time: 50 minutes
525-395 cals per serving

1.2 litres (2 pints) chicken or vegetable stock
large pinch of saffron strands
50g (2oz) butter
1 onion, peeled and chopped
3 garlic cloves, peeled and chopped
10ml (2 tsp) chopped fresh thyme
350g (12oz) arborio rice
150ml (¼ pint) dry white wine
125g (4oz) ricotta cheese
50g (2oz) Parmesan cheese, freshly grated
salt and freshly ground black pepper
FOR THE SAGE BUTTER:
125g (4oz) butter
15ml (1 tbsp) chopped fresh sage
2 ripe tomatoes, skinned, deseeded and diced
15ml (1 tbsp) balsamic vinegar
TO GARNISH:
sage leaves

1 Put the stock and saffron in a saucepan and slowly bring to a gentle simmer.

2 Melt half the butter in a saucepan, add the onion and fry gently for 5 minutes, then add the garlic and thyme and fry for a further 5 minutes. Add the rice, stir for 1 minute, then pour in the wine and let bubble rapidly until it is totally evaporated.

3 Add a ladleful of stock to the rice and cook over a medium heat, stirring constantly until the liquid is absorbed. Continue to add stock, a ladleful at a time, until the rice is cooked.

4 Off the heat, stir in the ricotta and Parmesan; season with salt and pepper to taste. Spread out on a baking sheet and leave until cold.

5 Heat the remaining butter in a non-stick heavy-based frying pan, add the rice pressing flat to the edges and fry over a low heat for 10 minutes. Slide out onto a plate, invert the frying pan over the top, then flip back into the pan. Fry for a further 10 minutes until the underside is golden brown and crisp.

6 Meanwhile, for the sage butter, heat the butter in a small pan and sauté the chopped sage for 2-3 minutes until beginning to turn crisp; stir in the diced tomatoes and balsamic vinegar. Remove from the heat.

7 Turn the rice cake out onto a plate and cut into wedges. Serve drizzled with the sage butter and garnished with sage.

paella

The national dish of Spain, paella is traditionally cooked in a *paellera* – a large open shallow pan. This paella is based on a typical combination of seafood, chicken and chorizo.

Serves 6
Preparation time: 20 minutes
Cooking time: 40 minutes
700 cals per serving

150ml (¼ pint) dry white wine or water
10ml (2 tsp) chopped fresh thyme
salt and freshly ground black pepper
450g (1lb) fresh mussels in shells, cleaned
1.2 litres (2 pints) chicken stock
4 boneless chicken thighs, skinned and quartered
350g (12oz) squid, cleaned and cut into rings
225g (8oz) monkfish fillet, cut into 2.5cm (1 inch) pieces
6 raw king prawns or langoustines
60ml (4 tbsp) olive oil
1 large onion, peeled and chopped
225g (8oz) chorizo sausage, sliced
1 red pepper, halved, cored and deseeded
generous pinch of saffron strands
3 large ripe tomatoes, skinned and chopped
10ml (2 tsp) paprika
3 garlic cloves, peeled and crushed
350g (12oz) long-grain rice
125g (4oz) frozen peas, thawed

1 Put the wine and thyme in a large pan with a little pepper. Bring to the boil and add the mussels. Cover with a tight-fitting lid and steam for a few minutes until the shells open. Drain, reserving liquor; discard any unopened mussels.
2 Shell half of the mussels; set all aside. Add the reserved cooking liquor to the chicken stock.
3 Heat the olive oil in a paella pan or large deep frying pan over a medium high heat. Add the chicken pieces and cook, turning, for a few minutes until browned. Transfer to a plate; set aside. Add the onion to the pan and cook for 10 minutes or until softened. Add the chorizo and red pepper and cook for 3 minutes.
4 Add the saffron, tomatoes, paprika and garlic. Cook for 1 minute, then stir in the rice and a little salt. Cook for a few minutes until the rice looks transparent. Meanwhile, heat the stock.

5 Add about half of the stock to the rice mixture. Bring to a simmer and cook for 5 minutes. Add the remaining stock and place the chicken pieces, monkfish, squid and prawns on top. Simmer gently for about 15 minutes until the rice is tender; at this stage avoid stirring up the rice if possible. Towards the end of the cooking time, stir in the peas and mussels.
6 Check seasoning and serve, with lemon wedges.

vegetarian paella

Serves 4
Preparation time: 20 minutes
Cooking time: 50 minutes, plus resting
560 cals per serving

90ml (6 tbsp) olive oil
2 red peppers, halved, cored, deseeded and sliced
2 onions, peeled and chopped
4 garlic cloves, peeled and finely chopped
10ml (2 tsp) paprika
5ml (1 tsp) turmeric
2.5ml (½ tsp) cayenne pepper
350g (12oz) easy-cook Italian brown rice
1.2 litres (2 pints) vegetable stock
175g (6oz) French beans, halved
175g (6oz) frozen peas
30ml (2 tbsp) chopped fresh parsley
50g (2oz) black olives
salt and freshly ground black pepper

1 Heat 30 ml (2 tbsp) oil in a large, deep frying pan. Add the peppers and fry over a medium heat for 5-10 minutes until well browned and softened. Remove with a slotted spoon; set aside.
2 Add remaining oil to pan and fry the onions, garlic and spices for 10 minutes until golden. Add the rice, stir once, then pour in the stock. Bring to the boil and simmer for 15 minutes.
3 Meanwhile, blanch the beans in boiling water for 1 minute. Drain and refresh with cold water.
4 Add the peppers, beans and peas to the rice and stir through. Cook for a further 15 minutes until the rice and vegetables are tender. Remove from the heat and stir in the parsley and olives. Season well, cover with a lid and allow to stand for 5 minutes before serving.

vegetable biryani

Serve this fragrant Indian dish with dhal and a selection of chutneys.

Serves 4
Preparation time: 25 minutes
Cooking time: 40 minutes
670 cals per serving

350g (12oz) basmati rice
about 60ml (4 tbsp) ghee or oil
1 large onion, peeled and finely sliced
25g (1oz) unsalted pistachio nuts
25g (1oz) slivered blanched almonds
25g (1oz) raisins
2 large pinches of saffron strands
1 cinnamon stick
6 black peppercorns
6 cloves
4 cardamoms
5ml (1 tsp) ground cumin
5ml (1 tsp) cayenne pepper
3 garlic cloves, peeled and crushed
225g (8oz) waxy potatoes, peeled and cut into chunks
125g (4oz) French beans, halved
2 carrots, peeled and sliced
225g (8oz) cauliflower, cut into small florets
75g (3oz) shelled peas
150ml (¼ pint) thick yogurt
TO SERVE:
hard-boiled eggs (optional)
garam masala, to taste

1 Wash the rice in a sieve under cold running water; drain.
2 Heat the ghee or oil in a heavy-based saucepan or flameproof casserole. Add the onion and cook over a high heat for about 5 minutes or until golden brown. Remove with a slotted spoon and drain on kitchen paper; set aside for the garnish.
3 Add the nuts and raisins to the oil remaining in the pan and cook for 1 minute, or until the nuts are lightly browned. Remove with a slotted spoon and drain on kitchen paper; set aside.
4 Add the spices and garlic to the pan, adding a little extra ghee or oil to the pan if necessary. Add all of the vegetables and cook, stirring, for 2 minutes. Stir in the yogurt, a spoonful at a time. Add 60ml (4 tbsp) water, cover and simmer for 10 minutes or until the vegetables are tender.
5 Meanwhile, put the rice in another saucepan with 600ml (1 pint) water and salt to taste. Bring quickly to the boil, then lower the heat, partially cover and simmer for 10 minutes or until barely tender and the liquid is absorbed.
6 Add the rice to the vegetables, recover and simmer gently for 5-10 minutes or until the rice and vegetables are tender. Season with salt and pepper to taste.
7 Pile the rice and vegetable mixture on to a warmed serving platter and top with the nuts, raisins, fried onions, and hard-boiled eggs if using. Sprinkle with garam masala to taste and serve with dhal and chutneys.

types of rice

Some varieties of rice cook to a separate firm texture, some to a creamy consistency, while others cook to a sticky mass. Using the correct rice for a particular dish is therefore important.

BASMATI RICE is a superior variety of long-grain rice, originating from the foothills of the Himalayas. It has a characteristic, subtle fragrance and, once cooked, the rice grains are light, very fluffy, and quite separate. It is the perfect accompaniment to curries and other spicy Indian dishes. Both white and brown varieties of basmati rice are available.

ARBORIO RICE is the classic Italian risotto variety with plump medium grains. It absorbs lots of liquid during cooking and develops a creamy texture, whilst retaining a slight bite. Carnaroli is another good Italian risotto rice.

RED CAMARGUE RICE from the south of France is an attractive russet colour, with a texture like brown rice.

THAI FRAGRANT RICE is distinctively aromatic, and is now available from larger supermarkets. Provided that it's correctly cooked, this rice has a soft, light, fluffy texture, and is the ideal accompaniment to Thai dishes.

smoked sausage and prawn jambalaya

Serves 4
Preparation time: 5 minutes
Cooking time: 35 minutes
980 cals per serving

30ml (2 tbsp) sunflower oil
175g (6oz) onions, peeled and finely chopped
6 baby red peppers, halved, or 2 large red peppers, cored, deseeded and roughly chopped
225g (8oz) long-grain and wild rice mix
750ml (1¼ pints) vegetable stock
75ml (5 tbsp) ready-made creole sauce (see note)
150g (5oz) cooked, smoked pork sausages, sliced
125g (4oz) cooked, peeled king prawns
50g (2oz) shelled pistachio nuts
thyme and lemon wedges, to garnish

1 Heat the oil in a large, deep frying pan and fry the onions for about 10 minutes until very soft and golden brown. Add the peppers and fry for a further 2-3 minutes until glazed with the oil and beginning to soften.
2 Stir in the rice and fry for about 1 minute, then add the stock and creole sauce. Stir well and bring to the boil.
3 Cover the pan with a lid or foil and simmer for 10-15 minutes or until all the liquid has been absorbed. Check that the rice is tender. If not, top up the pan with a little extra stock and simmer uncovered for a few more minutes.
4 Add the sliced sausages and prawns and stir gently over a low heat for 3-4 minutes until heated through. Stir in the pistachio nuts. Serve garnished with thyme and lemon wedges.

Note Several creole sauces are available. Most are based on tomatoes, peppers and spices.

vegetable pilau

Serve this pilau as part of an Indian meal with a selection of dishes, or as as an accompaniment.

Serves 4-6
Preparation time: 10 minutes
Cooking time: 20 minutes
475-315 cals per serving

30ml (2 tbsp) oil
2-3 shallots, peeled and halved
1-2 garlic cloves, peeled and crushed
125g (4oz) button mushrooms, thickly sliced
175g (6oz) cauliflower florets, thickly sliced
1 bay leaf
2.5ml (½ tsp) turmeric
6 cloves
6 cardamoms
1 cinnamon stick, halved
1 dried red chilli
350g (12oz) white basmati rice
125g (4oz) peas
salt and freshly ground black pepper
25g (1oz) butter (optional)
handful of roughly chopped fresh coriander (optional)
finely grated rind of 1 lemon or lime
toasted flaked almonds, to garnish

1 Heat the oil in a heavy-based pan. Add the shallots and cook, stirring, for a few minutes until beginning to soften. Add the garlic, mushrooms and cauliflower and cook briefly, stirring over a high heat, until softened and tinged with brown.
2 Add the bay leaf and spices. Cook for 1-2 minutes, stirring all the time.
3 Add the rice, 600ml (1 pint) water, the peas and plenty of salt. Bring to the boil, then lower heat, cover and simmer gently for 10-15 minutes or until the rice is tender and the water absorbed.
4 Add the butter and coriander if using, and lemon or lime rind. Season with pepper. Leave, covered, to stand for 5 minutes before serving, garnished with toasted almonds.

Variations Almost any vegetables can be used instead of – or as well as – these. Try green beans, carrots, okra and courgettes.

puy lentil and rice pilaf

Serves 4-6
Preparation time: 20 minutes
Cooking time: About 40 minutes
390-260 cals per serving

125g (4oz) Puy lentils
125g (4oz) brown rice or red Camargue rice
60ml (4 tbsp) olive oil
2 large onions, peeled and sliced
2 garlic cloves, peeled and crushed
10ml (2 tsp) ground coriander
5ml (1 tsp) turmeric
5ml (1 tsp) ground cumin
5ml (1 tsp) ground cinnamon
1.25-2.5ml (¼-½ tsp) cayenne pepper
4 ripe tomatoes, skinned, deseeded and chopped
30ml (2 tbsp) lemon juice
25g (1oz) butter
60ml (4 tbsp) chopped fresh parsley
salt and freshly ground black pepper

1 Wash and drain the lentils and place in a saucepan. Add plenty of cold water to cover. Bring to the boil, partially cover and simmer gently for 25-30 minutes until the lentils are cooked. Drain and refresh under cold water; drain thoroughly.

2 In the meantime, wash and dry the rice and cook as for the lentils, allowing 30 minutes for brown rice, or 20 minutes for red rice. Drain, refresh and dry well.

3 Meanwhile, heat the oil in a heavy-based frying pan, add the onions and garlic and fry gently for 15 minutes. Add the spices and fry, stirring, for 3-4 minutes. Add the tomatoes, lemon juice and 60ml (4 tbsp) water. Cover and simmer for a further 20 minutes.

4 Stir in the cooked lentils and rice, add the butter and parsley and heat through for 2-3 minutes, stirring constantly. Season with salt and pepper to taste. Serve at once, with toasted pitta bread and yogurt or crème fraîche if wished.

courgette and cheese pilaf

This tempting vegetarian Middle Eastern bulghar dish has typical sweet and savoury flavours.

Serves 4
Preparation time: 20 minutes
Cooking time: 30 minutes
490 cals per serving

60ml (4 tbsp) olive oil
1 onion, peeled and chopped
2 garlic cloves, peeled and crushed
1 red chilli, deseeded and chopped
1 courgette, diced
225g (8oz) bulghar wheat
300ml (½ pint) vegetable stock
50g (2oz) raisins or sultanas
25g (1oz) pine nuts, toasted
salt and freshly ground black pepper
125g (4oz) mozzarella or fontina cheese, shredded
15ml (1 tbsp) chopped fresh mint

I Heat the oil in a deep frying pan or saucepan. Add the onion, garlic and chilli and fry for 5 minutes, then add the courgette and fry for a further 5-10 minutes until golden. Remove with a slotted spoon and set aside.

2 Add the bulghar wheat to the pan and stir over a low heat for 30 seconds until the grains are glossy. Add the stock and raisins or sultanas. Bring to the boil, cover and simmer for 5-10 minutes until the bulghar wheat is softened and the water absorbed.

3 Return the courgette and onion mixture to the pan and cook for a further 5 minutes until heated through. Add the pine nuts and season with salt and pepper to taste. Remove the pan from the heat and add the cheese. Cover and leave to stand for 5 minutes until the cheese is melted, then stir in the mint. Serve hot.

Note Serve this pilaf as part of a main meal with one or two other vegetarian dishes, or as an accompaniment to a vegetable stew or curry.

bulgar wheat and walnut patties

If you have been disappointed by veggie burgers in the past, try these – they taste delicious.

Serves 4
Preparation time: 35 minutes, plus soaking
Cooking time: 20 minutes
Suitable for freezing (see note)
450 cals per serving

FOR THE PATTIES:
175g (6oz) bulghar wheat
30ml (2 tbsp) olive oil
1 small onion, peeled and finely chopped
1 garlic clove, peeled and finely chopped
finely grated rind of 1 lemon
5ml (1 tsp) dried oregano
125g (4oz) mozzarella cheese, roughly chopped
50g (2oz) walnuts, toasted and ground
30ml (2 tbsp) chopped fresh mint
2.5ml (½ tsp) each ground cumin and cinnamon
1 large egg
salt and freshly ground black pepper
FOR THE TOMATO SAUCE:
400g (14oz) can chopped tomatoes
15ml (1 tbsp) olive oil
1 garlic clove, peeled and crushed
15ml (1 tbsp) chopped fresh basil
pinch of sugar

1 Place the bulghar wheat in a large bowl, cover with plenty of boiling water and set aside to soak for 20 minutes. Drain well.
2 Meanwhile, make the tomato sauce. Place all the ingredients in a pan, season and bring to the boil. Cover and simmer for 15 minutes. Set aside.
3 Heat the oil in a frying pan, add the onion, garlic, lemon rind and oregano and fry gently for 5 minutes. Add the bulghar wheat and stir-fry for 1 minute.
4 Transfer the mixture to a food processor. Add the mozzarella, ground walnuts, mint, spices and egg. Season liberally and process until smooth.
5 Divide the mixture into 8 equal portions and shape into patties, using floured hands. Dust each one lightly with flour. Reheat the tomato sauce.
6 Heat a shallow layer of oil in a heavy-based frying pan. When hot, fry the patties, two at a time, for 2-3 minutes on each side until golden. Drain on kitchen paper; keep hot while cooking the rest. Serve with the tomato sauce.

Note Open-freeze the cooled, cooked patties, then pack in a polythene bag, seal and freeze for up to 2 months. Freeze the sauce separately. Thaw at room temperature, then reheat the patties in a moderate oven for 15-20 minutes.

grains

Grains such as wheat, barley, corn, oats and rye are the edible seeds of different grasses and are familiar sold ground into different flours. Many of these grains are also used in other forms.

BUCKWHEAT is sold as a grain, although it is actually the seed of a plant related to rhubarb. It is processed into groats, which are often toasted.

BULGHAR WHEAT is partially processed cracked wheat which readily absorbs moisture and therefore cooks quickly. It has a mild, nutty taste and is used extensively in Middle Eastern cooking. You may also find it sold as pourgouri, bulghul and cracked wheat.

COUSCOUS is a form of processed semolina grains, pale yellow in colour, with a soft texture and mild flavour. It is a staple north African food.

POLENTA is fine ground cornmeal, which forms the basis of the traditional Italian accompaniment of the same name.

polenta with chorizo

This one-pot warming supper dish is perfect for a cold winter's evening.

Serves 4
Preparation time: 20 minutes
Cooking time: about 15 minutes
350 cals per serving

350g (12oz) broccoli, divided into small florets, stalks sliced
30ml (2 tbsp) olive oil
70g (2¾oz) chorizo sausage, very thinly sliced
1 large onion, peeled and chopped
1 litre (1¾ pints) vegetable or chicken stock
salt and freshly ground black pepper
200g (7oz) quick-cook polenta
finely grated rind of 1 lemon
5ml (1 tsp) paprika
60ml (4 tbsp) roughly chopped flat-leaf parsley
15ml (1 tbsp) balsamic vinegar
10ml (2 tsp) thin honey
10ml (2 tsp) chopped fresh rosemary

1 Cook the broccoli stalks in boiling water for 30 seconds. Add the florets and cook for 1 minute. Drain, refresh under cold water and leave to drain.
2 Heat 15ml (1 tbsp) oil in a frying pan and fry the chorizo gently for 2 minutes; remove from the pan. Add the broccoli to the pan and fry quickly for 4–5 minutes until beginning to colour; remove from the pan.
3 Add the remaining oil to the pan and fry the onion for 5 minutes until golden.
4 Meanwhile, bring the stock to the boil in a medium saucepan with 2.5ml (½ tsp) salt added. Pour in the polenta in a steady stream, whisking well so that lumps do not form. Cook over a very gentle heat for about 5 minutes, stirring with a wooden spoon until soft and smooth. Stir in the lemon rind, paprika and parsley; season with black pepper.
5 Add the chorizo, broccoli, balsamic vinegar, honey and rosemary to the onion and warm through for 1-2 minutes. Spoon the polenta on to serving plates, top with the chorizo mixture and pour over any pan juices.

grilled polenta with warm leeks and olives

Serves 4
Preparation time: 10 minutes, plus cooling
Cooking time: 25 minutes
350 cals per serving

750ml (1¼ pints) vegetable stock
salt and freshly ground black pepper
175g (6oz) quick-cook polenta
30ml (2 tbsp) chopped fresh mixed herbs, such as parsley, thyme and chervil
75g (3oz) Parmesan cheese, freshly grated
olive oil, for brushing
FOR THE TOPPING:
15ml (1 tbsp) olive oil
1 garlic clove, peeled and crushed
250g (9oz) trimmed baby leeks, sliced diagonally
200g (7oz) mixed green and black olives, stoned
flat-leaf parsley, to garnish

1 Bring the stock to the boil in a medium pan with 2.5ml (½ tsp) salt added. Pour in the polenta in a steady stream, whisking well so that no lumps form. Cook over a very gentle heat for about 5 minutes, stirring with a wooden spoon until the polenta is soft and smooth. Stir in the chopped herbs and cheese; season with pepper to taste.
2 Spoon the polenta into a shallow greased tin, about 18x25cm (7x10 inches), spreading it smoothly in a thick layer. Allow to cool, then cover with cling film and chill for 30 minutes until firm.
3 Cut the set polenta into 8 triangular slices. Brush both sides with oil, place on a baking sheet and cook under a medium high grill for 4 minutes on each side or until golden.
4 For the topping, heat the oil in a saucepan, add the garlic and cook for 30 seconds. Add the leeks and cook for 5 minutes. Add the olives and cook for a further 3-4 minutes. Season to taste.
5 Arrange the polenta slices on warmed serving plates and top with the leek and olive mixture. Garnish with parsley and serve.

couscous-stuffed peppers

Fresh mint and raisins lend a Middle Eastern flavour to these stuffed peppers.

Serves 4-6
Preparation time: 25 minutes
Cooking time: 30 minutes
435-290 cals per serving

6 red or yellow peppers
25g (1oz) butter
1 red onion, peeled and finely chopped
5ml (1 tsp) oil
2.5ml (½ tsp) salt
175g (6oz) quick-cook couscous
25g (1oz) raisins
25g (1oz) pine nuts
30ml (2 tbsp) chopped fresh mint
15ml (1 tbsp) balsamic vinegar
salt and freshly ground black pepper
1 egg yolk
FOR THE DRESSING:
60ml (4 tbsp) olive oil
15ml (1 tbsp) white wine vinegar
15ml (1 tbsp) chopped fresh mint

1 Make a slit in the side of each pepper and carefully remove the core and seeds.
2 Melt the butter in a small pan, add the onion and cook until softened.
3 Bring 250ml (8fl oz) water to the boil in a saucepan. Add the oil and salt. Take off the heat, add the couscous, stir once, then cover and leave to stand for 5 minutes. Stir in the onion, raisins, nuts, mint and balsamic vinegar. Season well and stir in the egg yolk to bind the mixture.
4 Using a teaspoon, three-quarters fill the peppers with the couscous mixture; do not over-fill as the couscous will swell during baking. Brush the peppers with oil and bake at 200°C/fan oven 190°C (400°F) Mark 6 for 30-35 minutes until tender.
5 Meanwhile put the ingredients for the dressing in a screw-topped jar and shake to combine.
6 Serve the stuffed peppers warm or cold, with the dressing spooned over.

couscous-stuffed aubergines

These tasty aubergines are equally good hot or cold, with their fresh-tasting coriander dressing.

Serves 2
Preparation time: 30 minutes
Cooking time: 20-30 minutes, plus reheating
320 cals per serving

2 aubergines, each about 250g (9oz)
30ml (2 tbsp) lemon juice
sea salt and freshly ground black pepper
50g (2oz) quick-cook couscous
6 sun-dried tomatoes in oil, drained and chopped
25g (1oz) ready-to-eat dried apricots, chopped
8 fresh mint sprigs, chopped
15ml (1 tbsp) pine nuts, chopped
4 spring onions, trimmed and chopped
FOR THE CORIANDER DRESSING:
150ml (¼ pint) yogurt
1cm (½ inch) piece fresh root ginger, peeled and grated
1 garlic clove, peeled and crushed
finely grated rind of 1 lime, plus a squeeze of juice
30ml (2 tbsp) chopped fresh coriander

1 Cut the aubergines in half lengthways and score the cut sides deeply, without damaging the skins. Place, scored-side up, on a baking sheet. Rub in the lemon juice and sprinkle with a little sea salt. Bake at 200°C/fan oven 190°C (400°F) Mark 6 for 20-30 minutes until soft and tender.
2 Meanwhile, put the couscous in a bowl, pour on 150ml (¼ pint) boiling water and leave to soak.
3 Scoop out the flesh from the aubergines and chop finely. Fork through the soaked couscous to separate the grains, then add the chopped aubergine, sun-dried tomatoes, apricots, mint, pine nuts and spring onions. Mix gently, using a fork, until evenly combined and season to taste.
4 Combine the ingredients for the dressing, adding lime juice to taste. Chill until required.
5 Spoon the filling into the aubergine shells, piling it up well. If serving hot, reheat in the oven for 15 minutes. If serving cold, allow to cool. Serve the aubergines drizzled with the coriander dressing and accompanied by a tomato salad.

salmon with couscous

This flavourful warm salad is perfect for an early summer supper. Use fresh broad beans during May when they are in season.

Serves 4
Preparation time: 15 minutes, plus soaking
Cooking time: 20 minutes
595 cals per serving

225g (8oz) fresh or frozen broad beans
250g (9oz) couscous
salt and freshly ground black pepper
60ml (4 tbsp) olive oil
4 thick salmon fillets, each about 150g (5oz), skinned
juice of 2 limes
4 spring onions, trimmed and finely sliced
45ml (3 tbsp) chopped fresh mint
lemon zest and chopped mint, to garnish

1 Cook the broad beans in boiling water for 5-10 minutes until just tender; drain and set aside. When cool enough to handle, slip the beans out of their leathery outer skins (if you have time).
2 Put the couscous in a bowl with 2.5ml (½ tsp) salt. Pour on 300ml (½ pint) boiling water and 15ml (1 tbsp) olive oil. Stir once, then cover and leave to stand for 10 minutes.
3 Season the salmon fillets and place on the grill rack. Cook under a medium-high grill for 4-5 minutes each side until just cooked through to the centre. Set aside to cool slightly.
4 Fluff the couscous with a fork, add the lime juice, spring onions, mint and remaining olive oil. Season well.
5 Flake the salmon and gently fold into the couscous with the broad beans. Serve garnished with lemon zest and chopped mint.

grills, roasts & gratins

Innovative ways to grill
meat, fish and poultry, new
ideas to enhance the Sunday
roast and easy gratins for
fast midweek suppers

seafood and lime kebabs

Serves 4
Preparation time: 25 minutes, plus marinating
Cooking time: 6 minutes
200 cals per serving

225g (8oz) raw king prawns, peeled and deveined
550g (1¼lb) monkfish fillet, cut into 2.5 cm (1 inch)
    cubes
3 limes, each cut into 8 wedges
FOR THE MARINADE:
juice of ½ lime
1 garlic clove, peeled and crushed
30ml (2 tbsp) chilli oil
30ml (2 tbsp) teriyaki sauce

1 Place the king prawns and monkfish in a bowl.
   Mix the marinade ingredients together and pour
   over the fish. Turn to coat, cover and leave in a
   cool place to marinate for up to 1 hour.
2 Lift the seafood from the marinade and thread
   on to 8 skewers, interspersing with lime wedges.
3 Cook the kebabs under a grill or on a griddle for
   3 minutes, turning once and brushing with the
   marinade. Serve at once, with a salad.

mediterranean grilled sardines

Sardines taste particularly good grilled, griddled or
barbecued with strong Mediterranean flavours.

Serves 4
Preparation time: 15 minutes
Cooking time: 20 minutes
510 cals per serving

45ml (3 tbsp) olive oil
2 red onions, about 300g (11oz), peeled, halved and
    divided into petals
2 garlic cloves, peeled and crushed
2 red peppers, about 375g (12oz), halved, cored
    deseeded and cut into chunks
225g (8oz) courgettes, cut into small chunks
salt and freshly ground black pepper
900g (2lb) sardines (about 16), cleaned
olive oil and lemon juice, for drizzling

1 Heat the oil in a large frying pan or griddle, add
   the onions and fry for 2-3 minutes or until
   almost soft. Add the garlic and peppers and
   stir-fry for 5 minutes, then add the courgettes
   and stir-fry for 4-5 minutes or until almost soft.
   Keep warm.
2 Season the sardines and cook under a hot grill or
   on the griddle for 3-4 minutes on each side or
   until cooked in the centre.
3 Drizzle the sardines with a little oil and lemon
   juice and serve with the vegetables.

tikka prawn skewers

These quick and easy kebabs can be grilled, or
cooked on a griddle or barbecue if you prefer.

Serves 2
Preparation time: 10 minutes, plus marinating
Cooking time: 6 minutes
310 cals per serving

200g (7oz) raw king or tiger prawns
FOR THE TIKKA MARINADE:
30ml (2 tbsp) yogurt
30ml (2 tbsp) double cream
30ml (2 tbsp) medium Madras curry paste
15ml (1 tbsp) mango chutney
5ml (1 tsp) lemon juice
salt and freshly ground black pepper
FOR THE RAITA:
150ml (¼ pint) yogurt
50g (2oz) cucumber, diced
30ml (2 tbsp) chopped fresh mint
1 garlic clove, peeled and crushed

1 Pre-soak 4-6 wooden skewers in cold water for
   20 minutes. Mix the marinade ingredients
   together in a bowl, add the prawns and turn to
   coat. Cover and leave to marinate in a cool place
   for about 15 minutes. Mix the raita ingredients
   together in a serving bowl, cover and refrigerate
   until needed.
2 Thread the prawns on to the skewers and place
   on a baking sheet lined with foil. Cook under a
   hot grill. Alternatively, cook in a griddle pan or
   on the barbecue for 2-3 minutes on each side.
3 Serve the prawn skewers with rice, mango
   chutney, toasted naan bread and the raita.

salmon with caper and lemon butter sauce

Serve this sublime combination with new potatoes, green beans and baby spinach.

Serves 4
Preparation time: 15 minutes
Cooking time: 5-6 minutes
575 cals per serving

4 salmon fillets, with skin, each about 175g (6oz)
15ml (1 tbsp) oil
salt and freshly ground black pepper
FOR THE SAUCE:
125g (4oz) butter
20ml (4 tsp) lemon juice
10ml (2 tsp) white wine vinegar
2 large egg yolks
15-30ml (1-2 tbsp) capers, rinsed and chopped

1 First make the sauce. Slowly melt the butter in a pan over a low heat. Pour the lemon juice and vinegar into another pan and bring to the boil.

2 Meanwhile, whizz the egg yolks in a blender or food processor for 10 seconds, then, with the motor running, add the hot vinegar mixture. Increase the heat under the butter and bring to the boil. Again with the motor running, trickle the hot butter on to the egg. When it is all incorporated the sauce should be the thickness of lightly whipped cream. Spoon into a small bowl and fold in the capers to taste. Set aside.

3 Meanwhile, season the salmon and place skin-side down on a foil-lined grill pan. Brush with the oil and grill for about 1 minute. Turn skin-side up and grill under a high heat for a further 4-5 minutes until the skin is crisp and golden and the salmon is just cooked through. Lift on to warm plates and top with the butter sauce.

grilled herrings with spinach and almond stuffing

Herrings are perfect for grilling – their oily, silvery skins turning beautifully crisp, charred and appetising. For convenience, prepare them in advance, ready for grilling at the last moment.

Serves 4
Preparation time: 15 minutes
Cooking time: About 15 minutes
400 cals per serving

4 herrings, cleaned and boned
FOR THE STUFFING:
25g (1oz) butter
1 onion, peeled and finely chopped
25g (1oz) blanched almonds or pine nuts, roughly chopped
125g (4oz) young spinach leaves, stalks removed
25g (1oz) medium oatmeal
75g (3oz) mature Cheddar cheese, grated
salt and freshly ground black pepper
TO FINISH:
10ml (2 tsp) balsamic or wine vinegar
lemon wedges, to serve

1 To make the stuffing, melt the butter in a frying pan, add the onion and almonds and fry for 3 minutes. Stir in the spinach and cook until just wilted. Remove from the heat and stir in the oatmeal. Cool slightly, then add the cheese and a little seasoning.
2 Score the herrings several times on each side. Sprinkle the balsamic vinegar inside the cavities and over the skins.
3 Spoon the prepared stuffing into the cavities and secure the opening with wooden cocktail sticks.
4 Line the grill pan with lightly oiled foil and place the herrings in the pan. Grill under a moderate heat for 15 minutes, turning halfway through cooking. Transfer the herrings to warmed serving plates and serve with lemon wedges and a tomato salad.

Note If fresh spinach isn't available use 50g (2oz) frozen, thawing it thoroughly and squeezing out all excess moisture.

grilled halibut with stir-fried vegetables

Serves 4
Preparation time: 15 minutes
Cooking time: 8-10 minutes
280 cals per serving

1 large courgette, trimmed
1 red pepper, halved, cored and deseeded
4 halibut steaks, each about 175g (6oz)
melted butter, for brushing
15ml (1 tbsp) oil
25g (1oz) butter
15ml (1 tbsp) sun-dried tomato paste
10ml (2 tsp) chopped thyme
10ml (2 tsp) chopped chervil
salt and freshly ground black pepper
chervil sprigs, to garnish

1 Cut the courgette and red pepper into matchstick strips.
2 Brush the halibut steaks with melted butter and grill under a medium heat for 4-5 minutes each side until cooked through, basting with melted butter from time to time to prevent the fish from becoming dry.
3 Meanwhile, heat the oil and butter in a frying pan and stir-fry the courgette and red pepper strips for about 2 minutes. Stir in the sun-dried tomato paste, chopped herbs and seasoning.
4 Spoon the stir-fried vegetables onto warmed serving plates and place the grilled halibut steaks on top. Garnish with chervil and serve at once.

Variations Use turbot or salmon steaks in place of halibut. Substitute tarragon for chervil.

grilling fish

Grilling is one of the best methods of cooking fish. Not only is it wonderfully quick, it also produces delicious, moist fish with a crisp skin. Oily fish, such as sardines, herring and red mullet work particularly well. White fish fillets need to be basted frequently with oil or butter during cooking to keep them moist.

grilled cod with sweet chilli glaze

This sweet, spicy glaze can be applied to other fish varieties. Cod is hard to beat, with its large flakes and firm texture, but an oil-rich fish, such as mackerel, is fine too.

Serves 4
Preparation time: 10 minutes
Cooking time: 5 minutes
260 cals per serving

1 red chilli, deseeded and finely chopped
10ml (2 tsp) dark soy sauce
grated rind and juice of 1 lime
1.25ml (¼ tsp) ground allspice, or 6 allspice berries, crushed
50g (2oz) light soft brown sugar
4 thick cod fillets, with skin, about 175g (6oz) each (see note)
lime wedges, to garnish

1 Mix the chilli, soy sauce, lime rind and juice, allspice and sugar together in a small bowl.
2 Place the cod fillets skin-side down on a foil-lined grill pan and grill for about 1 minute. Turn skin-side up and grill for 1 minute.
3 Spoon the chilli glaze on top of the fish. Return to the grill for a further 2-3 minutes until the skin is crisp and golden.
4 Serve garnished with lime wedges. Accompany with Saffron Mash (see page 268) and steamed green beans.

Note You can now get thick-cut cod fillets from selected supermarkets or ask your fishmonger to cut thick fillets. They work better for this recipe.

preparing chillies

As a general rule, the smaller the chilli the hotter it is, but removing the seeds and membrane cuts down the heat. Look for bird's eye chillies which are tiny and fiery, and just one is enough to add a pleasant heat to most recipes. Protect your hands with rubber gloves when handling chillies; the smallest amount of chilli juice can cause severe irritation to the skin.

baked monkfish boulangère

Monkfish is a delicious firm-fleshed fish with a 'meaty texture'. Here monkfish fillets are sandwiched together with a herb and garlic stuffing, then wrapped in Parma ham to seal in the juices and keep the fish moist during baking.

Serves 6-8
Preparation time: 40 minutes
Cooking time: 1 hour 10 minutes
330-220 cals per serving

3 lemons
50g (2oz) fresh white breadcrumbs
75ml (5 tbsp) chopped flat-leafed parsley
2 garlic cloves, peeled and crushed
30-45ml (2-3 tbsp) olive oil
salt and freshly ground black pepper
1kg (2¼lb) monkfish tail, filleted into 4
12 slices prosciutto or Parma ham
75g (3oz) butter
900g (2lb) new potatoes, scrubbed and quartered
350g (12oz) onions, peeled and thinly sliced
5ml (1 tsp) dried thyme
thyme sprigs, to garnish

1 Grate the rind of 2 lemons. Place in a food processor with the breadcrumbs, parsley, garlic, 30ml (2 tbsp) oil and seasoning. Process until well mixed, adding extra oil if the mixture seems dry.
2 Lay 2 monkfish fillets flat-side up on a board. Sprinkle with the crumb mixture and top with the other monkfish fillets to make 2 parcels.
3 Wrap each parcel in Parma ham, to enclose completely. Tie at 5cm (2 inch) intervals with fine string; set aside.
4 Use 25g (1oz) butter to liberally grease a large roasting tin.
5 Cut the remaining lemon into quarters and add to the roasting tin with the potatoes and onions. Season, sprinkle with thyme and dot with the remaining butter. Bake at 200°C/fan oven 190°C (400°F) Mark 6 for 50 minutes or until golden brown, stirring occasionally.
6 Lay the fish parcels on top of the potatoes. Cover with foil and bake for 20-25 minutes. Garnish with thyme and serve.

lemon and honey spatchcocked poussins

This is a delicious way to flavour succulent poussins. Serve them with a crisp leafy salad.

Serves 4
Preparation time: 15 minutes
Cooking time: About 30 minutes
170 cals per serving

2 spatchcocked poussins, each about 700g (1½lb)
FOR THE GLAZE:
30ml (2 tbsp) thin honey
30ml (2 tbsp) wholegrain mustard
30ml (2 tbsp) dark soy sauce
5ml (1 tsp) sweet chilli sauce
finely grated rind of 1 lemon
15ml (1 tbsp) lemon juice
salt and freshly ground black pepper
4-8 lemon slices

1 Mix all the glaze ingredients together in a bowl, then brush all over the poussins. Lay, skin-side down, on a grill rack and grill under a medium heat for 15 minutes, brushing with more glaze as necessary.
2 Turn the poussins over and brush with more glaze. Grill for a further 15 minutes or until the poussins are cooked through and the juices from the thigh run clear when pierced with a skewer. If the poussins brown too quickly during cooking, lower the position of the grill pan.
3 Remove any skewers from the poussins and split each one in two along the length of the breast bone. Transfer to warmed plates, garnishing with the lemon slices and pour over any pan juices.

Note Spatchcocked poussins are split, flattened and skewered so that they can be grilled quickly and evenly. Selected supermarkets sell spatchcocked poussins; alternatively ask your butcher to prepare them for you.

maple-glazed chicken wings with sweetcorn

Serves 4
Preparation time: 15 minutes
Cooking time: 20 minutes
240 cals per serving

16 chicken wings
3 fresh corn cobs
60ml (4 tbsp) tomato ketchup
30ml (2 tbsp) maple syrup
15ml (1 tbsp) mushroom ketchup or Worcestershire
  sauce
1 garlic clove, peeled and crushed
30ml (2 tbsp) lemon juice
salt and freshly ground black pepper
60ml (4 tbsp) roughly chopped fresh parsley
TO SERVE:
soured cream flavoured with snipped chives

1 Cut the tips off the chicken wings. Strip the leaves and 'silk' from the corn, then add to a pan of cold water. Bring to the boil and simmer for 5 minutes. Drain and refresh under cold running water. Using a serrated knife, cut each cob into 4 pieces.
2 Thread the chicken wings and corn cobs onto 4 long metal skewers.
3 Mix the tomato ketchup, maple syrup, mushroom ketchup or Worcestershire sauce, garlic, lemon juice and seasoning together in a bowl. Brush the kebabs liberally with this sauce.
4 Place on the grill rack. Cook under a medium-high grill for 20 minutes, turning and basting with more sauce occasionally until the kebabs are browned and the chicken wings are crispy.
5 Roll each kebab in chopped parsley. Serve at once, with the soured cream and chive dip.

sticky baked sesame chicken

Orange marmalade makes an unusual base for this marinade – which is also suitable for sausages and lamb chops.

Serves 4
Preparation time: 5 minutes, plus marinating
Cooking time: 35 minutes
140 cals per serving

8 chicken thighs, with skin
salt and freshly ground black pepper
FOR THE MARINADE:
2 garlic cloves, peeled and finely chopped
2.5cm (1 inch) piece fresh root ginger, peeled and
    finely chopped
45ml (3 tbsp) orange marmalade
45ml (3 tbsp) dark soy sauce
TO GARNISH:
30ml (2 tbsp) sesame seeds
shredded spring onion (optional)

1　Mix the garlic, ginger, orange marmalade and soy sauce together in a large bowl. Add the chicken thighs. Stir to coat, then cover and set aside for 15 minutes.
2　Season the chicken thighs with salt and pepper and place in a single layer in a roasting tin. Roast at 220°C/fan oven 210°C (425°F) Mark 7 for 35 minutes until cooked through, basting and moving the chicken around from time to time, so that it cooks evenly. Lift the chicken out of the tin and transfer to a warm serving dish; keep hot.
3　Skim the fat off the juices in the roasting tin, then bring to the boil on the hob and allow to bubble for 30 seconds. Spoon the juices over the chicken thighs and sprinkle with the sesame seeds.
4　Serve topped with shredded spring onion if desired, and accompanied by rice or oven-roasted potatoes and a salad.

Note To test if the chicken thighs are cooked, pierce the thickest part with a metal skewer for 10 seconds. If it's hot to the touch when removed, the chicken is ready.

fast oven-roast chicken

All recipes serve 4

GARLIC CHICKEN　Mix together 50g (2oz) soft butter, the finely grated rind of 1 lemon and 2 crushed garlic cloves. Cut a deep pocket in each of 4 chicken breasts (with skin) and stuff with a portion of the garlic butter. Cook at 190°C/fan oven 180°C (375°F) Mark 5 for about 30 minutes. Pop under a hot grill to brown the skin if necessary.

ROAST STUFFED CHICKEN BREASTS　Make up a bought stuffing mix and push a little under the skin of each of 4 chicken breasts. Drizzle with olive oil, lemon juice and seasoning. Roast at 200°C/fan oven 190°C (400°F) Mark 6 for 30 minutes or until cooked through.

CHICKEN AND BACON ROLLS　Take 4 skinless 175g (6oz) chicken breasts, flatten with a rolling pin and spread 15ml (1 tbsp) of Boursin cheese over each breast. Wrap in bacon, secure with cocktail sticks and brush with olive oil. Roast at 200°C/fan oven 190°C (400°F) Mark 6 for 30 minutes. Remove the cocktail sticks and serve.

SPICED BUTTER CHICKEN　Mix 5ml (1 tsp) harissa or dried chilli flakes with 75g (3oz) salted butter. Roast four 175g (6oz) chicken breasts (with skin) at 200°C/fan oven 190°C (400°F) Mark 6 for 20-30 minutes. Place the chicken under the grill to brown and crisp the skin. Top with the spiced butter and serve on hot couscous, with a salad.

roasting chicken

In general, free-range, organic and corn-fed chickens are tastier than standard fresh or frozen chickens. Whichever type of bird you buy, freshness is most important, so check the 'use-by' date. Look for a bird with a good plump breast and a firm unblemished skin.

- Remove the giblets and reserve for making gravy. If you're stuffing a whole bird, put the stuffing in the neck end only – just before cooking. If you stuff the body cavity it slows down the heat penetration and means there's more chance of an undercooked result, with potential health risks. Don't pack the stuffing too tight, as it will expand on cooking and you don't want the skin to split or the stuffing to ooze out. Cook any excess separately in a small dish.
- If you don't want stuffing, put half a lemon, a few fresh herbs and a few peeled garlic cloves in the body cavity for flavour. At this stage, it's a good idea to truss the bird with string so that it keeps its shape, or simply fold the wings under the body, then tie the legs together with a piece of string or secure with a skewers.
- Weigh the whole bird and calculate the cooking time, allowing 20 minutes per 450g (1lb) plus 20 minutes. Put the bird in a roasting tin, season with salt and pepper and smear the breast with butter or oil or cover with a few rashers of fatty bacon. Roast in a preheated oven at 190°C/fan oven 180°C (375°F) Mark 5 for the calculated time or until the juices run clear when the thickest part of the thigh is pierced with a skewer or fork. Baste with the accumulated juices from time to time during roasting to keep the meat moist. If the breast shows signs of browning too quickly, cover it with a piece of foil.
- Chicken portions can be roasted at the same temperature – allow 30-45 minutes depending on their size. Poussins will take 45 minutes to 1 hour, depending on size. Like a whole chicken, the juices will run clear when cooked.

french-style roast chicken

Roasting chicken in this way ensures that it is deliciously moist and tender. Don't be put off by the large quantity of garlic – it cooks down to a sweet-tasting purée that gives body to the gravy.

Serves 4
Preparation time: 10 minutes
Cooking time: About 1¼ hours
470 cals per serving

1 oven-ready chicken, about 1.4kg (3lb), with giblets (see note)
1 carrot, peeled
1 onion, peeled
1 bouquet garni
2 fresh tarragon sprigs
½ lemon
125g (4oz) butter, melted
6 garlic cloves (unpeeled)
salt and freshly ground black pepper
FOR THE BEURRE MANIÉ:
10ml (2 tsp) butter
10ml (2 tsp) plain white flour

1 Put the chicken giblets in a pan with the carrot, onion, bouquet garni and 600ml (1 pint) water. Bring to the boil, cover and simmer for 1 hour while the chicken is cooking.
2 Meanwhile, weigh the chicken and calculate the cooking time, allowing 20 minutes per 450g (1lb), plus 20 minutes. Put the tarragon and lemon in the cavity. Lay the bird on its side in a rack in a roasting tin. Brush with melted butter. Roast at 200°C/fan oven 190°C (400°F) Mark 6 for 20 minutes of the cooking time.
3 Turn chicken so the other side is uppermost, brush with butter and roast for 20 minutes.
4 Turn the chicken, so the breast is uppermost. Brush with more butter. Scatter the garlic cloves in the roasting tin. Roast for the remainder of the time, or until the juices run clear when the thickest part of a thigh is pierced with a skewer.
5 Transfer the chicken to a warm platter; leave to rest in a warm place for 10 minutes. To make the gravy, skim off the fat from the roasting tin. Retrieve the garlic cloves, slip out of their skins back into the tin and mash with a fork. Strain the giblet stock into the pan; bring to the boil.

6 For the beurre manié, blend the butter with the flour. Whisk into the gravy, a piece at a time, to thicken. Simmer for a few minutes, whisking. Season with salt and pepper to taste.

7 Serve the chicken with the gravy and seasonal vegetables of your choice.

Note If you are unable to buy a bird with giblets, make or buy fresh chicken stock for the gravy.

chicken roasted in a lemon vinaigrette

Serves 6
Preparation time: 10 minutes
Cooking time: 40 minutes
360 cals per serving

2 lemons
175g (6oz) shallots or onions, peeled and thickly sliced
6 chicken supremes or 12 boneless thighs, with skin
salt and freshly ground black pepper
30ml (2 tbsp) balsamic vinegar
30ml (2 tbsp) sherry vinegar
60ml (4 tbsp) thin honey
150ml (¼ pint) olive oil

1 Grate the rind and squeeze juice of 1 lemon; set aside. Thinly slice the other lemon. Scatter the lemon slices and shallots over the base of a small roasting tin (see note). Lay the chicken on top and season generously.

2 Whisk together the grated lemon rind and juice, vinegars, honey and oil in a bowl. Pour the lemon vinaigrette over the chicken.

3 Roast at 200°C/fan oven 190°C (400°F) Mark 6, basting regularly, for 35 minutes or until the chicken is golden and cooked through. Transfer the chicken to a serving dish and keep warm.

4 Place the roasting tin with its juices on the hob over a medium heat. Bring to the boil and let bubble for 2-3 minutes or until syrupy. Spoon over the chicken to serve.

Note The roasting tin should be just large enough to hold the chicken comfortably in a single layer.

mediterranean baked chicken

This is an ideal dish to prepare well ahead as the chicken can be left to marinate in the red wine.

Serves 6
Preparation time: 15 minutes
Cooking time: 1 hour 10 minutes
Suitable for freezing
785 cals per serving

6 large chicken portions, about 2kg (4½lb) in total
60ml (4 tbsp) olive oil
sea salt
10ml (2 tsp) roughly crushed black peppercorns
175g (6oz) pitted black olives, such as Kalamata
6 garlic cloves (unpeeled)
225g (8oz) shallots, peeled and roughly chopped
4 bay leaves
6 large thyme sprigs
300ml (½ pint) red wine
thyme and oregano sprigs, to garnish

1 Skewer the chicken joints and put them in a large enamelled roasting tin. Spoon on the oil and sprinkle with the salt and crushed peppercorns.

2 Scatter the olives, garlic cloves and shallots over the chicken, then tuck in the bay leaves and thyme. Pour the red wine over the chicken and leave to marinate for 5-6 hours or overnight.

3 Drain off the red wine and set aside. Bake the chicken and flavourings at 220°C/fan oven 210°C (425°C) Mark 7 for 1 hour or until cooked through to the centre, moving the joints around halfway through so they cook evenly.

4 Place the reserved wine in a large pan, add the juices from the cooked chicken and bring to the boil. Allow to bubble for 5 minutes or until syrupy. Remove the bay leaves and thyme sprigs from the roasting tin.

5 Put the chicken on a large warm serving platter with the olives, garlic and shallots. Spoon the syrupy wine on top and garnish with thyme and oregano to serve.

Note Skewering the chicken will help it to keep its shape during cooking.

chicken breasts stuffed with mushrooms

These chicken breasts can be stuffed in advance, ready to bake when required.

Serves 6
Preparation time: 25 minutes, plus chilling
Cooking time: 25-30 minutes
500 cals per serving

30ml (2 tbsp) olive oil
1 shallot, peeled and very finely chopped
125g (4oz) small open cup mushrooms, diced
40g (1½oz) mild creamy goat's cheese
2 thin slices prosciutto or Parma ham, diced
45ml (3 tbsp) chopped fresh parsley
salt and freshly ground black pepper
125g (4oz) butter
30ml (2 tbsp) chopped fresh basil
squeeze of lemon juice
6 chicken breast fillets, with skin

1 Heat the oil in a heavy-based frying pan, add the shallot and cook gently until softened but not browned. Add the mushrooms and continue cooking until they are softened.
2 Take off the heat, let cool slightly, then add the goat's cheese, Parma ham and half of the parsley. Mix well; season generously. Leave until cold.
3 To make the herb butter, beat 75g (3oz) of the butter until soft, then add the remaining parsley, basil, lemon juice and salt and pepper. Shape into a cylinder on a sheet of greaseproof paper and wrap in the paper. Chill until firm.
4 When the stuffing is cold, carefully loosen the skin from each chicken breast, making sure you keep it attached along one long side. Carefully spoon the stuffing under the skin. Tie the chicken into a neat parcel with string, or secure the skin with a fine wooden skewer. Lay the chicken in a roasting tin, stuffed-side uppermost.
6 Melt the remaining butter and brush over the chicken. Season with salt and pepper. Roast at 200°C/fan oven 190°C (400°F) Mark 6 for 25-30 minutes or until cooked right through.
7 Cut the herb butter into thin slices. Transfer the chicken breasts to warmed serving plates and top with the herb butter. Serve immediately.

chicken tarragon burgers

Chicken and tarragon is a classic mix and these burgers are delicious topped with melting Roquefort butter.

Serves 2
Preparation time: 30 minutes, plus chilling
Cooking time: 12 minutes
250 cals per serving

2 shallots, peeled and finely chopped
225g (8oz) minced chicken
15ml (1 tbsp) chopped fresh tarragon
25g (1oz) fresh white breadcrumbs
1 egg yolk
sea salt and freshly ground black pepper
oil, for brushing
FOR THE ROQUEFORT BUTTER:
50g (2oz) Roquefort cheese
25g (1oz) unsalted butter, softened

1 First prepare the Roquefort butter. Beat the cheese and butter together until evenly blended, then season with pepper to taste. Shape into a cylinder on a sheet of greaseproof paper and wrap in the paper. Chill until firm.
2 Put the shallots, chicken, tarragon, breadcrumbs and egg yolk in a bowl. Mix well, then beat in about 75ml (3fl oz) cold water to bind the mixture and season with salt and pepper.
3 Lightly oil a foil-lined baking sheet. Divide the chicken mixture into 4 portions, shape into burgers and place on the foil. Using the back of a wet spoon, flatten each portion to a thickness of 2.5cm (1 inch). Cover and chill for 30 minutes.
4 Grill the burgers for 5-6 minutes on each side or until cooked through, brushing occasionally with oil.
5 Serve topped with slices of Roquefort butter, a green salad and chips or good quality crisps sprinkled with paprika.

Note Any leftover Roquefort butter can be stored in the fridge for up to 1 week.

spiced duck with port and berry sauce

Serves 6
Preparation time: 10 minutes
Cooking time: 1¼ hours
1150 cals per serving

6 duck breasts, each about 225g (8oz)
salt and freshly ground black pepper
1.25ml (¼ tsp) ground allspice
2.5ml (½ tsp) ground cinnamon
FOR THE PORT AND BERRY SAUCE:
20ml (4 tsp) vegetable oil
175g (6oz) onion, peeled and roughly chopped
45ml (3 tbsp) caster sugar
45ml (3 tbsp) red wine vinegar
150ml (¼ pint) port
450ml (¾ pint) red wine
450ml (¾ pint) fresh chicken stock
1 each cinnamon stick, bay leaf and clove
175g (6oz) frozen mixed berries, such as redcurrants, blackcurrants, raspberries and cranberries, thawed and drained
flat-leafed parsley, to garnish

1 Score the fat of the duck breasts; set aside.
2 To make the sauce, heat the oil in a saucepan, add the onion and cook gently for 10 minutes or until soft. Add the sugar and cook on a high heat until golden. Add the vinegar and bubble until totally reduced. Add the port, bubble and reduce by one third, then add the red wine and reduce by half. Add the stock, cinnamon, bay leaf and clove. Bring to the boil and bubble for 25 minutes or until reduced by half; strain and set aside.
3 To cook the duck, heat a heavy-based frying pan until hot. Add the duck breasts, skin-side down and cook, covered, for 10 minutes or until the skin is brown. Transfer to a roasting tin, turning the duck breasts skin-side up. Season with salt, pepper, allspice and cinnamon.
4 Cook at 220°C/fan oven 210°C (425°F) Mark 7; allow 10 minutes for rare; 15 minutes for medium rare; 20 minutes for well done. Set aside.
5 Add any juices to the reserved sauce, bring to the boil and add the berries. Check the seasoning. Serve the duck breasts sliced, on a pool of the berry sauce, garnished with parsley.

walnut crusted fillet steaks

An easy entertaining dish to prepare ahead.

Serves 6
Preparation time: 30 minutes, plus cooling
Cooking time: 15-20 minutes
750 cals per serving

350g (12oz) walnut pieces, roughly chopped
125g (4oz) pickled walnuts, drained and chopped
50g (2oz) can anchovies, drained
2 garlic cloves, peeled
15ml (1 tbsp) thick soy sauce
about 45ml (3 tbsp) olive oil
salt and pepper
1-1.1kg (2¼-2½lb) piece fillet of beef (not from the thick end)
30ml (2 tbsp) sunflower or corn oil
60ml (4 tbsp) white wine
300ml (½ pint) well-flavoured beef stock
60ml (4 tbsp) chopped fresh parsley

1 Mix all of the walnuts together; set aside one half. Put the rest in a blender or processor with the anchovies, garlic, soy sauce and olive oil. Blend until smooth. Stir in the reserved walnuts and season with salt and pepper; the paste should be thick and lumpy.
2 Cut the beef fillet into 6 thick steaks. Heat the oil in a heavy-based frying pan until almost smoking. Fry the steaks, one at a time, quickly on all sides to brown and seal. Allow to cool. Top each steak thickly with walnut paste. Cover and refrigerate until ready to cook.
3 To make the gravy, deglaze the frying pan with the wine, stirring to scrape up the sediment. Add the stock, bring to the boil and bubble for 2-3 minutes until reduced slightly. Check seasoning. Pour into a bowl; cool. Chill until required.
4 Bring the steaks to room temperature about 15-20 minutes before cooking.
5 Place the steaks on a baking sheet. Bake in the oven at 200°C/fan oven 190°C (400°F) Mark 6 for 10-15 minutes, depending on thickness and preference for rare or medium cooked steaks. Meanwhile reheat the gravy in a small pan.
6 Serve the steaks, sprinkled with chopped parsley and accompanied by the gravy.

beef fillet with chilli pepper butter

Thick slices of beef fillet topped with a delicious melting spiced butter.

Serves 6
Preparation time: 20 minutes, plus chilling
Cooking time: 25 minutes
590 cals per serving

1.1kg (2lb) piece fillet of beef (not from the thick
    end), at room temperature
olive oil, for basting
salt and freshly ground black pepper
12 large garlic cloves (unpeeled)
FOR THE FLAVOURED BUTTER:
1 medium red pepper
1 large red chilli
225g (8oz) unsalted butter, softened
5ml (1 tsp) mild chilli powder or chilli sauce
60ml (4 tbsp) freshly grated Parmesan cheese
TO GARNISH:
snipped chives

1. Trim the meat and tie at intervals to retain its shape. Rub all over with olive oil and seasoning.
2. To make the flavoured butter, grill the red pepper and chilli under a high heat until charred (about 15 minutes for the pepper, less for the chilli). Cover, allow to cool slightly, then skin, halve, core and deseed. Purée the pepper and chilli in a food processor. Add the butter, chilli powder or sauce, Parmesan and plenty of pepper. Process until evenly blended. Turn on to cling film, shape into a log, wrap and chill for at least 1 hour until firm.
3. Place the meat in a roasting tin, tuck the garlic cloves around and roast at 230°C/fan oven 220°C (450°F) Mark 8 for 25 minutes for medium rare. Leave to rest in a warm place for 10 minutes.
4. To serve, cut 12 thick slices of chilli butter. Carve the meat into 12 chunky slices, arrange on warm plates and set the flavoured butter slices on top. Garnish with the roasted garlic cloves and chives. Serve with mashed potatoes flavoured with horseradish and snipped spring onions.

roast topside of beef with fruity stuffing

This excellent alternative to the traditional Sunday roast is stuffed with spinach, raisins, olives, smoked ham and sweet peppers. The herb marinade creates a rich gravy.

Serves 6
Preparation time: 35 minutes, plus marinating
Cooking time: 1-1¼ hours
435 cals per serving

1.4kg (3lb) piece topside or top rump
salt and freshly ground black pepper
15ml (1 tbsp) balsamic vinegar
30ml (2 tbsp) white wine vinegar
45ml (3 tbsp) olive oil
45ml (3 tbsp) chopped fresh coriander or thyme, or 10ml (2 tsp) dried mixed Italian herbs
1 red pepper, cored, quartered and deseeded
1 yellow pepper, cored, quartered and deseeded
75g (3oz) fresh spinach, cooked and excess water squeezed out, or 150g (5oz) frozen leaf spinach, thawed and drained
75g (3oz) pitted black olives
50g (2oz) smoked ham
75g (3oz) raisins or sultanas

1 Make a deep incision along the length of the beef to create a large pocket, season liberally with pepper and place in a shallow dish.
2 Mix the balsamic vinegar, wine vinegar, olive oil and herbs together. Pour over the beef and into the pocket. Leave to marinate in a cool place for about 4 hours or preferably overnight.
3 Cook the peppers, skin-side up, under a hot grill until the skins are charred. Cool, then remove the skins.
4 Roughly chop the spinach, olives and ham. Mix together in a small bowl with the raisins and season with salt and pepper to taste.
5 Line the pocket of the beef with the peppers, reserving 2 pepper quarters for the gravy. Spoon the spinach mixture into the pocket and spread evenly. Reshape the meat and tie at intervals with string.
6 Place in a shallow roasting tin (just large enough to hold the joint). Pour on the marinade and cook at 190°C/fan oven 180°C (375°F) Mark 5 for 1 hour for rare beef, or 1¼ hours for medium rare, basting occasionally. Transfer the beef to a warmed platter, cover with foil and leave to rest in a warm place while preparing the gravy.
7 Skim off the excess fat from the roasting tin. Bring the pan juices to the boil and add 120ml (4fl oz) water; let bubble for 2-3 minutes. Finely chop the remaining pepper pieces and add to the gravy.
8 Carve the beef into slices and serve with gravy and vegetables of your choice.

Note Topside tends to be tough if well done, so it is best cooked rare or medium rare.

fillet of beef wrapped in spinach

Pork fat keeps this roast beautifully succulent and imparts a delicious flavour.

Serves 6
Preparation time: 45 minutes, plus cooling
Cooking time: 40 minutes
770 cals per serving

1kg (2¼lb) piece fillet of beef
sea salt and freshly ground black pepper
15ml (1 tbsp) oil
225g (8oz) large leaf spinach, stalks removed
350g (12oz) finely minced pork fat
10ml (2 tsp) cayenne pepper
10ml (2 tsp) dried rosemary
30ml (2 tbsp) chopped fresh chives
2.5ml (½ tsp) ground nutmeg
FOR THE WILD MUSHROOM SAUCE:
25g (1oz) butter
225g (8oz) mixed wild mushrooms, such as chanterelles
450ml (¾ pint) red wine
600ml (1 pint) fresh beef stock
50g (2oz) unsalted butter, chilled and cubed
TO GARNISH:
flat-leafed parsley

1 Trim the beef of any excess fat, then season with pepper. Heat the oil in a heavy-based frying pan and brown the beef evenly on all sides. Remove and set aside.

2 Put the spinach in a large bowl, pour on boiling water to cover and leave for 30 seconds. Drain, plunge into iced water, then drain and dry well.

3 With a fork, mix together the pork fat, cayenne pepper, rosemary and chives; add salt to taste. (Don't do this in a food processor – it must remain chunky.)

4 Wrap the browned beef in the spinach leaves, then season with salt, pepper and nutmeg. Place in a roasting tin and spread the pork fat mixture over the top and sides, pressing well into the spinach.

5 Roast at 230°C/fan oven 220°C (450°F) Mark 8 for 15 minutes then reduce the temperature to 200°C/fan oven 190°C (400°F) Mark 6 and cook for a further 20 minutes for rare, 25 minutes for medium, or 30 minutes for well done.

6 Meanwhile, make the sauce. Melt the butter in a heavy-based frying pan. Add the mushrooms and cook over a high heat for 3-4 minutes, stirring frequently. Remove the mushrooms and set aside. Add the wine and stock to the pan, bring to the boil and bubble for 15 minutes or until the liquid has reduced by half. Add any juices from the mushrooms.

7 Transfer the meat a warmed platter, cover with foil and leave to rest for 5-10 minutes. In the meantime, bring the sauce to the boil, add the mushrooms and whisk in the butter; adjust the seasoning.

8 Carve the meat into thick slices and serve with the mushroom sauce.

tapenade roast beef

The pungent flavours of anchovy tapenade melt into the meat, giving a deliciously different taste.

Serves 4
Preparation time: 10 minutes
Cooking time: 35-40 minutes, plus resting
380 cals per serving

50g (2oz) can anchovy fillets, drained
30ml (2 tbsp) capers
15ml (1 tbsp) Dijon mustard
60ml (4 tbsp) roughly chopped fresh parsley
about 15 fresh mint leaves
2 garlic cloves, peeled
15ml (1 tbsp) balsamic vinegar
45ml (3 tbsp) extra-virgin olive oil
900g (2lb) rolled topside of beef
15ml (1 tbsp) plain flour
600ml (1 pint) beef stock
150ml (¼ pint) red wine
salt and freshly ground black pepper

1 Put the anchovies in a food processor with the capers, mustard, herbs, garlic and balsamic vinegar, process until finely chopped. With the motor running, mix in 15ml (1 tbsp) olive oil.

2 Untie the topside and trim away any excess fat. Make a deep cut along the length of the beef to create a pocket. Spread half of the anchovy mixture inside the pocket. Fold the meat back to enclose and tie at intervals with string.

3 Heat the remaining oil in a roasting tin or flameproof roasting dish. Add the meat and brown well on all sides, then roast at 220°C/fan oven 210°C (425°F) Mark 7 for 25 minutes for medium-rare, 30 minutes for medium.

4 Spread the remaining anchovy mixture over the meat; return to the oven for 5-10 minutes. Transfer to a warm platter, cover with foil and leave to rest in a warm place for 10-15 minutes.

5 Blend the flour into the pan juices and cook, stirring, over a low heat for 1 minute. Whisk in the stock, wine and any anchovy mixture that has fallen from the meat. Bring to the boil and bubble for 10 minutes or until reduced by half. Adjust the seasoning – allowing for the saltiness of anchovies.

6 Slice the beef thickly. Serve with the sauce and accompaniments of your choice.

grilled lamb steaks and aubergine with mint pesto

Serves 4
Preparation time: 20 minutes
Cooking time: 8 minutes
890 cals per serving

4 lamb leg steaks
1 medium aubergine
olive oil, for basting
salt and freshly ground black pepper
balsamic vinegar, for sprinkling
FOR THE ALMOND AND MINT PESTO:
60g (2oz) unblanched almonds
25g (1oz) fresh mint leaves
25g (1oz) fresh parsley leaves
250ml (8fl oz) extra-virgin olive oil
75g (3oz) Parmesan cheese, freshly grated
5ml (1 tsp) lemon juice

1 First make the pesto. Spread the almonds in a shallow roasting tin and roast in the oven at 180°C/fan oven 170°C (350°F) Mark 4 until well browned. Cool, then place in a food processor with the mint and parsley. Process until roughly chopped, adding a little oil. Alternatively roughly chop by hand. Stir in the remaining oil, Parmesan and lemon juice.

2 Slice the aubergine to give 8 good slices. Brush these, and the lamb steaks with olive oil. Season well with salt and pepper.

3 Lay the lamb steaks and aubergines on the grill rack and grill for 3-5 minutes per side until tender.

4 Serve each lamb steak on 2 aubergine slices. Sprinkle with a little balsamic vinegar and drizzle with the almond and mint pesto. Serve with grilled plum tomato halves, garnished with mint and topped with any remaining pesto.

rack of lamb with minted cucumber salsa

Tender, juicy spring lamb is roasted to golden crispness on the outside while rosy pink inside. Serve with seasonal vegetables.

Serves 6
Preparation time: 35 minutes
Cooking time: 20-30 minutes
400 cals per serving

3 racks of spring lamb, each with 6 bones
30ml (2 tbsp) brandy
salt and freshly ground black pepper
a little sunflower oil, for brushing
FOR THE SALSA:
1 medium cucumber
2 pickled dill cucumbers, finely diced
1 small red onion, peeled and finely diced
45ml (3 tbsp) chopped fresh mint
FOR THE SAUCE:
150ml (¼ pint) medium dry white wine
10ml (2 tsp) plain flour
finely grated rind and juice of 2 oranges
45ml (3 tbsp) mint jelly

1 Trim the lamb of fat if not already done, leaving a thin covering to baste the meat during cooking. Rub with the brandy and seasoning. Cover and set aside for 30 minutes.
2 To make the salsa, peel the cucumber, if preferred, then halve lengthwise, scoop out the seeds and dice the flesh. Mix with the other ingredients and season with salt and pepper to taste. Cover and chill.
3 Stand the racks of lamb in a roasting tin. Brush with a little oil and roast in the oven at 200°C/fan oven 190°C (400°F) Mark 6 for 20-30 minutes, depending on how pink you like your lamb. Remove from the oven and transfer to a warm dish. Cover with foil and leave to rest in a warm place for 10 minutes before carving – this makes the lamb more juicy and easier to carve.
4 Meanwhile make the sauce. Set the roasting tin over a medium heat and pour in the wine. Bring to the boil, scraping up the sediment from the bottom of the pan. Boil until well reduced, then whisk in the flour. Cook, stirring, for 1 minute then add the mint jelly, orange rind and juice.

5 Bring to the boil, then simmer for 1-2 minutes until syrupy. Season with salt and pepper to taste. Strain if you prefer a smooth sauce.
6 Cut the lamb into cutlets, allowing 3 per person. Arrange on warmed plates. Spoon a little cucumber salsa on top of each cutlet and pour a little sauce around them. Serve the remaining sauce separately.

spiced lamb kebabs

Serves 4
Preparation time: 20 minutes, plus marinating
Cooking time: 15-20 minutes
365 cals per serving

900g (2lb) shoulder or leg of lamb
2 purple-skinned onions
1 lemon, cut into 8 wedges
olive oil, for basting
FOR THE YOGURT MARINADE:
200ml (7fl oz) Greek yogurt
finely grated rind of 2 lemons
15ml (1 tbsp) lemon juice
10ml (2 tsp) harissa
5ml (1 tsp) ground coriander
5ml (1 tsp) ground cumin
15ml (1 tbsp) sweet paprika
1.25ml (¼ tsp) ground ginger
1.25ml (¼ tsp) freshly grated nutmeg
1 garlic clove, peeled and crushed

1 Trim the lamb of any excess fat and cut into large chunks; place in a non-metallic bowl. Mix all the marinade ingredients together and pour over the meat, turning to ensure that it is well coated. Cover and leave to marinate for at least 2 hours, or in the refrigerator overnight.
2 Cut each onion into 6 wedges, keeping the root end intact, then peel. Trim the root ends, but make sure each onion wedge holds together.
3 Thread the lamb cubes, onion wedges and lemon wedges onto 4 long flat metal skewers. Grill under a high heat for about 15-20 minutes, turning frequently and basting with olive oil until cooked, crusty and slightly charred.
4 Serve immediately, on a bed of steamed couscous or rice scattered with coriander leaves.

lamb with mushroom and garlic stuffing

Serves 8
Preparation time: 20 minutes, plus cooling
Cooking time: 2½-3 hours
560 cals per serving

225g (8oz) brown mushrooms
6 large garlic cloves, peeled
60ml (4 tbsp) olive oil
1 leek, trimmed and chopped
45ml (3 tbsp) chopped fresh oregano
salt and freshly ground black pepper
2.3kg (5lb) boned leg of lamb
45-60ml (3-4 tbsp) redcurrant jelly
10ml (2 tsp) wine vinegar
150ml (¼ pint) red wine
300ml (½ pint) lamb stock
herb sprigs, to garnish

1 Place the mushrooms and garlic in a food processor and finely chop. Heat the oil in a frying pan. Add the mushrooms, garlic and leek and fry for about 10 minutes until the juices have evaporated and the mixture is the consistency of a thick paste. Stir in the oregano and season with salt and pepper. Leave to cool.
2 Open out the lamb and pack the stuffing down the centre. Fold the meat over the stuffing to enclose and tie at intervals with string. Place the lamb, seam-side down, in a roasting tin.
3 Roast the lamb in the oven at 180°C/fan oven 170°C (350°F) Mark 4 for 25 minutes per 450g (1lb) plus 25 minutes for medium; 30 minutes per 450g (1lb) plus 30 minutes for well done.
4 Meanwhile, melt the redcurrant jelly in a small saucepan with the wine vinegar. Thirty minutes before the end of the roasting time, brush the lamb with the redcurrant glaze. Repeat several times before the end of the cooking time.
5 Lift the lamb on to a warmed serving platter; leave to rest in a warm place. Drain off the fat from the roasting tin and stir in the wine and stock. Bring to the boil and boil until slightly reduced. Strain the gravy, if preferred, into a warm sauceboat.
6 Remove the string from the lamb. Surround with herbs and serve accompanied by the gravy, and vegetables of your choice.

roast lamb with harissa

Our recipe for the North African chilli condiment harissa makes more than you'll need for the lamb. Spoon any extra into a screw-top jar, cover with a thin layer of olive oil and store in a cool place for up to 2 weeks. Harissa is delicious tossed through salads or pasta.

Serves 6
Preparation time: 40 minutes
Cooking time: 1 hour 40 minutes
785 cals per serving

1.8kg (4lb) boned leg of lamb, bones reserved
30ml (2 tbsp) oil
salt and freshly ground black pepper
1 bunch of fresh rosemary sprigs
1 bunch of fresh thyme sprigs
350g (12oz) shallots, peeled, root left intact and blanched
1 head of garlic, divided into cloves (unpeeled)
300ml (½ pint) dry white wine
600ml (1 pint) fresh lamb or chicken stock
FOR THE HARISSA:
2 large red peppers, about 400g (14oz) in total
4 large fresh red chillies, deseeded and roughly chopped
6 garlic cloves, peeled
15ml (1 tbsp) ground coriander
15ml (1 tbsp) caraway seeds
10ml (2 tsp) salt
60ml (4 tbsp) olive oil
TO GARNISH:
roasted chillies
thyme sprigs

1 To make the harissa, grill the peppers, turning occasionally, until the skins are blackened and the flesh is soft, then cover and leave to cool. Peel away the skins and remove the core and seeds.
2 Place the chillies in the food processor with the garlic, coriander and caraway seeds and work to a rough paste. Add the peppers, salt and olive oil and whizz for 1-2 minutes or until smooth.
3 To prepare the lamb, spread the bone cavity with about 45ml (3 tbsp) harissa. Roll up and secure with wooden cocktail sticks or sew up, using a trussing needle and thread.

4 Heat the oil in a roasting pan over a moderate heat and brown the lamb on all sides; this should take about 5 minutes.

5 Season, place the rosemary and thyme under the lamb and add the bones to the roasting tin. Roast at 200°C/fan oven 190°C (400°F) Mark 6 for 1 hour for pink lamb, or 1½ hours for well done. Baste the lamb from time to time and add the shallots and garlic to the roasting pan 45 minutes before the end of the cooking time.

6 Transfer the lamb to a serving platter with the shallots and garlic. Cover loosely with foil and leave to rest in a warm place.

7 Skim any fat off the sediment in the roasting tin. Add the wine, bring to the boil and bubble until reduced by half. Add the stock, return to the boil and bubble until reduced by half. Adjust the seasoning and strain.

8 Remove the cocktail sticks or thread from the lamb and garnish with roasted chillies and the thyme. Serve with the shallots, garlic, gravy, soft polenta and Roasted Ratatouille (see page 265).

Note The harissa can be made up to 1 week ahead. Spoon into a screw-topped jar and cover the surface with a layer of olive oil. Seal and refrigerate.

pork escalopes with double cheese crust

Lean, tender pork escalopes topped with a cheesy crumb crust and grilled to perfection.

Serves 4
Preparation time: 10 minutes
Cooking time: 10 minutes
370 cals per serving

4 pork escalopes, each about 125g (4oz)
freshly ground black pepper
1½ slices white bread, processed into breadcrumbs
50g (2oz) mature Cheddar or Gruyère cheese, coarsely grated
25g (1oz) butter, melted
75g (3oz) soft goat's cheese, such as Chavroux
lemon slices, to garnish

1 Put the pork escalopes between 2 sheets of greaseproof paper and bat out thinly with a rolling pin. Season with plenty of pepper.
2 Mix together the breadcrumbs, grated cheese and melted butter.
3 Lay the pork escalopes on the grill rack and grill for 3-4 minutes, fairly close to the heat, until the meat changes colour and feels firm.
4 Spread the goat's cheese roughly over the pork, leaving it thick in places. Sprinkle the breadcrumb mixture on top and pop under the grill, slightly further away from the heat, for 3-4 minutes or until the cheese is bubbling and the breadcrumbs are golden. Transfer to warmed plates. Garnish with lemon slices and serve with stir-fried broccoli.

Note Taking time to bat out the meat thinly cuts down on the cooking time and makes a larger surface area for the cheese crust.

roast pork with fennel, garlic and apple

If your favourite part of roast pork is the crisp crackling then this recipe is for you!

Serves 6
Preparation time: 40 minutes
Cooking time: 1 hour 45 minutes
740 cals per serving

1.4kg (3lb) boned lion of pork, with skin
45ml (3 tbsp) olive oil, plus extra for oiling
30ml (2 tbsp) fennel seeds
7 garlic cloves
30ml (2 tbsp) chopped fresh rosemary
salt and freshly ground black pepper
450g (1lb) Spanish onions, peeled and finely sliced
2 sharp apples, such as Granny Smith
15ml (1 tbsp) soft brown sugar
500ml (1 pint) dry cider

1 Deeply score the pork loin skin, using a very sharp knife (eg Stanley knife). Remove the scored skin from the loin, leaving only a thin layer of fat. Rub a little oil into the skin; set aside.
2 Pound the fennel seeds in a pestle and mortar until broken down. Peel 5 garlic cloves and add to the mortar with the rosemary and 2.5ml (½ tsp) salt; pound again. Mix in the olive oil.
3 Turn the pork loin fat-side down and smear with the fennel seasoning. Wrap the scored skin over the seasoned side. Tie at intervals to keep the fat in place. Sprinkle the skin liberally with salt.
4 Place the onions, remaining garlic and apples in a roasting tin; sprinkle with the sugar. Place the pork on a rack over the top. Roast at 240°C/fan oven 230°C (475°F) Mark 9 for 30-40 minutes until the skin begins to blister. Lower setting to 200°C/fan oven 190°C (400°F) Mark 6 and roast for a further 50-60 minutes or until cooked through (check the onion mix doesn't burn).
5 Remove onion mixture from the tin; set aside. Add the cider to the roasting tin, bring to the boil and bubble until reduced by a third. Return the onion mixture to the tin, bring to the boil and simmer for 2-3 minutes; check seasoning.
6 Discard string from meat, lift off the crackling and cut into strips. Cut pork into thick slices and serve with the crackling, onion mix and juices.

pork with autumn fruits

Serves 6
Preparation time: 20 minutes, plus marinating
Cooking time: 45 minutes
475 cals per serving

225g (8oz) mixed dried fruit salad (pears, apples, apricots and prunes), roughly chopped
300ml (½ pint) medium white wine or cider
300ml (½ pint) apple or pear juice
60ml (4 tbsp) sunflower oil
1 onion, peeled and finely chopped
60g (2oz) walnuts, roughly chopped
salt and freshly ground black pepper
large pinch of saffron threads
2 pork fillets (tenderloins)
4 slices Parma ham
2.5ml (½ tsp) mild chilli seasoning

1 Soak the dried fruits in the wine and fruit juice for at least 6 hours, preferably overnight.
2 Heat half the oil in a pan, add the onion and cook gently for 7 minutes until soft and golden.
3 Drain the fruits, reserving the liquid, then mix with the onion and nuts; season to taste. Soak the saffron in 30ml (2 tbsp) hot water.
4 Slice each pork fillet along its length, not quite through, and open out like a book. Place between sheets of greaseproof paper and lightly flatten with a rolling pin – not too thinly.
5 Lay the Parma ham on top of the pork to cover it. Spoon the fruit mixture down the middle of each fillet. Bring the sides of the meat over the stuffing to enclose; tie with string at intervals.
6 Heat the remaining oil in a roasting tin, add the pork fillets and brown all over. Mix the reserved liquor with the saffron and chilli, pour over the meat and scatter any remaining stuffing around. Cover with foil and roast at 190°C/fan oven 180°C (375°F) Gas Mark 5 for 30 minutes. Roast, uncovered, for a further 10 minutes.
7 Lift the meat and fruit onto a warmed serving dish with a slotted spoon; cover and keep warm. Put the roasting tin on a medium heat. Add a little extra wine if there isn't enough liquid for a sauce, scraping up any sediment. Bring to the boil and boil to reduce slightly; check seasoning.
8 Slice the meat thickly and serve with the extra fruit and sauce.

pumpkin and cheese bake

Few will be able to resist this dish of potatoes, pumpkin and cheese baked in a melting crème fraîche sauce – perfect for bonfire night!

Serves 4
Preparation time: 15 minutes
Cooking time: 45 minutes
655 cals per serving

450g (1lb) new potatoes, halved
450g (1lb) pumpkin, peeled and thinly sliced
1 large onion, about 175g (6oz), peeled and finely sliced
salt and freshly ground black pepper
125g (4oz) thinly sliced smoked ham
225g (8oz) buttery cheese, such as taleggio, gruyère or fontina, thinly sliced
300ml (½ pint) crème fraîche

1 Cook the potatoes, pumpkin and onion together in a pan of salted water for 3-4 minutes, then drain. Transfer to a shallow flameproof casserole and roughly mix in the ham and cheese.
2 Beat a little cold water into the crème fraîche to give a thick pouring consistency. Season with pepper, then pour over the vegetables. Place the casserole on the hob and bring to the boil.
3 Transfer to the oven and cook, uncovered, at 220°C/fan oven 210°C (425°F) Mark 7 for 40 minutes or until bubbling and golden. Two or three times during cooking, stir the crust that forms on top into the dish to add to the flavour. To check that the dish is cooked, press the tip of a knife into the centre of a potato, which should be tender. Serve with warm baguette and a green salad if wished.

Variations
- For a vegetarian version, omit the ham and add an extra 125g (4oz) potatoes or pumpkin.
- Sweet potatoes and celeriac are delicious alternatives, too – simply peel and slice the sweet potato thinly and the celeriac a little thicker. Boil with the potatoes and pumpkin.

roasted vegetables with salsa verde

Oven-roasted Mediterranean vegetables enhanced with a robust, fresh-tasting herb and garlic sauce. Serve with plenty of crusty bread to mop up the delicious juices.

Serves 4
Preparation time: 35-40 minutes
Cooking time: 40-50 minutes
415 cals per serving

2 small aubergines
1 red pepper
1 yellow pepper
2 courgettes
8 garlic cloves (unpeeled)
90ml (6 tbsp) extra-virgin olive oil
15ml (1 tbsp) chopped fresh herbs, such as rosemary, sage and thyme
6 ripe plum tomatoes, quartered
salt and freshly ground black pepper
FOR THE SALSA VERDE:
60ml (4 tbsp) chopped fresh parsley
30ml (2 tbsp) chopped fresh mint
2 garlic cloves, peeled and crushed
1 red chilli, halved and deseeded
5ml (1 tsp) Dijon mustard
7.5ml (1½ tsp) lemon juice
120ml (4fl oz) extra-virgin olive oil

1 First prepare the salsa verde. Place of all the ingredients, except the oil, in a food processor and work until fairly smooth. Add the olive oil, process briefly and season with salt and pepper to taste. Transfer to a bowl, cover and set aside to infuse.
2 Remove a thin slice from each side of the aubergines and discard, then cut each one lengthwise into 5 mm (¼ inch) thick slices. Place on a lightly oiled large baking sheet.
3 Halve, core and deseed the peppers, then cut into thick strips. Cut the courgettes into 1cm (½ inch) slices. Put the courgettes, peppers and garlic cloves in a roasting tin large enough to hold them in a single layer.

4 Mix the oil and herbs together and drizzle half of this mixture over the vegetables, turning to coat them evenly. Brush the aubergine slices with the herb-flavoured oil.

5 Place the roasting tin on the top shelf of the oven at 230°C/fan oven 220°C (450°F) Mark 8, with the aubergines on the second shelf. Roast for 30 minutes, stirring the vegetables in the roasting tin halfway through cooking.

6 Add the plum tomatoes to the roasting tin and stir well. Turn the aubergine slices and brush with the remaining olive oil. Return the roasting tin and aubergines to the oven; cook for a further 10-20 minutes until tender. Allow to stand for a few minutes before serving, drizzled with the salsa verde.

mushroom, spinach and roasted potato bake

A tasty, nutritious vegetable bake, scented with thyme and enriched with a creamy cheese sauce.

Serves 6
Preparation time: 45 minutes
Cooking time: 35 minutes
775 cals per serving

900g (2lb) small potatoes, scrubbed
90ml (6 tbsp) olive oil
25g (1oz) dried porcini mushrooms (optional)
2 onions, peeled and roughly chopped
450g (1lb) mixed mushrooms, such as shiitake and brown cap, roughly chopped
2 garlic cloves, peeled and crushed
30ml (2 tbsp) tomato paste
60ml (4 tbsp) sun-dried tomato paste
10ml (2 tsp) chopped fresh thyme
300ml (½ pint) white wine
300ml (½ pint) vegetable stock
300ml (½ pint) double cream
400g (14oz) trimmed spinach leaves, roughly chopped
175g (6oz) gruyère cheese, grated
75g (3oz) Parmesan cheese, freshly grated
salt and freshly ground black pepper
2 eggs, beaten
300ml (½ pint) Greek yogurt

1 Quarter the potatoes and put in a large roasting tin. Drizzle with 60ml (4 tbsp) oil and turn to coat. Roast at 200°C/fan oven 190°C (400°F) Mark 6 for 40 minutes or until tender and golden.
2 Meanwhile, soak the porcini, if using, in warm water to cover for 20 minutes. Drain and chop.
3 Heat the remaining 30ml (2 tbsp) oil in a large heavy-based pan. Add the onions and cook gently for 10 minutes until soft. Increase heat, add the fresh mushrooms and garlic and cook for 5 minutes.
4 Stir in the tomato pastes, porcini mushrooms if using, and the thyme and wine. Bring to the boil and simmer for 2 minutes. Add the stock and cream, bring back to the boil and let bubble for 20 minutes or until well reduced and syrupy.
5 Transfer the mixture to a 2.3 litre (4 pint) ovenproof dish. Stir in the potatoes, spinach, gruyère and half of the Parmesan. Season well.
6 In a bowl, beat the eggs with the yogurt and seasoning; spoon over the vegetables. Top with the remaining Parmesan and bake at 200°C/fan oven 190°C (400°F) Mark 6 for 30-35 minutes, until golden and bubbling. Serve with a leafy salad and warm bread.

baked tomatoes stuffed with pesto rice

Pesto, melting mozzarella and a crisp Parmesan topping give stuffed tomatoes a new lease of life.

Serves 4
Preparation time: 20 minutes
Cooking time: 30 minutes
185 cals per serving

50g (2oz) long-grain rice
4 large beef tomatoes, each about 225g (8oz)
30ml (2 tbsp) pesto
50g (2oz) mozzarella cheese, shredded
25g (1oz) Parmesan cheese, freshly grated
salt and freshly ground black pepper
basil leaves, to garnish

1 Cook the rice according to the packet instructions; drain and set aside.
2 Meanwhile, cut a thin sliver from the base of each tomato so that it will sit flat. Cut a slightly thicker slice from the top of each one, then scoop out the seeds and pulp, taking care to avoid cutting through the skins; discard the seeds.
3 Finely chop the tomato pulp and stir into the rice with the pesto, mozzarella and half of the Parmesan. Season with salt and pepper to taste.
4 Spoon the rice mixture into the hollowed-out tomato skins and scatter over the remaining Parmesan. Place in a small roasting dish and bake at 220°C/fan oven 210°C (425°F) Mark 7 for 20 minutes until bubbling and golden. Garnish with basil and serve hot or warm, with a green salad and crusty bread.

summer vegetable moussaka

Ready-made canned ratatouille is easily transformed into this instant vegetarian supper.

Serves 4
Preparation time: 10 minutes
Cooking time: 35 minutes
325 cals per serving

15ml (1 tbsp) olive oil
2 garlic cloves, peeled and sliced
225g (8oz) button mushrooms, quartered
two 390g (13½oz) cans ratatouille
150g (5oz) baby spinach leaves
salt and freshly ground black pepper
1 egg
2.5ml (½ tsp) freshly grated nutmeg
250g (9oz) Greek yogurt
20g (¾oz) Parmesan cheese, freshly grated

1 Heat the oil in a large frying pan, add the garlic and mushrooms and cook briskly over a high heat for 2 minutes.
2 Add the ratatouille, then bring to the boil and simmer for 5 minutes.
3 Stir the baby spinach through the mixture, then season with salt and pepper to taste. Spoon into a 2 litre (3½ pint) ovenproof dish and spread evenly.
4 For the topping, in a bowl, lightly whisk the egg together with the nutmeg, seasoning and yogurt.
5 Spoon the topping over the vegetable mixture, then sprinkle with grated Parmesan. Bake at 200°C/fan oven 190°C (400°F) Mark 6 for 35 minutes or until golden brown. Serve with plenty of bread and a leafy salad.

Note Most supermarkets stock cans of ratatouille, though you may prefer to make your own if you have sufficient time.

casseroles & braises

Superb aromatic casseroles
and richly flavoured meat
and poultry braises, cooked
until meltingly tender

braised provençale seafood with fennel

Serves 4
Preparation time: 20 minutes
Cooking time: 40 minutes
320 cals per serving

60ml (4 tbsp) extra-virgin olive oil
1 large onion, peeled and finely chopped
1 large head of fennel, finely chopped
2 garlic cloves, peeled and chopped
2 fresh thyme sprigs
grated rind of ½ orange
60ml (4 tbsp) Pernod
400g (14oz) can tomatoes
10ml (2 tsp) chilli sauce
300ml (½ pint) fish stock
225g (8oz) monkfish fillet
1 large red mullet or small hake, filleted
225g (8oz) tuna steak
salt and freshly ground black pepper
25g (1oz) pitted black olives, chopped
30ml (2 tbsp) chopped fresh parsley

1 Heat the oil in a large sauté pan, add the onion,
fennel, garlic, thyme and orange rind and fry for
5 minutes until softened and lightly golden. Add
the Pernod and reduce by half.
2 Stir in the tomatoes, crushing them down with a
potato masher, then add the chilli sauce and fish
stock. Bring to the boil, cover and simmer for
30 minutes until rich and thickened slightly.
3 Meanwhile, cut all the fish into large, equal-sized
cubes. Add to the stew, cover and simmer gently
for a further 5 minutes or until the fish is just
cooked. Season with salt and pepper to taste.
4 Serve sprinkled with the olives and parsley.
Accompany with plenty of crusty bread.

Variations
• Use other fish – such as swordfish in place of the
tuna and snapper instead of red mullet.
• Omit the Pernod and fry 5ml (1 tsp) fennel seeds
with the onion.

navarin of monkfish

An attractive, delicate fish stew featuring firm monkfish and a medley of spring vegetables – asparagus tips, baby carrots and broad beans.

Serves 4-6
Preparation time: 15-25 minutes
Cooking time: 25 minutes
445-300 cals per serving

1kg (2¼lb) monkfish
25g (1oz) butter
30ml (2 tbsp) sunflower oil
225g (8oz) baby carrots, scrubbed
1 onion, peeled and sliced
1 garlic clove, peeled and crushed
225g (8oz) asparagus tips, trimmed
salt and freshly ground black pepper
60ml (4 tbsp) plain white flour
150ml (¼ pint) dry white wine
175g (6oz) shelled fresh or frozen broad beans,
    skinned if preferred
300ml (½ pint) fish stock
15ml (1 tbsp) lemon juice
45ml (3 tbsp) double cream
30ml (2 tbsp) chopped fresh chervil
chervil sprigs, to garnish

1 Fillet the monkfish by cutting down either side of the central bone. Remove any membrane and cut the fish into large chunks. (Use the bone and trimmings for the stock.)
2 Heat half the butter and oil in a deep sauté pan. Add the carrots, onion, garlic and asparagus; cook gently until just beginning to brown. Remove from the pan; set aside.
3 Season the fish with salt and pepper, and lightly dust with flour. Melt the remaining butter and oil in the pan, add the fish and brown on all sides. Remove and set aside.
4 Add the wine to the hot pan, scraping up any residue from the bottom. Simmer for 2 minutes, then return the vegetables and fish to the pan.
5 Add the broad beans, then pour in the fish stock. Bring to the boil, cover and simmer for about 15 minutes, until the fish is cooked.
6 Lastly, stir in the lemon juice, cream and chervil. Serve at once, garnished with chervil and accompanied by buttered baby new potatoes.

fish puttanesca

Fish is so quick, healthy and simple to cook, it makes an ideal mid-week supper. You could use any other white fleshed fish – such as haddock, monkfish, brill or halibut. Serve with a leafy salad.

Serves 4
Preparation time: 10 minutes
Cooking time: About 35 minutes
300 cals per serving

350g (12oz) new potatoes
salt and freshly ground black pepper
350g (12oz) jar ready-made tomato sauce (for pasta)
150g (5oz) button mushrooms, sliced
450g (1lb) cod or haddock fillet, cut into chunks
50g (2oz) pitted black olives
30ml (2 tbsp) chopped fresh basil
45ml (3 tbsp) freshly grated Parmesan cheese
basil leaves, to garnish

1 Cook the new potatoes in boiling salted water until just tender, about 20 minutes. Drain and put to one side.
2 Pour the tomato sauce into a shallow flameproof casserole or gratin dish. Stir in the potatoes, mushrooms and 50ml (2fl oz) water. Bring to the boil and allow to bubble for 1-2 minutes.
3 Scatter the cod chunks and olives on top of the sauce. Season with pepper, then sprinkle with the basil and Parmesan. Cook in the oven at 200°C/fan oven 190°C (400°F) Mark 6 for 10-15 minutes until the fish is cooked.

guinea fowl with madeira and spiced oranges

If you're thinking of cooking chicken for a special meal consider using guinea fowl, which are cooked in the same way. These lean golden birds have a superb, slightly gamey flavour. For convenience, prepare this casserole a day in advance; keep in the refrigerator overnight.

Serves 6
Preparation time: 30 minutes
Cooking time: 1¼ hours
Suitable for freezing
600 cals per serving

4 tangerines, halved
15ml (1 tbsp) oil
25g (1oz) butter
6-8 guinea fowl joints or corn-fed chicken joints, 2kg (4½lb) in total
225g (8oz) shallots or button onions, peeled, with the root end intact
225g (8oz) streaky bacon, cut into thin strips or lardons
50g (2oz) kumquats, halved
2.5cm (1 inch) piece fresh root ginger, peeled and coarsely grated
2 garlic cloves, peeled and crushed
30ml (2 tbsp) plain flour
300ml (½ pint) Madeira
600ml (1 pint) fresh chicken stock
1 cinnamon stick
45ml (3 tbsp) redcurrant jelly
200g (7oz) vacuum-packed chestnuts (optional)
salt and freshly ground black pepper
chopped flat-leafed parsley, to garnish

1 Squeeze the juice from 1 tangerine and set aside. Heat the oil and butter in a deep flameproof casserole and brown the guinea fowl or chicken joints in batches on both sides. Remove with a slotted spoon and set aside. Add the shallots or button onions, bacon or lardons, halved tangerines and kumquats to the pan and cook, stirring, until brown. Stir in the ginger and garlic and cook for 1 minute.
2 Stir in the flour, Madeira and stock. Return the joints to the casserole, then add the cinnamon stick, tangerine juice and redcurrant jelly.

3 Bring to the boil, then cover and cook at 170°C/fan oven 160°C (325°F) Mark 3 for 50-60 minutes or until tender. (The cooking time is determined by the thickness of the joints, rather than their weight.)
4 Discard the cinnamon stick. Lift the guinea fowl out of the sauce on to a warmed platter, cover with foil and keep warm. Bring the sauce to the boil, add the chestnuts, if using, and bubble for 10 minutes or until the liquid is reduced by half. Check the seasoning.
5 Pour the sauce over the guinea fowl, garnish with parsley and serve with fragrant couscous (see page 271).

Note Harissa is a north African spice paste based on hot red chillies, olive oil, garlic and spices.

spiced poussin with saffron and figs

When poussin or chicken is cooked in this way and served with couscous it's called a tagine and traditionally requires 9 different spices. This quick version uses just 5 spices but is still packed with flavour. Use a flameproof casserole large enough to hold the poussins side by side. Serve with fragrant couscous (see page 271).

Serves 4
Preparation time: 15 minutes
Cooking time: 1¼ hours
350 cals per serving

2 poussins, each about 350g (12oz)
30ml (2 tbsp) sunflower oil
6 small onions, peeled and quartered (see note)
2.5cm (1 inch) piece fresh root ginger, peeled and finely chopped
5ml (1 tsp) coriander seeds, crushed
large pinch of saffron strands
5ml (1 tsp) turmeric
1 cinnamon stick
250g (9oz) ready-to-eat dried figs
salt and freshly ground black pepper

1 Heat the oil in a flameproof casserole and fry the onions for about 10 minutes or until soft and golden. Add the ginger and fry for 1-2 minutes. Stir in the coriander seeds, saffron, turmeric and cinnamon stick and fry together for a further 1-2 minutes.

2 Place the poussins in the casserole, breast-side down, and cook until lightly browned. Scatter the figs around and pour in 600ml (1 pint) boiling water. Season with plenty of salt and pepper. Cover the casserole tightly and cook at 190°C/fan oven 180°C (375°F) Mark 5 for 1 hour until the poussins are very tender – the flesh should be falling off the bone. Discard the cinnamon stick.

3 Lift the poussins, figs and onions from the cooking liquid with a slotted spoon and place in an ovenproof dish. Cover and keep warm in a low oven until ready to serve. (Use the stock for the fragrant couscous to accompany.)

Notes
• Poussin has sweet, tender meat and cooks within the hour. The bones can be cut easily with kitchen scissors – just split each poussin in half along the breastbone and backbone before serving.
• When you peel onions for recipes such as these, leave on the root end and just trim it. That way, even if you quarter the onions the pieces will stay in shape and not fall apart during cooking.

chicken casserole with black-eye beans

This satisfying winter stew relies on a good mix of root vegetables, lentils and beans for flavour.

Serves 4-6
Preparation time: 15-20 minutes
Cooking time: About 1 hour
Suitable for freezing
580-390 cals per serving

1.4kg (3lb) chicken, jointed, or 4 chicken quarters, halved
salt and freshly ground black pepper
30ml (2 tbsp) plain flour
30-45ml (2-3 tbsp) olive oil
2 onions, peeled and roughly chopped
2 parsnips, peeled and cut into chunks
2 large carrots, peeled and cut into chunks
2 large potatoes, peeled and cut into chunks
125g (4oz) split red lentils
2 bay leaves
2 garlic cloves (optional)
425g (15oz) can black-eye beans, drained and rinsed
2 courgettes, sliced
45ml (3 tbsp) chopped fresh parsley

1 Season the chicken pieces with salt and pepper and toss in the flour to coat lightly.
2 Heat 30ml (2 tbsp) oil in a flameproof casserole and brown the chicken in batches on all sides; remove and set aside.
3 Fry the onions, parsnips, carrots and potatoes in the casserole, adding a little extra oil if necessary, until lightly browned.
4 Return the chicken to the casserole and add the lentils, bay leaves, garlic if using, and 900ml (1½ pints) water. Cover with a tight-fitting lid and simmer gently, stirring occasionally, for 45 minutes or until the chicken is tender and the lentils are soft and mushy.
5 Add the black-eye beans and courgettes. Season and cook for a further 15 minutes or until the courgettes are just tender.
6 If the sauce is too thin, retrieve a few spoonfuls of vegetables, mash them with a potato masher and return to the stew to thicken it slightly. Sprinkle with the chopped parsley to serve.

italian chicken cassoulet

This sustaining dish is a meal in itself. For a less rich version, leave out the sausages and/or beans.

Serves 8
Preparation time: 30 minutes
Cooking time: 2 hours
Suitable for freezing (without Parma ham)
1175 cals per serving

40ml (8 tsp) black olive tapenade
8 chicken quarters, each about 350g (12oz)
4 garlic bulbs, split vertically
4 fennel bulbs, quartered
150ml (¼ pint) olive oil
450g (1lb) Toulouse or other spicy sausages
freshly crushed black peppercorns and sea salt
8 fresh rosemary sprigs, plus extra for garnish
120ml (8 tbsp) lemon juice (2-3 lemons, squeezed shells cut into chunks and reserved)
900ml (1½ pints) fresh chicken stock
three 395g (14oz) cans cannellini beans, drained
140g (5oz) packet prosciutto or Parma ham
rosemary sprigs, to garnish

1 Tuck 5ml (1 tsp) of tapenade under the skin of each chicken quarter; set aside. Put the garlic in a large roasting tin with the fennel and 60ml (4 tbsp) oil. Toss well and roast at 220°C/fan oven 210°C (425°F) Mark 7 for 30 minutes.
2 Heat 45ml (3 tbsp) oil in a large, non-stick frying pan. Fry the chicken in batches, skin-side down, for about 4 minutes until deep brown, then turn over and fry for 1 minute.
3 Put the chicken, skin-side up, in two large roasting tins or wide, shallow flameproof dishes.
4 Lower the heat under the frying pan, add the sausages and brown evenly. Add to the chicken with the roasted fennel and garlic, plenty of seasoning, the rosemary, lemon juice and lemon shells. Drizzle with the remaining olive oil.
5 Cook at 220°C/fan oven 210°C (425°F) Mark 7 for 45 minutes, swapping the roasting tins around halfway through. Add the stock and cannellini beans. Return to the oven for 15 minutes, then lay the Parma ham on top and cook for a further 10 minutes or until the ham is crisp and the chicken is cooked through. Garnish with rosemary to serve.

chicken with citrus and pesto sauce

Try to use fresh stock for this recipe (available from the supermarket chilled cabinet), as the flavour is far superior to the stock cube option.

Serves 6
Preparation time: 40 minutes
Cooking time: 1 hour 20 minutes
Suitable for freezing (stage 3)
860 cals per serving

30ml (2 tbsp) olive oil
6 corn-fed chicken portions
1 onion, peeled and finely chopped
225g (8oz) shallots, peeled
2 garlic cloves, peeled and crushed
600ml (1 pint) fresh chicken stock
15ml (1 tbsp) chopped fresh thyme
900g (2lb) new potatoes
salt and freshly ground black pepper
225g (8oz) trimmed baby carrots
225g (8oz) asparagus tips
225g (8oz) French beans
225g (8oz) broad beans
150ml (¼ pint) double cream
2 large egg yolks
juice of 3 lemons
FOR THE PESTO SAUCE:
40g (1½oz) fresh dill, roughly chopped
40g (1½oz) fresh mint, roughly chopped
2 garlic cloves, peeled and chopped
50g (2oz) pine nuts, toasted
100ml (3½oz) olive oil

1 First make the pesto sauce. Put the dill, mint and garlic in a food processor and process for 10 seconds. Add the pine nuts and olive oil; whizz for 10 seconds. Season generously with salt and pepper, cover and set aside.

2 Heat the oil in a large flameproof casserole and brown the chicken in batches for 8 minutes or until the skin is golden. Remove from casserole and drain off the fat, reserving 15ml (1 tbsp).

3 Wipe the casserole clean. Return the reserved fat to the casserole, add the chopped onion and whole shallots and cook gently for 5 minutes or until soft and golden. Add the garlic and cook for 1 minute.

4 Add the stock, thyme and potatoes to the casserole, place the chicken on top and season. Bring to the boil. Cover and cook at 200°C/fan oven 190°C (400°F) Mark 6 for 30 minutes. Add the carrots, re-cover and cook for a further 30 minutes or until the chicken is cooked.

5 Meanwhile, blanch the asparagus, broad beans, and French beans in a large pan of boiling water for 2-3 minutes. Drain and immediately refresh in a bowl of iced water. Drain and pat dry, then slip the broad beans out of their skins. Add to the casserole and warm through for 2-3 minutes.

6 Using a slotted spoon, transfer the chicken and vegetables to a large serving dish; keep warm. Mix the cream, egg yolks and lemon juice together in a bowl and whisk in a large ladleful of the hot chicken stock. Pour into the casserole and stir over a low heat until the sauce thickens; do not boil. Season and pour over the chicken. Serve topped with the pesto sauce.

normandy chicken fricassée

A rich, creamy casserole flavoured with cider, bay, smoked bacon and mushrooms, served with golden sautéed apples.

Serves 8
Preparation time: 40 minutes
Cooking time: 45-50 minutes
480 cals per serving

8 large chicken quarters, halved
45ml (3 tbsp) plain white flour
salt and freshly ground black pepper
450g (1lb) button onions
75g (3oz) butter
225g (8oz) smoked bacon, derinded and chopped
45ml (3 tbsp) olive oil
300ml (½ pint) dry cider
300ml (½ pint) fresh chicken stock
2 bay leaves
8 small eating apples, such as Cox's
450g (1lb) small open cup mushrooms
15ml (1 tbsp) Dijon mustard
150ml (¼ pint) crème fraîche
chopped parsley, to garnish

1 Toss the chicken pieces in the seasoned flour to coat on all sides.

2 Put the onions in a bowl, add boiling water to cover and leave to soak for a few minutes. Drain and peel, leaving the root end attached.

3 Heat half of the butter in a large flameproof casserole dish. Add the bacon and onions and cook until golden brown. Remove from the pan with a slotted spoon and set aside. Add the oil to the pan, increase the heat, then brown the chicken in batches on all sides.

4 Return all the browned chicken pieces to the casserole dish along with any excess flour. Add the cider, chicken stock, bay leaves and seasoning and bring to the boil. Stir to loosen any sediment from the bottom of the casserole, then lower the heat, cover tightly and simmer gently for 25 minutes.

5 Meanwhile, core the apples and peel them if preferred. Heat the remaining butter in a heavy-based frying pan. Add the apples and cook until golden brown on the outside, shaking the pan occasionally to ensure that they brown evenly. Lower the heat, add 30ml (2 tbsp) water, then cover the pan and cook very gently for about 10 minutes or until the apples are cooked but not soft and collapsed.

6 Add the bacon, onions and mushrooms to the chicken. Re-cover and cook for a further 15-20 minutes or until the chicken is cooked right through. Skim off excess fat. Stir in the mustard, crème fraîche and salt and pepper.

7 Serve the fricassée with the apples, sprinkled generously with chopped parsley.

Note If preferred, use 2 chickens, each about 1.6kg (3½lb), jointed.

Variation For a simple fricassée, omit the apples.

buying poultry

Most supermarkets and butchers offer a wide variety of poultry. Free-range birds – which have been raised predominantly on a grain diet and allowed access to open air runs – are now widely available. Organic chickens are also obtainable. These are more expensive than ordinary poultry, but invariably tastier and preferred by many consumers.

OVEN-READY CHICKENS are sold completely eviscerated, fresh or frozen, with or without giblets. They range from 1.4-3.2kg (3-7lb). Pre-basted birds are also available. Allow at least 375g (12oz) per person.

CORN-FED CHICKENS have a distinctive yellow colour and characteristic flavour because they are reared on a diet of maize.

POUSSINS are 4-6 week-old chickens, weighing 450-675g (1-1½lb). A poussin serves 1 or 2. These tender birds can be stuffed and roasted; or spatch-cocked (split and flattened), then grilled or barbecued.

CHICKEN PORTIONS are available in many forms. In addition to chicken quarters, breast fillets, thighs and drumsticks, look out for goujons (strips of breast meat); escalopes (skinned and flattened breast fillets); supremes (breast fillets, with the wing bone attached).

handling and storing poultry

All poultry contains low levels of salmonella and campylobacter – the bacteria which can cause food poisoning if they multiply. It must therefore be handled and stored hygienically. Always get poultry home and into a refrigerator as soon as possible after buying. If the bird contains giblets take them out and store in a separate container. Wash your hands before and after handling poultry – and never use the same utensils for preparing raw poultry and cooked foods.

- If you buy frozen poultry, defrost it at cool room temperature rather than in the fridge. Frozen poultry must be fully thawed before cooking.
- Always ensure poultry is cooked thoroughly. To test, pierce the thickest part of the thigh with a skewer; only if the juices run clear – not at all pink – is the poultry cooked. Refrigerate leftover meat as soon as possible and eat within 2 days.

chicken and coriander chicken

Rich with coconut and scented with coriander, this is an easy curry – perfect if you're having friends to supper and there's little time to cook. Warm naan bread is an ideal accompaniment.

Serves 4
Preparation time: 10 minutes
Cooking time: 45 minutes
600 cals per serving

30ml (2 tbsp) roughly chopped fresh coriander
4 skinless chicken supremes (see note)
45ml (3 tbsp) vegetable oil
1 large onion, about 225g (8oz), finely chopped
350g (12oz) sweet potato, peeled and chopped
30ml (2 tbsp) mild curry paste (see note)
400ml (14fl oz) can coconut milk (see note)
400g (14 oz) can chopped tomatoes
salt and freshly ground black pepper
coriander leaves and lime halves, to garnish

1 Tuck a little fresh coriander in the centre of each piece of chicken, then roll up and secure with a wooden cocktail stick. (Or, to save time, simply add the coriander to the sauce in step 3).
2 Heat the oil in a deep frying pan or a shallow flameproof casserole, then fry the onion and sweet potato for about 10 minutes until the onion is soft. Add the curry paste and cook, stirring, for 3-4 minutes.
3 Add the coconut milk, tomatoes and chicken. Cover and simmer very gently for about 30 minutes or until the chicken is tender. If the pieces aren't completely covered in the sauce, turn the chicken over halfway through cooking. Adjust the seasoning. Serve garnished with coriander sprigs and lime halves.

Notes
- Chicken supremes have the little wing bone still attached. If you can't find them, use breasts or fillets and reduce the cooking time by 5 minutes.
- Curry pastes vary in heat and flavour and there are dozens to choose from.
- If you can't find canned coconut milk, dissolve a 200g (7oz) block of creamed coconut in 400ml (14fl oz) warm water.

stoved garlic chicken

Serves 4
Preparation time: 20 minutes
Cooking time: About 1¼ hours
555 cals per serving

900g (2lb) old potatoes, preferably King Edward's
salt and freshly ground black pepper
75g (3oz) butter
1 oven-ready free-range chicken, about 1.4kg (3lb), jointed into 8 pieces
45ml (3 tbsp) olive oil
8 garlic cloves, peeled
finely grated rind of 1 lemon
10ml (2 tsp) chopped fresh thyme
10ml (2 tsp) chopped fresh rosemary
1 bay leaf
300ml (½ pint) well-flavoured hot chicken stock

1 Peel the potatoes. Cut half of them into 5 mm (¼ inch) thick slices and immerse in a bowl of salted cold water. Slice the rest of the potatoes thinly and place in another bowl of salted cold water; set aside.
2 Melt 50g (2oz) butter in a frying pan until foaming and brown the chicken joints evenly all over.
3 Drain the thickly sliced potatoes, pat dry with kitchen paper, then toss with half of the olive oil and arrange in a thick layer over the base of a deep ovenproof casserole.
4 Lay the chicken joints on top of the potatoes and pour over any pan juices. Tuck the garlic cloves all around the chicken and scatter over the lemon rind. Sprinkle with the thyme and rosemary and tuck in the bay leaf. Season well with salt and pepper.
5 Drain the thinly sliced potatoes, pat dry, toss with the remaining oil and arrange over the chicken. Pour in the boiling stock, set over a moderate heat and bring slowly back to the boil. Cover with a tight-fitting lid and bake at 190°C/fan oven 180°C (375°F) Mark 5 for 1 hour.
6 Melt the remaining butter and brush over the potato topping. Bake, uncovered, for a further 15-20 minutes to brown the potatoes. Serve with steamed Savoy cabbage or spinach and carrots.

duck breast boulangère

Serves 6
Preparation time: 20 minutes
Cooking time: 45 minutes
500 cals per serving

900g (2lb) old potatoes
50g (2oz) butter
5 juniper berries, bruised
2 bay leaves
salt and freshly ground black pepper
300ml (½ pint) duck or chicken stock
3 heads of garlic, halved horizontally
3 magret duck breasts, each 350g (12oz)
150ml (¼ pint) red wine

1 Peel and thinly slice the potatoes; immerse in a bowl of cold water. Grease a 25cm (10 inch) shallow round ovenproof pan (or flameproof baking dish) liberally with a large knob of the butter. Drain the potatoes and pat dry on kitchen paper.

2 Spread half the potatoes over the base of the pan or dish. Dot with half the remaining butter, scatter over the juniper berries and bay leaves, and season well. Cover with the remaining potatoes, finishing with a neat layer of overlapping slices.

3 Pour in the hot stock and set the garlic heads, cut-side uppermost, around the edge of the dish. Place over a moderate heat and bring to the boil. Bake in the oven at 220°C/fan oven 210°C (425°F) Mark 7 for 45 minutes.

4 Meanwhile, score the fat side of the duck. Sprinkle with salt and rub well into the cuts.

5 About 25 minutes before the potatoes will be cooked, preheat a heavy-based frying pan over a medium high heat, then fry the duck breasts, fat-side down, for 4 minutes. Turn the duck breasts over and cook for 1 minute.

6 Lift the duck breasts out of the pan, and set on top of the potatoes, in between the garlic. Pour the fat from the frying pan over the potatoes and garlic. Return to the oven for 15 minutes; the duck will be medium rare. Pour the wine into the sediment in the frying pan and bubble to reduce by half.

7 Allow to rest in a warm place for 10 minutes, then carve the duck breasts into thick slices. Cut the potato cake into wedges and place on warmed serving plates with a roast garlic half alongside. Arrange the duck on the bed of potatoes and pour on a little of the red wine gravy. Scoop out and spread the garlic on each duck slice as you eat.

thai-style beef curry

Serves 4
Preparation time: 30 minutes
Cooking time: 40-45 minutes
505 cals per serving

450g (1lb) sirloin steak
4 cloves
5ml (1 tsp) each coriander and cumin seeds
seeds from 3 cardamom pods
2.5cm (1 inch) fresh root ginger, peeled
2 garlic cloves, peeled and roughly chopped
1 small onion, peeled and roughly chopped
30ml (2 tbsp) sunflower oil
15ml (1 tbsp) sesame oil
15ml (1 tbsp) Thai red curry paste
5ml (1 tsp) turmeric
225g (8oz) potatoes, peeled and quartered
4 tomatoes, quartered
5ml (1 tsp) sugar
15ml (1 tbsp) light soy sauce
300ml (½ pint) coconut milk
150ml (¼ pint) beef stock
4 fresh red chillies, bruised
50g (2oz) cashew nuts

1 Cut the steak into 3cm (1¼ inch) cubes.
2 Put the cloves, coriander, cumin and cardamom seeds in a small heavy-based frying pan over a high heat for 1-2 minutes until the spices release their aroma. Cool slightly, then grind to a powder in a spice grinder or blender.
3 Roughly chop the ginger and put in a blender or food processor with the garlic and onion. Purée to form a smooth paste. Heat the two oils together in a deep frying pan. Add the onion purée with the curry paste and stir-fry for 5 minutes, then add the roasted ground spices and turmeric; fry for a further 5 minutes.
4 Add the beef to the pan and fry for 5 minutes until browned on all sides. Add all of the remaining ingredients, except the cashews. Bring to the boil, lower the heat and simmer gently, covered, for 20-25 minutes until the beef is tender and the potatoes are cooked.
5 Stir in the cashews and serve with plain boiled rice or noodles and stir-fried vegetables.

Variation For a vegetarian Thai curry, replace the steak with 450g (1lb) root vegetables, such as celeriac and sweet potato. Add with the potatoes and cook for 25-30 minutes.

rich braised beef with herb and mustard dumplings

This is a revival of a wonderful traditional method of braising. The luting paste seals the casserole tightly and ensures no juices are lost – the result is a rich, intensely flavoured gravy. As with most stews, this is best served the next day.

Serves 6
Preparation time: 35 minutes
Cooking time: 3 hours
Suitable for freezing
465 cals per serving

two 440ml (15fl oz) cans stout (Guinness)
¾ oz (20g) dried porcini mushrooms or ceps, rinsed
1.4kg (3lb) thick-cut shin of beef or skirt
3 large onions, peeled and thickly sliced
450g (1lb) large carrots, peeled and cut into large chunks
125g (4oz) lardons or cubed pancetta
few fresh thyme sprigs
6 fresh parsley stalks
1 bay leaf
6 allspice berries, crushed
1 clove garlic, peeled and bruised
90ml (6 tbsp) mushroom ketchup
salt and freshly ground black pepper
FOR THE LUTING PASTE:
225g (8oz) plain white flour
150ml (¼ pint) water (approximately)
TO SERVE:
Herb and Mustard Dumplings (optional, see right)

1 Pour the stout into a shallow pan, bring to the boil and fast-boil until reduced by half; cool. Soak the mushrooms in 45ml (3 tbsp) boiling water for 20 minutes. Meanwhile, trim the beef and cut into large chunks.

2 Mix the onions and carrots together and scatter over the base of a heavy casserole (with a tight-fitting lid). Strain the mushrooms, reserving the soaking liquid, and scatter them over the vegetables. Lay the beef on top and scatter over the lardons.

3 Wrap the herbs, allspice and garlic in a small square of muslin and tie with string; bury this bouquet garni in the middle of the casserole. Pour over the cooled, reduced stout, then add the mushroom ketchup and strained mushroom liquid. Season with a little salt and plenty of pepper. Cover, set over a low heat and slowly bring to the boil.

4 Meanwhile, make the luting paste. Mix the flour with enough water to make a smooth pliable dough. Wet the edges of the lidded casserole with a little water. Roll the dough into a long sausage and press around the join of the lid and casserole to form a seal. Bake at 150°C/fan oven 140°C (300°F) Mark 2 for 3 hours.

5 Break the luting paste seal and discard the muslin bag. Stir the stew carefully, check the seasoning and serve topped with the dumplings, or accompanied by mashed potato and cabbage or other seasonal green vegetable.

herb and mustard dumplings

Mix 175g (6oz) self-raising flour with a pinch of salt, 75g (3oz) beef or vegetable suet, 5ml (1 tsp) mustard powder, finely grated rind of ½ lemon and 30-45ml (2-3 tbsp) chopped fresh parsley. Stir in just enough iced water to bind to a soft dough. Divide the dough into 12 equal pieces and lightly roll into balls with floured hands. Drop into a shallow pan of simmering stock and simmer for 30 minutes, then lift out with a slotted spoon, drain and serve with a rich beef (or lamb) stew.

carbonnade de boeuf

Slices of lean stewing beef and caramelised onions are cooked in beer in this French classic. For a darker stew, use half light ale and half sweet stout.

Serves 6
Preparation time: 35 minutes
Cooking time: About 2½ hours
Suitable for freezing
475 cals per serving

1.4kg (3lb) chuck steak, trimmed
50g (2oz) beef dripping
700g (1½lb) onions, peeled, halved and thinly sliced
4 garlic cloves, peeled and crushed
30ml (2 tbsp) light brown sugar
45ml (3 tbsp) plain white flour
600ml (1 pint) light ale or lager
300ml (½ pint) beef stock
1 bay leaf
2 large fresh thyme sprigs
salt and freshly ground black pepper
30ml (2 tbsp) wine or cider vinegar
chopped parsley, to garnish

1 Cut the meat into pieces, about 5cm (2 inches) square and 1cm (½ inch) thick. Heat the beef dripping in a large heavy-based frying pan and brown the meat in batches over a high heat. With a slotted spoon, transfer to a large casserole.

2 Add the onions to the pan and cook for 10 minutes, stirring until they begin to soften. Add the garlic and sugar, mix well and cook gently for 10 minutes or until they begin to brown and caramelise.

3 Stir in the flour, then gradually add the beer, stirring. Bring to the boil, scraping up any sediment from the bottom of the pan, then pour over the beef in the casserole.

4 Add the stock, onions, herbs and plenty of pepper; stir lightly to mix. Bring to a simmer, then cover tightly and cook at 150°C/fan oven 140°C (300°F) Mark 2 for about 2 hours.

5 Stir in the vinegar and cook for a further 30 minutes or until the meat is very tender. Check seasoning. Serve garnished with chopped parsley.

beef casserole with olives

Serves 6
Preparation time: 40 minutes
Cooking time: About 2¼ hours
Suitable for freezing
835 cals per serving

1.1kg (2½lb) stewing steak
90ml (6 tbsp) oil
350g (12oz) unsmoked streaky bacon lardons
450g (1lb) onions, peeled and roughly chopped
3 large garlic cloves, peeled and crushed
30ml (2 tbsp) tomato paste
100ml (3½fl oz) brandy
15ml (1 tbsp) plain flour
150ml (¼ pint) red wine
300ml (½ pint) hot beef stock
1 bouquet garni
225g (8oz) flat mushrooms, quartered
125g (4oz) black olives
salt and freshly ground black pepper
FOR THE PARSLEY CROÛTES:
small handful flat-leafed parsley
15ml (1 tbsp) chopped chives
90ml (6 tbsp) fresh white breadcrumbs
5ml (1 tsp) capers
30ml (2 tbsp) lemon juice
75ml (5 tbsp) olive oil, plus extra for drizzling
1 small ciabatta, cut into 5mm (¼ inch) slices

1 Cut the beef into 4cm (1½ inch) cubes. Heat half the oil in a large flameproof casserole and brown the beef in batches; remove. Fry the bacon in the casserole until golden brown; remove.

2 Add remaining oil and fry the onions until golden brown. Add the garlic, fry for 30 seconds, then mix in the tomato paste. Add the brandy and reduce by half. Stir in the flour, then the wine and bubble for 1 minute. Return all meat to the casserole; add the stock and bouquet garni.

3 Cover and cook at 170°C/fan oven 160°C (325°F) Mark 3 for 1½ hours or until tender. Add the mushrooms; cook for 5 minutes.

4 For the croûtes, whizz the herbs, breadcrumbs, capers, lemon juice and olive oil in a blender to combine. Drizzle the ciabatta slices with olive oil, toast under the grill, then top with the herb mix.

5 Just before serving, remove bouquet garni from the casserole and stir in the olives. Check the seasoning. Serve topped with the parsley croûtes.

red lamb curry with pumpkin and coconut

Serves 4
Preparation time: 10 minutes
Cooking time: 1 hour 20 minutes
470 cals per serving

15ml (1 tbsp) vegetable oil
600g (1¼lb) boneless leg of lamb, trimmed and cut
    into 2.5cm (1 inch) cubes
225g (8oz) red onion, peeled and chopped
125g (4oz) creamed coconut
10ml (2 tsp) red Thai curry paste
2.5cm (1 inch) piece fresh root ginger, peeled and
    chopped
salt
225g (8oz) peeled, deseeded pumpkin
60ml (4 tbsp) mango chutney
basil leaves and fried red onion rings, to garnish

1 Heat the oil in a heavy-based pan and fry the lamb over a high heat until deep golden brown. Lower the heat, add the onion and fry, stirring, for 5-10 minutes until the onion is softened and golden.

2 Meanwhile, pour 600ml (1 pint) boiling water over the creamed coconut and leave to dissolve.

3 Add the curry paste and ginger to the lamb and fry, stirring, for a further 1-2 minutes. Stir in the coconut liquid and bring to the boil. Season with salt, then cover and simmer on a very low heat for 30 minutes.

4 Cut the pumpkin into thin wedges and stir into the curry with the chutney. Cook gently, covered, for a further 30 minutes or until the lamb and pumpkin are tender. Serve garnished with basil and onion rings, accompanied by basmati rice.

Note If you can't find block creamed coconut, use 600ml (1 pint) canned coconut milk.

italian braised lamb shanks

Lamb shanks are braised long and slow in a rich tomato sauce until meltingly tender. Tossed with pasta and fresh Parmesan, this is Italian comfort food at its best.

Serves 6-8
Preparation time: 30 minutes
Cooking time: About 3½ hours
Suitable for freezing
660-495 cals per serving

2 half leg knuckles of lamb, each about 1.2-1.4kg
   (2½-3lb)
30ml (2 tbsp) olive oil
30ml (2 tbsp) dried porcini mushrooms, or 125g (4oz)
   fresh mushrooms
75g (3oz) butter
300g (10oz) onion, peeled and diced
175g (6oz) carrot, peeled and diced
175g (6oz) celery, finely chopped
9 sun-dried tomatoes, finely chopped
150g (5oz) spicy Italian sausage, sliced
600ml (1 pint) red wine
400g (14oz) passata or creamed tomatoes
600ml (1 pint) vegetable stock
salt and freshly ground black pepper
125g (4oz) dried pasta shapes
chopped parsley, to garnish
freshly grated Parmesan cheese, to serve

1 Place the lamb knuckles in a roasting tin and drizzle over 15ml (1 tbsp) oil. Roast at 240°C/fan oven 230°C (475°F) Mark 9 for 35 minutes.
2 If using dried porcini, soak in hot water to cover for 30 minutes, then drain, reserving the soaking liquor. Finely chop the soaked or fresh mushrooms if using.
3 Melt the butter with the remaining oil in a large flameproof casserole, add the onion, carrot and celery and cook, stirring, for 10-15 minutes until soft and golden. Stir in the mushrooms (with soaking liquid if relevant); cook for a further 2-3 minutes.
4 Add the sun-dried tomatoes and spicy sausage to the casserole with the wine, passata and stock. Bring to the boil, lower the heat and simmer for 10 minutes.
5 Lift the lamb from the roasting tin, place in the casserole and cover with a tight-fitting lid.
6 Reduce the oven setting to 170°C/fan oven 160°C (325°F) Mark 3. Place the casserole in the oven and cook for a further 2½-3 hours until the lamb is very tender – almost falling off the bone.
7 Lift the lamb on to a warm deep platter. Cover with foil and keep warm. Skim off the fat from the cooking liquor and check seasoning. Place the casserole on a medium heat. Stir in the pasta and simmer for 10 minutes, or until it is tender.
8 Spoon the pasta and sauce around the lamb and sprinkle with parsley. Serve with Parmesan.

lamb braised with artichokes and new potatoes

Fresh artichokes impart a superb flavour to this dish, although frozen or canned artichoke hearts can be used when fresh ones are not in season.

Serves 6
Preparation time: 30 minutes
Cooking time: 2 hours
650 cals per serving

1.4kg (3lb) boned shoulder of lamb
45ml (3 tbsp) olive oil
3 onions, peeled and finely sliced
4 fresh thyme sprigs
1 large fresh rosemary sprig
2 fresh bay leaves
finely grated rind and juice of 1 orange
900ml (1½ pints) well-flavoured lamb or vegetable
   stock
salt and freshly ground black pepper
12 fresh baby artichokes, or 12 frozen prepared
   artichoke hearts, thawed, or 400g (14oz) can
   artichoke hearts in brine, drained and rinsed
lemon juice, for brushing
600g (1¼lb) small new potatoes, scrubbed
175g (6oz) Greek black olives (pitted if preferred)
50g (2oz) butter, softened
30ml (2 tbsp) plain flour
30ml (2 tbsp) finely chopped fresh thyme

1. Trim the lamb and cut into large cubes. Heat the oil in a heavy flameproof casserole and quickly fry the meat in batches until browned on all sides; remove and set aside.

2. Lower the heat, add the onions and cook, stirring, for 10 minutes or until softened and lightly browned. Return the meat to the casserole and add the thyme, rosemary, bay leaves, orange rind and juice, stock and seasoning. Bring to the boil, cover and simmer gently for 1½ hours (see note).

3. To prepare fresh artichokes, break off the tough outside leaves starting at the base until you expose a central core of pale leaves. Slice off the tough green or purple tips. With a small sharp knife, pare the dark green skin from the base and down the stem. Cut in half, unless very small. Brush all cut surfaces with lemon juice to prevent discoloration.

4. Add the new potatoes to the casserole with the olives and fresh artichoke hearts; re-cover and cook for a further 30 minutes. If using frozen or canned artichoke hearts, add 5 minutes before the end of cooking.

5. Work the butter and flour together to make a beurre manié. Strain the liquid from the meat into a saucepan; keep the meat warm in the casserole. Gradually whisk the beurre manié into the liquid, bring to the boil and simmer gently for 10 minutes. Check the seasoning.

6. Remove the bay leaves and any twigs of herbs from the meat. Pour the sauce over the lamb, stir in the chopped thyme and serve.

Note Alternatively, cook the casserole in the oven at 170°C/fan oven 160°C (325°F) Mark 3.

lamb tagine

Serve this fragrant Moroccan dish with couscous.

Serves 8
Preparation time: 20 minutes, plus marinating
Cooking time: About 1½ hours
Suitable for freezing
410 cals per serving

1.4kg (3lb) boneless leg or shoulder of lamb
10ml (2 tsp) ground ginger
10ml (2 tsp) ground coriander
2.5ml (½ tsp) saffron strands
75ml (5 tbsp) olive oil
salt and freshly ground black pepper
275g (10oz) pearl onions or shallots
1 garlic clove, peeled and crushed
15ml (1 tbsp) plain flour
15ml (1 tbsp) tomato paste
450ml (¾ pint) lamb or chicken stock
150ml (¼ pint) sherry
30ml (2 tbsp) chopped fresh coriander
30ml (2 tbsp) chopped fresh parsley
1 bay leaf
1 cinnamon stick
75g (3oz) stoned dates
15ml (1 tbsp) honey
coriander leaves, to garnish

1. Cut the lamb into 4cm (1½ inch) cubes. Place in a bowl with the ginger, ground coriander, saffron and 15ml (1 tbsp) oil. Season, cover and leave to marinate in the refrigerator for at least 4 hours, preferably overnight.

2. Immerse the onions in boiling water for 2 minutes; drain, refresh in cold water and peel.

3. Heat 15ml (1 tbsp) oil in a heavy-based flameproof casserole and brown the lamb in batches, using more oil as necessary. Add the garlic and stir over the heat for 1 minute.

4. Return the lamb to the casserole. Stir in the flour and tomato paste, then add the onions, stock, sherry, herbs and cinnamon stick. Season with salt and pepper. Bring to the boil, cover and cook at 180°C/fan oven 170°C (350°F) Mark 4 for 1¼ hours, stirring occasionally.

5. Discard cinnamon and bay leaf. Add dates and honey and return to oven for 15-20 minutes. Garnish with coriander and serve with couscous.

spiced pork with cranberries and orange

Cranberries, orange and cinnamon cut through the richness of braised pork to delicious effect.

Serves 6
Preparation time: 50 minutes, plus overnight marinating
Cooking time: 1 hour
Suitable for freezing
560 cals per serving

1.1kg (2½lb) pork tenderloin fillets
finely grated rind and juice of 1 orange
15ml (1 tbsp) chopped rosemary
15ml (1 tbsp) chopped thyme
1 garlic clove, crushed
salt and freshly ground black pepper
300ml (½ pint) red wine
24 button onions or shallots
125g (4oz) sugar
45ml (3 tbsp) port
225g (8oz) fresh or frozen cranberries
60ml (4 tbsp) olive oil
1 cinnamon stick
30ml (2 tbsp) plain flour
30ml (2 tbsp) finely chopped celery leaves
150ml (¼ pint) light stock
30ml (2 tbsp) chopped fresh parsley
25g (1oz) butter (preferably unsalted)

1 Tie the pork fillets with string to form a neat shape. Place in a non-metallic dish with the orange rind, 60ml (4 tbsp) of the orange juice, herbs, garlic, pepper and red wine. Cover and leave to marinate in the refrigerator overnight.

2 Peel the onions, leaving root ends intact to keep them whole. Heat the sugar gently in a heavy-based pan until dissolved, then cook to a golden caramel. Add the port and cranberries; set aside.

3 Lift the pork from the marinade and pat dry with kitchen paper; reserve the marinade. Heat half the oil in a flameproof casserole and add the cinnamon. Add the pork and brown well on all sides; take out and set aside.

4 Add the onions to the casserole, with a little extra oil if necessary and fry, stirring, over a moderate heat, for 8-10 minutes until brown. Stir in the flour, celery leaves and reserved marinade. Add the stock and bring to the boil. Simmer gently for 1-2 minutes, then return the pork to the pan.

5 Cover and cook at 170°C/fan oven 160°C (325°F) Mark 3 for 20-25 minutes until the juices run clear when the pork is pierced with a skewer.

6 Transfer the pork to a warmed dish; keep warm. Boil the sauce for 5-10 minutes to reduce until syrupy. Add 150ml (¼ pint) to the cranberry mixture, bring to the boil, then add to the remaining sauce with the parsley; adjust the seasoning.

7 Carve the pork into slices and serve with the sauce. Accompany with sautéed celery and a potato gratin.

buying pork

Pork is an ideal meat for busy cooks, as it is quick to prepare and cook, and it absorbs flavours well. Contrary to popular belief, it's a healthy choice because pigs are now reared to have much less fat then they used to have.

When selecting pork, look for pink, smooth, velvety flesh with firm white fat and pale bones. Pork skin should be pale pinky-fawn, smooth and without hair. Avoid any meat that looks damp, oily or waxy.

pork steaks with gorgonzola

This recipe is also excellent using beef steaks instead of pork.

Serves 4
Preparation time: 5 minutes
Cooking time: 35 minutes
860 cals per serving

4 pork steaks, each about 175g (6oz)
salt and freshly ground black pepper
15ml (1 tbsp) olive oil
400g (14oz) shallots, peeled and quartered
2 garlic cloves, peeled and finely chopped
300ml (½ pint) white wine
300ml (½ pint) double cream
200g (7oz) Gorgonzola cheese, crumbled

1 Season the pork steaks with salt and pepper.
2 Heat the oil in a large, heavy-based frying pan. Fry the pork steaks for 3-4 minutes until deep golden brown, then turn over and cook on the other side. Remove and set aside.
3 Add the shallots and garlic to the pan and fry gently for 5 minutes or until soft. Pour in the wine, bring to the boil and bubble until reduced by half. Add the cream, bring to the boil and bubble to reduce until syrupy. Stir 150g (5oz) of the crumbled cheese into the sauce.
4 Place the pork steaks in an ovenproof dish, pour the sauce over the top, then sprinkle with the remaining cheese. Cook at 180°C/fan oven 170°C (350°F) Mark 4 for 10 minutes. Serve immediately, with green beans.

Note When you peel the shallots, leave the root end intact to ensure they will hold together once cut into quarters.

pork and spinach pots

Serves 4
Preparation time: 20 minutes
Cooking time: 50 minutes
435 cals per serving

15ml (1 tbsp) oil
125g (4oz) onion, peeled and roughly chopped
2 garlic cloves, peeled and crushed
450g (1lb) good-quality lean minced pork
5ml (1 tsp) ground cinnamon
10ml (2 tsp) ground coriander
50g (2oz) ready-to-eat dried apricots, diced
45ml (3 tbsp) Worcestershire sauce
300ml (½ pint) tomato juice
1 beef stock cube
15ml (1 tbsp) sun-dried tomato paste
salt and freshly ground black pepper
300g (11oz) frozen leaf spinach, thawed
15g (½oz) butter
30ml (2 tbsp) double cream
freshly grated nutmeg

FOR THE TOPPING:
50g (2oz) slice brioche loaf or roll
50g (2oz) gruyère cheese, coarsely grated
30ml (2 tbsp) chopped fresh chives
TO GARNISH:
thyme sprigs

1 Heat the oil in a flameproof casserole, add the onion and garlic and cook for about 4 minutes until starting to soften. Add the minced pork, increase the heat and cook, stirring, for 5 minutes until golden brown. Add the cinnamon and coriander; cook, stirring, for 1 minute.

2 Add the apricots, Worcestershire sauce, tomato juice, stock cube, sun-dried tomato paste, 150ml (¼ pint) water and plenty of seasoning. Stir well and bring to the boil. Cover and cook at 170°C/fan oven 160°C (325°F) Mark 3 for 30-40 minutes.

3 Meanwhile, prepare the topping. Roughly break the brioche up into coarse crumbs. Mix the grated cheese with the brioche, chives and plenty of seasoning. Set aside.

4 Squeeze out all excess liquid from the spinach. Heat the butter in a pan, add the spinach and cream; stir over a moderate heat until hot. Season to taste with salt and pepper and nutmeg.

5 Divide the spinach among four 200ml (7fl oz) ovenproof dishes, spoon the pork mixture on top and sprinkle with the brioche crumb mixture.

6 Stand the ovenproof dishes on a baking sheet and cook at 190°C/fan oven 180°C (375°F) Mark 5 for 10 minutes or until the topping is golden brown. Serve garnished with thyme sprigs and sprinkled with crushed pepper.

lemon braised pork chops with cumin

Serves 4
Preparation: 20 minutes
Cooking time: 45 minutes
420 cals per serving

4 pork chops
30ml (2 tbsp) plain flour
10ml (2 tsp) ground cumin
2.5ml (½ tsp) ground coriander
salt and pepper
30ml (2 tbsp) olive oil
2 onions, peeled and thinly sliced
300ml (½ pint) white wine
2.5ml (½ tsp) sugar
1 lemon, thinly sliced
225g (8oz) chestnut or brown cap mushrooms,
    quartered

1 Trim the pork chops of any excess fat. Sift the
   flour with the cumin, coriander, salt and pepper.
   Turn the chops in the spiced flour to coat.
2 Heat the oil in a frying pan, add the chops and
   brown on both sides; transfer to a plate.
3 Add the onions to the pan and cook gently for
   10 minutes until soft and golden. Add the wine
   and sugar. Bring to the boil and allow to bubble
   for 5 minutes until reduced and slightly syrupy.
4 Lay the lemon slices in a shallow ovenproof
   dish. Add the onions and wine, then lay the
   chops on top. Cover with foil. Bake at 190°C/fan
   oven 180°C (375°F) Mark 5 for 20 minutes.
5 Add the mushrooms, pushing them into the
   gaps between the chops. Bake, uncovered, for a
   further 15 minutes. Serve with baked potatoes.

wine-braised sausages with lentils

Sausages are enjoying a renaissance, with
supermarkets stocking a number of premium
brands and many butchers offering their own
special recipes.

Serves 4
Preparation time: 10 minutes
Cooking time: 30 minutes
530 cals per serving

15ml (1 tbsp) oil
450g (1lb) good meaty sausages
2 red onions, peeled and finely chopped
6 baby red peppers, halved and deseeded, or 2 large
    peppers, deseeded and thickly sliced
150ml (¼ pint) light stock
200ml (7fl oz) red wine
420g (15oz) can green lentils, rinsed and drained
salt and freshly ground black pepper
chopped parsley, to garnish

1 Heat the oil in a large flameproof casserole, add
   the sausages and brown for 4-5 minutes.
2 Add the onions to the pan and fry for about
   7 minutes until soft. Stir in the peppers and fry
   until slightly browned.
3 Pour in the stock and red wine and bring to the
   boil. Let the mixture bubble for 2 minutes. Stir
   in the lentils and season with salt and pepper.
   Cover tightly, then simmer gently on the hob for
   about 15 minutes or until most of the liquid has
   been absorbed and the peppers are quite soft.
4 Garnish with chopped parsley to serve.

sausages in red onion marmalade

This onion marmalade goes well with roast pork, duck and game, too. It is also delicious if you replace the sugar with 15ml (1 tbsp) crème de cassis.

Serves 4
Preparation time: 5 minutes
Cooking time: About 1 hour
860 cals per serving

50g (2oz) butter
900g (2lb) good quality sausages
3 large red onions, about 700g (1½lb), peeled and
    thinly sliced
15ml (1 tbsp) chopped fresh thyme
225ml (8fl oz) red wine
50ml (2fl oz) red wine vinegar
15ml (1 tbsp) sugar
salt and freshly ground black pepper
flat-leafed parsley, to garnish

1 Melt half the butter in a roasting tin or a 2 litre (3½ pint) shallow flameproof dish, then add the sausages and fry until lightly browned. Lift out and set aside. Gently fry the onions in the butter remaining in the pan for 10-15 minutes or until soft.

2 Stir in the thyme, wine, vinegar, sugar and seasoning. Bring to the boil and allow to bubble for 2 minutes or until reduced by half.

3 Place the sausages on top of the onions (so they continue to brown in the oven), then bake uncovered at 200°C/fan oven 190°C (400°F) Mark 6 for about 45 minutes, stirring occasionally. The onions should be soft, golden and glazed with the pan juices. If the juices are too concentrated, stir in 50ml (2fl oz) boiling water.

4 Garnish with flat-leafed parsley and serve with mashed potato or soft polenta.

african sweet potato and spinach stew

A richly flavoured vegetarian stew based on a typical African dish.

Serves 4-6
Preparation time: 20 minutes
Cooking time: 40-45 minutes
Suitable for freezing
305-205 cals per serving

60ml (4 tbsp) groundnut oil
1 onion, peeled and chopped
2 garlic cloves, peeled and crushed
10ml (2 tsp) grated fresh root ginger
1.25ml (¼ tsp) cayenne pepper
15ml (1 tbsp) mild or medium curry paste
350g (12oz) peeled sweet potatoes, cubed
300ml (½ pint) passata
300ml (½ pint) vegetable stock
225g (8oz) button mushrooms
225g (8oz) spinach leaves, roughly shredded
60ml (4 tbsp) peanut butter
30ml (2 tbsp) chopped fresh coriander
salt and freshly ground black pepper
chopped coriander, to garnish
Greek yogurt or soured cream, to serve

1 Heat 45ml (3 tbsp) oil in a saucepan, add the onion, garlic, ginger and cayenne and fry gently for 10 minutes. Add the curry paste; cook, stirring, for 1 minute.
2 Add the sweet potatoes, stir to coat with the onion mixture and fry for 3-4 minutes. Add the passata and stock. Bring to the boil, cover and simmer for 15-20 minutes until the potatoes are almost tender.
3 Meanwhile, heat the remaining oil in a frying pan, add the mushrooms and stir-fry for 4-5 minutes until golden and beginning to release their juices. Add to the potatoes with the shredded spinach and cook for a further 5 minutes or until the vegetables are tender.
4 Mix a few spoonfuls of the stew juices with the peanut butter to soften it, then stir back into the pan. Add the coriander, season with salt and pepper to taste and heat through.
5 Scatter over plenty of coriander and serve at once, with yogurt or soured cream.

spring vegetable stew

A wonderfully fresh-tasting stew of baby vegetables, fresh peas and broad beans, scented with garden herbs.

Serves 4
Preparation time: 30 minutes
Cooking time: 25-30 minutes
255 cals per serving

225g (8oz) new potatoes, scrubbed
salt and freshly ground black pepper
75g (3oz) unsalted butter
4 shallots, peeled and thinly sliced
1 garlic clove, peeled and crushed
10ml (2 tsp) chopped fresh thyme
5ml (1 tsp) grated lime rind
6 baby leeks, sliced into 5cm (2 inch) lengths
125g (4oz) baby carrots, scrubbed
125g (4oz) freshly podded peas
125g (4oz) freshly podded broad beans
300ml (½ pint) vegetable stock
1 little gem lettuce, shredded
60ml (4 tbsp) chopped fresh herbs, such as chervil, chives, mint and parsley
chervil sprigs, to garnish

1 Put the potatoes into a saucepan with plenty of cold water to cover. Add a little salt, bring to the boil, cover and cook for 5 minutes. Drain and immediately refresh under cold water.
2 Meanwhile, melt half of the butter in a large sauté pan, add the shallots, garlic, thyme and lime rind and fry gently for 5 minutes until softened and lightly golden. Add the leeks and carrots and sauté for a further 5 minutes.
3 Stir in the potatoes, peas and broad beans, then pour in the stock. Bring to the boil, cover and simmer gently for 10 minutes. Remove the lid and cook, uncovered, for a further 5-8 minutes until all the vegetables are tender.
4 Add the shredded lettuce to the stew with the chopped herbs and remaining butter. Heat through, stirring, until the butter is melted. Check the seasoning and serve at once, garnished with chervil sprigs.

okra and fennel tagine

A spicy Moroccan vegetable stew of okra, baby courgettes, fennel and plum tomatoes.

Serves 4-6
Preparation time: 15 minutes
Cooking time: 40 minutes
160-110 cals per serving

2.5ml (½ tsp) saffron strands
30ml (2 tbsp) olive oil
2 onions, peeled and roughly chopped
3 garlic cloves, peeled and crushed
5ml (1 tsp) ground ginger
5ml (1 tsp) turmeric
5ml (1 tsp) caraway seeds
2.5ml (½ tsp) ground cloves
10ml (2 tsp) paprika
finely grated rind and juice of 1 lemon
300ml (½ pint) vegetable stock
1 large fennel bulb, trimmed
handful of fresh coriander or parsley
3 fresh oregano sprigs
salt and freshly ground black pepper
425g (15oz) can plum tomatoes
350g (12oz) okra
8 baby courgettes, about 225g (8oz)
handful of black olives
harissa sauce, to serve (see note)

1 Put the saffron in a small bowl, pour on 150ml (¼ pint) warm water and leave to soak.
2 Heat the oil in a large casserole dish, add the onions and garlic and sauté until softened. Add the spices and cook, stirring constantly, for 2 minutes. Stir in the lemon rind and juice, the saffron with its soaking liquid, and the stock. Slowly bring to the boil.
3 Meanwhile, cut the fennel into 6 wedges. Roughly chop half of the herbs. Add the fennel and chopped herbs to the casserole and season liberally with salt and pepper. Lower the heat, cover and simmer gently for about 15 minutes until the fennel is softened.
4 Meanwhile drain the tomatoes, being careful not to break them up. Trim the stalk ends of the okra if necessary, being careful not to cut right through into the pod itself. Halve the baby courgettes lengthwise.

5 Add the tomatoes, okra and baby courgettes to the casserole. Simmer gently for 10-15 minutes until the okra and courgettes are cooked. Check the seasoning.
6 Add the remaining fresh herbs and the olives. Serve immediately, with harissa sauce and plenty of bread, rice or couscous to mop up the juices.

Note Harissa sauce is a hot pepper sauce available from delicatessens and selected supermarkets. It is a traditional accompaniment to many North African dishes.

Variation Add 150ml (¼ pint) thick yogurt with the tomatoes and okra, for a milder flavour.

vegetable and chick pea balti

French beans, butternut squash and tomatoes are included in this tempting, aromatic curry. Serve with plenty of naan bread and poppadoms.

Serves 6
Preparation time: 30 minutes
Cooking time: 1¼ hours
Suitable for freezing
245 cals per serving

1 large onion, peeled and chopped
4 garlic cloves, peeled and chopped
4 red chillies, deseeded and chopped
10ml (2 tsp) grated fresh root ginger
60ml (4 tbsp) sunflower oil
10ml (2 tsp) ground coriander
5ml (1 tsp) each ground cinnamon, paprika, fenugreek, turmeric and mustard powder
2.5ml (½ tsp) ground cumin
3 cardamom pods, bruised
450g (1lb) ripe tomatoes, chopped
350g (12oz) peeled potatoes, cut into cubes
350g (12oz) peeled butternut squash, cut into cubes
30ml (2 tbsp) lemon juice
400g (14oz) can chick peas, drained
225g (8oz) French beans, halved
salt and freshly ground black pepper
coriander leaves, to garnish

1. Put the onion, garlic, chillies and ginger in a blender or food processor and blend until fairly smooth.
2. Heat the oil in a saucepan, add the onion mixture and fry gently for 10 minutes until lightly golden, then stir in all of the ground spices and cardamon pods. Add the tomatoes and fry for a further 5 minutes.
3. Add the potatoes and butternut squash to the pan with the lemon juice and chick peas.

4. Pour in 450ml (¾ pint) water and stir well. Bring to the boil, partially cover the pan and simmer gently for 30-45 minutes until the potatoes are tender.
5. Add the French beans to the pan and cook for a further 5-10 minutes until tender. Season with salt and pepper to taste.
6. Scatter over the coriander leaves and serve the balti accompanied by warm naan bread and spicy poppadoms.

quick suppers

These mouth-watering meals
are effortless to prepare and
packed with flavour to set
the tastebuds tingling

bruschetta of mushrooms with poached eggs

Toasted country-style bread topped with thyme scented field mushrooms and poached egg.

Serves 4
Preparation time: 10 minutes
Cooking time: 10 minutes
300 cals per serving

4 thick slices country bread, such as pugliese or pain de campagne
2 garlic cloves, peeled
50g (2oz) butter
450g (1lb) field mushrooms, thinly sliced
10ml (2 tsp) chopped fresh thyme
4 eggs
salt and freshly ground black pepper
TO GARNISH:
rocket or other salad leaves

1 Grill the bread on both sides until golden, then immediately rub all over with the garlic; keep warm in a low oven.
2 Melt the butter in a large frying pan and stir-fry the mushrooms with the thyme over a high heat for 4-5 minutes until golden and starting to release their juices. Cover and keep warm.
3 Poach the eggs either in an egg poacher or in a pan of gently simmering water – allowing 3 minutes for a soft yolk, up to 5 minutes for a firm yolk.
4 Place a slice of garlic bread on each warmed serving plate. Spoon on the mushrooms and pan juices, then top each serving with a poached egg. Serve at once, garnished with rocket or other salad leaves.

egg safety

The young, elderly, pregnant women and those suffering from immune deficiency diseases should avoid raw or lightly cooked eggs, due to the possible risk of salmonella.

pan-fried mushroom and feta omelette

More substantial than a traditional omelette, this is enriched with mushrooms, sun-dried tomatoes, garlic, and melting feta cheese.

Serves 4
Preparation time: 5 minutes
Cooking time: 15 minutes
325 cals per serving

4 large eggs
freshly ground black pepper
50g (2oz) butter
225g (8oz) portabello or other large mushrooms, thinly sliced
3 garlic cloves, peeled and sliced
50g (2oz) sun-dried tomatoes, roughly chopped
100g (3½oz) feta cheese, crumbled
thyme sprigs, to garnish

1 Beat the eggs with 30ml (2 tbsp) cold water and season with pepper. (Salt isn't needed as feta cheese and sun-dried tomatoes are both salty.)
2 Melt the butter in an 18cm (7 inch) diameter non-stick omelette pan (suitable for use under the grill). Add the mushrooms and garlic and fry until the mushrooms are deep golden brown and starting to crisp at the edges. Add the sun-dried tomatoes and stir over the heat for 1-2 minutes.
3 Roughly spread the mushroom mixture over the base of the omelette pan. Pour the beaten egg over the mushrooms, gently swirling the pan to spread it evenly. Leave to set undisturbed on a low heat for 1-2 minutes, then sprinkle with the feta.
4 Place the pan under a preheated hot grill for about 1-2 minutes or until the eggs are lightly cooked and the feta cheese is just beginning to melt.
5 Sprinkle the omelette with pepper and scatter with sprigs of fresh thyme to garnish. Cut into wedges and serve immediately.

Note Portabello mushrooms are giant cup mushrooms with meaty flesh which fry successfully without exuding excess liquid. They are available from major supermarkets.

scrambled eggs with asparagus and smoked salmon

Serves 2
Preparation time: 15 minutes
Cooking time: 5 minutes
560 cals per serving

125g (4oz) asparagus tips
salt and freshly ground black pepper
6 eggs
25g (1oz) butter
50g (2oz) crème fraîche
15ml (1 tbsp) chopped fresh chives
125g (4oz) smoked salmon, cut into strips
TO SERVE:
warm buttered toast
few extra chives
60ml (4 tbsp) salmon caviar (optional)

1 Blanch the asparagus tips in lightly salted boiling water for 2 minutes. Drain, refresh under cold water and pat dry. Cut into 2.5cm (1 inch) lengths.

2 Beat the eggs together thoroughly in a bowl and season with a little salt and plenty of pepper.

3 Melt the butter in a non-stick saucepan over a low heat and add the eggs, stirring with a fork. Cook for a further 1 minute until the eggs are just starting to set, then stir in the crème fraîche and chives.

4 When the eggs are scrambled to a creamy consistency, fold in the blanched asparagus and smoked salmon.

5 Serve the scrambled eggs on warm buttered toast topped with extra chives, and caviar if wished.

227

cherry tomato and mozzarella frittata

Serves 2-3
Preparation time: 10 minutes
Cooking time: 8-10 minutes
590-395 cals per serving

6 eggs
30ml (2 tbsp) chopped fresh basil
15ml (1 tbsp) chopped fresh mint
15ml (1 tbsp) chopped fresh chives
5ml (1 tsp) celery salt
salt and freshly ground black pepper
30ml (2 tbsp) extra-virgin olive oil
175g (6oz) cherry tomatoes, halved
50g (2oz) pitted black olives (optional)
125g (4oz) mozzarella cheese, diced
25g (1oz) rocket leaves
Parmesan cheese shavings, to serve

1 In a bowl, beat the eggs with the herbs, celery salt, ordinary salt and plenty of pepper; set aside.
2 Heat half the oil in a large non-stick frying pan (suitable for placing under a grill). Add the tomatoes and stir-fry for 30 seconds or until starting to soften. Add to the egg mixture with the olives if using, mozzarella cheese and rocket leaves; stir lightly to mix. Clean the frying pan.
3 Heat the remaining oil in the clean frying pan. Swirl in the egg mixture and cook over a medium heat for 5-6 minutes until almost cooked through.
4 Place under a preheated grill for a further 1-2 minutes until the top is set. Let cool slightly, then serve topped with Parmesan shavings.

artichoke and rocket frittata

If you are lucky enough to have a good local Italian delicatessen, try their marinated baby artichokes for this recipe.

Serves 4
Preparation time: 10 minutes
Cooking time: 20 minutes
350 cals per serving

45ml (3 tbsp) olive oil
1 onion, peeled and chopped
400g (14oz) can artichoke hearts, drained
10 large eggs
salt and freshly ground black pepper
25g (1oz) rocket leaves

1 Heat the olive oil in a large non-stick frying pan, add the onion and fry gently for about 10 minutes or until soft and translucent.
2 Meanwhile halve the artichokes and leave to dry on kitchen paper. In a bowl, beat the eggs with 50ml (2fl oz) cold water and season with salt and pepper.
3 Increase the heat under the frying pan, add the artichoke hearts and fry until lightly coloured. Add the beaten eggs and stir with a flat-edged wooden spoon to mix. Reduce the heat and cook the frittata undisturbed until lightly set; this should take 7-8 minutes.
4 Scatter the rocket leaves over the top of the frittata and serve from the pan, cut into wedges.

frittata

The Italian equivalent to the French omelette, a frittata isn't turned during cooking, but cooked on one side only, until the eggs are set. A frittata is a good way of using leftover vegetables or meat, and makes an easy supper served with a salad.

fried halloumi salad with olive salsa

Serves 4
Preparation time: 20 minutes
Cooking time: 2 minutes
425 cals per serving

3 ripe plum tomatoes, chopped
½ small red onion, peeled and thinly sliced
½ green pepper, deseeded and diced
¼ cucumber, sliced
60ml (4 tbsp) extra-virgin olive oil
juice of ½ lemon
250g (9oz) halloumi cheese
30ml (2 tbsp) plain white flour
2.5ml (½ tsp) dried oregano
FOR THE OLIVE SALSA:
75g (3oz) pitted black olives
15ml (1 tbsp) capers, rinsed
1 garlic clove, peeled and crushed
30ml (2 tbsp) chopped fresh parsley
15ml (1 tbsp) chopped fresh basil
60ml (4 tbsp) extra-virgin olive oil
15ml (1 tbsp) balsamic vinegar
salt and freshly ground black pepper

1 Start by making the olive salsa. Finely chop the olives and mix with the capers, garlic, herbs, oil and vinegar. Season with salt and pepper to taste; set aside until required.
2 In a large bowl combine the tomatoes, onion, pepper and cucumber. Add 30ml (2 tbsp) of the oil and the lemon juice and stir well, adding a little salt and pepper.
3 Cut the halloumi into 12 slices and dust with flour. Heat the remaining olive oil in a frying pan and fry the halloumi slices in batches for 1 minute on each side until golden. Drain on kitchen paper.
4 Divide the tomato salad between plates, sprinkling with oregano. Arrange a few cheese slices on each serving and spoon over the olive salsa. Serve at once.

stir-fried prawns with pak choi

Pak choi, a Chinese member of the cabbage family, is full of nutrients and delicious stir-fried with prawns and Thai flavourings.

Serves 4
Preparation time: 20 minutes
Cooking time: 6 minutes
165 cals per serving

225g (8oz) pak choi or Chinese mustard cabbage
30ml (2 tbsp) vegetable oil
2 garlic cloves, peeled and thinly sliced
1 lemon grass stalk, cut in half and bruised
2 kaffir lime leaves, torn into small pieces
1 small red onion, peeled and thinly sliced
1 hot red chilli, deseeded and thinly sliced
4cm (1½ inch) piece fresh root ginger, peeled and cut into long thin shreds
15ml (1 tbsp) coriander seeds, lightly crushed
450g (1lb) large raw prawns, peeled and deveined (see note)
175g (6oz) mangetout, trimmed and halved diagonally
30ml (2 tbsp) Thai fish sauce
juice of 1 lime, or to taste
fried sliced red chilli, to garnish

1 Trim the pak choi or Chinese mustard cabbage, discarding any damaged or discoloured leaves. Tear the leaves into manageable sized pieces.
2 Heat the oil in a wok or large frying pan. Add the garlic, lemon grass, lime leaves, onion, chilli, ginger and coriander, and stir-fry for 2 minutes.
3 Add the raw prawns, mangetout and pak choi or Chinese mustard cabbage to the pan and stir-fry for 2–3 minutes until the vegetables are cooked but still crisp and the prawns are pink and opaque.
4 Add the Thai fish sauce and lime juice, and heat through for 1 minute. Discard the lemon grass. Serve immediately while the vegetables are crisp, garnished with sliced red chilli.

Note If raw prawns are unobtainable, you can use cooked ones instead, adding them at stage 4 to simply heat through.

kedgeree with herb butter

This simple combination of basmati rice, lightly poached smoked haddock, boiled eggs and subtle spices makes a delicious supper, lunch or brunch. The cockles and lemony herb butter provide additional flavour.

Serves 3-4
Preparation time: 10 minutes
Cooking time: About 20 minutes
720 540 cals per serving

450g (1lb) smoked haddock
150ml (¼ pint) milk
225g (8oz) basmati rice
75g (3oz) cooked shelled cockles (optional)
5ml (1 tsp) coriander seeds, finely crushed
3 hard-boiled eggs, quartered
30ml (2 tbsp) double cream
45-60ml (3-4 tbsp) chopped fresh chives
salt and freshly ground black pepper
FOR THE HERB BUTTER:
50g (2oz) butter
5-10ml (1-2 tsp) lemon juice
30ml (2 tbsp) chopped fresh tarragon, dill or chervil
TO GARNISH:
lemon wedges and extra herbs

1 Place the smoked haddock in a shallow pan with the milk. Cover and simmer gently for about 8 minutes until cooked through. Drain, reserving 30-45ml (2-3 tbsp) of the juices. Roughly flake the fish, discarding the skin and any bones.
2 Cook the rice in plenty of boiling salted water for 10 minutes or until just tender. Drain, rinse with boiling water; drain well.
3 Return the rice to the pan and add the flaked haddock, reserved cooking juices, cockles if using, coriander seeds, hard-boiled eggs, cream and chives. Season lightly with salt and pepper and heat through gently for 2 minutes.
4 Meanwhile, for the herb butter, melt the butter and stir in the lemon juice, herbs and a little seasoning. Pour into a warmed jug.
5 Spoon the kedgeree onto warmed serving plates and garnish with lemon wedges and extra herbs. Serve at once, accompanied by the herb butter.

skate with tomatoes and courgettes

Lemon, capers, olives and thyme enhance fish to delicious effect. This recipe is also suitable for salmon fillets.

Serves 4
Preparation time: 10 minutes
Cooking time: 10 minutes
300 cals per serving

4 skate wings, skinned, about 1.4kg (3lb) in total
salt and freshly ground black pepper
30ml (2 tbsp) plain flour
100ml (3½fl oz) oil
3 garlic cloves, peeled and crushed
225g (8oz) tomatoes, deseeded and roughly chopped
125g (4oz) courgettes, finely sliced
finely grated rind and juice of 1 lemon
60ml (4 tbsp) capers, drained
15ml (1 tbsp) chopped thyme
50g (2oz) olives, pitted and halved

1 Lightly coat the skate with seasoned flour. Heat 30ml (2 tbsp) oil in a large frying pan and cook the fish for 1-2 minutes each side until golden brown. Remove from the heat; set aside.
2 Heat the remaining oil in another pan. Add the garlic, tomatoes, courgettes and lemon rind. Stir over a medium heat for 2-3 minutes. Add the lemon juice, capers, thyme, olives and seasoning.
3 Spoon the courgette mixture over the fish and cook on a low heat for 4-5 minutes or until the fish is just tender. Serve at once.

pan-fried red mullet with citrus and basil

Red mullet, with its silvery pink skin is one of the most attractive fish, and has an excellent flavour.

Serves 4
Preparation time: 10 minutes, plus marinating
Cooking time: 10 minutes
430 cals per serving

4 red mullet, each about 225g (8oz), filleted
90ml (6 tbsp) olive oil
10 peppercorns, crushed
2 oranges
1 lemon
30ml (2 tbsp) plain white flour
15g (½oz) butter
2 anchovies
15g (½oz) shredded fresh basil
salt and freshly ground black pepper

1 Place the fish fillets in a shallow dish, in a single layer. Drizzle over the olive oil and sprinkle with the peppercorns. Peel one of the oranges, removing all of the skin and white pith, then cut into thin slices. Lay the orange slices over the fish. Cover and leave to marinate in the refrigerator for 4 hours.
2 Halve the lemon. Remove the skin and white pith from one half, then slice thinly. Squeeze the juice from the other half and reserve.
3 Using a fish slice, lift the fish out of the marinade (reserving the marinade) and pat dry on kitchen paper. Season with salt and pepper, then dust lightly with flour.
4 Heat 45ml (3 tbsp) of the marinade in a sauté pan or frying pan. Add the red mullet and fry for 2 minutes on each side; remove and set aside. Discard the oil remaining in the pan.
5 Melt the butter in the pan with the remaining marinade. Add the anchovies and crush to dissolve. Add the juice of the remaining orange and the reserved lemon juice. Season and cook until slightly reduced. Lastly, stir in the basil.
6 Pour the citrus sauce over the fish and garnish with the orange and lemon slices. Serve at once, with steamed couscous or rice and a salad.

salmon au poivre

Serves 4
Preparation time: 15 minutes, plus infusing
Cooking time: 6-8 minutes
695 cals per serving

4 salmon fillets, each about 150g (6oz)
30ml (2 tbsp) olive oil
15ml (1 tbsp) black peppercorns, roughly crushed
5ml (1 tsp) sea salt
FOR THE LEMON AND HERB HOLLANDAISE:
30ml (2 tbsp) lemon juice
45ml (3 tbsp) dry white wine
1 bay leaf
6 white peppercorns
3 egg yolks
175g (6oz) unsalted butter, melted
15ml (1 tbsp) chopped fresh chervil
salt
TO GARNISH:
chervil sprigs

1 Wash the salmon and pat dry, then brush with a little of the oil. Mix the peppercorns with the sea salt and use to coat the salmon. If possible, set aside to infuse for 1 hour.

2 To make the sauce, put the lemon juice, wine, bay leaf and white peppercorns in a small pan and boil until the liquid is reduced to 15ml (1 tbsp). Strain into the food processor bowl. Stir in 15ml (1 tbsp) cold water and the egg yolks. Whizz for 3-4 minutes until pale and frothy.

3 With the motor running, gradually add the hot butter through the feeder tube until the sauce is thickened. Stir in the chervil and salt to taste. Thin with a little hot water if the sauce is too thick. Pour into a heatproof bowl; keep warm over a pan of hot water.

4 Heat the remaining oil in a heavy-based frying pan. Add the salmon fillets, skin-side down, and cook for 3 minutes, then turn and cook for a further 2-3 minutes. Remove from pan and let rest for a few minutes before serving, garnished with chervil and accompanied by the sauce.

stir-fried chicken with spinach, cherry tomatoes and pine nuts

Serves 4
Preparation time: 10 minutes
Cooking time: 6 minutes
305 cals per serving

450g (1lb) skinless chicken breast fillets
30ml (2 tbsp) corn oil
450g (1lb) ripe cherry tomatoes, halved
225g (8oz) young ready-prepared spinach
salt and freshly ground black pepper
30ml (1 tbsp) balsamic vinegar
50g (2oz) pine nuts, toasted

1 Cut the chicken into strips. Heat the oil in a large wok or non-stick frying pan until very hot. Stir-fry the chicken strips in two batches for 2-3 minutes until golden brown. Return all the chicken to the pan.
2 Toss in the cherry tomatoes and stir-fry until they begin to disintegrate slightly. Add the spinach and stir-fry until it just wilts. Season with salt and pepper to taste.
3 Drizzle the balsamic vinegar around the edge of the pan and allow to evaporate.
4 Stir in the toasted pine nuts and serve at once, on a bed of thin pasta tossed in a little chilli oil.

Variation Use almonds instead of pine nuts.

grilled chicken with pesto butter

Serves 4
Preparation time: 10 minutes
Cooking time: 20-30 minutes
370 cals per serving

4 chicken breast fillets or supremes, with skin
salt and freshly ground black pepper
75g (3oz) butter, softened
45ml (3 tbsp) pesto
lemon juice, for sprinkling

1 Make 3-4 deep cuts on each side of the chicken breasts. If using supremes, make several cuts on the skin side. Season well.
2 Gradually work the pesto into the butter. Spread half of the butter over the chicken skin and sprinkle with a little lemon juice.
3 Lay the chicken on the grill rack and grill for about 10 minutes. Turn the portions over, spread with the remaining butter and sprinkle lightly with lemon juice. Grill for 10 minutes or until cooked through. (Some portions may take 5-10 minutes longer, depending on size and shape.)
4 Serve the chicken with any accumulated pan juices poured over.

chicken, bean and spinach curry

Serves 4
Preparation time: 10 minutes
Cooking time: 20 minutes
435 cals per serving

15ml (1 tbsp) sunflower oil
350g (12oz) skinless chicken breast fillets, cut into strips
1 garlic clove, peeled and crushed
300-350g (10-12oz) jar ready-made curry sauce
400g (14oz) can aduki beans, drained and rinsed
175g (6oz) ready-to-eat dried apricots
150g (5oz) natural bio yogurt (see note)
125g (4oz) ready-prepared fresh spinach

1 Heat the oil in a large saucepan, add the chicken and garlic and fry until golden.
2 Add the curry sauce, aduki beans and apricots, then cover and simmer gently for 15 minutes or until the chicken is tender.
3 Over a low heat, stir in the yogurt, keeping the curry hot without boiling, then add the spinach and stir over the heat until it just begins to wilt. Serve immediately.

Note Bio yogurt is the best choice for this curry as it's not as acidic as standard natural yogurt. For an extra creamy curry sauce, stir in a little cream with the yogurt.

lime and sesame chicken

Serves 4
Preparation time: 15 minutes, plus marinating
Cooking time: 10 minutes
270 cals per serving

4 chicken breast fillets, cut into bite-sized strips
2 lemon grass stalks, finely chopped
finely grated rind of 1 lime
juice of 2 limes
4 plump garlic cloves, peeled and crushed
225g (8oz) shallots, peeled and thinly sliced
30ml (2 tbsp) Thai fish sauce
10ml (2 tsp) light brown muscovado sugar
1 small red chilli, deseeded and finely chopped
30ml (2 tbsp) oil
15ml (1 tbsp) sesame oil
15ml (1 tbsp) sesame seeds
a little oil, for stir-frying
lime wedges, to garnish

1 Mix together all the ingredients (except the oil for frying) in a large non-metallic bowl. Cover and leave to marinate in the refrigerator for 2-3 hours.
2 Wipe the surface of a large wok with a little oil and place over a high heat until smoking hot.
3 Stir-fry the chicken mixture, in batches, for 3-4 minutes until golden brown and cooked through. Return all the chicken to the wok and toss together over the heat for 1 minute.
4 Serve immediately, with lime wedges and rice.

chicken goujons with a cheese and herb crust

These scrumptious chicken morsels are a great favourite with children.

Serves 4
Preparation time: 15 minutes
Cooking time: 10 minutes
300 cals per serving

125g (4oz) ciabatta, roughly chopped
75g (3oz) Stilton or Gorgonzola cheese, crumbled
salt and freshly ground black pepper
90ml (6 tbsp) mayonnaise
2 garlic cloves, peeled and crushed
45ml (3 tbsp) chopped fresh tarragon
4 skinless chicken breast fillets, about 450g (1lb) in
    total, cut into 7.5cm (3 inch) strips
15ml (1 tbsp) oil
tarragon sprigs, to garnish
lemon wedges, to serve

1 Put the bread in a food processor and process to crumbs. Transfer to a bowl, stir in the cheese and season with salt and pepper; set aside.
2 In another bowl, mix the mayonnaise with the garlic, tarragon and seasoning. Set aside a third of the mayonnaise. Add the chicken strips to the remaining 60ml (4 tbsp) and turn to coat well.
3 Toss the chicken strips in the crumbs to coat evenly. Place in an even layer on a baking sheet and drizzle with oil.
4 Cook under a preheated grill for 4-5 minutes on each side. Serve garnished with tarragon and accompanied by the remaining mayonnaise and lemon wedges.

mustard and vinegar chicken

If you can't find fresh basil for this sauce, mix 60ml (4 tbsp) chopped fresh flat-leafed parsley with 40ml (8 tsp) ready-made pesto and 100ml (3½fl oz) olive oil. Continue from step 2.

Serves 4
Preparation time: 15 minutes
Cooking time: 25 minutes for thighs, 15 minutes for
    breasts
675 cals per serving

8 chicken thighs or 4 chicken breasts, with skin
FOR THE SAUCE:
50g (2oz) fresh basil leaves
6 anchovy fillets
60ml (4 tbsp) red wine vinegar
20ml (4 tsp) Dijon mustard
175ml (6fl oz) olive oil
TO GARNISH:
basil sprigs

1 To make the sauce, put the basil leaves in a food processor with the anchovy fillets, vinegar and mustard and whizz for about 10 seconds to make a rough purée. With the motor running, slowly pour in the olive oil through the funnel, processing until incorporated. Reserve 90ml (6 tbsp) of the sauce for cooking; pour the remainder into a small serving bowl.
2 Place the chicken skin-side down in the grill pan and brush lightly with half of the reserved sauce. Heat the grill to its highest setting.
3 Grill the chicken, about 5cm (2 inches) from the heat element, allowing 12 minutes for thighs, 7 minutes for breasts. Turn the chicken skin-side up and brush with the remaining sauce. Baste with the cooking juices – which will look a little curdled but don't worry! Cook for a further 12 minutes; 7 minutes for breasts; or until the chicken is golden and cooked through. To crisp the skin, move the chicken closer to the heat.
4 Serve with the pan juices poured over. Garnish with basil and accompany with the sauce.

Note Because of the colour of the sauce, it's easiest to test if this chicken is cooked by making a deep cut in the flesh down to the bone.

duck breast with green peppercorn sauce

Succulent magret duck breasts are pan-fried, then braised in a creamy wine sauce, spiked with green peppercorns.

Serves 4
Preparation time: 10 minutes
Cooking time: 20 minutes
580 cals per serving

2 large magret duck breasts, each about 350g (12oz)
salt and freshly ground black pepper
15ml (1 tbsp) green peppercorns in brine, drained
150ml (¼ pint) dry vermouth or white wine
175ml (6fl oz) crème fraîche
30ml (2 tbsp) chopped fresh parsley

1 Lightly score the fat side of the duck breasts with a sharp knife and rub a little salt into the cuts. Rinse the peppercorns thoroughly, drain and crush lightly.
2 Heat a heavy-based frying pan until medium hot, then lay the duck breasts in the pan, fat-side down. Fry for about 4 minutes; this will release a large amount of fat. Turn the duck breasts over and seal the meat side for 1 minute. Pour off the excess fat from the pan.
3 Pour in the vermouth or wine around the duck breasts and stir in the green peppercorns. Cover and simmer very gently for 15 minutes.
4 Transfer the duck breasts to a warmed plate and leave to rest in a warm place. Whisk the cream into the pan juices, bring to the boil and let bubble for 2 minutes. Return the duck and any juices to the pan. Stir in the parsley and simmer for a further 1 minute. Check the seasoning.
5 Halve the duck breasts and place on warmed serving plates. Pour on the green peppercorn sauce and serve immediately, with vegetables of your choice.

mustard and peppered beef stroganoff

Fast to cook and full of flavour, steak is a great chioce when you have little time to cook, and this is a particularly good dish if you're suddenly faced with unexpected guests.

Serves 4
Preparation time: 10 minutes
Cooking time: 15 minutes
575 cals per serving

350g (12oz) rump steak, cut into thick strips
freshly ground black pepper
15ml (1 tbsp) mustard seeds, roughly ground
125g (4oz) unsalted butter
225g (8oz) shiitake or chestnut mushrooms, quartered if large
60ml (4 tbsp) brandy
200ml (7fl oz) crème fraîche
5ml (1 tsp) anchovy essence
30ml (2 tbsp) wholegrain mustard
30ml (2 tbsp) chopped fresh tarragon
snipped chives, to garnish

1 Toss the steak strips in pepper and ground mustard seeds to coat. Heat 75g (3oz) butter in a heavy-based frying pan until hot and sizzling, then cook the steak strips in 3 batches, each for 1-2 minutes. Remove from the pan and keep warm.
2 Heat the remaining butter in the pan and cook the mushrooms for 2-3 minutes. Add the brandy and bubble for 1 minute, then add the crème fraîche and bubble until syrupy. Stir in the anchovy essence, wholegrain mustard and tarragon. Season with pepper to taste.
3 Return the beef to the sauce and bring to a gentle simmer. Serve with pasta or rice, garnished with chives.

Note If you can't find shiitake mushrooms, use brown-cap or flat mushrooms instead.

warm steak escalopes and tomato salad

This delicious combination of sweet tomatoes, peppery rocket and tender beef is easy to assemble, making it ideal for a light lunch or supper. If you can't find ricotta, use soft goat's cheese or instead.

Serves 4
Preparation time: 20 minutes
Cooking time: 5 minutes
460 cals per serving

30ml (2 tbsp) wine vinegar
105ml (7 tbsp) olive oil
15ml (1 tbsp) chopped fresh parsley
15ml (1 tbsp) chopped fresh chives
5ml (1 tsp) caster sugar
50g (2oz) black olives, finely chopped
sea salt flakes and freshly ground black pepper
375g (12oz) plum tomatoes, finely sliced
50g (2oz) shallots, peeled and finely chopped
four 125g (4oz) fillet steaks
250g (9oz) tub ricotta cheese
flat-leafed parsley sprigs, to garnish
rocket and toasted ciabatta, to accompany

1 Combine the wine vinegar, 75ml (5 tbsp) of the oil, the herbs, sugar and olives in a small bowl and season well. Place the tomatoes in a shallow dish with the shallots and spoon the dressing over. Set aside while you prepare the steaks.

2 Place the steaks between sheets of greaseproof paper and gently flatten with a rolling pin to form very thin escalopes; season with pepper.

3 Heat the remaining oil in a large heavy-based frying pan. Fry the steaks in batches over a high heat for 30 seconds on each side.

4 Arrange the tomato salad on 4 serving plates and top each serving with a large spoonful of ricotta cheese. Arrange the steak escalopes on top of the tomatoes, garnish with parsley sprigs and serve immediately, surrounded by rocket leaves and accompanied with toasted ciabatta slices.

choice beef cuts

FILLET STEAKS Beef fillet is extremely lean and tender and although expensive, there's no waste. The tail end tapers, making it cheaper and suitable for recipes where meat is cut into strips. Look for deep red meat with an even marbling of fat – this is important in all cuts, as the fat will melt into the meat during cooking, making it more tender as a result.

SIRLOIN AND RUMP STEAKS As with fillet steak, look for deep red meat. Usually sold cut into steaks with an even layer of creamy-white fat, sirloin and rump are suitable for recipes where meat is pan-fried or grilled. Choose the best cut you can afford.

MINCED BEEF Look at the colour – the darker it is, the leaner the mince will be. Nowadays, the percentage of fat is usually declared on the packaging – 85% lean minced beef is common.

cooking steaks to perfection

- The best type of pan to use is a heavy-based, cast iron one as a domestic grill doesn't get hot enough to seal the outside of the steak quickly, so all the delicious juices seep into the grill pan.
- To test whether a steak is cooked, press the flesh gently. If the steak is soft and gives easily, it is rare. Steak with a firmer outside but plenty of give in the centre is cooked to medium. If well done, the steak will be firm with no give. The longer a steak is cooked, the tougher it becomes and will then require a lot of slow cooking before it reverts to a tender piece of meat.

teriyaki beef stir-fry

Serves 4
Preparation time: 20 minutes, plus marinating
Cooking time: 5 minutes
240 cals per serving

450g (1lb) piece fillet of beef
225g (8oz) carrots, peeled
½ cucumber, deseeded
4-6 spring onions, trimmed
30ml (2 tbsp) vegetable or groundnut oil
FOR THE TERIYAKI MARINADE:
60ml (4 tbsp) Japanese soy sauce (Kikkoman)
60ml (4 tbsp) mirin or medium sherry
1 garlic clove, peeled and finely chopped
2.5cm (1 inch) piece fresh root ginger, peeled and
   finely chopped
TO SERVE:
sesame seeds, for sprinkling
a little wasabi paste (optional)
deep-fried Japanese pickled ginger (optional, see note)

1 Slice the beef as thinly as possible, then cut into
  1cm (½ inch) wide strips. Mix the ingredients for
  the marinade together in a bowl, add the beef
  and turn to coat. Cover and leave to marinate in
  a cool place for 30 minutes, or preferably
  overnight.
2 Cut the carrots and cucumber into matchstick
  strips. Thinly slice the spring onions on the
  diagonal. Drain the meat, reserving any
  marinade.
3 Heat the oil in a wok or large frying pan until
  smoking. Add the vegetables and fry over a high
  heat for 2 minutes until the edges are well
  browned; remove and set aside.
4 Add the beef to the wok and stir-fry over a very
  high heat for 2 minutes. Return the vegetables to
  the pan, adding any reserved marinade. Stir-fry
  briefly, until heated through. Sprinkle with
  sesame seeds.
5 Serve immediately, on a bed of egg noodles
  tossed in a little sesame oil. Add a little wasabi
  paste and top with fried pickled ginger.

Note Japanese pickled ginger is available in jars
from larger supermarkets and oriental stores. Drain
well before deep-frying in hot oil for about 1-2
minutes until crisp and golden.

pan-fried steak with broad bean pesto

A perfect recipe for a special quick supper. Any
leftover broad bean pesto would be delicious stirred
into pasta or spread on to toasted Italian bread to
accompany a bowl of steaming soup.

Serves 4
Preparation time: 20 minutes
Cooking time: 10 minutes
520 cals per serving

225g (8oz) broad beans, thawed if frozen, cooked and
   skinned if preferred
1 garlic clove, peeled and crushed
50g (2oz) Pecorino or Parmesan cheese, freshly grated
15-30ml (1-2 tbsp) lemon juice, or to taste
10ml (2 tsp) creamed horseradish sauce
15ml (1 tbsp) chopped fresh mint
120ml (4fl oz) extra-virgin olive oil, plus extra for
   frying
4 rump steaks, each 175g (6oz)
salt and freshly ground black pepper
225g (8oz) cherry tomatoes
Parmesan cheese shavings, to garnish

1 Place the broad beans, garlic, cheese, lemon
  juice, horseradish and mint in a food processor.
  Pulse for about 30 seconds or until well blended.
  With the machine running, gradually add the
  olive oil. Turn the pesto into a bowl and set
  aside.
2 Season the steaks with pepper. Brush a frying
  pan or heavy-based ridged, cast-iron pan with
  oil. Heat until very hot, then cook the steaks
  quickly for about 1 minute on each side for rare,
  2 minutes for medium, 3-4 minutes for well
  done, depending on the thickness of the steak.
  (See cooking steaks to perfection, page 239.)
  Transfer to a warm plate and keep warm. Cook
  the whole cherry tomatoes in the hot frying pan
  for 1-2 minutes.
3 To serve, spoon the pesto over the steaks and
  serve with the cherry tomatoes. Garnish with
  shavings of Parmesan.

Note You can prepare the broad bean pesto in
advance, then cover it with a little olive oil and
store in the fridge for up 3 days.

scotch beef collops

'Collop' is derived from the French 'escalope'. It is a slice of boneless meat cut across the grain. Meat cut across the grain cooks faster and is more tender.

Serves 4
Preparation time: 10 minutes
Cooking time: 15-20 minutes
390 cals per serving

8 'minute' steaks, each 75g (3oz)
flour, for coating
salt and freshly ground black pepper
50g (2oz) unsalted butter
grated rind of ½ lemon
pinch of ground mace
150ml (¼ pint) white wine
1 egg yolk
45ml (3 tbsp) double cream
roughly chopped parsley, to garnish

1 Trim the steaks if necessary and, using a rolling pin, beat out thinly between two sheets of greaseproof paper. Lightly dust the steaks with seasoned flour.

2 Melt the butter in a large frying pan and, when foaming, brown the steaks well on both sides in two batches.

3 Return all the steaks to the pan and add the lemon rind, mace and wine. Bring to the boil, then simmer uncovered for about 5 minutes until tender. Transfer the meat to a serving dish; keep warm.

4 Boil the sauce to reduce slightly. Beat the egg yolk and cream together in a bowl, then stir into the sauce and heat through, without boiling, until slightly thickened; season with salt and pepper to taste. Strain.

5 Garnish with parsley and serve with the sauce, new potatoes and a green vegetable.

spiced lamb chops with mango salsa

Lamb chops marinated in a spicy yogurt mixture, then grilled and served with a piquant mango salsa.

Serves 4
Preparation time: 15 minutes, plus marinating
Cooking time: 15 minutes
350 cals per serving

15ml (1 tbsp) oil
175g (6oz) onion, peeled and finely chopped
10ml (2 tsp) cumin seeds
15ml (1 tbsp) coriander seeds
15ml (1 tbsp) mustard seeds
2.5ml (½ tsp) cayenne pepper
salt and freshly ground black pepper
300ml (½ pint) Greek yogurt
4 lamb chops, each about 175g (6oz)
1 large ripe mango, peeled, stoned and roughly
    chopped
15ml (1 tbsp) chopped fresh parsley
15ml (1 tbsp) chopped fresh mint
15ml (1 tbsp) lemon juice
lemon wedges, to serve

1 Heat the oil in a small frying pan, add the onion and cook, stirring, for 7 minutes or until soft. Add the cumin, coriander and mustard seeds and cook for 1 minute. Allow to cool.

2 Place the onion mixture in a shallow, non-metallic dish with the cayenne pepper, salt, pepper and 150ml (¼ pint) yogurt. Add the chops, turn to coat in the mixture, then cover and leave to marinate in the refrigerator for several hours if time, or overnight.

3 To make the salsa, combine the mango with the remaining yogurt, parsley, mint, lemon juice and seasoning.

4 Secure each chop with a wooden cocktail stick and grill for 3-5 minutes on each side.

5 Serve the lamb chops with any pan juices poured over and accompanied by the mango salsa and lemon wedges.

crisp crumbed lamb cutlets

For a simple midweek supper, buy lamb cutlets; if cooking a special meal for friends, buy French-trimmed rack of lamb and slice off thick cutlets.

Serves 4
Preparation time: 20 minutes
Cooking time: 10 minutes
205 cals per serving

75g (3oz) breadcrumbs, made from day-old bread
40g (1½oz) prosciutto or Parma ham, finely chopped
45ml (3 tbsp) freshly grated Parmesan cheese
salt and freshly ground black pepper
8 lamb cutlets, trimmed, or 2 French-trimmed racks of
    lamb, about 350g (12oz) each, divided into cutlets
2 eggs, beaten
45ml (3 tbsp) oil
3 large garlic cloves, peeled

1 Mix together the breadcrumbs, Parma ham and Parmesan cheese, then spread out on a large plate and set aside. Season the lamb and brush lightly with the beaten egg (see note). Press the lamb into the breadcrumbs to coat evenly, but lightly.

2 Heat the oil in a large non-stick frying pan, add the garlic cloves and heat gently until golden brown, then discard the garlic.

3 Fry the lamb in the garlic-infused oil over a low to moderate heat for 4-5 minutes on each side until deep golden brown and crisp. Turn and fry the fat edge for 1-2 minutes.

4 Serve the cutlets with a tomato relish, new potatoes and a salad or green vegetable.

Note Use a pastry brush to lightly brush the egg over the chops; too much egg will result in an over-thick crust of crumbs.

lamb noisettes with tarragon sauce

Noisettes are cut from the boned loin. They are more expensive than cutlets but cook quickly, without waste.

Serves 4
Preparation time: 25 minutes
Cooking time: 25 minutes
670 cals per serving

30ml (2 tbsp) olive oil
8 lamb noisettes, each about 125g (4oz)
175g (6oz) onion, peeled and finely chopped
15ml (1 tbsp) tarragon vinegar
150ml (¼ pint) white wine
150ml (¼ pint) double cream
300ml (½ pint) lamb or chicken stock
salt and freshly ground black pepper
15ml (1 tbsp) chopped fresh tarragon
tarragon sprigs, to garnish

1 Heat 15ml (1 tbsp) oil in a frying pan and brown the noisettes, in batches, for 2 minutes each side or until the fat is crisp.
2 Transfer the lamb noisettes to a roasting tin and cook at 200°C/fan oven 190°C (400°F) Mark 6 for 10 minutes for medium-rare, 15 minutes for well done.
3 Meanwhile, heat the remaining oil in the cleaned pan, add the onion and cook for 5-7 minutes until soft but not coloured. Add the vinegar and wine, bring to the boil and bubble for 2 minutes. Add the cream and stock; bubble for 10 minutes or until syrupy. Check the seasoning.
4 Remove the string from the lamb. Add the chopped tarragon and roasting juices to the sauce; warm through.
5 Serve the lamb garnished with tarragon and accompanied by the sauce.

spiced lamb steaks with aubergines

Griddled coriander-crusted lamb steaks and pan-fried aubergines flavoured with cumin, served piled on to toasted pitta bread.

Serves 2
Preparation time: 10 minutes
Cooking time: 23 minutes
665 cals per serving

1 large aubergine
45ml (3 tbsp) olive oil, plus extra for cooking
5ml (1 tsp) cumin seeds
1 garlic clove, peeled and crushed
2 boneless lamb steaks, 300g (11oz) in total
5ml (1 tsp) ground coriander
sea salt and freshly ground black pepper
TO SERVE:
toasted pitta or other flat bread
1 small red onion, peeled and sliced into rings
coriander leaves, to garnish
lemon wedges

1 Cut the aubergine into 2.5cm (1 inch) cubes. Heat 45ml (3 tbsp) oil in a frying pan and fry the aubergine for 8 minutes or until beginning to soften. Add the cumin seeds and garlic, increase the heat and fry the mixture for 5 minutes or until the aubergine is cooked and golden. Remove from the heat and set aside.
2 Meanwhile, cut each lamb steak into half. Coat with the ground coriander and season with salt and pepper.
3 Using kitchen paper, smear a griddle or heavy-based frying pan with olive oil and heat. Add the lamb steaks and fry on a moderate to high heat for 4-5 minutes on each side.
4 Pile the lamb and aubergines on to warm pitta bread. Garnish with onion rings and coriander leaves and accompany with lemon wedges.

stir-fried pork with chinese greens

This stir-fry is really quick to make, using ready-prepared vegetables.

Serves 6
Preparation time: 5 minutes
Cooking time: 10 minutes
200 cals per serving

350g (12oz) lean pork, cut into strips (see note)
60ml (4 tbsp) rice wine or dry sherry
30ml (2 tbsp) soy sauce
2.5ml (½ tsp) thin honey
45ml (3 tbsp) oil
450g (1lb) pak choi or other Chinese greens, shredded
2 x 300g (11oz) bags fresh stir-fry vegetables (see note)
15ml (1 tbsp) Chinese five spice paste

1 Toss together the pork, rice wine, soy sauce and honey with 15ml (1 tbsp) oil. (If time, leave the pork to marinate for 1 hour at this stage).

2 Lift the pork from the marinade, using a slotted spoon; reserve marinade. Heat a wok or large deep frying pan until very hot. Add 15ml (1 tbsp) oil to the wok, add half of the pork and stir-fry for about 1 minute or until beginning to brown; remove and set aside. Stir-fry the remaining pork.

3 Wipe out the wok, add the remaining oil and heat. Add all the vegetables with the Chinese five spice paste andand fry for a further 3-4 minutes. Return the pork and reserved marinade to the wok, bring to the boil and let bubble for 1-2 minutes. Serve immediately.

Notes
- Most supermarkets sell stir-fry pork strips – neat lengths of pork with no waste and little fat.
- Ready-prepared bags of shredded vegetables are available from supermarkets.

fried yellow bean pork with cashews

Serves 4
Preparation time: 10 minutes
Cooking time: 10 minutes
520 cals per serving

6 cardamom pods, split
2.5cm (1 inch) piece fresh root ginger, finely chopped
15ml (1 tbsp) Chinese five-spice powder
450g (1lb) pork fillet (tenderloin), thinly sliced
30ml (2 tbsp) oil
225g (8oz) small oyster mushrooms
125g (4oz) leek or spring onions, sliced
3 garlic cloves, peeled and sliced
30ml (2 tbsp) yellow bean sauce
pared rind and juice of 1 small orange
50g (2oz) toasted cashew nuts

1 Rub the split cardamom pods, ginger and five-spice powder into the pork; set aside.
2 Heat half the oil in a wok or frying pan and fry the mushrooms quickly for about 1 minute; lift out with a slotted spoon before they begin to wilt.
3 Add the remaining oil to the pan and, when hot, toss in the pork, leek and garlic. Stir-fry over a high heat for 5 minutes.
4 Return the mushrooms to the pan and add the yellow bean sauce, orange rind and juice, and the cashew nuts. Cook, stirring, over a high heat until all of the ingredients are coated in sauce and hot through. Serve immediately.

pork with rosemary

Serves 2
Preparation time: 10 minutes
Cooking time: 7 minutes
290 cals per serving

200g (7oz) pork fillet (tenderloin)
25g (1oz) butter
150ml (¼ pint) medium dry white wine
10ml (2 tsp) finely chopped fresh rosemary
salt and freshly ground black pepper

1 Put the pork fillet between two sheets of greaseproof paper and beat with a rolling pin to flatten. Cut into thick diagonal slices.
2 Melt the butter in a heavy-based frying pan, add the pork and cook over a high heat until golden brown. Remove from the pan; keep warm.
3 Add the wine to the pan, bring to the boil and bubble for 2-3 minutes or until reduced by at least half. Add the chopped rosemary and return the pork to the pan. Toss together and season with salt and pepper to taste. Serve with pasta and baby spinach.

pork steaks with sage and apple

This recipe is loosely based on the traditional Italian dish of saltimbocca, which uses veal, prosciutto, sage and white wine.

Serves 4
Preparation time: 5 minutes
Cooking time: 10 minutes
380 cals per serving

4 pork shoulder steaks, each about 150g (5oz)
4 thin slices prosciutto or Parma ham
6 fresh sage leaves
freshly ground black pepper
15ml (1 tbsp) oil
150ml (¼ pint) pure unsweetened apple juice
50g (2oz) chilled butter, diced
squeeze of lemon juice

1 Lay a slice of prosciutto and a sage leaf on each pork steak, then secure to the meat with a wooden cocktail stick. Season with pepper.
2 Heat the oil in a heavy-based frying pan and fry the pork for about 3-4 minutes on each side until golden brown.
3 Pour in the apple juice – it will sizzle and start to evaporate immediately. Scrape the sediment from the bottom of the pan and let the liquid bubble until reduced by half. Lift the pork out on to a warm plate.
4 Add the butter to the pan and swirl until melted into the pan juices. Add lemon juice to taste and pour over the pork to serve.

stir-fried vegetables with hoisin and tofu

Tofu is roasted in a spicy glaze, then tossed with a medley of stir-fried vegetables. For a quicker version, omit the tofu and simply serve the stir-fried vegetables with rice or egg noodles.

Serves 4
Preparation: 15 minutes
Cooking time: 20 minutes
410 cals per serving

275g (10oz) packet tofu, drained
30ml (2 tbsp) hoisin sauce
30ml (2 tbsp) dark soy sauce
30ml (2 tbsp) sherry vinegar
15ml (1 tbsp) chilli sauce
15ml (1 tbsp) thin honey
10ml (2 tsp) sesame oil
45ml (3 tbsp) sunflower oil
2 carrots, peeled and thinly sliced
175g (6oz) broccoli, cut into small florets
125g (4oz) shiitake mushrooms, halved
1 leek, trimmed and sliced
4 spring onions, trimmed and sliced
125g (4oz) mangetout, halved
toasted sesame seeds, to garnish

1 Cut the tofu into 2.5cm (1 inch) cubes and place in a shallow roasting dish.
2 For the glaze, combine the hoisin sauce, soy sauce, vinegar, chilli sauce, honey and sesame oil in a bowl. Pour two thirds over the tofu and toss to coat. Bake on the top shelf of the oven at 230°C/fan oven 220°C (450°F) Mark 8 for 20 minutes, stirring halfway through.
3 In the meantime, heat the sunflower oil in a wok or large frying pan. When hot, add the carrots, broccoli and mushrooms and stir-fry for 3 minutes. Add the leek, spring onions and mangetout and stir-fry for a further 2 minutes.
4 Stir 45ml (3 tbsp) water into the remaining glaze and add to the wok. Cook gently for 3-4 minutes until the vegetables are tender. Stir in the roasted tofu and serve at once, sprinkled with the sesame seeds.

parmesan polenta with minted summer vegetables

Serves 4
Preparation time: 10 minutes
Cooking time: 15 minutes
645 cals per serving

FOR THE PARMESAN POLENTA:
900ml (1½ pints) vegetable stock
125g (4oz) polenta
45ml (3 tbsp) double cream
125g (4oz) Parmesan cheese, finely grated
30ml (2 tbsp) chopped fresh mint
salt and freshly ground black pepper
FOR THE MINTED VEGETABLES:
50g (2oz) butter
50g (2oz) shallots, peeled and finely chopped
2 garlic cloves, peeled and thinly sliced
125g (4oz) baby carrots, scrubbed
125g (4oz) fresh broad beans, skinned, or fresh peas
125g (4oz) asparagus tips or French beans, halved
15ml (1 tbsp) caster sugar
30ml (2 tbsp) chopped fresh mint
10ml (2 tsp) grainy mustard
15ml (1 tbsp) white wine vinegar

1 To make the Parmesan polenta, bring 600ml (1 pint) stock to the boil in a large saucepan, then reduce to a simmer. Add the polenta in a slow, steady stream, stirring all the time over the heat for about 5 minutes until thick.
2 Stir in the remaining stock and cream, then cook, stirring, for a further 10 minutes, until the polenta resembles mashed potato. Add the Parmesan cheese and chopped mint, then season well. Remove from the heat and keep warm.
3 To prepare the minted vegetables, melt the butter in a large saucepan and add the shallots and garlic. Cook gently for 5 minutes, then add the vegetables, sugar and 50ml (2fl oz) water. Bring to the boil, cover and cook for about 5 minutes until the vegetables are tender and the liquid becomes syrupy.
4 Toss the hot vegetables with the chopped mint, mustard and wine vinegar. Season generously, with salt and pepper to taste. Serve immediately, with the soft polenta.

spring green, lentil and red pepper stir-fry

Serves 4
Preparation time: 10 minutes
Cooking time: 10 minutes
270 cals per serving

30ml (2 tbsp) dark soy sauce
15ml (1 tbsp) lime juice
15ml (1 tbsp) chilli sauce
15ml (1 tbsp) preserved stem ginger syrup
350g (12oz) spring greens or curly kale
1 large red pepper, halved, cored and deseeded
30ml (2 tbsp) sunflower oil
10ml (2 tsp) sesame oil
1 red onion, peeled and thinly sliced
2.5cm (1 inch) fresh root ginger, peeled and grated
1 garlic clove, peeled and crushed
400g (14oz) can green lentils, drained
30ml (2 tbsp) sesame seeds, toasted

1 Mix the soy sauce, lime juice, chilli sauce and ginger syrup together in a small bowl with 45ml (3 tbsp) water; set aside.
2 Remove the tough stalks from the greens or kale, then shred the leaves and blanch in a large pan of lightly salted boiling water for 1 minute. Drain, refresh under cold water and dry on kitchen paper. Thinly slice the red pepper.
3 Heat the sunflower and sesame oils together in a wok or large frying pan. When hot, add the red pepper, onion, ginger and garlic, and stir-fry over a high heat for 3 minutes.
4 Add the greens or kale, lentils and the soy mixture. Stir well, cover and cook over a low heat for 3-4 minutes until the vegetables are tender. Scatter over the sesame seeds and serve at once.

Note If you haven't any preserved ginger to hand, use thin honey instead of ginger syrup.

vegetable accompaniments

Imaginative, colourful side dishes, designed to bring out the full flavour of fresh seasonal vegetables

roasted asparagus salad

Roasting is a great way to cook asparagus. As there is no water added, the exquisite flavour of the vegetable is not diluted.

Serves 4-6
Preparation time: 10 minutes, plus cooling
Cooking time: About 20 minutes
275-180 cals per serving

700g (1½lb) asparagus spears
90ml (6 tbsp) olive oil
45ml (3 tbsp) lemon juice
coarse sea salt and freshly ground black pepper
TO SERVE:
rocket leaves
lemon wedges
Parmesan cheese shavings (optional)

1 Trim the asparagus spears and use a potato peeler to peel the bottom 5cm (2 inches) of each stalk.
2 Lay the asparagus in a shallow roasting tin and spoon over 60ml (4 tbsp) of the olive oil; toss to mix. Roast at 200°C/fan oven 190°C (400°F) Mark 6 for about 20 minutes until just tender, turning the asparagus spears once during cooking. Allow to cool.
3 To serve, spoon the remaining olive oil over the asparagus and sprinkle with the lemon juice. Season with coarse sea salt and freshly ground black pepper and toss lightly. Serve with rocket leaves and lemon wedges. Sprinkle with shavings of Parmesan cheese, if desired.

Note The cooking time applies to stalks of medium thickness and should be increased if you are using fatter asparagus stems.

spicy grilled aubergines

Baby aubergines are ideal for this recipe. If you are lucky enough to obtain some allow one per person, otherwise one aubergine half should be ample as an accompaniment.

Serves 4
Preparation time: 25 minutes, plus standing
Cooking time: 15-20 minutes
125 cals per serving

2 medium aubergines, or 4 baby ones
salt and freshly ground black pepper
2 garlic cloves, peeled and finely chopped
1 green chilli, deseeded and finely chopped
15ml (1 tbsp) chopped fresh rosemary
finely grated rind and juice of 1 lemon
45ml (3 tbsp) chopped fresh parsley
olive oil, for basting

1 Halve the aubergines lengthwise and deeply score the flesh in a criss-cross pattern, cutting almost, but not quite through to the skin. Sprinkle generously with salt and leave to degorge for 20 minutes.
2 Meanwhile, mix the green chilli, garlic, rosemary, lemon rind and parsley together in a small bowl.
3 Rinse the aubergines thoroughly and pat dry with kitchen paper. Brush the scored sides with olive oil and place, cut-side uppermost, on the grill rack. Grill – not too close to the heat – for 10 minutes (see note).
4 Spread with the herb mixture and drizzle with a little more olive oil. Position closer to the heat and grill for a further 5-10 minutes or until the aubergines are tender, brushing with oil occasionally. Sprinkle with a little lemon juice and olive oil to serve.

Notes
• If you're short of time you could omit the degorging, but it does draw out any bitter juices and reduces the amount of oil the aubergines absorb during cooking.
• If the aubergines are quite plump, increase the initial cooking time to 15-20 minutes.

marinated artichokes with mint and dill

This accompaniment also makes a good Italian antipasta dish, served with prosciutto, olives etc.

Serves 4
Preparation time: 30 minutes, plus marinating
Cooking time: 15 minutes
200 cals per serving

8 medium globe artichokes
juice of 1½ lemons
100ml (3½ fl oz) extra-virgin olive oil
2 garlic cloves, peeled and chopped
6 coriander seeds, bruised
1 fresh rosemary sprig, bruised
60ml (2fl oz) dry white wine
salt and freshly ground black pepper
15ml (1 tbsp) chopped fresh mint
15ml (1 tbsp) chopped fresh dill

1 First, prepare the artichokes. Take an artichoke and snap off the stalk, peel away the tough outer leaves around the base until the pale inner heart remains. Cut across the top of the base and scrape away the prickly choke inside. Immerse in a bowl of cold water with the juice of 1 lemon added. Repeat with the rest of the artichokes, then drain and pat dry.

2 Heat half of the olive oil in a large frying pan or flameproof casserole, add the artichoke bases and and sauté over a high heat for 4-5 minutes until just turning golden. Add the garlic, coriander seeds, rosemary, wine, 30ml (2 tbsp) water and salt and pepper. Cover and braise over a low heat for 8-10 minutes until tender. Remove from the heat.

3 Add the remaining olive oil and juice from the remaining lemon half. Leave to cool. Scatter over the mint and dill and leave to marinate for 1 hour before serving.

buying and storing vegetables

Most supermarkets now stock organic vegetables grown without the use of pesticides or artificial fertilisers, although they do tend to be more expensive. Whether or not you buy organic produce, look for bright, firm vegetables. Avoid any that are shrivelled or bruised.

- Resist buying the largest specimens, especially when choosing roots. In general, the younger and smaller the vegetable, the sweeter and more tender it will be, although some baby vegetables lack flavour because they are so immature. Don't buy potatoes with a green tinge, as these are unfit for eating.
- To enjoy them at their best, vegetables should be eaten as soon as possible after picking or buying, but most will keep for a few days in a cool, dark place. Store green vegetables and salad ingredients in the salad drawer of the fridge. Root vegetables can be stored in a cool, dark place, such as a wire rack in a cool larder, for up to 1 week. Exposure to light turns potatoes green, so they must be kept in the dark.

preparing and cooking vegetables

Clean all vegetables thoroughly before cooking. Brush or shake off any loose dirt, then wash thoroughly (except mushrooms). The easiest way to clean leeks is to slit them lengthwise and rinse under cold running water. Mushrooms are best wiped with damp kitchen paper.

- As soon as vegetables are peeled they begin to lose vitamins so, where possible, prepare at the last minute. Alternatively, if the produce is organic and the skins are edible, simply don't peel. Non-organic produce is better peeled; washing alone is not enough to remove all traces of residual chemicals. Never prepare vegetables hours in advance and leave them immersed in cold water as water-soluble vitamins will be lost.
- Vegetables can be steamed, boiled, sautéed, stir-fried, roasted, braised or grilled. To minimise the loss of water-soluble vitamins, cook in the minimum amount of water (if boiling), and use the cooking water as stock or to make a sauce. Avoid overcooking at all costs. In general, vegetables are their best cooked until *al dente*, tender but still retaining some bite.

broad beans in a creamy herb sauce

Homegrown broad beans are in season from late May to the end of June. Young, fresh baby broad beans with pale green tender pods are best for this dish. Alternatively, you can use frozen baby beans, slipping them out of their skins before cooking.

Serves 4-6
Preparation time: 20 minutes
Cooking time: 20 minutes
385-260 cals per serving

50g (2oz) butter
2 garlic cloves, peeled and finely chopped
4 shallots, peeled and finely chopped
450g (1lb) shelled fresh or frozen broad beans
150ml (¼ pint) vegetable stock
200ml (7fl oz) double cream
30ml (2 tbsp) chopped fresh chervil or chives
30ml (2 tbsp) chopped fresh parsley
grated rind of 1 lemon
salt and freshly ground black pepper

1 Melt the butter in a saucepan, add the garlic and shallots and cook gently for 3 minutes. Stir in the broad beans and stock. Bring to the boil, cover and simmer gently for 12-15 minutes, until the beans are tender. Drain, reserving the liquid.
2 Pour the reserved cooking liquid into a blender or food processor, add 60ml (4 tbsp) of the beans and blend to a purée, gradually adding the cream through the feeder tube to make a smooth sauce. Return to the pan.
3 Add the rest of the broad beans, chopped herbs, lemon rind and salt and pepper to taste. Reheat gently to serve.

runner beans with hazelnut butter

Serves 4-6
Preparation time: 15 minutes
Cooking time: 20 minutes
210-140 cals per serving

700g (1½lb) young tender runner beans, trimmed
salt and freshly ground black pepper
50g (2oz) butter
50g (2oz) hazelnuts, chopped
lemon juice, to taste

1 Slice the runner beans on the diagonal. Add to a pan of boiling salted water, return to the boil and cook for 3-4 minutes, until tender.

2 Meanwhile, melt the butter in a frying pan, add the hazelnuts and fry until golden.

3 Drain the beans and toss with the nuts and lemon juice to serve.

Note To preserve the bright green colour of the beans, splash with half a cupful of cold water after draining them.

thai-style mangetout and bean sauté

Serves 4
Preparation time: 10 minutes
Cooking time: 6 minutes
90 cals per serving

15ml (1 tbsp) groundnut oil
5ml (1 tsp) sesame oil
125g (4oz) green beans, trimmed and sliced
225g (8oz) mangetout, trimmed
125g (4oz) bean sprouts, rinsed and drained
1 bunch of spring onions, trimmed and sliced
1 garlic clove, peeled and crushed
1 red chilli, deseeded and finely chopped
15ml (1 tbsp) rice vinegar
15ml (1 tbsp) dark soy sauce
15ml (1 tbsp) caster sugar
salt and freshly ground black pepper

1 Heat the two oils in a wok or large frying pan until starting to smoke. Immediately add the green beans and stir-fry for 3 minutes. Add the mangetout, beans sprouts and spring onions; stir-fry for a further 1 minute.

2 Add the remaining ingredients and stir-fry over a low heat for a further 1 minute or so, until the vegetables are tender. Adjust the seasoning and serve at once.

Variations

- Vary the vegetables according to whatever you have to hand: carrot julienne, courgette slices, red and yellow peppers are suitable alternatives.
- Omit the chilli and scatter with chopped fresh coriander to serve.

brussels sprouts with chestnuts and onions

Serves 8-10
Preparation time: 20 minutes
Cooking time: 45 minutes
225 cals per serving

125g (4oz) butter
450g (1lb) small red onions, preferably red, peeled and quartered
grated rind of 1 lemon
900g (2lb) Brussels sprouts, trimmed
salt and freshly ground black pepper
450g (1lb) vacuum-packed cooked, peeled chestnuts

1 Melt half the butter in a roasting tin. Add the onions and lemon rind and roast below the centre of the oven at 190°C/fan oven 180°C (375°F) Mark 5 for 35 minutes or until golden.
2 Meanwhile, cook the brussels sprouts in boiling salted water for 3-4 minutes; drain well.
3 Stir in the chestnuts, brussels sprouts, remaining butter and seasoning. Return to the oven for a further 5-10 minutes until piping hot.

braised bok choi

Serves 4
Preparation time: 10 minutes
Cooking time: 20 minutes
150 cals per serving

25ml (1fl oz) dark soy sauce
grated rind and juice of ½ orange
30ml (2 tbsp) rice wine or medium sherry
5ml (1 tsp) grated fresh root ginger
1 garlic clove, peeled and crushed
1 red chilli, deseeded and chopped
10ml (2 tsp) caster sugar
1 whole star anise
12 small bok choi, halved lengthways

1 Place all the ingredients, except the bok choi, in a wide pan with 60ml (4 tbsp) water, bring to the boil, cover and simmer for 15 minutes.
2 Add the bok choi, cover and simmer for a further 5 minutes until tender. Serve at once.

sicilian-style broccoli

Enhanced with piquant capers, parsley, sultanas and a crunchy pine nut and breadcrumb mix, this stir-fried broccoli makes a particularly good accompaniment to grilled fish.

Serves 4
Preparation time: 15 minutes
Cooking time: 10 minutes
260 cals per serving

700g (1½lb) broccoli
salt and freshly ground black pepper
60ml (4 tbsp) extra-virgin olive oil
25g (1oz) breadcrumbs
25g (1oz) pine nuts
2 garlic cloves, peeled and crushed
25g (1oz) sultanas
15ml (1 tbsp) lemon juice
4 anchovy fillets, drained and chopped
15ml (1 tbsp) drained capers
30ml (2 tbsp) chopped fresh parsley

1 Cut the broccoli into small florets and peel and slice the base of the stalks. Blanch in a large pan of lightly salted boiling water for 1 minute. Drain and immediately refresh under cold water. Drain and dry well.
2 Heat 15ml (1 tbsp) of the oil in a frying pan and stir-fry the breadcrumbs and pine nuts for 2-3 minutes until crisp and golden; remove and set aside.
3 Heat the remaining oil in a wok or large frying pan, add the garlic followed by the broccoli and stir-fry for 3 minutes. Add the sultanas, lemon juice and 30ml (2 tbsp) water and cook for a further 5-6 minutes until the broccoli is tender.
4 Stir in the anchovies, capers and parsley. Serve scattered with the pine nut mixture.

grilled chicory and radicchio with orange

Serves 4
Preparation time: 15 minutes
Cooking time: 10 minutes
230 cals per serving

1 orange
2 plump heads of chicory, halved lengthways
1 large firm radicchio, quartered lengthways
olive oil, for basting
125g (4oz) fresh soft goat's cheese, crumbled
a little chopped fresh thyme (optional)
pepper
30ml (2 tbsp) pine nuts, toasted

1 Over a bowl to catch the juice, peel and segment the orange, discarding all pith and membrane.
2 Place the chicory and radicchio in a grill pan, cut-side up, and brush liberally with olive oil. Cook under a high grill, as close to the heat as possible, for about 3-4 minutes until beginning to char and soften. Turn, baste with more olive oil and cook for a further 2-3 minutes.
3 Transfer to a gratin dish, carefully turning again. Lay the orange segments on top and sprinkle with the reserved orange juice. Scatter the goat's cheese on top. Brush with oil, sprinkle with thyme if using, and season with pepper.
4 Grill until the cheese is bubbling and golden brown. Sprinkle with the pine nuts to serve.

braised red cabbage

Serves 6
Preparation time: 25 minutes
Cooking time: About 3 hours
210 cals per serving

1.4kg (3lb) red cabbage
450g (1lb) red onions, peeled and finely sliced
salt and freshly ground black pepper
50g (2oz) butter
5cm (2 inch) fresh root ginger, peeled and grated
105ml (7 tbsp) light brown muscovado sugar
105ml (7 tbsp) red wine vinegar

1 Discard the outer leaves from the cabbage, then shred finely, discarding the core. Layer the cabbage and onions in a casserole, seasoning as you do so.
2 Melt the butter in a small pan and fry the ginger for 2-3 minutes. Off the heat, stir in the sugar and vinegar, then pour the mixture evenly over the cabbage.
3 Cover tightly and cook in the oven at 150°C/fan oven 140°C (300°F) Mark 2 for about 3 hours, stirring occasionally, until tender. Adjust the seasoning before serving.

braised celery with pancetta and cheese

Serves 4-6
Preparation time: 10 minutes
Cooking time: 25 minutes
400-265 cals per serving

1 head of celery, trimmed (450g/1lb trimmed weight)
125g (4oz) smoked pancetta or rindless streaky bacon, diced
25g (1oz) butter
1 large onion, peeled and chopped
2 garlic cloves, peeled and crushed
150ml (¼ pint) single cream
salt and freshly ground black pepper
125g (4oz) gruyère cheese, grated

1 Separate the celery stalks and cut into 5cm (2 inch) lengths, on the diagonal.
2 Preheat a large flameproof sauté pan, add the pancetta and stir over a high heat until it releases its fat and browns. Remove with a slotted spoon and set aside.
3 Add the butter to the pan and, as soon as it melts, add the onion and garlic. Fry gently for 10 minutes until softened, then stir in the celery and cook for a further 5 minutes.
4 Return the pancetta to the pan, add the cream and bring to the boil. Cover and simmer for 5 minutes; season with salt and pepper to taste.
5 Scatter the cheese over the celery and place under a hot grill for 1-2 minutes until golden. Serve at once.

cabbage with horseradish

Serves 4
Preparation time: 10 minutes
Cooking time: 5 minutes
110 cals per serving

½ small white cabbage, about 400g (14oz)
200g (7oz) spring greens, stalks removed
15g (½oz) butter
15ml (1 tbsp) olive oil
1 bunch spring onions, trimmed and sliced
65g (2½oz) fresh horseradish, peeled and finely grated
salt

1 Cut the white cabbage into wedges, discarding the core. Finely shred the cabbage and spring greens in a food processor.
2 Melt the butter in a large wok or frying pan with the oil. Add the cabbage and spring greens and fry gently, stirring constantly, for 2 minutes until softened.
3 Add the spring onions, grated horseradish and a little salt and cook for a further 3 minutes, stirring, until softened but still retaining a bite.
4 Transfer to a warming serving bowl and serve at once.

Note This is an excellent accompaniment to serve with grilled pork steaks or chops, or sausages.

patty pans with balsamic vinegar

Serves 4
Preparation time: 10 minutes
Cooking time: 10 minutes
180 cals per serving

450g (1lb) patty pans, preferably a mixture of green and yellow
45-60ml (3-4 tbsp) extra-virgin olive oil
1 garlic clove, peeled and crushed
1 small red chilli, deseeded and finely diced
25g (1oz) raisins
30ml (2 tbsp) small French capers, washed
30ml (2 tbsp) balsamic vinegar
pinch of brown sugar
salt and freshly ground black pepper
25g (1oz) flaked almonds, toasted
15ml (1 tbsp) chopped fresh basil

1 Halve or quarter the patty pans. Heat the oil in a frying pan, add the patty pans, garlic and chilli and stir-fry for 5-6 minutes, until the patty pans are lightly browned on all sides.

2 Add the raisins, capers, vinegar, sugar and a splash of water. Season with plenty of salt and pepper and simmer, covered, over a low heat for a further 3-5 minutes until the patty pans are tender.

3 Remove from the heat, stir in the toasted almonds and basil and check the seasoning. Serve at once.

Notes
- Patty pans are an attractive variety of small summer squash with scalloped edges, and a flavour similar to baby courgettes.
- This accompaniment is also delicious served cold, as a side salad.

roasted fennel with lemon and thyme

Roasting fennel bulbs with lemon and a sprinkling of sugar until caramelised brings out the full, sweet flavour of this aromatic vegetable.

Serves 4-6
Preparation time: 10 minutes
Cooking time: 1 hour
190-120 cals per serving

700g (1½lb) fennel (about 3 bulbs)
1 lemon, halved
45ml (3 tbsp) olive oil
50g (2oz) butter, melted
5ml (1 tsp) caster sugar
salt and freshly ground black pepper
2 large fresh thyme sprigs

1 Quarter the fennel lengthwise and place, cut-side up, in a roasting tin.
2 Squeeze the juice from the lemon halves over the fennel, then drizzle with the olive oil and melted butter. Add the empty lemon halves to the tin. Sprinkle with the sugar and season generously with salt and pepper. Add the thyme sprigs.
3 Cover with a dampened piece of non-stick baking parchment. Bake at 200°C/fan oven 190°C (400°F) Mark 6 for 30 minutes. Remove paper and bake for a further 20-30 minutes or until the fennel is tender and slightly charred.

leeks with toasted cheese sauce

Serves 4
Preparation time: 15 minutes
Cooking time: About 10 minutes
155 cals per serving

700g (1½lb) small leeks, trimmed
salt and freshly ground black pepper
25g (1oz) butter
25g (1oz) plain white flour
125g (4oz) soft cheese flavoured with garlic and herbs
15g (½oz) Parmesan cheese, freshly grated

1 Place the leeks in a pan of cold salted water, bring to the boil and simmer for 2-3 minutes or until just tender. Drain the leeks and reserve 300ml (½ pint) of the cooking liquid.
2 Melt the butter in a saucepan, stir in the flour, then blend in the reserved liquor. Bring to the boil, stirring constantly. Add the soft cheese, season and heat through, stirring.
3 Arrange the leeks in a shallow flameproof dish, then spoon the cheese sauce over the top and sprinkle with the Parmesan. Grill for 1-2 minutes until bubbling and golden. Serve immediately.

grilled mushrooms with herb and garlic butter

Serve these mushrooms as a simple side dish, with grilled meat or other vegetables.

Serves 4-6
Preparation time: 10 minutes, plus chilling
Cooking time: 10 minutes
280-185 cals per serving

125g (4oz) butter, softened
2 garlic cloves, peeled and crushed
30ml (2 tbsp) chopped fresh herbs, such as chives, chervil, parsley and thyme
5ml (1 tsp) grated lemon rind
salt and freshly ground black pepper
12 field mushrooms, trimmed
15ml (1 tbsp) olive oil

1 Cream the butter, garlic, herbs, lemon rind and a little salt and pepper together in a bowl. Cover and chill in the refrigerator for at least 30 minutes to allow the flavours to develop.
2 Brush the mushrooms lightly with oil, arrange gill-side down on a grill pan and grill under a high heat for 5 minutes. Meanwhile, cut the flavoured butter into small pieces.
3 Turn the field mushrooms gill-side up. Dot with the butter and grill for 4-5 minutes until the mushrooms are tender and sizzling. Serve immediately.

Variation Flavour the butter with chopped basil, garlic and chopped sun-dried tomatoes.

summer vegetable stir-fry

Vary the vegetables for this stir-fry as you like, but always blanch harder ones first. For a winter vegetable stir-fry, use cauliflower and broccoli florets, carrot sticks, 2-3 spring onions, sliced, and a little chopped fresh root ginger.

Serves 4-6
Preparation time: 15 minutes
Cooking time: 7-8 minutes
160-110 cals per serving

125g (4oz) baby carrots, trimmed
125g (4oz) baby courgettes
30ml (2 tbsp) sunflower oil
2 garlic cloves, peeled and roughly chopped
1 large yellow pepper, halved, cored, deseeded and cut into broad strips
125g (4oz) patty pans (optional), halved
125g (4oz) thin asparagus spears, trimmed
125g (4oz) cherry tomatoes, halved
salt and freshly ground black pepper
30ml (2 tbsp) balsamic or sherry vinegar
5ml (1 tsp) sesame oil
15ml (1 tbsp) sesame seeds, toasted

1 Blanch the carrots in boiling salted water for 2 minutes; drain and pat dry. Halve the courgettes lengthwise.
2 Heat the sunflower oil in a wok or deep frying pan until smoking, then stir-fry the garlic for 20 seconds. Add the carrots, yellow pepper, courgettes, patty pans and asparagus. Stir-fry over a high heat for 1 minute.
3 Add the tomatoes and seasoning. Stir-fry for 3-4 minutes until the vegetables are just tender. Add the balsamic vinegar and sesame oil, toss well and sprinkle with the toasted sesame seeds. Serve immediately.

minted peas with cucumber

This is a lovely way to bring out the full flavour of fresh peas, though frozen peas can be used.

Serves 4-6
Preparation time: 5 minutes
Cooking time: About 10 minutes
350-230 cals per serving

450g (1lb) shelled fresh peas
salt and freshly ground black pepper
50g (2oz) butter
1 bunch of spring onions, trimmed and sliced
175g (6oz) cucumber, halved lengthwise, deseeded and thickly sliced
150ml (¼ pint) crème fraîche
45ml (3 tbsp) dry vermouth, such as Noilly Prat
30ml (2 tbsp) chopped fresh mint
pinch of sugar
mint sprigs, to garnish

1 Add the peas to a pan of boiling salted water and cook for 5-10 minutes, until tender; drain.
2 Meanwhile, heat the butter in a frying pan, add the spring onions and cucumber and sauté for 3 minutes. Add the crème fraîche and vermouth. Bring to the boil and bubble for 2-3 minutes.
3 Add the peas, mint and sugar. Season generously and toss to mix. Serve garnished with mint.

creamed spinach

Serves 6
Preparation time: 15 minutes
Cooking time: 5 minutes
75 cals per serving

900g (2lb) spinach leaves, stalks removed
60ml (4 tbsp) crème fraîche
salt and freshly ground black pepper

1 Cook the spinach with just the water clinging to the leaves after washing in a covered pan for 3-4 minutes or until just wilted.
2 Stir in the crème fraîche and season with salt and pepper to taste. Serve at once.

baby carrots with basil

Young carrots are best in the summer months when they have a delicious, sweet flavour which develops into an earthier taste as they mature. Scrape with the edge of a knife instead of peeling, and cook them whole to maximise their flavour.

Serves 6
Preparation time: 5 minutes
Cooking time: 5-10 minutes
90 cals per serving

700g (1½lb) baby carrots
salt and freshly ground black pepper
75ml (5 tbsp) double cream
60ml (4 tbsp) roughly torn fresh basil

1 Trim the carrots and peel if necessary, leaving on a tuft of stalk. Cook in boiling salted water for about 5-7 minutes, until almost tender. Drain thoroughly.
2 Return the carrots to the pan and add the cream and basil. Lower the heat and cook for about 2 minutes, stirring occasionally.
3 Season generously with salt and pepper and serve at once.

Variation Omit the cream and basil. At stage 2, add 5ml (1 tsp) soft brown sugar, a large knob of butter and a squeeze of lemon juice. Toss over a high heat until the carrots are well glazed. Sprinkle with chopped parsley or mint to serve.

vital vegetables

From a nutritional angle, vegetables are invaluable. In particular, they are an excellent source of vitamins A, B, C and E, and minerals, including iron, calcium and phosphorous; the exact content depending upon the variety. Low in fat and cholesterol, yet high in fibre, vegetables provide an important source of roughage. Starchy varieties, such as potatoes are also a good source of energy, but most vegetables are low in calories. Many varieties provide some protein too.

baked baby beets

Serves 6
Preparation time: 15 minutes
Cooking time: 1¼-1½ hours
90 cals per serving

1.25kg (2¾lb) baby beetroot
15g (½oz) butter
salt and freshly ground black pepper
chopped parsley or chives, to garnish

1 Trim the beetroot and carefully rinse in cold water, making sure you do not tear the skins.
2 Rub a large piece of foil with the butter. Place the beetroot on the buttered foil, season and wrap well to form a parcel. Bake at 200°C/fan oven 190°C (400°F) Mark 6 for 1¼ -1½ hours or until soft and the skin comes away easily.
3 Leave for a minute or two, until cool enough to handle, then rub off the skins. Sprinkle the beetroot with parsley or chives to serve.

honey-glazed shallots

Serves 4
Preparation time: 15 minutes, plus standing
Cooking time: 25 minutes
95 cals per serving

450g (1lb) shallots
25g (1oz) butter
15ml (1 tbsp) thin honey
juice of ½ lemon
15ml (1 tbsp) Worcestershire sauce
15ml (1 tbsp) balsamic vinegar
salt and freshly ground black pepper

1 Soak the shallots in cold water to cover for 20 minutes. Drain and peel away the skins.
2 Put the shallots in a pan with just enough cold water to cover. Bring to the boil, lower the heat and simmer for 5 minutes. Drain well.
3 Return the shallots to the pan and add all the remaining ingredients. Stir to coat the shallots with the glaze. Cover and cook gently, stirring occasionally, until the shallots are tender.
4 Remove the lid and bubble for 2-3 minutes until the liquid is reduced and syrupy.

roasted ratatouille

Serves 6
Preparation time: 15 minutes
Cooking time: 1 hour
235 cals per serving

400g (14oz) red peppers, halved, cored, deseeded
    and roughly chopped
700g (1½lb) aubergines, trimmed and cut into chunks
450g (1lb) onions, peeled and cut into wedges
4-5 garlic cloves (unpeeled)
150ml (¼ pint) olive oil
5ml (1 tsp) fennel seeds
sea salt flakes and freshly ground black pepper
200ml (7fl oz) passata
thyme sprigs, to garnish

1 Place the red peppers, aubergines, onions, garlic, olive oil and fennel seeds in a roasting tin, season with salt and pepper and toss well. Roast at 240°C/fan oven 230°C (475°F) Mark 9 for 30 minutes or until the vegetables are charred and beginning to soften, tossing frequently during cooking.

2 Stir the passata through the roasted vegetables and return to the oven for about 30 minutes, stirring from time to time. Garnish with sprigs of thyme to serve.

Notes
- If you can't find fennel seeds, use cumin seeds instead.
- Passata is puréed, sieved tomatoes with a concentrated flavour, readily available in jars and cartons from supermarkets.

sesame-fried swede

Serves 4
Preparation time: 15 minutes
Cooking time: 20 minutes
130 cals per serving

900g (2lb) swede
15ml (1 tbsp) sunflower oil
5ml (1 tsp) sesame oil
1 garlic clove, peeled and crushed
10ml (2 tsp) grated fresh root ginger
1 red chilli, deseeded and finely chopped
4 ripe tomatoes, deseeded and diced
30ml (2 tbsp) dark soy sauce
pinch of sugar
salt and freshly ground black pepper
15ml (1 tbsp) toasted sesame seeds
coriander leaves, to garnish

1 Cut the swede into 2.5cm (1 inch) cubes. Heat the two oils in a frying pan and stir-fry the swede for 5 minutes until starting to brown on all sides.
2 Add the garlic, ginger and chilli and fry gently for a further 5 minutes.
3 Stir in the diced tomatoes, soy sauce, sugar and 30ml (2 tbsp) water. Cover and cook for 10 minutes until the swede is tender. Season with salt and pepper to taste.
4 Sprinkle over the toasted sesame seeds and coriander leaves. Serve at once.

Note When buying swede, choose small ones if available. Large specimens are likely to be coarse-textured and may be woody.

Variation Sprinkle with chopped toasted almonds instead of sesame seeds.

winter vegetables roasted with cardamom

This is a wonderful partner to any winter meat or poultry dish. Cardamom pods add a hint of aroma, without being too overpowering.

Serves 6-8
Preparation time: 20 minutes
Cooking time: About 1 hour
355-265 cals per serving

350g (12oz) carrots, peeled
350g (12oz) parsnips, peeled
350g (12oz) celeriac, peeled
350g (12oz) sweet potato, peeled
150ml (¼ pint) olive oil
4 cardamom pods, lightly crushed
15ml (1 tbsp) soft brown sugar
coarse sea salt and freshly ground black pepper

1 Quarter the carrots and parsnips lengthwise. Cut the celeriac and sweet potato into chunks.
2 Heat the olive oil in a roasting tin, add the vegetables and toss well. Roast in the oven at 200°C/fan oven 190°C (400°F) Mark 6 for 30 minutes, turning twice during cooking.
3 Add the cardamom pods and sugar to the vegetables, turning them to coat well. Bake for a further 30 minutes until well browned and soft, but not disintegrating. Season generously with salt and pepper, then serve.

celeriac mash

An excellent accompaniment for roast pork and game, and rich casseroles.

Preparation time: 15 minutes
Cooking time: 30 minutes
250 cals per serving

900g (2lb) celeriac, peeled and roughly chopped
900g (2lb) potatoes, peeled and roughly chopped
salt and freshly ground black pepper
150ml (¼ pint) double cream
150ml (¼ pint) milk

1 Add the celeriac and potatoes to a pan of salted water. Bring to the boil and cook for 20-30 minutes or until both are tender; drain.
2 Return to the pan and mash with a potato masher. Warm the cream and milk and beat into the mash over a low heat. Season generously with salt and pepper, then serve.

buying potatoes

The many varieties of potatoes fall into two categories: early or new potatoes, and maincrop varieties. Home-grown new potatoes are available from May to August, though imported produce gives us year round availability. Maincrop British potatoes or 'old potatoes' are lifted during September and October and stored for sale over the next 8 months.

- In general, new potatoes have a firm, waxy texture, which does not break up during cooking. They are therefore ideal for boiling, sautéeing and salads. Old potatoes have a floury texture which does soften on cooking; these are generally better for mashed potatoes, roasting and baking (in their jackets). Both types can be used to make chips.
- Individual potato varieties have their own characteristics; some maincrop varieties, for example, are better for baking than boiling and vice versa. Refer to packet directions or ask your supplier for advice. Good all-round maincrop varieties are King Edward, Maris Piper, Desirée, Romano, Cara and Pentland Hawk. The Pink Fir Apple variety is fine-flavoured with an unusual texture for a maincrop potato – being firm and waxy it is more like a new potato and is ideal for salads.
- Jersey Royals with their creamy, tender flesh and fine flavour have long been regarded as the 'king' of new potatoes. Other varieties to look out for are Belle de Fontenay, Charlotte, Maris Bard and Pentland Javelin.
- Choose potatoes with smooth, firm skins. Don't buy potatoes with a green tinge, as these are unfit for eating. New potatoes generally have skins that can be rubbed off. Buy new potatoes in small quantities and use them fairly quickly. To prepare, scrub or scrape new potatoes. Peel old potatoes (unless you are baking them in their jackets).

new potatoes with peas and broad beans

Serves 4
Preparation time: 5 minutes
Cooking time: 20 minutes
275 cals per serving

700g (1½lb) small new potatoes
salt and freshly ground black pepper
200g (7oz) shelled fresh peas
200g (7oz) shelled fresh broad beans
40g (1½oz) butter
pinch of sugar
45ml (3 tbsp) chopped fresh flat-leaf parsley

1 Cook the new potatoes in a large pan of boiling salted water for about 15 minutes until tender; drain and set aside.
2 In the meantime, place the peas and broad beans in a large frying pan with the butter, sugar and 75ml (5 tbsp) water. Bring to the boil, cover and simmer for 10 minutes.
3 Add the potatoes and simmer, uncovered, until all the liquid has evaporated. Season well and stir in the chopped parsley. Serve at once.

flavoured mash

For a delicious, creamy mash, cook 900g (2lb) maincrop, peeled potatoes in boiling salted water. Drain and mash with 50g (2oz) butter (preferably unsalted) and 30-45ml (2-3 tbsp) warm milk. Try the following ideas for flavoured mash:

SAFFRON MASH Omit milk. Soak a pinch of saffron strands in 30ml (2 tbsp) boiling water. Beat the saffron and liquid into the mashed potatoes with the butter. Sprinkle with coarse salt to serve.

SPRING ONION AND CHIVE MASH Chop 3-4 spring onions and stir into the creamy mash with a handful of snipped chives.

ROSEMARY AND GORGONZOLA MASH Add 2 sprigs of rosemary to the potato cooking water; discard after draining. Stir 75g (3oz) crumbled gorgonzola cheese into the potatoes after mashing.

rösti with garlic and thyme

Thin potato sticks are tossed with garlic and thyme and cooked in a frying pan to a golden, crisp cake. This is a good accompaniment to serve with roast meats and chicken.

Serves 6
Preparation time: 20 minutes
Cooking time: 35-40 minutes
240 cals per serving

700g (1½lb) potatoes
6 garlic cloves, peeled and crushed
30ml (2 tbsp) chopped fresh thyme
salt and freshly ground black pepper
125g (4oz) unsalted butter

1 Peel the potatoes and immerse in a bowl of cold water. Drain the potatoes, slice thinly, then cut into thin sticks, a little thicker than matchsticks. Place in a bowl; it won't matter if they discolour a little.
2 Add the garlic and thyme to the potato matchsticks and toss well. Season liberally.
3 To clarify the butter, slowly melt the butter in a small pan, then skim off any impurities from the surface. Keep warm.
4 Pour 30ml (2 tbsp) of the butter into a heavy-based 25cm (10 inch) non-stick frying pan, suitable for oven use (or moule à manque tin). Transfer the potato sticks to the pan, spread evenly and press down to form a 'cake'. Pour over the remaining butter. Cook over a moderate heat for 5 minutes or until the underside is golden.
5 Press the potatoes down firmly once more and cover with a lid or a buttered sheet of foil. Bake at 200°C/fan oven 190°C (400°F) Mark 6 for 25-30 minutes, or until the potatoes are tender when pierced with a sharp knife and the underside is a deep golden brown.
6 Place a plate on top of the potato cake, invert onto the plate and slide back into the pan. Cook over a medium heat for 5 minutes, until golden and crisp. Loosen the cake with a palette knife, place a warmed plate over the pan and invert the potato cake onto the plate. Serve at once.

croquette potatoes

Easy to make, these are delicious served with fish.

Serves 8
Preparation time: 20 minutes, plus chilling
Cooking time: About 30 minutes
Suitable for freezing (see note)
265 cals per serving

700g (1½lb) large floury potatoes, peeled and cut into
    chunks
salt and pepper
60ml (4 tbsp) milk
25g (1oz) butter
2 eggs, lightly beaten
30ml (2 tbsp) chopped fresh chives
30ml (2 tbsp) chopped fresh parsley or tarragon
TO FINISH:
seasoned plain white flour, for coating
2 eggs, beaten
125g (4oz) day-old white breadcrumbs
butter and oil, for frying
parsley or tarragon sprigs, to garnish

1 Cook the potatoes in a large pan of boiling
   salted water for about 15 minutes until tender;
   drain and dry off over a low heat. Mash with the
   milk and butter until smooth; season generously.
   Stir in the beaten eggs and chopped herbs.
2 Spread the mixture in a shallow non-stick tin,
   cover and allow to cool, then chill for at least
   4 hours or overnight.
3 Divide the mixture into about 16 pieces and roll
   into small barrel shapes. Roll in seasoned flour,
   dip in egg, then roll in the breadcrumbs to coat
   all over.
4 Heat a thin layer of butter and oil in a frying
   pan and fry the croquettes in batches, turning
   occasionally, until golden brown and crisp.
   Drain on kitchen paper and keep warm while
   cooking the remainder.
5 Serve the croquette potatoes piping hot,
   garnished with parsley or tarragon.

Note Open-freeze the cooled, cooked croquettes,
then wrap. Reheat from frozen on a wire rack over
a baking sheet at 200°C/fan oven 190°C (400°F)
Mark 6 for about 25 minutes.

creamy baked potatoes with mustard seeds

These tempting jacket potatoes are an excellent accompaniment to beef casseroles and pies.

Serves 6
Preparation time: 15-20 minutes
Cooking time: 1¼ hours
Suitable for freezing (stage 3)
330 cals per serving

6 baking potatoes, about 1.4kg (3lb) in total
30ml (2 tbsp) sunflower oil
15ml (1 tbsp) coarse sea salt
4-5 large garlic cloves (unpeeled)
50g (2oz) butter
90ml (6 tbsp) crème fraîche
30ml (2 tbsp) mustard seeds, toasted and lightly crushed
salt and freshly ground black pepper
oregano or parsley sprigs, to garnish

1 Prick the potato skins, rub with oil and sprinkle with salt. Place on a baking sheet and bake at 200°C/fan oven 190°C (400°F) Mark 6 for 40 minutes. Add the garlic cloves and cook for 20 minutes.
2 Slice the tops off the potatoes and scoop out the flesh into a warm bowl, leaving 1cm (½ inch) shells.
3 Squeeze the garlic out of the skins and add to the potato flesh with the butter, crème fraîche and mustard seeds. Mash together and season generously with salt and pepper. Pile the mixture back into the hollowed-out potato skins.
4 Return to the oven for 20-25 minutes or until hot through to the centre. Serve garnished with oregano or parsley sprigs.

Note If frozen, thaw overnight at cool room temperature, then bake at 200°C/fan oven 190°C (400°F) Mark 6 for 20-25 minutes.

potato gratin

A deliciously creamy gratin of potatoes flavoured with garlic, herbs and a hint of saffron.

Serves 4-6
Preparation time: 15-20 minutes
Cooking time: 1¼ hours
Suitable for freezing
460-305 cals per serving

450ml (¾ pint) milk
150ml (¼ pint) double cream
2 bay leaves, bruised
2 fresh rosemary sprigs, bruised
2 strips of lemon zest, bruised
pinch of saffron strands
900g (2lb) even-sized, small waxy potatoes
1 small onion, peeled and grated
2 garlic cloves, peeled and finely chopped
25g (1oz) butter, diced
salt and freshly ground black pepper

1   Put the milk, cream, bay leaves, rosemary and lemon zest into a saucepan. Bring slowly to the boil, remove from the heat, stir in the saffron and set aside to infuse for 10 minutes.
2   Meanwhile, peel the potatoes, then cut into thin even slices, preferably using a mandolin or a food processor fitted with a fine slicing blade.
3   Arrange a layer of potatoes over the base of a 1.5 litre (2½ pint) gratin dish. Scatter over some of the onion, garlic and butter; season well. Repeat the layers, finishing with potatoes and a few pieces of butter.
4   Strain the infused cream over the potatoes, pressing the herbs and lemon to extract as much flavour as possible. Cover the dish with foil, place on a baking sheet and bake at 200°C/fan oven 190°C (400°F) Mark 6 for 1 hour.
5   Remove the foil and bake for a further 15-20 minutes until the potatoes are softened and the top is golden brown.

soft polenta

Preparation time: 20 minutes
Cooking time: 35-40 minutes
275 cals per serving

900ml (1½ pints) milk
1.25ml (¼ tsp) salt
125g (4oz) instant polenta
60ml (4 tbsp) olive oil
75g (3oz) Parmesan cheese, finely grated
15ml (1 tbsp) chopped fresh rosemary
15ml (1 tbsp) chopped fresh thyme
salt and freshly ground black pepper

1   Bring the milk to the boil in a large pan with the salt added. Remove from the heat and add the polenta in a slow, steady stream. Return to the heat and stir for 5 minutes or until smooth and the mixture comes away from the side of the pan.
2   Remove from the heat and stir in the olive oil, grated Parmesan and chopped herbs. Season with salt and pepper to taste. Serve immediately.

fragrant couscous

Serves 4
Preparation time: 15 minutes
265 cals per serving

150ml (¼ pint) chicken or vegetable stock
250g (9oz) couscous
5ml (1 tsp) harissa or 1 large red chilli, deseeded
50g (2oz) blanched almonds, toasted
50g (2oz) raisins
30ml (2 tbsp) chopped flat-leaf parsley
45ml (3 tbsp) chopped fresh mint

1   Bring the stock to the boil in a saucepan. Take off the heat and stir in the couscous, harissa or chilli, and the almonds and raisins.
2   Cover with foil and leave to soak for 10 minutes. Fluff up the couscous grains with a fork and remove the chilli, if using. Fork through the chopped parsley and mint to serve.

cooking for crowds

Sensational, prepare-ahead
party foods, from original
canapés to smart celebration
buffets, plus hints for stress-
free entertaining

canapés & party nibbles

Canapés are perfect for drinks parties as they can be made ahead and simply warmed through prior to serving. Similarly nibbles, such as palmiers, spiced nuts and marinated olives, can be prepared in advance. Larger supermarkets and delicatessens stock ready-prepared party foods, including dips. A colourful platter of crunchy crudités and a selection of tasty dips always looks attractive.

Allow about 5 canapés per person if guests are going on to have dinner; cater for approximately 10 'bites' each if they are not – with nuts, olives, dips and 'dunks' as extras.

cheese palmiers

Makes 48
Preparation time: 20 minutes
Cooking time: 12-14 minutes
Suitable for freezing
250-215 cals per palmier

two 375g (13oz) packets puff pastry
50g (2oz) Parmesan cheese, freshly grated
paprika, for sprinkling
sesame seeds, for sprinkling

1 Roll out 1 packet of pastry on a lightly floured surface to a 30x25cm (12x10 inch) rectangle. Sprinkle evenly with a little cheese and paprika.
2 Fold the long sides halfway towards the centre, sprinkle with cheese and paprika, then fold again, so the sides meet in the middle. Sprinkle with paprika, then fold in half again, concealing the first folds; press down lightly.
3 Cut across the roll into 24 equal pieces. Place the palmiers, cut-side down, on a large dampened baking sheet. Flatten slightly with a palette knife or the palm of your hand. Sprinkle with sesame seeds. Repeat with the other packet of pastry.
4 Bake, one sheet at a time, at 220°C/fan oven 210°C (425°F) Mark 7 for 8 minutes until golden brown. Carefully turn the palmiers and bake for a further 6-8 minutes until crisp and golden brown. Transfer to wire racks to cool.

spiced nuts

Makes 450g (1lb)
Preparation time: 20 minutes
Cooking time: 30 minutes
195 cals per 25g (1oz)

45ml (3 tbsp) sunflower oil
15ml (1 tbsp) curry powder or garam masala
350g (12oz) mixed skinned nuts, such as almonds, pecans, hazelnuts
125g (4oz) mixed pumpkin and sunflower seeds
5ml (1 tsp) coarse sea salt

1 Heat the oil in a roasting tin and stir in the curry powder. Cook, stirring, for 30 seconds. Add the nuts and seeds and stir to coat.
2 Roast at 150°C/fan oven 140°C (300°F) Mark 2 for 30 minutes, stirring from time to time. On removing from the oven, toss with the salt.
3 Serve warm from the oven, or cool completely and store in an airtight tin for up to 2 weeks.

marinated olives

Prepare these olives at least a month in advance to allow time for them to absorb the flavours.

Makes 600g (1¼lb)
Preparation time: 20 minutes, plus maturing
50 cals per 25g (1oz)

200g (7oz) each black, green and stuffed olives
30ml (2 tbsp) coriander seeds
finely pared zest of 1 orange, shredded
few fresh coriander sprigs
about 600ml (1 pint) extra-virgin olive oil

1 Using a rolling pin, strike each olive gently (except the stuffed ones), to split but not crush it. Arrange in layers in a 1.2 litre (2 pint) glass jar, sprinkling with coriander seeds and orange zest. Tuck a few sprigs of coriander down the side.
2 Warm the olive oil in a saucepan to release the aroma, then pour sufficient into the jar to cover the olives completely. Tapping the jar to release air bubbles, seal tightly and allow to cool. Leave to mature in a cool dark place for 1 month.

lingonberry and camembert tartlets

Lingonberry, the Swedish relative of the cranberry, makes a sauce that marries well with cheese. Lingonberry sauce is available from selected supermarkets and delicatessens, but cranberry sauce can be used if preferred.

Makes 15
Preparation time: 30 minutes
Cooking time: 6 minutes
160 cals per tartlet

4 filo pastry sheets
100g (3½oz) butter, melted
100g (3½oz) ripe Camembert or Brie, cut into
    15 pieces
125g (4oz) wild lingonberry sauce, or cranberry sauce

1 Using a sharp knife, cut each filo pastry sheet into 15 x 5cm (2 inch) squares.
2 Place a filo square on a board, brush with melted butter, then place another filo square on top at an angle and brush again with butter. Apply two more squares, at an angle, brushing each with butter to create a star effect. Gently press the filo into a mini tartlet tin. Repeat to make 14 more tartlet cases.
3 Place a piece of cheese in each of the filo cases. Place on a baking sheet and bake at 200°C/fan oven 190°C (400°F) Mark 6 for 5-6 minutes or until the pastry is golden brown and the cheese is melted.
4 Place a heaped spoonful of lingonberry or cranberry sauce in each tartlet, then serve.

Note When working with filo, it is important to keep the pastry covered with a damp cloth until ready to use, otherwise it will dry out.

lime and gin marinated salmon

Use Japanese sushi rice for this recipe – its high starch content gives just the right amount of stickiness. The salmon must be very fresh.

Makes 15
Preparation time: 30 minutes, plus overnight marinating and cooling
Cooking time: 12 minutes
55 cals per canapé

30ml (2 tbsp) gin
grated rind of 1 lime
15ml (1 tbsp) sea salt flakes
15ml (1 tbsp) pink peppercorns, lightly crushed
150g (5oz) salmon fillet, skinned
150g (5oz) Japanese rice for sushi, washed and drained (see note)
30ml (2 tbsp) rice vinegar
15ml (1 tbsp) caster sugar
15 slices Japanese pickled ginger (see note)
15ml (1 tbsp) wasabi paste (see note)
snipped chives, to garnish

1. In a shallow dish, mix together the gin, lime rind, sea salt flakes and peppercorns. Add the salmon to the marinade, turn to coat, cover and refrigerate overnight.
2. Pour 350ml (12fl oz) water into a large pan and add the rice. Bring to the boil, cover and simmer for 10-12 minutes. Off the heat, stir in the rice vinegar and sugar. Leave until cool, then cover.
3. Using a sharp carving knife, cut the salmon into 30 very thin slices (there's no need to remove seasonings).
4. Wet your hands and mould the rice into 15 walnut-sized balls; flatten to form discs. Top each rice disc with 2 slices of marinated salmon, a slice of pickled ginger and a little wasabi paste. Garnish with chives to serve.

Notes
- Japanese sushi rice and pickled ginger are available from selected supermarkets.
- Wasabi is a condiment made from Japanese horseradish, available from oriental food stores and selected supermarkets. You can buy it ready-made in a tube or as a powder that you mix with water to make a paste. Use wasabi sparingly as it's very hot.

marinated scallops wrapped in bacon

Small, delicate queen scallops grilled within a protective bacon wrapping and served with lime and coriander flavoured mayonnaise.

Makes 15
Preparation time: 30 minutes, plus marinating
Cooking time: 10-12 minutes
210 cals per canapé

15 queen scallops
2.5cm (1 inch) piece fresh root ginger, peeled and
    finely chopped
2 garlic cloves, peeled and crushed
60ml (4 tbsp) thin honey
30ml (2 tbsp) soy sauce
8 rashers streaky bacon, derinded
30ml (2 tbsp) vegetable oil
FOR THE LIME MAYONNAISE:
175g (6oz) mayonnaise
30ml (2 tbsp) chopped fresh coriander
grated rind of 1 lime
15ml (1 tbsp) lime juice
salt and freshly ground black pepper

1 First make the lime mayonnaise. Mix all the ingredients together in a bowl, then cover and refrigerate until required.
2 Place the scallops in a bowl. Mix together the ginger, garlic, honey and soy sauce and pour over the scallops. Cover and leave to marinate in a cool place for 1-2 hours (no longer or the scallops will become tough).
3 Pre-soak 15 wooden cocktail sticks in cold water for 15 minutes to prevent them scorching under the grill. Stretch the bacon rashers using the back of a knife and cut in half. Wrap a half rasher around each scallop and secure with a cocktail stick.
4 Place the scallops on a lightly oiled grill rack, brush with oil and grill for 10-12 minutes or until golden brown. Serve hot, accompanied by the lime mayonnaise for dipping.

Note For convenience, prepare ahead to the end of step 3. Cover and chill the mayonnaise and scallops separately for up to 12 hours.

smoked salmon and dill roulades

A creamy smoked trout pâté spiked with horseradish, wrapped in slices of smoked salmon.

Makes 50-60
Preparation time: 30 minutes, plus chilling
Suitable for freezing
40-35 cals per canapé

300g (10oz) smoked rainbow trout fillets
grated rind and juice of 1 lemon
75ml (5 tbsp) horseradish sauce
125g (4oz) cream cheese
salt and freshly ground black pepper
150ml (¼ pint) double cream, lightly whipped
450g (1lb) thinly sliced smoked salmon
60ml (4 tbsp) chopped fresh dill
salad leaves, to serve

1 Put the trout in a food processor with the lemon rind, horseradish and cream cheese. Pulse until the mixture is just smooth.
2 Turn into a bowl. Add 30ml (2 tbsp) lemon juice, and season with salt and pepper to taste. Fold in the whipped cream.
3 Fit a large piping bag with a 2cm (¾ inch) plain nozzle and fill with the smoked trout mixture.
4 Cut 12cm (5 inch) wide strips of smoked salmon and lay each one on a piece of cling film. Pipe the trout mixture along the length of each strip. Roll up the smoked salmon to enclose the filling, using the cling film to help. Chill in the refrigerator for at least 1 hour.
5 To serve, cut the salmon on the diagonal into 2.5cm (1 inch) lengths, using a very sharp knife. Dip the ends into the chopped dill. Serve on a bed of salad leaves.

Note If the roulades are too soft to cut, firm up in the freezer for 10-15 minutes.

mini shellfish and saffron tarts

Makes 60
Preparation time: 50 minutes, plus chilling
Cooking time: 20 minutes
Suitable for freezing
65 cals per canapé

FOR THE PASTRY:
350g (12oz) plain flour
175g (6oz) butter
75g (3oz) Parmesan cheese, freshly grated
2 eggs, lightly beaten
45ml (3 tbsp) iced water
FOR THE FILLING:
1 egg, beaten
pinch of saffron strands
150ml (¼ pint) double cream
75ml (3 tbsp) chopped fresh chives
salt and freshly ground black pepper
225g (8oz) cooked peeled prawns, roughly chopped,
    or white crab meat, flaked
TO GARNISH:
chives

1 To make the pastry, put the flour, butter and cheese into a food processor and process until the mixture resembles fine crumbs. Add the eggs and iced water. Pulse until the dough comes together to form a ball. Wrap in cling film and chill for 30 minutes.
2 Roll out the pastry thinly on a lightly floured surface. Stamp out rounds with a 5cm (2 inch) plain cutter and use to line 60 mini tartlet tins. Prick the bases well and chill for 30 minutes.
3 Bake in the oven at 200°C/fan oven 190°C (400°F) Mark 6 for 10 minutes or until the tartlet cases are golden.
4 Meanwhile, prepare the filling. Whisk together the egg, saffron, cream and chives; season with salt and pepper.
5 Divide the shellfish between the pastry cases and top each with a teaspoonful of the saffron cream. Bake in the oven for 5-10 minutes. Serve immediately, garnished with chives.

Note If frozen, thaw overnight at cool room temperature. Reheat at 200°C/fan oven 190°C (400°F) Mark 6 for 5-10 minutes.

chicken and salsa verde crostini

Chicken and piquant salsa verde are a sublime combination and these impressive canapés couldn't be easier to make.

Makes 15
Preparation time: 20 minutes, plus chilling
Cooking time: 2 minutes
100 cals per crostini

FOR THE SALSA VERDE:
45ml (3 tbsp) each roughly chopped fresh coriander,
    mint and basil leaves
1 garlic clove, peeled and roughly chopped
30ml (2 tbsp) Dijon mustard
3 anchovy fillets
15ml (1 tbsp) capers
50ml (2fl oz) olive oil
juice of ½ lemon
FOR THE CROSTINI:
1 loaf walnut bread, cut into 1cm (½ inch) slices
30ml (2 tbsp) olive oil
15ml (1 tbsp) sea salt flakes
175g (6oz) cooked chicken breast
125g (4oz) sun-dried tomatoes in oil, drained
50g (2oz) walnuts, toasted and finely chopped
flat-leafed parsley, to garnish

1 To make the salsa verde, process all the ingredients in a blender or food processor until smooth. Cover and chill.
2 To make the crostini, cut the bread slices into 2.5cm (1 inch) pieces. Place on a baking sheet, brush with olive oil and sprinkle with sea salt. Lightly toast on both sides under a hot grill.
3 Slice the chicken into 15 pieces. Cut the sun-dried tomatoes into 15 pieces, too.
4 To serve, place a chicken slice on each crostini base, top with a spoonful of salsa verde and a slice of sun-dried tomato, then garnish with a sprinkling of toasted walnuts and parsley.

Note Prepare ahead to end of step 3. Refrigerate the salsa verde and store the crostini bases in an airtight container for up to 2 days. To serve, lay the crostini bases on a baking sheet and crisp in the oven at 200°C/fan oven 190°C (400°F) Mark 6 for 5-10 minutes. Cool, then complete recipe.

aromatic duck bites

Succulent roast duck and crisp vegetables enhanced
with Chinese flavourings to delicious effect.

Makes 15
**Preparation time: 20 minutes, plus overnight marinating
   and cooling**
Cooking time: 20 minutes
70 cals per bite

6 star anise
2.5cm (1 inch) piece fresh root ginger, peeled and
   finely chopped
150ml (¼ pint) rice wine or sherry
60ml (4 tbsp) dark soy sauce
1 large duck breast, about 225g (8oz)
10ml (2 tsp) sea salt flakes
freshly ground black pepper
2 spring onions, trimmed and finely chopped
75g (3oz) pear, cored and finely chopped
30ml (2 tbsp) plum sauce
30ml (2 tbsp) chopped fresh coriander
20cm (8 inch) piece cucumber
spring onion curls, to garnish (see note)

1 In a small bowl, mix together the star anise,
  ginger, rice wine and soy sauce. Score the duck
  fat, then place the duck breast in the marinade.
  Turn to coat with the mixture, then cover and
  chill overnight.
2 Remove the duck from the marinade and rub the
  skin with the sea salt and pepper. Heat a heavy-
  based frying pan and cook the duck, fat-side
  down, for 5 minutes. Turn the duck over and
  cook for a further 1 minute.
3 Place the duck in a small roasting tin and cook,
  skin-side up, at 200°C/fan oven 190°C (400°F)
  Mark 6 for about 15 minutes. Allow to cool.
4 In a bowl, mix together the spring onions, pear,
  plum sauce and coriander. Cover and chill.
5 Cut the cucumber into 15 x 1cm (½ inch) slices.
  Thinly slice the duck breast and place one piece
  on each slice of cucumber. Top with a spoonful
  of the plum sauce mixture and garnish with
  spring onion curls to serve.

Note To make spring onion curls, shred the spring
onions into 9cm (3½ inch) strips. Place in a bowl of
cold water and chill for at least 4 hours until
curled. Drain and dry on kitchen paper.

cajun sticky chicken wings

These sticky wings are slightly spicy – and irresistible. If you haven't time to prepare the wings as in step 1, don't worry – it isn't essential. Remember to provide a dish for the bones and wipes or a finger bowl for sticky fingers!

Serves 15
Preparation time: 30 minutes
Cooking time: 50 minutes
50 cals per chicken wing

15 chicken wings, about 700g (1½lb) in total
5ml (1 tsp) coriander seeds
2.5ml (½ tsp) cardamom seeds
grated rind of ½ lemon
10ml (2 tsp) paprika
5ml (1 tsp) dried chilli flakes
15ml (1 tbsp) ground mixed spice
30ml (2 tbsp) golden syrup
75ml (5 tbsp) tomato ketchup

1 Remove the chicken wing tips at the joint and discard. Using a small, sharp, pointed knife, cut through the skin and scrape the meat from either side of the bone. Hold the tip of the bone and push the meat down to the base joint. Repeat with the remaining chicken wings.
2 In a small heavy-based saucepan, dry-fry the coriander and cardamom seeds for a few minutes until golden, then crush using a pestle and mortar. Transfer to a bowl, add the lemon rind, paprika, dried chilli flakes, mixed spice, golden syrup and tomato ketchup and mix well.
3 Place the chicken wings in a large non-stick roasting tin. Pour the spice mixture over the chicken and toss until thoroughly coated.
4 Bake at 220°C/fan oven 210°F (425°F) Mark 7 for 45 minutes, turning the chicken from time to time or until charred and sticky. Serve immediately.

Note To prepare ahead, complete up to the end of step 3. Cover and chill for up to 24 hours.

mini koftas

Make these bite-sized koftas well in advance of the party, freeze and reheat on the day.

Makes about 50
Preparation time: 20 minutes
Cooking time: 10 minutes
Suitable for freezing (koftas only, see note)
20 cals per kofta

1 small onion, peeled and quartered
1 garlic clove, peeled
2.5cm (1 inch) piece fresh root ginger, peeled
5ml (1 tsp) ground cumin
5ml (1 tsp) ground coriander
45ml (3 tbsp) vegetable oil
450g (1lb) lean minced beef
45ml (3 tbsp) chopped fresh coriander
salt and freshly ground black pepper
1 small egg, beaten
FOR THE RAITA:
300ml (½ pint) Greek yogurt
5cm (2 inch) piece cucumber, grated
45ml (3 tbsp) chopped fresh coriander

1 First, mix the raita ingredients together in a bowl, season, cover and let stand for 30 minutes.
2 To make the koftas, put the onion, garlic and ginger in a blender or food processor and chop finely. Add the spices and process until mixed.
3 Heat 15ml (1 tbsp) oil in a frying pan, add the onion paste and cook over a medium heat for 2-3 minutes, stirring. Allow to cool.
4 Put the minced beef in a bowl and break it up with a fork. Add the chopped coriander, seasoning and cooled onion paste; mix thoroughly. Add just sufficient beaten egg to bind; don't add too much or the mixture will be too sticky.
5 Using lightly floured hands, shape the mixture into bite-sized balls. Heat the remaining oil in a large frying pan and fry the koftas, in batches if necessary, for about 5 minutes until browned on all sides and cooked through, shaking the pan to ensure they cook evenly. Drain on kitchen paper.
6 Skewer the koftas on to wooden cocktail sticks. Serve hot, with the raita.

Note Thaw overnight at room temperature, then reheat at 200°C (400°F) Mark 6 for 10 minutes.

mixed satay

Satay sticks of tender meat and prawns make great canapés – just be sure to make plenty as they are always popular. If preferred use skinless chicken breast fillets in place of pork.

Makes about 36
Preparation time: 30 minutes, plus marinating
Cooking time: 6-10 minutes
80-85 cals per satay

350g (12oz) pork fillet
350g (12oz) rump steak
12 large raw prawns
squeeze of lemon juice
1 garlic clove, peeled and crushed
5ml (1 tsp) salt
15ml (1 tbsp) soft dark brown sugar
10ml (2 tsp) ground coriander
10ml (2 tsp) ground cumin
5ml (1 tsp) turmeric
60ml (4 tbsp) coconut milk
melted ghee or oil, for brushing
FOR THE PEANUT SAUCE:
75g (3oz) unsalted peanuts, toasted
1 garlic clove, peeled
30ml (2 tbsp) Thai red curry paste
400ml (14fl oz) coconut milk
pinch of hot chilli powder
30ml (2 tbsp) soft dark brown sugar
squeeze of lemon juice
TO GARNISH:
lime or lemon wedges

1 Cut the pork into 2.5cm (1 inch) slices on the diagonal, along the length of the fillet. Put the pork slices between two sheets of cling film and, using a meat mallet or rolling pin, beat until fairly thin. Cut each slice into 2 or 3 strips, about 2.5cm (1 inch) across.

2 Cut the rump steak into thin strips, roughly the same size as the pork.

3 Peel the prawns, leaving the tail end attached. Using a small sharp knife, make a shallow slit along the outer curve from the tail to the head end and remove the dark intestinal vein. Wash under cold running water, then drain and dry with kitchen paper.

4 Put the meat and prawns in a shallow glass dish and sprinkle with the lemon juice. In a small bowl, mix the garlic with the salt, sugar and spices. Stir in the coconut milk to make a fairly dry paste.

5 Spoon the spice paste over the meat and prawns and rub it all over them. Cover and leave to marinate for at least 30 minutes, preferably overnight.

6 To make the peanut sauce, put the peanuts, garlic and Thai curry paste in a food processor or blender with a little of the coconut milk. Process until almost smooth. Add the rest of the coconut milk with the chilli powder, sugar and lemon juice. Work until blended, then transfer to a saucepan.

7 Bring to the boil and cook for 2 minutes, then lower the heat and simmer gently for about 10 minutes, stirring occasionally. If the mixture becomes too thick, thin with a little water; keep warm.

8 Thread each prawn and piece of meat on to a (pre-soaked) bamboo skewer and brush with ghee or oil. Cook under a very hot grill for 6-10 minutes, turning frequently until the prawns are pink; the beef is still just pink in the centre and the pork is cooked right through.

9 Arrange the satay on a serving platter, with lime or lemon wedges. Serve accompanied by the peanut sauce.

quick canapés

- Serve olives, cubed feta cheese and a pinch of dried chilli flakes in bowls with cocktail sticks.
- Serve tortillas with a chilli salsa, made by adding chilli sauce and Worcestershire sauce to a can of chopped tomatoes.
- Pile extra toppings on to thin crusted pizza, cook in a hot oven and serve in tiny squares.
- Grill garlic bread slices until golden, then cut into rough chunks and serve warm in a basket.
- Use a small pastry cutter to cut out discs from a quiche. Put them on a baking sheet, sprinkle with grated cheese and warm through in the oven. Garnish with fresh herbs.

buffet menu for 12

Parma Ham Nibbles

· · · · · · ·

Roast Beef Roulades

Boned Stuffed Chicken

Garden Salad with Crisp Crumbs

New Potato Salad with Mint Dressing

· · · · · · ·

Summer Fruit Whip

Chocolate and Raspberry Torte

parma ham nibbles

Good quality Parma ham, sliced and rolled around complementary foods is an easy-to-prepare, substantial bite to serve with a glass of champagne before the meal. Skewer rolled-up slices of Parma ham on cocktail sticks with cubes of sweet Charentais melon, slices of pecorino cheese, basil leaves, or some good pitted olives. The best Parma ham is freshly sliced and not too salty or too wet.

roast beef roulades

Makes about 24
Preparation time: 45 minutes
Cooking time: 1 hour, plus cooling
235 cals per serving

1.25kg (2¾lb) sirloin of beef
4 garlic cloves, peeled and cut into slivers
10ml (2 tsp) each celery salt, ground mace and
   roughly crushed black peppercorns
550g (1¼lb) large onions, peeled
50g (2oz) fresh horseradish, peeled and roughly
   grated (optional)
150ml (¼ pint) olive oil
3 large, long aubergines, each about 225g (8oz)
sea salt
30ml (2 tbsp) wasabi paste (see note, page 276)
125g (4oz) rocket or baby spinach leaves
oregano sprigs, to garnish

1 Make small incisions all over the beef and insert the garlic slivers. Mix together the celery salt, ground mace and black peppercorns and rub 15ml (1 tbsp) of the mixture all over the beef.
2 Heat a heavy-based frying pan and sear the beef on all sides. Transfer to a roasting tin. Cut the onions into wedges and place around the meat. Sprinkle with the reserved seasoning, horseradish and 15ml (1 tbsp) oil. Cook at 200°C/fan oven 190°C (400°F) Mark 6 for 15 minutes per 450g (1lb) plus 15 minutes for rare beef; allow an extra 5 minutes per 450g (1lb) for medium.
3 Remove the beef from the roasting tin and set aside for at least 4 hours until cool. Meanwhile, thinly slice the aubergines lengthways and brush the slices lightly with the remaining olive oil. Heat a large non-stick frying pan and cook the aubergine slices in batches until golden on both sides; remove and allow to cool.
4 To assemble the roulades, thinly slice the beef. Lay a few aubergine slices on a clean surface, grind over a little sea salt and place a slice of beef on top of each. Spread each slice of beef with a little wasabi and top with a few rocket or spinach leaves. Roll up tightly from the short end and secure with cocktail sticks, if wished.
5 Serve on a large platter, garnished with oregano.

Note You can prepare the roulades a day in advance. Cover and chill until required.

boned stuffed chicken

This is the kind of recipe that gives you a glowing sense of achievement as the first slice is carved! Boning a chicken is not difficult, especially if you have a step-by-step guide to follow. Alternatively, you may be able to order a boned chicken from your butcher. The bird's skin must not be pierced otherwise the stuffing may leak out during cooking.

Serves 10-12
Preparation time: 1 hour, plus boning and chilling
Cooking time: 1½-1¾ hours
305-255 cals per serving

1 chicken, about 1.6kg (3½lb), boned
125g (4oz) butter
1 small onion, peeled and finely chopped
2 small leeks, thinly sliced
2 garlic cloves, peeled and finely chopped
1 large courgette, coarsely grated
50g (2oz) long-grain white rice
50g (2oz) macadamia nuts or skinned hazelnuts, toasted
1 small eating apple
50g (2oz) farmhouse or well-flavoured Cheddar cheese, grated
50g (2oz) seedless raisins
finely grated rind and juice of 1 lemon
75g (3oz) fresh white breadcrumbs
120ml (8 tbsp) chopped fresh mixed herbs, such as parsley, chives and thyme
salt and freshly ground black pepper
1 egg
4-6 large thick slices ham
flat-leafed parsley, to garnish

1 Spread out the boned chicken, flesh-side uppermost, on a clean surface and cover with cling film. Using a rolling pin, slightly flatten the thickest areas to give a fairly even thickness all over. Refrigerate while making the stuffing.

2 Heat half of the butter in a heavy-based pan, add the onion, leeks and garlic and cook, stirring, for 2-3 minutes until beginning to soften. Cover tightly and cook gently for a further 10 minutes or until the leeks are quite soft. Add the courgette and cook for 2 minutes.

3 Meanwhile, cook the rice in boiling salted water until just tender. Drain in a sieve and rinse with plenty of boiling water.

4 Mix together the softened vegetables, rice and nuts. Peel the apple and grate the flesh into the mixture. Add the cheese, raisins, lemon rind and juice, with the breadcrumbs and herbs. Season with plenty of salt and pepper. Add just enough beaten egg to bind the stuffing – don't make it too wet.

5 Lay the chicken, flesh-side uppermost, on a clean surface and spoon a third of the stuffing down the centre. Lay 2-3 slices of ham on top, overlapping them slightly to cover the mixture. Repeat with half of the remaining stuffing and the remaining slices of ham. Top with the remaining stuffing.

6 Fold the chicken over the stuffing and sew the edges together with fine cotton string to enclose the filling and make a neat shape. Lay it on a double sheet of muslin and roll up the chicken in the muslin, keeping it fairly tight and in a neat shape. Tie the ends with string.

7 Place in a roasting tin and smear the remaining butter on top of the muslin. Roast at 180°C/fan oven 170°C (350°F) Mark 4 for 1½-1¾ hours, basting occasionally. To test, push a skewer right through the middle – the juices should run clear; if at all pink, return to the oven for 15 minutes, then test again.

8 Leave to cool, wrapped in the muslin, then refrigerate overnight. Serve cut into thick slices, garnished with parsley.

garden salad with crisp crumbs

Baby carrots, fresh garden peas or broad beans could also be used in this tasty, versatile salad. The spicy chorizo sausage crumb topping makes the salad more substantial, but it can be omitted for a vegetarian version.

Serves 12
Preparation time: 45 minutes, plus cooling
Cooking time: 5 minutes
230 cals per serving

175g (6oz) asparagus tips or French beans, trimmed
  and thickly sliced on the diagonal
175g (6oz) sugar snaps, halved on the diagonal
1 cucumber, peeled, halved, deseeded and sliced on
  the diagonal
3 bunches watercress, divided into sprigs
1 fennel bulb, quartered and thinly sliced
225g (8oz) red or yellow cherry tomatoes, halved
1 large red onion, peeled and finely sliced
FOR THE CRISP CRUMBS:
30ml (2 tbsp) olive oil
2 garlic cloves, peeled and crushed
125g (4oz) chorizo sausage, chopped
75g (3oz) fresh white breadcrumbs, preferably from
  ciabatta
grated rind of 1 lemon
30ml (2 tbsp) chopped flat-leafed parsley
FOR THE DRESSING:
juice of 1 lemon
5ml (1 tsp) Dijon mustard
salt and freshly ground black pepper
5ml (1 tsp) caster sugar
120ml (4fl oz) olive oil
TO GARNISH:
lemon zest shreds

1 To make the crisp crumbs, heat the olive oil in a frying pan, add the garlic, chorizo sausage and breadcrumbs and cook for 3-4 minutes or until golden. Add the lemon rind and parsley and cook for a further 1 minute. Remove and drain on kitchen paper.
2 To make the dressing, shake the ingredients together in a screw-topped jar or whisk together in a bowl until thoroughly combined.

3 To prepare the salad, cook the asparagus or French beans and sugar snaps in boiling salted water for 1 minute. Drain and refresh in cold water, then drain again.
4 Place the asparagus or beans, sugar snaps, cucumber, watercress, fennel, tomatoes and red onion in a large salad bowl. Just before serving, add the dressing and toss to mix. Top with the crumb mixture and garnish with lemon zest.

new potato salad with mint dressing

Jersey Royals make a delicious summery potato salad. The flavours of the fresh mint dressing are absorbed as the potatoes cool.

Serves 12
Preparation time: 45 minutes, plus cooling
Cooking time: 5 minutes
170 cals per serving

2kg (4½lb) Jersey Royal new potatoes, scrubbed and
  halved or quartered if large
handful of fresh mint sprigs
FOR THE DRESSING:
60ml (4 tbsp) white wine vinegar
100ml (3½fl oz) olive oil
90ml (6 tbsp) chopped fresh mint
5ml (1 tsp) caster sugar
salt and freshly ground black pepper
TO SERVE:
30ml (2 tbsp) chopped fresh mint
45ml (3 tbsp) chopped fresh flat-leafed parsley

1 Cook the potatoes in a large pan of boiling salted water with the mint sprigs added for about 15 minutes until tender.
2 Meanwhile, whisk the dressing ingredients together in a small bowl.
3 Drain the cooked potatoes, turn into a bowl and immediately toss with the mint dressing. Allow to cool, then cover and chill. Just before serving, check the seasoning and toss with the freshly chopped mint and parsley.

summer fruit whip

This is a delicious way to enjoy summer berry fruits. Spoon into tall glasses and keep chilled until ready to serve.

Serves 6
Preparation time: 15 minutes, plus chilling
Cooking time: 5 minutes
290 cals per serving

225g (8oz) strawberries
225g (8oz) raspberries
125g (4oz) redcurrants
15ml (1 tbsp) kirsch
50g (2oz) caster sugar
30ml (2 tbsp) water
300ml (½ pint) double cream
2 egg whites

1 Place all the fruits in a saucepan with the kirsch, sugar and 30ml (2 tbsp) water. Heat slowly, then simmer for 5 minutes until the fruits are softened. Strain off and reserve half of the juice. Set aside until cold.
2 Whip the cream in a bowl until it just holds its shape. Fold in the cooled fruit, reserving a few spoonfuls for decoration.
3 Whisk the egg whites in a clean bowl until soft peaks form, then fold into the mixture until evenly incorporated. Spoon into glasses and chill until ready to serve.
4 Top each serving with the reserved fruit and a little juice. Serve with crisp dessert biscuits.

choosing the wine

Special family gatherings demand a reasonably straightforward selection of wines which will appeal to everyone. If you intend to serve dishes like the boned stuffed chicken and horseradish-spiked beef roulades, opt for bold New World whites and reds, such as a fruity Chardonnay and a good Shiraz Cabernet.

chocolate and raspberry torte

This elegant gâteau makes an exquisite dessert to finish a special buffet meal with a flourish.

Makes 12 slices
Preparation time: 45 minutes, plus overnight chilling
Cooking time: 12-15 minutes
375 cals per slice

5 eggs
150g (5oz) caster sugar
125g (4oz) plain white flour
25g (1oz) cocoa powder
FOR THE FILLING:
4 egg yolks
50g (2oz) caster sugar
10ml (2 tsp) vanilla extract
60ml (4 tbsp) cornflour
450ml (¾ pint) milk
90ml (6 tbsp) Grand Marnier or other orange liqueur
300ml (½ pint) double cream
175g (6oz) raspberries
100g (3½oz) plain chocolate, grated or finely chopped
2 pieces preserved stem ginger in syrup, about 25g
    (1oz), finely chopped
TO FINISH:
cocoa powder, for dusting

1 Grease and line a 23cm (9 inch) spring-release cake tin, and a 26x16cm (10½x6½ inch) shallow rectangular tin. Put the eggs and sugar in a large heatproof bowl set over a pan of hot water. Whisk until the mixture is pale and creamy and leaves a trail when the whisk is lifted from the bowl. Remove from the heat and whisk until cool.
2 Sift the flour and cocoa powder over the mixture, then carefully fold in, using a large metal spoon. Spoon a thin layer of the mixture into the rectangular tin, to give an 8mm (⅜ inch) depth. Turn the remainder into the spring-release tin. Bake both cakes at 200°C/fan oven 190°C (400°F) Mark 6 for 12-15 minutes until just firm. Leave to cool.

3 For the filling, beat the egg yolks, sugar, vanilla, cornflour and a little of the milk together in a bowl until smooth. Put the remaining milk in a heavy-based pan and bring to the boil, then pour on to the yolk mixture, stirring constantly. Return to the pan and heat gently, stirring until thickened; do not boil. Turn into a bowl, cover the surface with dampened greaseproof paper to prevent a skin forming and leave to cool.

4 Cut the round cake horizontally into two layers and fit one back into the cleaned round tin, cut-side down. Trim off the edges of the rectangular cake, then cut into 4cm (1½ inch) wide strips.

Fit these around the side of the tin to make a sponge case. Using a teaspoon, drizzle 45-60ml (3-4 tbsp) of the orange liqueur evenly over both round cake layers.

5 Whip the cream in a bowl until thickened, but not peaking. Fold in the cooled custard, raspberries, chocolate, ginger and remaining liqueur. Turn the mixture into the chocolate case and level the surface. Lay the reserved sponge on top, cut-side up. Refrigerate overnight.

6 To serve, carefully release the side of the tin and invert the torte on to a large flat plate. Serve dusted with cocoa powder.

buffet menu for 15

This stylish celebration menu is straightforward to make and easily adapted to cater for a larger crowd – up to 80 guests – simply increase the quantities accordingly.

Sesame Chilli Prawns

Asparagus with Dill Sauce

Egg Mayo Focaccia

. . . .

Baked Spiced Salmon

Italian Chicken Salad

Bacon, Parmesan and Anchovy Salad

Saffron Roasted Vegetable Couscous

. . . .

Ginger and Mint Fruit Salad

Chocolate Cherry Gâteau

catering for crowds

- If you're catering for large numbers, have several serving points for the buffet food and drinks. This avoids bottlenecks and delays.
- Never leave food in a hot room or marquee for any length of time before serving – keep it chilled for as long as possible.
- Keep cold food tightly covered until it's served and, if possible, add garnishes at the last minute, too.
- Pre-slice meat or quiche into portions for easy serving. If you don't, the whole spread could be a mess within minutes.
- Plan to leave at least one person on hand at the buffet table to help serve. It will speed things up and answer the inevitable 'What's that?' question.

sesame chilli prawns

Prepare these a day ahead and refrigerate. Bring to room temperature 30 minutes before serving.

Makes 40
Preparation time: 40 minutes
25 cals per prawn

40 cooked tiger prawns, about 450g (1lb)
75ml (5 tbsp) sweet chilli sauce
75g (3oz) toasted sesame seeds

1 Peel the prawns, leaving the tail end attached.
2 Hold each prawn by the tail and dip into the chilli sauce, then into the sesame seeds to coat.
3 Place the prawns on a tray lined with cling film, cover loosely and chill until required.

asparagus with dill sauce

Makes 40
Preparation time: 15 minutes
Cooking time: 1 minute
20 cals per 'bite'

200g (7oz) thin asparagus (about 40 spears)
sea salt
FOR THE SAUCE:
90ml (6 tbsp) Dijon mustard
30ml (2 tbsp) soft brown sugar
30ml (2 tbsp) chopped fresh dill
salt and freshly ground black pepper

1 Whisk the ingredients for the sauce together in a bowl, seasoning with salt and pepper to taste.
2 Steam the asparagus or plunge into boiling salted water for 1 minute; it should be firm to the bite. Drain and refresh in iced water. Drain well.
3 Arrange the asparagus on platters, sprinkle with sea salt and serve with the dipping sauce.

Note Make the sauce well ahead (leaving out dill), cover and chill. Cook the asparagus up to 4 hours ahead, cover and chill. Bring to room temperature 30 minutes before serving; add dill to the sauce.

egg mayo focaccia

Small rounds of toasted focaccia with a savoury watercress and hard-boiled egg topping.

Makes 40
Preparation time: 45 minutes
Cooking time: 25 minutes
50 cals per focaccia

2 focaccia loaves, sliced
50g (2oz) butter, melted
6 eggs, hard-boiled and shelled
75ml (5 tbsp) mayonnaise
1 bunch of watercress, finely chopped
5ml (1 tsp) Dijon mustard
5ml (1 tsp) anchovy essence
freshly ground black pepper
shredded spring onion, to garnish

1 Stamp out 40 x 4cm (1½ inch) rounds from the focaccia slices. Brush with the melted butter and place on a baking sheet. Bake at 200°C/fan oven 190°C (400°F) Mark 6 for 15 minutes until golden, turning halfway through cooking.
2 Put the hard-boiled eggs in a bowl with the mayonnaise, watercress, mustard, anchovy essence and pepper to taste. Crush with a potato masher until finely chopped and well mixed.
3 Place 5ml (1 tsp) of the egg mixture on each toast round and garnish with spring onions. Finish with a sprinkling of pepper.

Note Prepare the toasts 2 days in advance and store in an airtight tin. Make the egg mixture a day ahead and keep refrigerated. To use, crisp the toasts on a baking sheet in the oven at 200°C/fan oven 190°C (400°F) Mark 6 for 5 minutes. Cool before completing the recipe.

baked spiced salmon

This looks spectacular served on a bed of banana leaves, which you can buy from oriental super-markets – trim to size and lightly oil before use.

Serves 15
Preparation time: 10 minutes, plus cooling
Cooking time: 15 minutes
169 cals per serving

1 salmon fillet, about 1.4kg (3lb)
10ml (2 tsp) each mild chilli powder, ground cumin, ground coriander and ground ginger
5ml (1 tsp) garlic granules
5ml (1 tsp) sea salt
sea salt flakes, for sprinkling

1 Remove any small, residual bones from the salmon with tweezers. Line a large roasting tin with a sheet of foil. Mix together the spices, garlic granules and salt. Rub this mixture over the surface of the salmon, then cut it into 15 pieces on the diagonal.
2 Place the fish in the roasting tin and cook at 200°C/fan oven 190°C (400°F) Mark 6 for 10-15 minutes or until just cooked to the centre. Leave to cool.
3 Serve on a platter lined with banana leaves if available, and sprinkled with sea salt flakes.

Note Prepare ahead to the end of stage 1 a day in advance. Cover and chill overnight. Bring to room temperature 30 minutes before serving.

italian chicken salad

Prepare this salad a day in advance and keep in the refrigerator until ready to slice and serve.

Serves 15
Preparation time: 1 hour
Cooking time: 35 minutes
Suitable for freezing
100 cals per serving

grated rind of 2 lemons
40g (1½oz) fresh parsley sprigs
40g (1½oz) fresh basil leaves
60ml (4 tbsp) capers, drained and rinsed
3 large garlic cloves, peeled
15ml (1 tbsp) olive oil
salt and freshly ground black pepper
10 skinless chicken breast fillets
25g (1oz) unsalted butter, melted
½ quantity Caesar Dressing (see right)
basil sprigs, to garnish

1 Put the lemon rind, parsley, basil, capers, garlic and olive oil in a blender or food processor and blend to a paste. Season with salt and pepper.
2 Place a chicken breast between two sheets of greaseproof paper and bat out thinly, using a rolling pin, until doubled in surface area, taking care not to rip the flesh. Repeat with the other breast fillets.
3 Place the chicken fillets, smooth side down, on a clean surface and season with salt and pepper. Spread each one with 15ml (1 tbsp) of the herb and garlic paste. Roll up and secure with wooden cocktail sticks.
4 Put the rolled chicken fillets in a roasting tin and pour on the melted butter. Cover the tin with foil. Bake at 200°C/fan oven 190°C (400°F) Mark 6 for 30-35 minutes, moving the chicken around in the tin after 20 minutes, to ensure it cooks evenly. Leave to cool, then remove the cocktail sticks. Cover and chill until ready to serve.
5 Slice each breast diagonally into 4 to 5 pieces. Pile the chicken on to a platter, drizzle with the caesar dressing and garnish with basil to serve.

bacon, parmesan and anchovy salad

Prepare the croûtons for this salad well ahead and store in an airtight container. Refresh in a moderately hot oven for 5 minutes, before use.

Serves 15
Preparation time: 50 minutes
Cooking time: 15 minutes
275 cals per serving

150ml (¼ pint) olive oil
175g (6oz) ciabatta, cut into 2.5cm (1 inch) cubes
5ml (1 tsp) sea salt flakes
12 rashers streaky bacon, derinded
50g (2oz) Parmesan cheese
4 little gem lettuces, separated into leaves
50g (2oz) rocket leaves
100g (3½oz) marinated fresh anchovies
½ quantity Caesar Dressing (see below)

1 Pour half of the oil into a frying pan and heat gently until a cube of bread dropped in sizzles. Add half of the ciabatta cubes and toss over the heat for 2-3 minutes or until golden. Remove with a slotted spoon and drain on kitchen paper. Fry the rest of the bread in the remaining oil; drain. Toss the croûtons in the salt; leave to cool.
2 Grill the bacon for 3-4 minutes on each side until golden and crisp. Drain and cool on kitchen paper, then break into pieces.
3 Using a vegetable peeler, finely pare the Parmesan to make shavings.
4 In a large bowl, toss the lettuce and rocket leaves with the croûtons, bacon and anchovies. Drizzle the dressing over the salad, toss lightly and scatter with the Parmesan shavings to serve.

caesar dressing

Put 2 eggs, 2 peeled garlic cloves, the juice of 1 lemon, 20ml (4 tsp) Dijon mustard and 10ml (2 tsp) balsamic vinegar in a food processor and blend until smooth. Then, with the motor running, gradually incorporate 300ml (½ pint) sunflower oil; season to taste. Transfer to a jug, cover and refrigerate for up to 2 days until needed.

saffron roasted vegetable couscous

It's always a good idea to have a vegetarian choice on your party menu. This one doubles up as a side dish for the salmon.

Serves 15
Preparation time: 20 minutes, plus standing
Cooking time: 1 hour 10 minutes
170 cals per serving

3 fennel bulbs, trimmed
3 red onions, peeled
105ml (7 tbsp) olive oil
700g (1½lb) aubergine
700g (1½lb) courgettes
3 red peppers, halved, cored and deseeded
30ml (2 tbsp) thin honey
salt and freshly ground black pepper
generous pinch of saffron threads
500g (1lb 2oz) packet instant couscous
extra-virgin olive oil, for drizzling

1 Cut the fennel and onions into wedges and place in two large roasting tins. Mix 30ml (2 tbsp) oil into each batch. Roast at 240°C/fan oven 230°C (475°F) Mark 9 for 15 minutes.
2 Meanwhile, cut the aubergine, courgettes and red peppers into large pieces, add to the roasting tins, then drizzle each batch with 15ml (1 tbsp) honey and 15ml (1 tbsp) of the remaining oil; season generously and toss well. Roast for 50-55 minutes or until golden brown and tender, tossing the vegetables from time to time and swapping the positions of the tins halfway through cooking. Transfer to a bowl and leave to cool.
3 Put the saffron in a bowl and pour on 600ml (1 pint) boiling water; leave to stand for about 20 minutes.
4 Put the couscous in another bowl with 5ml (1 tsp) salt and the remaining oil. Pour on the saffron liquid, cover and leave to stand for 10 minutes. Fork through to separate the grains.
5 Stir the vegetables through the couscous; check seasoning. Drizzle with a little olive oil to serve.

Note Prepare to end of stage 4 a day ahead. Cover and chill couscous and vegetables separately.

chocolate and cherry gâteau

A delicious, moist chocolate cake, topped with cherries and a wickedly rich chocolate ganache.

Makes 12-15 slices
Preparation time: 1 hour, plus soaking and chilling
Cooking time: 45 minutes
Suitable for freezing (stage 7)
520-415 cals per slice

350g (12oz) fresh cherries, stoned, or 400g (14oz) pitted cherries, drained
45ml (3 tbsp) dark rum
50g (2oz) blanched almonds, toasted
50g (2oz) plain white flour
125g (4oz) good quality plain dark chocolate, in pieces
3 eggs, separated
125g (4oz) butter, softened
125g (4oz) caster sugar
FOR THE CHOCOLATE GANACHE:
225g (8oz) good quality plain dark chocolate, in pieces
450ml (¾ pint) double cream
TO DECORATE:
chocolate curls (see right)
cocoa powder

1 Put the cherries in a bowl with 30ml (2 tbsp) rum; leave to soak for 6 hours or overnight.
2 Grease a 23cm (9 inch) deep round cake tin and line the base with non-stick baking parchment. Place the almonds in a food processor with the flour and process until finely ground.
3 Melt the chocolate with 45ml (3 tbsp) water in a bowl over a pan of simmering water. Remove from the heat, add the egg yolks and remaining rum and beat until smooth.
4 Beat the butter and sugar together in a bowl until light and fluffy. Stir in the chocolate mixture, then fold in the flour. Whisk the egg whites in a clean bowl until they form soft peaks, then fold into the chocolate mixture.
5 Pour the mixture into the prepared tin. Bake at 180°C/fan oven 170°C (350°F) Mark 4 for 30-35 minutes or until the cake is cooked. Leave in the tin for 10 minutes, then turn out on to a wire rack to cool completely.

6 To make the ganache, put the chocolate in a bowl. Slowly bring the cream to the boil in a small pan. Pour over the chocolate and leave to stand for 5 minutes, then stir until melted and smooth; cool. Using an electric whisk, beat the ganache until lighter in colour and thick.

7 Return the cake to the cleaned tin. Scatter the cherries and any juice over the surface. Spoon the ganache on top, spread smoothly, then cover and chill for at least 2 hours.

8 Decorate with chocolate curls and dust liberally with cocoa powder. Serve cut into thin slices, with cream, if wished.

chocolate curls

Use fine quality dark chocolate with at least 70% cocoa solids. Melt the chocolate in a bowl over a pan of barely simmering water, making sure it doesn't become too hot and that no moisture gets into the chocolate. Spread the melted chocolate in a thin layer on a marble slab or other clean, smooth surface. When it has just set, push a large knife across the chocolate at an angle of about 25° to scrape off curls. Store in an airtight container between sheets of greaseproof paper in a cool place for up to 1 week.

ginger fruit salad

This refreshing, fruit salad is the ideal finale to a large gathering. For best results, make it the day before to allow the flavours to develop.

Serves 15
Preparation time: 50 minutes, plus chilling
Cooking time: 30 minutes
145 cals per serving

70cl bottle (1¼ pints) ginger wine
225g (8oz) caster sugar
25g (1oz) piece fresh root ginger, peeled
3 large mangoes, halved, stoned and peeled
3 large papaya, halved, deseeded and peeled
2 Charentais melons, halved, deseeded and peeled
450g (1lb) seedless red grapes
30ml (2 tbsp) chopped fresh mint (optional)
small mint sprigs, to decorate

1 Place the ginger wine, sugar and ginger in a pan with 600ml (1 pint) water and heat gently until the sugar has dissolved. Increase the heat and bring to the boil, then turn down and simmer gently for 20-30 minutes. Leave to cool.

2 Roughly chop the mangoes, papaya and melons. Place in a large serving bowl with the grapes. Strain the cooled syrup over the fruit and toss gently to mix. Cover and chill for at least 2 hours.

3 To serve, add the chopped mint if using. Decorate with mint sprigs.

chilling drinks

Chill large quantities of wine in plastic tubs or bins lined with plastic sacks and filled with ice and water. Ice can be delivered or bought from supermarkets and off-licences. A 12.6kg (28lb) bag of ice should chill a case of wine in approximately 1 hour – allow longer on hot days.

barbecues & picnics

Outdoor feasts are a great way to relax and entertain. These tempting new ideas will give your barbecues and picnics maximum appeal

fish wrapped in vine leaves

hot tips for a perfect barbecue

- Light the barbecue at least 30 minutes, preferably an hour in advance to ensure it is hot enough and to allow the flames to die down before you begin cooking. Barbecues need a draught to get going, so choose a spot that's not too sheltered, nor totally exposed. The barbecue is ready for cooking when the embers are covered with a layer of ash.
- Line the ash tray with foil, shiny side up, to reflect heat and make cleaning easier afterwards.
- Use flavoured wood chips and rosemary or thyme sprigs to add extra flavour.
- Hinged metal barbecue holders are useful for cooking fish or chops.
- Long metal or wooden skewers are invaluable for threading shellfish, fish, meat, poultry and vegetables. To prevent burning, soak wooden skewers in cold water for at least 20 minutes before using.
- If you're cooking for large numbers of people, switch on your oven to keep food warm.
- Take ingredients out of the fridge about 30 minutes before cooking to ensure food cooks quickly and thoroughly.
- Don't choose the leanest cuts of meat to barbecue; instead, opt for chops and steaks that have some fat on them as this will help to keep the meat succulent.
- Brush all food with oil and baste with any remaining marinade to keep it moist.
- A fresh, seasonal salad and some salsas and dips with good-quality bread are all that's needed to accompany barbecue food.
- Instead of elaborate puddings, serve fresh, seasonal fruit with ice cream, succulent fresh fruit tarts or quick puddings which can be cooked on the barbecue after the main meal.

Small, whole fish are delicious cooked on the barbecue and vine leaves provide an ideal protective wrapping. For convenience, prepare up to 6 hours ahead; keep chilled.

Serves 6
Preparation time: 30 minutes
Cooking time: 14 minutes
50 cals per serving

6 small whole fish, such as red snapper, tilapia or
    rainbow trout, cleaned, each 175-225g (6-8oz)
salt and freshly ground black pepper
2 lemons, sliced
olive oil, for brushing
227g (8oz) packet vine leaves (see note)
lemon wedges, to serve

1 Rinse the fish, pat dry and season inside. Place 2 halved lemon slices in each cavity, then brush the fish with oil. Wrap each fish in vine leaves and tie with wet string. Brush again with oil.
2 Cook the fish on a hot barbecue for 5-7 minutes on each side, depending on thickness. Serve with lemon wedges.

Note Vine leaves are sold in Middle Eastern shops and larger supermarkets.

fish steaks with a difference

Liven up tuna, salmon or swordfish steaks with these ideas. Each is sufficient for 4 fish steaks.

SUN-DRIED TOMATO MARINADE Mix together 50g (2oz) melted butter with 30ml (2 tbsp) sun-dried tomato paste, 10ml (2 tsp) lemon juice and seasoning. Brush the marinade over the fish steaks from time to time during cooking.

WASABI MAYONNAISE Stir 10ml (2 tsp) Japanese wasabi paste into 90ml (6 tbsp) mayonnaise. Use as a sauce to top barbecued fish steaks.

steam-grilled oriental salmon

Oriental flavours work well with salmon. Here, the cooking juices and soy sauce keep the fish deliciously moist within its parcel. Pak choi – available in larger supermarkets – is the ideal size for this recipe. For convenience, prepare the parcels up to a day ahead; keep chilled.

Serves 4
Preparation time: 15 minutes
Cooking time: 10 minutes
300 cals per serving

sesame oil, for greasing
4 salmon fillets, each about 150g (5oz) and 2.5cm (1 inch) thick
60ml (4 tbsp) soy sauce
200g (7oz) pak choi or spinach
2.5cm (1 inch) piece fresh root ginger, peeled and coarsely grated
4 spring onions, trimmed and sliced

1 Lightly grease 4 large sheets of foil, about 35cm (14 inches) square, with sesame oil. Put a salmon fillet in the centre of each and drizzle with 15ml (1 tbsp) soy sauce.
2 Put the pak choi or spinach leaves, ginger and spring onions on top of the salmon fillets and fold the foil over neatly but loosely to form parcels, sealing the edges well so they can be turned over. Make sure the parcels are large enough to allow for the expansion of air that takes place as the salmon begins to cook.
3 Place the parcels on a barbecue or hot grill and cook for about 4-5 minutes on each side.
4 Pierce the sealed parcels before handing them to your guests, to release the hot steam. Allow guests to open their own parcels at the table. Serve with fragrant Thai rice.

five quick barbecue sauces

All these sauces are fantastic to accompany barbecued fish, poultry or meat, or try them as dips with crunchy vegetables and bread.

MANGO MAYONNAISE Halve, stone and peel 1 large mango, then mash the flesh in a bowl. Mix in 10ml (2 tsp) chopped fresh coriander, 5ml (1 tsp) grated fresh root ginger and the juice of 1 lime. Season well. Slowly whisk in 200ml (7fl oz) sunflower oil until thick and well-emulsified. Serve with barbecued chicken or gammon.

CRUSHED AVOCADO DRESSING Halve, stone, peel and chop 1 large avocado and toss in 60ml (4 tbsp) lemon juice. Blend to a purée with 100ml (3½fl oz) olive oil and 30ml (2 tbsp) water; season well. Serve with barbecued chicken or fish, or a salad.

MUSTARD AND CAPER SAUCE Mash the yolks of 2 hard-boiled eggs with 10ml (2 tsp) smooth Dijon mustard, add 30ml (2 tbsp) white wine vinegar and slowly whisk in 120ml (8 tbsp) olive oil. Add 30ml (2 tbsp) chopped capers, 15ml (1 tbsp) diced shallot and a pinch of sugar. Season well. Serve with barbecued fish, beef, pork or sausages.

ROAST NUT AND HERB PESTO In a blender, whizz together 50g (2oz) flat-leafed parsley, 1 thick slice stale bread (crusts removed), 30ml (2 tbsp) lemon juice and 1-2 peeled garlic cloves until well combined. Blend in 50g (2oz) toasted almonds and 200ml (7fl oz) olive oil. Serve with barbecue chicken or grilled vegetables.

SMOKY PEPPER MAYONNAISE Grill 1 red pepper until charred, then skin, core, deseed and roughly chop. Whizz in a blender with 1 peeled garlic clove and 250ml (8fl oz) mayonnaise. Stir in 10ml (2 tsp) chilli oil and 30ml (2 tbsp) lemon juice. Serve with barbecued pork, beef or sausages.

fiery mango chicken

A spicy yogurt marinade gives chicken a juiciness that helps to keep it moist over the fierce heat of the barbecue.

Serves 4
Preparation time: 15 minutes
Cooking time: 10 minutes
330 cals per serving

60 ml (4 tbsp) hot mango chutney (see note)
grated rind and juice of 1 lime
60ml (4 tbsp) yogurt
30ml (2 tbsp) chopped fresh coriander
1 small green chilli, deseeded and finely chopped (optional)
4 chicken breast fillets, with skin
1 large ripe mango, peeled
oil, for brushing
salt and freshly ground black pepper
lime halves, to serve

1 Mix together the mango chutney, lime rind and juice, yogurt, coriander, and chilli if using.
2 Put each chicken breast, skin side down on a board, cover with greaseproof paper and beat lightly with a rolling pin to flatten slightly. Cut each chicken breast into 3 pieces and place in the yogurt mixture. Turn to coat thoroughly. Cover and leave to marinate in the refrigerator for up to 24 hours until ready to cook.
3 Cut the mango into 4 thick pieces, discarding the stone. Brush lightly with oil and season well. Barbecue for about 2 minutes on each side; the fruit should be lightly charred but still firm. Put on to one side.
4 Barbecue the chicken slices for about 3 minutes on each side until golden. Serve with the mango and lime halves.

Note If you do not have the hot version, use ordinary mango chutney and add 2.5ml (½ tsp) Tabasco to the marinade.

barbecued chicken

Try these great barbecue recipes for chicken portions. Use thighs, breasts or poussin halves. Each marinade is sufficient for 4 chicken portions.

GINGER AND RED CHILLI MARINADE Peel and grate a 5cm (2 inch) piece fresh root ginger and 1 small onion. Combine with 1 finely chopped large red chilli, 2 crushed garlic cloves, 15ml (1 tbsp) soy sauce, 30ml (2 tbsp) oil and 30ml (2 tbsp) honey. Spread over the chicken portions; leave to marinate for 30 minutes. Barbecue for 4-5 minutes each side.

HOT DEVILLED SAUCE Combine 15ml (1 tbsp) olive oil with 30ml (2 tbsp) mango chutney, 15ml (1 tbsp) tomato ketchup, 5ml (1 tsp) Worcestershire sauce, 15ml (1 tbsp) Dijon mustard, 5ml (1 tsp) paprika, 30ml (2 tbsp) dark soft brown sugar and 45ml (3 tbsp) orange juice. Season and pour over the chicken; leave to marinate for 30 minutes. Barbecue for 4-5 minutes each side.

YOGURT AND SAFFRON MARINADE Beat 200ml (7fl oz) Greek yogurt with 2 crushed garlic cloves, a pinch of saffron strands, 15ml (1 tbsp) chopped fresh mint and 30ml (2 tbsp) olive oil. Season and pour over the chicken; cover and leave to marinate in the fridge for at least 1 hour. Barbecue for 4-5 minutes each side.

cracked peppercorn steaks with aïoli

A rocket leaf salad and salt-baked new potatoes (see below) would be perfect accompaniments to these barbecued steaks.

Serves 4
Preparation time: 15 minutes, plus marinating
Cooking time: 8 minutes
585 cals per serving

3 garlic cloves, peeled and crushed
15ml (1 tbsp) olive oil
30ml (2 tbsp) mixed peppercorns
30ml (2 tbsp) Dijon mustard
4 sirloin steaks, each 150g (5oz)
200ml (7fl oz) mayonnaise
30ml (2 tbsp) lemon juice
salt and freshly ground black pepper
rocket salad, to serve

1 Mix 1 crushed garlic clove with the olive oil, crushed peppercorns and mustard. Spread the mixture on both sides of the steaks. Leave to marinate for at least 15 minutes.
2 To make the aïoli, mix the remaining crushed garlic with the mayonnaise, lemon juice and seasoning.
3 Barbecue or grill the steaks for 3-4 minutes on each side then allow them to rest in a warm place for 5 minutes before serving. Serve with the aïoli.

salt-baked new potatoes

Toss 550g (1¼lb) par-boiled new potatoes with 30ml (2 tbsp) olive oil and 15ml (1 tbsp) sea salt flakes in a roasting tin. Cook at 200°C/fan oven 190°C (400°F) Mark 6 for 40 minutes or until the potatoes are cooked through and crisp.

lamb chops with olive tapenade

Pernod works well in this marinade as it cuts through the fattiness of the lamb. If you dislike the flavour of aniseed, you could use lemon juice or dry white wine instead.

Serves 4
Preparation time: 5 minutes, plus marinating
Cooking time: 10 minutes
710 cals per serving

90ml (6 tbsp) olive oil
60ml (4 tbsp) ready-made tapenade
30ml (2 tbsp) Pernod or Ricard
2 garlic cloves, peeled and crushed
8 loin lamb chops, each about 100g (3½oz)
salt and freshly ground black pepper
lemon wedges, to serve

1 Mix the oil, tapenade, Pernod or Ricard and crushed garlic together and rub all over the lamb chops; season with pepper. Leave to marinate for at least 30 minutes.
2 Barbecue or grill the lamb for 4-5 minutes on each side. Cook the slices of fennel or courgette for 5 minutes.
3 Serve the lamb with lemon wedges, and barbecued slices of fennel and courgettes.

Note For convenience, prepare the chops ahead and marinate in the refrigerator overnight.

spiced lamb in pitta

Serves 4
Preparation time: 20 minutes, plus chilling
Cooking time: 10 minutes
575 cals per serving

1 small green pepper, halved, cored, deseeded and
  chopped
½ small onion, peeled and chopped
3 garlic cloves, peeled
10ml (2 tsp) ground cumin
45ml (3 tbsp) olive oil
15ml (1 tbsp) chopped fresh mint
550g (1¼lb) lean minced lamb
salt and freshly ground black pepper
450g (1lb) ripe tomatoes, roughly chopped
30ml (2 tbsp) chopped flat-leafed parsley
4 large pitta breads
TO SERVE:
lemon wedges, Greek yogurt and mint sprigs

1 Put the green pepper in a food processor with
   the onion, garlic, cumin and olive oil. Pulse to
   form a coarse paste. Add the chopped mint.
2 Mix the paste and minced lamb together; season
   well. Using wet hands, shape the mixture into
   16 small patties. Arrange on a baking sheet and
   chill for 30 minutes.
3 Toss the tomatoes with the chopped parsley and
   season well; place in a serving bowl.
4 Barbecue or grill the lamb patties for 4-5 minutes
   on each side. Wrap the pitta breads into cone
   shapes and secure with a cocktail stick. Fill with
   3-4 patties, a drizzle of yogurt and mint sprigs.
   Serve accompanied by the tomato salad and
   lemon wedges.

Note Prepare ahead to the end of stage 2 for
convenience.

jamaican spiced pork steaks

Add a tropical flavour to your summer barbecue with these spicy chops – allspice and rum give them a real Jamaican taste!

Serves 4
Preparation time: 20 minutes, plus marinating
Cooking time: 17 minutes
410 cals per serving

2 garlic cloves, peeled and crushed
2 small red chillies, finely chopped
5ml (1 tsp) ground allspice
30ml (2 tbsp) dark rum
30ml (2 tbsp) tomato ketchup
4 pork steaks, each about 200g (7oz)
50g (2oz) butter, softened
2 spring onions, trimmed and chopped
salt and freshly ground black pepper
4 corn-on-the-cobs

1 Mix the garlic, chopped chillies (including seeds), allspice, rum and tomato ketchup together in a bowl. Spoon the marinade all over the pork steaks and leave to marinate in a cool place for at least 30 minutes.
2 Mix the softened butter with the spring onions and plenty of black pepper; set aside.
3 Par-cook the corn cobs in a pan of boiling salted water for 2 minutes; drain.
4 Cook the pork steaks on the barbecue for about 5 minutes on each side or until firm to the touch and golden brown. Place the corn cobs on the barbecue for about 4-5 minutes, turning frequently, until cooked through.
5 Serve the pork steaks with the corn, smothered with the flavoured butter.

Note Prepare to the end of stage 2 a day ahead; cover and chill the pork and butter separately.

five barbecue marinades

All meats benefit from marinating for at least 1 hour before barbecuing, as it takes time for the flavour of a marinade to penetrate the food.

PINEAPPLE AND COCONUT MARINADE Blend ¼ peeled, chopped pineapple with the scooped-out flesh of ½ lime until smooth. Add a 200ml (7fl oz) carton coconut milk and 5ml (1 tsp) Tabasco sauce. Use for marinating chicken or pork pieces.

TAMARIND GLAZE Mix 45ml (3 tbsp) fresh tamarind paste with with 30ml (2 tbsp) thin honey and 15ml (1 tbsp) dark soy sauce. Use for marinating pork chops or steaks.

LEMON AND OLIVE OIL MARINADE Mix together the coarsely grated rind and juice of 1 lemon with 30ml (2 tbsp) roughly chopped fresh rosemary and 90ml (6 tbsp) olive oil. Use for marinating lamb, chicken and fish.

MUSTARD AND BEER MARINADE Mix 60ml (4 tbsp) grainy mustard with 150ml (¼ pint) beer. Use for marinating beef steaks and pork.

SPICY TOMATO MARINADe Mix 120ml (8 tbsp) tomato ketchup with 30ml (2 tbsp) soy sauce, 30ml (2 tbsp) chilli sauce and 60ml (4 tbsp) red wine. Add 10ml (2 tsp) Jamaican jerk seasoning. Use for marinating pork, chicken or sausages.

herb sausages with mustard dip

Par-boiling sausages might sound like a strange thing to do but it saves a lot of time and reduces the risk of them burning on the barbecue.

Serves 4-6
Preparation time: 10 minutes
Cooking time: 11 minutes
840 560 cals per serving

12 good-quality sausages
12 rashers smoked streaky bacon
30ml (2 tbsp) fresh thyme leaves
60ml (4 tbsp) grainy mustard
120ml (8 tbsp) mayonnaise
salt and freshly ground black pepper
250g (9oz) small tomatoes
watercress sprigs, to serve

1 Put the sausages in a pan of boiling water, bring to the boil and simmer gently for 3 minutes, then drain and leave to cool.
2 Stretch the bacon rashers with the back of a knife, then lay flat and sprinkle with the thyme leaves. Wrap each cold sausage in a bacon rasher (so the thyme is next to the sausage) and spear with a soaked cocktail stick to secure.
2 Mix the mustard and mayonnaise together in a bowl and season with salt and pepper.
3 Barbecue or grill the sausages for 7-8 minutes, turning frequently, until well browned and cooked through. Barbecue the tomatoes for about 1 minute or until the skins begin to burst.
4 Remove the cocktail sticks from the sausages and serve with the mustard dip, grilled tomatoes and watercress sprigs.

Note For convenience, prepare to the end of stage 3 a day in advance; cover and chill the sausages and mayonnaise separately.

Variation You can use any sturdy herb instead of thyme; oregano and rosemary are good alternatives.

barbecued pork

Try these tasty barbecue recipes for pork. Each is sufficient to serve 4.

FIVE-SPICE PORK In a shallow dish, combine 2 crushed garlic cloves with 5ml (1 tsp) Chinese five-spice powder, 60ml (4 tsp) hoisin sauce, 45ml (3 tbsp) soft brown sugar and 30ml (2 tbsp) each light soy sauce and orange juice. Add 450g (1lb) cubed pork fillet (tenderloin) and leave to marinate for 30 minutes. Thread on to wooden skewers with pieces of yellow pepper and shiitake mushrooms; cook for 3-4 minutes each side.

MUSTARD SAGE AND APPLE MARINATED PORK Stir 15ml (1 tbsp) chopped fresh sage into 30ml (2 tbsp) Dijon mustard with 50ml (2fl oz) apple juice and 15ml (1 tbsp) each cider vinegar and oil; season. Place 4 pork chops in a shallow dish, pour on the marinade and leave to marinate for 30 minutes. Barbecue for 4-5 minutes each side.

CARAMELISED PEPPERCORN PORK CHOPS Roughly crush 30ml (2 tbsp) mixed peppercorns and combine with 60ml (4 tbsp) each soft brown sugar and wholegrain mustard. Beat into 50g (2oz) softened butter and season with salt and pepper. Barbecue 4 pork chops on one side only for 4-5 minutes; turn, spread with the flavoured butter and cook the other side until tender.

five barbecue side salads

Every one of these salads can be prepared quickly or in advance.

CREAMY POTATO SALAD Mix 90ml (6 tbsp) mayonnaise with 30ml (2 tbsp) crème fraîche, 30ml (2 tbsp) white wine vinegar, 2 finely chopped shallots, 60ml (4 tbsp) finely chopped gherkins and 30ml (2 tbsp) olive oil. Cook 550g (1¼lb) new potatoes in boiling salted water until tender; drain. While still warm, cut into large chunks and toss with the flavoured mayonnaise. Season and allow to cool.

ROASTED RED PEPPER AND HERB PASTA SALAD Skin, deseed and slice 2 roasted, large red peppers. Cook 350g (12oz) pasta shapes until *al dente*. Meanwhile, mix 90ml (6 tbsp) olive oil with 1 crushed garlic clove, 10ml (2 tsp) Dijon mustard and 30ml (2tbsp) balsamic vinegar. Drain the pasta and toss with the dressing while still warm. Allow to cool, then add the sliced peppers and 45ml (3 tbsp) chopped mixed fresh herbs.

FRUITY COUSCOUS SALAD Put 225g (8oz) couscous in a bowl, pour on 600ml (1 pint) boiling vegetable stock and set aside. When cold, add 45ml (3 tbsp) each chopped fresh mint and parsley, 75g (3oz) chopped ready-to-eat dried apricots, 75g (3oz) sultanas, the finely grated rind of 1 orange and 45ml (3 tbsp) olive oil; season and toss to mix.

CRUNCHY AVOCADO SALAD Drain a 400g (14oz) can mixed beans. Add 1 chopped red onion, 1 diced green chilli (optional), 4 diced celery sticks and 2 diced avocados. Toss in 60ml (4 tbsp) lemon juice and 60ml (4 tbsp) olive oil. Season well. Add plenty of chopped coriander to serve.

SPICY RICE NOODLE SALAD Cook 250g (9oz) rice noodles according to packet instructions; drain and refresh in iced water. Blanch 175g (6oz) small broccoli florets, 175g (6oz) mangetout and 175g (6oz) baby corn in boiling water for 1 minute; drain and refresh in iced water. Drain and toss all ingredients together with 10ml (2 tsp) sesame oil, 30ml (2 tbsp) plum sauce and 60ml (4 tbsp) dark soy sauce. Serve sprinkled with sliced spring onions and diced red chillies.

grilled sweet potatoes with feta and olives

Sweet potatoes barbecue extremely well and are a good match for this tangy feta cheese relish.

Serves 4
Preparation time: 15 minutes
Cooking time: 15 minutes
350 cals per serving

1 large sweet potato, about 500g (1lb 2oz), peeled
60ml (4 tbsp) olive oil, plus extra for brushing
salt and freshly ground black pepper
200g (7oz) feta cheese
10ml (2 tsp) herbes de Provence
50g (2oz) pitted black olives, chopped
1 garlic clove, peeled and crushed
flat-leaf parsley, to garnish

1 Cut the sweet potato into 8 wedges lengthways. Add them to a pan of boiling water, bring to the boil, then simmer for 3 minutes. Drain, rinse in cool water, then drain and dry well. Brush lightly with olive oil, season and barbecue for 10-15 minutes or until well browned on all sides and cooked through.
2 Mash the feta cheese, herbes de Provence, black olives, garlic and olive oil together in a bowl.
3 Serve the barbecued sweet potato wedges topped with the feta cheese mixture and sprinkled with chopped parsley.

mediterranean flavours

The aromatic dried herb mix – Herbes de Provence – enhances barbecued or grilled food to delicious effect. It is made up of dried rosemary, thyme, basil, bay and savoury. Just mix with olive oil and coarse salt, then rub over lamb chops or chicken portions before barbecuing for a wonderful Mediterranean flavour.

sumptuous barbecue salad

Serves 8
Preparation time: 30 minutes
Cooking time: 1 hour
430 cals per serving

2 garlic cloves, peeled and crushed
30ml (2 tbsp) balsamic vinegar
10ml (2 tsp) chopped fresh thyme
150ml (¼ pint) olive oil
900g (2lb) small new potatoes
salt and freshly ground black pepper
450g (1lb) French beans, trimmed
225g (8oz) baby fennel
12 quail's eggs
400g (14oz) can cannellini beans, drained
175g (6oz) streaky bacon rashers, derinded
300g (11oz) cherry tomatoes, halved
125g (4oz) baby spinach leaves
50g (2oz) pitted black olives

1 To make the dressing, put the garlic, balsamic vinegar and thyme in a bowl, then whisk in 90ml (6 tbsp) olive oil.
2 Place the potatoes in a roasting tin, drizzle with the remaining oil and season generously. Cook at 200°C/fan oven 190°C (400°F) Mark 6 for 50 minutes-1 hour or until golden and tender.
3 Cook the French beans and fennel in boiling salted water for 3-4 minutes; drain and refresh in iced water.
4 Place the quail's eggs in a pan, cover with cold water, bring to the boil and cook for 2 minutes; drain. Cover with cold water; peel when cold.
5 Rinse the cannellini beans and drain well. Grill the bacon until crisp, then crumble.
6 To serve, combine all of the salad ingredients in a large serving bowl. Pour on the dressing and toss lightly to serve.

Note For convenience, prepare the salad to the end of stage 5, about 3-4 hours ahead.

strawberry and redcurrant tart

A classic French tart with short pastry, a creamy vanilla filling and a glazed fruit topping.

Serves 6
Preparation time: 1 hour, plus chilling
Cooking time: 50 minutes
Suitable for freezing (stage 3)
675 cals per serving

FOR THE PASTRY:
250g (9oz) plain white flour
100g (3½oz) unsalted butter
100g (3½oz) icing sugar
1 egg
2-3 drops vanilla extract
FOR THE FILLING:
3 large eggs
75g (3oz) caster sugar
45ml (3 tbsp) plain white flour
45ml (3 tbsp) cornflour
450ml (¾ pint) milk
10ml (2 tsp) vanilla extract
700-900g (1½-2lb) medium strawberries
125g (4oz) redcurrants
TO FINISH:
90ml (6 tbsp) redcurrant jelly, to glaze (optional)
icing sugar, for dusting

1 To make the pastry, put the flour, butter and icing sugar in a food processor and process until the mixture resembles fine crumbs. Add the egg and vanilla extract and pulse briefly until the mixture just comes together. You may need to add a few drops of cold water if the dough is a little dry. Gather the pastry together, knead gently on a lightly floured surface, then wrap and chill for 30 minutes.

2 Roll out the pastry on a lightly floured surface and use to line a 2.5cm (1 inch) deep, 23cm (9 inch) loose-based tart tin. Prick the pastry base all over and line with greaseproof paper and baking beans. Chill for 15 minutes.

---

five fast barbecue puddings

All of these can be prepared ahead – ready to put on the barbecue at the end of your meal.

BARBECUE BANOFFEE Make long slits in 4 peeled bananas. Fill the slits with 75g (3oz) roughly chopped vanilla fudge and place each one on a large square of buttered foil. Spoon 15ml (1 tbsp) rum or brandy over each banana and fold the foil over the bananas to make loose parcels. Barbecue for about 4-5 minutes. Serve with thick cream or vanilla ice cream.

BAKED PLUMS Put 8 halved, stoned plums on a large piece of buttered foil. Sprinkle with 30ml (2 tbsp) kirsch or other fruit liqueur, 30ml (2 tbsp) sugar and add a split vanilla pod. Fold the foil over the plums to make a secure parcel and barbecue for 10 minutes. Serve with lightly barbecued brioche slices and mascarpone sweetened with a little sugar.

BROWNIE AND STRAWBERRY KEBABS Spear 8 chunks of chocolate brownie and 8 large strawberries on skewers and barbecue for 3 minutes, turning occasionally. Serve with whipped cream.

GRILLED FIGS Split 12 fresh figs in half and spread each half with 5ml (1 tsp) mild goat's cheese. Sprinkle with chopped fresh thyme and drizzle each with a little thin honey. Place on the barbecue for about 5 minutes to warm through.

GRILLED COCONUT CAKE WITH FRUIT Grill 4 thick slices of coconut or Madeira cake until lightly charred. Serve with thick Greek yogurt and roughly chopped fresh fruit, dusted with icing sugar.

3 Place the flan tin on a baking sheet and cook at 200°C/fan oven 190°C (400°F) Mark 6 for 15-20 minutes. Remove the paper and beans and cook for a further 10-15 minutes until the pastry base is golden. Allow to cool a little, then carefully unmould and cool on a wire rack.

4 Meanwhile, make the filling. Beat the eggs and sugar together in a large bowl until well combined. Sift the flour and cornflour into a separate bowl and beat in a little of the milk to make a smooth paste. Stir into the whisked egg mixture until smooth.

5 Heat the remaining milk in a pan until almost boiling and pour on to the egg mixture, stirring all the time. Return the egg mixture to a clean pan and cook over a low heat, stirring continuously, until the mixture comes to the boil. Simmer, stirring, for 1 minute.

6 Take off the heat, add the vanilla extract and cover the surface closely with a disc of dampened greaseproof paper to prevent a skin forming. Allow to cool, then chill.

4 To assemble, whisk the custard briefly until smooth, then spoon into the cooled pastry case. Trim the stalk end of the strawberries so they stand upright and arrange, cut-side down, on top of the custard. Arrange small sprigs of redcurrants between the strawberries.

5 To glaze the tart if required, melt the redcurrant jelly in a small pan over a low heat, stirring until smooth. Add a tiny amount of water to the jelly if it's too thick. Leave to cool a little, then brush the glaze generously over the fruit.

6 Dust the tart with a little sifted icing sugar just before serving.

Note For convenience, prepare and bake the pastry case and make the custard a day in advance. Keep the custard chilled. Fill the tart and glaze shortly before serving.

Variation Use other fruits instead of the strawberries and redcurrants, such as raspberries, grapes, kiwi and pineapple.

salmon and herb pasties

Crammed with salmon, prawns and fragrant summer herbs, these luxurious pasties make perfect outdoor eating.

Serves 6
Preparation time: 40 minutes, plus chilling
Cooking time: 25 minutes
Suitable for freezing (stage 5)
880 cals per pasty

FOR THE PASTRY:
350g (12oz) plain white flour
salt and freshly ground black pepper
250g (9oz) butter, frozen for 1 hour
FOR THE FILLING:
450g (1lb) salmon fillet, skinned and cubed
25g (1oz) flat-leafed parsley, finely chopped
15g (½oz) fresh mint leaves, finely chopped
1 large garlic clove, peeled and crushed
100g (3½oz) cooked peeled prawns (optional)
2 lemons
25g (1oz) butter
125g (4oz) leeks, finely sliced
1 large egg, lightly beaten
30ml (2 tbsp) mascarpone
TO FINISH:
dried crushed chillies or coarse sea salt flakes

perfect picnics

Many of these tempting recipes – especially the cakes – are suitable for freezing, so plan ahead and make the most of warm summer weather, as and when it appears. Use the excellent picnic foods in major supermarkets stock to supplement your own cooking. The following are always popular:

• Italian bread sticks, crisps and savoury biscuits.
• Flavoured focaccia, split and filled with your favourite fillings. Try grilled vegetables with mozzarella; avocado and crisp, grilled bacon; or smoked chicken, endive and mayonnaise.
• Ripe summer fruits, such as Italian peaches, cherries, strawberries and apricots.

1 To make the pastry, sift the flour into a bowl, add 2.5ml (½ tsp) salt and a little pepper. Coarsely grate the frozen butter into the flour and mix lightly. Using a fork, stir in enough cold water to form a dough, approximately 150ml (¼ pint). Gather the dough together into a ball, wrap in cling film and chill for 30 minutes.

2 For the filling, put the salmon, herbs, garlic, and prawns if using in a bowl. Using a zester; pare the rind from the lemons in strips and add to the salmon mixture. Melt the butter in a frying pan, add the leeks and cook briskly, stirring, for 10 minutes until just golden. Allow to cool.

3 Add the cooked leeks to the salmon mixture and toss to mix. Season with salt and pepper to taste, then set aside. Divide the chilled pastry into 12 equal pieces.

4 On a floured surface, roll out 6 pieces of pastry and cut out 12cm (5 inch) circles; roll out the remaining pieces and cut six 15cm (6 inch) circles, using suitable sized saucers as guides.

5 Brush the edges of the smaller circles with beaten egg and place two heaped tablespoonfuls of filling in the centre of each one. Postion the larger circles on top, press the pastry edges together to seal, then flute decoratively. Cut a cross in the middle of each pasty and fold back the tips of each cross. Transfer the pasties to a non-stick baking sheet.

6 Spoon 5ml (1 tsp) mascarpone into each pasty, then chill for 30 minutes. Preheat a baking sheet in the oven at 200°C/fan oven 190°C (400°F) Mark 6 for 5 minutes. Brush the pasties with egg and sprinkle with crushed chillies or sea salt. Place on the hot baking sheet, loosely cover with foil and bake for 20 minutes. Remove the foil and cook for a further 5 minutes or until golden. Transfer to a wire rack to cool.

Note The pasties can be baked from frozen; allow an extra 10-15 minutes after removing the foil.

filo pastries with feta and herb filling

These Greek-style filo pastries with their herby feta and pine nut filling are perfect for picnics.

Makes 20-24
Preparation time: 30 minutes
Cooking time: 20-25 minutes
100-75 cals per pastry

225g (8oz) packet filo pastry
olive oil, for brushing
FOR THE FILLING:
300g (10oz) feta cheese
60ml (4 tbsp) pine nuts, toasted
30ml (2 tbsp) chopped fresh parsley or coriander
15ml (1 tbsp) chopped fresh dill
½ egg, lightly beaten
pinch of freshly grated nutmeg
freshly ground black pepper

1 First prepare the filling. Crumble the cheese into a bowl and add the nuts, herbs, egg, nutmeg and pepper to taste. Mix well.
2 Cut the filo pastry sheets into strips, measuring about 10x25cm (4x10 inches). Keep covered with a damp cloth while not in use to prevent them drying out.
3 Working with 3 or 4 filo strips at a time, brush with oil and place a heaped teaspoonful of filling at the top right-hand corner of each strip. Fold the corner down to make a triangle and continue to flip the filled triangle down the length of the filo strip to wrap in the pastry. Place the filo triangles on a greased baking sheet and brush with a little more oil. Repeat to use all of the filo strips and filling.
4 Bake the filo pies in the oven at 190°C/fan oven 180°C (375°F) Mark 5 for 20-25 minutes or until crisp and deep golden. Serve warm or cold.

Variation For the filling, mix 3 chopped hard-boiled eggs with 50g (2oz) chopped olives, 3 diced anchovy fillets or sun-dried tomatoes, 30ml (2 tbsp) pine nuts and 30ml (2 tbsp) chopped parsley.

chicken panino

You need a medium, rustic round loaf with a crisp crust for this recipe. The Italian *paglieno* – available from Italian delicatessens and larger supermarkets – is ideal. Make sure that you pack the filling in well, so that the loaf holds together when cut. Serve panino as part of a picnic.

Serves 8
Preparation time: 40 minutes, plus overnight chilling
Cooking time: 10 minutes
300 cals per serving

1 large crusty loaf
FOR THE FILLING:
1 large aubergine, sliced
salt and freshly ground black pepper
3 large courgettes, thinly sliced
chilli oil or virgin olive oil, for brushing
6 red peppers, halved, cored and deseeded
2 beef tomatoes, sliced
225g (8oz) Parma ham or thin-sliced smoked ham
about 275g (10oz) thinly sliced cooked chicken
few marinated artichokes (optional), sliced
few sun-dried tomatoes (optional)
few stoned olives (optional)
generous handful of rocket or large basil leaves

1 To prepare the filling, sprinkle the aubergine slices liberally with salt and layer in a colander. Leave to degorge the bitter juices for 30 minutes.
2 Meanwhile, brush the courgette slices with a little oil and cook under a hot grill for 2 minutes each side until tinged with brown and softened, but still remaining some bite. Season with salt and pepper and leave to cool.
3 Rinse the aubergine slices thoroughly, drain and pat dry, then brush with a little oil. Cook under a hot grill for a few minutes each side until tender. Season and leave to cool.
4 Lay the peppers, cut-side down, in a grill pan and cook until the skins are charred. Cover with a cloth and leave until cool enough to handle, then peel off the skins. Leave to cool completely.
5 Cut a large slice from the rounded top of the bread and set aside. Carefully remove the soft bread from inside the loaf, leaving a 2.5-4cm (1-1½ inch) shell within the crust. Brush the inside of the loaf with oil.
6 Layer the filling ingredients in the bread shell, seasoning well and drizzling each layer with a little oil. Arrange the ingredients to give a good contrast of colours between the layers.
7 Replace the bread lid. Wrap the whole loaf in foil. Refrigerate with a weight on top overnight.
8 The next day, unwrap the loaf and cut into wedges, using a serrated knife, to serve.

raspberry palmiers

Ideal for picnics, these attractive pastries are excellent served with fresh soft fruits, such as strawberries or raspberries.

Makes 16
Preparation time: 20 minutes, plus chilling
Cooking time: 15 minutes
145 cals per palmier

225g (8oz) ready-made puff pastry
30ml (2 tbsp) raspberry jam
25g (1oz) caster sugar
125g (4oz) raspberries
icing sugar, for dusting

1 Roll out the pastry to a 30cm (12 inch) square on a surface dusted with icing sugar. Cut the pastry into two long strips, each measuring 15x30cm (6x12 inches).
2 Spread the pastry strips with the jam, then sprinkle with the caster sugar. Scatter the raspberries on top, crushing them slightly. Roll up each end of one strip tightly, towards the centre until the rolls meet in the middle; press lightly. Repeat with the other strip. Chill for 30 minutes.
3 Place the pastry rolls on the surface with the long edges towards you, then cut into 5mm (¼ inch) slices. Place on non-stick baking trays, spacing at least 7.5cm (3 inches) apart.
4 Dust liberally with icing sugar and bake at 200°C/fan oven 190°C (400°F) Mark 6 for 15 minutes or until golden. Transfer to a wire rack to cool. Dust with icing sugar and serve with mixed berry fruits and cream if you like.

coconut squares

These scrumptious, moist cakes are gluten-free and therefore suitable for anyone who has an allergy to wheat.

Makes 12
Preparation time: 10 minutes
Cooking time: 35 minutes
Suitable for freezing
415 cals per cake

75g (3oz) butter
200g (7oz) demerara sugar
175g (6oz) ground rice
2 eggs
pinch of salt
1-2 drops vanilla extract
75g (3oz) desiccated coconut
75g (3oz) chopped hazelnuts
45ml (3 tbsp) apricot or raspberry jam
extra jam, warmed, to glaze

1 Grease a 28x18cm (11x7 inch) baking tin (or a tin with similar dimensions).
2 Cream the butter and 75g (3oz) of the sugar together in a bowl until light and fluffy. Stir in 150g (5oz) of the ground rice. Spread the mixture into the prepared tin and bake at 180°C/fan oven 170°C (350°F) Mark 4 for 15 minutes. Leave in the tin to cool for a few minutes.
3 Lightly beat the eggs in a bowl. Add the remaining sugar and ground rice, the salt, vanilla extract, desiccated coconut and chopped hazelnuts; mix well.
4 Spread the jam over the cooked base, then cover with the coconut mixture. Bake in the oven for 20 minutes.
5 Allow to cool slightly, then brush with a little warmed jam. Cut the cake into squares. Leave in the tin to cool completely before removing. Store the coconut squares wrapped in greaseproof paper in an airtight container for up to 5 days.

double chocolate muffins

Homemade muffins have a deliciously light texture. Chunks of dark and white chocolate are folded into this mixture to give melt-in-the-mouth morsels of pure delight!

Makes 14
Preparation time: 15 minutes
Cooking time: 25 minutes
Suitable for freezing
370 cals per muffin

300g (10oz) plain chocolate
125g (4oz) white chocolate
375g (13oz) self-raising white flour
15ml (1 tbsp) baking powder
65g (2½oz) cocoa powder
75g (3oz) light muscovado sugar
1 egg
1 egg yolk
10ml (2 tsp) vanilla extract
90ml (6 tbsp) sunflower oil
375ml (13fl oz) milk
icing sugar, for dusting (optional)

1 Line 14 deep bun tins or muffin tins with paper muffin cases. Break up 175g (6oz) of the plain chocolate and melt in a heatproof bowl set over a saucepan of simmering water.
2 Roughly chop the remaining plain and white chocolate. Sift the flour, baking powder and cocoa powder into a bowl. Stir in the sugar.
3 In another bowl, beat together the egg, egg yolk, vanilla extract, sunflower oil, milk and melted chocolate. Add to the dry ingredients with the chopped chocolate and stir together quickly until the flour is only just incorporated; do not over-mix.
4 Spoon the mixture into the paper cases, piling it up in the centre. Bake at 220°C/fan oven 210°C (425°F) Mark 7 for 25 minutes or until the muffins are well risen and craggy in appearance. Transfer to a wire rack and dust lightly with icing sugar, if desired. Serve warm or cold.

Variation Sift 5ml (1 tsp) ground cinnamon or mixed spice with the dry ingredients.

cherry chip cookies

These melt-in-the-mouth cookies are perfect for picnics.

Makes 12-14 cookies
Preparation time: 20 minutes, plus cooling
Cooking time: 10-12 minutes
Suitable for freezing
210-180 cals per cookie

75g (3oz) unsalted butter, softened
25g (1oz) caster sugar
50g (2oz) light soft brown sugar
few drops of vanilla extract
1 egg, lightly beaten
175g (6oz) self-raising white flour, sifted
finely grated rind of 1 orange
125g (4oz) white chocolate, roughly chopped
125g (4oz) glacé cherries, roughly chopped
icing sugar, for dusting (optional)

1. Put the butter, caster and brown sugars, and the vanilla extract in a large bowl and beat thoroughly until well combined, using an electric whisk. Gradually beat in the egg until the mixture is light and fluffy.

2. Lightly fold in the flour, orange rind, chopped chocolate and glacé cherries, using a metal spoon. Drop tablespoonfuls of the mixture on to greased baking sheets, spacing apart to allow for spreading. Bake at 180°C/fan oven 170°C (350°F) Mark 4 for 10-12 minutes; the biscuits should be soft under a crisp crust.

3. Leave the cookies on the baking sheet for 1 minute, then transfer to a wire rack to cool. Dust with icing sugar before serving if you like. Pack the cookies in a rigid plastic container to take on a picnic.

Note Use natural glacé cherries, available from selected supermarkets, for these cookies.

festive cooking

Sensational Christmas recipes, including prepare-ahead dishes, to carry you through the festivities with ease and style

marinated salmon salad with lime and coriander

This sophisticated starter is the perfect way to start a Christmas dinner. Make sure you buy very fresh salmon. The acidity of the marinade effectively 'cooks' the salmon, giving it an opaque appearance.

Serves 4
Preparation time: 20 minutes, plus chilling
235 cals per serving

225g (8oz) salmon fillet, skinned and chilled
mixed salad leaves, such as rocket, lamb's lettuce or frisée
50g (2oz) cucumber, peeled, deseeded and finely chopped
1 bunch spring onions, trimmed and roughly chopped
1 large green chilli, deseeded and finely chopped
FOR THE MARINADE:
grated rind and juice of 3 limes
60ml (4 tbsp) olive oil
2 tomatoes, skinned, deseeded and diced
60ml (4 tbsp) chopped fresh coriander
10ml (2 tsp) caster sugar
salt and freshly ground black pepper
TO GARNISH:
pared lime rind

1 To make the marinade, combine the lime rind and juice, oil, tomatoes, coriander, sugar and seasoning in a small bowl. Cover and set aside.

2 Using a sharp knife, cut the salmon fillet on the diagonal into wafer-thin slices. Place in a large, non-metallic shallow dish, pour over the marinade, then cover and chill for up to 3 hours or until the salmon is pink and opaque.

3 To serve, put the salad leaves on individual plates, then top with the salmon slices and marinade juices. Arrange the chopped cucumber, spring onions and chilli on top of the salmon, then garnish with pared lime rind.

festive starters

An easy, light starter is essential if you are serving a traditional Christmas dinner with all the trimmings. The following simple appetisers are ideal:

- Finely sliced oak-smoked salmon, served with thin slices of pumpernickel or wholemeal bread, lime wedges and rocket leaves.
- Parma ham draped over wedges of melon, papaya slices or quartered figs.
- A selection of canapés and marinated olives served casually with pre-lunch drinks (see pages 274-8).

festive nut and cranberry terrine

A vegetarian alternative to the traditional turkey.

Serves 8
Preparation time: 45 minutes, plus cooling
Cooking time: 45-50 minutes
490 cals per serving

FOR THE FILLING:
125g (4oz) long-grain rice
60ml (4 tbsp) olive oil
1 onion, peeled and finely chopped
1 leek, thinly sliced
4 celery sticks, thinly sliced
60ml (4 tbsp) chopped mixed fresh herbs, such as
    sage, parsley and thyme
40g (1½oz) fresh white breadcrumbs
40g (1½oz) walnuts, toasted and roughly ground
125g (4oz) dolcelatte cheese, crumbled
1 egg, lightly beaten
125ml (4fl oz) crème fraîche
salt and freshly ground black pepper
FOR THE HOT WATER CRUST PASTRY:
225g (8oz) plain white flour
pinch of salt
100ml (3½fl oz) water
40g (1½oz) white vegetable fat
15g (½oz) butter
FOR THE TOPPING:
125g (4oz) redcurrant jelly
5ml (1 tsp) lemon juice
15ml (1 tbsp) water
125g (4oz) cranberries
bay leaves, to garnish

1 Cook the rice in boiling salted water according
   to the pack instructions until just tender; refresh
   under cold water, drain thoroughly and set aside.
2 Heat the oil in a frying pan, add the onion, leek,
   celery and herbs and fry gently for 10 minutes
   until softened; transfer to a bowl. Add the rice
   and remaining filling ingredients; stir until well
   combined and season well; set aside to cool.
3 For the pastry, sift the flour and salt into a bowl
   and make a well in the middle. Heat the water,
   fat and butter in a pan until the liquid comes to
   the boil. Pour into the well and work into the
   flour, using a wooden spoon, until smooth.

4 When cool enough to handle, bring the dough
   together with your hands and knead lightly until
   smooth. Roll out on a lightly floured surface to a
   25x20cm (10x8 inch) rectangle and use to line a
   900g (2lb) loaf tin, pressing the dough into the
   corners; trim the overhanging pastry and reserve.
5 Spoon the filling into the pastry case and
   smooth the surface. Divide the pastry trimmings
   in half and roll each piece into a long thin rope.
   Plait the two lengths together.
6 Dampen the edges of the pastry in the tin and
   top with the pastry plait, pressing down gently.
   Bake at 220°C/fan oven 210°C (425°F) Mark 7 for
   45-50 minutes until golden and a skewer
   inserted into the centre comes out hot. Leave to
   cool.
7 For the topping, heat the redcurrant jelly in a
   small pan with the lemon juice and water until
   melted, then simmer for 3 minutes. Remove
   from the heat and stir in the fruit.
8 Unmould the pie on to a plate. Spoon on the
   cranberry topping and leave to set. Garnish with
   bay leaves and serve cold, cut into slices.

cranberry, orange and port sauce

Serves 8-10
Preparation time: 15 minutes
Cooking time: 20 minutes
115-90 cals per serving

2 large oranges
450g (1lb) cranberries
125g (4oz) caster sugar
150ml (¼ pint) port

1 Grate the rind from the oranges, then peel and
   segment, discarding all white pith and pips.
2 Put the cranberries and orange rind in a heavy-
   based pan and cook over a low heat for
   5 minutes or until the cranberry skins begin to
   split. Using a slotted spoon, transfer the
   cranberries to a bowl.
3 Add the sugar and port to the pan. Dissolve over
   a low heat, then bring to the boil. Bubble to
   reduce by half, then pour over the cranberries.
   Allow to cool, then stir in the orange segments.

lemon and herb roasted turkey

Cooking the turkey with a little wine in the roasting tin ensures it stays succulent and moist.

Serves 8-10
Preparation time: 25 minutes
Cooking time: 3 hours, plus resting
685-545 cals per serving

4.5kg (10lb) oven-ready turkey, with giblets
salt and freshly ground black pepper
1 large bunch fresh thyme
1 large bunch fresh rosemary
3 lemons (preferably unwaxed), cut into chunks
450g (1lb) Spanish onions, peeled and cut into chunks
450g (1lb) stuffing of your choice (see right)
125g (4oz) butter, softened
375g (13oz) pancetta or thin sliced streaky bacon
150ml (¼ pint) white wine
FOR THE GRAVY:
60ml (4 tbsp) plain flour
150ml (¼ pint) white wine
1.1 litres (2 pints) turkey or chicken stock
TO SERVE:
thyme and rosemary sprigs, to garnish
Cranberry, Orange and Port Sauce (see page 317)
Traditional Bread Sauce (see page 319)

1 To make carving easier, remove wishbone from the turkey: loosen the skin at the neck end, ease your fingers up between the skin and the breast and, using a sharp knife, remove wishbone. Take out the giblets and reserve. Season the inside of the turkey, then stuff with thyme, rosemary and a few pieces of lemon and onion. Spoon the cold stuffing into the neck end only, neaten, tuck the skin underneath and secure with metal skewers.

2 Place the turkey in a large roasting tin, spread with the butter and arrange the slices of pancetta or bacon on the breast. Put the remaining lemon and onion around the turkey and add the wine to the tin. Cover with a loose tent of foil.

3 Roast at 190°C/fan oven 180°C (375°F) Mark 5 for about 3 hours, basting from time to time. If the legs are tied together tightly, loosen after the first hour so they cook through more evenly. Remove foil 45 minutes before the end of the cooking time, lift off the pancetta and set aside. Return the turkey to the oven to continue cooking. To test the turkey, insert a skewer deep into the thigh – the juices should run clear. If not, roast until they do.

4 Tip the turkey so the juices run into the tin, then place the turkey on a carving board. Place the pancetta back on the breast, cover the turkey with foil and leave to rest in a warm place for 30 minutes. Meanwhile, make the gravy.

5 Strain the juices from the turkey and skim off the fat, reserving 45ml (3 tbsp). Put the reserved fat in the roasting tin and stir in the flour to make a smooth paste. Cook, stirring, on a medium heat until the flour turns russet brown. Off the heat, add the wine, stir until smooth, then stir in the turkey juices and stock. Bring to the boil and bubble for 5-10 minutes until reduced by half and thickened; skim. Season and strain.

6 Serve the turkey with the roasted lemons, onions, fresh herbs, pancetta, stuffing, gravy, sauces, and vegetables of your choice.

homemade stock

Simmer the turkey giblets (less the liver) or 5 chicken wings in a pan with 2.3 litres (4 pints) water, a few slices of onion, celery and leek and seasoning, for 2 hours until reduced by half. Strain, cool and chill.

couscous and herb stuffing

Makes about 450g (1lb)
Preparation time: 20 minutes, plus standing
Cooking time: 6 minutes
115-95 cals per serving

30ml (2 tbsp) oil
225g (8oz) onions, peeled and roughly chopped
1 garlic clove, peeled and crushed
100g (3½oz) couscous
salt and freshly ground black pepper
5ml (1 tsp) paprika
grated rind of 1 lemon
15ml (1 tbsp) chopped fresh herbs
1 medium egg

1 Heat the oil in a pan and gently fry the onion for 5 minutes until soft but not coloured. Add the garlic and cook for 30 seconds.
2 Meanwhile, put the couscous in a heatproof bowl with 5ml (1 tsp) salt and pepper to taste. Pour on boiling water to cover the couscous by 5mm (¼ inch). Cover and leave in a warm place for 20 minutes, then fluff up with a fork.
3 Stir the onions and remaining ingredients through the couscous and season. Allow to cool. Cover and chill for up to 2 days until needed.
4 Use to stuff turkey; or cook in a buttered 450g (1lb) loaf tin, covered with foil, at 200°C/fan oven 190°C (400°F) Mark 6 for 45 minutes.

salami and sour cherry stuffing

Makes 450g (1lb)
Preparation time: 15 minutes
Cooking time: 30 minutes, plus standing
260-210 cals per serving

75g (3oz) wild rice
salt and freshly ground black pepper
30ml (2 tbsp) oil
125g (4oz) onion, peeled and roughly chopped
70g (2¾oz) sliced salami
40g (1½oz) dried sour cherries
1 egg

1 Cook the rice in boiling water for 20 minutes or until just tender. Drain and rinse with hot water. Turn on to a plate and set aside for 20 minutes.
2 Heat the oil in a saucepan, add the onion and cook gently for 5 minutes until soft but not coloured. Place in a bowl.
3 Grill the salami until crisp; drain on kitchen paper. When cold, break into large pieces, add to the onion with the cherries, egg and rice. Season and mix well. Cover and chill for up to 2 days until needed.
4 Use to stuff the turkey, or cook separately in a buttered 450g (1lb) loaf tin, covered with foil at 200°C/fan oven 190°C (400°F) Mark 6 for 45 minutes.

traditional bread sauce

Serves 8-10
Preparation time: 10 minutes
Cooking time: 10 minutes, plus standing
215-170 cals per serving

1 small onion, peeled, halved and studded with
   6 cloves
900ml (1½ pints) milk
2 bay leaves
10 peppercorns
2 fresh thyme sprigs
150g (5oz) fine fresh white breadcrumbs
25g (1oz) butter
90ml (6 tbsp) double cream
freshly grated nutmeg
salt and freshly ground black pepper

1 Put the onion in a pan with the milk, bay leaves, peppercorns and thyme. Bring to the boil, remove from the heat and leave to infuse for 30 minutes.
2 Strain the milk into a clean pan, bring to the boil and stir in breadcrumbs. Return to the boil, stirring, and simmer for 5 minutes or until the sauce has thickened. Stir in the butter and cream. Add nutmeg and seasoning to taste.

creamy brussels sprouts

This creamy accompaniment make a delicious change from plain boiled Brussels sprouts.

Serves 8-10
Preparation time: 15 minutes
Cooking time: 25 minutes, plus infusing
170-135 cals per serving

600ml (1 pint) milk
1 thick slice onion
1 thick slice celery
6 peppercorns
1 small bay leaf
1.1kg (2½lb) Brussels sprouts, lightly trimmed
salt and freshly ground black pepper
40g (1½oz) butter
40g (1½oz) plain flour
½ whole nutmeg, grated – about 5ml (1 tsp)
60ml (4 tbsp) single cream
oregano sprigs, flat-leafed parsley and grated
    nutmeg, to garnish

1 Place the milk in a saucepan with the onion, celery, peppercorns and bay leaf. Bring to the boil, remove from the heat and leave to infuse for 20-30 minutes.
2 Meanwhile, cook the sprouts in a pan of boiling salted water until just tender. Drain and plunge into a bowl of icy cold water. Drain again and dry well.
3 Strain the milk. Melt the butter in a heavy-based saucepan. Off the heat, add the flour and stir until smooth. Stir in the milk and mix until smooth. Return to the heat and bring to the boil, stirring. Simmer for 1-2 minutes, add the grated nutmeg and season with salt and pepper to taste. Float the cream on top.
4 In a food processor, pulse the sprouts briefly until roughly chopped. Combine with the sauce.
5 When ready to serve, stir the sprout mixture in a pan over a low heat until hot. Serve garnished with herbs and sprinkled with grated nutmeg.

Note You can prepare the dish in advance to the end of stage 4. Allow the sauce to cool before combining with the sauce.

red thai turkey curry

For an easy supper dish, rustle up this spicy Thai curry with the turkey leftovers. You can adjust the spiciness to suit your taste.

Serves 6
Preparation time: 35 minutes
Cooking time: 25 minutes
285 cals per serving

45ml (3 tbsp) vegetable oil
450g (1lb) onions, peeled and finely chopped
200g (7oz) French beans, trimmed
125g (4oz) baby corn, halved on the diagonal
2 red peppers, halved, cored, deseeded and cut into thick strips
15ml (1 tbsp) red Thai curry paste, or to taste
1 red chilli, deseeded and finely chopped
1 lemon grass stalk, trimmed and very finely chopped
4 kaffir lime leaves, bruised
30ml (2 tbsp) finely chopped fresh root ginger
1 garlic clove, peeled and crushed
400ml (14fl oz) can coconut milk
600ml (1 pint) chicken or turkey stock
450g (1lb) cooked turkey, cut into strips
150g (5oz) bean sprouts
chopped fresh coriander, to garnish

1 Heat the oil in a large frying pan or wok. Add the onions and cook for 4-5 minutes or until softened. Add the French beans, baby corn and red peppers and stir-fry for 3-4 minutes.
2 Add the curry paste, chilli, lemon grass, kaffir lime leaves, ginger and garlic and cook, stirring, for a further 2 minutes. Remove from the pan and set aside.
3 Add the coconut milk and stock to the pan, bring to the boil and bubble vigorously for 5-10 minutes or until reduced by a quarter.
4 Return the vegetables to the pan and add the turkey and bean sprouts. Bring to the boil and cook for 1-2 minutes. Serve immediately, sprinkled with chopped coriander.

winter vegetable roast with chestnuts

Any seasonal root vegetables can be used in this tasty accompaniment, but make sure you include some which are colourful.

Preparation time: 20 minutes
Cooking time: 50 minutes
290 cals per serving

1.4kg (3lb) mixed root vegetables, such as carrots, sweet potato, parsnips, celeriac, turnips, squash or salsify, and pumpkin
150g (5oz) shallots, peeled with root intact
60ml (4 tbsp) olive oil
salt and freshly ground black pepper
150g (5oz) spicy sausages, such as merguez, twisted in half and cut in two
125g (4oz) vacuum-packed chestnuts

1 Peel the vegetables and cut into rough chunks, keeping the sweet potato and pumpkin in larger pieces. Cut the shallots in half lengthways if large.
2 Place all the vegetables in a roasting tin, drizzle with the olive oil and season with salt and pepper. Cook on the top shelf of the oven at 200°C/fan oven 190°C (400°F) Mark 6 for 25 minutes.
3 Add the sausages and return to the oven for a further 15 minutes, stirring occasionally. Finally, add the chestnuts, stir to mix and roast for a further 15 minutes or until the vegetables are golden brown.

turkey and ham pie
with chestnuts

This pie works well with ready diced packs of raw turkey from the supermarket; it is also an excellent way of using up Christmas leftovers. The flavourful juices are laced with cream, and cranberries provide a piquant contrast. All are encased under a crumbly potato pastry crust.

Serves 8-10

Preparation time: 50 minutes, plus cooling

Cooking time: 40 minutes for filling; 40 minutes baking

Suitable for freezing

945-755 cals per serving

FOR THE PIE FILLING:

900g (2lb) boneless turkey (preferably a mixture of breast and thigh meat), chopped

45ml (3 tbsp) plain white flour

salt and freshly ground black pepper

50g (2oz) butter

2 large onions, peeled and chopped

750ml (1¼ pints) chicken stock

freshly grated nutmeg

350g (12oz) cooked ham, chopped

350g (12oz) vacuum-packed chestnuts

15ml (1 tbsp) chopped fresh thyme

150g (5oz) fresh or frozen cranberries

150ml (¼ pint) double cream

FOR THE PASTRY:

1 large potato, peeled and diced

450g (1lb) plain white flour

125g (4oz) butter, in pieces

150g (5oz) white vegetable fat, in pieces

TO FINISH:

beaten egg, to glaze

coarse salt, for sprinkling

1 Toss the turkey meat in seasoned flour to coat. Melt the butter in a large frying pan. Add half of the turkey and fry quickly on all sides until golden. Remove with a slotted spoon and set aside; fry the rest of the turkey; remove.

2 Add the onions to the pan and cook gently for 10 minutes until soft. Stir in the stock, plenty of nutmeg and seasoning; cook, stirring, until thickened. Combine the turkey, ham, chestnuts and thyme in a flameproof casserole and pour on the stock mixture. Cover and cook very gently for 30 minutes. Stir in the cranberries and cream.

3 Using a slotted spoon, transfer the mixture to a 2 litre (3½ pint) shallow pie dish. Place a pie funnel in the centre and add enough of the cooking juices to half fill the dish; reserve any remaining liquid. Allow the filling to cool.

4 Meanwhile, make the pastry. Cook the potato in boiling salted water until tender; drain well and mash. Sift the flour into a bowl and rub in the fats, using fingertips. Add the potato and stir with a round-bladed knife, adding a little cold water to mix to a smooth, firm dough. Wrap in cling film and chill for 30 minutes.

5 Roll out the pastry on a lightly floured surface and use to cover the pie. Make a hole in the centre and decorate with a pastry rose and leaves shaped from the trimmings if liked. Brush with beaten egg to glaze and scatter with a little coarse salt. Bake at 200°C/fan oven 190°C (400°F) Mark 6 for about 40 minutes until the pastry is crisp and golden.

6 Serve hot, with seasonal vegetables and any reserved cooking juices in a sauceboat.

roasted vegetables and turkey on focaccia

Serves 6
Preparation time: 30 minutes
Cooking time: 1 hour 10 minutes
400 cals per serving

900g (2lb) red onions, peeled, quartered and
    separated into 'petals'
150ml (¼ pint) olive oil
3 red and 3 yellow peppers, halved, deseeded and cut
    into wedges
6 large garlic cloves (unpeeled)
200g (7oz) cherry tomatoes
30ml (2 tbsp) balsamic vinegar
sea salt flakes and freshly ground black pepper
30ml (2 tbsp) white wine vinegar
1 ciabatta or focaccia loaf, thickly sliced
300g (10oz) cooked turkey, cut into thick strips
basil sprigs, to garnish

1 Put the onion in a large roasting tin with 30ml
   (2 tbsp) olive oil and toss to coat. Roast at
   220°C/fan oven 210°C (425°F) Mark 7 for
   10 minutes, add the peppers and garlic cloves,
   mix thoroughly and return to the oven for about
   50 minutes or until the vegetables are charred
   and soft. Add the cherry tomatoes and roast for
   10 minutes. Remove from the oven and mix in
   the balsamic vinegar and seasoning; keep warm.
2 Pour the wine vinegar and 90ml (6 tbsp) olive oil
   into a small bowl, season and whisk thoroughly
   to make a dressing; set aside.
3 Toast the focaccia or ciabatta bread slices on one
   side. Turn, brush the second side with the
   remaining olive oil and toast until brown and
   crisp. Sprinkle with sea salt flakes.
4 Add the cooked turkey strips to the warm
   roasted vegetables, then toss in the dressing.
   Serve immediately, on the toasted focaccia,
   garnished with basil sprigs and sprinkled with
   crushed peppercorns.

the ultimate rich christmas pudding

Serves 8-10
Preparation time: 30 minutes
Cooking time: 6 hours, plus 2 hours reheating
400-325 cals per serving

125g (4oz) sultanas
125g (4oz) currants
125g (4oz) dark muscovado sugar
50g (2oz) seedless raisins
50g (2oz) chopped mixed peel
50g (2oz) plain white flour
75g (3oz) shredded suet (beef or vegetarian)
125g (4oz) fresh white breadcrumbs
5ml (1 tsp) ground mixed spice
2.5ml (½ tsp) salt
grated rind of 1 lemon
200g (7oz) sharp apple, such as Granny Smith, cored
   and coarsely grated
15ml (1 tbsp) black treacle
2 large eggs
50g (2oz) chopped almonds (optional)
90ml (6 tbsp) ginger wine or milk
2.5ml (½ tsp) bicarbonate of soda
60ml (4 tbsp) brandy

1 Grease and base-line a 1.1 litre (2 pint) pudding basin. Place all of the ingredients, except the brandy, in a mixing bowl and stir well. Spoon the mixture into the basin and smooth the surface.

2 Press a circle of buttered greaseproof paper on to the surface. Cover the basin with a sheet of foil, pleated across the middle. Secure with string, just under the rim.

3 Place an upturned, old heatproof saucer in the base of a large saucepan. Stand the pudding basin on the saucer, pour in sufficient boiling water to come two thirds of the way up the side of the basin, then cover the saucepan with a tight-fitting lid. Simmer gently for 6 hours, topping up the saucepan with boiling water from time to time, as necessary. Allow to cool completely. Store in a cool, dark place for at least 6 weeks to mature.

4 To reheat, place the pudding basin in a saucepan as above, and simmer for 2 hours or until hot through. To serve, turn out the pudding on to a serving plate. Warm the brandy in a pan, ignite it and pour over the pudding. Serve with brandy butter, fresh custard or ice cream.

Variation For a lighter Christmas pudding, use half of the quantity of suet.

traditional mince pies

Makes 12
Preparation time: 30 minutes, plus standing
Cooking time: 20 minutes
Suitable for freezing (stage 4)
260 cals per pie

FOR THE PASTRY:
225g (8oz) plain white flour
pinch of salt
150g (5oz) butter
30ml (2 tbsp) caster sugar
1 egg yolk
FOR THE FILLING:
225-300g (8-10oz) luxury mincemeat
TO FINISH:
1 egg white, lightly beaten
caster sugar, for sprinkling

1   To make the pastry, sift the flour and salt into a large bowl and rub in the butter using your fingertips until the mixture resembles coarse breadcrumbs. Stir in the sugar.
2   Mix the egg yolk with 45ml (3 tbsp) cold water, then add to the dry ingredients and mix to a dough. Knead gently until smooth, wrap in cling film and chill for 30 minutes.
3   On a lightly floured surface, roll out half of the pastry to a 3mm (⅛ inch) thickness. Using a 7.5-9cm (3-3½ inch) fluted cutter, stamp out 12 circles of pastry. Gently press these into patty tins or individual tartlet tins; the pastry should just protrude above the tins to allow for shrinkage when cooked. Spoon the mincemeat into the pastry cases; do not overfill.
4   Roll out the remaining pastry and stamp out 12 circles or stars, using a 6cm (2½ inch) fluted or star cutter. Dampen the edges of the pastry in the tins, then top with the smaller pastry circles. Press edges together to seal. Decorate plain tops with leaves cut from the trimmings, if wished.
5   Brush the tops with egg white, then sprinkle lightly with caster sugar. Bake at 190°C/fan oven 180°C (375°F) Mark 5 for about 20 minutes. Leave in the tins for 5 minutes, then transfer to a wire rack. Serve warm, dusted with icing sugar and accompanied by brandy butter or cream.

Note The uncooked mince pies can be glazed and baked from frozen; allow an extra 10-15 minutes.

pineapple, date and kumquat salad

An ideal dessert to offer as an alternative to a rich Christmas pudding, this pretty fruit salad is made with seasonal oranges, kumquats, pineapple and fresh dates. The kumquats are poached in an acacia honey syrup and acquire a wonderful flavour.

Serves 6
Preparation time: 35 minutes
Cooking time: 15 minutes
330 cals per serving

75ml (5 tbsp) acacia honey
50g (2oz) soft brown sugar
300ml (½ pint) Earl Grey tea, strained
225g (8oz) kumquats, halved
2 oranges
1 medium pineapple
12 fresh dates, halved and stoned
125g (4oz) walnut halves

1   Put the honey, sugar and tea into a saucepan, bring to the boil and boil for 1 minute. Add the kumquats to the syrup and simmer, uncovered, for about 10 minutes until tender. Leave to cool in the syrup.
2   Peel the oranges, removing all the rind and white pith. Slice them crosswise and place in a bowl.
3   Using a sharp knife, cut the top and bottom off the pineapple. Cut away the skin and the brown 'eyes'. Quarter the pineapple lengthwise and cut out the core. Cut the flesh into large chunks. Carefully mix with the oranges.
4   Stir in the dates and walnuts. Drain the kumquats and set aside; strain the syrup and pour over the fruit in the bowl. Cover and chill in the refrigerator for 1 hour.
5   Spoon the fruit salad into a serving bowl and scatter the poached kumquats on top. Serve with whipped cream.

the ultimate christmas cake

A moist cake full of Christmas flavours. If you're short of time, leave the mixture in a cool place until the following day to bake; this will also ensure the cake has a flat top. Brush the surface very lightly with cold water before baking to prevent a hard crust forming.

Makes 16-20 slices
Preparation time: 1½ hours, plus maturing
Cooking time: 2 hours
Suitable for freezing (stage 5)
660-530 cals per slice

300g (10oz) raisins, preferably large ones
200g (7oz) sultanas
225g (8oz) currants
75g (3oz) candied peel
75g (3oz) glacé cherries
200ml (7fl oz) brandy
300g (11oz) plain white flour
pinch of salt
5ml (1 tsp) ground cinnamon
freshly grated nutmeg
150g (5oz) unsalted butter, softened
150g (5oz) soft dark brown (muscovado) sugar
4 eggs, separated
5ml (1 tsp) cocoa powder
pinch of bicarbonate of soda
TO FINISH:
60ml (2fl oz) brandy
28cm (11 inch) round cake board
90ml (6 tbsp) thin honey or apricot jam
450g (1lb) white almond paste
cornflour, for dusting
about 900g (2lb) ready-to-roll icing
1 metre silver braid
silver leaf, to decorate (optional)

1 Place all the dried fruit in a bowl with the candied peel, glacé cherries and brandy. Stir well, cover and leave to macerate in a cool place for 1-2 days, stirring occasionally.

2 Grease a deep 20cm (8 inch) round cake tin and line with a double thickness of greaseproof paper. Sift the flour with the salt, cinnamon and a little nutmeg.

3 Beat the butter in a bowl until creamy, using a food mixer if available, or electric hand whisk. Add the sugar gradually, beating well between each addition until light and fluffy. Beat in the egg yolks one at a time, then fold in half of the flour mixture. Fold in the macerated fruit with its soaking liquid, then incorporate the remaining flour.

4 In another bowl, whisk the egg whites until foamy. Add to the cake mixture with the cocoa powder and bicarbonate of soda; stir until evenly mixed.

5 Turn the mixture into the prepared tin, smooth the top and bake at 150°C/fan oven 140°C (300°F) Mark 2 for 2 hours or until a skewer inserted in the centre comes out clean. Leave in the tin for 30 minutes, then transfer to a wire rack to cool.

6 When cold, wrap the cake in greaseproof paper and foil, and store in a cool place for up to 6 weeks (or a minimum of 1 week). Every week for the first 4 weeks, prick the base of the cake and spoon over 15ml (1 tbsp) brandy. For the last 2 weeks, leave to dry.

7 Place the cake on the cake board. Warm the honey and brush a thin layer over the cake. Roll out the almond paste on a surface dusted with cornflour to a 30cm (12 inch) round. Position over the cake and press lightly on to the top and sides; trim away the excess at the base. Leave in a cool place to dry for 1-2 days.

8 Thinly roll out 225g (8oz) of the icing on a surface lightly dusted with cornflour to a 30cm (12 inch) round. Position over the cake and press lightly on to the top and sides; trim away excess icing at the base.

9 Cut a greaseproof paper triangle template, with 2 equal long sides measuring 20cm (8 inches), and a base measurement of 4cm (1½ inches). Roll out the remaining icing thinly and use the template to cut about 22 triangles; re-roll trimmings to cut more triangles as necessary.

10 Position the triangles on the cake with the narrow points to the centre, overlapping them and tucking in excess icing as you go. Secure silver braid around the base of the cake. Roll the icing trimmings into balls, covering some of them with silver leaf if using. Arrange on top of the cake, pressing gently, to secure. Position a few balls on the board to finish.

panettone

This classic Italian favourite is really a cross between a bread and a cake. Light, yet buttery and rich, it is studded with dried fruit and candied peel. Because of the high butter content, panettone keeps well. It is normally eaten with coffee, or a glass of dessert wine, Marsala or sherry.

Makes 10-12 slices
Preparation time: 25 minutes, plus rising
Cooking time: 35 minutes
Suitable for freezing
415-320 cals per serving

450g (1lb) strong plain white flour
10ml (2 tsp) salt
75g (3oz) caster sugar
1½ x 7g sachet fast-action dried yeast
finely grated rind of 1 lemon
finely grated rind of 1 orange
1 egg
4 egg yolks
150ml (¼ pint) warm milk
175g (6oz) unsalted butter, softened
75g (3oz) chopped mixed candied orange and citron peel
125g (4oz) raisins

1 Line a 15cm (6 inch) deep cake tin with a double layer of non-stick baking parchment which extends 12cm (5 inches) above the rim.
2 Sift the flour and salt into a bowl and stir in the sugar, yeast and citrus rinds. Make a well in the centre. Beat the egg and egg yolks together and add to the well with the warm milk. Mix to an elastic dough, adding a little more flour if necessary, but keeping the dough quite soft. Work in the softened butter.
3 Cover with cling film and leave to rise for 2-4 hours until doubled in volume.
4 Knock back the dough and knead in the chopped peel and raisins. Place in the prepared tin and cut a deep cross on the top with a very sharp knife. Cover and leave to rise until the dough is 2.5cm (1 inches) above the top of the tin.
5 Bake at 200°C/fan oven 190°C (400°F) Mark 6 for 15 minutes, then lower the heat to 180°C (350°F) Mark 4 and bake for a further 40 minutes until well risen and golden. Leave in the tin for 10 minutes, then transfer to a wire rack to cool.
6 To serve, cut off the top and slice horizontally. To store, replace the top, wrap the whole panettone in cling film or foil and refrigerate. Bring to room temperature to serve.

kugelhopf

Traditionally eaten at Christmas in Austria and Germany, this yeast cake is best eaten within 2 days. If you have any left over, toast or use to make a luxury bread and butter pudding.

Makes 12 slices
Preparation time: 45 minutes, plus overnight chilling and
**   rising**
Cooking time: 50-55 minutes
Suitable for freezing
390 cals per serving

200g (7oz) seedless raisins
45ml (3 tbsp) light rum
10ml (2 tsp) fast-action dried yeast
300g (11oz) strong plain white flour
4 eggs
100ml (3½fl oz) milk
225g (8oz) unsalted butter, softened
75g (3oz) caster sugar
pinch of salt
finely grated rind of 1 lemon
100g (3½oz) split blanched almonds, lightly toasted
icing sugar, for dusting
glacé fruits, nuts and dragées (optional), to decorate

1 Soak the raisins in the rum overnight.
2 Place the yeast and flour in a food mixer. Whisk the eggs and milk together lightly in a bowl. With the machine running on a slow speed, pour in the egg mixture and mix for approximately 10 minutes or until the dough is smooth, shiny and elastic. (Or mix by hand.)
3 Meanwhile, beat the butter, sugar, salt and lemon rind together in a bowl. With the machine running, gradually add this mixture to the dough until evenly incorporated. Turn into a large bowl, cover with cling film and refrigerate overnight.
4 Generously butter a 2 litre (3½ pint) kugelhopf ring mould, then press a third of the almonds on to the sides of the mould; refrigerate.
5 Roughly chop the remaining almonds and knead into the dough by hand, with the raisins and rum. Carefully place in the prepared mould. Cover and leave in a warm place until the dough has risen to within 2cm (¾ inch) of the top of the mould.
6 Bake below the centre of the oven at 200°C/fan oven 190°C (400°F) Mark 6 for 10 minutes. Lower the setting to 190°C/fan oven 180°C (375°F) Mark 5. Cover the kugelhopf with greaseproof paper and bake for a further 40-45 minutes or until the kugelhopf sounds hollow when the mould is tapped.
7 Leave in the tin for 15 minutes, then turn out on to a wire rack to cool. Serve dusted with icing sugar and decorated with glacé fruits, nuts and dragées if wished.

christmas stollen

A richly fruited, lightly spiced festive yeast bread with moist, almond paste through the middle.

Makes 10 slices
Preparation time: 20 minutes, plus rising
Cooking time: 40 minutes
Suitable for freezing
320 cals per serving

350g (12oz) strong plain white flour
2.5ml (½ tsp) salt
2.5ml (½ tsp) ground mixed spice
50g (2oz) unsalted butter, diced
7g sachet fast-action dried yeast
25g (1oz) caster sugar
125g (4oz) mixed sultanas, currants and raisins
25g (1oz) glacé cherries or ready-to-eat dried apricots, chopped
25g (1oz) chopped mixed peel
50g (2oz) chopped almonds
1 small egg, beaten
120-150ml (4-5fl oz) warmed milk
125g (4oz) ready-made almond paste
icing sugar, for dusting

1 Sift the flour, salt and spice into a bowl and rub in the butter. Stir in the rest of the ingredients, except the almond paste, adding sufficient warm milk to mix to a soft dough.
2 Turn on to a lightly floured surface and knead for about 10 minutes, then shape into a ball. Place in an oiled bowl, cover with cling film and leave to rise in a warm place for 2 hours or until doubled in size.
3 Knock back the dough, then shape into a long oval, about 1cm (½ inch) deep.
4 Roll the almond paste into a log, a little shorter than the length of the oval. Make a slight indentation along the length of the dough. Lay the almond paste in this groove and fold the dough over to enclose it; press the edges together to seal.
5 Transfer to a lightly oiled large baking sheet, cover and leave to rise for a further 30 minutes.
6 Bake at 180°C/fan oven 170°C (350°F) Mark 4 for 40 minutes or until deep golden. Transfer to a wire rack to cool. Serve dusted with icing sugar. Eat within 1-2 days.

traditional scottish shortbread

This rich, buttery shortbread really should melt in the mouth. Make sure all of the ingredients are at room temperature before you start.

Makes 18-20
Preparation time: 20 minutes, plus chilling
Cooking time: 15-20 minutes
270-180 cals per piece

225g (8oz) butter
125g (4oz) caster sugar
225g (8oz) plain white flour
125g (4oz) ground rice or rice flour
pinch of salt
golden or coloured granulated sugar, for coating
caster sugar, for sprinkling

1 Cream the butter and sugar together in a bowl until pale and fluffy. Sift the flour, rice flour and salt together on to the creamed mixture and stir in, using a wooden spoon, until the mixture resembles breadcrumbs.
2 Gather the dough together with your hand and turn on to a clean surface. Knead very lightly until it forms a ball, then lightly roll into a sausage, about 5cm (2 inches) thick. Wrap in cling film and chill in the refrigerator until firm.
3 Unwrap the roll and slice into discs, about 7-10mm (⅓-½ inch) thick. Pour golden or coloured granulated sugar on to a plate and roll the edge of each disc in the sugar. Place the biscuits, cut-side up, on two baking sheets, lined with greaseproof paper.
4 Bake at 190°C/fan oven 180°C (375°F) Mark 5 for 15-20 minutes, depending on thickness, until very pale golden. On removing from the oven, sprinkle the shortbread with caster sugar. Leave on the baking sheet for 10 minutes, then transfer to a wire rack to cool.

panforte de siena

This Italian rich, spicy, thin 'cake' is packed with candied peel, honey and nuts. It is typically served in thin slices, after dinner or with coffee.

Makes 12 slices
Preparation time: 45 minutes
Cooking time: 35 minutes
265 cals per slice

125g (4oz) whole blanched almonds
125g (4oz) whole skinned hazelnuts
125g (4oz) candied orange peel, finely chopped
125g (4oz) candied citron peel, finely chopped
50g (2oz) plain white flour
1.25ml (¼ tsp) ground coriander
1.25ml (¼ tsp) ground white pepper
1.25ml (¼ tsp) ground nutmeg
1.25ml (¼ tsp) ground cloves
5ml (1 tsp) ground cinnamon
125g (4oz) granulated sugar
225g (8oz) thin honey
25g (1oz) butter
icing sugar, for dusting

1 Grease and line a 20cm (8 inch) springform cake tin with non-stick baking parchment, or edible rice paper. Spread the almonds and hazelnuts on a baking tray and bake at 180°C/fan oven 170°C (350°F) Mark 4 for 10-15 minutes until golden brown. Allow to cool slightly, then chop roughly and place in a bowl. Lower the oven setting to 150°C/fan oven 140°C (300°F) Mark 2.
2 Add the orange and citron peel to the nuts. Sift in the flour together with the spices. Stir to mix.
3 Put the sugar, honey and butter in a heavy-based pan and heat gently, stirring occasionally, until dissolved. Bring to the boil and boil steadily until the syrup registers 117°C (242°F) on a sugar thermometer (the soft ball stage). Quickly stir in the nut mixture, pour into the prepared tin and smooth the surface with an oiled potato masher; work quickly otherwise the mixture will set.
4 Bake for 35 minutes; it won't be set at this stage. Transfer the tin to a wire rack; the panforte will harden as it cools. When cold, carefully remove tin and peel away baking parchment (if used).
5 Store in an airtight tin for up to 1 month. Serve dredged with icing sugar and cut into thin slices.

chocolate truffles

These luscious liqueur-laced chocolate truffles make ideal Christmas gifts. You can either coat them in melted chocolate or simply roll in cocoa powder, chopped nuts or grated coconut. Store in the refrigerator until ready to serve.

Makes about 24
Preparation time: 30 minutes, plus chilling
Suitable for freezing
65 cals per truffle

225g (8oz) good quality bitter, plain or milk chocolate
90ml (3fl oz) double cream
45ml (3 tbsp) brandy, rum, orange liqueur, coffee
    liqueur, coconut liqueur, or vanilla essence
TO FINISH:
cocoa powder, chopped nuts, dessicated or grated
    coconut, chocolate vermicelli or grated chocolate,
    for coating

1 Grate the chocolate into a small heatproof bowl and add the cream. Stand the bowl over a pan of simmering water until the chocolate begins to melt. Stir well until smooth and remove from the heat. Leave to cool for about 20-30 minutes to room temperature; the mixture should have thickened considerably.

2 Beat in the brandy, rum, liqueur or vanilla. Using an electric whisk, beat for about 5 minutes until the mixture is light, fluffy and paler in colour. It should be firm enough to stand in peaks. Spoon into a shallow tin, cover and refrigerate for at least 2 hours until quite firm.

3 To make simple rolled truffles, sprinkle a tray with cocoa powder and place even-sized teaspoonfuls of truffle mixture on the tray. Dust your hands with a little cocoa powder and quickly roll the mixture into uneven balls. If preferred roll the truffles in chopped nuts, coconut, chocolate vermicelli or grated chocolate. Place on waxed paper and refrigerate for at least 2 hours.

4 Place the truffles in paper cases and pack in boxes. Store in the refrigerator for up to 3 days.

Variations

DIPPED TRUFFLES Roll the truffle mixture into neat 2.5cm (1 inch) balls, place on a tray and freeze overnight until rock hard. Spear, one at a time, on to a cocktail stick, then dip in melted white, plain or milk chocolate turning to coat. Place on a tray lined with non-stick baking parchment and refrigerate for at least 2 hours until set.

DECORATED DIPPED TRUFFLES Pipe a contrasting colour of chocolate over the dipped truffles or apply a little edible gold leaf, to decorate. Alternatively, press a toasted flaked nut, sliver of crystallised ginger, or quartered cherry onto the setting chocolate.

puddings

Delectable desserts to grace
all menus, from tangy fruit
desserts and light creamy
concoctions to irresistible
baked puddings and tarts

winter fruit compote with prune cream

Dried fruits are soaked overnight in tea and ginger syrup, scented with cinnamon and cloves, then served with a delicious prune cream.

Serves 6
Preparation time: 15 minutes, plus overnight soaking
315 cals per serving

1 large piece preserved stem ginger in syrup, diced
45ml (3 tbsp) ginger syrup (from ginger jar)
600ml (1 pint) English Breakfast tea
30ml (2 tbsp) caster sugar
pared zest of 1 lemon
3 cloves
2.5cm (1 inch) piece cinnamon stick
350g (12oz) mixed dried fruits, such as cranberries, sultanas, apricots, figs, pears
FOR THE PRUNE CREAM:
125g (4oz) ready-to-eat pitted prunes
50ml (2fl oz) Armagnac
200ml (7fl oz) crème fraîche

1 Put the diced ginger, syrup, tea, sugar, lemon zest and spices in a saucepan and bring to the boil. Remove from the heat, add the mixed dried fruits and stir well. Transfer to a bowl, set aside to cool, then cover and leave in the refrigerator overnight.
2 To make the prune cream, place the prunes in a bowl, add the Armagnac and set aside to soak for 2 hours until all the brandy is absorbed. Transfer to a blender or food processor and work until smooth. Put the crème fraîche in a bowl and beat in the prune purée. Cover and chill until required, or freeze for 1 hour prior to serving if preferred.
3 Spoon the ginger fruits and syrup into individual bowls and serve topped with a spoonful of the prune cream.

Note Most larger supermarkets and healthfood shops now stock a good variety of luxury dried fruits, especially during the winter.

poached pears with fudge sauce

Fresh pears are delicious poached and served with an indulgent fudge sauce. The cooking time will depend on the ripeness of the pears – they will appear transluscent when cooked.

Serves 4
Preparation time: 15 minutes, plus cooling
Cooking time: 20-25 minutes
225 cals per serving

225g (8oz) granulated sugar
2 cinnamon sticks
600ml (1 pint) water
4 medium, firm pears
FOR THE SAUCE:
50g (2oz) butter
75g (3oz) light soft brown muscovado sugar
30ml (2 tbsp) golden syrup
60ml (2fl oz) double cream
TO SERVE:
Brandy Snaps (see page 371, optional)

1 Put the sugar in a heavy-based saucepan (see note) with the cinnamon and water. Heat gently until the sugar dissolves, then bring to the boil and boil for 2 minutes.
2 Peel the pears, leaving them whole with the stalks intact. Using the tip of a potato peeler, scoop out the core end from the base of each pear.
3 Immediately add the pears to the sugar syrup, packing them in as snugly as possible. Cover the pears with a disc of greaseproof paper, then position the lid. Simmer for 20-25 minutes until tender, turning the pears in the syrup occasionally. Set aside.
4 To make the sauce, put the butter, brown sugar, syrup and cream in a pan. Heat gently until melted and smooth, then bring to the boil and bubble for 1 minute.
5 Lift the poached pears out of the syrup and place on serving plates. Spoon the warm fudge sauce over the pears and serve at once, with brandy snaps or other dessert biscuits.

Note Use a pan just large enough for the pears to fit in upright, to ensure they cook evenly.

poached figs with macaroons and mascarpone

Serves 4
Preparation time: 10 minutes, plus cooling
Cooking time: 20 minutes
390 cals per serving

300ml (½ pint) sweet red wine
60ml (2fl oz) crème de cassis
75g (3oz) caster sugar
2 strips of lemon zest
2 strips of orange zest
6 cloves
1 cinnamon stick, roughly broken
3 allspice berries, bruised
12 large figs
8 macaroons, lightly crushed
125g (4oz) mascarpone

1 Put the wine, cassis, sugar, citrus zests and spices in a heavy-based saucepan and heat gently to dissolve the sugar.
2 Add the figs, heat slowly and simmer gently for 20 minutes or until the figs are tender. Transfer the figs to a bowl, using a slotted spoon.
3 Return the syrup to the boil and let bubble to reduce by half. Strain the syrup over the figs and allow to cool.
4 To serve, place 3 figs in each bowl, spoon on some of the syrup and add a spoonful of mascarpone to each portion. Scatter over the crushed macaroons.

Note Purple and pale green skinned fresh figs are both widely available. With their fragile skins, figs are easily damaged and should be handled carefully. Look for firm, unblemished fruit which yields slightly to the touch.

peaches and blueberries with mascarpone ice cream

Serves 4
Preparation time: 15 minutes, plus freezing ice cream
Cooking time: 5 minutes
790 cals per serving

25g (1oz) unsalted butter
25g (1oz) soft brown sugar
3 firm ripe peaches, stoned and sliced
225g (8oz) blueberries
pared zest and juice of 1 orange
pared zest and juice of 1 lemon
6 cardamom pods, seeds extracted and bruised
FOR THE MASCARPONE ICE CREAM:
450g (1lb) mascarpone
15ml (1 tbsp) lemon juice
125g (4oz) icing sugar
3 egg yolks
30ml (2 tbsp) Marsala or Grand Marnier

1 To make the ice cream, beat all the ingredients together in a bowl until smooth. Freeze the mixture, either in an ice-cream maker according to the manufacturer's instructions, or in a freezerproof container beating at hourly intervals until the ice cream is frozen, to prevent ice crystals forming and ensure an even-textured result.

2 Put the butter and brown sugar in a pan over a low heat until melted and smooth, then add the peaches, blueberries, citrus zests and cardamom seeds. Heat gently for 5-10 minutes until the peaches and blueberries are just softened. Set aside to cool slightly.

3 Divide the fruit between individual bowls and serve warm, with a scoop of the ice cream.

Note Use a pestle and mortar to crack open the cardamom pods, then to bruise the seeds. Alternatively crush on a chopping board, using the base of a heavy pan.

Variations Use blackberries or raspberries instead of the blueberries.

baked apples with cinnamon ice cream

Serves 8
Preparation time: 30 minutes, plus freezing ice cream
Cooking time: 1 hour
570 cals per serving

8 large, crisp dessert apples, such as Granny Smith's
50g (2oz) unsalted butter
50g (2oz) caster sugar
finely pared zest of 1 lemon
2 cinnamon sticks, broken
200ml (7fl oz) Vin Santo or other dessert wine
FOR THE CINNAMON ICE CREAM:
450ml (¾ pint) double cream
450ml (¾ pint) milk
4 cinnamon sticks, broken
6 egg yolks
125g (4oz) caster sugar

1 To make the ice cream, put the cream, milk and cinnamon sticks in a saucepan and slowly bring to the boil. Remove from the heat and leave to infuse for 20 minutes, then return to the heat and bring to the boil.

2 Beat the egg yolks and sugar together in a bowl, pour on the hot cream mixture, stirring, then strain back into the pan. Heat gently, stirring until thickened enough to coat the back of a wooden spoon; do not boil.

3 Turn into a bowl and leave to cool. Freeze in an ice-cream maker according to the manufacturer's directions, or in a freezerproof container, beating from time to time to break down the ice crystals.

4 Cut a thin slice from the base of each apple so they stand upright. Scoop out the cores through the bases, leaving stalks intact. Stand the apples in a baking dish and dot with the butter, sugar, lemon zest and cinnamon. Drizzle with the wine. Cover dish with foil and bake at 180°C/fan oven 170°C (350°F) Mark 4 for 30 minutes.

5 Remove the foil and return to the oven for a further 20-30 minutes until the apples are tender.

6 Transfer the apples to a dish and pour the cooking juices into a pan. Boil rapidly for 4-5 minutes until reduced and syrupy.

7 Serve the apples warm, drizzled with the sauce and accompanied by the ice cream.

summer pudding

Vary the fruits for this quintessential British pudding according to availability. Blackberries, blueberries, cherries and plums are all suitable. The total weight of fruit should be 900g (2lb).

Serves 6-8
Preparation time: 35 minutes, plus chilling
Cooking time: 5 minutes
Suitable for freezing
180-135 cals per serving

450g (1lb) raspberries
225g (8oz) redcurrants
225g (8oz) blackcurrants
75g (3oz) caster sugar
8 large slices close-textured white bread, 5mm
    (¼ inch) thick (preferably one-day old)
redcurrant sprigs, to decorate

1 Place the raspberries in a saucepan with the redcurrants, blackcurrants, sugar and 45ml (3 tbsp) water. Bring to a gentle simmer over a low heat, then cook gently for 3-4 minutes until the juices begin to run. Remove from the heat and set aside.

2 Remove the crusts from the bread slices, then cut a round of bread from one slice to fit the base of a 1.5 litre (2½ pint) pudding basin. Cut the remaining slices in half lengthwise.

3 Arrange the bread slices around the side of the pudding basin, overlapping them slightly at the bottom, so they fit neatly and tightly together. Position the round of bread to cover the base.

4 Spoon about 100ml (3½fl oz) of the juice from the fruit into a jug; set aside. Spoon the fruit and remaining juice into the bread-lined pudding basin. Cover completely with the remaining bread slices, trimming them to fit as necessary.

5 Cover the pudding with a saucer, that fits just inside the top of the pudding basin, then set a 2kg (4lb) weight on the saucer. Chill the pudding in the refrigerator overnight.

6 To unmould the pudding, remove the weight and saucer, then invert the serving plate over the pudding basin. Hold the two firmly together, invert and shake firmly (up and down).

7 Spoon the reserved juice over the pudding and decorate with redcurrant sprigs. Serve cut into wedges, with cream.

blueberry fritters with apple sauce

Serves 8
Preparation time: 20 minutes
Cooking time: 3-4 minutes
370 cals per serving

250ml (9fl oz) water
50g (2oz) butter
pinch of salt
25g (1oz) caster sugar
125g (4oz) plain white flour
25g (1oz) ground almonds
3 eggs
125g (4oz) blueberries
oil, for deep-frying
FOR THE SAUCE:
25g (1oz) butter
600ml (1 pint) apple juice
TO FINISH:
icing sugar, for dusting

1 To make the batter, put the water, butter, salt and sugar into a saucepan and bring to the boil. Stir in the flour and beat over a low heat until the mixture comes away from the sides of the pan. Remove from the heat and beat in the ground almonds, then the eggs, one at a time. Fold in the blueberries.

2 For the sauce, melt the butter in a saucepan, then add the apple juice. Bring to the boil and boil rapidly until reduced by half and slightly thickened.

3 Heat a 5cm (2 inch) depth of oil in a deep, heavy saucepan until it registers 180°C (350°F) on a sugar thermometer. Cook the fritters in batches. Drop small spoonfuls of the batter into the hot oil and deep-fry for 1-2 minutes until puffed and golden. Drain on kitchen paper and keep warm in a low oven until all the fritters are cooked.

4 Serve the blueberry fritters as soon as possible, dusted with icing sugar and accompanied by the warm apple sauce and thick cream.

baked fruit charlotte with orange sabayon

An assortment of berries baked in a buttery brioche crust and served with a delicious orange sabayon sauce.

Serves 4
Preparation time: 30 minutes
Cooking time: 25 minutes
560 cals per serving

50g (2oz) unsalted butter
1 small orange
125g (4oz) blackberries
50g (2oz) caster sugar
2.5ml (½ tsp) ground mixed spice
1 large or 6 individual brioches (one-day old)
75g (3oz) raspberries
75g (3oz) strawberries, hulled
FOR THE ORANGE SABAYON:
4 egg yolks
60ml (4 tbsp) caster sugar
juice of ½ orange
15ml (1 tbsp) Grand Marnier

1 Base-line 4 individual moulds, such as timbales or custard cups, then grease generously using most of the butter.
2 Finely grate the rind of the orange. Put the blackberries, sugar, spice, 60ml (2fl oz) water and half of the orange rind in a pan. Bring to a simmer and cook gently for 5 minutes; let cool.
3 Cut the brioche into thin slices. Cut out 4 small rounds to fit the base of the moulds and 4 larger ones, the diameter of the rims. Cut the remaining slices into strips. Press the smaller rounds into the base of the moulds; line the sides with strips.
4 Peel and segment the orange, discarding all white pith, and place in a bowl. Stir in the cooked blackberry mixture, raspberries and strawberries. Spoon into the lined moulds.
5 Press the 4 larger brioche circles on top and brush with the remaining melted butter. Place on a baking sheet and bake at 200°C/fan oven 190°C (400°F) Mark 6 for 25 minutes, covering the tops with foil after about 10 minutes.
6 Meanwhile, make the sabayon. Whisk the egg yolks, sugar and remaining orange rind in a bowl until pale. Place over a pan of simmering water, add the orange juice and liqueur and whisk until frothy and doubled in volume; keep warm.
7 Leave the puddings to stand for 5 minutes, then carefully unmould on to warm plates and serve with the sabayon.

date and walnut pudding with chocolate sauce

This moist, steamed pudding – with its chocolate fudge sauce – is winter comfort food at its best.

Serves 8
Preparation time: 20 minutes, plus standing
Cooking time: 2 hours
540 cals per serving

125g (4oz) butter, softened
125g (4oz) caster sugar
3 eggs, beaten
175g (6oz) self-raising white flour
45ml (3 tbsp) milk
75g (3oz) walnuts, toasted and roughly chopped
175g (6oz) stoned dates, roughly chopped
FOR THE CHOCOLATE FUDGE SAUCE:
50g (2oz) unsalted butter
50g (2oz) soft light brown sugar
50g (2oz) plain chocolate, in pieces
100ml (3½fl oz) double cream

1 Put the butter, sugar, eggs, flour and milk in a bowl and beat with an electric beater until smooth. Fold in the nuts and dates.
2 Spoon into a greased 1.2 litre (2 pint) pudding basin and smooth the surface. Place a greased and pleated sheet of greaseproof paper over the bowl, then apply a pleated layer of foil; secure tightly under the rim with string.
3 Sit the basin on a trivet in a large saucepan and add enough boiling water to come halfway up the side of the basin. Cover the pan and steam the pudding for 2 hours, checking the water level from time to time and topping up with boiling water as necessary. Lift the pudding out of the pan and leave to rest for 15 minutes.
4 Meanwhile, make the sauce. Place the butter, sugar and chocolate in a pan and heat gently until the chocolate is melted. Add the cream and let bubble for 3 minutes until thickened.
5 To serve, unmould the pudding on to a warmed plate. Cut into wedges and serve with the chocolate fudge sauce poured over.

marmalade pudding with whisky sauce

Serves 8
Preparation time: 20 minutes
Cooking time: 40-45 minutes
550 cals per serving

5 large oranges
90ml (6 tbsp) thin-cut marmalade
175g (6oz) butter
175g (6oz) caster sugar
3 eggs
175g (6oz) self-raising white flour
FOR THE SAUCE:
75g (3oz) butter
75g (3oz) caster sugar
45ml (3 tbsp) whisky
30ml (2 tbsp) marmalade

1 Finely grate the rind and squeeze the juice from 1 orange. Squeeze the juice from another two. Peel and segment the other 2 oranges, discarding all pith; set aside.
2 Grease eight 150ml (¼ pint) individual pudding moulds, base-line with non-stick baking parchment and dust with a little flour. Spoon two thirds of the marmalade into the moulds.
3 Cream the butter with the sugar and orange rind in a bowl until light and fluffy. Beat in the eggs, one at a time. Fold in the flour, 30ml (2 tbsp) orange juice and remaining marmalade.
4 Divide the mixture between the moulds and level the surface. Cover with pleated non-stick baking parchment and foil. Secure with string.
5 Stand the pudding moulds in a small roasting tin. Pour boiling water around to come halfway up the sides of the moulds. Cover the tin with foil. Bake at 190°C/fan oven 170°C (375°F) Mark 5 for about 40 minutes until firm to the touch.
6 To make the sauce, melt the butter and sugar together in a small, heavy-based pan over a low heat. Then cook, stirring, over a medium heat for 5 minutes to a golden caramel. Add the whisky and bubble for 1 minute. Add the reserved orange juice and bubble gently for 15 minutes or until syrupy. Off the heat, stir in the marmalade and reserved orange segments.
7 To serve, loosen the puddings and turn out on to warm plates. Spoon over the whisky sauce.

peach brown betty

Fresh peach slices layered with a lightly spiced buttery crumb mixture and baked in ramekins.

Serves 4
Preparation time: 15 minutes
Cooking time: 30 minutes
295 cals per serving

2 firm peaches
50g (2oz) unsalted butter
50g (2oz) caster sugar
30ml (2 tbsp) double cream
75g (3oz) fresh wholemeal breadcrumbs
25g (1oz) soft brown sugar
15g (½oz) plain white flour
5ml (1 tsp) ground mixed spice
whipped cream and grated nutmeg, to serve

1 Halve the peaches and remove the stones, then cut each half into thin slices.
2 Place the butter, caster sugar and cream in a small pan and heat gently until the butter is melted and the sugar dissolved.
3 Divide half of this buttery mixture between 4 ramekin dishes and top with a layer of peach slices.
4 In a bowl, mix together the breadcrumbs, soft brown sugar, flour and mixed spice. Spoon half of the breadcrumb mixture over the peaches.
5 Cover with the remaining peach slices and top with a layer of breadcrumb mixture. Drizzle over the rest of the buttery mixture. Bake at 190°C/fan oven 180°C (375°F) Mark 5 for 30 minutes until bubbling.
6 Leave to stand for 5 minutes, then turn out on to dessert plates and serve topped with cream, sprinkled with a little nutmeg.

tarte tatin

This classic French dessert is cooked upside down, then inverted to serve, so the apples sit atop the rich pastry base.

Serves 8
Preparation time: 30 minutes, plus cooling
Cooking time: 40-45 minutes
535 cals per serving

FOR THE PASTRY:
225g (8oz) plain flour
150g (5oz) butter
1.25ml (¼ tsp) salt
50g (2oz) icing sugar
1 egg
few drops of vanilla extract
FOR THE FILLING:
125g (4oz) butter
1-1.2kg (2-2½lb) large eating apples, preferably Cox's
200g (7oz) caster sugar
juice of ½ lemon

1   To make the pastry, put all the ingredients in a food processor and process briefly until the mixture resembles coarse crumbs. Knead lightly to a smooth dough on a lightly floured surface. Wrap in cling film and chill for 20 minutes.
2   For the caramel, melt the butter in a 25cm (10 inch) tatin mould or heavy-based shallow cake tin (not loose-based). Peel, quarter and core the apples. Sprinkle the sugar evenly over the melted butter, then tightly pack the apples in the tin.
3   Cook over a gentle heat for about 15 minutes until well caramelised, turning the apples around halfway through cooking. Sprinkle with the lemon juice. Allow to cool.
4   Roll out the pastry to a round, 2.5cm (1 inch) larger all round than the top of the tarte tatin tin. Lay over the top of the cooked apples, tucking the edges of the pastry down the side of the tin. Prick the pastry with the tip of a sharp knife. Bake at 220°C/fan oven 210°C (425°F) Mark 7 for 25-30 minutes until the pastry is golden brown all over.
5   Leave in the tin for 10 minutes, then turn out on to a serving plate. Serve warm, with cream, custard or ice cream.

pineapple, apple and almond puddings

Attractive individual baked puddings topped with caramelised apple slices and served with a cardamom-scented custard.

Serves 6
Preparation time: 20 minutes
Cooking time: 35-40 minutes
Suitable for freezing
230 cals per serving

1 Granny Smith's apple, cut into 6 slices
75g (3oz) caster sugar, plus extra for dusting
50g (2oz) plain white flour
5ml (1 tsp) baking powder
pinch of salt
50g (2oz) butter, diced
50g (2oz) ground almonds
100g (3½oz) cooking apple, peeled, cored and diced
100g (3½oz) pineapple, peeled, cored and diced
1 large egg, lightly beaten
1.25ml (¼ tsp) almond extract
TO DECORATE:
mint sprigs
crystalised violets (optional)
crushed cardamom seeds (optional)

1   Grease and base-line 6 individual 150ml (¼ pint) pudding basins or ramekins and dust the sides with flour. Using a pastry cutter the same size as the base of the moulds, stamp out circles from the apple slices. Dust with sugar and fry in a hot, non-stick frying pan until caramelised on both sides. Place an apple slice in the base of each mould.
2   Sift the flour, baking powder and salt into a bowl, then rub in the butter until the mixture resembles fine crumbs. Stir in the sugar and ground almonds. Add the cooking apple, pineapple, egg and almond extract and stir until evenly combined.
3   Spoon the mixture into the prepared moulds to half-fill and stand on a baking tray. Bake at 180°C/fan oven 170°C (350°F) Mark 4 for 35-40 minutes or until the puddings are golden and firm in the centre.

4 Leave to stand for 15 minutes, then carefully run a knife around the inside of each mould to loosen the puddings and turn out on to serving plates. Decorate with mint, crystallised violets and cardamom seeds if using. Serve with cardamom custard (see right), or ordinary custard if you prefer.

Note To freeze, allow the cooked puddings to cool completely, then turn out and freeze in a rigid container. Defrost at room temperature, then reheat at 180°C/fan oven 170°C (350°F) Mark 4 for 5-10 minutes. Finish as above.

cardamom custard

Put 200ml (7fl oz) semi-skimmed milk, 200ml (7fl oz) double cream, the crushed seeds from 3 cardamom pods and 1 vanilla pod in a heavy-based pan. Bring slowly to the boil. Take off the heat and leave to infuse for 20 minutes, then strain. In a bowl, beat 2 large egg yolks with 20g (¾oz) caster sugar. Pour on the infused milk, whisking, then return to the pan and cook over a low heat, stirring constantly, until the custard is slightly thickened and creamy; do not boil.

chocolate and cherry amaretti tart

Chocolate and cherries are, of course, a classic combination. Tart morello cherries give this flan a wonderful depth of flavour.

Serves 8
Preparation time: 30 minutes, plus chilling
Cooking time: 1 hour 20 minutes
Suitable for freezing
765 cals per serving

400g (14oz) bottled or canned pitted morello cherries, drained
45ml (3 tbsp) brandy, sloe gin or amaretto liqueur
FOR THE PASTRY:
150g (5oz) butter, softened
50g (2oz) icing sugar
1 small egg, beaten
225g (8oz) plain white flour
FOR THE FILLING:
100g (3½oz) good quality plain chocolate (70% cocoa solids)
125g (4oz) butter, softened
125g (4oz) caster sugar
3 large eggs, beaten
125g (4oz) ground almonds
25g (1oz) self-raising white flour
50g (2oz) amaretti biscuits, crushed
75g (3oz) silvered or flaked almonds
TO FINISH:
icing sugar, for dusting

chocolate for baking

When you're making a pudding or cake where chocolate is the main ingredient and the dominant taste, it's most important to use a fine quality brand. You could ruin the taste if you use a cheap variety. Generally, sweet milk chocolate with a low content of cocoa solids should be avoided, as should synthetic-tasting 'cooking chocolate' or 'cake covering'. Instead, choose a bittersweet, plain, or semi-sweet chocolate that has at least 70% cocoa solids – very often, these are stocked in the confectionery section along with the sweets and eating chocolates and are labelled as continental or luxury chocolate.

1 Put the morello cherries in a bowl, add the brandy, sloe gin or liqueur and leave to stand for 30 minutes.

2 Meanwhile, make the pastry. Put the butter, icing sugar and egg in a food processor and whizz until almost smooth. Add the flour and process until the mixture just begins to form a dough. Turn out on to a floured work surface and knead lightly until smooth, then wrap in cling film and chill for 30 minutes.

3 Roll out the pastry on a lightly floured surface and use to line a 24cm (9½ inch) fluted, loose-based flan tin. Chill for a further 20 minutes.

4 Line the pastry case with greaseproof paper and baking beans and bake blind at 200°C/fan oven 190°C (400°F) Mark 6 for 15 minutes. Remove paper and beans and bake for a further 5 minutes. Lower the setting to 150°C/fan oven 140°C (300°F) Mark 2.

5 For the filling, melt the chocolate in a heatproof bowl over a pan of simmering water; stir until smooth and set aside to cool.

6 In a bowl, beat together the butter and sugar until pale and fluffy. Gradually beat in the eggs, alternately with the ground almonds and flour. Finally, fold in the cooled melted chocolate and crushed amaretti biscuits.

7 Spoon about one third of the mixture over the base of the pastry case. Spoon the cherries evenly over the surface, then cover with the remaining filling, spreading it carefully. Sprinkle the almonds over the top. Bake in the oven for about 1 hour until the tart forms a thin crust on top; it should be quite soft underneath.

8 Leave to stand for about 10 minutes, then carefully remove the flan from the tin. Serve warm, dusted with icing sugar.

italian ricotta tart

This decadent tart is an adaptation of the traditional Italian *gran pastiera* tart. Containing arborio rice rather than wheat, it has a delicate orange and cinnamon flavour.

Serves 6-8
Preparation time: 50 minutes, plus chilling
Cooking time: 1 hour
715-535 cals per serving

FOR THE PASTRY:
250g (9oz) plain white flour
100g (3½oz) chilled butter, diced
100g (3½oz) icing sugar, sifted
grated rind of 1 orange
1 egg yolk
1.25ml (¼ tsp) vanilla extract

FOR THE FILLING:
75g (3oz) arborio or carnaroli (risotto) rice
750ml (1¼ pints) milk
15g (½oz) butter
50ml (2fl oz) brandy
30ml (2 tbsp) orange flower water
grated rind and juice of 1 orange
75g (3oz) raisins
2.5ml (½ tsp) ground cinnamon
1 vanilla pod, split
500g (1lb 2oz) ricotta cheese
125g (4oz) caster sugar
2 eggs, separated

TO SERVE:
Icing sugar, for dusting
caramelised oranges (optional, see right)

1 To make the pastry, put the flour, butter, icing sugar and orange rind in a food processor and whizz until the mixture resembles coarse crumbs. Add the egg yolk, vanilla and a few drops of cold water and pulse to a dough. Wrap in cling film and chill for 30 minutes.

2 Roll out two thirds of the pastry on a lightly floured surface and use to line a deep 23cm (9 inch) loose-based fluted flan tin. Prick the base and line with greaseproof paper and baking beans. Bake blind at 200°C/fan oven 190°C (400°F) Mark 6 for 15 minutes. Remove paper and beans and bake for a further 5-10 minutes until the base is cooked.

3 Meanwhile, make the filling. Put the rice in a saucepan with 600ml (1 pint) milk. Add the butter, brandy, orange flower water, orange rind and juice, raisins, cinnamon and vanilla pod. Bring slowly to the boil and simmer, stirring occasionally, for 20 minutes or until the rice is cooked and creamy. Take off the heat and stir in the remaining milk; remove the vanilla pod.

4 Beat the ricotta cheese, caster sugar and egg yolks together in a bowl until light and fluffy, then fold into the rice.

5 Whisk the egg whites in a clean bowl to stiff peaks, then gently fold into the rice and ricotta mixture. Spoon the filling into the pastry case and level the surface.

6 Roll out the remaining pastry, cut into 5mm (¼ inch) strips and arrange in a lattice on top of the tart. Bake at 180°C/fan oven 170°C (350°F) Mark 4 for 20 minutes, then increase the temperature to 190°C/fan oven 180°C (375°F) Mark 5 and cook for a further 15 minutes. The pastry should be golden and the filling just set. Leave to cool slightly in the tin for 10-15 minutes, then carefully remove.

7 Dust the tart with icing sugar and serve warm, with caramelised oranges if you like.

caramelised oranges

Pare strips of zest from 1 orange, using a citrus zester. Peel and thinly slice 3 oranges, discarding all white pith. Dissolve 175g (6oz) sugar in 600ml (1 pint) water in a heavy-based pan over a low heat. Increase the heat and boil steadily for 5 minutes. Add the orange slices and zest strips. Bring to the boil, then simmer gently for 15 minutes. Transfer the orange slices and zest to a bowl with a slotted spoon. Cook the syrup for a further 20 minutes or until pale golden. Pour over the fruit and allow to cool.

caramelised citrus tart with dark berry ice

Crisp, melt-in-the-mouth pastry filled with silky lime custard and served with a delicious dark berry sorbet – a sensational dessert for a special occasion.

Serves 8
Preparation time: 50 minutes, plus freezing sorbet
Cooking time: 1 hour 50 minutes
875 cals per serving

FOR THE PASTRY:
250g (9oz) plain white flour, sifted
100g (3½oz) butter, chilled and diced
100g (3½oz) icing sugar, sifted
1 egg, lightly beaten
1 egg white, lightly beaten

FOR THE FILLING:
finely grated rind of 4 limes
juice of 6 limes
juice of 2 lemons
8 medium eggs
200g (7oz) caster sugar
600ml (1 pint) double cream

FOR THE DARK BERRY ICE:
75g (3oz) caster sugar
500g (1.1lb) frozen mixed berries (strawberries, raspberries, blackberries etc)

FOR THE CANDIED LIMES:
2 limes, frozen for 2 hours
125g (4oz) granulated sugar

FOR THE CARAMELISED TOPPING:
icing sugar, for dusting
grated lime rind, to decorate

1 First make the berry ice. Put the sugar and 100ml (3½fl oz) water in a small pan and dissolve over a low heat. Put the berries in a food processor, pour on the hot syrup and whizz to a purée. Freeze, either in an ice-cream maker according to the manufacturer's instructions, or in a freezer container beating at hourly intervals until the sorbet is frozen, to prevent ice crystals forming and ensure an even-textured result.

2 To make the pastry, place the flour, butter and icing sugar in a food processor and process until the mixture forms fine crumbs.

3 Add the beaten whole egg and process briefly, adding a few drops of chilled water if necessary for the dough to come together in a ball. Wrap the dough in cling film and chill for at least 30 minutes.

4 Roll out the pastry on a lightly floured surface to a 30cm (12 inch) circle and use to line a 5cm (2 inch) deep, 20cm (8 inch) loose-based flan tin. Chill for 20 minutes. Line with greaseproof paper and baking beans and bake blind at 200°C/fan oven 190°C (400°F) Mark 6 for 15 minutes. Remove paper and beans. Return to the oven for 10-15 minutes, then brush the inside of the pastry case with beaten egg white to seal; return to the oven for 2-3 minutes.

5 To make the filling, measure the citrus juice: you should have 175ml (6fl oz) in total. In a large bowl, whisk the eggs gently for 30 seconds, then add the sugar and cream and whisk until evenly combined. Finally, whisk in the lemon and lime juice with the grated lime rind. The mixture will thicken suddenly at this point – don't be alarmed!

6 Pour the filling into the cooled pastry case. Bake at 150°C/fan oven 140°C (300°F) Mark 2 for 1 hour or until just set. Leave to cool in the tin for 20 minutes (see note), then unmould.

7 To make the candied limes, cut the limes into very thin slices using a sharp, serrated knife. Put the sugar and 100ml (3½fl oz) water in a heavy-based pan and dissolve over a low heat, then add the lime slices. Poach for 15 minutes then drain, reserving the syrup. Set aside until cool.

8 To caramelise the surface, cut the tart into 8 slices and place on a baking sheet. Chill for 1 hour in the freezer. Cover the pastry edges with foil to prevent them burning. Dust each slice liberally with sifted icing sugar and place under a hot grill for 2-3 minutes until the icing sugar caramelises. Serve with the sorbet and lime slices, sprinkled with lime rind and drizzled with the reserved lime syrup.

Note The set lime custard might crack slightly but this won't be apparent once the surface is caramelised. To reduce the risk of cracking, cover the surface with a round of non-stick baking parchment, cut to fit exactly. Remove the paper when the tart is completely cool.

crème fraîche crèmets with red fruit sauce

A delicate blend of crème fraîche and creamy mascarpone set in a pool of tart berry sauce.

Serves 6
Preparation time: 20 minutes, plus draining
Cooking time: 3-5 minutes
370 cals per serving

300ml (½ pint) crème fraîche
225g (8oz) mascarpone, or cream cheese
30ml (2 tbsp) caster sugar
2 egg whites
FOR THE RED FRUIT SAUCE:
25g (1oz) blackcurrants
50g (2oz) redcurrants
50g (2oz) caster sugar
125g (4oz) raspberries
TO DECORATE:
4 mint sprigs
icing sugar, for dusting (optional)

1 Line six 150ml (¼ pint) perforated moulds with muslin. Place the crème fraîche, mascarpone and sugar in a large bowl and beat until smooth and light.
2 In a clean bowl, whisk the egg whites until holding soft peaks, then fold into the crème fraîche mixture.
3 Spoon the mixture into the muslin-lined moulds; place on a tray. Leave to drain in a cool place for at least 8 hours, or overnight.
4 To make the sauce, place the black and red currants in a small pan with the sugar, and cook over a low heat for 3-5 minutes until just soft. Press the raspberries through a fine sieve into a bowl, then stir in the black and red currant mixture. Leave to cool.
5 To serve, turn out the crèmets on to plates and spoon around the red fruit sauce. Serve at once, decorated with mint sprigs. Dust with a little icing sugar, if desired.

Note Special heart-shaped moulds with draining holes are available from kitchen shops. Shallow 200ml (7fl oz) crème fraîche pots make good substitutes; puncture 8 holes in the base of each one with a skewer.

maple and walnut mille feuille

Crisp layers of filo pastry interleaved with vanilla pastry cream, walnuts, pistachios, dates and maple syrup. Assemble within 2 hours of serving.

Serves 8
Preparation time: 30 minutes, plus chilling
Cooking time: 6-8 minutes
455 cals per serving

4 filo pastry sheets, about 50x28cm (20x11 inch)
25g (1oz) unsalted butter, melted
FOR THE FILLING:
3 egg yolks
50g (2oz) caster sugar
5ml (1 tsp) vanilla extract
60ml (4 tbsp) cornflour
pinch of freshly grated nutmeg
300ml (½ pint) milk
150ml (¼ pint) double cream
50g (2oz) pistachio nuts
150g (5oz) broken walnuts, finely chopped
75g (3oz) dried dates or figs, finely chopped
pinch of ground cloves
125ml (4fl oz) maple syrup
TO FINISH:
icing sugar, for dusting

1 Cut each filo sheet widthways into 3 rectangles. Arrange 3 rectangles on lightly greased baking sheets, crumpling to make slightly narrower rectangles. Sprinkle with a little melted butter. Top each with another rectangle, again crumpling slightly and sprinkling with more butter. Repeat with the remaining rectangles.
2 Bake at 200°C/fan oven 190°C (400°F) Mark 6 for 6-8 minutes until golden. Cool on the baking sheets.
3 For the filling, beat the egg yolks with the sugar, vanilla, cornflour, nutmeg and a little of the milk. Put the remaining milk and cream in a heavy-based saucepan and bring to the boil. Pour over the yolk mixture, beating well. Return to the pan and cook over a low heat, stirring, until thickened enough to coat the back of the wooden spoon. Pour into a bowl, cover the surface with a disc of damp greaseproof paper and leave to cool.

4 Put the pistachio nuts in a small bowl, cover with boiling water, leave for 3 minutes, then drain. Rub the nuts between sheets of kitchen paper to remove the skins, then chop finely. Mix the pistachios, walnuts, dates or figs and cloves together in a bowl with all but 30ml (2 tbsp) of the maple syrup.

5 Lay one filo layer on a serving plate and sprinkle with 15ml (1 tbsp) syrup. Spoon over half the walnut mixture, then half of the pastry cream. Repeat these layers and top with the remaining filo. Refrigerate until needed.

6 Dust generously with icing sugar and cut into slices to serve.

orange and chocolate cheesecake

This velvety orange and vanilla cheesecake tops a melt-in-the-mouth chocolate biscuit. It freezes brilliantly and is perfect for a special occasion.

Serves 12
Preparation time: 45 minutes, plus cooling
Cooking time: 2 hours 10 minutes
Suitable for freezing (stage 5)
820 cals per serving

FOR THE BASE:
250g (9oz) plain white flour
150g (5oz) muscovado sugar
45ml (3 tbsp) cocoa powder
225g (8oz) chilled butter, cut into pieces
FOR THE FILLING:
finely grated rind and juice of 2 oranges
4 x 200g (7oz) tubs cream cheese
250g (9oz) tub mascarpone
4 eggs
225g (8oz) caster sugar
30ml (2 tbsp) cornflour
2.5ml (½ tsp) vanilla extract
1 vanilla pod, split
TO DECORATE:
3-4 large oranges
150g (5oz) kumquats, sliced and deseeded
2 passion fruit
50g (2oz) dark chocolate

1 Lightly grease and base-line a 23cm (9 inch) spring-release cake tin. Put the flour, muscovado sugar, cocoa powder and 175g (6oz) of the butter in a food processor and process briefly until the mixture resembles fine breadcrumbs. Melt the remaining butter, pour into the processor and pulse until the mixture comes together.

2 Press the mixture evenly on to the base of the prepared tin, using the back of a metal spoon. Bake at 180°C/fan oven 170°C (350°F) Mark 4 for 35-40 minutes or until lightly puffed; don't allow the biscuit to overbrown, or it will have a bitter flavour. Allow to cool. Reduce the oven setting to 150°C/fan oven 140°C (300°F) Mark 2.

3 Meanwhile, make the filling. Measure the orange juice; you'll need about 150ml (¼ pint). Put the cream cheese, mascarpone, eggs, sugar, cornflour, grated orange rind and vanilla extract into a large bowl. Using a hand whisk, beat well until the mixture is smooth and evenly combined.

4 Scrape the seeds from the vanilla pod into the cheese mixture. Beat in the orange juice and continue whisking until evenly blended.

5 Pour the mixture over the cooled biscuit base. Bake for about 1½ hours or until pale golden brown, slightly risen and just set around the edge (the middle should still be wobbly; it will set as it cools). Leave the cheesecake to cool inside the switched-off oven for about 1 hour. Remove and allow to cool completely.

6 Just before serving, unclip the tin and transfer the cheesecake to a plate. To decorate, peel and segment the oranges, discarding all white pith and pips. Arrange the orange segments and kumquat slices on top of the cheesecake. Scoop the seeds and pulp from the passion fruit and drizzle over the citrus fruit. Using a potato peeler, shave curls from the chocolate and scatter over the top of the cheesecake to decorate.

Note If you are making the cheesecake ahead, keep it in a cool place rather than the fridge. Over-chilling tends to make the texture too firm.

raspberry and lemon bavarois

Serves 8-10
Preparation time: 1 hour, plus chilling
Cooking time: 25 minutes
395-320 cals per serving

FOR THE SPONGE BASE:
2 eggs, beaten
50g (2oz) caster sugar
50g (2oz) plain flour, sifted
FOR THE LEMON BAVAROIS:
450ml (¾ pint) milk
grated rind and juice of 2 lemons
1 vanilla pod, split and seeds extracted
5 egg yolks
150g (5oz) caster sugar
20ml (4 tsp) powdered gelatine
300ml (½ pint) whipping cream
225g (8oz) raspberries
FOR THE RASPBERRY SAUCE:
225g (8oz) raspberries
15ml (1 tbsp) lemon juice
25-50g (1-2oz) icing sugar, to taste
TO DECORATE:
mint sprigs

1 For the sponge, grease and line a 23cm (9 inch) springform cake tin. Whisk the eggs and sugar together in a bowl set over a pan of simmering water until pale and doubled in volume. Off the heat, fold in the flour.

2 Pour into the cake tin and bake at 180°C/fan oven 170°C (350°F) Mark 4 for 25 minutes until risen and firm to the touch. Leave in the tin for 10 minutes, then turn on to a wire rack to cool.

3 Grease and line the side of a 20cm (8 inch) springform tin. Trim the edges of the cooled sponge slightly, then press on to the base of the smaller tin.

4 For the bavarois, put the milk, lemon rind and vanilla seeds into a saucepan and slowly bring to the boil. Meanwhile, beat the egg yolks and sugar together in a bowl until pale, then whisk in the hot milk. Return to the pan and cook, stirring, over a low heat, until thick enough to lightly coat the back of the spoon.

5 Soften the gelatine in 60ml (4 tbsp) water, then stand the bowl over a pan of simmering water until the gelatine is dissolved. Mix in a little custard, then stir back into the rest. Stir in the lemon juice. Let cool slightly.

6 Whip the cream in a bowl until it holds its shape; fold into the custard. Stand the bowl over a basin of iced water and cool until on the point of setting, stirring occasionally.

7 Scatter most of the raspberries over the sponge, reserving a few for decoration. Pour on the custard and chill for 4 hours until firm.

8 For the sauce, purée the raspberries and lemon juice together in a blender or food processor, then pass through a sieve to remove the pips. Stir in the icing sugar.

9 To serve, carefully unmould the bavarois on to a plate. Decorate with the reserved raspberries and mint sprigs. Serve with the raspberry sauce.

tropical lemon mousse

These tangy lemon mousses make a refreshing finale to a special dinner party.

Serves 6
Preparation time: 45 minutes, plus freezing
Cooking time: 15 minutes
Suitable for freezing (stage 5)
335 cals per serving

10ml (2 tsp) powdered gelatine
pared zest of 2 lemons
175ml (6fl oz) lemon juice
120ml (4fl oz) double cream
5 medium eggs, separated
175g (6oz) caster sugar
20g (¾oz) plain flour
FOR THE STRAWBERRY SAUCE:
225g (8oz) strawberries
30-45ml (2-3 tbsp) icing sugar
TO SERVE:
1 small pineapple, peeled, cored and sliced
6-8 kiwi fruit, peeled and thickly sliced
few strawberries and mint sprigs, to decorate
icing sugar, for dusting

1 Grease six 200ml (7fl oz) ramekins or other individual moulds. Spoon 45ml (3 tbsp) cold water into a bowl and sprinkle on the gelatine; leave to soften. Place the lemon zest, lemon juice and double cream in a saucepan, slowly bring to the boil, then remove from the heat and set aside to infuse.

2 In a bowl, beat the egg yolks and 40g (1½oz) caster sugar together until thick and light, then mix in the flour until smooth. Strain the lemon cream mixture into the bowl. Mix until smooth, then return to the clean saucepan.

3 Cook, stirring, for about 30 seconds until the mixture comes to the boil. Remove from the heat. Add the gelatine and stir until melted. Cover and set aside.

4 Put the remaining caster sugar in a small heavy-based saucepan with 100ml (3½fl oz) water and dissolve over a low heat. Bring to the boil and bubble for 10 minutes or until the temperature registers 117°C (240°F) on a sugar thermometer. When the syrup is almost at the correct temperature, whisk the egg whites until stiff. Pour in the sugar syrup in a steady stream, whisking constantly, and whisk on a low speed until the mixture is cool. Fold the mixture into the custard.

5 Pour the lemon mousse into the ramekins, smooth the tops and chill for 2-3 hours or until set. To make the strawberry sauce, whizz the strawberries and icing sugar in a food processor to a purée, then sieve to remove the seeds.

6 To serve, arrange the pineapple and kiwi fruit on individual plates. Unmould the mousses and set on top of the fruit. Spoon the strawberry sauce around the plate, then decorate with strawberries and mint. Dust with icing sugar.

Variation Half an hour before serving, place the mousses in the freezer to harden. Unmould on to a baking sheet and place under a hot grill until lightly browned. Return to the freezer for 15 minutes if necessary. Serve as above.

syllabub with poached plums

Ripe plums are poached in dessert wine, then topped with a creamy syllabub, which is lightly infused with rosemary for a distinctive flavour.

Serves 8
Preparation time: 25 minutes, plus chilling
Cooking time: 12 minutes
350 cals per serving

40-60g (1½-2½oz) caster sugar (depending on sweetness of plums)
175ml (6fl oz) dessert wine
700g (1½lb) ripe red plums, stoned and quartered
450ml (¾ pint) double cream
2-3 rosemary sprigs

1 Put the sugar and wine in a saucepan and heat gently, stirring until the sugar dissolves. Add the plums, cover and simmer very gently for 5-10 minutes until they are softened but not pulpy. (The poaching time will vary, depending on the texture of the plums).
2 Drain the plums, reserving 200ml (7fl oz) syrup; if necessary make up to this quantity with a little extra wine.
3 Put 150ml (¼ pint) of the cream in a saucepan with the rosemary sprigs and bring almost to the boil. Remove from the heat and leave to infuse for 15 minutes. Spoon the plums into 8 tall serving glasses.
4 Strain the infused cream into a large bowl and add the rest of the cream. Whip until just holding its shape, then slowly whisk in the reserved syrup, until the mixture is thick enough to leave a trail when the whisk is lifted.
5 Spoon the cream over the plums. Chill the syllabubs for at least 2 hours before serving.

sparkling fruit jellies

Small seedless grapes and flavourful fresh raspberries set in a sparkling wine jelly.

Serves 8
Preparation time: 10 minutes, plus chilling
105 cals per serving

75cl (1¼ pint) bottle demi-sec sparkling wine
300ml (½ pint) red grape juice
25ml (5 tsp) powdered gelatine
125g (4oz) small seedless grapes, halved
225g (8oz) raspberries

1 Pour the sparkling wine into a bowl. Put 60ml (4 tbsp) of the grape juice in a small heatproof bowl, sprinkle on the gelatine and leave to soak for 1 minute, then stand the bowl over a pan of simmering water until the gelatine is dissolved. Stir in the remaining grape juice, then stir this mixture into the wine.
2 Divide the grapes and raspberries between 8 stemmed glasses, pour in enough of the wine mixture to cover them and chill until just set.
3 Pour on the remaining wine mixture and chill for a further 3-4 hours until set.

Variations
• Use a dry sparkling wine in place of the demi-sec.
• Use cranberry juice instead of grape juice.
• Replace the raspberries with small strawberries.

dissolving gelatine

Powdered gelatine must be properly dissolved in a little liquid before adding to a mixture. Sprinkle powdered gelatine on to the liquid (rather than add the liquid to the gelatine). Leave to soften for 5-10 minutes until spongy, then stand the bowl over a pan of simmering water until fully dissolved and translucent. Always add dissolved gelatine to a mixture which is at room temperature or warm. If added to a cold mixture, it will set on contact in fine threads and spoil the texture of the dish.

exotic almond jelly with orange salad

This almond-scented soft-set milk jelly – served with a contrasting orange and pomegranate salad – is a far cry from old-fashioned blancmange.

Serves 4
Preparation time: 20 minutes, plus chilling
Cooking time: 5-10 minutes
240 cals per serving

500ml (18fl oz) milk
15ml (1 tbsp) powdered gelatine
25g (1oz) caster sugar
2.5ml (½ tsp) almond extract
FOR THE ORANGE SALAD:
3 oranges
75g (3oz) caster sugar
150ml (¼ pint) water
3 cardamon pods, bruised
juice of lemon
½ pomegranate

1 Pour 150ml (¼ pint) of the milk into a small saucepan, sprinkle over the gelatine and leave to soak for 1 minute. Stir in the sugar and heat very gently until the sugar and gelatine are completely dissolved. Pour into 4 dampened 200ml (7fl oz) individual moulds and chill for several hours until set.

2 For the fruit salad, finely pare the zest from 1 orange, using a zester or potato peeler, then cut into thin julienne strips. Halve the orange and squeeze the juice.

3 Put the orange juice and zest, sugar and water in a pan. Stir to dissolve the sugar, add the cardamom pods, then boil for 5-10 minutes until reduced and very syrupy. Stir in the lemon juice and remove from the heat.

4 Meanwhile, peel the remaining oranges, removing all pith, and cut into thin slices. Place in a shallow dish and pour over the syrup; set aside to cool. Discard the cardamom pods.

5 Unmould the jellies on to serving plates and surround with the orange salad. Scatter over the pomegranate seeds to serve.

ricotta, ginger and chocolate mousse

Serves 4
Preparation time: 15 minutes, plus chilling
Cooking time: 6-8 minutes
535 cals per serving

225g (8oz) ricotta cheese
25g (1oz) icing sugar
25g (1oz) crystallised stem ginger, finely chopped
50g (2oz) good quality plain chocolate (70% cocoa solids), finely chopped
200ml (7fl oz) double cream, whipped
2 egg whites
cocoa powder, for dusting
FOR THE GINGER ALMOND BISCUITS:
25g (1oz) butter
25g (1oz) caster sugar
25g (1oz) golden syrup
25g (1oz) plain flour, sifted
2.5ml (½ tsp) ground ginger
few drops of almond extract
15g (½oz) flaked almonds

1 Line four 200ml (7fl oz) individual pudding basins or similar moulds with a layer of muslin.

2 Press the ricotta through a fine sieve into a bowl and beat in the icing sugar, ginger and chocolate. Fold in the whipped cream. Whisk the egg whites in a clean bowl until soft peaks form, then fold in.

3 Spoon the mixture into the moulds; level the surface. Cover and chill in the refrigerator for 3-4 hours.

4 For the biscuits, melt the butter, sugar and syrup together in a pan over a low heat. Off the heat, beat in the flour, ginger and almond extract. Finally stir in the flaked almonds.

5 Drop four teaspoonfuls of the biscuit mixture on to a baking sheet lined with oiled baking parchment, spacing them well apart to allow for spreading. Bake at 180°C/fan oven 170°C (350°F) Mark 4 for 6-8 minutes until lightly golden. Leave for a few seconds, then carefully lift off and transfer to a wire rack to cool. Repeat with the remaining mixture.

6 To serve, unmould the mousses on to plates and dust with cocoa powder. Serve with the ginger almond biscuits.

honey mousse with pepper biscuits

For optimum flavour, use a good quality fragrant honey for these individual mousses, such as acacia or orange blossom.

Serves 4-6
Preparation time: 15 minutes, plus chilling
Cooking time: 4-5 minutes
560-375 cals per serving

10ml (2 tsp) powdered gelatine
2 large eggs, separated
25g (1oz) caster sugar
50g (2oz) thin honey
juice of ½ lemon
300ml (½ pint) double cream
FOR THE PEPPER BISCUITS:
1 egg white
pinch of salt
50g (2oz) caster sugar
25g (1oz) plain flour
25g (1oz) unsalted butter, melted
1.25ml (¼ tsp) ground black pepper

1 Put 45ml (3 tbsp) water into a small pan, sprinkle on the gelatine and leave to soak for 1 minute, then heat gently until dissolved.
2 Whisk the egg yolks, sugar, honey and lemon juice together in a bowl until pale and creamy. Whip the cream until it just holds its shape, then fold into the honey mixture. Stir a little of this mixture into the gelatine, then fold this back into the mousse.
3 Whisk the egg whites in a clean bowl until standing in peaks, then fold into the honey cream. Spoon into individual serving dishes and chill for 2 hours until firm.
4 For the biscuits, in a bowl whisk together the egg white, salt and sugar, then beat in the flour, butter and pepper. Drop 2 heaped teaspoonfuls of the batter on to an oiled non-stick baking sheet, spacing them well apart and spread into rounds, about 10 cm (4 inches) in diameter. Bake at 200°C/fan oven 190°C (400°F) Mark 6 for 4-5 minutes until golden at the edges. Immediately lift off and curl over a rolling pin. Leave until set, then carefully remove. Repeat to make 12.
5 Serve the mousses with the biscuits.

chocolate, prune and armagnac mousse

Look out for Agen prunes from France for this divine mousse – they have a particularly fine flavour. Good quality chocolate is essential!

Serves 6
Preparation time: 20 minutes, plus soaking and chilling
295 cals per serving

50g (2oz) pitted prunes
50ml (2fl oz) Armagnac
125g (4oz) good quality plain chocolate (minimum 70% cocoa solids)
1 large egg, separated
25g (1oz) caster sugar
200ml (7fl oz) whipping cream
ground cinnamon, for sprinkling

1 Put the prunes into a bowl and pour on the Armagnac; set aside to soak for at least 2 hours until the prunes have absorbed most of the liquid and doubled in size. Transfer the prunes and liquid to a blender or food processor and work to a smooth purée.
2 Melt the chocolate in a small heatproof bowl over a pan of barely simmering water; stir until smooth and remove from the heat.
3 Beat the egg yolk and sugar together in a bowl until pale, then stir in the melted chocolate and prune mixture.
4 Whip the cream in a bowl until it just holds its shape, then fold into the prune mixture. Whisk the egg white in a clean bowl until firm peaks form, then fold into the mousse until evenly incorporated.
5 Spoon into small pots or small ramekins and chill in the refrigerator for 2 hours before serving, with dessert biscuits.

panna cotta with balsamic strawberries

This classic Italian dessert is soft set with a wonderful creamy texture. Strawberries in a balsamic syrup are the perfect foil.

Serves 6
Preparation time: 10 minutes, plus chilling
Cooking time: 5 minutes
520 cals per serving

600ml (1 pint) double cream
1 vanilla pod, split and seeds extracted
pared zest of 1 lemon
50g (2oz) caster sugar
30ml (2 tbsp) amaretto di Saronno liqueur
10ml (2 tsp) powdered gelatine
FOR THE BALSAMIC STRAWBERRIES:
350g (12oz) strawberries, halved
60ml (2fl oz) light red wine, such as Fleurie
30ml (2 tbsp) balsamic vinegar
15ml (1 tbsp) thin honey

1 Put 450ml (¾ pint) of the cream in a heavy-based pan with the seeds from the vanilla pod, lemon zest and sugar. Slowly bring to the boil, then strain into a bowl.
2 Put the liqueur in a small heatproof bowl, sprinkle on the gelatine and leave until spongy, then stand the bowl over a pan of simmering water until the gelatine is dissolved. Stir a little of the cream into the gelatine mixture, then stir back into the rest of the cream; leave to cool.
3 Whip the remaining cream in a bowl until soft peaks form and fold into the cooled cream. Divide the mixture between 6 individual 150ml (5fl oz) moulds and chill for several hours until just set.
4 Put the strawberries in a pan with the wine, vinegar and honey and heat gently for 1 minute to soften the strawberries. Using a slotted spoon, transfer the strawberries to a bowl, then boil the liquid rapidly for 3-4 minutes until syrupy. Let cool slightly, then pour over the strawberries.
5 To unmould, dip the moulds briefly in hot water, then turn the panna cotta out on to individual plates and serve at once, with the strawberries.

crema catalana

This caramel-topped creamy custard, infused with lemon and fennel, is a speciality from Catalonia in Spain. The accompanying fruit can be macerated in dessert wine rather than cassis if preferred.

Serves 6
Preparation time: 10 minutes, plus infusing and
    overnight chilling
Cooking time: 10 minutes
Suitable for freezing (stage 4)
630 cals per serving

450ml (¾ pint) milk
200ml (7fl oz) double cream
pared zest of 1 lemon
5ml (1 tsp) fennel seeds, crushed
6 egg yolks
175g (6oz) caster sugar
30ml (2 tbsp) cornflour
1.25ml (¼ tsp) ground cinnamon
FOR THE BERRIES IN CASSIS:
450g (1lb) strawberries
200g (7oz) blueberries
20ml (4 tsp) caster sugar
60ml (1 tbsp) crème de cassis
juice of ½ lemon

1 Place the milk, cream, lemon zest and crushed fennel in a heavy-based saucepan. Heat to boiling point, then set aside to infuse for 30 minutes.
2 Beat the egg yolks, 125g (4oz) of the sugar and the cornflour together in a small bowl until light and fluffy.
3 Strain the infused milk on to the egg yolk mixture, a little at a time, stirring constantly. Pour back into the clean saucepan. Cook over a low heat, stirring constantly, until the cream thickens and almost comes to the boil; this will take about 6-8 minutes. Immediately, remove from the heat.
4 Pour into six 150ml (¼ pint) ramekins or custard pots. Allow to cool, then cover loosely with foil and place in the fridge overnight to set.
5 Halve or quarter the strawberries, depending on size and place in a bowl with the blueberries. Sprinkle with the caster sugar, cassis and lemon juice. Toss together, then cover and chill.

6 Preheat grill until very hot. Mix the remaining 50g (2oz) sugar with the cinnamon and sprinkle evenly over the custards. Place under the hot grill until the sugar has caramelised. Allow to stand for at least 20 minutes before serving, with the macerated fruit.

summer fruit brûlée

A medley of summer fruits concealed under a blanket of whipped cream and yogurt, topped with crisp caramelised sugar. An excellent quick and easy dessert to round off a casual dinner.

Serves 4
Preparation time: 15 minutes, plus standing
Cooking time: 3-4 minutes
280 cals per serving

1 ripe nectarine, halved, stoned and thinly sliced
350 g (12oz) mixed summer berries, such as
    strawberries, blackberries, raspberries and
    redcurrants
30ml (2 tbsp) ruby port
150ml (¼ pint) double cream
125g (4oz) Greek yogurt
few drops of vanilla extract
25g (1oz) demerara sugar

1 Put the nectarine and summer berries in a bowl, add the port and stir to mix. Leave to stand for 1-2 hours if possible. Transfer to a 900 ml (1½ pint) gratin dish.
2 Whip the cream in a bowl until it holds its shape, then fold in the yogurt together with the vanilla extract. Spread the cream mixture over the fruit, to cover completely.
3 Scatter the demerara sugar over the cream and grill under a high heat as close to the heat source as possible for 3-4 minutes until the sugar is golden brown and caramelised. Leave to stand for 5 minutes, then serve.

pistachio praline floating islands

Soft pillows of poached meringue, speckled with pistachio praline and floating on a delicate custard, make an impressive dessert.

Serves 4-6
Preparation time: 30 minutes, plus chilling
Cooking time: 18-20 minutes
520-350 cals per serving

FOR THE PRALINE:
50g (2oz) unskinned pistachio nuts
50g (2oz) caster sugar
FOR THE FLOATING ISLANDS:
2 eggs, separated
150g (5oz) caster sugar
300ml (½ pint) single cream
300ml (½ pint) milk

1 To make the praline, put the pistachios and sugar in a small heavy-based pan over a low heat and stir until the sugar melts and begins to caramelise. Cook until deep brown in colour, then immediately pour on to an oiled baking sheet. Leave to cool and harden, then grind to a coarse powder in a food processor or blender.
2 To make the meringue, whisk the egg whites in a bowl to soft peaks. Gradually whisk in 75g (3oz) of the caster sugar until the mixture is very stiff and shiny. Quickly and carefully fold in all but 30ml (2 tbsp) of the praline.
3 Place the cream, milk and remaining sugar in a medium saucepan and bring to a gentle simmer. Spoon 5-6 small rounds of meringue mixture into the pan and cook gently for 2-3 minutes, or until they have doubled in size and are quite firm to the touch. Remove with a slotted spoon and drain on kitchen paper. Repeat with the remaining mixture to make 12-18 meringues, depending on size.
4 Whisk the egg yolks into the poaching liquid. Heat gently, stirring all the time, until the custard thickens slightly to the consistency of double cream; do not boil.
5 Strain custard into a serving dish, or individual dishes, and position the meringues on top. Cool, then chill for 30 minutes, or up to 2-3 hours. Sprinkle with the reserved praline to serve.

raspberry and redcurrant pavlova

A medley of soft fruits nestling in whipped cream on a luscious deep, mallowy meringue.

Serves 8
Preparation time: 30 minutes
Cooking time: 1¼-1½ hours
220 cals per serving

3 egg whites
175g (6oz) caster sugar
5ml (1 tsp) cornflour, sifted
5ml (1 tsp) white wine vinegar
2.5ml (½ tsp) vanilla extract
FOR THE FILLING:
300ml (½ pint) double cream or half Greek yogurt and half double cream
450g (1lb) mixed soft fruits, such as strawberries, raspberries and redcurrants
TO DECORATE:
chocolate curls (see page 293)

1 Line a baking sheet with non-stick baking parchment and draw a 23cm (9 inch) circle on the paper; turn the paper over.
2 For the meringue, whisk the egg whites in a bowl until stiff. Whisk in the sugar a third at a time, whisking well between each addition until stiff and very shiny. Fold in the cornflour, vinegar and vanilla extract.
3 Pile the meringue on to the marked circle, making a substantial hollow in the centre.
4 Bake at 130°C/fan oven 120°C (250°F) Mark ½ for 1¼-1½ hours or until slightly browned and dry but a little soft in the centre; press lightly with a finger to test. Leave to cool slightly, then peel off paper. At this stage the meringue will probably crack and sink a little.
5 To make the filling, whip the cream until thick and, if using, mix with the yogurt; spoon on top of the Pavlova. Scatter the soft fruits on top and decorate with chocolate curls.

brandied prune ice cream

Serve this wonderfully indulgent ice cream in brandy snap baskets.

Serves 8
Preparation time: 40 minutes, plus soaking and freezing
Cooking time: 20 minutes
310 cals per serving

125g (4oz) pitted ready-to-eat prunes, roughly
    chopped
50g (2oz) large seedless raisins
90ml (6 tbsp) brandy
5 egg yolks
75g (3oz) caster sugar
300ml (½ pint) milk
300ml (½ pint) double cream
1 vanilla pod, split
TO SERVE:
brandy snap baskets (page 371, optional)
chopped prunes
marrons glacés (optional)
toasted pecans and almonds

1 Put the prunes and raisins in a bowl with the brandy. Cover and leave to soak for at least 6 hours or overnight.
2 Beat the egg yolks and sugar together in a bowl. Put the milk, cream and vanilla pod in a large, heavy-based saucepan and slowly bring to the boil, then gradually pour on to the egg yolk mixture. Return to the saucepan and cook, stirring, over a very low heat for about 10 minutes or until the custard begins to thicken; do not boil.
3 Remove the custard from the heat and immediately pour through a fine sieve into a cold bowl. Cool quickly, then freeze. Once the mixture has started to freeze and thicken, stir in the marinated prunes and raisins, together with any liquid, then return to the freezer.
4 Scoop the ice cream into serving dishes or brandy snap baskets. Decorate with prunes, marrons glacés if available, toasted pecans and almonds. Serve immediately.

passion fruit and coconut meringue gâteau

Crisp, light coconut meringue rounds layered with a fragrant passion fruit cream.

Serves 10
Preparation time: 25 minutes, plus cooling
Cooking time: 1¼ hours
320 cals per serving

4 egg whites
225g (8oz) caster sugar
10ml (2 tsp) vanilla extract
50g (2oz) desiccated coconut
FOR THE FILLING:
12 passion fruit
60ml (4 tbsp) white rum
250g (9oz) Greek yogurt
300ml (½ pint) double cream
30ml (2 tbsp) icing sugar
TO DECORATE:
passion fruit quarters
lychees or mango slices
toasted coconut shavings

1 Line 3 baking sheets with non-stick baking parchment, then draw a 23cm (9 inch) circle on each; invert the paper.
2 Whisk the egg whites in a bowl until stiff. Gradually beat in the sugar, a tablespoonful at a time, beating well after each addition, until the meringue is stiff and glossy. Fold in the vanilla extract and coconut.
3 Spoon on to the marked circles, peaking the meringue around the edges. Bake at 140°C (275°F) Mark 1 for about 1¼ hours until crisp, switching the baking sheets halfway through to ensure even cooking. Leave to cool.
4 Halve 8 passion fruit and scoop the pulp into a sieve over a bowl. Press the juice into the bowl and stir in the rum and yogurt. Whip the cream and icing sugar until peaking; fold in the yogurt.
5 Place one meringue on a plate and spread with half of the cream mixture. Scoop the seeds from 2 passion fruit around edge of cream. Add a second meringue round, the remaining cream and scooped passion fruit. Top with the final meringue. Decorate with passion fruit, lychees or mango and coconut shavings to serve.

mochacino ice cream

Serves 6-8
Preparation time: 20 minutes
775-580 cals per serving

600ml (1 pint) double cream
300ml (½ pint) milk
6 egg yolks
50g (2oz) caster sugar
150ml (¼ pint) strong espresso coffee, cooled
50g (2oz) chocolate chips
FOR THE CHOCOLATE SAUCE:
75g (3oz) plain chocolate
few drops of vanilla extract
60ml (2fl oz) water
TO FINISH:
150ml (¼ pint) whipping cream
ground cinnamon, for dusting

1 Heat the cream and milk together in a heavy-based pan just to the boil. Meanwhile, beat the egg yolks and sugar together in a bowl until pale. Pour on the hot cream mixture, whisking. Return to the pan and heat gently, stirring until the custard thickens enough to lightly coat the back of a wooden spoon.

2 Strain the custard into a freezerproof container, stir in the coffee and set aside to cool. When cold, stir in the chocolate chips.

3 Freeze the mixture in an ice-cream maker according to the manufacturer's directions, or in a freezer container, beating at hourly intervals until frozen, to ensure an even-textured result.

4 About 30 minutes before serving, transfer the ice cream to the refrigerator to soften and make the sauce. Put the chocolate, vanilla extract and water in a saucepan and heat gently until the chocolate is melted. Bring to the boil and let bubble for a few minutes until thickened; set aside to cool slightly.

5 Whip the cream in a bowl until almost holding its shape. Scoop the ice cream into individual bowls. Top with a little whipped cream, then pour on the chocolate sauce and finish with a dusting of cinnamon. Serve at once.

baking

Moist, fruity muffins, gooey
traybakes, original cakes and
a wonderful selection of
breads to fill your kitchen
with enticing aromas

cranberry muffins

Bursting with tangy cranberries, these moist muffins are perfect for a winter brunch.

Makes 12
Preparation time: 15 minutes, plus cooling
Cooking time: 15-18 minutes
Suitable for freezing
190 cals per muffin

125g (4oz) fresh or frozen cranberries (see note)
25g (1oz) icing sugar, sifted
300g (10oz) plain white flour
10ml (2 tsp) baking powder
150g (5oz) light muscovado sugar
grated rind of 1 large orange
1 egg
5ml (1 tsp) vanilla extract
250ml (8fl oz) milk
50g (2oz) unsalted butter, melted
icing sugar, for dusting

1 Line a 12-hole muffin or deep bun tin tray with paper muffin cases (or simply grease if using a non-stick tray). Toss the cranberries in the icing sugar to coat.
2 Sift the flour and baking powder together into a bowl. Stir in the sugar, orange rind and cranberries.
3 In another bowl, beat together the egg, vanilla, milk and butter. Add to the dry ingredients and stir until the ingredients are just mixed together; do not over-mix.
4 Spoon into the prepared muffin tins and bake at 200°C/fan oven 190°C (400°F) Mark 6 for 15-18 minutes until risen and just firm. Transfer to a wire rack and leave to cool.
5 Serve the muffins warm or cold, dusted with icing sugar.

Note If using frozen cranberries, allow to defrost at room temperature and dry thoroughly on kitchen paper before tossing in the icing sugar.

wholemeal banana muffins

High-fibre muffins topped with dried banana chips and walnuts in a sticky orange glaze.

Makes 6
Preparation time: 15 minutes, plus soaking
Cooking time: 20-25 minutes
Suitable for freezing
370 cals per muffin

50g (2oz) raisins
grated rind and juice of 1 orange
125g (4oz) plain wholemeal flour
25g (1oz) wheatgerm
45ml (3 tbsp) caster sugar
10ml (2 tsp) baking powder
pinch of salt
1 egg, beaten
50ml (2fl oz) milk
50ml (2fl oz) sunflower oil
2 ripe bananas, about 225g (8oz) peeled weight
FOR THE TOPPING:
75ml (5 tbsp) orange marmalade
50g (2oz) dried banana chips
50g (2oz) roughly chopped walnuts

1 Line 6 muffin tins with paper muffin cases or grease non-stick muffin tins well. Place the raisins in a bowl, add the orange juice and leave to soak for 1 hour.
2 Mix the flour, wheatgerm, sugar, baking powder, salt and orange rind together in a bowl. Make a well in the centre.
3 In another bowl, combine the egg, milk and oil. Pour into the flour mixture and stir until just mixed. Drain the raisins, reserving 15ml (1 tbsp) juice. Roughly mash the banana and stir into the mixture with the raisins; don't over-mix.
4 Two-thirds fill each muffin case with the mixture. Bake at 200°C/fan oven 190°C (400°F) Mark 6 for 20-25 minutes or until a skewer inserted into the centre comes out clean. Transfer to a wire rack to cool slightly.
5 For the topping, gently heat the orange marmalade with the reserved orange juice until melted. Simmer for 1 minute, then add the banana chips and chopped walnuts. Spoon on top of the muffins. Serve while still warm.

pear and cinnamon buns

A twist on old-fashioned rock buns, these are dotted with dried pears and sultanas, and topped with a sugary lemon glaze after baking.

Makes 14
Preparation time: 10 minutes, plus cooling
Cooking time: About 15 minutes
Suitable for freezing (stage 2)
215 cals per bun

225g (8oz) self-raising white flour
2.5ml (½ tsp) ground cinnamon
125g (4oz) unsalted butter, in pieces
75g (3oz) caster sugar
125g (4oz) dried pears, roughly chopped
150g (5oz) sultanas
1 egg
90ml (3fl oz) milk
finely grated rind of 1 lemon
FOR THE GLAZE:
juice of 1 lemon
50g (2oz) caster sugar
15ml (1 tbsp) preserving sugar or crushed sugar cubes

1 Sift the flour and cinnamon together into a bowl. Rub in the butter, using fingertips, until the mixture resembles fine breadcrumbs. Add the sugar, pears, sultanas, egg, milk and lemon rind; mix to a soft dough.
2 Spoon into about 14 small mounds on a greased large baking sheet. Bake at 190°C/fan oven 180°C (375°F) Mark 5 for about 15 minutes until risen and golden.
3 Meanwhile make the glaze. Heat the lemon juice, sugar and 30ml (2 tbsp) water in a small heavy-based pan until the sugar is dissolved. Bring to the boil and boil for 3 minutes until syrupy.
4 On removing the buns from the oven, spoon on the glaze and sprinkle with the sugar. Transfer to a wire rack to cool.

Note These buns are best eaten within 1-2 days. If frozen, apply the glaze after thawing.

Variation Use a mixture of dried peaches and apricots instead of the pears.

syrupy semolina halva

Makes 10 slices
Preparation time: 30 minutes, plus cooling
Cooking time: 30 minutes
Suitable for freezing (stage 3)
485 cals per slice

125g (4oz) unsalted butter, softened
125g (4oz) light muscovado sugar
2 oranges
2 lemons
30ml (2 tbsp) lemon juice
2 eggs
175g (6oz) semolina
5ml (1 tsp) baking powder
125g (4oz) ground almonds
30ml (2 tbsp) poppy seeds
TO FINISH:
300g (10oz) caster sugar
300ml (½ pint) freshly squeezed orange juice
2 cinnamon sticks, halved

1 Grease and base-line a shallow 23 cm (9 inch) square tin. Grate the rind from 1 orange and 1 lemon.
2 Cream the butter and sugar together until pale and fluffy. Add the orange and lemon rind, lemon juice, eggs, semolina, baking powder, ground almonds and poppy seeds. Beat until well mixed, then turn into the prepared tin; level the surface.
3 Bake at 220°C/fan oven 210°C (425°F) Mark 7 for about 20 minutes until slightly risen and turning golden. Leave to cool in the tin, then peel off the paper and return to the tin.
4 Finely pare the zest from the other orange and lemon in strips using a citrus zester. Cut away all white pith from the oranges and lemons, then slice thinly. Put the sugar in a small heavy-based pan with the orange juice, cinnamon sticks and citrus zest. Heat gently until the sugar dissolves, then bring to the boil and boil for 3 minutes.
5 Remove the citrus zest and cinnamon from the syrup with a slotted spoon; reserve. Pour half of the syrup over the surface of the cake. Scatter the fruit, citrus zest and cinnamon sticks on top.
6 Boil the remaining syrup for about 5 minutes until starting to caramelise. Pour evenly over the fruit. Leave for several hours before cutting. Store in a plastic container for up to 5 days.

sticky orange flapjacks

Nutty sunflower seeds and tangy orange zest add a new dimension to this chewy traybake.

Makes 18
Preparation time: 15 minutes, plus cooling
Cooking time: 25-30 minutes
Suitable for freezing
300 cals per flapjack

2 small oranges
250g (9oz) unsalted butter, in pieces
250g (9oz) caster sugar
175g (6oz) golden syrup
425g (15oz) rolled oats
30ml (2 tbsp) sunflower seeds
45ml (3 tbsp) fine-cut orange marmalade

1 Grease a 28x20cm (11x8 inch) shallow baking tin (or a tin with similar dimensions).
2 Using a citrus zester, finely pare the zest from the oranges in fine strips.
3 Put the orange zest in a large heavy-based saucepan with the butter, sugar and syrup. Stir over a moderate heat until the butter is melted. Remove from the heat and stir in the rolled oats to coat evenly with the syrup mixture.
4 Turn the mixture into the prepared tin, level the surface and sprinkle with the sunflower seeds. Bake at 180°C/fan oven 170°C (350°F) Mark 4 for 25-30 minutes until deep golden around the edges; the mixture will still be very soft in the centre. Leave in the tin until almost cold.
5 Heat the marmalade with 15ml (1 tbsp) water in a small pan until syrupy. Brush this glaze over the flapjack and leave to set.
6 Remove the flapjack from the tin, place on a board and cut into 18 bars. Store in an airtight container for up to 1 week.

Variations

FRUIT AND NUT FLAPJACKS Omit the orange zest, sunflower seeds and marmalade. Add 125g (4oz) luxury mixed dried fruit and 75g (3oz) chopped and toasted mixed nuts with the oats.

PEAR AND CINNAMON FLAPJACKS Omit the orange zest, sunflower seeds and marmalade. Add 5ml (1 tsp) ground cinnamon with the sugar, and 150g (5oz) roughly chopped dried pears with the oats.

cherry chocolate fudge brownies

Deliciously rich, moist brownies dotted with glacé cherries and coated with a kirsch-flavoured chocolate ganache.

Makes 12
Preparation time: 20 minutes, plus cooling
Cooking time: 50 minutes
Suitable for freezing
470 cals per serving

150g (5oz) unsalted butter
200g (7oz) good quality plain chocolate (70% cocoa
    solids)
175g (6oz) caster sugar
10ml (2 tsp) vanilla extract
5 medium eggs
175g (6oz) plain white flour
3.75ml (¾ tsp) baking powder
250g (9oz) glacé cherries, halved
FOR THE GANACHE:
150g (5oz) good quality plain chocolate (70% cocoa
    solids)
30ml (2 tbsp) kirsch
60ml (4 tbsp) double cream
icing sugar mixed with cocoa powder, for dusting

1 Grease and base-line an 18cm (7 inch) square cake tin, 5cm (2 inches) deep. Put the butter and chocolate in a bowl over a pan of simmering water; leave until melted. Remove from the heat and stir until smooth. Allow to cool.

2 Whisk the sugar, vanilla extract and eggs together in a bowl until thick, pale and frothy. Stir in the melted chocolate mixture.

3 Sift the flour and baking powder together over the mixture then lightly fold in, together with the glacé cherries. Pour the mixture into the prepared tin. Bake at 180°C/fan oven 170°C (350°F) Mark 4 for 40 minutes or until just set. Leave to cool slightly in the tin, then transfer to a wire rack.

4 To make the ganache, put the chocolate and kirsch in a heatproof bowl over a pan of simmering water. Once melted, add the cream and 60ml (4 tbsp) water; stir well. Pour the icing over the brownie and leave to set.

5 Cut into squares and dust with icing sugar and cocoa powder. Serve with cream if you like.

almond fudge crumbles

Makes 24
Preparation time: 15 minutes, plus cooling
Cooking time: 12 minutes
Suitable for freezing
130 cals per biscuit

200g (7oz) plain white flour
pinch of salt
2.5ml (½ tsp) bicarbonate of soda
125g (4oz) unsalted butter, in pieces
125g (4oz) light muscovado sugar
1 egg
5ml (1 tsp) almond extract
75g (3oz) flaked almonds, broken into pieces
50g (2oz) vanilla fudge (see note), finely diced
FOR THE TOPPING:
25g (1oz) flaked almonds, lightly crumbled
25g (1oz) vanilla fudge, chopped
icing sugar, for dusting

1 Sift the flour, salt and bicarbonate of soda into a bowl. Rub in the butter, using the fingertips, until the mixture resembles coarse crumbs. Add the sugar, egg, almond extract, flaked almonds and fudge and mix to a fairly firm dough.

2 Turn on to a lightly floured surface and roll into a cylinder, 23cm (9 inches) long. Cut the dough into 24 slices. Place the rounds, slightly apart, on 2 lightly greased baking sheets.

3 For the topping, scatter the crumbled almonds and chopped fudge on top of the biscuits and press down lightly to adhere. Bake at 190°C/fan oven 180°C (375°F) Mark 5 for about 12 minutes until turning golden around the edges.

4 Leave on the baking sheets for 5 minutes, then transfer the biscuits to a wire rack to cool. Store in an airtight tin for up to 1 week. Serve dusted with icing sugar.

Note Either use a slab of vanilla or 'cream' fudge, or individually wrapped sweets.

double chocolate cookies

Chunky, crumbly and rich with chocolate, these delicious biscuits closely resemble home-baked American style cookies.

Makes 18
Preparation time: 15 minutes, plus cooling
Cooking time: 12-15 minutes
Suitable for freezing
215 cals per cookie

125g (4oz) white chocolate
125g (4oz) plain dark chocolate
125g (4oz) unsalted butter, softened
125g (4oz) caster sugar
1 egg
5ml (1 tsp) vanilla extract
125g (4oz) porridge oats
150g (5oz) plain white flour
2.5ml (½ tsp) baking powder

1 Chop the white and plain chocolate into small chunks, no larger than 1cm (½ inch).
2 Cream the butter and sugar together in a bowl until pale and creamy. Add the egg, vanilla extract and oats. Sift in the flour and baking powder and mix until evenly combined. Stir in the chocolate chunks.
3 Place dessertspoonfuls of the mixture on 2 lightly greased baking sheets, spacing well apart. Flatten each one slightly with the back of a fork.
4 Bake at 180°C/fan oven 170°C (350°F) Mark 4 for 12-15 minutes until risen and turning golden. Leave on the baking sheets for 5 minutes, then transfer to a wire rack to cool. Store in an airtight tin for up to 1 week.

Variations

TOASTED PINE NUT COOKIES Cream an extra 25g (1oz) sugar with the butter. Replace the chocolate with 40g (1½oz) toasted pine nuts.

TRIPLE CHOCOLATE COOKIES Replace 15g (½oz) flour with cocoa powder.

cranberry biscuits

These are very easy to make, as the dough is simply cut into slices and baked – no fiddling with cutters, or wastage. Dried cranberries are widely available in supermarkets or you can use other dried fruit instead, such as apricots or sultanas.

Makes 24
Preparation time: 20 minutes, plus chilling
Cooking time: 20 minutes
75 cals per biscuit

125g (4oz) butter, chilled
50g (2oz) caster sugar
25g (1oz) dried cranberries
125g (4oz) plain white flour
75g (3oz) ground rice

1 Put the butter and sugar in a food processor and process until well combined. Add the dried cranberries, flour and ground rice and pulse briefly until the mixture begins to come together.
2 Turn out onto a lightly floured surface and bring the dough together with your hands. Shape into an oblong, measuring about 12x7.5cm (5x3 inches), and approximately 2cm (¾ inch) thick. Wrap in cling film and chill in the refrigerator for about 30 minutes.
3 Unwrap the dough and cut into 3mm (⅛ inch) slices. Place slightly apart on a non-stick baking sheet. Bake at 200°C/fan oven 190°C (400°F) Mark 6 for 8-10 minutes or until lightly golden. Leave to cool before removing from the baking sheet. Store in an airtight tin for up to 4 days.

florentines

These enticing Italian chewy biscuits are rich with fruit and nuts. This version also includes sunflower seeds. After baking, the edges of the florentines are rolled in melted chocolate. As an alternative, spread the chocolate over the backs of the biscuits and mark into wavy lines, using a fork.

Makes 12
Preparation time: 15 minutes, plus cooling
Cooking time: 8-10 minutes
170 cals per biscuit

65g (2½oz) unsalted butter
50g (2oz) caster sugar
30ml (2 tbsp) double cream
25g (1oz) sunflower seeds
20g (¾oz) chopped mixed candied peel
20g (¾oz) sultanas
25g (1oz) glacé cherries, roughly chopped
40g (1½oz) flaked almonds, lightly crushed
15g (½oz) plain white flour
TO FINISH:
125g (4oz) plain dark chocolate, in pieces

1 Melt the butter in a small heavy-based pan. Add the sugar and heat gently until dissolved, then bring to the boil. Take off the heat and stir in the cream, sunflower seeds, candied peel, sultanas, cherries, almonds and flour. Mix well until evenly combined.

2 Placed heaped teaspoonfuls of the mixture on 2 lightly greased baking sheets, spacing well apart to allow plenty of room for spreading.

3 Bake, one sheet at a time, at 180°C/fan oven 170°C (350°F) Mark 4 for about 6-8 minutes until the biscuits have spread considerably and the edges are golden brown.

4 Immediately push the edges into the centre, using a large plain metal biscuit cutter, to create neat rounds. Bake for a further 2 minutes or until deep golden.

4 Leave the florentines on the baking sheet for 2 minutes to firm up slightly, then transfer to a wire rack to cool.

5 Melt the chocolate in a heatproof bowl over a pan of simmering water; stir until smooth.

6 Roll the edges of the biscuits in the chocolate and place on a sheet of non-stick baking parchment until set. Store in an airtight tin.

Note If the biscuits solidify before you've had the time to use the cutter, return to the oven for a further 30 seconds.

Variation Dip the biscuits into melted white chocolate, rather than plain chocolate.

melting chocolate

The most important thing to remember when melting chocolate is to treat it gently. Break it up into small pieces and place it in the top half of a double boiler or in a heatproof bowl over a pan of gently simmering water – the water should not be boiling. Make sure the bowl doesn't touch the water. Heat slowly without stirring until the chocolate is soft, then stir until smooth. Remove the chocolate from the heat once all of it has melted.

- Don't try to hurry up the melting process, and never allow the chocolate to overheat. Avoid letting any moisture or steam come into contact with it, or the chocolate may seize and harden.
- While it is still of pouring consistency, melted chocolate can be combined with other ingredients – but make sure any liquids you mix with it are at a similar temperature. Melted chocolate can be allowed to set and melted again, but each time it is reused it will get thicker. If you do want to re-melt it, mix it with the same amount of fresh chocolate.

brandy snaps

Makes 12-16
Preparation time: 25 minutes, plus cooling
Cooking time: 8-10 minutes
Suitable for freezing
165-125 cals per biscuit

75g (3oz) butter
75g (3oz) caster sugar
45ml (3 tbsp) golden syrup
75g (3oz) plain white flour
5ml (1 tsp) ground ginger
30ml (2 tbsp) brandy
15ml (1 tbsp) lemon juice
150ml (¼ pint) double cream, whipped, to serve
    (optional)

1 Lightly oil several wooden spoon handles.
2 Put the butter, sugar and syrup in a heavy-based
   pan and warm gently until evenly blended. Let
   cool for 2-3 minutes. Sift in the flour and ginger,
   and add the brandy and lemon juice. Mix
   thoroughly until smooth.

3 Taking 15ml (1 tbsp) of mixture at a time, spoon
   on to baking sheets lined with non-stick baking
   parchment, allowing plenty of room for
   spreading, and no more than 3 per baking sheet.
4 Bake, one sheet at a time, at 190°C/fan oven
   180°C (375°F) Mark 5 for 8-10 minutes or until
   golden brown – the texture will be lacy. On
   removing from the oven, leave for about 15
   seconds to firm up slightly, then loosen with a
   palette knife and roll around the spoon handles.
5 Place on a wire rack and leave until set, then
   twist gently to remove and leave to cool
   completely and crisp up. Just before serving, fill
   with whipped cream, if desired, using a piping
   bag fitted with a 1cm (½ inch) nozzle.

Note If biscuits set too hard on the baking sheet
to roll, return to oven for a few moments to soften.

Variation To make brandy snap baskets, bake
heaped tablespoonfuls of the mixture to make
larger rounds. Once cooked, mould over upturned
ramekins to form baskets. Lift off once set. Use as
containers for ices and creamy desserts.

fruited honey teabread

This moist teabread is richly flavoured with tea-soaked dried apricots, prunes and raisins.

Makes 10 slices
Preparation time: 10 minutes, plus overnight soaking and cooling
Cooking time: 1-1¼ hours
Suitable for freezing
320 cals per slice

50g (2oz) ready-to-eat dried apricots, roughly chopped
50g (2oz) ready-to-eat prunes, roughly chopped
225g (8oz) raisins
150g (5oz) dark muscovado sugar
300ml (½ pint) strong black tea, strained
125g (4oz) plain wholemeal flour
125g (4oz) self-raising white flour
5ml (1 tsp) baking powder
5ml (1 tsp) ground cinnamon
75g (3oz) brazil nuts, roughly chopped
2 eggs
125g (4oz) thin honey
extra honey, warmed, to glaze (optional)

1 Mix the apricots, prunes, raisins and sugar together in a bowl. Pour on the tea, cover and leave to soak overnight.
2 Grease and line a 900g (2lb) loaf tin. Sift the flours, baking powder and cinnamon together into a bowl. Add the soaked fruits and liquid, brazil nuts, eggs and honey. Mix well until evenly combined.
3 Turn into the prepared loaf tin and bake at 180°C/fan oven 170°C (350°F) Mark 4 for 1-1¼ hours, or until firm and a skewer inserted into the centre comes out clean, covering loosely with foil after about 20 minutes to prevent overbrowning if necessary.
4 Leave to cool in the tin. Drizzle with a little extra honey to glaze if liked. Store in an airtight container for up to 1 week.

Variation Use roughly chopped walnuts instead of brazil nuts.

apple and ginger teabread

Fresh apples and preserved stem ginger are a perfect partnership here.

Makes 8-10 slices
Preparation time: 20 minutes
Cooking time: 1-1¼ hours
Suitable for freezing
410-330 cals per slice

4 crisp, tart dessert apples, such as Granny Smith's
15ml (1 tbsp) lemon juice
125g (4oz) unsalted butter
75g (3oz) light muscovado sugar
200g (7oz) golden syrup
300g (10oz) self-raising white flour
2.5ml (½ tsp) baking powder
2.5ml (½ tsp) ground cinnamon
2.5ml (½ tsp) ground cloves
1 egg
75g (3oz) preserved stem ginger in syrup, drained and finely chopped
45ml (3 tbsp) golden syrup, warmed, to serve (optional)

1 Grease and line a 900g (2lb) loaf tin. Peel, core and thinly slice the apples and immerse in a bowl of cold water with the lemon juice added to prevent discoloration.
2 Put the butter, sugar and syrup in a saucepan and heat until melted. Allow to cool slightly.
3 Sift the flour, baking powder and spices together into a bowl. Add the syrup mixture and egg; stir until well combined.
4 Thoroughly drain the apple slices on kitchen paper. Add three quarters of them and all but 15ml (1 tbsp) of the chopped ginger to the cake mixture; stir until evenly combined.
5 Turn the mixture into the prepared loaf tin and smooth the surface. Scatter over the reserved apple slices and ginger. Bake at 170°C/fan oven 160°C (325°F) Mark 3 for 1-1¼ hours until just firm and a skewer inserted into the centre comes out clean.
6 Leave in the tin for 15 minutes, then spoon over the syrup. Allow to cool completely before slicing. Eat within 4-5 days.

coconut and cherry loaf

Packed with the tropical flavour of coconut, this scrumptious cake is difficult to resist.

Serves 8
Preparation time: 20 minutes, plus cooling
Cooking time: 50 minutes
Suitable for freezing (stage 3)
410 cals per serving

150g (5oz) unsalted butter, softened
75g (3oz) caster sugar
3 medium eggs, separated
75g (3oz) desiccated coconut
125g (4oz) self-raising white flour, sifted
125g (4oz) glacé cherries, roughly chopped
FOR THE TOPPING:
75g (3oz) strawberry jam, warmed and sieved
75g (3oz) glacé cherries, roughly chopped
TO DECORATE:
50g (2oz) desiccated coconut

1 Grease and base-line a 900g (2lb) loaf tin. Using an electric whisk, beat the butter and sugar together in a bowl until light and fluffy. Add the egg yolks slowly, beating well between each addition. Fold in the coconut, flour and cherries.

2 Whisk the egg whites in a clean bowl until they form soft peaks. Using a large metal spoon, beat one spoonful of the egg white into the cake mix to lighten it, then gently fold in the rest.

3 Pour the mixture into the prepared loaf tin. Bake at 170°C/fan oven 160°C (325°F) Mark 3 for 45-50 minutes, until firm and a skewer inserted into the centre comes out clean, covering the loaf with foil if it appears to be browning too quickly. Leave to cool completely in the tin.

4 For the topping, brush the top of the loaf with the jam, top with the cherries and sprinkle with coconut. Leave to set. Cut into slices to serve.

Variation As an alternative decoration, pare thin slices of fresh coconut, with a swivel peeler, sprinkle with a little sugar and grill until lightly browned. Scatter over the glaze.

cherry, lemon and almond cake

Makes 18 slices
Preparation time: 20 minutes, plus cooling
Cooking time: About 50 minutes
Suitable for freezing
335 cals per slice

300g (10oz) glacé cherries, rinsed and dried
150g (5oz) self-raising white flour, plus 15ml (1 tbsp)
250g (9oz) unsalted butter, softened
250g (9oz) caster sugar
finely grated rind of 2 lemons
5 eggs, separated
150g (5oz) ground almonds
45ml (3 tbsp) milk
25g (1oz) slivered or flaked almonds
FOR THE GLAZE:
100g (3½oz) caster sugar
100ml (3½fl oz) water
juice of 2 lemons
5ml (1 tsp) almond extract

1   Grease and line a 23cm (9 inch) square cake tin. Halve the cherries and toss in 15ml (1 tbsp) flour.
2   Cream the butter and sugar together in a bowl until light and fluffy. Stir in the lemon rind and egg yolks.
3   Sift in the flour. Add the ground almonds and milk and fold in, using a large metal spoon.
4   Whisk the egg whites in a clean bowl to soft peaks; fold a quarter into the creamed mixture to lighten it, then carefully fold in the remainder.
5   Turn the mixture into the prepared tin. Scatter over the cherries and almonds. Bake at 180°C/ fan oven 170°C (350°F) Mark 4 for about 50 minutes until golden and just firm. Leave to cool in the tin.
6   For the glaze, put the sugar and water in a small heavy-based pan and heat gently until dissolved. Bring to the boil, add the lemon juice and almond extract and boil rapidly for 5 minutes until syrupy. Let cool, then spoon over the cake. Store in an airtight container for up to 5 days.

Note Buy natural glacé cherries for baking – these are available from most supermarkets.

coffee pecan layer cake

Makes 10 slices
Preparation time: 30 minutes, plus cooling
Cooking time: 20-25 minutes
Suitable for freezing (stage 3)
570 cals per slice

175g (6oz) self-raising white flour
7.5ml (1½ tsp) baking powder
175g (6oz) unsalted butter, softened
175g (6oz) light muscovado sugar
3 eggs
30ml (2 tbsp) instant coffee, dissolved in
15ml (1 tbsp) hot water
100g (3½oz) pecan halves, chopped
FOR THE FILLING:
75g (3oz) unsalted butter, softened
175g (6oz) icing sugar
2.5ml (½ tsp) vanilla extract
FOR THE FROSTING AND DECORATION:
225g (8oz) caster sugar
pinch of cream of tartar
1 large egg white
15ml (1 tbsp) instant coffee, dissolved in
10ml (2 tsp) hot water
pecan halves, to decorate

1 Grease and base-line three 18cm (7 inch)
   sandwich tins.
2 Sift the flour and baking powder into a bowl.
   Add the butter, sugar, eggs and coffee and whisk
   until pale and creamy. Stir in the chopped nuts.
3 Divide between the prepared tins and level the
   surface. Bake at 180°C/fan oven 170°C (350°F)
   Mark 4 for 20-25 minutes until just firm to the
   touch. Transfer to a wire rack and leave to cool.
4 To make the filling, beat the butter, icing sugar
   and vanilla extract together in a bowl with 5ml
   (1 tsp) boiling water until pale and creamy. Use
   to sandwich the cake layers on a serving plate.
5 To make the frosting, heat the sugar and cream
   of tartar in a small heavy-based saucepan with
   60ml (4 tbsp) water until dissolved. Bring to the
   boil and boil, without stirring, until the syrup
   registers 116°C (240°F) on a sugar thermometer.
6 Meanwhile, whisk the egg white in a bowl until
   stiff. Pour on the sugar syrup in a thin stream,
   whisking all the time until the frosting is glossy
   and peaking. Stir in the coffee. Spread the
   frosting over the cake and decorate with pecans.

lemon angel cakes

Rosewater and cardamom add an exotic perfume to
this light, low-fat cake.

Makes 15-18 slices
Preparation time: 20 minutes, plus cooling
Cooking time: 35 minutes
Suitable for freezing
35-40 cals per slice

50g (2oz) plain white flour
15ml (1 tbsp) cornflour
100g (3½oz) caster sugar
5 large egg whites
1.25ml (¼ tsp) salt
2.5ml (½ tsp) cream of tartar
2.5ml (½ tsp) vanilla extract
2.5ml (½ tsp) rosewater
seeds from 3 large cardamom pods, finely crushed
grated rind of 1 lemon
icing sugar, for dusting

1 Grease and base-line an 18cm (7 inch) square
   cake tin with non-stick baking parchment. Sift
   the flour, cornflour and 50g (2oz) of the caster
   sugar together into a bowl; set aside.
2 In a clean bowl, whisk the egg whites with the
   salt, cream of tartar, vanilla extract, rosewater
   and 15ml (1 tbsp) cold water until stiff. Gradually
   whisk in the remaining sugar and continue to
   whisk until stiff and glossy. Sift the flour mixture
   over the egg whites and carefully fold in with the
   crushed cardamom seeds and lemon rind. Spoon
   into the prepared tin and level the surface.
3 Bake at 170°C/fan oven 160°C (325°F) Mark 3 for
   35 minutes or until firm to the touch and the
   cake has shrunk from the sides of the tin. Loosen
   the sides with a palette knife and invert on to a
   wire rack, leaving the tin over the cake as it
   cools.
4 Cut the cake into slices and dust with icing sugar.
   Serve with fromage frais or crème fraîche and
   fresh berries or pineapple if you like.

butterscotch nut gâteau

Makes 12 slices
Preparation time: 35 minutes, plus chilling
Cooking time: 15 minutes
580 cals per slice

125g (4oz) brazil nuts
5 eggs
150g (5oz) caster sugar
150g (5oz) plain white flour
FOR THE FILLING:
100g (3½oz) unsalted butter
200g (7oz) dark muscovado sugar
45ml (3 tbsp) cornflour
300ml (½ pint) milk
600ml (1 pint) double cream
10ml (2 tsp) vanilla extract

1 Set aside 12 nuts for decoration; finely chop the remainder. Line 3 baking sheets with non-stick baking parchment and draw a 25cm (10 inch) circle on each. Grease the circles.
2 Whisk the eggs and sugar together in a heatproof bowl over a pan of hot water until thick and pale, and the whisk leaves a trail when lifted. Remove from the heat and whisk until cool.
3 Sift the flour over the mixture. Add the chopped nuts and fold in, using a large metal spoon. Spread the mixture over the marked circles. Bake at 180°C/fan oven 170°C (350°F) Mark 4 for 15 minutes or until just firm. Leave to cool.
4 For the filling, melt the butter in a pan, add the sugar, stir until dissolved, then boil for 1 minute. Add 50ml (2fl oz) boiling water; stir until smooth.
5 Blend the cornflour with a little of the milk. Put the remaining milk in a saucepan with 150ml (¼ pint) of the cream and bring to the boil. Pour over the cornflour mixture, stirring. Add to the butter mixture and cook, stirring, until smooth and thickened. Transfer to a bowl and leave to cool. Set aside 45ml (3 tbsp) for decoration.
6 Trim the sponges to neat 25cm (10 inch) rounds. Dampen and line the sides of a 25cm (10 inch) loose-based cake tin. Lay one sponge in the tin.
7 Whip the remaining cream in a bowl with the vanilla until holding its shape. Spread half over the sponge in the tin. Cover with a third of the butterscotch mixture.
8 Repeat these layers then top with the final sponge and the remaining butterscotch. Chill for at least 2 hours.
9 Carefully unmould the gâteau. Position the nuts around the edge. Drizzle reserved butterscotch on top of the gâteau. Chill until required.

summer berry cake

Any combination of summer berries can be used here – try blackberries, strawberries and black or white currants. Don't worry if the berries sink during baking – this won't affect the flavour.

Makes 8 slices
Preparation time: 40 minutes, plus cooling
Cooking time About 1 hour
435 cals per serving

2 eggs
1 egg yolk
pinch of salt
150g (5oz) butter, softened
150g (5oz) caster sugar
150g (5oz) self-raising white flour, sifted
grated rind and juice of 1 lemon
125g (4oz) mixed raspberries and blueberries
FOR THE TOPPING:
25g (1oz) white sugar cubes, roughly crushed
25ml (5 tsp) bottled lemon juice
225g (8oz) caster sugar
icing sugar, for dusting
fresh berries, to decorate

1 Grease and base-line a 900g (2lb) loaf tin. Lightly beat the eggs and egg yolk with the salt.
2 Cream the butter and sugar together in a bowl until light and fluffy. Beat in the eggs, gradually.
3 Fold in the flour, lemon rind and 30ml (2 tbsp) of the lemon juice. Fold in the berries.
4 Spoon the mixture into the prepared tin and bake at 170°C/fan oven 160°C (325°F) Mark 3 for 50 minutes – 1 hour. Leave in the tin for 5 minutes, then transfer to a wire rack to cool.
5 Mix together the reserved fresh lemon juice, bottled lemon juice and caster sugar. Spoon over the cake, then sprinkle with the crushed sugar. Set aside for 1 hour or until set.
6 Dust with icing sugar and top with berries. Serve with crème fraîche or yogurt.

iced rosemary cake

A sweet orange glaze is the perfect foil for this delicately rosemary-scented Madeira cake.

Makes 12 slices
Preparation time: 20 minutes
Cooking time: About 1 hour
Suitable for freezing (stage 4)
325 cals per slice

3 tender fresh rosemary sprigs, each about 10cm (4 inches)
175g (6oz) unsalted butter, softened
175g (6oz) caster sugar
10ml (2 tsp) vanilla extract
3 eggs, beaten
225g (8oz) self-raising white flour
30ml (2 tbsp) milk
FOR THE GLAZE:
225g (8oz) icing sugar
finely grated rind of ½ orange
15ml (1 tbsp) orange juice
TO DECORATE:
rosemary sprigs

1 Grease and line a 15cm (6 inch) round, deep cake tin. Strip the leaves from the rosemary stalks and chop finely. Set aside half for the glaze.

2 Cream the butter, sugar and remaining rosemary together in a bowl until pale and creamy. Stir in the vanilla extract.

3 Beat in the eggs, a little at a time, adding a little flour to prevent curdling. Sift the remaining flour over the mixture. Add the milk and fold in.

4 Turn into the prepared tin and level the surface. Bake at 180°C/fan oven 170°C (350°F) Mark 4 for 50 minutes to 1 hour until firm and a skewer inserted into the centre comes out clean.

5 Meanwhile, put the remaining rosemary in a small pan with 30ml (2 tbsp) water. Heat gently for 2 minutes; set aside to infuse until cool.

6 Sift the icing sugar into a bowl and add the orange rind and juice. Strain the rosemary juice into the bowl and mix to the consistency of pouring cream, adding a little water if necessary.

7 Leave the cake to cool for 5 minutes, then run a knife between the cake and lining paper. Pour on the icing and leave to cool completely before removing paper. Decorate with rosemary.

almond and apricot roulade

This irresistible roulade is flecked with grated marzipan and moistened with amaretto liqueur, for a superb almondy flavour. In perfect contrast, fresh, juicy apricots and crème fraîche are encased inside. Make the sponge a day in advance if you like, but fill shortly before serving.

Serves 8
Preparation time: 20 minutes, plus standing
Cooking time: 20 minutes
380 cals per serving

FOR THE ROULADE:
25g (1oz) flaked almonds
5 eggs, separated
150g (5oz) caster sugar
5ml (1 tsp) vanilla extract
125g (4oz) white almond paste, grated
45ml (3 tbsp) plain white flour
45ml (3 tbsp) amaretto liqueur
FOR THE FILLING:
300g (10oz) crème fraîche
6 ripe apricots, halved, stoned and cut into slivers
caster or icing sugar, for dusting

1   Grease a 33x23 cm (13x9 inch) Swiss roll tin and line with greased non-stick baking parchment. Scatter the flaked almonds evenly over the paper.
2   In a large bowl, whisk the egg yolks with 125g (4oz) of the sugar until pale and fluffy. Stir in the vanilla extract and grated almond paste. Sift the flour over the mixture, then lightly fold in, using a large metal spoon.
3   Whisk the egg whites in another bowl, until stiff but not dry. Gradually whisk in the remaining sugar. Using a large metal spoon, fold a quarter of the egg whites into the almond mixture to loosen it, then carefully fold in the remainder.
4   Turn into the prepared tin and gently ease the mixture into the corners. Bake at 180°C/fan oven 170°C (350°F) Mark 4 for about 20 minutes or until well risen and just firm to the touch. Cover with a sheet of non-stick baking parchment and a damp tea-towel. Leave until cool.

5   Remove the tea-towel and invert the roulade (and paper) onto a baking sheet. Peel off the lining paper. Sprinkle another piece of baking parchment with caster sugar and flip the roulade onto it. Drizzle with the amaretto liqueur.
6   Spread the roulade with the crème fraîche and scatter over the apricots. Starting from one of the narrow ends, carefully roll up the roulade, using the paper to help. Transfer to a plate and dust with caster or icing sugar to serve.

Note The roulade will probably crack during rolling – this is an appealing characteristic!

Variations
- For the filling, use 300ml (½ pint) whipped cream instead of the crème fraîche.
- Replace the apricots with strawberries or raspberries. Use kirsch or Grand Marnier instead of amaretto liqueur.

chocolate roulade

A melt-in-the-mouth baked chocolate mousse mixture rolled around vanilla-scented cream, served sliced and scattered with chocolate curls.

Serves 10
Preparation time: 30 minutes, plus chilling
Cooking time: 20-25 minutes
Suitable for freezing (stage 8)
325 cals per serving

175g (6oz) good quality plain dark chocolate (70% cocoa solids), in pieces
150ml (¼ pint) water
6 eggs, separated
175g (6oz) caster sugar
FOR THE FILLING:
300ml (½ pint) whipping cream
5ml (1 tsp) caster sugar
2.5ml (½ tsp) vanilla extract
TO DECORATE:
cocoa powder, for dusting
chocolate curls (optional, see page 293)

1. Grease and line a 38x28cm (15x11 inch) Swiss roll tin with non-stick baking parchment.
2. Melt the chocolate with the water in a small heatproof bowl over a pan of gently simmering water. Stir until smooth; set aside.
3. Whisk the egg yolks and sugar together in a bowl, using an electric whisk, until pale and thick. Beat in the melted chocolate.
4. In a clean bowl, whisk the egg whites until they just hold a soft peak. Stir a quarter of the egg white into the chocolate mixture to loosen it, then carefully fold in the remainder, using a large metal spoon; do not overmix.
5. Immediately pour into the prepared tin and spread into the corners. Bake at 180°C/fan oven 170°C (350°F) Mark 4 for 20-25 minutes until well risen and springy to the touch.
6. Cover the roulade with a damp tea-towel and leave in the tin until cold. Once cold, cover the cloth with cling film, then refrigerate for at least 6 hours or overnight.
7. For the filling, whip the cream in a bowl until it starts to thicken. Add the caster sugar and vanilla extract and continue to whip until it just holds its shape.
8. Lightly dust a large sheet of greaseproof paper with caster sugar. Uncover the roulade, then carefully turn out on to the greaseproof paper. Cut 5mm (¼ inch) off the two short sides to neaten. Spread the cream over the roulade. Roll up tightly from a long side, using the paper to help. (Don't worry if the sponge cracks.)
9. Transfer to a plate, sprinkle with cocoa and serve decorated with chocolate curls.

spiced almond easter cake

This has a layer of sticky almond paste running through the middle and a delicious fresh spicy flavour that improves with keeping. Homemade almond paste tastes wonderful and can be made in minutes, but if you're pressed for time, use 125g (4oz) ready-made almond paste.

Makes 10 slices
Preparation time: 45 minutes
Cooking time: 1¾ hours
Suitable for freezing (stage 5)
450 cals per slice

FOR THE ALMOND PASTE:
50g (2oz) ground almonds
40g (1½oz) icing sugar
25g (1oz) caster sugar
grated rind of 1 lemon
15ml (1 tbsp) beaten egg (see cake)
FOR THE CAKE:
300g (11oz) plain white flour
10ml (2 tsp) baking powder
pinch of salt
2.5ml (½ tsp) ground coriander
2.5ml (½ tsp) ground cloves
5ml (1 tsp) ground ginger
5ml (1 tsp) ground cinnamon
175g (6oz) unsalted butter, softened
grated rind of 1 lemon
225g (8oz) light muscovado sugar
4 medium eggs, beaten, less 15ml (1 tbsp)
TO DECORATE:
90-120ml (6-8 tbsp) apricot glaze or jam
15ml (1 tbsp) kirsch or Grand Marnier
8-10 kumquats
few ready-to-eat dried apricots or mango slices
4-5 physalis fruit
1 metre wide gold ribbon

1 Line a deep 23cm (9 inch) round cake tin with greaseproof paper. For the almond paste filling, in a small bowl, mix the ingredients together to a smooth paste, then cover and chill.
2 To make the cake, sift the flour, baking powder, salt and spices together. Beat the butter and lemon rind together in a bowl until creamy. Beat in the sugar, a spoonful at a time.

3 Beat in the eggs, a little at a time, until the mixture is light and fluffy, adding 15ml (1 tbsp) flour with the last addition. Using a large metal spoon, fold in the flour and spices.
4 Spoon half of the cake mixture into the prepared tin; smooth the surface. Roll out the almond paste on a sheet of greaseproof paper sprinkled with icing sugar to a 20cm (8 inch) round. Use the paper to help lift the almond paste on top of the mixture in the tin. Spoon the remaining cake mixture on top of the almond paste layer and smooth.
5 Bake at 150°C/fan oven 140°C (300°F) Mark 2 for approximately 1¾ hours, covering with greaseproof paper if the cake appears to be overbrowning. Leave in the tin for 30 minutes, then turn out on to a wire rack to cool completely.
6 To decorate the cake, warm the apricot glaze, add the kirsch, kumquats and apricots or mango slices and spoon on top of the cake. Leave for about 30 minutes until set. Open the physalis fruit and arrange around the edge of the cake. Tie the ribbon around the side to finish.

testing when a cake is cooked

Once the cake is in the oven resist the temptation to open the door – a sudden gush of cold air will make it sink in the middle. Instead wait until the cooking time is almost up before testing. If your cake appears to be browning too quickly, cover with greaseproof paper towards the end of cooking.

- To test a baked sponge, carefully remove from oven and touch the centre with one hand – it should feel spongy and give very slightly. A whisked sponge cake should just be shrinking from the sides of the tin. If necessary return cake to the oven for a few minutes, closing the door gently so that vibration does not cause the cake to sink in the centre.
- To test a fruit cake, take it out of the oven, insert a skewer into the centre and remove: it should come away cleanly. If any mixture is sticking to the skewer, return to the oven for a little longer.
- Apart from very light sponges, all cakes are best left to stand in their tin for several minutes after baking to firm up slightly.

seeded multigrain loaf

Enriched with sunflower, poppy and sesame seeds, this wonderfully moist, granary bread has a delicious nutty taste.

Makes 2 loaves; each 12 slices
Preparation time: 20 minutes, plus rising
Cooking time: 30-35 minutes
Suitable for freezing
115 cals per slice

225g (8oz) strong plain wholemeal flour
350g (12oz) strong granary flour
125g (4oz) rye flour
25g (1oz) butter, diced
10ml (2 tsp) salt
7g sachet fast-action dried yeast (see note)
5ml (1 tsp) caster sugar
40g (1½oz) rolled oats or barley, or millet flakes
30ml (2 tbsp) each sesame seeds, poppy seeds and
    sunflower seeds
450ml (¾ pint) warm water
30ml (2 tbsp) malt extract
TO FINISH:
egg beaten with a little water, to glaze
few extra sesame, poppy and sunflower seeds

1 Mix the wholemeal, granary and rye flours together in a large bowl. Rub in the butter, then stir in all the remaining dry ingredients.
2 Make a well in the centre and gradually work in the warm water and malt extract to form a soft dough.
3 Knead the dough for 10 minutes, then transfer to an oiled bowl, cover with oiled cling film and leave to rise in a warm place for 2 hours or until doubled in size.
4 Lightly oil two 900g (2lb) loaf tins. Knock back the dough, divide in half and shape each one into an oblong.
5 Press into the prepared tins, cover loosely and leave to rise for 30 minutes until the dough reaches the top of the tins.
6 Carefully brush each loaf with egg glaze and scatter over some extra seeds. Bake at 220°C/fan oven 210°C (425°F) Mark 7 for 30-35 minutes until the breads are risen and golden brown. Leave in the tins for 10 minutes, then transfer to a wire rack to cool.

Note If available, use 20g (¾oz) fresh yeast instead of dried. Blend with the sugar, 150ml (¼ pint) of the water and 60ml (4 tbsp) of the wholemeal flour until smooth; leave to froth in a warm place for 10 minutes. Add at stage 2.

kneading bread dough

After mixing, bread dough must be kneaded vigorously to strengthen the gluten in the flour, make the dough elastic and ultimately to achieve a good rise. If you omit this stage, the dough will not rise. There's nothing difficult about kneading and, contrary to popular belief, it doesn't take long to do by hand – 5-10 minutes should be long enough.

  Turn the dough onto a floured surface, fold it firmly towards you, then quickly and firmly push it down and away from you with the heel of your hand. Give it a quarter turn and continue kneading until the dough feels elastic and smooth: it shouldn't be sticky.

  As an alternative to kneading by hand, you can use a large mixer with a dough hook attachment, or a food processor. In either case, avoid overloading machine.

rising bread dough

Shape the kneaded dough into a ball and place in a clean bowl. Cover with a clean tea-towel, an oiled polythene bag or oiled cling film to prevent a skin forming. Leave in a warm place until the dough has doubled in size and springs back when pressed. The time it takes to rise will depend on the ambient temperature. If you put the bowl near a warm oven or in an airing cupboard, rising can take as little as 30 minutes, while at cooler temperatures it may take over an hour. Don't be tempted to put it somewhere hot to speed things up; you will end up with a badly shaped, uneven-textured loaf, or you could even kill the yeast.

herbed cheese stick

Savoury batons with an enticing aroma of fresh rosemary and herbes de Provence.

Makes 2 loaves; each serves 4
Preparation time: 20 minutes, plus rising
Cooking time: 25 minutes
Suitable for freezing
240 cals per serving

450g (1lb) strong plain white flour
5ml (1 tsp) salt
½ x 7g sachet fast-action dried yeast
15ml (1 tbsp) dried herbes de Provence
25g (1oz) gruyère cheese, finely grated
250-300ml (9-10 fl oz) warm water
30ml (2 tbsp) olive oil
50g (2oz) sultanas
2 fresh rosemary sprigs

1 Sift the flour and salt into a bowl and stir in the yeast, herbs and cheese. Make a well in the centre and gradually work in sufficient warm water and the oil to make a soft dough. Knead for 10 minutes.

2 Turn the dough on to a lightly floured surface and knead in the sultanas. Shape into a ball and place in an oiled bowl. Cover with a tea-towel and leave to rise in a warm place for 1 hour or until doubled in size.

3 Knock back the dough on a lightly floured surface, divide in half and shape each piece into a baton. Place on a large baking sheet and sprinkle with flour. Slash along the length of each stick and top with the rosemary sprigs. Cover loosely and leave to rise for a further 30 minutes.

4 Bake at 220°C/fan oven 210°C (425°F) Mark 7 for 25 minutes until risen and golden. Transfer to a wire rack to cool slightly. Serve warm.

apricot and hazelnut loaf

Flavoured with toasted hazelnuts and dried apricots, this granary bread is exceptionally good.

Makes 2 loaves; each 12 slices
Preparation time: 20 minutes, plus rising
Cooking time: 30-35 minutes
Suitable for freezing
125 cals per slice

450g (1lb) strong granary flour
225g (8oz) strong plain white flour
10ml (2 tsp) salt
25g (1oz) butter, diced
75g (3oz) hazelnuts, toasted and chopped
75g (3oz) ready-to-eat dried apricots, chopped
7g sachet fast-action dried yeast
30ml (2 tbsp) molasses
350ml (12fl oz) warm water
milk, for brushing

1 Put the flours into a large bowl. Add the salt, then rub in the butter. Stir in the hazelnuts, dried apricots and dried yeast.
2 Make a well in the centre and gradually work in the molasses and warm water to form a soft dough.
3 Knead for 8-10 minutes until smooth, then transfer the dough to an oiled bowl. Cover with a tea-towel and leave to rise in a warm place for 1-1½ hours until doubled in size.
4 Preheat a large baking sheet on the top shelf of the oven set at 220°C/fan oven 210°C (425°F) Mark 7. Knock back the dough, then divide in half. Shape each portion into a small flattish round and place on a floured baking sheet. Cover loosely and leave to rise for a further 30 minutes.
5 Using a sharp knife, cut several slashes on each round, brush with a little milk and transfer to the heated baking sheet. Bake for 15 minutes, then reduce the oven setting to 190°C/fan oven 180°C (375°F) Mark 5 and bake for a further 15-20 minutes or until the bread is risen and sounds hollow when tapped underneath. Transfer to a wire rack to cool.

schiacciata

An Italian pizza-style flat bread with a tasty sage, garlic and olive oil topping.

Makes 2; each serves 4
Preparation time: 15 minutes, plus rising
Cooking time: 15-20 minutes
Suitable for freezing
265 cals per serving

450g (1lb) strong plain white flour
½ x 7g sachet fast-action dried yeast
5ml (1 tsp) sea salt
2.5ml (½ tsp) caster sugar
30ml (2 tbsp) extra-virgin olive oil
250-300ml (8-10fl oz) warm water
FOR THE TOPPING:
60ml (4 tbsp) extra-virgin olive oil
2 garlic cloves, peeled and crushed
15ml (1 tbsp) chopped fresh sage
sea salt

1 Sift the flour into a large bowl and stir in the yeast, salt and sugar. Make a well in the centre and gradually work in the oil and sufficient warm water to form a soft dough.
2 Knead for 8-10 minutes until smooth and elastic, then transfer the dough to a greased bowl. Cover with a tea-towel and leave to rise in a warm place for 1-1½ hours until doubled in size.
3 Preheat a large baking sheet on the top shelf of the oven set at 220°C/fan oven 210°C (425°F) Mark 7. Knock back the risen dough, divide in half and roll each piece out to a 25x12cm (10x5 inch) oval. Transfer to a well-floured baking sheet, cover loosely and leave to rise for a further 30 minutes.
4 To prepare the topping, in a small bowl, mix the oil with the garlic, sage and a little salt.
5 Make 4 deep slashes along each oval and transfer to the preheated baking sheet. Quickly drizzle over the garlic oil and bake for 15-20 minutes until the bread is risen and golden. Transfer to a wire rack to cool. Serve warm.

parmesan and chive rolls

These tasty cheese and herb rolls are particularly good served with soups.

Makes 8
Preparation time: 20 minutes, plus rising
Cooking time: 15-20 minutes
Suitable for freezing
270 cals per roll

450g (1lb) strong plain white flour
5ml (1 tsp) salt
7g sachet fast-action dried yeast
pinch of sugar
60ml (4 tbsp) chopped fresh chives
65g (2½oz) Parmesan cheese, freshly grated
300ml (½ pint) milk
25g (1oz) butter

1 Sift the flour and salt into a bowl and stir in the yeast, sugar, chives, and all but 15g (½oz) of the cheese.
2 Heat the milk and butter in a small pan until the butter is melted; cool slightly until tepid. Gradually add to the dry ingredients and work together to form a soft dough.
3 Knead for 8-10 minutes until smooth, then transfer to a greased bowl. Cover with a tea-towel and leave to rise in a warm place for 1 hour.
4 Knock back the dough and divide into 8 pieces. Shape into balls, flatten slightly and place on an oiled large baking sheet. Cover loosely with oiled cling film and leave to rise for 30 minutes.
5 Sprinkle the remaining Parmesan over the rolls and bake at 220°C/fan oven 210°C (425°F) Mark 7 for 15-20 minutes until risen and golden. Cool on a wire rack.

focaccia

Makes 2; each serves 6
Preparation time: 30 minutes, plus rising
Cooking time: 20-25 minutes
Suitable for freezing
275 cals per serving

700g (1½lb) strong plain white flour
pinch of salt
7g sachet fast-action dried yeast
450ml (¾ pint) warm water
45ml (3 tbsp) extra-virgin olive oil
TO FINISH:
60ml (4 tbsp) olive oil
coarse sea salt or crystal salt, for sprinkling

1 Sift the flour and salt into a large bowl, stir in the yeast and make a well in the centre. Gradually work in the warm water and olive oil to form a soft dough.
2 Knead for 10 minutes until smooth and elastic, then place in a greased bowl. Cover with a tea-towel and leave to rise in a warm place for 1½-2 hours until doubled in size. If too soft, knead in a little more flour.
3 Lightly oil two shallow 25cm (10 inch) metal pizza tins or pie plates. Knock back the dough and divide in half. Roll out each piece to a 25cm (10 inch) circle. Place in the oiled tins. Cover with a damp tea-towel and leave to rise for 30 minutes.
4 Using your fingertips, make deep dimples all over the surface of the dough. Drizzle with the olive oil, sprinkle generously with salt and spray with water. Bake at 200°C/fan oven 190°C (400°F) Mark 6 for 20-25 minutes, spraying with water twice during cooking. Transfer to a wire rack and allow to cool slightly. Serve warm, the same day.

Variations

OLIVE AND SUN-DRIED TOMATO FOCACCIA Drain 50g (2oz) sun-dried tomatoes in oil, slice and knead into the dough at stage 2. Scatter 225g (8oz) black or green olives over the dough at stage 4.

SAGE AND ONION FOCACCIA Knead 15-20 chopped fresh sage leaves into the dough at stage 2. Sprinkle the focaccia with extra sage leaves and 2 thinly sliced red onions at stage 4 before baking.

olive bread

Speckled with black olives, these irresistible rolls are brushed with fruity olive oil and sprinkled with coarse sea salt for additional flavour.

Makes 6 rolls
Preparation time: 15 minutes, plus rising
Cooking time: 15-20 minutes
Suitable for freezing
310 cals per roll

450g (1lb) strong plain white flour, plus 25g (1oz)
10ml (2 tsp) salt
7g sachet fast-action dried yeast
pinch of caster sugar
5ml (1 tsp) dried rosemary (optional)
300ml (½ pint) warm water
30ml (2 tbsp) olive oil
125g (4oz) pitted black olives, finely chopped
extra-virgin olive oil, for brushing
coarse sea salt, for sprinkling

1 Sift all but 25g (1oz) of the flour with the salt into a bowl and stir in the yeast, sugar, and rosemary if using. Make a well in the centre and add the warm water and olive oil; work to a soft dough. Knead for 10 minutes until smooth.

2 Pat the olives dry and add to the dough with the extra 25g (1oz) flour; knead in gently. Shape into a ball, then transfer the dough to a greased bowl. Cover with a tea-towel and leave to rise in a warm place for 1 hour.

3 Knock back the dough and divide into 6 pieces. Shape into balls, then press lightly to form flat rolls, about 12cm (5 inches) in diameter. Transfer to a baking sheet, cover loosely with oiled cling film and rise for a further 30 minutes.

4 Make finger indentations over each roll, then brush with olive oil and sprinkle with sea salt. Bake at 220°C/fan oven 210°C (425°F) Mark 7 for 15-20 minutes until risen and golden. Cool on a wire rack.

glossary of cookery terms

A brief guide to cooking methods, terms and ingredients used in the recipes featured in this book

ACIDULATED WATER Water to which lemon juice or vinegar has been added in which fruit or vegetables, such as pears or Jerusalem artichokes, are immersed to prevent discoloration.

AL DENTE Italian term used to describe food, especially pasta and vegetables, which are cooked until tender but still firm to the bite.

ANTIPASTO Italian selection of cold meats, fish, salads etc. served as a starter.

ARROWROOT Fine, white powder used as a thickening agent for sauces. Unlike cornflour, arrowroot gives a clear gloss.

AU GRATIN Describes a dish which has been coated with sauce, sprinkled with breadcrumbs or cheese and browned under the grill or in the oven. Low-sided gratin dishes are used.

BAIN-MARIE Literally, a water bath, used to keep foods, such as delicate custards and sauces, at a constant low temperature during cooking. On the hob a double saucepan or bowl over a pan of simmering water is used; for oven cooking, the baking dish(es) is placed in a roasting tin containing enough hot water to come halfway up the sides.

BAKING BLIND Pre-baking a pastry case before filling. The pastry case is lined with greaseproof paper and weighted down with dried beans or ceramic baking beans.

BAKING POWDER A raising agent consisting of an acid, usually cream of tartar and an alkali, such as bicarbonate of soda, which react to produce carbon dioxide. This expands during baking and makes cakes and breads rise.

BALSAMIC VINEGAR Italian oak-aged vinegar, dark brown in colour with a superior sweet, mellow flavour.

BARD To cover the breast of game birds or poultry, or lean meat with fat to prevent the meat from drying out during roasting.

BASTE To spoon the juices and melted fat over meat, poultry, game or vegetables during roasting to keep them moist. The term is also used to describe spooning over a marinade.

BEAT Method of incorporating air into an ingredient or mixture by agitating it vigorously with a spoon, fork, whisk or electric mixer. Also used to soften ingredients.

BÉCHAMEL Classic French white sauce, used as the basis for other sauces and savoury dishes.

BEURRE MANIÉ Equal parts of flour and butter kneaded together to form a paste. Used for thickening soups, stews and casseroles. It is whisked into the hot liquid a little at a time at the end of cooking.

BIND To mix beaten egg or other liquid into a dry mixture to hold it together.

BLANCH To immerse food briefly in fast-boiling water to loosen skins, such as tomatoes, or to remove bitterness, or to destroy enzymes and preserve the colour, flavour and texture of vegetables (especially prior to freezing).

BONE To remove the bones from meat, poultry, game or fish, so it can be stuffed or simply rolled before cooking.

BOUQUET GARNI Small bunch of herbs – usually a mixture of parsley stems, thyme and a bay leaf – tied in muslin and used to flavour stocks, soups and stews.

BRAISE To cook meat, poultry, game or vegetables slowly in a small amount of liquid in a pan or casserole with a tight-fitting lid. The food is usually browned first, in oil.

BROCHETTE Food cooked on a skewer or spit.

BRÛLÉE A French term, literally meaning 'burnt' used to refer to a dish with a crisp coating of caramelised sugar.

BUTTERFLY To split a food, such as a large prawn or poussin, almost in half and open out flat, so that it will cook more quickly.

CALORIE Strictly a kilocalorie, this is used in dietetics to measure the energy value of foods.

CANAPÉ Small appetiser, usually consisting of a pastry or bread base with a savoury topping, served with drinks.

CAPER Small bud of a Mediterranean flowering shrub, usually packed in brine. Small French capers in balsamic vinegar are considered to be the best.

CARAMELISE To heat sugar or sugar syrup slowly until it is brown in colour; ie forms a caramel.

CARBONADE Rich meat braise which includes beer.

CASSEROLE Strictly speaking, a dish with a tight-fitting lid used for slow-cooking meat, poultry and vegetables. Now applied to the food cooked in this way.

CHARCUTERIE French term for cooked pork products, including hams, sausages and terrines.

CHILL To cool food in the refrigerator.

CHINE To sever the rib bones from the backbone, close to the spine. This is done to meat joints, such as loin of pork or lamb, to make them easier to carve into chops after cooking.

CLARIFY To remove sediment or impurities from a liquid. Stock is clarified by heating with egg white, while butter is clarified by melting and skimming. Butter which is clarified will withstand a higher frying temperature.

TO CLARIFY BUTTER Heat until melted and all bubbling stops. Remove from the heat and let stand until the sediment has sunk to the bottom, then gently pour off the fat, straining it through muslin.

COCONUT MILK Used in curries and other ethnic dishes. Available in cans from larger supermarkets and ethnic stores. Alternatively creamed coconut sold compressed in blocks can be reconstituted to make coconut milk.

COMPOTE Mixture of fresh or dried fruit stewed in sugar syrup. Served hot or cold.

CONCASSÉ Diced fresh ingredient, used as a garnish. The term is most often applied to skinned, seeded tomatoes.

COULIS A smooth fruit or vegetable purée, thinned if necessary to a pouring consistency.

COURT BOUILLON Aromatic cooking liquid containing wine, vinegar or lemon juice, used for poaching delicate fish, poultry or vegetables.

CONSISTENCY Term used to describe the texture of a mixture, eg firm, dropping or soft.

CREAM OF TARTAR Also known as tartaric acid, this is a raising agent which is also an ingredient of baking powder and self-raising flour.

CREAM To beat together fat and sugar until the mixture is pale and fluffy, and resembles whipped cream in texture and colour. The method is used in cakes and puddings which contain a high proportion of fat and require the incorporation of a lot of air.

CRÊPE French term for a pancake.

CRIMP To decorate the edge of a pie, tart or shortbread by pinching it at regular intervals to give a fluted effect.

CROQUETTE Seasoned mixture of cooked potato and fish, meat, poultry, or vegetables shaped into a small roll, coated with egg and breadcrumbs and shallow-fried.

CROÛTE Circle or other shaped piece of fried bread, typically used as a base for serving small game birds.

CROÛTONS Small pieces of fried or toasted bread, served with soups and salads.

CRUDITÉS Raw vegetables, usually cut into slices or sticks, typically served with a dip or sauce as an appetiser.

CRYSTALLISE To preserve fruit in sugar syrup.

CURDS The part of milk which coagulates when natural fermentation takes place or when a curdling agent, such as rennet, is added.

CURDLE To cause sauces or creamed mixtures to separate once the egg is added, usually by overheating or over-beating.

CURE To preserve fish, meat or poultry by smoking, drying or salting.

DARIOLE Small, narrow mould with sloping sides used to make individual puddings.

DAUBE Braising meat and vegetables with stock, often with wine and herbs added.

DEGLAZE To heat stock, wine or other liquid with the cooking juices left in the pan after roasting or sautéing, scraping and stirring vigorously to dissolve the sediment on the base of the pan.

DÉGORGE To draw out moisture from a food, eg salting aubergines to remove bitter juices.

DICE To cut food into small cubes.

DRAW To remove the entrails from poultry or game.

DREDGE To sprinkle food generously with flour, sugar, icing sugar etc.

DRESS To pluck, draw and truss poultry or game. The term is also used to describe tossing a salad in vinaigrette or other dressing.

DRIPPING Fat obtained from roasting meat.

DROPPING CONSISTENCY Term used to describe the required texture of a cake or pudding mixture just before cooking. Test for it by taking a spoonful of the mixture and holding the spoon on its side above the bowl. The mixture should fall of its own accord within 5 seconds.

DRY To preserve food by dehydration. Rice, pasta, pulses and dried fruit are treated in this way.

DUST To sprinkle lightly with flour, cornflour, icing sugar etc.

EMULSION A mixture of two liquids which do not dissolve into one another, eg oil and vinegar. Vigorous shaking, whisking or heating will emulsify them, as in a vinaigrette.

EN CROÛTE Term used to describe food which is wrapped in pastry before cooking.

EN PAPILLOTE Term used to describe food which is baked in a greaseproof paper or baking parchment parcel and served from the paper.

ENZYME Organic substance in food which causes chemical changes. Enzymes are a complex group. Their action is usually halted during cooking.

ESCALOPE Thin slice of meat, such as pork, veal or turkey, cut from the top of the leg, usually pan-fried.

EXTRACT Concentrated flavouring which is used in small quantities, eg yeast extract, vanilla extract.

FERMENT Chemical change deliberately or accidentally brought about by fermenting agents, such as yeast or bacteria. Fermentation is utilised for making bread, yogurt, beer and wine.

FILLET Term used to describe boned breasts of birds, boned sides of fish, and the undercut of a loin of beef, lamb, pork or veal.

FILO PASTRY A popular type of Greek pastry manufactured in wafer-thin sheets and sold in packets or boxes. It must be kept covered to prevent it drying out.

FINES HERBES Classic French mixture of chopped herbs, ie parsley, tarragon, chives and chervil.

FLAKE To separate food, such as cooked fish, into natural pieces.

FLAMBÉ Flavouring a dish with alcohol, usually brandy or rum, which is then ignited so that the actual alcohol content is burned off.

FOLDING IN Method of combining a whisked or creamed mixture with other ingredients by cutting and folding so that it retains its lightness. A large metal spoon or plastic bladed spatula is used.

FROSTING To coat leaves and flowers with a fine layer of sugar to use as a decoration. Also an American term for icing cakes.

FRY To cook food in hot fat or oil. There are various methods: shallow-frying in a little fat in a shallow pan; deep-frying where the food is totally immersed in oil; dry-frying in which fatty foods are cooked in a non-stick pan without extra fat; see also Stir-frying.

GALETTE Cooked savoury or sweet mixture shaped into a round.

GARNISH A decoration, usually edible, such as parsley or lemon, which is used to enhance the appearance of a savoury dish.

GELATINE An animal-derived gelling agent sold in powdered form, and as leaf gelatine. Used in jellies, mousses and cold soufflés.

GELAZONE A vegetarian gelling agent sold in powdered form in sachets, and used as a substitute for gelatine.

GHEE Clarified butter widely used in Indian cookery.

GLAZE A glossy coating given to sweet and savoury dishes to improve their appearance and sometimes flavour. Ingredients for glazes include beaten egg, egg white, milk and syrup.

GLUTEN A protein constituent of grains, such as wheat and rye, which develops when the flour is mixed with water to give the dough elasticity.

GRATE To shred hard food, such as cheese and carrots, with a grater or food processor attachment.

GRIDDLE A flat, heavy, metal plate used on the hob for cooking scones or for searing savoury ingredients.

GRIND To reduce foods such as coffee beans, nuts and spices to small particles using a food mill, pestle and mortar, electric grinder or food processor.

GUT To clean out the entrails from fish.

HANG To suspend meat or game in a cool, dry place for a number of days to tenderise the flesh and develop flavour.

HULL To remove the stalk and calyx from soft fruits, such as strawberries.

INFUSE To immerse flavourings, such as aromatic vegetables, herbs, spices and vanilla, in a liquid to impart flavour. Usually the infused liquid is brought to the boil, then left to stand for a while.

JULIENNE Fine 'matchstick' strips of vegetables or citrus zest, sometimes used as a garnish.

KNEAD To work dough by pummelling with the heel of the hand.

KNOCK BACK To knead a yeast dough for a second time after rising, to ensure an even texture.

LARD To insert small strips of fat or streaky bacon into the flesh of game birds and dry meat before cooking. A special larding needle is used.

LIAISON A thickening or binding agent based on a combination of ingredients, such as flour and water, or oil and egg.

MACERATE To soften and flavour raw or dried foods by soaking in a liquid, eg soaking fruit in alcohol.

MANDOLIN(E) A flat wooden or metal frame with adjustable cutting blades for cutting vegetables.

MARINATE To soak raw meat, poultry or game – usually in a mixture of oil, wine, vinegar and flavourings – to soften and impart flavour. The marinade may also be used to baste the food during cooking.

MEDALLION Small round piece of meat, usually beef or veal.

MINCE To cut food into very fine pieces, using a mincer, food processor or knife.

MOCHA Term which has come to mean a blend of chocolate and coffee.

PARBOIL To boil a vegetable or other food for part of its cooking time before finishing it by another method.

PARE To finely peel the skin or zest from vegetables or fruit.

PASSATA A purée of plum tomatoes, used in many Italian dishes. Available ready-made from supermarkets.

PÂTE The French word for pastry, familiar in pâte sucrée, a sweet flan pastry.

PÂTÉ A savoury mixture of finely chopped or minced meat, fish and/or vegetables, usually served as a starter with bread or toast and crudités.

PATTY TIN Tray of cup-shaped moulds for cooking small cakes and deep tartlets. Also called a bun tin.

PESTLE AND MORTAR Heavy marble or porcelain bowl with a heavy grinding tool for grinding herbs, spices etc.

PESTO A paste-like sauce made from puréed herbs and oil, used to flavour pasta and vegetables. A classic pesto is made from basil, pine nuts, garlic and olive oil.

PITH The bitter white skin under the thin zest of citrus fruit.

PIZZA STONE A clay stone for pizza-baking which reproduces the intense heat of a professional pizza oven.

PLUCK To remove the feathers from poultry and game.

POACH To cook food gently in liquid at simmering point, so that the surface of the liquid is just trembling.

PROVE To leave bread dough to rise after shaping.

PURÉE To pound, sieve or liquidise fruit, vegetables or fish to a smooth pulp. Purées often form the basis for soups and sauces.

QUENELLES Fish, meat or poultry which has been blended to a fine paste, shaped into ovals, then poached in a liquid.

REDUCE To fast-boil stock or other liquid in an uncovered pan to evaporate water and concentrate the flavour.

REFRESH To cool hot vegetables very quickly by plunging into ice-cold water or holding under running water in order to stop the cooking process and preserve the colour.

RENDER To melt fat slowly to a liquid, either by heating meat trimmings, or to release the fat from fatty meat, such as duck or goose, during roasting.

ROAST To cook meat by dry heat in the oven.

ROULADE Soufflé or sponge mixture rolled around a savoury or sweet filling.

ROUX A mixture of equal quantities of butter (or other fat) and flour cooked together to form the basis of many sauces.

RUB-IN Method of incorporating fat into flour by rubbing between the fingertips, used when a short texture is required. Used for pastry, cakes, scones and biscuits.

SALSA Piquant sauce made from chopped fresh vegetables and sometimes fruit.

SAUTÉ To cook food in a small quantity of fat over a high heat, shaking the pan constantly – usually in a sauté pan (a frying pan with straight sides and a wide base).

SCALD To pour boiling water over food to clean it, or loosen skin, eg tomatoes. Also used to describe heating milk to just below boiling point.

SCORE To cut parallel lines in the surface of food to improve its appearance or help it cook more quickly.

SEAR To brown meat quickly in a little hot fat before grilling or roasting.

SEASONED FLOUR Flour mixed with a little salt and pepper, used for dusting meat, fish etc before frying.

SHRED To grate cheese or slice vegetables into very fine pieces or strips.

SIEVE To press food through a perforated sieve to obtain a smooth texture.

SIFT To shake dry ingredients through a sieve to remove lumps.

SIMMER To keep a liquid just below boiling point.

SKIM To remove froth, scum or fat from the surface of stock, gravy, stews, jam etc. Use either a skimmer, a spoon or absorbent kitchen paper.

SPRING-RELEASE CAKE TIN Also known as a springform pan, this is a round cake tin with a spring-release side and removable base which is clamped in. Used for cakes and desserts which are not to be inverted.

STEAM To cook food in the steam of rapidly boiling water.

STEEP To immerse food in warm or cold liquid to soften it, and sometimes to draw out strong flavours.

STERILISE To destroy bacteria in foods by heating.

STEW To cook food, such as tougher cuts of meat, slowly in flavoured liquid which is kept at simmering point.

STIR-FRY To cook small even-sized pieces of food rapidly in a little fat, tossing constantly over a high heat, usually in a wok.

SUET Hard fat of animal origin used in pastry and steamed puddings. A vegetarian alternative is available.

SWEAT To cook chopped or sliced vegetables in a little fat without liquid in a covered pan over a low heat.

SWISS ROLL TIN Shallow, rectangular tin, available in several different sizes, used for baking sponges which are filled and rolled after baking – such as roulades.

SYRUP, SUGAR A concentrated solution of sugar in water used to make sorbets, granitas, fruit juices etc.

TEPID The term used to describe temperature at approximately blood heat, ie 37°C (98.7°F).

THERMOMETER, SUGAR/FAT Used for checking the temperature of boiling sugar syrups, and fat for deep-frying. Dual purpose thermometers are obtainable.

TRUSS To tie or skewer poultry or game into shape prior to roasting.

UNLEAVENED Bread made without a raising agent.

VANILLA SUGAR Sugar in which a vanilla pod has been stored to impart its flavour.

WHIPPING (WHISKING) Beating air rapidly into a mixture either with a manual or electric whisk.

WOK Large Chinese pan with a rounded base and sloping sides, used for stir-frying.

ZEST The thin coloured outer layer of citrus fruit which contains essential oil.

ZESTER Small bevelled tool with five holes drawn across citrus fruit to remove the zest in fine strips.

index